THE WAR ON TERRORISM
AND THE TERROR OF GOD

THE WAR ON TERRORISM
and the
TERROR OF GOD

LEE GRIFFITH

WILLIAM B. EERDMANS PUBLISHING COMPANY
GRAND RAPIDS, MICHIGAN / CAMBRIDGE, U.K.

Wm. B. Eerdmans Publishing Co.
255 Jefferson Ave. S.E., Grand Rapids, Michigan 49503 /
P.O. Box 163, Cambridge CB3 9PU U.K.

Paperback edition 2004

Printed in the United States of America

08 07 06 05 04   7 6 5 4 3 2

www.eerdmans.com

Library of Congress Cataloging-in-Publication Data

Griffith, Lee.
The war on terrorism and the terror of God / Lee Griffith.
p.   cm.
Includes bibliographical references (p.   ) and indexes.
ISBN 0-8028-2860-4 (pbk.: alk. paper)
1. Terrorism — Religious aspects — Christianity.
2. Pacifism — Religious aspects — Christianity.   I. Title.

BT736.15.G75   2002
261.8′73 — dc21
                              2001055749

Unless otherwise noted, the Scripture quotations in this publication are from
the New Revised Standard Version Bible, copyright © 1989 by the
Division of Christian Education of the National Council of
Churches of Christ in the U.S.A., and used by permission.

Some sections of this book have previously appeared
in different form as articles in *The Other Side*,
300 W. Apsley St., Philadelphia, PA 19144.
The author and publisher wish to thank
The Other Side for permission
to use this material.

For my mother
with thanks for what
she tried to teach me
about the love of learning
and the love of life

Contents

Preface

The skies of New York City were clear and bright on September 11, 2001, when it started raining human beings. So many lives were lost that day at the World Trade Center, at the Pentagon, in a field near Pittsburgh. But the scale of the tragedy must not obscure the reality that each life lost was of inestimable value, was irreplaceable — that each life lost was sacred because each was a gift from God. Including the lives of the terrorist hijackers? Yes, theirs, too.

In an instant, the phrase "the war on terrorism" entered everyday discourse with a new and urgent meaning. In this book I do not seek to exploit that urgency. Indeed, the title of this book was chosen and the first draft was completed almost a full year before the events of September 11. With the exception of these two paragraphs at the beginning and a postscript at the end, the manuscript has not been altered to cover these most recent exchanges of terror and counterterror. Therefore, it should be noted that in all places except the postscript, references to the attack on the World Trade Center refer to the 1993 bombing and not to the attack of September 11. It is my hope — but also my fear — that the perspectives expressed in this book have remained cogent following recent events.

*. * *

To no small degree, this book had its origins in a cruise missile attack launched by the United States on August 20, 1998, a military assault that is already fading in the memories of many Americans. Less than two weeks before, on August 7, the U.S. embassies in Nairobi, Kenya and Dar es Salaam, Tanzania had been destroyed by explosives in coordinated attacks. Of the 213 people killed in Kenya, the 11 people killed in Tanzania, and the hundreds injured in the combined attacks, most were bystanders, Africans who had no conceivable relationship to whatever grievances had motivated the assaults. Clearly, the destruction of the embassies was an act of "terrorism" — violent, sudden, and designed to instill fear.

On August 20, President Clinton announced the U.S. response, which was also violent, sudden, and designed to instill fear. Cruise missiles had been launched against "terrorist training camps" in Afghanistan and against the Al-Shifa pharmaceutical plant in Khartoum, Sudan, a plant the U.S. claimed was producing "precursors" to nerve gas. We do not know and will likely never know how many people were killed by the cruise missile attack on Afghanistan. In Khartoum, the attack took place when the pharmaceutical plant was unoccupied, so the only deaths resulting from that attack were the Sudanese who were deprived of the medical supplies that Al-Shifa did in fact produce. U.S. government officials were convinced that there were links between Al-Shifa and the Saudi militant, Osama bin Laden, but the United States has never provided convincing evidence that the plant was involved in producing "precursors" to nerve gas or any other weapons. As international reporters wandered through the rubble of the plant on the morning after the attack, angry Sudanese protesters were videotaped as they denounced the "American terrorists."

Were the Sudanese wrong to portray the United States as engaging in terrorism? How is it possible to portray Americans as "terrorists" when the U.S. is the primary underwriter of "the war against terrorism"? As the old adage has it, one person's terrorist is another person's freedom fighter. But if terrorists can assume the guise of freedom fighters, is it also possible that terrorism can assume the guise of a war against terrorism?

Questions only proliferate regarding the source and the very definition of "terrorism" when attention is turned from the cruise missile target in Sudan to the targets in Afghanistan. What were these "terrorist training camps" and how did they come to be located in Afghanistan? The camps were in Afghanistan because they had been established there with covert and overt U.S. assistance in the 1980s. The Afghan government was allied with the Soviet Union, and in order to overthrow that government and drive Soviet troops from Afghanistan, the CIA and agencies within the Pentagon recruited, trained, and subsidized teams of "freedom fighters" to mount an insurgency. Recruits were drawn from as far away as Algeria and Egypt, as well as from Pakistan and from within Afghanistan itself. The methods of the insurgents included guerrilla raids, attacks on civilian targets, and torture of captives, but the freedom fighters succeeded in driving out the Soviets. Flush with such success, the recruits for the war in Afghanistan discovered that there were battles to be fought elsewhere as well. Now that Soviet imperialism was on the run, perhaps U.S. imperialism could also be thwarted. Links have been traced between the "freedom fighters" of Af-

1993

ghanistan and "terrorist" attacks in Algeria, Egypt, the World Trade Center in New York City, the U.S. embassies in Kenya and Tanzania, and elsewhere, including among more recent attacks, the suicide bombing of the *USS Cole*. The cruise missiles that were launched against Afghanistan on August 20, 1998 were aimed with relative ease since the United States was attacking some of the very camps the U.S. had helped build and subsidize. Was this an aberration or are there other instances in which the United States and other powers are plagued by terrorists whom they themselves have helped create? Are "terrorists" ad hoc assortments of violent individuals and non-state organizations that are bent on generating fear through random, bloody attacks? Or does the phenomenon of terror have more to do with the calculations of the powerful, with the intentional sowing and inevitable reaping of whirlwinds whipped up by the powers that be? Indeed, if the term "terrorism" is to function as anything other than a propagandistic label, is it possible that terrorism can also come in the guise of the legally sanctioned violence of powerful nation states?

The questions raised above will be revisited throughout this book, but I must acknowledge that what initially set me to writing was not an academic interest in questions of foreign policy or history or ethics. I was (and am) interested in protesting violence — all violence, but especially that violence which the governing authorities of the United States inflict in my name by means of the resources I provide to those authorities. I am made complicit in such violence. Try as one might to "come out of Babylon," there is no avoiding such complicity; it is in the very air (spirit) that we breathe. Even a refusal of federal income taxes does not deny the governing authorities the taxes that are paid somewhere along the marketing line in every purchase we make, in all we consume. There can be no pretense to righteousness or lack of complicity. One can only confess — and protest.

But the types of protests that are possible have been circumscribed by governments that have become increasingly savvy at initiating military actions without any need for public accountability. Whatever happened to the "declaration of war"? For the U.S., the absence of any such constitutionally mandated declaration in the last 55 years might lead the naïve to believe that the United States has enjoyed a prolonged period of peace. In fact, since the end of World War II, the United States has been involved in dozens of wars and invasions and covert interventions as well as uncounted bombing runs and missile attacks. The longest of these military actions, the U.S. War in Vietnam, also evoked the most sustained protest. History has demonstrated that the War in Vietnam has not left U.S. military and political leaders more reluctant to engage in military intervention or more likely to renounce pretenses to policing the world. Rather, the lessons from Vietnam have been that those military actions least likely to provoke public protest are those that are quick — "mini-wars" played out in a matter of weeks, days, or even (as in the case of cruise missile attacks) minutes — and those in which U.S. casualties are few (Grenada, Panama, the Persian Gulf) or none (Kosovo, the surrogate Contra war in Nicaragua), even though a huge number of people of other nationalities may be killed (hundreds of thousands of Iraqis in the Persian Gulf War). An example of a military action unlikely to provoke protest is the cruise missile attack of August 20, 1998 — a "mini-war" that was over before we knew it had begun, with no American casualties. What is there to protest?

This book is a protest against the cruise missile attacks on Sudan and Afghanistan. It is a protest against the terrorist bombers of embassies as well as the mighty powers who are indistinguishable from terrorists when they bomb and burn people and buildings in retaliation for grievances real and imagined, with little sense of any moral, political, or legal accountability. It is a protest against the hypocrisy of nations that organize and subsidize "freedom fighters" to do their violent bidding but then call them "terrorists" when they attack targets that were not part of the original deal. But this book is also a protest against the next terrorist attack and against the devastation of human lives that will take place when the bomb is set off or the nerve gas is released by a guerrilla band which imagines that in so doing it is saving the world (or some corner of it) or that it is doing the will of God. And it is a protest against the next little or big war launched by the U.S. or some other nation, be it the quick military action that is over before objections can be raised, or some other type of war which, though never legally declared, is nonetheless tediously proclaimed to be the will of God or the salvation of the world.

Whether in the proclamations of freedom fighters, terrorists, presidents, or other lords and princes, the references to God are not entirely gratuitous. Though the human proclivity for violence has reached a feverish pitch, there is still an awareness that bloodshed is a sufficiently serious matter that it should not be precipitated without cause. What better cause than the will of God? With varying degrees of sincerity, world leaders on the eve of battle make a show of consulting with "spiritual advisors" and of invoking the name of God. It is a practice not lost on the organizations that have been labeled "terrorist," many of which (as we shall see) have incorporated God into the very names of their organizations. In nations in which the majority of believers are Christian, the church must bear the responsibility for the ease with which the name of God has been co-opted into the service of carnage. The preaching of many churches has lent greater credibility to an image of a God who intervenes in history through warfare rather than a God who intervenes in history through resurrection and the renunciation of death. As if God were somehow prone to mighty swings of mood, the terror of God has been segregated from the love of God, and the terror of God has been vested with greater credibility. Beware when humans view themselves as instruments of that terror.

While the claim of divine sanction for violence is among the crudest forms of blasphemy, this is not to suggest that questions of faith and questions of violence are unrelated. Decisions to engage in bloodshed may entail political, economic, social, or interpersonal crises, but above all, such decisions entail a spiritual malady. The physical killing is preceded by a death somewhere in the "soul." The choice of death rather than life is not a decision without spiritual consequence (Deuteronomy 30:15-20). The apostasy of violence lies in its denial of God's ability to accomplish anything without the trigger that is about to be pulled, without the missile that is about to be fired. Violence is inevitably a renunciation rather than an affirmation of the will and freedom of God.

And so a consideration of the terror that people inflict on one another necessarily entails a consideration of faith. Karl Barth once called upon believers to read Bible and newspaper side by side. An understanding of current events sheds new light on the hermeneutical context from which the reader approaches the biblical text, but more importantly, the juxtaposition of newspaper and Bible makes more readily apparent the manner in which the biblical word demythologizes our contemporary ideologies and social and political circumstances. A reading of Barth's *Church Dogmatics* reveals that Barth added a dialogue with church history into the mix of newspaper and Bible. The encounter with the biblical word is less individual than communal. It is within community — both the living communion of saints as well as the host of witnesses who have gone before us — that we come to understand our own idiosyncratic readings of Scripture and faith alongside other readings that have borne good fruit or not. Ideally, the dialogue with history illuminates those paths we need not travel again because they end not in the glory of God but the glory of war — the crusades, the jihad, the violent revolutions that strive (still again) to incarnate the reign of righteousness, the temporal battles of Armageddon that demonically pursue the eradication of all that is demonic. Ideally too, the dialogue with history also illuminates and beckons us onto the dangerous paths of discipleship that have been traveled by saints who have renounced all terrorism (whether legally sanctioned or not), saints whose only allegiance is to those who suffer — the poor, the rejected and abused, the disposable people, the crucified Christ.

The following chapters are arranged as a dialogue with newspaper, history, and Bible. The first section of each chapter engages the "newspaper," the current and recent events in the convoluted world of terror and counterterror. The second section of each chapter offers a relevant case study from church history.

In some chapters, the choice of historical events may seem obvious and predictable (such as the overview of the crusades as an example of ethical dualism in Chapter 3), while other choices may become sensible only as the story is told (such as the account in Chapter 4 of the hidden dangers of terror in the apocalypticism of the abolitionist movement). The third section of each chapter offers exegesis and/or theological reflection on biblical texts. Of course, in books as in life, it is neither easy nor particularly desirable to create compartments for study and reflection that are segmented one from another. In the following chapters, history enters into the consideration of current events and vice versa, and it is my hope that biblical reflection finds expression not only at the end of each chapter but throughout.

It seems arrogant in the extreme to set such a task for oneself, to study terror from the perspective of current events *and* history *and* biblical theology. We live in the age of experts, and I am not one. Indeed, our age of increasingly compartmentalized knowledge and study has given rise to a new discipline and a class of scholars known as "terrorism experts." I am not one of those either. But if we laypeople are deprived of the specialized knowledge and modes of thought that belong to the experts, perhaps we are also spared the prejudices of expertise. We bring different sets of prejudices. I have already acknowledged my own prejudice in favor of nonviolence, and while that acknowledgment deprives me of any claim to detached objectivity, I hope nonetheless that I have been fair in the manner in which I have utilized all of the references cited in this book.

Writers incur debts, and mine are not few. I am indebted to those teachers with whom I once visited frequently (in classroom or soup kitchen or jailhouse) but who are now visited mostly by raids of letters or newsletters, phone calls or only thoughts: Dale Aukerman, Dan and Phil Berrigan, Dale Brown, Joan Cavanaugh, Gene Clemens, Don Durnbaugh, Paul Grout, Bill Wylie Kellermann, Cliff and Arlene Kindy, Liz McAlister, Ed Plum, Ladon Sheats, and Scott Wright. It might also become apparent in this book that I am indebted to some teachers I have met only once — Bill Stringfellow — or never at all except in the witness of their writings and their lives — Will Campbell, Dorothy Day, Jacques Ellul. Of course, none of these teachers living or dead should be saddled with blame for my failings in this book or in life.

I am indebted to Michael R. Cinquanti, who offered constant encouragement for my writing. Even though (or perhaps because) his faith differs from my own, he persistently offers challenges and comments that are spurs to further reflection. For his insights, for his nonviolence, and for more, I am thankful.

I am indebted to coworkers and clients at the community mental health program where I work. As I was absent at odd times of two days here or three days there to complete my habitually tardy chapters, they were profoundly patient and good-humored.

I am indebted to Darlene Gee-Woodfin and Denise and Tom Kaufmann, who have persisted throughout my absence in the small and ragtag demonstration at the National Warplane Museum. Darlene, Denise, and Tom have demonstrated that it is vital to respond to the substantial needs of veterans, but it is a cheapening of the experience of those veterans whenever war is glorified. Museums that claim to recollect history have a responsibility to show not only the marvels of bombers and jet fighters in flight, but also the bloodied victims who are left in their wake. It is an assault on the biblical text when military air shows are called "the wings of eagles" (Isaiah 40:31). For their presence at the air shows, and for their presence at Southport Prison when it was slated to become New York's death house, and for their presence when the governor came to town, and for their presence when the bombs rained down on Belgrade, I am thankful for Mary Skinner, Pat Breux, Darlene, Denise, Michael, Tom, and others in this motley crew who keep faith by not keeping silence.

And I am indebted to those old friends (Warren Drabek, Matt Barlow) and new (Bryan Horch) who do not write me off when I become a hermit with the feeble excuse that "I am writing."

As he was commenting favorably on the work of Christoph Blumhardt, Karl Barth once wrote, ". . . our cause, our hope is at the moment served better with prayers than with treatises." The comment reminds me of other debts I have incurred. I must ask forgiveness for putting into my work too much of treatise and too little of prayer. There are always and forever too few prayers.

CHAPTER I

The Meaning of Terror

Does not the ear test words as the palate tastes food?

JOB 12:11

The Ideology in a Definition

It is to our benefit that Job did not suffer in silence, nor was the "patience of Job" all that it was cracked up to be. He protests and argues about why God should have permitted or even decreed his fall from considerable social and economic height. More than any other figure in the Hebrew Bible, Job identifies God as the source of "terrors" (Job 6:4). Job finds scant solace from his friends who persist in reminding him that it is usually the wicked who have terror nipping at their heels (18:11). Job seeks escape in sleep but then, Job says to God, "you scare me with dreams and terrify me with visions . . ." (7:14).

It is this very image of God as the source of terrors which is at issue in the book of Job. Like Job, the book itself is struggling and arguing. It is a struggle for a new model of God,[1] and while the argument is left unfinished, there are glimpses of a God who is not terrifying. It is the God who delighted "when the morning stars sang together and all the heavenly beings shouted for joy" (38:7). Job the patriarch is accustomed to a certain understanding of how justice ought to work.[2] Job the patriarch is familiar with the legal codes by which rewards and punishments are meted out, but God is not a patriarch.[3] If Job sees a God of terror (the book of Job seems to be saying to Job the man), then he has not seen deeply enough or far enough or long enough, for this is a God of snows and

1

constellations, of mountain goats and lions, of ostriches and bear cubs, of fish and lotuses (Job 38-41).

But the theme of God as the source of terror is a persistent one. The image of God as cosmic patriarch who inflicts or at least permits atrocity is revealed in such anguishing questions as "Why would God allow that child to die?" Why indeed? We need to argue with such a God and with such an image of God. It is the argument of the patriarch Abraham against the patriarchal God (Genesis 18:22-33). It is the argument with God of the Jewish people both before and since the Holocaust.[4] Why would God allow this to happen? From differing perspectives, many have sought to struggle with this question of theodicy and with this God who seems too silent.[5] With whom do we struggle? The God of love (1 John 4:16) or the God of terrors (Job 6:4) or somehow both?

No matter how one evaluates Job's estimation of the source of the terror he experiences, his description of the terror itself is lucid and arresting. Does it not give pause to read Job's lament over being scared "with dreams" and terrified "with visions" (7:14)? We are not accustomed to hearing about the dreams of saints and prophets being invaded by terror. Instead, prophets dream of righteous faith and reconciled communities. Prophets have visions of the geography of justice, as when "every valley shall be exalted, every hill and mountain shall be made low, the rough places shall be made plain, and the crooked places shall be made straight and the glory of the Lord will be revealed and all flesh shall see it together."[6]

Yet, Job reminds us, not all dreams and visions are benign. There are also dreams and visions of terror. Indeed, the perpetrators of some of the greatest terrors in history have never lacked dreams and visions. These visions have filled the killing fields of Kampuchea and the ovens of Auschwitz. These dreams have launched ships that brought death to the native people of North America, ships that brought slaves out of Africa. These are the visions and dreams of terrorism.

Today, to see a geography shaped by the dreams and visions of terrorism, we might look to Lebanon. Few areas of the planet are free from terror or the threat of terror, but in recent history, it is the tortured land of Lebanon that has played unwilling host to the greatest number of opposing groups who have been labeled "terrorist." In a manner that seems a mockery of spirituality, these groups have also been labeled "Muslim" and "Jewish" and "Christian." What's in a name? In the names of the militia groups and the bands of guerrillas that have roamed Lebanon past and present, there is little cognizance of the human suffering that has been inflicted. Rather, the names of these groups speak of exalted dreams. There is Hope (*Amal,* "Hope") and Faith (*Al Dawa,* "Call to Faith" and *Hezbollah,* "Party of God"). There is Liberation — poor Lebanon has been visited by so much Liberation (among others, the Arab Liberation Front, the Democratic Front for the Liberation of Palestine, and from time to time, the Palestine Liberation Organization). And there is even Salvation (the National Salvation Front).

All of the aforementioned groups have been called "terrorist" organizations, but this too is a name that gives pause, a name that may conceal more than it reveals. Who are "terrorists"? How are they to be identified? Is terrorism that which is perpetrated by non-state or subnational groups in contrast to the legally sanctioned violence of the nation state?

In fact, most of the groups that have precipitated terror in Lebanon are pervaded by the veiled (at times, very thinly veiled) influence of various nation states. Amal, for example, was initially founded by Iranian Imam Musa Sadr, but close ties between Amal and Syria developed after the Libyan government was implicated in the disappearance of Musa Sadr and the support of Iran shifted to Hezbollah. Due to conflicts with Palestinian guerrillas operating in the south of Lebanon, Amal did not oppose the Israeli invasion of 1982.

The Phalange militia provides another example of a Lebanese group with strong ties to a number of governments.[7] Founded in the 1930s in imitation of Fascist, paramilitary Phalangists in Spain and Italy, the Lebanese Phalangist Party sought to preserve the dominant position of Maronite Christians in Lebanon. When segments of the Palestine Liberation Organization moved to Lebanon following their expulsion from Jordan in 1970, the United States and Israel supported the Phalange militia in an effort to oppose the PLO. When their position was threatened in a 1975 civil war, the Phalangists invited intervention by Syria, which occurred on June 1, 1976. In an effort to maintain their own dominance, the Syrians did not confine their support to the Phalange. On some occasions, the Syrian military also supported the Druze militia who were opponents of the Phalange. The Phalange militia welcomed the 1982 Israeli invasion of southern Lebanon during which an estimated 20,000 people were killed. As many as two thousand of those people were killed at the Sabra and Shatila refugee camps where Phalangists conducted a two-day massacre in reprisal for the murder of their leader, Bashir Gemayel.

In these brief sketches of only two of the groups that have brought terror to Lebanon, note the direct and indirect involvement of Iran, Iraq, Israel, Jordan, Libya, Syria, and the United States. Some speak of "state-sponsored terrorists" as if the word "sponsored" somehow insulated the states from being terrorists themselves. Some have also spoken of Lebanon as being in a condition of "sheer anarchy." It is not true. The Lebanese people have not suffered an absence of power but the presence of an obscene quantity of power — too many guns and bombs, too many groups offering violent visions of faith and hope and salva-

3

tion, too many nation states bringing too many weapons and invasions and cynical manipulations of the mini-saviors they "sponsor." This is not anarchy. It is a vulgar overabundance of raw power.

Still, mention of the nation state evokes a sense of solidity, legality, and order, whereas mention of "terrorists" evokes images that are the antithesis of civilization. Is it this, perhaps, which distinguishes the violence of the state from mere terrorism? Perhaps terrorists do not fight fairly, striking out as they do at noncombatant targets with unconventional weapons secreted away in the trunks of cars and on the bodies of suicidal zealots. Perhaps, unlike the ordered responses of the state, terror strikes at random.

After her release by hijackers in Beirut, Lebanon, Judy Brown of Delmar, New Jersey said, "They kept yelling about New Jersey. I was afraid to tell them where I was from. Why were they so mad at New Jersey?"[8] It was not the state of New Jersey that had provoked the anger of the hijackers, but the U.S. battleship *New Jersey,* which was anchored off the coast of Lebanon hurling bombs the size of cars into the Muslim sections of Beirut. This bombing was in turn a response to the killing of 241 U.S. Marines in a 1983 "Islamic Jihad" suicide truck bombing of the temporary Marine barracks at the Beirut Airport. This series of events illustrates the difficulty faced by those who would seek to classify "terrorism" as a distinguishable and uniquely abhorrent category of violence. First, the randomness of the violence is called into question, at least by the perpetrators. The hijacking was in response to the *New Jersey* shelling, which was in response to the truck bombing, which was in response to attacks by U.S. Marines, which were in response to. . . . Trust me, the provocations (real and imagined) can be traced into the mists of Lebanese history. Were it not for the deadly consequences, the best analogy for these wranglings back and forth would be to a childhood spat over "who started it." Given the deadly consequences, the apt analogy is that drawn by Dom Helder Camara — the downward spiral, the "spiral of violence" in which each atrocity flows from the one that precedes it.[9]

If "terrorist" actions are not distinguishable by some supposed randomness, what of the claim that terrorists target noncombatants? On this point too, the events in Lebanon provide no reassurance. American and European media freely applied the term "terrorism" to the truck bombing of the U.S. Marine barracks on October 23, 1983 and the bombing on the same day of the French military headquarters in Beirut. Regarding the 241 Marines and the 56 French soldiers who were killed, it must be emphasized that their lives were sacred and the suffering of their survivors is incalculable. Ultimately, the effort to differentiate between combatants and noncombatants entails the crude suggestion that, in times of war, some lives are more expendable than others. By international agreement, in times of conflict, some human beings are "fair game" in ways that others are not. It is the cynical compromise of those who would seek to outlaw "war crimes" without outlawing the crime of war itself. Nonetheless, according to these differentiations between combatants and noncombatants, the U.S. Marines and the French soldiers were clearly the former. Meanwhile, the shelling of Muslim neighborhoods by the *New Jersey* did not differentiate between soldiers and civilians. While there were doubtless members of militia groups residing in these neighborhoods, the bombs could not set them apart from the children or the grandparents or the other women and men who were clearly noncombatants. If the defining feature of terrorism is the civilian identity of those who are targeted, then the "terrorists" in Beirut were not those who bombed military barracks but those who lobbed car-sized bombs into city neighborhoods.

But, some might object, while shelling from a battleship is certainly deadly, it is a conventional form of military engagement. Perhaps terrorism can be distinguished from other forms of military action by its reliance on exotic weapons and tactics which leave us all vulnerable — truck bombings, kidnappings, hijackings. This protest against unconventional forms of violence has a long history among imperial powers. It was one of the complaints the British lodged against the rebels in their North American colonies. While the British fought in a "civilized" manner, marching in line and firing on command, the insurgents utilized guerrilla tactics. In effect, the rebels refused to stand and fight. Unconventional tactics were also applied against Tory sympathizers. Some were tarred and feathered, some were lynched, and others were slaughtered in raids.[10] It is why to this day a monument still stands by the harbor in Saint John, New Brunswick, dedicated to those who fled terror and tyranny, i.e., those 18th-century refugees who fled the United States and sought freedom in Canada.

The question still looms: What distinguishes terrorism from other forms of violence? In Lebanon, the land of terror, we are brought no closer to an answer. There is only the downward spiral of violence inflicted with a plethora of weaponry (standard or not matters little to the victims) on combatants and noncombatants alike by a welter of nation states and militias and freedom fighters and liberation fronts. And there are the dreams of death, the glorious visions of death inflicted or suffered in a holy cause.

Robin Morgan, founder of the Sisterhood is Global Institute, went to Lebanon in 1986. While there, she met a woman named Ghanima who was the mother of fifteen children. Eight of her children were gone, either disappeared or killed. Two of her sons had died as members of this or that faction of the Palestinian cause; Ghanima did not know which groups they fought for or against. As Robin Morgan spoke with her, a Palestinian man approached to pay his respects to this "Mother of Martyrs," but an angry Ghanima would have none of it. She whirled around and yelled at him, "To what have you given birth? Who have you nursed at your breast? In God's name, I swear I will give you no more martyrs! *I am done with being a mother of martyrs!*"[11]

O Brother Job, the terrors are with us still. The raiders still come and the firepower falls from the sky; the winds still rage and the edge of the sword is bloody (Job 1:13-19). While some suffer these horrors, others try to sleep. Are these terrifying dreams by which the sleep is invaded a warning from God (Job 33:14-18)?[12] While the source of the dreams is unclear, in Lebanon, the violence can be traced to its sources. When we follow the trail and trace the violence back, we do not find God. We find a mad confluence of godlets. We find principalities and powers, imperial nation states and barely organized guerrilla fronts, all self-exalted, all petty, and all appealing to as much inhumanity as humans can muster. It is called *liberation* and *martyrdom*. It is called *defense* and *justice*. Call it what you will. It is terrorism.

*　　　*　　　*

Terror is not a rational phenomenon. It possesses people, body, mind, and spirit. In the extreme, it even disables the so-called "fight or flight" response and leaves people "paralyzed by fear." While the fear of death may seem like a nearly universal experience, it comes in phobic guises that seem trivial except to those who suffer these fears of spiders, of heights, of the dark, of lightning. An entire dissertation on the small chance of being hit by lightning is of little comfort to one who genuinely has the fear. Terror is not a rational phenomenon and, like the unclean spirit that possessed the Gerasene demoniac (Mark 5:9; Luke 8:30), the sources of human terror are legion.

Unlike terror itself, terror*ism* entails an element of calculation, an effort to generate and harness the irrational whirlwind of human fear. Terror*ism* is the intentional effort to generate fear through violence or the threat of violence and the further effort to harness these fears in pursuit of some goal. Given the prevalence of violence on our planet, the question immediately arises: Which perpetrators of violence in pursuit of which goals? To cite only the goal-oriented threat of violence is to cast a very large net indeed. Governments generate fear and threaten violence (both judicially and militarily) with the intended goal of maintaining political and economic systems. Some men perpetrate or threaten violence in relationships with the goal of maintaining dominance. Planetary ecosystems are under violent assault from corporate interests intent on maintaining profit margins, and if the prophets are believed (e.g., Habakkuk 2:17; 3:10), the earth itself experiences terror and violence. The list could be endless. Which perpetrators of violence with which goals merit the label "terrorist"?

Whatever other usefulness it may have, the concept of "terrorism" has given birth to a veritable industry.[13] A portion of this industry sells hardware (bulletproof vehicles, alarms, detection devices, and other gadgets) to corporate executives, governmental officials, and other wealthy clients who may fear kidnapping or worse, but the bulk of this industry is comprised of experts who are consulted for evaluations of terrorist threats and prognostications of future directions in the world of terrorism. The identity of these experts is revealing. In one survey of the sixteen terrorism experts most frequently consulted by the U.S. media, Edward Herman found that eleven had affiliation with the federal government (CIA, Pentagon, or State Department).[14] It is hardly surprising that the groups identified as "terrorist" by such experts are overwhelmingly those groups that oppose U.S. foreign policy. If there is mention of "state sponsorship of terrorism," the references are to Castro's Cuba or Hussein's Iraq or Qaddafi's Libya. Regarding Botha in South Africa, Pinochet in Chile, Roberto D'Aubuisson in El Salvador, or Rios Montt in Guatemala, records of horrendous violence have been either ignored or categorized as "counterterrorism."[15] What are the criteria by which nations, groups, or individuals are included or excluded under such categorizations?

To be fair, it should be noted that there are fields of study besides "terrorism" in which experts fail to agree on a shared definition of precisely what it is on which they are experts. Nonetheless, the lack of definitional agreement among terrorism experts is pronounced. One survey of 109 definitions of "terrorism" found that 22 different elements were cited in these definitions, but only three of the elements were cited by a majority.[16] The three elements appearing in the majority of the definitions by the experts were as follows: (1) terrorism entails the use of violence or force, (2) the violence is utilized in pursuit of political goals, and (3) the violence is intended to generate fear. Yet, these apparently simple elements of a definition are not without contention.

To assert that terrorism is the use of violence for political goals is to ignore the religious motivation that has been claimed by a substantial number of violent groups, past and present. Admittedly, in the annals of violence, religious and political motivations freely mix. Bruce Hoffman, director of the Center for the Study of Terrorism and Political Violence and author of *Inside Terrorism*, asserts that terrorism is "ineluctably political in aims and motives,"[17] but he nonetheless includes a chapter on "Religion and Terrorism" in his book. As historical examples of terrorism, Hoffman and others cite the Zealots and the Sacarii of first-century Judea.[18] The Sacarii were named for the type of daggers they used in attacking (often in broad daylight) Jewish religious officials who were allied with the Romans. Another religious group cited in the history of terrorism is the 11th- and 12th-century Islamic Fedayeen ("self-sacrificers") of the Shi'a Ismaili sect. The ferocity with which the Fedayeen opposed both Christian crusaders and Sunni rulers of the Abbasid dynasty contributed to false reports that the Fedayeen were "Hashshishin," i.e., acting under the influence of hashish; it is the birth of the word "assassin."[19] The word "Thug" derives from another religious group, an Indian sect of devotees to Kali, the Hindu goddess of creation and destruction, death and rebirth. Over a span of centuries, on days that were set aside for the worship of Kali, Thugs would lie in wait and murder random travelers as human sacrifices to the goddess.[20]

And so, while a majority of experts assert that political motives are integral to the very definition of terrorism, suspect religious groups are sufficiently plentiful that another expert argues that, prior to the 19th century, religion served as the *only* justification for terrorism.[21] Such marked disagreements on fundamental issues of definition have elicited a number of concessions from terrorism experts. Brian Jenkins admits that what constitutes terrorism "seems to depend on one's point of view," and Bruce Hoffman of the Center for the Study of Terrorism and Political Violence admits that the terrorist label is "unavoidably subjective."[22] It is quite possible that Walter Laqueur, chairman of the International Research Council of the Center for Strategic and International Studies, has written and published more on the subject of terrorism than any of the other experts. Yet, Laqueur frankly concedes the impossibility of arriving at a definition and even questions the value of the effort.[23] Laqueur once said, "Terrorism is like pornography. No one can really define it, but everyone recognizes it when they see it."[24]

Perhaps Walter Laqueur is correct. Although he may not have intended his observation to imply that the victims of violence should do the defining, what better experts are there? They recognize it when they see it. Both the U.S. Marines subjected to the truck bombing in Beirut and the Lebanese citizens subjected to U.S. shelling — they knew terrorism when they saw it. The women who are subjected to rape and abuse, the African Americans who are subjected to racist attack, the gay men and lesbians who are beaten in homophobic rage — they all know terrorism when they see it. Hutus and Tutsis, Palestinians and Israelis, Iraqis and Kuwaitis, Serbs and Croats — they all see it and they know. No matter the identity of the perpetrators or the class of the weaponry or the nature of the motivation, it is terrorism.

*   *   *

One of the few matters on which most terrorism experts agree is that the contemporary prominence of the term "terrorism" can be traced to the French Revolution.[25] It is an interesting agreement. While the modern attribution of "terror" is frequently in reference to the activities of guerrillas and subnational militia groups who lack the governmental apparatus of the state, the 18th-century Terror in France was the product of an efficient and bureaucratic state. While modern charges of terrorism are lodged against groups that supposedly strike at random with weapons that are crude and imprecise, the Terror in France was very calculating in its choice of human targets and the victims were dispatched by means of a new weapon of high sophistication and total precision — the guillotine. Today, to be called a "terrorist" is to be maligned, but the Terror in France was associated with progress, virtue, and order.

In his classic study, *The Anatomy of Revolution,* Crane Brinton surveyed the French, American, English, and Russian revolutions and found they all contained periods of varying length and severity that might fairly be characterized as "Reigns of Terror." These are periods of revolutionary paranoia in which all citizens must prove that they are not allied with the old regime or with counterrevolutionaries. It is a time when, as Brinton notes, "Political indifference, that mainstay of the modern state, becomes impossible. . . ."[26] Ironically, the Terror comes only *after* the revolution has already *become* the state. Armed with the newly acquired machinery of the state and imbued with "the habit of violence"[27] instilled by the revolutionary struggle itself, the revolution-turned-state seeks to consolidate its position of power. Those who were so recently subversive become attuned to seeking out subversives.[28] As noted by Jacques Ellul, it is the paradoxical end result that "revolt and revolution, which strike at the state, serve to fortify it."[29]

While there were similar periods following the American, English, Russian, and other revolutions, the Terror in France plays a more prominent role in the history of terrorism due in part to the candor with which some Jacobins wore the label *"Terroriste."* Among them was Robespierre, a man who, prior to his ascension to power, held no small number of viewpoints that were progressive and humane. He spoke in favor of justice for the poor, emancipation of slaves, and an end to persecution of Jews. He also favored (considerable irony here) abolition of the death penalty.[30] Even after his 1793 assumption of leadership of the primary organ of Terror, the Committee of Public Safety, Robespierre retained his commitment to "virtue," a commitment he shared with the numerous other revolutionary leaders marked by an "unmistakably puritanical or ascetic" streak.[31] If sacrifice is required for personal virtue, then how much more sacrifice is required for national virtue. If the price of freedom is paid with blood, then blood is the food by which freedom will be sustained.[32] With the zeal of the newly converted, Robespierre put aside his earlier opposition to the death penalty in favor of a new understanding of justice that was swift as the guillotine:

If virtue is the mainstay of a democratic government in time of peace, then in time of revolution a democratic government must rely on *virtue* and *terror*. . . . Terror is nothing but justice, swift, severe and inflexible; it is an emanation of virtue. . . . It has been said that terror is the mainstay of a despotic government. . . . The government of the revolution is the despotism of liberty against tyranny.[33]

In defending the actions of the Revolutionary Tribunal, Georges Jacques Danton suggested that the Terror was charitable in that it spared ordinary citizens the trouble of having to deal with counterrevolutionaries: "Let us be terrible so that the people will not have to be."[34] Later, Danton would discover that even his own revolutionary credentials were not beyond suspicion; he was among the thousands who were sent to the guillotine.[35]

The concentration of state power during the Terror was more extreme than anything the monarchy ever managed. The power of the departments of France was curtailed, agents from the Committee of Public Safety were dispatched throughout the country, and all federalists were identified as enemies of the Revolution.[36] The "Equality" that had been touted by the revolutionaries was finally achieved in the identity of those who were executed. The condemned included not only those of nobility and wealth, but also common working people who were denounced by grudging neighbors, and poor people who were charged with depraving public virtue. But the scaffold was not a mere "Fraternity," for even though the Revolution had not brought basic political rights to women, it brought many women to the guillotine; these included not only prominent women like Marie Antoinette, but also poor, rural women who were charged with providing sanctuary for suspects. In one of his final letters before he was executed, a health officer named Dufresne wrote that ". . . France is nothing but a giant scaffold in which the strong kill off the weak in the name of the Law. . . . Our plight is such that I dare to believe that we have fallen to the level of America."[37] The Terror did not end with Robespierre; it merely took on a Thermidorian guise, for within a few days of the fall of Robespierre, over a hundred of his associates were executed.[38]

When there was a pause in the bloodshed, the shedding of ink continued apace as political theorists debated the source and blame for the Terror in France. In the context of this debate, it was Edmund Burke who first popularized the use of the word "terrorist" in English. He characterized the French revolutionaries as "Thousands of those Hell hounds called Terrorists . . . let loose on the people."[39] Significantly, what Burke criticized about the terrorists in France did not focus on their violence, for as Burke himself argued in *A Vindication of Natural Society*, "All empires have been cemented in blood." Nor was

10

he particularly critical of the extreme centralization of state power under the terrorists of France, for Burke himself was a supporter of the monarchy in his native Britain and he viewed the state as having been established by God for nothing less than the moral perfection of humanity. Like the revolutionaries in France, Burke emphasized "virtue," but he theorized that it was only to be realized through a process of moderate reform that respected traditions and social order. Virtue had little to do with revolutions and nothing to do with egalitarianism, which Burke described as a crime.[40] It was this which qualified the terrorists of France as hell hounds: their lack of moderation, their ripping away of traditions, their crass egalitarianism. Scratch an ideologue, wrote Burke, and you find a terrorist.[41] He believed that the division of society into social classes ranging from the aristocracy to the poor was a "natural" phenomenon. While extolling the virtue of social order, he apparently paid little heed to the social disorder of abject poverty. Regarding starvation during one period of economic hardship in England, Burke noted that only a few of the poor had died, far less than the number that might have died during similar economic troubles in previous generations.[42] Of course, this arithmetical view of starvation could only be offered by one who was not among the poor.

Burke had his critics. An entirely different view of the state and revolution was offered by Thomas Paine in *Rights of Man,* a tract that was written in no small degree as a response to Burke. Against the priority that Burke assigned to the social order as bequeathed by tradition, Paine asserted "the rights of the living" as opposed to "the authority of the dead." The ire of critics less civil than Paine was provoked when Burke deigned to contrast good social order with "the swinish multitude." A whole host of popular pamphlets circulated under names like "Hog's Wash," "Brother Grunter," and "Porculus." One titled *Address to the Hon. Edmund Burke from the Swinish Multitude* (1793) observed that there's more than one type of pig: "Whilst ye are . . . gorging yourselves at troughs filled with the daintiest wash; we, with our numerous train of *porkers,* are employed, from the rising to the setting sun, to obtain the means of subsistence, by . . . picking up a few acorns."[43] If one chooses to attack "the multitude," there should be little surprise when the response is voluminously negative.

What was more surprising was that Burke's characterization of terrorists stuck. Since Burke believed that the state had been instituted by God to serve the moral regeneration of humanity, then the state itself was not involved in terrorism, even though his attack was upon French terrorists who had managed to concentrate political, military, economic, and juridical power in a highly centralized state. Burke associated terrorism with disorder, even though his attack was upon French terrorists who used the guillotine to enforce a very rigid understanding of public order and virtue. In short, while Burke lifted the words "terror" and "terrorist" from the French milieu, the definitions he attached to those words were not descriptive of the Reign of Terror in France; they were instead descriptive of any who acted in opposition to the high value Burke placed on the state and on tradition.

Written in 1790 before the reign of Robespierre, Burke's *Reflections on the Revolution in France* was already highly critical of events across the Channel. *Reflections* was also reflective of Burke's reverence for the state: "We have consecrated the state, that no man should approach to look into its defects or corruptions but with due caution, that he should never dream of beginning its reformation by its subversion; that he should approach to the faults of the state as to the wounds of a father, with pious awe and trembling solicitude."

Even though the Terror in France was state terror, it was Edmund Burke who bequeathed us the definition of "terrorists" as those who are lacking sufficient awe for Father State. Terrorists see the wounds of the state and, rather than exercising caution, they practice subversion. Terrorists approach the state without piety or trembling. Such were the claims of Edmund Burke. Preoccupied as he was with the dangers posed by impious subversives and swinish multitudes, Burke paid scant attention to the possible dangers posed by a wounded state.

Burke's characterization of "terrorists" as anti-state subversives gained prominence and it functioned as propaganda, with the label of "terror" being hung on all manner of groups who were actively opposed to the established political or economic order. Independent of any particular level of violence or even in the absence of any violence at all, dangerous ideas could qualify one as a terrorist — and much more so if the ideas found expression in action. The earliest Luddites, for example, employed no violence against people. Faced with the threat to their livelihood posed by the approach of industrial capitalism, a group of Nottingham weavers broke into a building on November 4, 1811 and destroyed lace-making machines and frames. When they attempted to repeat the action a week later, the owner of the business was waiting along with several armed guards, and a Luddite named John Wesley was shot and killed. The magistrates of Nottingham quickly denounced this "terror," by which they meant not the murder of John Wesley but the smashing of machines.[44] Parliament responded to the terror with uncharacteristic speed. On March 5, 1812, the death penalty was approved as the punishment for the breaking of machines.

Also smeared with charges of terrorism were the Lazzarettiani of 19th-century Italy. While this group was clearly opposed to the state, the Italian monarchy, and oppressive taxation, it was equally clear to all but those in power that the group was not involved in violent sedition. Their leader, Davide

Lazzaretti, was a millenarian who founded egalitarian communities and espoused doctrines reminiscent of those of Joachim de Fiore. He advocated tax resistance and also "peace and compassion." Lazzaretti came to be viewed by his followers (and he came to view himself) as a messiah who would usher in "The Republic of God." On August 18, 1878, as Lazzaretti descended from Monte Amiata with 3,000 hymn-singing followers, the Italian *carabinieri* met them and opened fire. Lazzaretti was among the dead. Other leading Lazzarettiani were rounded up and charged with planning violent revolution and plotting attacks upon the rich, but in fact they had done no such thing. As E. J. Hobsbawm observed, while millenarians may be opposed to the state, they are not schooled in revolutionary techniques of gathering weaponry and setting up barricades. In fact, they "are not makers of revolution. They expect it to make itself, by divine revelation, by an announcement from on high, by a miracle. . . ."[45]

If the magistrates and other rulers of 19th-century Italy seemed paranoid, it may have been in part a reaction to the increasing activism of anarchists. Michael Bakunin spent considerable time preaching anarchism in Italy, and prominent Italian anarchists included Carlo Cafiero, Andrea Costa, Errico Malatesta, and Carlo Pisacane. It is Pisacane who is credited with having devised the phrase "propaganda by the deed."[46] It was Pisacane's contention that the propaganda value of carrying out revolutionary acts was far superior to the propaganda value of merely speaking or writing. In Pisacane's view, the lack of mass support for revolution should not be used as an argument for passivity. Propaganda by the deed would serve to build revolutionary fervor to the point of combustion. Partly inspired by the theories of Pisacane, Italian anarchists plotted several insurrections in the 1870s but all were so ineffective that the anarchists were treated leniently when they were arrested and tried.[47] More repressive measures were utilized against the anarchists of Italy after an assassination attempt against King Umberto I in 1878. Links between the assailant and anarchist groups were never proven, but during the four decades that followed, there was an international wave of assassinations and attempted assassinations by both anarchists and those who claimed anarchist affiliation. Left dead were Tsar Alexander II, Archduke Ferdinand, President Sadi Carnot of France, President William McKinley of the United States, Empress Elisabeth of Austria, a prime minister of Spain, another king of Italy. The list of attempted assassinations is longer still.

Reading the sordid record of violence, it is difficult to believe that there could be such creatures as nonviolent anarchists, but such there were and are. Some anarchists oppose state power precisely because of the violence the state perpetrates. Noteworthy figures in the history of nonviolent anarchism include

William Lloyd Garrison and Dorothy Day in the United States, Leo Tolstoy in Russia, Mohandas Gandhi in India, and Gustav Landauer in Bavaria.[48]

But it was those anarchists who advocated and practiced violent "propaganda by the deed" who captured the attention of the public and of the historians of terrorism. It was as if this group was ready-made to fit Burke's criteria of the terrorists who scheme subversion of wounded Father State. If the French Revolution marked the popularization of the term "terrorism," then the application of the term to anarchism marked the second of what historians of terrorism call "several interpretive phases."[49] Some violent practitioners of "propaganda by the deed" doubtless would have felt complimented by Walter Laqueur's exaggerated sense of anarchism as the "high tide of terrorism in Western Europe."[50]

Arguably, Michael Bakunin was the leading anarchist figure of 19th-century Europe. Unlike others prominent in the history of anarchism (e.g., Godwin, Proudhon, Kropotkin), Bakunin always seemed to have a clearer sense of what it was he wished to destroy than of that which he wished to build. He opposed Marxism and bourgeois capitalism alike.[51] He wished to smash the state and, since he viewed God as the transcendent power behind the state, he willed the destruction of God as well. Reversing Voltaire's saying that, if God did not exist, it would be necessary to invent him, Bakunin introduced his book, *God and the State*, with the words, "If God really existed, it would be necessary to abolish him."[52]

In 1842, Bakunin wrote, "The urge to destroy is also a creative urge."[53] One period of Bakunin's life in which he expressed far more of the destructiveness than of the creativity was during his 1869 association with the Russian fanatic, Sergei Nechaev. The probable author of both *Principles of Revolution* and *Catechism of a Revolutionary*, Nechaev ends up advocating little more than nihilism. "Our business is destruction," he wrote, "terrible, complete, universal, and merciless."[54] No wonder that Bakunin soon repudiated Nechaev. No wonder too that, in a recent foreword to the *Catechism*, Nicholas Walter described it as a "revolting rather than revolutionary document."[55]

Groups are ordinarily as anxious to repudiate the label of "terrorist" as their opponents are to smear them with it. Such was not the case, however, with anarchist participants in a Russian group called *Narodnaya Volya*, or People's Will. If not well-loved, the group is well-cited by historians of terrorism. Organized in 1879, People's Will vowed to oppose the authority of the state with "the means of William Tell." The group was responsible for a series of explosions and for the March 1, 1881 assassination of Tsar Alexander II. One member of the People's Will Executive Committee, a wealthy landowner named Gerasim Romanenko, advocated "terroristic revolution" in a book with the remarkably candid title, *Terrorism and Routine.* In an almost Burkean contempt for the multitudes, Romanenko described the "masses" as undisciplined. With a bow to the theories of Auguste Blanqui in France, Romanenko asserted the need for elite, intellectual leadership so that the revolutionary movement would not become mired in everyday routine. Nicholas Morozov, another member of the People's Will Executive Committee, was also quite open in his advocacy of terrorism. Lacking Robespierre's tribunals, revolutionaries could utilize terrorist attacks as a "ministry of justice of the revolution." New recruits would be more fully committed by engaging in terrorist acts that involved murder and the risk of death. It is terrorism, wrote Morozov, which separates those who passionately love the revolution from the "purely Platonic" rhetoric of liberals.[56] Such love of violence often leads to nihilism, sometimes under the guise of apocalypse. It is therefore not surprising that a 1907 book by Morozov was titled *Revelation in Thunder and Storm: The Birth of Apocalypse.* One author notes similarity to the 1918 poem by Alexander Blok, "The Twelve," in which the concluding image is that of a revolutionary Christ leading apostles replete with weaponry into St. Petersburg.[57]

The People's Will barely survived the government repression that followed the assassination of Alexander II, but it saw a brief revival in 1886 in the form of a group organized by Lenin's older brother, Alexander Ulyanov. The group was called the Terrorist Fraction of the People's Will and, apart from flirtations with the linguistics of "terror" in revolutionary France, this was likely the first group anywhere to designate its own members as "terrorists."[58] The Terrorist Fraction was short-lived, its main claim to fame being an unsuccessful attempt on the life of Alexander III. A host of Russian conspiratorial groups followed, all utilizing similar tactics of violence. By 1905, the noted anarchist Peter Kropotkin was repeatedly denouncing such groups and such tactics. No pacifist he, the early Kropotkin had endorsed the use of "dagger, gun, and dynamite" in the service of propaganda by the deed.[59] But he came to believe that such tactics were counterproductive, serving merely to spread human misery and to create the impression that anarchists were merely engaged in terrorism. Such an impression was in fact created for many historians of terrorism.

With the waning of the anarchist movement of the late 19th and early 20th centuries, the next major "phase of terrorism" is identified with the anti-colonial and ethno-nationalist movements of the middle and late 20th century. One might think that this skips rather blithely over the horrors of Nazi, Fascist, and Stalinist regimes, but it must be recalled that in the definitions of many terrorism experts, Father State is exempted from the "terrorist" label. This is not to suggest that the experts are insensitive to the horrors that governments perpetrate, but due to the perception of terrorism as a non-state phenomenon, Walter Laqueur writes in *Terrorism* more about "Nazi terrorism" before Hitler became Chancellor and about Nazi "counterterrorism" than he does about the Holocaust, which presumably, as a horror perpetrated by the state, would not qualify as "terrorism."[60] It must be emphasized that Laqueur later wrote a sensitive and perceptive book on the Holocaust, which adds to the impression that its relative exclusion from his earlier book was due only to the fact that the Holocaust did not fall under the rubric of "terrorism."[61] Acknowledging the "Great Terror" of Stalin and the horrors of Nazi and Fascist rule, Bruce Hoffman cuts the definitional distinctions finely. If a government utilizes political violence against people of another country, it is warfare; a government utilizing political violence against its own citizens, writes Hoffman, is "generally termed 'terror' in order to distinguish that phenomenon from 'terrorism', which is understood to be violence committed by non-state entities."[62] Of course, when it comes to owning the labels that are applied to them, not all individuals or groups are as obliging as the Terrorist Fraction of the People's Will. Benito Mussolini would have none of the terror label, with or without the "ism." "Terror?" he asked sardonically. "Never. It simply is social hygiene, taking those individuals out of circulation like a doctor would take out a bacillus."[63]

It is not surprising in the least that a plethora of terrorist groups would be found among the anti-colonial and nationalist struggles of the 20th century. This is certainly not owing to any greater propensity for violence among colonized people. It is owing to definition. When outside rule is inflicted on a nation or a tribe or a community and "terrorism" is defined as violence by a "non-state entity," then *ipso facto*, if any individual from among a colonized people picks up a gun with a political idea in his or her head, he or she is a "terrorist." This is sleight of hand, and it is not uncommon in the study of so-called "terrorism."[64] The actions of a European power in invading and colonizing another nation is not terrorism because it is an action by a state, but any violent objections from colonized people are now grist for study as "terrorism." How people became "non-state entities" is really outside the purview of study. Whether people even wish to be a state entity (as some Native Americans did not) has no relevance. And so, we are told, groups ranging from the African National Congress (once "terrorist," but no longer so) to the Zapatistas engage in terrorism, not due to any particular level of violence they employ, but due to their political status (or lack thereof).

None of this is to deny that anti-colonial and nationalist struggles have entailed horrendous violence from all sides. From all sides also, there have been frequent efforts to justify this violence and sporadic efforts to glorify it. Such glorification is evident in Jean-Paul Sartre's preface to Frantz Fanon's *The Wretched of the Earth*. Sartre intended to take the side of oppressed people, but

16

when he wrote of them that "Hatred, blind hatred . . . is their only wealth," it reads like libel.[65] And when he wrote that "violence, like Achilles' lance, can heal the wounds that it has inflicted," it reads like sophistry.[66]

Of the virtues of violence for oppressed people, Fanon himself wrote, "At the level of individuals, violence is a cleansing force. It frees the native from his inferiority complex and from his despair and inaction; it makes him fearless and restores his self-respect."[67] Fanon reaped some richly merited critiques from a number of quarters. From a history of terrorism perspective, Walter Laqueur noted that there was nothing new here, in evidence of which he cited the words of Patrick Pearse, leader of the 1916 Dublin Easter Rising: "Bloodshed is a cleansing and sanctifying thing, and the nation which regards it as the final horror has lost its manhood."[68] James Billington wondered whether Fanon's ruminations about self-esteem and catharsis derived more from his Western training as a psychiatrist than from the real experience of oppressed people.[69] Of the disorders Fanon diagnosed and of the reassertion of "manhood" he prescribed, Robin Morgan observed, "Fanon's diagnoses, his analysis, his *perception,* were totally circumscribed by his gender."[70] And from the perspective of nonviolent activism, there must be a strong challenge to Fanon's claim that oppression "will only yield when confronted by greater violence."[71] When Fanon died (1961), he would have known about the U.S. civil rights struggle and about the nonviolent movement for Indian independence and about the host of additional historical instances in which strikes, boycotts, demonstrations, tax refusals, and other nonviolent actions have constituted not only viable resistance to oppression but also an assertion of human dignity and self-respect.[72]

Despite the considerable leeway for criticism, however, Frantz Fanon cannot be dismissed as a mere apologist for terror, for he offers reminders that are both disconcerting and worthy of a hearing. He reminds us that it is quite easy for the comfortable to denounce the violence of the wretched of the earth while simultaneously subsidizing and benefiting from the violence that keeps them in a wretched state. He reminds us of the ease with which terror is ignored until it strikes close to home, and he reminds us of the many terrorized homes that are not our own. He reminds us of the church which has too often ignored the violence of the powerful while admonishing all others to turn the other cheek and to forgive trespasses,[73] the church which "does not call the native to God's ways but to the ways of the white man, of the master, of the oppressor."[74] He reminds us of the official pronouncements and media redactions that count some murders as "terrorism" and others as "foreign policy."

In defining "terrorism," the Friends Committee on National Legislation has said forthrightly that which many terrorism experts have denied:

Terrorism is a tactic, whether used by an established government, a revolutionary group, or an individual. The characterization of an action as "terrorism" depends on *what* is done, not on *who* does it. Terrorism includes threats or acts of violence ranging from deprivation of basic human rights, to property destruction, physical violence, torture and murder. Terrorist acts are consciously chosen and committed for purposes that go beyond the violence itself. Terrorist acts are usually undertaken for an identifiable political goal, as distinguished from crimes committed for personal gain or private vengeance or because of mental derangement. The political goals might be to punish or retaliate against an enemy or dissident elements or to destabilize an opposing government or organization.[75]

It is a definition with merit, although some qualms persist. Primary among the misgivings is the unqualified inclusion of "property destruction" as terrorism. It seems fair to say that people are terrorized by the fire-bombing of churches or homes, even if no people are physically injured in the bombing. It seems less clear that anyone is terrorized by the destruction of a draft card or even by the large-scale destruction of draft files (e.g., the 1968 raid on the Selective Service Office in Catonsville, Maryland, which contrasted the burning of paper draft files with the napalming of human beings). Likewise, it is doubtful that anyone is terrorized by damage inflicted on weaponry (e.g., the Plowshares actions which have damaged missiles and bombers while not threatening or inflicting injury on any person). That misgiving aside, the Friends offer a definition with merit. By noting that terrorist acts "usually" have political goals, the possibility is left open that some terror is perpetrated in which religious or economic motivation commingles with the political. And by emphasizing that terrorism is to be defined by *what* is done and not by *who* does it, the possibility remains open that, in some instances, charges of "terrorism" may function as something other than mere propaganda.

To be sure, the charge of terrorism has most often functioned as the tool of the propagandist, a tool that seeks to differentiate one's own righteous or justifiable or necessary violence from the sheer barbarism of an opponent.[76] At times the propaganda entails projection, as when European settlers labeled Native Americans "savages." At other times, the propaganda weaves together disparate events to present an intricate (if not paranoid) vision of conspiracy; such was the Reagan-era claim that there was a "global terror network" directed from Moscow.[77]

If the concept of "terrorism" is to have any meaning beyond its utility to the propagandist, there will be a need to abandon the claim of the experts that terrorism is perpetrated only by "non-state entities." In *The Demon Lover*, Robin

Morgan does not whitewash the terrorist acts of the state, and she provides a more helpful designation for those "non-state entities." Morgan writes of the terror perpetrated by both "the State-that-is" and "the State-that-would-be."[78] It rings true, does it not? How often the state claims to resist terror by creating a still greater terror. And how often violence is pursued in the name of liberation by an organization that wishes nothing so much as to assume the political power it denounces. The king is dead; long live the king.

E. V. Walter is a scholar who offers no exemption for the state in his study of terrorism. Walter distinguishes between the "siege of terror," which is violence by a movement seeking to replace established power, and the "regime of terror," which is violence perpetrated by powerholders.[79] Walter also notes that within an otherwise non-terrorist environment, there may arise a "zone of terror" aimed at a specific group, e.g., prisoners or slaves, racial or ethnic minorities, poor people, people with physical or mental illnesses.

As noted, Walter writes as a scholar. He aims for objectivity in his survey of historical and sociological sources and, to some degree, he writes impassively. It is perhaps because of this that his observations are occasionally chilling. Such is the case when he writes, "Terror is not confined to anomalous circumstances or exotic systems. It is potential in ordinary institutions. . . ."[80] As we will come to see as well, terrorist acts are not only committed by exotic individuals. It is potential in ordinary people.

Changing Allegiance, Changing Meaning

If one allows for the possibility that the use of violence is morally justifiable only in certain circumstances, one should not be surprised by the frequency with which those circumstances arise. If one allows for the possibility that certain wars may be just, one should not be surprised by the ample opportunities that history provides for just such just wars. If one allows for the possibility of using violence (or perhaps being used by it), then the only questions that remain are these: Violence against which enemies? (The demonic ones? Are there not demons all around?) What type of violence? (Are there "types"? Can a violence be found that will spare the innocent? If so, can the innocent be found?) For what purpose? (To save the world? To save our hides? In either case, to be saviors?) The answers may depend, of course, on whether one is attacker or attacked, a distinction that can also be quite subjective. Once one justifies the use of violence, one should not be surprised to find that the line between just warrior and terrorist can be very fine indeed — fine to the point of subjectivity, fine to the point of apparition.

In *The City of God*, Augustine of Hippo retells a tale from Cicero. The story, perhaps apocryphal but instructive nonetheless, recounts a confrontation between Alexander the Great and a recently captured pirate:

> The king asked the fellow, "What is your idea, in infesting the sea?" And the pirate answered, with uninhibited insolence, "The same as yours, in infesting the earth! But because I do it with a tiny craft, I'm called a pirate: because you have a mighty navy, you're called an emperor."[81]

The story is intriguing, not least because of the identity of the one who retells it. It was Augustine of Hippo who first formulated the "just war doctrine" which, with various permutations, is still alluded to as a basis for participation in war by Christians and others.[82] The nature of the doctrine was shaped in part by Augustine's allegiance to empire, in his case, the Roman Empire. He did not, after all, devise a theory of "just piracy"[83] or "just terrorism,"[84] let alone a theory of just revolution. What were "just" were just the imperial wars. Augustine's was an allegiance with historical consequence. As one observer has described this consequence, "The dominant tradition of the church has . . . tended to bless the state's use of violence while condemning violent revolution against the ruling authorities."[85]

By the time of Augustine, the Empire was already past its prime. The golden age of Rome was most often associated with the "Pax Romana" of Augustus Caesar. In the *Res Gestae*, Augustus himself wrote with considerable pride about how he was able to close the doors of the temple of Janus Quirinus on three different occasions, an action that was only permitted when the whole world was at peace. The source of this "peace" was evident in the Roman coinage of the era which prominently featured not only the goddess Pax, but also the goddess Victoria and Mars, the god of war, thus comprising a type of triumvirate — peace through victory in war.[86]

The Romans of an earlier era might have been pleased by Augustine's assertion that they had conferred benefits on the vanquished,[87] but to ask whether the Romans also viewed their wars as "just" may be anachronistic. At times there was a frank admission that justice counted for little, as when Pompey sought to establish Roman jurisdiction over the city of Messina in Sicily; to the reminder that Messina was protected by a state treaty with Rome, Pompey replied, "Cease quoting laws to us that have swords girt about us."[88] At times too, there was a candid and even boastful acknowledgment that the Pax Romana was established and maintained through nothing short of terrorism. Of Agricola's conquest of northern Britain, Tacitus wrote, "After he had terrorized them sufficiently, he paraded before them the enticements of peace."[89] And

Pliny praises Trajan with the words, "Now once more terror is in their midst; our enemies are afraid, and crave permission to obey commands."[90]

The vanquished may have disagreed with Augustine's estimation of the benefits the Romans conferred, but there was little disagreement that the Romans inflicted a brutal terror. All too rarely does history preserve the voices of the vanquished, but in his account of the conquests of Agricola, Tacitus quotes the words of the Caledonian, Calgacus:

> But today the boundary of Britain is exposed; beyond us lies no nation, nothing but waves and rocks and the Romans, more deadly still than they, for you find in them an arrogance which no reasonable submission can elude. Brigands of the world, they have exhausted the land by their indiscriminate plunder, and now they ransack the sea. The wealth of an enemy excites their cupidity, his poverty their lust of power. East and West have failed to glut their maw. They are unique in being as violently tempted to attack the poor as the wealthy. Robbery, butchery, rapine, the liars call Empire; they create a desolation and call it peace.[91]

Clear across the Empire from Britain, over a span of two centuries and more, the words of the oppressed were also preserved and at times were treated as holy writ. In Israel as in Britain, these voices from below testify to the coming of the Romans as a descent into terror. From the Dead Sea Scrolls, the first century B.C.E. *Commentary on Habakkuk* describes the "Kittim" or "Westerners" who bring "fear and terror."[92] Habakkuk wrote of the Chaldeans that "their own might is their god" (1:11), and the commentator wrote of the Kittim that they worship their standards, i.e., the military insignia mounted on a staff and bearing the symbol of a god. The reference to the standards is a clear indication that the Kittim are the Romans. The commentator writes that "their weapons are what they worship."[93]

In the first century C.E., the author of the Fourth Book of Ezra described the Roman occupiers as the last of four beasts:

> You, the fourth that has come, have conquered all the beasts that have gone before; and you have held sway over the world with much terror, and over all the earth with grievous oppression; and for so long you have dwelt on the earth with deceit. And you have judged the earth, but not with truth; for you have afflicted the meek and injured the peaceable; you have hated those who tell the truth, and have loved liars; you have destroyed the dwellings of those who brought forth fruit, and have laid low the walls of those who did you no harm. (4 Ezra 11:40-42)[94]

21

Unfortunately, the Romans were neither the first nor the last to bring terror to Palestine. Over centuries, due in large part to geographical location, Palestine was plagued by those with imperial designs. In Judea, the responses to invasions and occupations were richly varied, ranging from resistance to collaboration, from apocalyptic withdrawal from the world to apocalyptic engagement. Some of the varied responses to the oppressive reign of the Seleucid king, Antiochus IV Epiphanes, are discernible in the several writings that circulated under the name of "Maccabees." In particular, 1 Maccabees and 4 Maccabees, both telling of the same events, offer markedly contrasting portrayals of the faithful responses that might be expected of believers.

1 Maccabees recommends a blatantly military response to oppression. It recounts the military resistance of Mattathias, the overthrow of Antiochus by the sons of Mattathias, Judas Maccabeus and his brothers, and the establishment of the Hasmonean dynasty under John Hyrcanus. It was a response of meeting violence with violence. "The Jews also made engines of war to match theirs . . ." (1 Maccabees 6:52). It was a response of meeting terror from above with terror from below. "Then Judas and his brothers began to be feared, and terror fell on the Gentiles all around them" (1 Maccabees 3:25). It was a holy terror to which Mattathias had beckoned his followers when he cried, "Let every one who is zealous for the law and supports the covenant come out with me!" (1 Maccabees 2:27) And yet, even those who are meticulous defenders of the law find the need to compromise in times of war. When Mattathias learned of a slaughter that his enemies had perpetrated on the Sabbath, he and his forces resolved that they would fight even on the Sabbath (1 Maccabees 2:39-41). And later, even though the prophets had condemned alliances with Gentiles and the Torah had explicitly prohibited alliances with neighbors, Judas Maccabeus formed an alliance with (of all people) the Romans.[95] "Now Judas heard of the fame of the Romans, that they were very strong and were well-disposed toward all who made an alliance with them, that they pledged friendship to those who came to them, and that they were very strong" (1 Maccabees 8:1-2). Especially, that they were very strong.

Unknown to the author of 1 Maccabees (writing around 100 B.C.E.), these events would only add to the disaster. As the Hasmonean dynasty collapsed in corruption and violence, the Romans had been handed a foothold in Judea. The author of 4 Maccabees (written sometime between the middle of the first century B.C.E. and the middle of the following century) did know of subsequent events and that doubtless had some influence on the retelling of the history and the prescription for believers. The emphasis throughout 4 Maccabees is not on the resistance of those engaging in military escapades but on the resistance of the martyrs. There is reference to the lions and fiery furnaces by which the faithful were persecuted in the book of Daniel, which was also a writing in response to the terrors of Antiochus Epiphanes. In both Daniel and 4 Maccabees, ephemeral military victories are ignored in favor of the more fundamental question of what serves the ultimate victory of God. Hope does not lie in the Hasmoneans but in the faith of the martyrs. While 1 Maccabees offers effusive praise to the military might of the Romans (8:1-16), 4 Maccabees closes with an encomium on the mother of seven children who were slain by the tyrant. "By steadfastness you have conquered even a tyrant, and in word and deed you have proved more powerful than a man" (4 Maccabees 16:14). And then, in a remarkable inversion of the military meaning of victory, "O mother, who with your seven sons nullified the violence of the tyrant, frustrated his evil designs, and showed the courage of your faith!" (17:2).

Is victory achieved by those who inflict violence or those who suffer it? On the face of it, the question seems absurd. The answer of the Roman Empire (and of many before and since) was clear: Victoria and Pax require Mars. But through a remarkable period of Jewish and early Christian history, the response of some was quite different: Victory is won and violence is transformed, not by those who inflict it, but by those who suffer it. Such was the witness of the faithful woman of 4 Maccabees. And such was also part of the witness of another Jew, Jesus of Nazareth.[96]

Jesus was a disappointment to many, occasionally including his own disciples. For many in first-century Palestine, there was an abiding hope that the Messiah would appear as the Lion roaring out of the forest and leading the people in the destruction of the Roman Eagle (2 Esdras 12:31-33), or that the Messiah would be a new and mighty Davidic King who would break the nations with an iron rod (Psalm 2:9). Clearly, Jesus knew of this hope, and just as clearly, he renounced it.[97] Instead, in the parallel accounts of the Sermon on the Mount in Matthew 5 and Luke 6, Jesus admonished his followers to turn the other cheek, to love enemies, and to do good to persecutors. During the first three centuries of the church, this Sermon was one of the most quoted of any of the writings of the New Testament, becoming a sort of canon within the canon.[98]

The admonitions of the Sermon on the Mount were understood as literal, ethical guidance. The difficulty of following the path that the Sermon illuminates is evidenced by a phrase in the early Christian manual, the *Didache*. After quoting from the Sermon, the author of the *Didache* (or perhaps a later redactor) writes, "If you can bear the Lord's full yoke, you will be perfect. But if you cannot, then do what you can."[99]

In first-century Palestine, there was obvious scandal in the call of a Jewish sect (and a messianic sect at that) to love the Roman enemies. What happened to that scandal as the sect spread to other regions through the efforts of missionaries like Paul, himself a Roman citizen? Among believers within the new sect, the dilemma of potential conflicts between "God and country" would have been quite different for a Roman Gentile than for a Palestinian Jew. The issue of the identity and loyalty of one's citizenship quickly came to the fore. One option for resolution which was a distinctly minority position within the church until the 4th century was to give unqualified endorsement of one's status as a citizen of the Empire; this was the position of Clement of Rome who saw a harmonious parallel between the peace of the church and Pax Romana.[100] A very different view and one with wider support was the identification of the Roman Empire with the Beast of Daniel and Revelation; it was the view held by Hippolytus of Rome as well as Tertullian, who admonished Christians to pray for the Empire, but only because of the command to pray for enemies.[101] A view that was even more prominent, however, maintained that Christians held some of the rights and responsibilities of citizenship in various localities, but that this citizenship was provisional and secondary to the primary responsibility they held as citizens of the Kingdom of God. This view was eloquently expressed by the anonymous 2nd- or 3rd-century author of the *Epistle to Diognetus:*

> Do you think that [Jesus] was sent [by God], as might be supposed, to establish some sort of political sovereignty [*tyrannis*], to inspire fear and terror? Not so. But in gentleness and meekness has He sent him. . . . Christians are not distinguished from the rest of humanity either in locality or in speech or in customs. For they do not dwell off somewhere in cities of their own, neither do they use some different language. . . . But while they dwell in cities of Greeks and barbarians as the lot of each is cast . . . the constitution of their citizenship is nevertheless quite amazing and admittedly paradoxical. They dwell in their own countries, but only as sojourners. . . . *Every foreign country is a fatherland to them, and every fatherland is a foreign country.*[102]

The crux of the extent to which Christians should fulfill their responsibilities as provisional citizens of various localities came with two defining issues: whether Christians could honor the divinity of the emperor, and whether Christians could wield weapons of war. "No" was the resounding answer on both counts during the first three centuries of church history, with very few exceptions to prove the rule. There was overlap between the two concerns in that Roman soldiers were expected to participate in rituals considered idolatrous by Christians, but the renunciation of violence *per se* was equally clear. In *The Apostolic Tradition* of Hippolytus (c. 218), "military constables" and "magistrates" are to be admitted to the church community only if they refuse to kill, and any of those already baptized who decide to become soldiers "shall be sent away."[103] In his 2nd-century *Dialogue with Trypho,* Justin Martyr wrote, "We ourselves are well conversant with war, murder, and everything evil, but all of us throughout the whole wide earth have traded in our weapons of war."[104] The claim that such was the case for Christians "throughout the whole wide earth" may seem a trifle optimistic, but in effect, the claim was supported (and lamented) by the pagan philosopher Celsus.[105] He asserted that civilization would collapse if all refused military and public office as the Christians did. Celsus cited the words of Jesus that no one could serve two masters (Matthew 6:24) and he labeled the words "seditious."[106] If all did as the Christians, the emperor would stand "in utter solitude and desertion and the forces of the empire would fall into the hands of the wildest and most lawless barbarians."[107] In fact, in near-advocacy of nonviolent resistance, Tertullian warned the Empire that Christians could have chosen to do just that:

> Without taking up arms, without rebellion, simply by standing aside, by mere ill-natured separation, we could have fought you! . . . by sheer desertion! Beyond doubt, you would have shuddered at your solitude. . . . You would have had to look about for people to rule.[108]

Tertullian seemed to doubt that the terror brought by the wildest barbarians was much different than that brought by Rome. In *Against Celsus,* Origen expressed greater allegiance to Rome, but he noted that Christians served the emperor with prayers and not with weapons.

The persecutions came, and with them came a renewed affirmation that violence is not transformed by those who inflict it, but only by those who suffer it. The gruesome literalness of the transformation that Ignatius of Antioch foresaw was evident in his letter to Roman Christians asking them not to intervene to spare him from the lions: ". . . let me be the food of the beasts, through whom I can attain the presence of God. God's wheat am I and I shall be ground by the teeth of the beasts, that I may become the pure bread of Christ."[109] The perpetrators would reap nothing but shame. It was only the victims who could realize victory out of the terrorism of the persecution. And it was in fact described as terrorism. In *Scorpiace,* Tertullian writes that "terrorism has already arrayed with a crown the faith of martyrs," while a witness to the martyrdom of the slave woman Blandina writes of the witnesses present, "All of us were in terror."[110]

The reason cited for the martyrdom of Polycarp was his refusal to say that "Caesar is the lord" and his refusal to "swear by the emperor's genius."[111]

Through their martyrdom, the faithful were said to achieve a "victory" that was in sharp contrast to the victories of Caesar, but not infrequently, military imagery was employed. Clement of Alexandria issues a call "to desert to God's side" and to join "the soldiers of peace," and then he piles up the metaphorical equipment in preparation for battle: the trumpet of Christ, the armor of peace, the breastplate of righteousness, the shield of faith, the helmet of salvation, the sword of the spirit.[112]

While it is fair to say that the resounding testimony of the early church was one of nonviolence, by the beginning of the 4th century, there had already been some who had abandoned the peace position. As early as 173 c.e., there were some Christian recruits to the Thundering Legion from southern Armenia. In Syria in 202, Abgar IX, the king of Edessa, converted to Christianity, a move that divided the church in the region between those Christians who were willing to join the military of the newly converted king and those who continued to renounce all violence.[113] The persecutions of Christians in the empire were sporadic, but the history of one of these is suggestive of the possibility that there was a small number of Christians in the army. When the priests of Diocletian sought to perform their auguries, the animal innards were silent and the priests speculated that it was because of the presence of "profane men" in the court and in the military. After consulting with the oracle of Apollo at Miletus, beginning in February 303, Diocletian issued a series of edicts that mandated the offering of sacrifices and the destruction of churches. It is not clear whether Diocletian's order to his commanders to hunt down Christians in their ranks was based on the actual presence of Christians in the military or on the paranoia of the oracle at Miletus.[114]

The accession of Constantine marked dramatic changes — eventual changes of substance for the church and immediate changes of image for the empire.[115] Apart from changes of image, the empire retained its militarism, slavery, and power politics, but the more profound changes in the church marked the beginning of what some fairly call "the Constantinian fall of the church." After attributing his victory at the Battle of Milvian Bridge to the intercession of Jesus, Constantine "converted" to Christianity, albeit he retained some devotion to Apollo and to Mars, the god whose image appeared on his early coins.[116] In place of the symbols of the gods that had earlier adorned the military standards of the Romans, Constantine placed the cross. He bestowed upon himself the title of "Victor." As Roland Bainton comments, "This designation, which the pagans gave only to the gods and the Christians only to the martyrs, was assumed by the Christian emperor on the ground that what the martyrs had commenced with their blood, he had completed with his sword."[117] Calling himself a "bishop" to those outside the church, Constantine maintained that the most effective

26

method to convert barbarians was to expose them to the terror of the army, which fights with the blessing of God.[118] Of course, during his reign and for decades afterwards, there was not a Christian majority in the Roman army, thanks not to Constantine but to the pacifism of the early church.[119]

If the army lacked Christians, the church lacked a theology to buttress the actions of a newly converted emperor. Between the Council of Arles in 314 and the ultimate capitulation in the Theodosian Code of 438, the church underwent a series of tortured compromises with the earlier pacifist position. The first small steps onto this slipperiest of slopes held that perhaps Christians could hold positions as soldiers or magistrates provided that they only engaged in policing functions and provided too that their bishops found all of their actions to be in conformity with Christian standards. It was an anguishing ride down the slope to the Theodosian Code, which mandated that *only* Christians could be in the army. The Code was Christendom's version of the Diocletian auguries, a fretting that God may not be well disposed to an army corrupted by the presence of pagans.

Ambrose of Milan and Augustine of Hippo were two figures who played a powerful role in shaping a new theology for an imperial church. By far, Ambrose was the less subtle of the two. His allegiance to the empire was never in doubt, for prior to becoming bishop of Milan in 374, he had been governor of Aemilia and Liguria. Ordinarily, a governor would have been ineligible for the episcopate since a relic of the pacifist legacy of the early church held that church officials should not engage in bloodshed. Ambrose was not a baptized Christian at the time that a popular agitation arose for his assumption of the bishopric, and he showed his initial indifference to the call by proceeding with his official duties and ordering the administration of torture to suspects in criminal cases.[120] When he became bishop, he did not become more squeamish about the utility of violence. After reading the denunciation of torture and capital punishment written by Siricius, the bishop of Rome, a magistrate named Studius wrote to Ambrose and asked for advice. Ambrose responded that, even though it was the law of Rome which the Christian magistrate enforced, by doing so, the judge could serve as "God's avenger against those who do evil."[121] It was a quite remarkable melding, a claim that human terror could be used in service to the terror of God.

But for Ambrose, not all terror was equal. The violence that was used by the opponents of Rome he characterized as "the savagery of barbarian nations."[122] Gone was the suggestion of the *Epistle to Diognetus* that Christians dwell with equanimity among both Greeks and barbarians. Gone was the claim that all countries are equally foreign. Ambrose compared the barbarians to the forces of Satan, Gog and Magog, who "marched up over the breadth of the earth and surrounded the camp of the saints and the beloved city" (Revelation 20:9). This "deadly neighbour" had been able to invade the Danubian provinces only because of the Arian heresy which infested the region.[123] In a clear call for the cross to totally replace all other symbols on Roman military standards, Ambrose wrote, "Not eagles and birds must lead the army but thy name and religion, O Jesus."[124]

Symbols were important to Ambrose. He led the successful opposition to the proposal that the statue of the goddess Victoria be reintroduced into the Roman senate chamber. It was the goddess and paganism that he opposed, not the association between victory and military conquest. With a Christian as emperor, the victories to be won are not those of martyrs. When Theodosius wrote to Ambrose to inform him of a military victory, it was symbolically significant that Ambrose held the letter in his hand as he celebrated Eucharist so that the words of the emperor, said Ambrose, "should perform the function of a priestly offering."[125] Although the goddess Victoria was denied her place in the Roman senate, she was not dead. Winged and carrying wreath and palm, the portrait of this Valkyrie of Jupiter reappeared on Roman coins, albeit now she was an angel who also carried the cross of Christ in whose name the empire would win its subsequent victories.[126]

It was partly due to the influence of Ambrose that Augustine of Hippo became a Christian convert. Augustine's writing is the quintessence of what is meant by "natural theology." The revelation of God's will is not only to be read in Scripture, but also in the assorted fortunes of men and women, pagans and Christians, mighty lords and common slaves. While Augustine asserts that "God dispenses freely to good and evil alike,"[127] he peppers his writing with illustrations which suggest that he agrees with the observation of Job's friend that terror nips at the heels of the wicked (Job 18:11). One of the events that prevented him from putting the matter so simply was the visitation of terror to Rome itself when the city was sacked by the Visigoths under Alaric in 410. Ambrose had died over a decade before the event, so he had no need to offer theological explanation for why the forces of Gog and Magog should have realized such success. Augustine did.

Augustine was helped in the effort by the fact that the characterization of "barbarians" was already beginning to fray. Alaric the barbarian was a Christian (even if of questionable orthodoxy), and as he prepared his final assault on Rome, the city was defended by the barbarian general Stilicho and by troops who hailed from Gaul and Germanic regions.[128] Indeed, Augustine argues that the fury unleashed on Rome was likely mitigated by the invaders' familiarity with Christianity, even if it was of a suspect variety.[129] Still, his allegiance was clearly with Rome.[130]

Augustine wrote *The City of God* to defend against the charge that the collapse of Rome had been due to the advent of Christianity and the abandonment of the old gods.[131] There were actually two cities, wrote Augustine, the city of God and the earthly city, and events in this latter city could only ever hope to approximate the justice that will be found in the city of God. God is in charge of both cities, but the divine plan is more or less hidden in the various destinies that befall the earthly city. Augustine vacillates on the degree to which God's plan in history is decipherable, writing at one point that God "gives earthly dominion both to good men and to evil" in "an order completely hidden from us,"[132] but there was no hiding from Augustine the "prosperity bestowed by God on Constantine, the Christian emperor."[133] Likewise, regarding the opposite end of the social spectrum, there was not much hidden about the fact that "the condition of slavery is justly imposed on the sinner" and that such bondage was "the judgment of God, with whom there is no injustice, and who knows how to allot different punishments according to the deserts of the offenders."[134] But on many matters other than Constantine and slavery, Augustine was more subtle than some of his contemporaries. While he obviously believed that armies could serve to inflict punishment from God, he was writing to defend against the charge that Rome had fallen because of the Christians, and he therefore could not write as boldly as did Jerome in 396 when the invasions were beginning. "It is by reason of our sins that the barbarians are strong," wrote Jerome. It is God's anger that "vents its fury on us by the barbarians' mad attacks."[135] Augustine took greater care both in his references to Roman sins and in the degree to which terror could be read as a sign of divine displeasure. He knew that a reading of such signs can cut both ways.

As good citizens of the earthly city, Augustine argued, Christians need not shrink from participation in just wars. The taking of life was not inevitably wrong, for all of us must die. Of greater importance is the reward or punishment that follows death. "Why then should those who have lived well be dismayed by the terrors of death in any form?"[136] In his dispute with the Donatists, Augustine argued that violence could be utilized to good benefit, citing Luke 14:23, "compel people to come in." While instilling terror in others is less preferable than the conversions that can be won through love, still "those are certainly more numerous who are corrected by fear."[137] Augustine conceded that wars are evil, but while arguing against the pacifism of the Manichaeans in *Contra Faustum*, he wrote,

> The real evils in war are the love of violence, revengeful cruelty, fierce and implacable enmity, wild resistance, and the lust of power, and such like; and it is generally to punish these things, when force is required to inflict

the punishment, that, in obedience to God or some lawful authority, good men undertake wars.[138]

Augustine maintains that, in private life, the Christian should never utilize violence, not even in self-defense, not even to prevent robbery or rape. In warfare, however, it is possible to use violence while maintaining an attitude of love. To the modern reader who is accustomed to hearing the virtues of self-defense extolled above all other justifications for violence, Augustine's argument seems skewed. To the modern reader accustomed to associations between passions and violence and to denunciations of dispassionate, "cold-blooded killers," Augustine's advice to soldiers seems strange: "Let necessity, therefore, and not your will, slay the enemy who fights against you."[139] Herein lies the difference between the Christian soldier and the mere terrorist possessed by "revengeful cruelty." The Christian kills from necessity. The Christian kills with no will save a dispassionate love.

But perhaps the modern reader is not alone in finding the advice strange. Writing toward the end of the 4th century, Basil of Caesarea compared the violence of robbers and the violence of soldiers, and the robbers got the better end of the comparison. Basil wrote,

> He who makes use of a sword or any other such weapon has no excuse . . . for instance, the acts of robbers and the attacks of soldiers. For the former kill for the sake of money and to avoid exposure, and men in warfare proceed to slaughter openly, proposing neither to terrify nor to chastise but to kill their opponents.[140]

While Basil condemned the use of the sword, at least the terrorist has his or her passions as an excuse. Augustine proposed to remove the passions while preserving the use of the sword.

No matter the dispassion and the subtlety of his arguments, there can be no doubt that Augustine (like all before and since) was influenced by the time and place in which he lived. Would he have employed his considerable theological talents toward different conclusions had he lived in an era which still demanded the affirmation that "Caesar is lord"? Or is it possible (for us as well as for him) that he actually did live in such an era but that the affirmation of Caesar's lordship had been transformed so that it required less of ritualized assent? The persecutions never ended, but the identity of the victims changed. Augustine himself had a role to play in the persecution of Donatists and Manichaeans. When the state turned its persecuting fury away from the "orthodox," was it because of the changing allegiances of newly converted emperors, or was it because of the changing allegiances of the church? Were sacrifices still being offered unto Caesar? Can Augustine's "just war doctrine" be understood as exactly such a burnt offering?

Clovis was also a man of his time, the late 5th and early 6th centuries. He was king of the Franks, a military hero, and a newly converted Christian. When he first learned of the crucifixion of Jesus, he was outraged and he boldly claimed, "If I and my Franks had been there, it would never have happened." It was not only a matter of historical accident that Clovis was not there. It was a matter of Jesus' deciding when he told Peter, as he certainly told Clovis as well, "Put your sword back into its sheath" (John 18:11).[141]

Terror Is Not God

Some might count it as a benefit of polytheism that the dilemma of theodicy is mitigated. Human travails serve as a reminder that the gods who populate the heavens and the earth may not be altogether beneficent. Some gods or goddesses may manage to combine aspects that are both nurturing and terrifying (as is the case with Kali, cited above), but for Zoroastrians, Ahura Mazda and Ahriman, along with angels and demons, are engaged in a dualistic struggle between good and evil which is perpetual to the point of apocalypse.[142] Even when the gods are not evil, assorted figures in Roman and Greek pantheons serve as reminders that the gods can be fallible, even mortal, and that human joys and sufferings are impacted by these gods who are sometimes mere tricksters.[143] The departed gods leave behind spirits who work both for good and for ill, so send the scapegoat into the desert to Azazel (Leviticus 16:7-10; Isaiah 34:14) so that all may go well with you.

There are some who claim of both monotheism and polytheism that deities serve as mere projections of human needs and aspirations, conflicts and fears. Among philosophers and theologians, Ludwig Feuerbach was the primary proponent of the claim, asserting that God is an objectification of self-alienated humanity and suggesting that people can become more fully human by translating theology into anthropology. From an economic and political perspective, Karl Marx agreed, hypothesizing that theism of whatever variety was reflective of social condition and that, with the overcoming of human alienation from productivity and creativity, religion would fade as surely as the state would wither. Among psychological theorists, Sigmund Freud saw some kinship between the projections of religion and the more severe manifestations of hallucination and delusion as coping mechanisms for anxiety. In monotheism, Freud theorized, there is a projection and preservation of the child's simultaneous

31

fear and love for the father. Of course, the gods all antedate Feuerbach, Marx, and Freud, and many show no signs of withering, but the idea of projection cannot help but come to mind when we meet the gods named "Terror."[144]

Plato cites Socrates' definition of both fear and terror as the "expectation of evil."[145] The reference to "expectation" is suggestive of the interval between one's prior, calm disposition and the imminent arrival of potential harm for oneself or for loved ones. One has not yet suffered or escaped death, but there has been an irruption, an invasion from without — a battle joined, a lion spotted, a bump in the night. To experience this terror is to be "out of control." One feels at a loss to control the interval or the approaching danger or perhaps even oneself. Who, then, is in control? Is it a god who has brought this irruption from without, who controls the interval, who determines the outcome?

A number of polytheistic religions have designated a specific god who is in charge of the phenomenon of terror. A Neo-Punic inscription refers to a certain god as *b'l chrdt*, "lord of terror."[146] In the Greek context, Phobos is a powerful deity who is mentioned by both Homer and Hesiod. Sacrifices were offered to Phobos by Alexander and Theseus, and in militaristic Sparta, there was a temple dedicated to the god. Possessing the power to either precipitate or turn aside terror, the name of Phobos is invoked on amulets and the god is depicted as a grotesque creature on military shields.[147] Another Greek god, Pan ("all, everything"), was associated with nature and the countryside, but as Plato noted, there was always a dual quality to this god who had the face and torso of a man, but the horns and lower extremities of a goat.[148] Associated with the Roman god Faunus, Pan was not only the gentle god of shepherds and peaceful woodland, but also the god who could bring panic to the deep woods at night. It was the panic of Pan which was said to have routed the Persians at the battle of Marathon.[149]

Like Pan himself, panic also has a dual quality. While the more common understanding of panic and terror is associated with Plato's "expectation of evil," there is a different manifestation of panic that emerges in the context of profound spiritual experience, of encounter with the divine. The fear that urges retreat is still present, but now it is mixed with the attraction of reverence and awe. This back and forth, this retreat and attraction of "holy terror" is associated with trembling, with the writhing of birth pangs,[150] with dance.[151] This is the realm of the whirling dervish and the "holy roller." It is the realm of ecstatic spirituality that members of the American beat generation and early British rock musicians were surprised to discover still associated with Pan among the pipers of Jajouka in northwest Africa; the Pan pipers would play frenetically, and panicked dancing would ensue as a means of both summoning and reacting to the presence of deity. In the presence of the divine, people tremble, people swoon, people die. In this swoon may lie the basis of proskynesis and ritual bows of greeting and prayer.[152]

This sense of numinous, the experience of awe and reverence in the presence of the holy is fundamental to biblical references to the fear of God and the terror of God.[153] The human wonder and delight at theophany is accompanied by a strong sense of frailty and fear of death. Even the terrain in which God's appearance occurs is rendered "awesome," as Jacob discovered after his dream at Bethel (Genesis 28:17). At the burning bush, Moses kept his distance and hid his face for fear that he might see God (Exodus 3:5-6), and during the theophany at Sinai, the people were to be careful so as not even "to touch the edge" of the mountain (Exodus 19:12). It is as one who has survived both joy and terror that Hagar asks, "Have I really seen God and remained alive after seeing him?" (Genesis 16:13).

There is no distinctive vocabulary for the fear or terror of God in contrast to the more mundane fears that humans face. There are biblical references to the fears and terrors evoked by animals (Amos 3:8), by imminent battle (1 Samuel 13:7), by other individuals (for example, the fear evoked by Jehu in 2 Kings 10:4 or Uriah's fear of Jehoiakim in Jeremiah 26:21), or by the threat of punishment (Deuteronomy 17:12-13). A question arises about whether human authorities and powers can ever serve as instruments of God's terror. The text most often cited in response is Romans 13:1-7. Paul writes that "rulers are not a terror to good conduct, but to bad" (v. 3) and that the governing authority "is the servant of God to execute wrath on the wrongdoer" (v. 4). Historically, it is the text that has been misused most often to justify Christian participation in horrendous bloodshed, including the Nazi reign of terror.[154]

Regarding Romans 13 and any possible attribution of divine terror to human authorities, it must first be affirmed that there is rich variety in the biblical terrain, and any attempt to smooth out the theologies and perspectives of various biblical writers and redactors into a single "biblical view of the state" (or even a single "biblical view of divine terror") is doomed to failure and risks distortion of biblical texts in the process. Indeed, some apologists for state power may give prominence to the text of Romans 13 precisely because they find scant solace among some other biblical writers who are busily depicting state power as a rejection of God's rule (1 Samuel 8:6-18), as a pretext for crucifixion (John 19:15), as the beast of the final days (Revelation 13:1-8). But caution must be exercised before declaring even Paul an apologist for state power; it was the same Paul, after all, who faced persecution by civil authorities as well as religious ones and who characterized magistrates as "the unrighteous" (1 Corinthians 6:1).[155] Romans 13:1-7 must be read in the context of the ethical parenesis which calls the faithful to compassion, love, and peace (Romans 12;

13:8-10) as well as the eschatological context which reminds believers of the imminence of the only valid authority, the judgment of God (Romans 13:11-14; 14:10-13). In reference to governing authorities as "the servant of God," William Stringfellow discerns an allusion to that day when all of the rebellious principalities and powers will be truly subject to God. Stringfellow suggests that those theologians who have always emphasized the ethical relevance of Romans 13 and the eschatological relevance of Revelation 13 might profit by also learning to reverse those perspectives.[156]

While Paul refers to the "terror" of the rulers, it is clear that there is no melding of this terror with fear of God. For Paul, fear is "due" or "owed" only to God.[157] A similar position was taken by a later biblical writer: "Honor everyone. Love the family of believers. Fear God. Honor the emperor" (1 Peter 2:17). The honor to be given to the emperor (and to everyone else as well) was hardly sufficient in a setting that expected worship of the emperor, but the fear that was owed God was distinguished from the honor owed the emperor.

One of the instances in the Hebrew Bible in which "fear of God" was motivation for *dis*obedience of governing authorities can be found in the story of the Hebrew midwives, Shiphrah and Puah (Exodus 1:15-22). The king of Egypt ordered that all male children born to Hebrew women should be killed. "But the midwives feared God; they did not do as the king of Egypt commanded them, but they let the boys live" (v. 17). To fear God meant disobedience of the king.[158]

What was this "fear of God" that could motivate disobedience? Was it an emotional fear? Were Shiphrah and Puah caught between the rock of fearing punishment from the king of Egypt if they did not obey him and the hard place of divine retribution if they did? But if the reference is to the emotion of fear, how can one be commanded to have emotions? How is it possible to speak of an emotion being "owed" or being "due"? Obviously, this "fear of God" is something more than the simple trembling emotion of fear that is experienced in the presence of theophany. In and through biblical writings, the concept of "fear of God" undergoes change and development to the point at which (similar to that other emotion, love) it can in fact be owed.

Even in the primordial experience of theophany, the emotion of fear is a reaction from the human side independent of any particular divine will to instill it.[159] Where God is depicted as having the power to instill terror, there is still biblical clarity on the point that God is not terror and terror is not God. Indeed, in the account of the preparations for the entry into Canaan (Exodus 23:20-28), terror is depicted as a power which is independent of God but which God may somehow "send" (v. 27), like God sends the angel in front (v. 20), while God remains behind as a protective presence with the sojourners.[160]

34

While the "fear of God" may have its origin in the encounter with theophany, the language quickly became associated with obedience to God's law, walking with God, and loving God (Deuteronomy 10:12). In the Holiness Code, impartial social justice was a sign of fear of God (Leviticus 19:14-15; 25:39-43). No longer an emotional reaction, for the Deuteronomist this fear of God was to be learned (Deuteronomy 4:10; 31:12-13). No longer an expectation of evil, in wisdom literature, "The fear of the LORD is the beginning of knowledge . . ." (Proverbs 1:7). No longer a trembling in the face of death, "The fear of the LORD is life indeed; filled with it one rests secure and suffers no harm" (Proverbs 19:23).

Still, the ultimate wrath and terror of God are yet to be faced in the eschatological Day of Yahweh. Here we have a return of the trembling, the panic, the pains of labor (Psalm 48:4-6). The nations and peoples may plot, but God will terrify them (Psalm 2:1-6). This will be a Day when the fire of God's wrath will burn brightly and "the whole earth shall be consumed; for a full, a terrible end he will make of all the inhabitants of the earth" (Zephaniah 1:18).

And is this great terror of God the end? No, for equally eschatological, equally associated with the Day of Yahweh is the great "Fear not!"[161] It is the eschatological blessing of Deutero-Isaiah: "In righteousness you shall be established; you shall be far from oppression, for you shall not fear; and from terror, for it shall not come near you" (Isaiah 54:14). It is the promise of Zephaniah who, despite his fearsome vision, promises a remnant "and no one shall make them afraid" (3:13). It is the word of the angel to the shepherds, "Do not be afraid" (Luke 2:10). It is the word to the women at the empty tomb, "Do not be afraid" (Matthew 28:5).[162]

So terror does not have the final word. In part, this apparent reversal, this journey from "Fear" to "Fear not" is possible because creation itself is not grounded in fear. By contrast, in the creation myths of Mesopotamia, terror plays a prominent role.[163] There is combat among the gods and the earth itself is shaped from the dead body of Tiamat who has been slain by the god Marduk. Creation itself is based on violence.[164]

In Genesis, the world is created out of nothing save the breath, the spirit of God. In this there is hope — hope for love, hope for an end to terror.

CHAPTER II

Terror and the Death of Community

So then you are no longer strangers and aliens, but you are citizens
with the saints and also members of the household of God. . . .

EPHESIANS 2:19

Terrorism and Dehumanization

Political power can be wielded in a way that seeks to shape, subvert, or eradicate memory. When President Bush the elder and other political leaders lamented the "Vietnam syndrome" in America, their protest was against our memory of that war, a memory that entails stark, mental pictures of GIs holding cigarette lighters to thatched roofs, of a Vietcong suspect being shot in the head at point blank range, of a napalmed child crying as she ran naked toward the camera. We were urged to overcome this "syndrome," to abandon these memories of images of terror. In the subsequent American wars that have been fought in Panama, in Grenada, in Nicaragua through the Contra surrogates, there was tightened U.S. military control of the images that reached our television screens and our newspapers. By the time of the Gulf War, the media control was nearly complete. In the age of the so-called "information superhighway," Americans have access to more information about the U.S. Civil War than about the Persian Gulf War. Estimates of the number of Iraqi dead run into the hundreds of thousands, but for those who were not there, the remembered images of the Gulf War are remarkably antiseptic. There were no pictures to accompany the occasional news leaks of American bulldozers plowing the bodies of Iraqi soldiers into mass graves in the desert. Indeed, the sole image of the Gulf War in the memory of many Americans is that of video taken from the nose of a laser-guided bomb as it steadily approaches the smokestack of a nondescript building with no evidence of life in the target zone. As the camera is destroyed, we see no explosion but only the electronic snow of an interrupted transmission. It is antiseptic in the extreme. It is a remembered image of warfare as video game. Pictures taken by a machine mounted on a machine that will soon destroy machines. Warfare as a mere figment of cyberspace. The Vietnam syndrome is overcome when the memory of triumphant technology supplants the memory of the little sister who has been napalmed, when we are more familiar with computer memory than with the memory of human terrors suffered in war.

There was no effort to censor the pictorial images filled with anguish and blood that flowed from the bombings of the World Trade Center and the Oklahoma City Federal Building or the 1998 attacks on U.S. embassies in Kenya and Tanzania. Quite appropriately, the images were allowed to speak: "Look what these terrorists have done. Look how little human life has been respected." In contrast, when the Smithsonian Institution was preparing an exhibit to mark the fiftieth anniversary of the end of World War II, there were howls of protest at plans for the exhibit to include pictures of the victims of the U.S. atomic bombings of Hiroshima and Nagasaki. The memory of those who suffered at Hiroshima and Nagasaki was somehow a dangerous memory, a subversive memory. The American national mythos is messianic; it seeks to tell a story of freedom spread through self-sacrifice, not victories won through the spread of terror. To sustain the myth, Americans need to rewrite history just as surely as did Stalin to sustain his own version of communist orthodoxy. For the time being in America, the effort at historical rewrite meets greater resistance than was condoned in Stalinist Russia, but the Smithsonian controversy indicated the power of the encouragement to forget, to write the memories of the victims out of history.[1]

How does one accomplish such forgetting? If one seeks to forget events or people, is not the effort to forget itself a form of remembrance? It is, to be sure, a twisted form of remembrance. The denial of remembered traumas and the loss of the ability to integrate these memories is what psychologists call "dissociation." While dissociation may be an understandable reaction to trauma, it is not the path to healing. Whether the trauma is childhood abuse or the devastation of war, recovery requires remembrance and mourning.[2] The advice to "forgive and forget" is nonsensical. Forgiveness requires memory.[3]

When power subverts memory, then in the words of a Milan Kundera character, "the struggle of man against power is the struggle of memory against forgetting."[4] But the subversion of memory does not only come by means of censorship and control of the media. At times, memory is subverted not by depriving our consciousness of information and images, as was the case with the Gulf War and the Smithsonian exhibit, but by flooding our consciousness with a rapidly moving plethora of competing images. It is not governmental censorship but the media itself which is the tool of such subversion. What passes for "news" in the information age is a cacophonous presentation of images of genocide commingled with beer commercials and stock market reports and tidbits on the lives of the latest celebrities. While some stories preoccupy the media to the point of obsession (the O. J. Simpson trial, White House sex scandals), the depiction of other, more profound events flashes by with a rapidity that discourages any public engagement. As Kundera observes:

> The bloody massacre in Bangladesh quickly covered over the memory of the Russian invasion of Czechoslovakia, the assassination of Allende drowned out the groans of Bangladesh, the war in the Sinai Desert made people forget Allende, the Cambodian massacre made people forget Sinai, and so on and so forth until ultimately everyone lets everything be forgotten.[5]

And, as Kundera notes, the subversion of memory is ultimately in the service of death:

> This is the great private problem of man: death as the loss of self. But what is this self? It is the sum of everything we remember. Thus, what terrifies us about death is not the loss of the future but the loss of the past. Forgetting is a form of death ever present within life. . . . But forgetting is also the great problem of politics. When a big power wants to deprive a small country of its national consciousness, it uses the method of *organized forgetting*.[6]

It is not only national consciousness that is targeted by this "organized forgetting." When the writing of history entails the intentional exclusion of women or the poor or people of color or gay men and lesbians or heretics of whatever stripe, the human community itself is diminished. And as indigenous people and others have discovered, organized forgetting can include the eradication of culture through genocide.

The biblical call to "remembrance" is a renunciation of the death that accompanies organized forgetting. "Do this in remembrance of me" (Luke 22:19; 1 Corinthians 11:24). This is a call to subversion not of memory but of amnesia, as suggested by the Greek *anamnesis*. It is a call to activity, to a re-collecting and re-membering of Jesus in the form of the community that emerges from the sharing of bread and cup.[7] While some faiths hold that certain spaces or objects or rituals are holy, in Christianity, the community itself is the locus of sanctification.[8] It is this community that is called to stand against amnesia and organized forgetting.

But are there instances in which remembrance itself is a problem? Some of the most notorious, contemporary acts of terrorism — genocide in Rwanda, in Kurdistan, in the former Yugoslavia — are accompanied by news coverage that refers to "age-old hatreds." Are these instances in which there has been too much remembering, too little forgetting of historical animosities?

This view of ethnic conflicts as grounded in "age-old hatreds" may be based less in fact than in the triumphalist view of our own age as "the end of history."[9] In the perspective touted by some Western political leaders, with the collapse of communism and the emergence of the "new world order," the triumph of capitalism and a global free market economy will prove to be eventual panaceas for regional conflicts. If conflicts persist, it must be due to something primitive, to those "age-old hatreds" that have yet to evaporate in the profits of the new world paradise.[10] The only clouds on the bright horizon are due to these ethnic hatreds and to a few "rogue states" (e.g., Cuba, Iraq, Libya, North Korea). The U.S. State Department references to certain nations as rogue states is itself indicative of confidence in the direction (or the "end") of history. A "rogue" is a wandering beggar, a tramp, an elephant who travels apart from the rest of the herd. One way or another, these rogues will be brought into conformity with the herd.

Contrary to this portrayal of regional conflicts as sparked by age-old hatreds, many recent instances of war and even genocide have been sparked in settings where people of varied ethnic and religious backgrounds have lived together as neighbors and flourished in the same communities for generations. The breakdown of community had little to do with the ethnic and religious differences that had already been present for centuries. Nor can the collapse of community be attributed to the collapse of empire, although this too is a popular misperception. This view holds that, for example, the collapse of the Ottoman Empire caused the Armenian genocide, that the end of communist rule led to ethnic conflict in the Balkans, and that the end of colonial rule precipitated terror in Rwanda and Burundi. In this view, ethnic and religious animosities were seething just beneath the surface and it was only due to strong, central authority that bloodshed was averted as long as it was. Such a view seems opposed to pluralism; it cannot account for those many regions of the globe where differing racial, ethnic, and religious groups form peaceable communities, nor can it account for instances of largely peaceful parting of the ways, as was the case with the establishment of the post-communist Czech Republic and

Slovakia. Such a view also seems suggestive of authoritarian control as the prescription for situations of potential conflict.

Rather than serving as a force to control seething hatreds, more often than not, imperial and colonial powers fostered the collapse of pluralistic communities. Communal violence becomes possible or even likely when a disrupted sense of community is combined with economic insecurity, militarization, and racism or ethnocentrism. Colonialism brought all three. In colonized areas of the Americas, Asia, and Africa, European powers disrupted subsistence economies and extracted resources, introduced profuse quantities of weaponry, and (as we will see in the example of Rwanda) generated a heightened, bifurcated sense of ethnicity in the service of a "divide and conquer" form of governance. The neocolonialism of the "new world order" continues to spread economic insecurity among nations that have been impoverished, while Western powers and multinational corporations continue to find a free market for the massive quantities of weapons that flow into regions of insecurity. Few formulas could be designed more effectively to generate terror.

The analysis by W. E. B. Du Bois of an earlier colonial era might serve as a warning to those major economic powers in the new world order who continue to advocate high levels of military "preparedness" while competing with other powers to exploit "Third World" markets and resources. Besides sowing terror among the exploited nations, such simultaneous militarism and economic competition can boomerang to bring terror to the major powers as well. Such was the understanding of Du Bois of the origins of World War I:

> It was this competition for the labor of yellow, brown and black folks that was the cause of the World War. . . .
>
> Colonies, we call them, these places where "niggers" are cheap and the earth is rich; they are those outlands where like a swarm of hungry locusts white masters may settle to be served as kings, wield the lash of slave-drivers, rape girls and wives, grow rich as Croesus and send homeward a golden stream. . . .
>
> The cause of war is preparation for war; and of all that Europe has done in a century there is nothing that has equaled in energy, thought, and time her preparation for wholesale murder. The only adequate cause of this preparation was conquest and conquest, not in Europe, but primarily among the darker peoples of Asia and Africa; conquest, not for assimilation and uplift, but for commerce and degradation.[11]

Du Bois's reading of the situation was at considerable variance from that of the colonial powers of the northern hemisphere who represented colonialism as a humanitarian enterprise, an effort to bring Christianity and civilization to the deprived. The great explorer Henry Morton Stanley wrote with pride that one of his greatest achievements was telling the Emperor of Uganda about the Ten Commandments and thereby converting him to Christianity. Unfortunately for Stanley, a French officer happened to be visiting Uganda at the time and the officer later reported that the Emperor had only agreed to convert when Stanley told him that there were eleven commandments, the eleventh being "Honor and respect kings, for they are the envoys of God."[12] Unfortunately for the Emperor of Uganda, it was soon the kings of Europe whom the people were expected to honor. Like the native people of North America who supposedly "sold" Manhattan for beads and other trinkets, African leaders who were familiar with friendship treaties between villages would have been at a loss to understand how placing a mark on a paper written in a foreign language "sold" the land on which they lived. Through such subterfuge, King Leopold II of Belgium laid claim to the lands surrounding the Congo River. In the late 19th and early 20th centuries, *millions* of Africans died in the Belgian race to extract rubber and other goods through forced labor, kidnapping, and torture. The era in the Congo became known as the "rubber terror."[13]

In neighboring Rwanda, the sense of community life that included both Hutu and Tutsi was profoundly disrupted by colonialism. Ethnographers today agree that Tutsi and Hutu cannot properly be called separate ethnic groups.[14] Traditionally, the separate designations constituted a form of caste system with the Tutsi being the aristocratic rulers, but the class lines were permeable; Hutu could become Tutsi and vice versa.[15] Tutsi and Hutu are the same race, they speak the same language (Kinyarwanda, although many Rwandans are bilingual with post-colonial fluency in French), and both groups are predominantly Christian (primarily Roman Catholic, but with a fair representation of Seventh Day Adventists and other Protestants). In 1933, the Belgian colonial rulers brought an end to the permeability of the line that distinguished Tutsi from Hutu by issuing "ethnic" identity cards and instituting a system of apartheid.[16] While the Belgians initially favored the Tutsi, with growing pressure for Rwandan independence in the 1950s, the Belgians suddenly reversed their policy and installed a Hutu-led government. Contrary to popular misperceptions of age-old tribal and ethnic hatreds, the first systematic bloodshed between Hutu and Tutsi ever recorded anywhere was in Rwanda in 1959.[17] The shattering of community and the descent into terror continued when the colonial system of identity cards was retained following Rwandan independence. The identity cards became one of the bases for selecting victims in subsequent massacres, including the genocide of 1994.

But it took more than a colonial legacy of impoverishment and bifurcated sense of identity to precipitate genocide. Following independence, Hutu and Tutsi continued to live as neighbors, to worship together, to work together, to intermarry. The massacres of Tutsi in the early 1990s did not result from communal animosity but from intentional governmental decision. The Hutu-led government of General Juvenal Habyarimana was facing waning support as the result of economic reforms urged by foreign creditors; as with many of the "reforms" imposed on debtor nations today by the International Monetary Fund, the poorest people are the first to be targeted by reductions in government programs. Faced with a loss of popular support, Habyarimana was also faced by a 1990 invasion of Rwanda by troops of the Rwandan Popular Front, an organization of Rwandan refugees based in Uganda. The heightened militarization in times of warfare is highly conducive to genocide.[18] Arms flowed into the region from France, Belgium, Egypt, and South Africa, and France supplied troops to support the Hutu-led regime even after there was clear evidence of a government-sponsored slaughter of Tutsi.[19] French President Mitterand was quoted as saying, "In such countries, genocide is not too important."[20] On October 4, 1990, President Habyarimana staged a fake attack on his own capital of Kigali and depicted it as a real attack by the Rwandan Popular Front with the support of Tutsi "collaborators." The subsequent attacks on Tutsi were not the result of anarchy; they were the result of Rwandan government policy that encouraged and directed the attacks. Government officials encouraged Hutu to kill their Tutsi neighbors in fulfillment of *umuganda,* a remnant of colonial practice in which all residents were required to devote one day of unpaid labor per month to public service projects. International concern was placated by Rwandan government protestation that it could not be expected to curb fully the "ancient tribal hatreds" that were so familiar to former colonial powers. All the while, guns, grenades, machetes, and other arms were being distributed by the government to Hutu militia groups, and instructions for the terror were being broadcast from a private radio station operated by Habyarimana's wife. Instructions included the reminder that Tutsi babies should not be allowed to escape extermination. Meanwhile, the war with the RPF was going badly for Habyarimana, and as he was on the verge of being forced into negotiated settlement, Habyarimana was killed on April 6, 1994 when his plane was shot down, probably by extremists within his own army. The "Hutu power" government that replaced him in office accelerated the pace of the genocide against the Tutsi, and within the space of a few months, the people of Rwanda were literally decimated.[21]

From Rwanda, from the midst of all the terror, there are stories of courage and love. There are stories of Hutu who faced death themselves rather than join in the slaughter of their Tutsi neighbors.[22] There are stories of faithful Christians who remembered Jesus' call to a faith community that includes both Tutsi and Hutu. But the more prevalent responses of churches within Rwanda and of churches internationally were reflective of lukewarm faith or of no faith at all. It is true that some churches sent badly needed food and medical supplies (some of which was actually misused to support heavily armed "Hutu power" militia camps across the border in Zaire). It is true that some churches issued statements of concern, but beyond that, many churches outside of Rwanda seemed resigned to allowing governments to decide if and when and how to intervene to stop the genocide. Within Rwanda, some of the Tutsi who sought sanctuary in churches during the massacres found scant refuge. Some of the two thousand people who gathered for sanctuary at the Seventh Day Adventist hospital complex in Mugonero wrote to their Hutu pastor asking for his assistance. The pastor responded, "You must be eliminated. God no longer wants you."[23] It stands as a judgment against the church and against all advocates of nonviolence that there has been so little creativity and boldness in devising and practicing methods of nonviolent intervention into settings of widespread violence and even genocide.

From within these settings of terror, there has been powerful witness offered by some individuals (e.g., the nonviolent interventions of Desmond Tutu in South Africa which spared the lives of both blacks and whites; the defiant efforts of Father Dhelo of the Congo to provide refuge for Tutsi at his monastery in Mokoto, just across the border from Rwanda).[24] On the possibility of intervention from the outside, we must remember the faithful witness of church workers like the four women who formed a type of "rescue squad" in El Salvador at a time when the U.S.-sponsored Salvadoran regime was conducting a reign of terror against its own people; over 50,000 Salvadoran civilians were murdered, and on December 2, 1980, these four church women were murdered as well — Maura Clarke, Jean Donovan, Ita Ford, Dorothy Kazel.[25] When searching for options for nonviolent intervention from outside, we must also recall the creative and courageous efforts of members of Witness for Peace, who attempted through their presence to prevent armed attacks in Nicaragua and elsewhere in Central America.[26] We might also commend the missions of prayer, reconciliation, and release of captives undertaken by Daniel Berrigan and others on their trip to Hanoi during the Vietnam War, and undertaken by Jesse Jackson and others on their trip to Belgrade during the NATO bombing.

But these examples of faithful witness in the midst of violence suggest that there is a crisis of faith when churches commend military intervention as a response to ethnic conflict and/or genocide. Bloodshed is not indicative of a lack of militarized engagement. Not infrequently, those nations that offer "humanitarian" military intervention had previously been busy providing weapons to those very troops they now seek to disarm. In the United States, the supposed need for U.S. military involvement in such "humanitarian missions" has been used as an argument in favor of increased Pentagon spending. When such interventions fail even by military standards (for example, the U.S. military intervention in Somalia), that too is used as an argument for more Pentagon spending in order to assure greater readiness in the future. Even leaving aside a sordid history of direct American involvement in the slaughter of civilians (of Native Americans, of colonized people in the Philippines, of residents of Hiroshima and Nagasaki, of Vietnamese . . .), the U.S. government's interest in averting genocide is suspect for its selectivity. It was the day after President Ford and Henry Kissinger visited Djakarta that Indonesia launched an invasion of East Timor on December 7, 1975; while the United Nations General Assembly called for Indonesian withdrawal, the United States vetoed proposed actions in the Security Council. The resultant genocide in East Timor has spanned two decades.[27] American policy toward the Kurds is indicative of a similar selectivity in the concern to avert massacres. It was ostensibly to protect the lives of Kurds that a "no fly zone" was enforced by the U.S. in northern Iraq following the Gulf War, but when the U.S. was "tilting" in favor of Iraq during the Iran-Iraq war, there was scant U.S. protest of Iraqi chemical weapons attacks on Kurdish villages. Following the Gulf War, there was strong American condemnation of Saddam Hussein's treatment of the Kurds while the U.S. was simultaneously supplying weapons to Turkey for its own brutal war against its Kurdish citizens.[28] Since U.S. support for NATO attacks on Serbia was justified as a move to end the human suffering in Kosovo, what then does that say about the failure of the U.S. to act as hundreds of thousands died in recent warfare inside the Sudan and inside Algeria?

When there is human suffering on a massive scale, those who would seek to heed the Word of God must devise creative strategies for nonviolent intervention, perhaps strategies akin to the model of Witness for Peace. Two strategies that lack both creativity and engagement with the Word are (a) doing nothing, and (b) advocating military intervention. The befuddling and mixing of categories like "humanitarian relief" and "military intervention" may have served to ease the qualms of some as NATO lobbed cruise missiles into cities in Yugoslavia, but whether or not it made for effective war fighting, it only served to exacerbate the humanitarian crisis as refugees and foreign observers and relief agencies were expelled from Kosovo. Rather than advocating "humanitarian" military intervention, churches and others could do far more to avert massacres by actively seeking an end to all arms shipments and an end to all military interventions. The charge that such a stance would be "isolationist" is itself reflective of a militarized view of international engagement. A decision to stop policing and arming the world does not constitute isolationism if there is continuing involvement in cultural exchange and trade and *genuine* humanitarian efforts to provide food, medical supplies, relief workers, and conciliators in areas of need. *Nothing* creates more famine, disease, or homelessness than war, and nothing creates a more fertile environment for genocide. Contrary to any notion of our own age as "civilized" and contrary to the supposed "rules of warfare" imposed by the Geneva Convention, our time has seen a dramatic expansion of the slaughter and misery spread by war. Eighty percent of those killed during World War I were soldiers. During World War II, half of the casualties were civilian and half were military. Today, almost 90 percent of all deaths in war are civilians.[29] The churches, which have sometimes provided exemplary assistance in meeting the human needs of those who are suffering, have been far more timid in renouncing the militarism that plays such a powerful role in creating that suffering.

And churches need to bear additional responsibility for inattention to the Word of God. Remembrance — *anamnesis* — of Jesus has not been practiced. Instead there has been a great forgetting, a great amnesia. What but amnesia regarding both Jesus and the community which is his body could account for the fact that the greatest number of terrorist acts in recent years have been perpetrated by "Christians"? It was not "Muslim extremists" who brought horror to Rwanda; it was Christians killing other Christians. It was not some "demonic" cult group who planted bombs in Northern Ireland; it was Christians trading brutality with other Christians. It was not "atheistic communists" who instituted a reign of terror to enforce apartheid in South Africa; it was Christians kidnapping and torturing and murdering other Christians. This is certainly not to suggest that the outrage is less when Christians kill people of other faiths, but it is to suggest that the attribution of terror and genocide to "age-old ethnic and religious hatreds" is simply a ruse employed by the governments and opposition groups who plot these slaughters for purposes no nobler than temporary political and military gain. Even in the Balkans, history has seen far more of shared community than of animosity among Serb, Croat, Bosnian, Albanian, and other ethnic groups; the emergence of animosity required militarization and political leaders who peddled hate.[30] And even in the Balkans, violence between Serb Orthodox Christians and Croat Catholic Christians has been as vicious as that between Christians and Muslims.[31]

Massacre on a massive scale is not a sign of age-old hatreds that have prevented community formation; it is a sign of new hatreds that have been generated intentionally to disrupt and destroy communities that already existed. Why? Because strong, pluralistic communities constitute a threat to the unhindered exercise of political and military power. Terror can be both reflective of community disintegration and a means of fostering further disintegration by leaving people feeling unsafe, suspicious, and disconnected. Grotesque acts of terrorism that entail the dismemberment of human bodies are sometimes used to communicate the message that the community itself is being dismembered.[32]

In the pursuit of raw power, terror is an attack upon community and an attempt to eradicate even the memory of community. Of the Nazis, Elie Wiesel said, "They were trying to annihilate the memory of Israel."[33] Hitler thought that just such annihilation of memory was possible because, as he said, "No one remembers what the Turks did to the Armenians."[34] In order to oppose terrorism and genocide, whenever there is an effort at organized forgetting, we must remember.

We must remember the victims. It is a stand on behalf of life, it is a stand against the perpetrators of terror when we make room in our memory for the victims of violence, for this "great cloud of witnesses" (Hebrews 12:1). When a Commission of Inquiry finally got around to investigating the Belgian terror in the Congo in the early years of the 20th century, one of the witnesses was Lontulu of Bolima, a man who had suffered kidnapping, flogging, and being sent to forced labor in chains. When he spoke before the Commission, Lontulu brought with him 110 twigs representing the people from his village who had been killed in the terror. He arranged these into four piles for the leaders, the women, the men, the children. As he picked up the twigs one at a time, he spoke the name of each of the 110 people who had been murdered.[35] A similar service of memory was performed by the Mothers of Plaza de Mayo following the state terror in Argentina in the 1970s and early 1980s. In a supposed war against subversives (the period was known as the "Dirty War" in Argentina), the governor of Buenos Aires, General Iberico Saint-Jean, was remarkably candid about his goal: "first we will kill all the subversives; then we will kill their collaborators; then . . . their sympathizers, then . . . those who remain indifferent; and finally we will kill the timid."[36] With the Argentine state employing torture and summary execution, hundreds of people were made to "disappear." Near the end of the "Dirty War" and for years after, the Mothers of the Plaza de Mayo marched on the Plaza every Thursday to ask about the fate of their loved ones who had disappeared. Where are they? Who is responsible? How could we allow this terror to happen? The act of remembrance is a plea for justice. It was Stalin who said, "A single death is a tragedy, a million deaths is a statistic." He must be proven wrong with a million twigs, with a million days of marching.

We must remember community. For Mohandas Gandhi, the nonviolent campaign for Indian independence was of far less importance than the remembering of the pluralistic community that had been shattered by colonialism. While he himself chose a path of voluntary poverty, Gandhi recognized dispossession and economic exploitation as forces that destroy communities, and so he preached economic self-reliance for India and he allied himself with the outcastes and "untouchables" whom he called "Harijan," children of God. Gandhi was fond of quoting from the Gospels, especially while speaking to British colonial administrators, but he would also quote from the Vedas and the Gita while speaking to Muslims, and in Hindu worship services, he would read from the Holy Koran. When violence broke out between Hindus and Muslims, Gandhi fasted for suspension of the independence struggle because he believed that the maintenance and building of community were more important than political self-determination. He recognized that the hope for any viable community life in India could not rest on ethnocentrism or religious exclusivity. He recognized that communal solidarity provided the only nonviolent means with which to oppose tyranny and militarism. When governments intentionally precipitate ethnic conflict and terror (as in the Balkans, as in Rwanda), it is an effort to destroy the memory of those communities that constitute a countervailing power independent of the state. If communities are dismembered, both freedom and nonviolence are endangered. We must remember community.

We must remember Jesus. Wherever and whenever Jesus is not remembered, those who claim the name of Christian have shown a special proclivity to give allegiance to race or ethnicity, wealth or weaponry, empire or liberation army, or any of the other numerous powers laying claim to lordship. When there is failure to remember the one who died on the cross, crucifixion follows. When there is failure to remember the one who rose from the grave, the graves are filled. Terror is a sign of dismembered community. Terror is also a sign of spiritual crisis, of a faith that has failed. To remember Jesus, bread is broken, cup is shared, community is formed. *All* violence is an attack upon community. *All* violence by Christians is also an attack upon the memory of Jesus.

*   *   *

The very concept of memory entails paradox. To remember is a present event that seeks to re-collect portions of the past. It is an act of the will to leap back across short or long chronological distances and to have the present visited by that which has gone before. At times, however, memories "flood in" independent of any conscious will to remember. When memories come "out of the blue," it is as if the notion of re-collecting history is turned on its head. Rather than laying hold of the past, the past lays hold of us. The affirmation that "Jesus lives" is in part an acknowledgment that Jesus invades the present even in the absence of any particular human will to remember him. It is as if Jesus remembers us, recollects us. By bridging the chronological distance and invading the present from the past (and the future?), Jesus turns memory upside down and he re-members us. Contrary to some notions of sacramentalism, the admonition to "Do this in remembrance of me" is not a request by Jesus to perform a sacrifice or service so that he will not be forgotten. The service we are asked to perform for Jesus has to do with feeding the hungry, clothing the naked, visiting the prisoners (Matthew 25:31-46), but "Do this in remembrance of me" is not a service to be performed for the sake of Jesus. Jesus does not need us to remember him. *We* need us to remember him. And when our memory of Jesus fails (as it always seems to do), then it is Jesus who seeks us out and remembers *us*.

The paradox of chronological distance plays a role not only in communion with Jesus, but also in the very concept of human community. In the debate between Paine and Burke, Thomas Paine was certainly correct that community is established among the living, but Edmund Burke's emphasis on the value of what he called "tradition" is not to be denied. The saints and sinners who have gone before have a powerful influence on the community of the living. Across the expanse of time, we learn from them and argue with them, as those who follow us will do as well. In Native American spirituality, there are complementary calls to remember the future as well as the past; honor the ancestors *and* consider the impact that all of your words and deeds will have on the next seven generations. Like the pebble tossed into the lake, the smallest thoughtful or thoughtless deed produces ripples that travel far. Ideally, conscious community in the present recollects sisters and brothers from the past as well as the future.

If there is this sense in which community transcends time, may it be said to transcend geographical distance as well? Is there a sense beyond mere sentimentality in which we may be said to share human community with people the world over? The biblical account of creation is itself suggestive of kinship among all who are shaped from the dust of the ground (Genesis 2:7). This unity of creation, this Gaia "beckons us into communion."[37] What happens to ecology and to creatures half a world away is of concern to the full community of creation. But a dialectical tension is present here as well, for it is not only natural but it is also a *gift* that our sense of community is first and foremost local, shaped by a specific place and people. Any thought of "humanitarian intervention" half a world away can only fail if it is not based on the experience of having practiced compassion in a local place. Any notion of "global community" is doomed to abstraction if it is divorced from the original sense of communing with people and with nature in a specific place. The attempt to suppress or ignore differences in localities or human differences (ethnicity, race, religion) is less an encouragement of tolerance than an encouragement of uniformity. When addressing racism, for example, the encouragement to be "color blind" (which is both impossible and insulting to people of all colors) is indicative of a desire for uniformity. Current trends toward "globalism" in the economy and in technology are productive of uniformity (whether in militarism or fast food restaurants or mass communication) but destructive of community. As Wendell Berry notes, "Abstraction, of course, is what is wrong. The evil of the industrial economy (capitalist or communist) is the abstractness inherent in its procedures — its inability to distinguish one place or person or creature from another."[38]

Modern warfare aims for such abstraction by placing distance between the killer and the killed. Michel Foucault placed considerable emphasis on the body (both the biological and the social body) as the target in the exercise of political power and domination.[39] But he also noted a trend towards being free from contact or engagement with those bodies that are the subjects of domination.[40] With capital punishment, for example, a history of profuse and gruesome contact between executioner and victim in the form of torture, drawing and quartering, or beheading gave way in most settings to hangings and firing squads. In the United States, one of the few democracies still using the death penalty (and using it zealously, at that), it was considered "humane" progress when the contact between executioner and victim was reduced to a mere pinprick in the form of lethal injection. With the infliction of other violence as well, killing up close is considered by many to be suspect in ways that launching a cruise missile is not. In commenting on the massacre at My Lai, one author observed that even military personnel must wonder at the supposed ethical difference that distance makes: "How is it, the foot soldier must wonder, that to kill women and children at less than five hundred paces is an atrocity, at more than five hundred paces, it is an act of heroism?"[41]

In his classic work *On Aggression,* Konrad Lorenz offers biological and behavioral explanations for this vague sense that killing up close and killing at a distance are somehow to be judged differently. Lorenz argues that most species are possessed of certain "behavioral analogies to morality" that usually serve to prevent creatures from killing members of their own species. Subtle or ritualized displays of submission, appeasement, or affection serve as signals to inhibit aggression. These inhibitory behaviors are more successful at curbing aggression within some species than within others. For example, Lorenz notes that an objective observer would likely conclude that human "social organization is very similar to that of rats, which, like humans, are social and peaceful beings within their clans, but veritable devils toward all fellow members of their species not belonging to their own community."[42] If in fact the human species is possessed of any natural, visual signals that inhibit aggression, these are totally subverted by the distance modern weaponry places between the attacker and the victim. The distance grants permission for violence by dehumanizing people into mere "targets." And so, notes Lorenz, from a distance, "perfectly good-natured" people who would not dream of spanking a child can drop incendiary bombs which maim and kill dozens of children.[43]

If not "good-natured," Adolf Eichmann was judged by psychiatrists to be "normal." The fact that Eichmann could present himself as a man just doing his job was part of what Hannah Arendt called "the banality of evil."[44] He was a bureaucrat who ordinarily kept his physical distance from any actual killing and, if his later testimony is to be believed, he wanted to get away when he saw the killing up close. In his official capacity, he was taken to see the operation of a van being used to gas Jews:

> I couldn't bring myself to look closely, even once. I didn't look inside the entire time. I couldn't, no, I couldn't take any more. The screaming and, and, I was too upset. . . . Then I saw the most horrifying thing I have ever seen in my entire life.
>
> The van drove up to a long trench, the doors were opened and bodies thrown out. They still seemed alive, their limbs were so supple. They were thrown in, I can still remember a civilian pulling out teeth with some pliers and then I just got the hell out of there.[45]

Even in his own testimony, Eichmann's description shows concern for his own emotional "upset" and his desire to leave, not compassion for the victims, let alone any desire to intervene. He wished to return to the safe distance that facilitated his work.

There has never been any doubt that people are capable of barbarity at close range, but modernity has brought a proclivity to put more distance between attacker and victim. While technological developments foster claims (albeit false claims) that ours is an age of greater intimacy in the form of a "shrinking globe," a "world wide web," and a "global community," there is no technological drive towards greater intimacy between combatants when all hell breaks loose in the global neighborhood.

Not only geography, but also political and bureaucratic layers of governance can provide the distance that grants permission for violence. The bureaucratic layers serve to insulate political leaders from the consequences of their decisions. As Adam Hochschild observed of the governance by the Belgian King Leopold, who presided over the Congo while millions were killed:

> Unlike many other great predators of history, from Genghis Khan to the Spanish conquistadors, King Leopold II never saw a drop of blood spilled in anger. He never set foot in the Congo. There is something very modern

about that . . . as there is about the bomber pilot in the stratosphere, above the clouds, who never hears screams or sees shattered homes or torn flesh.[46]

Like the proverbial monkeys in a row, leaders can claim to have seen, heard, and spoken no evil. But further down the bureaucratic ladder, other functionaries can also claim immunity from ethical responsibility. Like Eichmann, other bureaucrats are just doing their jobs and following orders, and as long as the orders are issued legally, one must remain within the confines of the law. Besides, careers and paychecks cannot be abandoned with impunity, for families would suffer as a result. Maximilian Grabner, head of the Political Department at Auschwitz, said, "I only took part in the murder of some three million people out of consideration for my family."[47] Hannah Arendt notes that people are dehumanized by becoming mere cogs in the administrative machinery of this "rule of Nobody, which is what the political form known as bureaucracy truly is."[48] Whether or not the bureaucratic layers of organization mean that Nobody rules, they certainly mean that Nobody need take moral responsibility, including "the people" who supposedly rule in democratic societies. Like Eichmann, we might recoil in horror if we ever witnessed atrocities up close. Yet, good folks who would never dream of gassing people in a van or incinerating people with a cruise missile pay for that to be done with the price of taxes and silence.[49] All of the distancing by common folks, by military personnel, by governmental functionaries constitutes permission for violence. But the dehumanization of the victims of violence is accompanied by a profound dehumanization of self — or, more accurately, the creation of a second, "false" self who can shed blood and then step back into a "true" self who is good neighbor and loving parent.[50] Georges Bernanos observed that what should most rouse our concern is not the mad terrorist but the obedience within our neighbors and ourselves: "The horrors which we have seen, the still greater horrors which we will presently see, are not signs that rebels, insubordinate, untamable men, are increasing in constant numbers but rather that there is a constant increase, a stupendously rapid increase, in the number of obedient, docile men."[51]

In addition to geographical distance and bureaucratic insulation, racism and ethnocentrism can play powerful roles in granting permission for violence and, as noted earlier, governments sometimes peddle these hatreds in seeking to disrupt established communities. Colonial terror by European powers in Africa and elsewhere was abetted by a dehumanizing and dehumanized racist view of the enslaved people. Just as a wild animal may not respond to human kindness, there was a common view among the colonizers that terrorism was the only language their "uncivilized" subjects could understand. Charles Caudron was a rubber company agent convicted of murdering 122 Africans in the Congo; when his case was heard in an appeals court in 1904, his sentence was reduced in light of the mitigating circumstance that he was trying to supervise people who were "absolutely resistant to any idea of work" and who knew "no other means of persuasion than terror."[52] Recognizing the powerful role that racism can play in granting permission for violence, the U.S. government participated in a racist propaganda campaign against the Japanese during World War II (replete with depictions of the "Yellow Peril" as comprised of "little monkey men" and "lice" that needed to be exterminated), but the campaign was quickly abandoned as war's end brought new hopes that Japan could be shaped into a major market for American exports.[53]

Race hate plays a role in granting permission for violence among non-state groups as well. In the United States, the Aryan Nations and the Ku Klux Klan are just two obvious examples of groups with a history of perpetrating race-based violence. In the testimony of a number of former members of these groups, a dehumanized view of potential victims is essential to the perpetration of such violence. In 1980, Sibylle Vorderbrugge joined *Deutsche Aktionsgruppen,* a German neo-Nazi group headed by Manfred Roeder. In a campaign to rid Germany of foreigners, Vorderbrugge participated in the bombing of a hotel for Eritrean refugees near Stuttgart in which three people were injured, and an arson attack against a hostel in which Vietnamese refugees were sleeping. In the latter attack, two people were killed. Vorderbrugge reports that after the attack, she experienced shock that she had participated in an action that had caused deaths, but Roeder offered assurance that the victims were just "half-apes."[54]

The dehumanization that grants permission for violence may be based on criteria other than race. Mario Moretti of the Red Brigade was a key figure in planning the kidnapping and murder of former Italian Premier Aldo Moro. At his trial in November 1984, Moretti explained, "You know that we did not kidnap Moro the man, but [rather] his function."[55] This depersonalized notion of attacking people based on their "function" can be used with equal agility by zealots of the left and the right. After all, do we not all have our "functions"?

Another man who was doubtless kidnapped because of his function was Geoffrey Jackson. While he held the position of British Ambassador to Uruguay, Jackson was kidnapped in January 1971 and held for eight months by Tupamaro guerrillas. But his experience points to the possibility of some level of *re*humanization between people who had previously viewed each other as mere "functions." Jackson was held in a cellar and was watched by a changing guard of up to 30 different Tupamaros, most of whom were students, all of whom wore black hoods to conceal their faces. To pass the time, Jackson took to drawing sketches of these hooded people, sketches that depicted them shopping or sitting in classrooms or doing other ordinary things out in the world, always with hood in place. This mild mockery of their situation became a point of contact between captive and captors. They shared laughter and the Tupamaros asked for copies of the sketches. Jackson survived the eight-month ordeal, but he feared that many of his captors may have died in a 1972 Uruguayan military campaign against the Tupamaros.[56]

In addition to the ways in which distance, obedience, and various forms of dehumanization grant permission for violence, violence itself constitutes sanction for the perpetration of additional spirals of violence. Whatever else the use of violence teaches (whether it is the violence of domestic abuse, capital punishment, or slaughter in warfare), its primary lesson is that the use of violence itself is justifiable. Such a lesson is communicated even to those who are not immediate witnesses of violence, but some people who are later charged with terrorism have in fact been prior witnesses of atrocity. After noting that battered children are at higher risk of becoming abusive parents, Eqbal Ahmad notes that state terror can also play a role in breeding other forms of terrorism:

> Typically, the most notorious Zionist terrorist groups — the Stern and Irgun — were composed of youthful immigrants from Eastern Europe and Germany who had been victims of pogroms and the Holocaust. Similarly, the young Shias who hijacked [a] TWA aircraft were witnesses to violence since childhood; most are believed to be refugees in Beirut from Israel's bombings and invasions, since 1976, of southern Lebanon.[57]

Indeed, there is a growing body of evidence that, not only past exposure to violence, but even the very presence of weapons can serve to increase aggression. For forty years, Leonard Berkowitz, emeritus professor of psychology at the University of Wisconsin, has studied the "weapons effect," i.e., the manner in which the mere presence of a weapon such as a gun can increase aggressiveness among observers. To the claim that "Guns don't kill people, people kill people," Berkowitz responds, "The finger pulls the trigger. But the trigger may also pull the finger." Psychology professor Ann Frodi reached similar conclusions based on her behavioral experiments with high school students. Frodi measured increased aggressive behaviors among students when a weapon was placed within their field of vision. Berkowitz explains that "Guns aren't neutral. They create aggression that wouldn't exist in the absence of guns."[58] The very presence of weapons must be added to the list of those factors that grant permission for violence.

*   *   *

54

And so we have assembled a list (and an incomplete list, at that) of the ways in which violence may be sanctioned or even encouraged. We have examined the ways in which organized assaults upon community and memory can make the ground fertile for terror and genocide, especially when combined with militarization and economic deprivation. We have noted how dehumanization of others can predispose people to violence, and we have noted the impact of factors such as distance, racism, the proclivity to obey, the presence of weapons, and prior exposure to violence. But despite the lists of permissions and predispositions, we have still not explained (nor can we explain) how and why people actually cross the threshold to commit horrendous acts of terror.

As research for her book, *Shoot the Women First,* Eileen MacDonald conducted scores of interviews with women who had been or continued to be members of groups labeled as "terrorist" organizations. Reportedly, the advice to "shoot the women first" was given in the 1980s to recruits of West Germany's anti-terrorist squad and was offered by Interpol to other such agencies in Europe. Christian Lochte of Germany's anti-subversives intelligence-gathering network regarded it as good advice: "There are some examples where men waited a moment before they fired, and women shot at once. This is a general phenomenon with terrorists."[59] Whether Lochte's generalization is accurate or not, MacDonald is certainly correct in observing that women who use violence transgress traditional stereotypes. Women and other oppressed people have often been coached or forced into passivity, but with violence, said former Red Brigade member Susanna Ronconi, "You felt you were able to influence the world about you instead of experiencing it passively."[60] Ronconi is certainly not alone in the mistaken impression that there are only these two options — violence or passivity.

While posing the difficulty of seeking to explain the decision to engage in terror, MacDonald cites the shocking case of the young women who were suicide-bombers in Lebanon during the 1980s:

> Aged between seventeen and nineteen, many were filmed before setting out on their missions to blow themselves up along with their targets. On the videos that were released, they wore makeup and smiled for the cameras — and they sent shock waves into family living rooms around the world. In their western clothes, they looked just like ordinary kids; and yet they were about to kill, and die themselves, in the most horrifying circumstances. Experts opined that they had been brainwashed or drugged; these suggestions were quickly taken up by the media. Anything rather than believe that these girls were sane, deeply committed, and acting of their own free will. Whatever the truth, the image of these pretty, smiling teenagers,

intent on the kind of violence that few would even contemplate, was extraordinarily potent.[61]

This decision in favor of terror, whether it is made by women or by men, how does one explain it? There may in fact be some who are "brainwashed," like Kim Hyon Hui who blew up a passenger jet on orders from North Korea. There may be some suffering a variety of "Stockholm Syndrome," like Patty Hearst of the Symbionese Liberation Army. There may be some who are duped, such as Ann Murphy, the pregnant romantic partner of Hindawi, who unwittingly carried a suitcase full of explosives onto a passenger jet. There may be some children of privilege who see themselves as standing with the oppressed, like Astrid Proll of the Baader-Meinhof group who said, "You have got to remember that we were very well-armed social workers."[62] And there may be some who are merely longing for adventure, as also noted by Proll: "then the most fantastic thing in the world was not to be a rock star but a revolutionary."[63] But how does one explain the smiling faces of the teenaged suicide-bombers and of so many others?

The need to explain is not only a need experienced by outside observers. As one reads the statements of those who have engaged in violence, one detects rationalization and self-justification. In a virtual argument with self, those who have perpetrated violence can be heard distorting the very meaning of words such as "peace," "love," and "humanity." It is not only Big Brother, but it is also little brothers and sisters who can make war sound like peace.

Bassam Abu Sharif of the Popular Front for the Liberation of Palestine was editor of *Al Hadaf.* He had lost most of his eyesight and several of his fingers to a mail bomb. When he was interviewed by British journalist Gerald McKnight in 1973, Abu Sharif said of violence, "You must differentiate between the kind used to exploit people and that used in self-defence: legitimate violence. The bullets that I shoot are not the bullets used to exploit or subdue. They are just the opposite. They will remove exploitation. . . ."[64] Abu Sharif's predecessor at *Al Hadaf,* Ghassan Kanafani, was killed along with his young niece when a bomb planted by Israeli agents destroyed his car. Kanafani's Danish-born widow, Anni, asserted, "Love of life necessitates violence. Ghassan wasn't a pacifist. He was killed in the class struggle. . . ."[65]

A similar rationalizing approach to violence is discernible in the statements of Ruairi O'Bradaigh of the Irish Republican Army. After witnessing a fellow member of the IRA triggering a mine that killed several British soldiers, O'Bradaigh expressed admiration for the way in which his IRA comrade had crossed himself and asked that God might have mercy on the souls of the British soldiers just before making the connection to "blow them all to smithereens."[66] When asked about the charge that the IRA is a terrorist organization, O'Bradaigh replied:

> I don't disagree with terror, not at all. Because the British presence constitutes another sort of violence. It uses terror too. Counter-terror, call it what you like, is completely acceptable to me for that reason. It is one method of getting rid of the terror that causes it. . . . We all want peace. And brutal decisions have to be taken. The supreme driving force for those deeply and closely involved is the desire to end it, for all time.[67]

Of course, O'Bradaigh's view that terror can be ended by inflicting sufficient quantities of terror was shared by some within the British military and within the Ulster Defence Association. Indeed, Tommy Herron, one of the leaders of the UDA until the time of his violent death, asserted the need for the UDA to rely on terrorist tactics because the previous loyalist approach of "restraint and compassion" had merely elicited IRA terrorism.[68]

This love of life which requires killing. This terrorism which seeks to end terrorism and which is caused by terrorism. Beyond mere rationalizing, is this not doublespeak? Angel Bengochea was founder of an Argentine guerrilla group called ERP (People's Revolutionary Army). Following his death in an explosion in July 1964, his widow quoted him as having said, "We can only achieve what is human — a just society — in inhuman ways. We must dehumanise ourselves so that, by being inhuman, we can achieve what is human."[69] The statement serves as a reminder of the extent to which some people assume that the means employed (dehumanizing oneself and others) can be divorced from the ends sought (being human). The statement also serves as a reminder that if we ever have illusions of being either gods or devils, illusions of being either totally sinless or totally evil, we forfeit the one task that is clearly given to us — being human.

When violence is to be perpetrated up close, humanity itself sometimes intrudes on the rationalizing process. On August 29, 1969, TWA Flight 840 from Los Angeles to Tel Aviv made a scheduled stop in Rome where Leila Khaled and her accomplice, Salim, boarded in order to hijack the flight. Eventually, the plane was destroyed after the passengers had been evacuated, but the plan included the possibility that the plane would be blown up in flight. Khaled later reported that, as she waited in the lounge for the flight to depart, armed with grenade and pistol, she was given pause when she saw two little children happily playing as they waited to board Flight 840. While the response is not universal, the presence of children can evoke a protective response from adults.[70] For Khaled, the presence of children evoked the need for additional rationalizing, which was accomplished by conjuring the images of other children. "Then I remembered all the countless thousands of Palestinian children in the refugee camps. They were depending on me to tell the world about them. When I remembered their faces I was strengthened."[71] Strengthened for what? Strengthened for the possibility that she would be killing children in order to save children?

The presence of children also gave pause to the Russian Populists who plotted the assassination of Grand Duke Sergei. The assassins abandoned their first planned attempt to throw a bomb into the carriage of the Grand Duke when they discovered that his two young nephews were riding in the carriage with him. This true story serves as the basis of Albert Camus's play, *The Just Assassins,* a play that explores the dilemma faced by those who would dehumanize people for the sake of humanizing the social order. The one chosen to throw the bomb is Ivan Kaliayev, also known as Yanek the Poet. Dora Dulebov is the one member of the group of assassins who seems fully aware of the deadly nature of what it is they propose to do. When Yanek exalts the virtues of the revolution that will bring new possibilities for life, Dora reminds him that they are plotting a death. Yanek responds, "When we kill, we're killing so as to build up a world in which there will be no more killing. We consent to being criminals so that at last the innocent, and only they, will inherit the earth."[72] Dora reminds Yanek that he will not have the advantage of killing at a distance and that, after all, "A man is a man. Perhaps the Grand Duke has gentle eyes, perhaps you'll see him smiling to himself, scratching his ear." Yanek responds that he will not look, that he will not see, that "with God's help, my hatred will surge up just in time, and blind me." Besides, says Yanek in a fashion akin to the assassins of Aldo Moro, "It's not he I'm killing. I'm killing despotism."[73] Due to the presence of the two children in the Grand Duke's carriage, Yanek fails to throw the bomb. Unlike the hijacker Leila Khaled, Yanek has failed to evoke the images of other children to rationalize his act. This failure elicits rebuke from his fellow-assassin, Stepan: "Just because Yanek couldn't bring himself to kill those two, thousands of Russian children will go on dying of starvation for years to come."[74] Eventually, the Grand Duke was killed, and as we know in retrospect, thousands of Russian children went on dying of starvation. The Gospel reminder that the poor are always with us (Matthew 26:11; Mark 14:7; John 12:8) should at least spare the poor from the libel that our murders are inflicted for their sake.

But the question still looms: How do we explain the smiles of the suicide-bombers of Lebanon? These young terrorists, barely past the age of childhood themselves, were they brainwashed or drugged? Were they sick? The tendency to label the violence of others as "sick" is a powerful tool in the so-called "war on terrorism." The label identifies the violence of others as somehow more repugnant and more elusive of explanation than our own violence. A corresponding tactic is to label all the victims of the violence of these sick terrorists as "innocent" in contrast to our own violence, which is carefully calibrated and laser-guided to seek out only the "guilty." It is, of course, another version of rationalizing to say that our war is not against the people of Panama, or the people of Iraq, or the people of Yugoslavia, but against their "evil" leaders. When the smart bomb smoke clears and the bulldozers set to work, it is not evil that is buried; it is the people of Panama, Iraq, and Yugoslavia.[75]

While those who are ill might be treated with compassion, labeling an opponent as "sick" is in no way a pretext for mercy. As Susan Sontag noted in her book, *Illness as Metaphor,* some diseases are to be battled, to be attacked, to be cut out: "To describe a phenomenon as a cancer is an incitement to violence."[76] It is precisely this metaphor which Paul Johnson chose in an essay called "The Cancer of Terrorism."[77] It is precisely this metaphor which the Ulster Freedom Fighters chose when they issued a statement that sought to justify their violent struggle against the IRA: ". . . we would make it clear to our people, and indeed to the world, that our methods, although extreme, are necessary. When the cancer within the human body lies deep, the surgeon must cut accordingly."[78]

Apart from the violence implicit in the illness metaphor, the attempt to assign a mental illness to those who perpetrate terror does not stand up to scrutiny. Most "mad bombers" are not mad, and most people living with mental illness are no more violent than the rest of us despite media depictions to the contrary. It was once common practice in the crime coverage by broadcast and print media to engage in selective racial identification, as for example, "a black man was arrested today," but rarely "a white man was arrested today." Similarly, coverage of violent crime continues to highlight those instances in which suspects have a history of schizophrenia or bipolar disorder, but we never hear reports that "A man with no diagnosis of mental illness was arrested today in a murderous rampage." This is part of an effort to depict violence as something foreign to the mainstream, something peculiar to minorities or sick people or poor people, something found on Skid Row but not on Main Street and certainly not on Wall Street.

Bruce Hoffman of the Center for the Study of Terrorism and Political Violence remarks, "I have been studying terrorists and terrorism for more than twenty years. Yet I am still always struck by how disturbingly 'normal' most terrorists seem when one actually sits down and talks to them."[79] Likewise, Eileen MacDonald found that the women she interviewed were not "monsters," that in fact they "look and speak much like the next-door neighbor or the woman behind you in line at the checkout," and that they "do not much like talking about killing people."[80] As with those who interviewed Eichmann, what seems abnormal is this sense of normality. What seems unacceptable is this sense that those who could perpetrate evil are not somehow different from the rest of us in their very nature.

To the perennial question of whether human nature is fundamentally good or evil, Martin Luther King, Jr. offered the response that neither is the case. Drawing on insights from Jesus, Tolstoy, and Gandhi, King noted that all people have potential for loving acts of kindness or horrendous acts of terror.[81] We are all created in the image of God and we are all fallen. Our task, then, becomes one of seeking to appeal to that image of God, to that potential for love which persists in ourselves and others. There is no one who is not so created. There is no one without the image of God.

And there is no one who is not fallen. There is no one who is free from the potential for hatred and violence. There is a solid kinship between the violence inflicted up close and that which comes from a distance. There is no more need to explain the smiles of terrorists in Lebanon than there is to explain the smiles of presidents and senators, the smiles of Americans at Gulf War victory rallies, the smiles of citizens who pay the bills, the smiles of the silent. These are our smiles. Normal smiles. What is there to explain?

The Terror of Antisemitism

We are spray upon the ocean. We are mist. Each individual is a droplet who is lifted by power of wind or wave to linger for a moment, hovering so briefly above the ocean to which each shall return. The ocean alone is eternal, is Brahman, is God. Here there is Gautama and here Jesus. There is Mohammed and there Gandhi. All are gifts from the ocean and to the ocean they return. It is possible to be an adherent of one teacher or many, a devotee of one God or many or none at all, and still remain within the *dharma*, the way. Such, at least, is one reading of the pervasive tolerance within that wide and multifaceted tradition known as Hinduism.

While Hinduism has a well-deserved reputation as the spiritual tradition most tolerant (and even assimilative) of a rich variety of beliefs, all of the major world religions foster versions of tolerance for those whose faith may differ. In Islam, for example, special respect is accorded to Jews and Christians as "people of the Book" who, like Muslims, are monotheists and claim Abraham as father. Throughout history, it has more often been Islamic rule and not Christendom that has provided an environment of relative safety and freedom for Jews. In Iberia, Sephardic Judaism flourished under Muslim rulers, but after King

Ferdinand and Queen Isabella conquered Granada and established a unified, Christian Spain, there was a wholesale expulsion of Jews. The event was noted with apparent approval by Columbus in his account of his 1492 voyage: "In the same month when they expelled all Jews from the country, Your Highnesses commanded me to go with an adequate fleet to those parts of India."[82]

But if Islamic tolerance toward Judaism surpassed that of Christendom, tolerance alone has never been enough to forestall terror. Indeed, there can be an interdependence between periods of relative tolerance and periods of violence, as indicated by the occasional pogroms against Jews under Islamic rule in medieval Europe, with some Muslims joining in the charge that Jews were "Christ killers."[83] No matter the degree to which tolerance has been encouraged, it must be acknowledged that none of the major religious traditions on the planet has been free from complicity in fostering violence and terror. From among adherents of that most pacific of faiths, Jainism, there have arisen ferocious military commanders like Ganga Raja and Chamunda Raya Karnataka.[84] From among adherents of that most tolerant of faiths, Hinduism, there have arisen terrorists perpetrating sporadic bloodshed against Muslims and Sikhs. From among adherents of that most compassionate of faiths, Buddhism, there have arisen those who launched pogroms against Tamils in Sri Lanka, as well as a Dalai Lama who announced support for the thermonuclear weapons tests conducted by India's "Hindu nationalist" government.[85] And from among adherents of that most loving of faiths, Christianity, there have arisen holocausts.

As noted earlier in this chapter, some of the most virulent forms of hatred and terror emerge, not between groups that are diametrically opposed, but between groups that have once shared community (Serbs and Croats, Pakistanis and Indians, Hutu and Tutsi). If the community suffers disintegration, which often comes as the result of intentional political, military, or economic intrusion, any conflict that erupts may be most intense between those who were previously closest.[86] Conflicts may result from competition for control of land, economic resources, and political power, but also from competition for control of those symbols and forms of discourse that had previously served to unify the community.[87] The struggle for a monopoly over the interpretation of communal symbols may engender bloodshed on a scale that is anything but "symbolic."[88] Rosemary Radford Ruether discerns such a struggle in the origins of antisemitism in the church: "Hatred between groups who have no stake in a common stock of religiously sanctioned identity symbols can scarcely be as virulent as hatred between groups whose relations express a religious form of 'sibling rivalry.'"[89]

The debate among historians and theologians regarding the origins of antisemitism has been somberly joined by many in the decades since the Holocaust. While we cannot hope to trace the debate in full, concerns have emerged from this debate that touch not only on the origins of terror but also on the origins of Christianity. Some authors have exonerated Christianity by tracing the origins of antisemitism to Greek and Roman "paganism" and by asserting that Nazism and other anti-Jewish ideologies are not grounded in Christian theology.[90] In sharp contrast, some other authors have asserted, not only that the history of Christendom is filled with anti-Jewish terrors, but that the very origins of Christian antisemitism can be found in the New Testament itself.[91] Implicit in this latter position, however, there is another paradoxical and unintentional exoneration of Christians from responsibility for antisemitism.[92] If antisemitism is part and parcel of the faith that proclaims that Jesus is the Messiah, then the believer would seem to have only two options — abandon the faith or be antisemitic; the antisemitism could be excused as a refusal to abandon the faith. In fact, a tragically large number of Christian theologians, princes, and others throughout history have sought to exonerate themselves from responsibility for violence against Jews in precisely this way, that is, by claiming that New Testament faith requires opposition to Judaism.

"Jesus and Paul and Peter would have perished at Auschwitz. . . ."[93] Such is the reminder by Franklin Littell of the thoroughly Jewish identity of the major figures in the New Testament, an identity that was likely shared by all New Testament authors. A growing number of biblical scholars might agree with the observation that, "Simply put, we can now read the New Testament as a Jewish book."[94] Since most New Testament writings can be dated to the period between the mid and late first century c.e., the decisive split between the Christian movement and the larger Jewish community had not yet occurred. Therefore, prophetic discourse within the New Testament that might sound anti-Jewish to the modern ear can be better understood as "intra-Jewish polemic," often aimed at specific parties or authorities within Judaism.[95] The prophetic tradition of the Hebrew Bible indicates that intra-Jewish polemic can become quite vociferous. The Gospel of John portrays a scene in which Jesus engages in controversy in the temple with those who claim to be descendants of Abraham. In John's version, Jesus issues the harsh rebuke, "You are from your father the devil . . ." (John 8:44). But significantly, the statement is directed towards "the Jews who had *believed in him*" (8:31, emphasis added). The harsh rebuke is issued by the Jewish Jesus, not against his Jewish opponents, but against his Jewish followers, who were his only followers. Similar language ("sons of Belial") is used in the Dead Sea Scrolls as part of an intra-Jewish polemic.[96]

More than any other biblical writer, Paul has been invoked by theologians ranging from Martin Luther to some of the modern liberationists as evidence of an irreconcilable division between the primitive Christian community and

Judaism.[97] But actually, as E. P. Sanders notes in the conclusion of one of his several studies on the relationship between Paul and Judaism, "Paul's thought was largely Jewish, and his work as apostle to the Gentiles is to be understood within the framework of Jewish eschatological speculation. . . ."[98] A powerful strain within Jewish thought held that, in the final days before the establishment of God's reign, Gentiles would turn from idolatry and join with the people of God (Israel), but the basis of this turning would be eschatological and not halakic.[99] Thus, while Paul offered reassurance that there was no distinction between Jew and Gentile in the eschatological community (Romans 3:9; 3:22; Galatians 3:28), he nonetheless insisted that Gentiles should participate in this community as Gentiles and not as Torah-observant Jews (Romans 3:28-31; Galatians 5:2-6). His point was not a repudiation of some supposed Jewish legalism, but rather an assertion that Gentiles could witness to the coming of God's reign through the Jewish Messiah Jesus by participating as Gentiles in the Jewish community. It is thus a misnomer to speak of Paul's "conversion" as if he was changing "religions"; one might more properly speak of the "call" by which Paul is sent to the Gentiles, a call that is firmly within the prophetic tradition of Israel.[100] In writing to his Gentile readers in Rome, Paul makes it clear that his mission remains one of preaching God's good news of liberation for Israel (Romans 1:16; 11:25-32). Paul's change from persecuting the followers of Jesus to embracing them entailed a renewed and thoroughly Jewish understanding of eschatology as well as an awareness that, contrary to the strategy of persecution, "God did not work through the balance of terror. . . ."[101]

What, then, accounts for the origins of the antisemitic terror that has been so prominent during extensive periods of church history? The death of the community between the followers of Jesus and the rest of Judaism was not intrinsic to anything being preached by those within the Jesus movement of the first century, who were busily reminding Gentiles of the priority accorded to the salvation of the Jews (Romans 1:16). Nor was the demise of community demanded by anything within Judaism itself. Judaism has provided a "big tent" to serve as home for ornery and polemical parties including Sadducees, Pharisees, Essenes, and Zealots, to serve as home for the messianic movements of Bar Kochba, Sabbatai Zevi, and a profusion of others.[102]

As with the modern examples that have been cited (Rwanda, the Balkans), the bifurcated sense of identity between the Jesus movement and the rest of Judaism came on the heels of warfare, outside intervention, and economic disruption. Rome was the outside colonizing force that sought to crush any pretensions to self-rule for Jews or others. The warfare in Palestine came in waves known as the "Jewish wars," most prominent of which were the armed uprisings and Roman military repression of 66-73 c.e. and 133-136 c.e. The destruction of Jerusalem and the Temple in 70 C.E. provoked a crisis for all of Judaism and initiated the decline of the "Jewish Christian" community that had been forged by James, the brother of Jesus. As an expression of Jewish solidarity and as an eschatological sign of the Gentiles honoring Jerusalem, Paul had organized a great collection to be given to the poor in Jerusalem, but after 70 C.E., with the city and the Temple in ruins, there was diminished potential for such signs of solidarity and economic interdependence. With the Roman military victory, the Emperor Vespasian decreed that the half-shekel contribution which Jews the world over had previously given to the Jerusalem Temple should now be paid as a Jewish tax to the Capitoline Jupiter treasury in Rome.[103] The Temple had served as an important unifying symbol for Judaism, and with its destruction, imperial policies played an intrusive role in forcing questions of religious identity into the foreground. Who was Jewish? Who was "sufficiently Jewish" to claim the traditional Jewish exemption from the imperial system of worship and devotion to the spirit of the emperor? And more ominously, who was "sufficiently Jewish" to be subjected to the special taxes and penalties that were imposed upon a defeated people?

While the sense of community between the Jesus movement and the rest of Judaism was placed under severe strain by the war of 66-73 C.E. (by which time all of the genuine Pauline epistles, the Q source, and perhaps a Gospel or two had already been written), the final collapse came with the Roman military repression of 133-36 C.E. (by which time, with the possible exception of a few interpolations, all of the writings that came to be included in the New Testament had already been completed). The war of 133-36 marked the final disappearance of the Jewish Christian group that had once been led by James.[104] While the writings of the first century can be fairly characterized as intra-Jewish polemic, the second century sees a gradual shift towards writings that are clearly anti-Jewish or anti-Christian in character.[105]

As we have seen in more recent history, for terror to ensue, the animosities that result from communal disruption must be vested with political and/or military power. Christians acquired such power in the Constantinian era. As French historian Jules Isaac wrote, ". . . the fate of Israel did not take on a truly inhuman character until the 4th century A.D. with the coming of the Christian Empire."[106] Beginning in the 4th century, there is a dramatic increase in the number of accounts of Christian attacks on synagogues, attacks that were defended by church leaders such as Ambrose of Milan (see note 125 in the first chapter). These attacks upon Jews, however, were rarely understood as an effort to totally eliminate Judaism. The new imperial church needed Jews to continue existing as a rejected people so that their very rejection would testify to blessings bestowed upon the church. "The Jew was allowed to exist, indeed commanded to exist in the Christian era," writes Ruether, so that the Jew might inhabit "the negative space of divine reprobation. . . ."[107] Such motivation may have influenced Augustine's reading of Psalm 59 as advice for Christians in their relationship to Jews: Do not kill them, but scatter them.[108]

Thus there developed a perverse sense in Christendom that Judaism should be preserved so that Jews could be persecuted. The desire simultaneously to preserve and to persecute is illustrated by the medieval creation of the ghetto. The Fourth Lateran Council (1215) decreed that Jews should be segregated from Christians and that Jews should be required to wear distinctive dress and round, yellow "Jew badges" symbolizing the gold that the Jews had supposedly received to betray Jesus.[109] With Judaism simultaneously preserved but cursed as the religion of "Christ killers," the ghetto constituted a type of "social mark of Cain."[110] No matter the theological ruminations that may have ostensibly supported the creation of the ghetto, the continued presence of Jews as scapegoats served a unifying function for Christendom.[111] Those Christians who experienced uncomfortable doubts concerning their own faith could project those doubts onto the Jews who were "the very incarnation of disbelief in Jesus."[112] As the anxieties and guilt of Christian communities grew through a medieval period replete with religious wars and plentiful executions of witches and heretics, guiltier still were the deicidal Jews.[113]

With the Reformation, while there is no doubt about the continued persecution of the Jews, an ominous note of ambiguity is detectable in the writings of some church leaders on the question of whether the very existence of the Jewish community should be afforded continued protection by "the mark of Cain." In preaching to his congregation in 1539, Martin Luther noted that he could not hope to convert the Jews since Jesus himself had been unable to do so, "But I can close their mouths so that there will be nothing for them to do but lie upon the ground."[114] By the time of his 1543 invective, *Against the Jews and Their Lies,* Luther surrendered his ambiguity in favor of the blatant assertion that Christians "are at fault in not slaying them." The fault of Christians, wrote Luther, consisted of "not avenging" the "blood of our Lord," but significantly, Luther added that vengeance should also be exacted for the manner in which the Jews "curse, spit on and malign the Germans."

Luther's claim that the Germans were being victimized by the Jews was an early example of how nationalism and antisemitism could be mutually supportive. There is kinship between the antisemitism of the early, northern European nationalism associated with the Reformation era and the more recent nationalism, which held that "Germanness" and Judaism were antithetical. In a work that enjoyed wide circulation in the late 19th and early 20th centuries, *Die Judenfrage,* nationalist and socialist Eugen Dühring characterized the Jews as "foreign parasites" who merited only "terror and brute force."[115] The Jews had forfeited the mission that had been assigned to them, and now it was Germany that would fulfill the role of bringing redemption to humanity, a redemption the Jews could only forestall.[116] While nationalist antisemitism may be indifferent to or even opposed to Christian symbolism, Christendom provided the historical foundation on which such antisemitism could flourish.[117]

As Elie Wiesel has remarked, antisemitism is a "light sleeper."[118] What accounts for the persistence of antisemitic violence? While we have seen that terror can emerge from the death of community, modern genocide can hardly be attributed to communal disintegration, which was a *fait accompli* over 1,800 years ago. This is not to deny that there is an ongoing revisitation of tensions associated with the fact that there is a shared body of writings and symbols inherent to both Judaism and Christianity. Many of these tensions arise, however, from the tendency of some Christians to read the intra-Jewish polemic of the New Testament as anti-Jewish attack.

Contemporary antisemitism is best understood not as the residue of age-old hatreds inherent to Christianity, but as the expression of a different type of *Gemeinschaft*. Not all communities are benign. Some visions of community formation maintain that solidarity is achieved through the exercise of violence or the establishment of power over those outside of the community. Such was the vision of Martin Heidegger, who lent his considerable philosophical talents to the support of Nazism. With violence as an "ontological imperative," Heidegger theorized that the formation of a *Kampfgemeinschaft*, a fighting community, was demanded by the very nature of Being itself.[119] *Kampfgemeinschaft* might fairly characterize Nazism and other versions of violent antisemitism. Coincidentally, "a fighting community" might also be a fair description of street gangs who have no other reason for being than an ongoing struggle for turf — or a fair description of the military establishments of states the world over, including our own.[120] *Kampfgemeinschaft* is a community bonded by violence.

In contrast, both Judaism and Christianity are communities that are bonded solely by the Word of God. If it were not for this Word, these communities would not have been called into being, and it is this Word which these communities have to offer to the world. In reflecting on why the Jews of the Warsaw Ghetto lacked preparation for armed resistance against the Nazis, Alexander Donat reported that some "religious Jews" favored nonviolent defiance. He reported hearing a Jew make the following "unexpected argument":

> Try to imagine Jesus on the way to Golgotha suddenly stooping to pick up
> a stone and hurling it at one of the Roman legionnaires. After such an act,

could he ever have become the Christ? Think of Gandhi and Tolstoy, too. For two thousand years we have served mankind with the Word, with the Book. Are we now to try to convince mankind that we are warriors? We shall never outdo them at that game.[121]

While both Judaism and Christianity are communities bonded by the Word, there must be a surrendering of any notion of two communities vying for control of shared symbols, competing for control of the shared Word. We do not control the Word of God, rather it is the Word that calls out to us, that challenges us, that seeks to turn us about and to establish governance over us so as to free us from all of the other words of the numerous principalities and powers that claim dominion and divinity. It is only a dead word that can be controlled and owned. It is a living Word that breaks the confines of religious expectations (be they ever so holy and devout) to fill the world itself and to embrace all creatures in love. We happily wait for the fulfillment of such an unruly Word.

It is precisely this waiting that is a quality shared by both Jewish and Christian communities. Both are communities waiting for the fulfillment of God's Word. Jews await the Messiah, but Christians too await the return of Jesus.[122] Both Jews and Christians await the full manifestation of the "Kingdom of God."[123] In the Christian tradition, part of the messianic role of Jesus (and part of what distinguishes him from other biblical prophets) is his inauguration and establishment of the coming reign of God as already present and as already normative for disciples. Jesus is the invasion of the present by the new reality that God has promised for the future. The disciples are beckoned to practice now the loving of enemies, the turning of the cheek, the feeding of the hungry, the freeing of the captives, all of which are contra-indicated by the dangerous world in which we live, and all of which are normative under the reign of God. But paradoxically, this kingdom of God which is already present (Luke 17:21) is not yet fully realized. The paradox is evident when, in the space of a single chapter, the author of Luke can refer to the presence of the kingdom (11:20) and to the prayer of Jesus, "Your kingdom come" (11:2). And so we wait. Not passively, not without hope, but we wait, Jews and Christians alike. Indeed, all of creation groans and waits for adoption and redemption (Romans 8:18-25).

But as we wait, we are surrounded by terror. We are even surrounded by terror perpetrated in the name of Jesus — indeed, perpetrated on Jews in the name of a Jewish Christ. In Andre Schwarz-Bart's novel, *The Last of the Just*, there is a conversation between two young Jews who have met in Nazi-occupied Paris:

"Oh Ernie," Golda said, "you know them. Tell me why, *why* do the Christians hate us the way they do? They seem so nice when I can look at them without my star."

Ernie put his arm around her shoulders solemnly. "It's very mysterious," he murmured in Yiddish. "They don't know exactly why themselves. I've been in their churches and I've read their gospel. Do you know who the Christ was? A simple Jew like your father. A kind of Hasid."

Golda smiled gently. "You're kidding me."

"No, no, believe me, and I'll bet they'd have got along fine the two of them, because he was really a good Jew you know, sort of like the Baal Shem Tov — a merciful man, and gentle. The Christians say they love him, but I think they hate him without knowing it. So they take the cross by the other end and make a sword out of it and strike us with it! You understand, Golda," he cried suddenly, strangely excited, *"they take the cross and they turn it around, they turn it around, my God. . . ."*[124]

Violence is a form of proselytism which preaches that there is no God. The preachments of violence are more effective than televangelists, more zealous in winning converts than those who sell religion door to door. As we wait for God, terror surrounds us with a message offered as holy writ: "God is not."

In *Night*, Elie Wiesel writes of the experience of those at Auschwitz who were forced to witness the hanging of three prisoners, one of whom was a child. Where was God?

Behind me, I heard the same man asking:
"Where is God now?"
And I heard a voice within me answer him:
"Where is He? Here He is — He is hanging here on this gallows. . . ."[125]

But in fact, this is a strange and anguished affirmation of faith. In answering the question of where God is, it acknowledges the presence of God in the midst of terror, but never as the one who terrorizes and always as the one who suffers — the one who dies. In an age of terror, beware of the strong faith in a mighty God. Instead, permit faith to be tentative as life itself. Protest the silence of God, and if the silence is broken by a Word from God, ask if that God suffers.

Such seems to be part of the profound and anguished vision of faith offered by some who survived the Holocaust. Of the first night in the camp, surrounded by the smoke of the crematoria, Wiesel writes, "Never shall I forget those moments which murdered my God and my soul and turned my dreams to dust. Never shall I forget these things, even if I am condemned to live as long as God Himself. Never."[126] A God who is murdered. A God who lives. In Auschwitz on the Day of Atonement, should those who are starving fast? "I no longer accepted God's silence. As I swallowed my bowl of soup, I saw in the gesture an act of rebellion and protest against Him."[127] A God of silence. A God who elicits protest. Of prayer in Auschwitz: "And, in spite of myself, a prayer rose in my heart, to that God in whom I no longer believed."[128] This is an anguished and profound faith — a faith that struggles with God even as terror testifies to God's absence.

In his reflections on *Hope in Time of Abandonment*, Jacques Ellul cites a passage by the French novelist Monteilhet (from *Policiers pour la forme*) in which a child has been beaten:

I can still hear his cries. It's unbearable. It almost makes you believe in God. . . . Cries like that seem to call God back to life, much more surely than all the happiness in the world. There's a rare quality of silence surrounding certain atrocities, an end-of-the-world silence, more frightening even than instant justice. One has the impression that a presence has been withdrawn which could one day fill everything. That total absence of charity takes the form of the low-pressure areas which bring storms.[129]

One form of resisting terror is to offer prayers for the storm of God's love.

Strangers and Aliens

"Don't talk to strangers" is traditional parental instruction to children. On the face of it, the admonition would seem to constitute common sense advice intended to ensure greater safety for vulnerable children. But though it is common sense, it is advice that ignores the hard reality that the greatest threat of violence to children (and to adults as well) does not come from the stranger. While the random act of stranger-to-stranger violence receives a disproportionate share of media attention, murder, kidnap, assault, and sexual abuse are all more likely to come at the hands of an acquaintance.[130] Judging from crime statistics, children and adults are both far safer talking to strangers than talking to family members, coworkers, neighbors. Violence entails an odd intimacy. Nonetheless, fear is rarely molded by statistical analyses. The parental admonition to beware of strangers plays a far more powerful role in shaping the sense that terror is potential in all people outside of a small circle of family and friends. Always ready to strike, terror is lurking everywhere.[131]

The association between strangers and potential terror is not a new phenomenon. In the Hebrew Bible, *ger* is the word which is used to refer to strangers, sojourners, foreigners, and aliens, but linguistically, there are strong indications that *ger* may have roots in other Hebrew and Akkadian words meaning "to attack," "to be hostile," and "to be afraid."[132] But who is being hostile to whom? Who is experiencing the fear and who is provoking it? While the presence of a stranger can produce anxiety among those who are not acquainted with him or her, it is equally clear that the newcomer, the alien, is in a position of vulnerability. No matter the lofty idealism etched at the base of the Statue of Liberty, "aliens" in America today are often viewed as competitors for scarce jobs or as likely beneficiaries of the public dole. In addition to the economic threat, visions of other horrors that may come in the wake of aliens are fed by racist stereotypes. Are immigrants from Latin America and Asia bringing drugs? Are immigrants from Haiti and Africa bringing AIDS? Are immigrants from Arab countries bringing terrorism? If such fears are rampant among the "hosts," immigrants themselves have a basis for fearing that they will be met with hostility. Thus the links between "aliens" and "to be afraid" are more than linguistic.

In ancient Israel too, the *ger* was a figure who could be both subject and object of fear. While it was likely the case then as now that most refugees were driven out of their homelands by war or famine (e.g., Ruth 1:1), there are also accounts of individuals who sought refuge as the result of crimes they had committed elsewhere.[133] No matter the cause of their being driven from their homes, aliens were particularly vulnerable people. In ancient Israel, tenuous social and economic security was provided for most residents by the extended family, but aliens were people who had been severed from any support that might be offered by the *paterfamilias*. Without the extended family, there could be no inheritance and there could be no ownership of land.[134] And so in a repeated biblical formula (e.g., Exodus 22:21-22; Jeremiah 22:3), aliens are cited alongside widows and orphans as *personae miserae* who are cut off from family.

Who, then, will serve as family, not only for the widows and orphans, but also for the aliens who are both feared and frightened? Early in biblical tradition there is the affirmation that it is God who will serve as protector and family for those who have no other.[135] In Hebrew society, anyone who became so poor as to fall into servitude was to be redeemed by the next of kin known as the *go'el*. But what would happen to those who were so abandoned that they had no *go'el* to buy their freedom? The Sabbath and Jubilee Year proclamations (Leviticus 25:1-10; Deuteronomy 15) stipulated that on a regular basis (every seven years and every fifty) land should be redistributed and slaves and other captives should be set free. In effect, God served as *Go'el* for those who had no one to redeem them; the price of their freedom had already been paid when God led all of the Hebrew people out of captivity in Egypt.[136] Likewise, God would serve as next of kin for the alien who was separated from family. Like the Levites, who are without property due to their special calling, and like the widows and orphans, the alien must receive a portion of the tithe (Deuteronomy 14:28-29; 26:11-13) and must be allowed to glean the fields (Deuteronomy 24:19-21). God has already paid the price.

In biblical law, three of the earliest references to aliens appear in the Book of the Covenant (Exodus 22:21; 23:9, 12). Significantly, these laws stipulate no punishments in the motivation clauses. In contrast to other Near Eastern legal collections, there is a sense that these laws should be obeyed, not out of a fear of punishment, but out of a simple choosing of the right.[137] Regarding the laws pertaining to aliens, there is confidence that those who receive the laws will know what is right, for in fact, they themselves were once aliens. "You shall not oppress a resident alien; you know the heart of an alien, for you were aliens in the land of Egypt" (Exodus 23:9). This sense of being an alien and a stranger was traced back to the age of the patriarchs, for Abraham was *ger* at Hebron (Genesis 23:4). And later in Midian, Moses and Zipporah named their son Gershom (Exodus 2:22).

So the people of Israel were once aliens in the land of Egypt, but there may be an even more fundamental sense in which the people of Israel were once strangers and aliens to one another. In her detailed study of biblical laws related to the *ger,* Christiana van Houten writes that some of the earliest laws are "understandable in the sociopolitical context of pre-monarchic Israel. The laws do not evince a national consciousness, but only a clan consciousness. The alien thus is someone from another tribe, whether Israelite or non-Israelite."[138] How could an Israelite be an alien to another Israelite? The possibility is coherent within the revolt model of Israel's origins which has been most prominently espoused by George Mendenhall and Norman Gottwald.[139] The two earlier models that had stood alone as theories regarding the origins of Israel were: (1) the conquest model, which held that proto-Israelites had entered the land of Canaan quite suddenly and, by means of what must be described as a genocidal terror, had eliminated the native population; or (2) the migration model, which held that the proto-Israelites were nomads who gradually supplanted the Canaanite population in a migratory process that may have spanned generations. In neither of these models do the Canaanites fare well. In both of these models, there is the suggestion that the origin of Israel is steeped in thievery at best and terrorism at worst.

In contrast, the revolt model of Israel's origins does not posit the extermination or displacement of populations but rather portrays a grass-roots movement to shape an alternative "kingdom of God" that could replace the repres-

71

sive monarchies of the Canaanite city-states.[140] One of the challenges faced by the revolt model involves the difficulty of uncovering the pre-monarchic story of Israel's origins from biblical narratives that were largely written during and shaped by the period of Israel's monarchy.[141] The revolt model does not ignore the Exodus account of the Hebrew people being freed from slavery in Egypt; indeed, it was the proto-Israelites of the Exodus (whether a small contingent or multitude) who brought Yahwism to the land of Canaan, and it was the proclamation of Yahweh as the one who freed the poor from bondage that facilitated alliances with and among oppressed Canaanites.[142] The Amarna Letters and other sources indicate that the *hapiru* (semantically linked to "Hebrews") did not constitute an ethnic group, but rather were identified as outlaws, fugitives, and rebels.[143] The twelve tribes (more or less in assorted biblical texts) were comprised of the poor and rural populations of Palestine and the Transjordan who, along with the *hapiru* and the remnants of the Exodus community, united to reject the oppressive rule of the city-states in favor of the rule of God.[144] Extended families joined to form tribes, and through covenant, the tribes joined in a confederacy of free "people of Yahweh" who practiced mutual aid and resisted state control.[145] Many of those who joined this confederacy were in fact native to the land of Canaan. In the biblical depiction of an Israelite-Canaanite polarity, those who are referred to as "Canaanites" are probably those who remained loyal to the kings of the city-states and to the worship of Baal.[146] Eventually, "the Philistines emerged in Canaan as the heirs of Egyptian imperialism and of Canaanite city-state feudalism."[147] And eventually too, Israel itself succumbed to the desire "to have a king over us, so that we also may be like other nations . . ." (1 Samuel 8:19-20). With the emergence of the monarchy, the revolutionary, anti-statist themes of the origins of the Israelite confederacy were left behind, but these themes would reemerge later in Israel's prophetic and eschatological traditions.[148]

The revolt model offers a viable depiction of Israel's origins as entailing community formation without campaigns of terror or population displacement, but the model also offers insight into the "strangers and aliens" who emerge repeatedly in biblical texts. If the tribes of Yahweh included not only those who had been held captive in Egypt, but also oppressed people who were held captive to poverty in an assortment of monarchical city-states, and fugitive *hapiru* who were always in danger of being brought into captivity or worse, then this collectivity of the abused and the dispossessed was comprised of people who were alien one to another. What united them was a call from God. What united them was a God-given vision of a land of milk and honey (Deuteronomy 6:3).

This formative sense in which the people of Israel had been not only aliens in Egypt but also aliens and strangers one to another continued to shape the sensitivity towards other aliens throughout biblical history. Even in the midst of Priestly writings and Holiness Code with their concern for purity and avoidance of pollution, the alien is to be treated with justice, and moreover, the alien is to be loved: "When an alien resides with you in your land, you shall not oppress the alien. The alien who resides with you shall be to you as the citizen among you; you shall love the alien as yourself, for you were aliens in the land of Egypt: I am the LORD your God" (Leviticus 19:33-34). While scholars debate whether the core of Leviticus is best dated to the period before or after the Babylonian Exile, the experience of the Exile contributed to the persistent focus on the theme of the alien and stranger, for once again, contingents of the people of God were alienated from family, land, and community. In Babylon, in the heart of power, in the belly of the beast, how could the people sing (Psalm 137:1-4)? Writing out of the experience of Babylonian captivity, the prophet Ezekiel offers a sweeping vision of the new respect to be accorded the alien. No longer mere recipients of charity through tithings and gleanings, the aliens will be allotted an inheritance of land as full "citizens of Israel" (Ezekiel 47:21-23).[149] Therefore it is appropriate that the Septuagint translates the Hebrew *ger* as *proselytos*,[150] for the aliens are newcomers who are to be welcomed into the faith community of aliens.

This *ger*, this stranger who is a potential source of fear and terror may also be a messenger from God. And so, like Abraham by the oaks of Mamre, welcome the stranger with hospitality that overflows (Genesis 18:1-15). Though you are afraid, the stranger may bring you surprising and joyful news that makes you laugh (Genesis 18:15). Though you are unaware, this stranger who stands before you is the Christ (Matthew 25:31-40).

Biblical community was not shaped by the militarized unity of a terrorist campaign to exterminate the inhabitants of the promised land. Nor was biblical community shaped by those who shared allegiances in politics, theological doctrine, culture, or ethnicity. Biblical community was shaped as a gift from God and through a call from God to diverse people who were aliens one from another.

There is a sense in which we are all aliens wandering East of Eden (Genesis 3:23-24), fugitives one from another due to our own violence, our fratricide, our sororicide (Genesis 4:8-12).[151] But the biblical vision is one in which ultimately, our unity will be restored. In the eschatological vision of Isaiah 2, as the "proud and lofty" (2:12) cower and hide in "the caves of the rocks and the holes of the ground, from the terror of the LORD" (2:19), aliens from all nations will stream to the mountain of the Lord (2:2) and "nation shall not lift up sword against nation, neither shall they learn war any more" (2:4). It is a vision worth living in the meantime (which is the time in which we live). It is a vision worth living in Babylon (which is the place in which we live).[152] With such a vision, it may be possible to resist the effort of Babylon to define community for us. With such a vision, it may be possible to resist the effort of Babylon to enlist us in the never-ending series of wars against nations, against terrorism, against aliens — against humanity, against our brother Abel.

CHAPTER III

The Ethics of Terrorism

For thus says the LORD: *I am making you a terror to yourself and to all your friends. . . .*

JEREMIAH 20:4

Ethical Dualism

A Buddhist monk sat with his feet resting on a statue of the Buddha. A traveler came by and demanded that the monk remove his feet from the image of the "holy Buddha." The monk replied, "And where shall I put my feet that is not holy?"[1]

The story is typical of the many pithy stories and koans that circulate in some schools of Buddhism and aim for enlightenment through an instant flash of recognition. The story is also illustrative of the nondualistic — indeed, monistic — perspective that is widespread in Buddhism. The distinction between "I" and "Thou" is illusory, and in some sense, so too is the distinction between "good" and "evil."[2] There is no separate "I" who can designate other beings as evil. The war between good and evil need not rage forever. It may be gone in a flash — not the flash of nuclear holocaust that exterminates evil (and everything else as well), but the flash of compassionate enlightenment that recognizes there is no place to put our feet that is not holy.

Biblical writings do not often give voice to perspectives approximating philosophical monism, but neither can it be claimed that biblical faith is marked by dualism. The light/dark, truth/lie, life/death imagery of the Gospel of John notwithstanding, the Gospels do not portray Jesus as a messiah who takes his stand with the forces of righteousness to do battle with evil. Rather, Jesus abandons the righteous in favor of sinners and the capacity for *metanoia* that he discerns among them (Matthew 9:9-13; Mark 2:13-17; Luke 5:27-32). The canonical Gospels do not speculate on the illusory nature of individual identity or of suffering.[3] As Jesus weeps over Jerusalem (Luke 19:41-44), it is clear that the suffering wrought by violence and hatred is real. But as the apostle Paul discerns (Romans 8:18-23), the groans of the suffering are not a plea for retribution against evil but a plea for redemption, a plea that fills all of creation. The world is not ripe for conquest. The world is ripe for *metanoia* and redemption. Conquest comes through the infliction of suffering. Redemption comes through the Suffering Servant. These are sharply contrasting views of the world: a world filled with evil in need of conquest, or a suffering creation groaning for redemption. If we endorse the former, dualistic view, then we must set about to combat evil with any means at our disposal (unless, of course, we are part of the forces of evil, which we most assuredly are not). If, in contrast, we are able to sense that the suffering of others and even that the violence and the hatred and the faithlessness of others *and of ourselves* does not result from some great choosing of evil but rather from a groaning for redemption, then how can we view others *or ourselves* with anything but compassion? Then they (and we) are not irredeemable but only yet to be redeemed. Then they and we and all of creation ultimately belong to the Redeemer. Then, no matter where we place our feet, there is no place to aim our weapons that is not holy, that does not belong to the Redeemer.

It is more a result of captivity than of intentional deciding that the principality and power known as the United States has fallen into a dualistic view of the world as a place in which evil is running amok. Accompanying this, there is a growing American incapacity to address any problem without resorting to war. This is more than a matter of semantics. Behind the linguistic style that speaks of a war on crime, a war on poverty, a war on drugs, and a war on terrorism lies a style of being and acting. The enemies must be identified, not merely as abstract social problems to be solved, but as real flesh-and-blood enemies to be vilified (which is why the "war on poverty" so quickly turned into a war on the poor). The enemies must be defeated rather than being transformed, much less loved (which is why there is profligate spending for prisons and executions but scant resources for drug treatment). When there is a problem, America goes to war because the world is viewed as ripe for conquest rather than ripe for redemption.

In coordinated attacks on August 7, 1998, bombs destroyed the U.S. embassy buildings in Nairobi, Kenya and Dar es Salaam, Tanzania. Of the 11 people who were killed in Tanzania and the 213 killed in Kenya, many were Africans who just happened to be in the vicinity of the explosions. On August 20, the United States responded with coordinated attacks of its own. Cruise missiles were launched against the Al-Shifa pharmaceutical plant in Khartoum, Sudan (where, U.S. officials asserted, "precursors" to chemical weapons were being produced) and against "terrorist training camps" in Afghanistan. Osama bin Laden of the Al Qaeda organization was identified as the "mastermind" of the embassy bombings. As President Clinton declared a "war on terrorism," he called bin Laden "America's public enemy number one." Of course, this was not the first time that a "terrorist" had been so designated, nor was this America's first "war on terrorism."[4]

Of the previous wars on terrorism, one of the more prominent was announced by Secretary of State Alexander Haig on January 28, 1981, the day that 52 Americans returned from 444 days as hostages in Iran. Haig announced that, in place of the Carter administration focus on human rights, counterterrorism would be the cornerstone of the Reagan administration's foreign policy. It was an interesting choice of cornerstone. A 1980 CIA report indicated that the threat to American lives from the "nonstate entities" labeled as terrorist groups had actually been declining since 1975.[5] Indeed, the greatest threat to the lives of Americans from nongovernmental terrorist groups probably could be traced to the 19th century when thousands of indigenous people, Mexicans, and African Americans were killed by an assortment of "Indian hunters" and self-appointed "vigilante" groups such as the Texas Rangers and the Ku Klux Klan. But even this violence paled in comparison to the death toll exacted by government-sanctioned slavery and by the various "official" wars that the United States fought against Mexican and Native people. The actions of governments have always produced body counts that are exponentially higher than those of the most brutal terrorist organizations.[6]

Of course, doing ethics by body count is a highly questionable endeavor, although it is one that has figured prominently in American foreign policy. President Truman asserted that his decision to use atomic bombs against Hiroshima and Nagasaki was influenced by his calculations that fewer people would die in the bombings than in a continuation of the war in the Pacific. There is a surreal quality to such calculations that killing on a massive scale is the means to prevent killing on a scale which is really — well, massive. Such calculations are usually accompanied by the assertion (which is offered as self-evident) that our enemies have a quite low estimation of the value of human life. During the Vietnam War, Pentagon officials speculated repeatedly about the "Oriental" worldview which supposedly held that life was cheap. The American war effort was stalled because of the Vietnamese willingness to suffer heavy losses due to their low valuation of life. The American willingness to inflict heavy losses was due, then, to what?[7]

Since the end of World War II, civilian casualties caused by U.S. or allied forces are often depicted as resulting from aberration (as at My Lai) or accident (as in the attack on a bomb shelter in Iraq or the attack on the Chinese embassy in Yugoslavia). No matter the smartness of the bombs, protracted aerial bombardment is simply impossible without taking a high toll in human life. During the NATO attack on Yugoslavia, NATO spokesman Jamie Shea repeatedly found himself in the position of needing to explain the "regrettable" loss of life in a series of "accidents" — the bombing of Albanian refugees on a road in southern Kosovo, the destruction of a civilian bus in which 24 people died, attacks on residential areas in the towns of Merdare and Surdulica, the destruction of a hospital in Aleksinac, the bombing of a passenger train on a bridge over the Juzna Morava River. On the morning after a 2,000-pound, laser-guided bomb hit civilian homes, Jamie Shea exhorted reporters to remember that "We're there to protect the sanctity of human life, and we're up against an enemy who doesn't hold human life very dear at all."[8] On another occasion, Shea acknowledged that a Yugoslav television station had been targeted intentionally. While the loss of life was "regrettable," the station was destroyed because, as Shea reported without the slightest hint of irony, it broadcast "propaganda."[9]

So even when fought with weapons of "surgical precision," the assorted wars and police actions of the nation states have always exacted a higher toll in death and suffering than have the actions of more mundane terrorist organizations. It is violence with insult, however, when the violence is perpetrated by groups lacking the aura of legitimacy vested in the state.[10] Max Weber is representative of the many sociologists and ethnologists who understand the monopoly on the so-called "legitimate" use of violence as the essence of the development of state power.[11] As Eli Sagan puts it succinctly, "A king was a king because he could kill at will."[12] Thus, the insult that terrorist organizations add to injury is the manner in which their recourse to violence constitutes a challenge to the state's monopoly. As noted earlier, however, when a terrorist group aspires to assume the reins of political power, when a group is actually "the state-that-would-be," then the challenge to the state is not fundamental. Then, like violent revolutionaries of whatever stripe, non-state terrorist groups merely serve to reinforce the power of the state.

But there is a paradoxical dilemma for the state as it seeks to monopolize and centralize the utilization of violence. While political trends in complex, hierarchical societies favor limiting the legitimate initiation of violence to a small elite, technological trends in methods of warfare and accessibility of weaponry favor democratization of violence. The trends did not originate in recent times. In feudal societies ranging from Europe to Japan, military engagement was largely the prerogative of a warrior elite.[13] Warriors (knights in Europe and *samurai* in

Japan) constituted a hereditary class who represented the interests of the landed aristocracy. They were highly trained and expensively equipped with horses, armor, and an assortment of swords and lances. When the European warrior class was confronted by invading Mongols whose style of warfare was anything but elite, the invaders were promptly labeled as "barbarians." Similar to the earlier labels that Augustine and Ambrose applied to the invaders of Rome, "barbarians" was a label for those (like "terrorists") whose violence lacked all legitimacy. As Barbara Ehrenreich observes, however, the pillaging and plundering by the Mongol invaders was not that different from the manner in which the elite warriors were also supported by the toil of the non-warrior classes. Each in their own way, barbarian invaders and elite warriors were both parasitic.[14]

Between the 14th and 18th centuries, with the spread of missile warfare (e.g., the firing of arrows and bullets), the elite status of the warrior class was lost. Fielding highly trained fighters became less decisive than fielding quantities of troops who could absorb whatever the enemy had to fire at them. With early and imprecise firearms, skill in shooting counted for much less than the ability to rain down a large quantity of fire on enemy positions.[15] As missile warfare gave new importance to the quantity of available troops, mere peasants began to occupy the battlefields once populated by the elite. Thus, as kings and governments were seeking to centralize and monopolize the *authority* to utilize violence, historical trends in the techniques and instruments of warfare clearly have been in favor of a democratization of the *ability* to utilize violence.[16] This democratization means that, as Georges Sorel observed in his apologia for violence, even those with scant financial resources still "have at their disposal a much more efficacious means of action; they can inspire *fear*. . . ."[17]

One of the greater fears of political leaders and of citizenry as well is that the democratization of access to weaponry will extend to the point at which "weapons of mass destruction" (chemical, biological, or nuclear weapons) will come into the possession of non-state groups or even into the possession of certain disreputable states. The threat is not new. Indeed, terrorist attack with biological weapons has a long history, one example being the widespread murder of indigenous people in North America by means of "gifts" of blankets and other items intentionally infected with smallpox.[18] Regarding more recent weapons of mass destruction, concern over the possibility of nuclear terrorism can be traced to the dawn of the atomic age. In 1954, President Eisenhower proposed a reward of half a million dollars for the apprehension of any individuals in possession of atomic bombs.[19] Already in the 1950s, detectors were secretly being used at U.S. airports and ship terminals to expose the possible smuggling of nuclear materials.[20] Historical trends in the spread of weapons suggest that these efforts to deny subnational groups access to nuclear weapons will ultimately fail.

While advocates of the right to bear arms have been markedly expansive in their understanding of which arms properly belong in the hands of private citizens, even the most zealous of the lot have stopped short of advocating the spread of weapons of mass destruction. Thus, the peculiarly American anxiety over retaining freedom of access to weaponry is matched by an anxiety that some weapons (e.g., those of the nuclear variety) will be too freely accessible. But why is there this worry over the proliferation of nuclear weapons? The question (like the weapons themselves) seems absurd and surreal. Yet, the official position of the world's current nuclear powers is that these weapons are actually instruments of peace insofar as they make the consequences of war so horrible that aggression is effectively deterred. There is nothing inherent to the theory of nuclear deterrence which would suggest that proliferation is a bad thing. Indeed, if deterrence is a viable theory, would not peace be better assured if weapons of mass destruction were in the hands of all potential adversaries? If, on the other hand, such a scenario of mass proliferation is too frightening to contemplate, then the justification for *any* nation or group to possess nuclear weapons is undermined.

In seeking to address the quandary posed by the doctrine of deterrence, current members of the nuclear club have basically asserted that deterrence only works for those who are sane, responsible, and civilized. It is only the highly civilized who should possess these weapons that could obliterate life on the planet. Proliferation risks having the weapons fall into the hands of "madmen" and "terrorists" who lack familiarity with the way deterrence is supposed to work. This is essentially a version of dualism. The world is populated by the responsible and the mad, and thankfully, weapons of mass destruction are currently in the hands of those who will use them for only the best of reasons.

On November 30, 1950, White House personnel were sent scrambling to reassure apprehensive allies after President Truman let slip at a press conference the fact that he was contemplating the use of nuclear weapons in Korea.[21] Although it was portrayed as a presidential gaffe at the time, in retrospect, it is not at all clear that Truman simply blundered into his banter about the nuclear option in Korea. In addition to the alarmingly numerous times in which the U.S. seriously considered nuclear attacks,[22] there are more numerous instances in which the U.S. wanted adversaries to believe that the nuclear option was a live one. As William Schaap has observed, "Most people think that the only time the U.S. has used a nuclear weapon was against Japan, but if you are held up at gunpoint, the robber used a gun. And in that fashion, the U.S. has used nuclear weapons many times."[23] Indeed, the deterrent effectiveness of these weapons is dependent on the degree to which potential adversaries are convinced of the lowness of the threshold at which nuclear weapons will be launched. In strategic parlance, it is called "the madman factor."[24] In his books *On Thermonuclear War* and *Thinking About the Unthinkable,* nuclear strategist Herman Kahn compared the situation of the nuclear powers to that of adolescents involved in a game of "chicken." Gregg Herken summarizes Kahn's suggestion that "in order to win the game — in which two cars race toward a cliff until one driver becomes the first to jump out or veer away — a contestant should deliberately appear either drunk or crazy by staggering around the car before getting into it, and then throwing the steering wheel out of the window."[25] In short, while the nuclear powers are warning of the danger that weapons of mass destruction might fall into the hands of mad terrorists, those same powers are simultaneously seeking to effectuate deterrence by projecting an image of madness. Potential adversaries must be terrorized with the suspicion that we are mad enough to "go nuclear."[26]

It is no mere hyperbole to assert that nuclear states are engaged in terrorism. Such is even explicitly acknowledged in the phrase "balance of terror." Of the recent scholars who have attempted to resurrect just war thinking, Michael Walzer is to be admired for the consistency with which he refuses to exempt nation states from the charge of terrorism. The firebombing of German cities during World War II was terrorism, writes Walzer, and the terror was made no more just by the fact that the Nazis also bombed cities.[27] Since he is a defender of just war, Walzer's description of the bombings of Hiroshima and Nagasaki as American terrorism cannot be dismissed as the rantings of a pacifist. The American decision to murder civilians on a massive scale was not determined as a response to Japanese actions but in pursuit of the American military objective of attaining an unconditional surrender.[28] Walzer proceeds to write of nuclear deterrence that "the enterprise is immoral," comparing it to a theoretical scenario in which the police would announce that, henceforth, they will seek to prevent murder by executing not only the murderers, but all of their families and friends as well.[29] Unfortunately, Walzer concludes that the immoral enterprise of nuclear deterrence may temporarily fall under "the standard of necessity." But he does concede that "Nuclear weapons explode the theory of just war."[30]

Profound irony is evident in the fretting of the nuclear states that terrorists will intrude upon the balance of terror. Former Israeli Prime Minister Benjamin Netanyahu offered a frightening (and perhaps realistic) portrayal of the horrors that await us if nuclear weapons fall under the control of the "rising tide of Islamic terrorism."[31] Yet, he mentions no form of threat, attack, or manipulation that is not already fully available to the existing nuclear powers. Netanyahu has high praise for the Clinton administration's Omnibus Counter-Terrorism Act of 1995 and for U.S. efforts to keep nuclear technology out of the hands of "terrorist states." He comments that "Nuclear weapons in the hands of, say, the Dutch government are simply not the same as nuclear weapons in the hands of Qaddafi or the Ayatollahs in Tehran."[32] This dualistic view of the world as divisible into terrorist and non-terrorist states is actually a powerful contributor to the spread of nuclear technology and a plethora of weapons. Even if the Dutch government (to use Netanyahu's example) proved to be the paragon of virtue in international relations today, there is no way of assuring that the next twenty years will not bring a resurgence of Dutch imperialism or the rise of Dutch fascism — no way of assuring that the Netherlands will not come apart at the seams with Dutch weapons suddenly available to the highest bidders among national or subnational terrorist groups of the left, right, or middle. But we need not theorize about the future of Holland. We may instead look at the history of Iran, one of the states that Netanyahu labels as "terrorist." As Netanyahu himself points out, the Iranian nuclear program was started under the government of the Shah with West German assistance in plans for a nuclear plant at Busheir and French assistance in plans for reactors at Durkubin.[33] While the Shah may have been a terror to his own people, under his rule, Iran was not regarded as a terrorist state but as an ally of the West. Nuclear assistance to the Shah was inherited by what Netanyahu now calls "terrorist" Iran. As we will come to see, there are many such instances in which technologies and weapons that are given and bartered come back in haunting fashion.

Nation states are mortal creatures. There are no Reichs to last a thousand years, no empires on which the sun will never set.[34] Like the Soviet Union, like Rome, like Babylon, the United States will surely pass away. Like treasures, nations are consumed by moth and rust (Matthew 6:19). The life span of nations is much shorter than the half-life of most nuclear materials. A failure to acknowledge that the weapons we disperse *and the weapons we possess* will someday be held by other hands is simply hubris.

*   *   *

"So elemental is the human need to endow the shedding of blood with some great and even sublime significance that it renders the intellect almost entirely helpless," writes Martin van Creveld.[35] The effort to establish transcendent meaning for the shedding of blood is an enterprise that engages both mighty nations and tiny militias. Without some sense of transcendent cause, it may be impossible to marshal citizens or resources for military exploits because, after all, violence in and of itself is neither sublime nor inherently meaningful. Even ants wage wars.[36]

In fact, the effort to infuse violence with meaning is over half the battle. If blood is to be shed, people must be enlisted to the cause, or at least they must be rendered acquiescent. Shades of gray, reservations, self-examinations, confessions — these are all enemies of the nobility that must attach to violence in order for it to proceed.[37] This is the realm of ethical dualism in which the fate of freedom and justice, indeed, the fate of the world depends upon the ability to administer violence swiftly and efficaciously. The enemy must be demonized, and the 20th century offered up no clearer demon to whom the enemy could be compared than Adolf Hitler.

There is something appalling about the use of the Hitler analogy to justify military action, especially in view of the fact that the Nazis were quick to use demonizations of their own as pretext for violence, albeit the demons conspiring against the Reich were Bolsheviks and Jewish bankers. The nature of the lessons that people and nations have drawn from World War II were not foreordained. If Hitler analogies there must be, then why not analogies that point to the corrupting influence of militarism and the dangers of ethnocentrism and blind patriotism? Why not analogies that encourage disarmament and dismantling of the oppressive structures of the state? But such lessons and analogies are rarely drawn, in part because the drawing of them would entail imagining oneself in the role of the demon. Ethical dualism does not pose questions about how to avoid demonic actions oneself, but rather about how to oppose the demonic actions of others. For those who are persistently on the righteous side of duality, the clearest lesson to be drawn from World War II is the lesson of Chamberlain at Munich, i.e., the lesson that the greatest danger is not violent conflagration but "appeasement" of those who are evil. In fact, Neville Chamberlain's presumption that he was in a position to "allow" Hitler or anyone else to occupy Sudetenland betrays some imperial pretension itself, but in any event, nothing suggests that a different outcome at Munich would have altered Hitler's plans for expansion.[38] Nonetheless, "appeasement" entered the diplomatic vocabulary as a fate worse than war. And so the lesson of World War II cited by many political leaders is the need for stronger military force to be used at slighter provocation. Rather than making a Hitler analogy, Jacques Ellul was describing an empirical reality when he wrote the following: "That violence is so generally condoned today shows that Hitler won his war after all: his enemies imitate him."[39]

The portrayal of U.S. adversaries as "Hitler" began when Hitler himself was not long gone. Under Eisenhower, Secretary of State John Foster Dulles referred to Egyptian President Gamal Abdul Nasser as "Hitler of the Nile." The demonization process has become more rapid and more prevalent, however, since the demise of the Soviet Union. The continued maintenance of a huge military establishment is justified by accentuating the threat of terrorists and assorted Third World "Hitlers." Colonel Muammar Qaddafi of Libya was said to be suffering from "Hitlerite megalomania" and Panamanian President Manuel Noriega was said to possess pictures of Adolf Hitler (which he actually did possess in the form of a *Time/Life* photo history of World War II). In addition to being "the Butcher of Baghdad," Saddam Hussein was "worse than Hitler," said President Bush.[40] His successor, Bill Clinton, agreed with that characterization of Hussein, but Clinton was confronted by another Hitler still in the guise of Yugoslav President Slobodan Milosevic. Demonization, of course, can be a reciprocal process. Benjamin Netanyahu denounces the manner in which both American militias and "Islamic militants" characterize the U.S. federal government as "the Great Satan," but then Netanyahu himself proceeds to characterize these "terrorists" as "evil" and as "beasts of prey."[41]

Ethical dualism has consequences, not only for the demoni*zed* but for the demoni*zers* as well. For the United States, these serious consequences have included: (1) devoting massive resources to a military establishment, (2) increasing the haste with which the military option is utilized, (3) engaging in practices identical to those attributed to the demonized adversary, and (4) actually creating and conjuring those principalities and powers that are subsequently demonized as the source of terror.

1. Spending on the Quest for Security

By their very nature, demons are powerful creatures. But paradoxically, in order to muster resources and adrenaline for pending engagements, those who would battle demons portray the power of evil as magnified to near omnipotence. When doing battle with the demonic, one can never be too prepared or too strong. This also means that one should never allow oneself to feel secure. In the quest for strength and security, feelings of security are actually signs of complacency and are therefore subversive of the continuing quest for genuine security. It is, of course, a perpetual quest doomed to failure. Like any addiction, the quest for security creates its own need for the next "fix." If there are demons and Hitlers all around, then we are in a perpetual state of emergency.[42] There can be no "peace dividend" from the end of World War II or the demise of the Soviet Union, for what passes for "peace" is only possible when military readiness is sustained at wartime levels.[43]

This is a portrait of addiction: The United States spends more on the military than the next fifteen nations *combined*.[44] In 1999, both President and Congress supported large increases in a Pentagon budget that already totaled more than twice the military expenditures of Russia, China, Cuba, Iraq, Libya, North Korea, and Syria *combined*.[45] In the name of preparedness, the aircraft components and ammunition that the Pentagon keeps in *storage* costs more than the annual federal spending on community development, conservation, housing, mass transportation, occupational safety, and pollution control *combined*.[46] As if this huge expenditure of funds and resources was not sufficient, the United States called upon other nations to fund the U.S. war effort in the Persian Gulf and again in the former Yugoslavia.[47] These guns are not only for hire; they are also for sale. Some presidents have come to view the promotion of U.S. arms sales to friendly nations as virtually a part of the job description.[48] In 1991 alone, the year of the Gulf War, the U.S. authorized the sale of $63 billion worth of arms, military construction, and military training to over 140 different countries.[49] It is becoming commonplace that "peace treaties" brokered by the U.S. (such as that between Israel and Egypt) are sealed with promises of weapons sales and weapons gifts all around.

Like all addictions, the perpetual quest for security has hidden costs. The degradation of the planetary environment is being driven not only by the crass consumerism of the First World but also by wars and preparations for wars.[50] How can there be any meaningful national security when contaminated air and water are no respecters of national borders, when ozone depletion and greenhouse effects are oblivious to ethical dualities?[51]

But there are not only *acts* of violence and terror; there are also *states* of violence and terror in which people are forced to live.[52] It is structural violence when people are condemned to live with hunger, inadequate shelter, and treatable disease. Weapons play a role in determining who will live in such a state of terror and who will not, but moreover, militarism plays the premier role in determining that *anyone* should have to live in such a state. It is not only that war is the largest single contributor to the spread of hunger, disease, and homelessness; it is also that military establishments constitute wholesale theft from the planet and from the poor. While the food and medical treatments are available to save the lives of the fifteen million children who die annually of starvation and treatable disease, to do so would require a huge expenditure of funds — approximately the same huge amount that is currently devoted to global military spending each day.[53]

2. Hasty Resort to Force

Should one make deals with the devil? Should one negotiate with Hitler? When the adversary is demonized, any form of diplomatic contact evokes the specter of appeasement. The refusal to negotiate or to have any contact with demons becomes evidence of purity and resistance to contamination. Conversely, in ancient complex societies, spiritual powers surrounded the presence of the king, and even the most fleeting contact with him was a quite serious matter governed by taboos. Today, diplomatic contact with representatives of the nation state confers a "legitimacy" that must be carefully guarded and restricted. The phrase "We do not negotiate with terrorists" has served as clichéd justification to forestall the possibility of lending legitimacy to adversaries. Coincidentally, it also forestalls the possibility of pacific rather than military engagement. The phrase "We do not negotiate with terrorists" is utilized across the ideological spectrum. It has been used by the United States and Israel against the PLO,[54] by apartheid-era South Africa against the ANC, by the Soviet Union against Afghan rebels, by the Turks against the Kurds, by Yugoslavia against the Kosovo Liberation Army, by the British in Northern Ireland, by Russia in Chechnya. That even communication is forbidden is another example of the dehumanization that accompanies the designation of an adversary as "terrorist." If one may not speak with the demons (for to do so would risk contaminating oneself and conferring legitimacy on evil) and if the demons will not change their ways (and how could demons be anything other than demonic?), then warfare is foreordained as the only possible form of engagement.

Citizens are mobilized to risk life, limb, and treasure not against enemies who are horribly mistaken but against those who are horribly evil. The demonization of adversaries facilitates the shaping of the sufficient conformity of thought — the "groupthink" — which is a prerequisite to the mobilization of a populace for war. Political and military leaders are already amenable to a certain level of groupthink insofar as the need for secrecy in military action tends to radically limit the size and diversity of a decision-making group.[55] As psychologist Irving L. Janis observed, "In dealing with a rival nation, policy makers in an amiable group atmosphere find it relatively easy to resort to dehumanizing solutions. . . ."[56] But this amiable atmosphere of uniformity may prevail not only behind the doors where power brokers reach consensus. Among the American public, some observers have discerned that endorsement of freedom of expression coexists with a high degree of uniformity in political thought. Early in the history of the nation, Alexis de Tocqueville (an observer who was not unsympathetic to America) wrote, "I know no country in which, speaking generally, there is less independence of mind and true freedom of discussion than in America. . . . In America the majority has enclosed thought within a formidable fence."[57] John Pilger heard similar observations among a more recent group of visitors:

A group of Russians touring the United States before the age of *glasnost* were astonished to find, after reading the newspapers and watching television, that all the opinions on the vital issues were the same. "In our country," they said, "to get that result we have a dictatorship, we imprison people, we tear out their fingernails. Here you have none of that. So what's your secret — how do you do it?"[58]

Fortunately, the perceptions of the Russian visitors were somewhat skewed because not *all* American opinions conform to a narrow range. The Clinton administration was confronted with some nonconformity when cabinet officials including Secretary of State Albright were sent to Columbus, Ohio on February 18, 1998 for a "Town Meeting" to pitch administration plans for another round of bombing against Iraq. What was touted as a town meeting was actually a choreographed pretext for administration officials to give speeches, with the only form of audience participation coming by way of prescreened questions. The CNN-facilitated format was interrupted when a group of up to 300 antiwar activists unfurled a banner, gained access to microphones, and asked some questions that had not been screened — questions like, What human rights were being violated by Iraq that were not already being violated by U.S. allies such as Turkey, Saudi Arabia, and Indonesia? The event was memorable in part because of the way it was portrayed afterwards. The media generally depicted the town meeting as a "public relations disaster" for the Clinton administration. When it comes to war, support is welcomed but dissent is not permitted by the format. If dissenting opinion is expressed too vociferously, then war must become a matter of decision making by the professionals who have a better grasp of what is in the best interests of the nation. As Secretary Albright said after the Columbus "disaster," war "is not an issue that is going to be decided by public opinion polls — this is a national security issue."[59]

The need to *ignore* public opinion is rare, however, since the governing authorities can frequently *shape* public opinion by resorting to demonizations and lies which present violence as not only permissible but as inevitable and obligatory.[60] While the reality of demonic spirits is not to be denied, the effort to transform mere mortals into demons requires prevarication. The lies of the principalities and powers are occasionally inept and transparent, but more frequently, the lies are carefully crafted and dispersed through reliance on sophisticated public relations techniques.[61] Like justifications for violence, efforts to justify lying as an astute and necessary tactic play across the political spectrum. The words of Trotsky from the left might have been written just as easily by combatants on the right or in the center: "The life and death struggle is unthinkable without military craftiness, in other words, without lying and deceit."[62] Violence and lies need one another, contribute to one another, become one another. Perhaps it is for this reason that Mohandas Gandhi cited violence and lying as two examples of means that are never good in and of themselves. Lies and violence can never be good without appeal to some ulterior motive or end that would ostensibly justify them. Like all wars, the war on terrorism is firmly rooted in these: lies and violence.

The American people have seemed readier to forgive presidential deceit regarding "private" matters ("I didn't inhale . . ."; "I did not have sexual relations . . .") than unkept public promises on financial matters ("Read my lips: No new taxes"). But on matters of war and international intrigue, it would seem that the majority of the American people not only forgive but even expect that political leadership will engage in the dissemination of lies and deceit. In the latter half of the 20th century alone, we can cite both Republican and Democratic presidents lying about U-2 flights over Russia and the Bay of Pigs invasion of Cuba. There was presidential confirmation of a Gulf of Tonkin attack that never occurred and denial of Laotian and Cambodian bombings that did occur. We were blinded by the light at the end of the tunnel in Vietnam and enlisted into a "Star Wars" Strategic Defense Initiative the president knew to be a technical failure even as he announced its success. The CIA had no involvement in overthrowing Allende in Chile or in initiating the Contra guerrilla movement in Nicaragua. The U.S. does not assassinate foreign leaders, as Cuba's Fidel Castro almost found out and as the Congo's Patrice Lumumba did find out.

The point here has little to do with the moral character of American presidents. The point is not that we have elected a succession of liars to the presidency. More directly to the point is that all of us (presidents and commoners alike) are held captive in a system — a powerful principality — that thrives on lies and deceit. The evidence of our captivity lies in the ease with which the majority of Americans support *any* U.S. military action despite a half century of lies behind *every* U.S. military action. While public debate on military matters may sometimes be lively before the missiles cruise (as in 1990 during "Desert Shield," when a majority of Americans opposed attacking Iraq), our captivity is evident in the ease with which debate and divergent convictions are rendered irrelevant by merely commencing the killing (as during "Desert Storm," when over 90 percent of Americans supported the war). On August 20, 1998, President Clinton ordered the cruise missile attacks against Sudan and against "terrorist camps" in Afghanistan. While urging bipartisan support for the "war on terrorism," Representative Dick Armey stated, "We're a two-party system, but when it comes to U.S. military action, we're no longer a two-party system. We're a one-party system." It is the dream of tyrants, this one-party system, and it is achieved by merely commencing the killing. It is captivity.

Whether it functions at a conscious level or not, the bipartisan support elicited by military action could serve as incentive for political leaders to utilize force more quickly. The U.S. Constitution notwithstanding, the declaration of war has become an anachronism. An artifact of the war declaration requires that Congress be "consulted" regarding military action, but such consultations have come to mean little more than informing congressional leaders when attacks are already underway. The media have come to portray presidential decisions to use force as signs of "toughness" and "resolve," whereas reticence in exercising the military option is often a sign of "indecision."

Presidents have offered a variety of rationales for the speed with which they have resorted to violence. With memories of the Iranian hostage crisis hanging in the air, President Reagan raised the specter that Americans might be held hostage as justification for his invasion of Grenada, as did President Bush for his invasion of Panama.[63] President Clinton announced that he had to act quickly in ordering the cruise missile attacks against Sudan and Afghanistan in 1998 in order to stop further terrorist attacks that were already being planned;[64] ironically, after the attacks, administration officials urged Americans to be cautious and alert because terrorist reprisals were likely. It is typical of the spiral of violence that reprisals for terrorist attack evoke terrorist reprisals.[65] U.S. military reprisals for "terrorist" attacks were authorized by a 1984 National Security Directive.[66] As Michael Walzer notes in his reflections on just war, "No part of the war convention is so open to abuse, is so openly abused, as the doctrine of reprisals."[67] But no matter the potential for abuse, hasty retaliation has the advantage of effectuating an imminent judgment. Albert Camus wrote, "In the universe of religion . . . the final judgment is postponed; it is not necessary for crime to be punished without delay or for innocence to be rewarded. In the new universe, on the other hand, the judgment pronounced by history must be pronounced immediately. . . ."[68]

If it was ever so, war is no longer a last resort. In the buildup to the Persian Gulf War, speed was of the essence in order to prevent the collapse of the shaky coalition that had been assembled against Iraq. The Bush administration scrambled for a war rationale that would rally support. The argument that Kuwait should be returned to freedom did not play well because the Kuwaiti ruling elite had never been advocates of freedom.[69] The next argument, that U.S. jobs would suffer if oil imports lagged, was too crassly materialistic.[70] Finally, public support for war increased when administration officials argued that Saddam Hussein was a screwdriver twist away from having nuclear weapons. The vision of a demon with nuclear weapons led Congress to vote authorization for military action as "the last best hope for peace."[71] Members of Congress speculated that a vote in favor of military action might force Hussein to back down. This is the world of Orwell. A vote for war is a vote for peace.

3. Using the Tools of the Demons

Military history is filled with stories of nations matching and surpassing whatever sophisticated weaponry adversaries could concoct.[72] But the competition that is conducted on the frontier of high technology is also conducted in the gutter of lowdown tactics and most unsophisticated butchery. Enemies who must not be allowed advantage in missiles must also be denied the upper hand in surreptitious murder. Stephen Atkins discerns the melding of terror and counterterror:

> A manual prepared by the CIA and entitled *Psychological Operations in Guerrilla Wars* (a Spanish version appeared in October 1984) advocates "neutralization" of selected individuals in a coordinated counterterrorism campaign. . . . This sort of counterterrorism resembles the tactics of the terrorists themselves, and makes it difficult for outsiders to distinguish the good guys from the bad guys.[73]

Difficult indeed.

One method by which the good guys seek to distinguish themselves from the bad is through propagandistic interpretations of the motivations of different actors who are performing identical actions. Today, any nation that gives asylum to airline hijackers is a state sponsor of terrorism. In contrast, the U.S. was taking a stand for freedom when asylum was extended to anti-communist hijackers from Cuba and Eastern Europe in the 1950s and 60s.[74] When Saddam Hussein denied weapons inspectors access to certain Iraqi sites, it was called an outrage, but when the Chemical Weapons Convention Implementation Act of 1997 gave the U.S. president the right to deny access to inspectors, it was called a defense of sovereignty and national security.[75] When the Soviet Union shot down Korean Flight 007 in 1983, U.S. officials called it "cold-blooded murder." When the USS *Vincennes* shot down an Iranian airliner in 1988, U.S. officials called it a "tragic error."[76] It is likely that both incidents resulted from miscalculations in highly militarized, hair-trigger environments.

If might makes right, then the good guys can be distinguished from the bad by a simple tally of military forces, and the United States handily wins that tally. If not moral authority, such might certainly brings the military authority to set the agenda for countries near and far. In defending the American role in the overthrow of the democratically elected government of Salvador Allende in Chile, Secretary of State Henry Kissinger commented, "I don't see why we need to stand by and watch a country go communist because of the irresponsibility of its own people."[77] We have not stood by. Since the end of World War II, the

United States has been involved in either direct military intervention or the sponsorship of revolts, coups, and invasions in over 70 different nations.[78] Richard Barnet notes that Central America was once "almost a second home for the U.S. Marine Corps," but in recent years, "the use of military power has been much more subtle."[79] Such new subtlety involves the use of surrogate forces such as the Contras in Nicaragua. In testimony before Congress in 1985, even former CIA director Stansfield Turner acknowledged that support of the Contras must be "characterized as terrorism, as State-sponsored terrorism."[80] Surrogacy also operates through the funding and training of allied military and security personnel in institutions such as the U.S. Army School of the Americas at Fort Benning, Georgia. The SOA was supposedly closed in December 2000, but it simply reopened in January 2001 with the new name "Western Hemisphere Institute for Security Cooperation." In El Salvador, a majority of the officers implicated in village massacres were graduates of the School of the Americas.[81] Some U.S. surrogates operate under a much thicker veil of secrecy than did the Contras. We may never know about some of the actions authorized by U.S. intelligence agencies in the name of the American people, but there are occasional glimpses of terror. With Cuba the frequent target of U.S. violence, speculations abound about possible CIA involvement in an attack on a Cuban hotel, the destruction of a Cuban airliner, the use of chemical and biological agents against Cuban crops and livestock, but there was less speculation and more hard evidence in a 1976 Senate report disclosing U.S. involvement in over a dozen attempts to murder Fidel Castro.[82] There is also evidence that the CIA authorized a 1985 car bombing in Lebanon that left 80 people dead and 200 injured; the intended target who escaped the attack was Sheikh Fadlallah, a Shi'ite leader who had been implicated in acts of terrorism.[83] If all's fair in war, then is it not fair to use terrorism in the war on terrorism? If one is opposing a demon, a Hitler, a Great Satan, then all's fair.

In the battle of terrorism against terrorism, terrors that oppose one another need one another. In Argentina in the 1970s, the armed left needed a repressive state in order to garner support for revolution, and after a 1976 coup installed a repressive, right-wing government, the regime needed the threat of subversion to justify a brutal state terror. Long after armed leftists had been annihilated, the Argentine regime used "national security" as justification for torture and murder.[84]

Terrors that oppose one another train one another and learn from one another. Members of the rightist French OAS (Secret Army Organization) learned some of their terror techniques while being held as prisoners by leftists in Indochina. In turn, these methods were imparted by the OAS to the left-wing National Liberation Front of Algeria.[85]

Terrors that oppose one another become one another. Martin van Creveld writes:

> Given time, the fighting itself will cause the two sides to become more like each other, even to the point where opposites converge, merge and change places. . . . The principal reason behind this phenomenon is that war represents perhaps the most imitative activity known to man.[86]

4. Conjuring and Creating Our Own Demons

There's more than one way to create an adversary. One approach is simply to reject repeated overtures of friendship. Early in the histories of their respective struggles and even after they each assumed office, Ho Chi Minh, Fidel Castro, and Daniel Ortega all made repeated diplomatic approaches seeking friendly relations with the United States. Although Ho, Castro, and Ortega were all of socialist bent, none was allied with the Soviet Union until the United States adopted an unfriendly or blatantly aggressive stance. The case of Ho Chi Minh is especially illustrative of this tendency to drive potential friends into the "enemy camp," often for ill-defined ideological reasons. As he sought to force Japanese occupiers from his homeland, Ho Chi Minh was a strong supporter of the Allies during World War II. He was inspired by the story of America's struggle for independence from Britain, and so convinced was he that the U.S. would continue to support the cause of national liberation that he wrote numerous letters to President Truman asking the U.S. to mediate French withdrawal from Indochina. As he wrote the Vietnamese Declaration of Independence, Ho Chi Minh began, "All men are created equal. They are endowed by their Creator with . . ."[87] Dwight Eisenhower acknowledged that Ho Chi Minh would have won by large margins had free elections taken place in both north and south Vietnam. Ho Chi Minh was not an apostle of nonviolence and he did not merit the near-beatification accorded him by some in the American peace movement, but neither was he a demon. Literally millions of lives might have been spared if the United States had not made an enemy out of this man.

Also in Southeast Asia, there is one illustration of how the tortured calculus of geopolitics can occasionally cause the process of demonization to work in reverse. Of all those designated as "Adolf Hitler" by U.S. leaders, Pol Pot of Cambodia would be one of the more difficult to defend against the charge. The killing fields of Cambodia will remain a prominent example of the 20th century's many atrocities. Yet, when Vietnam invaded Cambodia to topple the Khmer Rouge regime, U.S. policy shifted to depict Pol Pot as less Hitleresque than originally portrayed. The American government began to support the ousted Khmer Rouge as an important source of Cambodian resistance to the invading Vietnamese.[88] In the shifting fortunes of power politics, once a Hitler, not necessarily always a Hitler.

In addition to the rejection of proffered friendships, there is another, more direct way in which America creates its own enemies and conjures its own terror. In a significant number of cases in which the U.S. demonizes groups or political leaders or nations, there had been prior relationships in which the newly demonized powers had actually been recipients of U.S. military largesse. This has led to some instances of U.S. troops fighting enemy troops armed with weapons supplied by the U.S. In other instances, the U.S. has trained anticommunist rebels in the use of guerrilla warfare techniques that were later employed against U.S. targets. As the world's greatest supplier of arms and military training and construction, it is naïve for the U.S. to claim immunity from the effects of these tools of violence that have been disseminated. Like Dr. Frankenstein, like Dr. Moreau, we create our own monsters.

In recent history, Saddam Hussein is the most frequently cited example of the U.S. contributing to the creation of its own demons. If Hussein was "Hitler" after Iraqi forces invaded Kuwait in August 1990, then prior to the invasion, he was clearly a Hitler supported by the U.S. In fact, many horrendous actions that President Bush later cited as evidence of Hussein's demonic character were actions performed by Hussein while he was being supported by the U.S. in his war against Iran. During the Iran-Iraq war, the U.S. supplied protection for Iraqi shipping through the Gulf and provided intelligence information to Hussein on the movement of Iranian troops. The 1988 Iraqi chemical weapons attack against the city of Halabja alone left four thousand dead, while an estimated twenty thousand Kurdish civilians were killed with poison gas. In opposing congressional moves to place sanctions on Iraq, both the Reagan and Bush administrations cited Saddam Hussein's bold stance against terrorism, the proffered example of which was his expulsion of the Abu Nidal organization from Iraq. Just a few years later, President Bush was telling the American people that the war against Iraq was a war to make the world "free from the threat of terror. . . ."[89]

The U.S. support for the anti-terrorist but soon-to-be-terrorist Hussein was motivated by a desire to oppose other terrorists in Iran. The government of Iran is another example of a demonized state that has benefited from American generosity with weapons. The "revolutionary" government of Iran inherited a considerable arsenal that the U.S. had supplied to the Shah, but even as the United States was busily demonizing the Shah's successors, weapons from the U.S. continued to find their way to Iran. The most notorious example was the Iran-Contra arms deal in which Iran would procure the release of American hostages in Lebanon in return for U.S. sale of weapons to Iran with the proceeds going to support Contra guerrillas in Nicaragua. Benjamin Netanyahu describes the scandal as a "setback" in "the West's battle against terrorism," and he quotes Secretary of State George Shultz as bemoaning the fact that the U.S. had "fallen into the trap" of making "deals with terrorists."[90] In fact, the affair was not a "setback" or a "trap" or an accident. It was a direct result of a view of the world as arms bazaar, and it involved the often knowing participation of those listed by Robin Morgan:

> . . . governments, private companies, corporations large and small, presidents, kings, sultans, the military, rabbis and mullahs, bankers, diplomats, attorneys, drug pushers, the global network of arms dealers, and machinations across thirteen different countries on five continents — all of them involved in selling arms to one set of terrorists in order to fund another set of terrorists, and all of them meanwhile denouncing terrorism.[91]

Even Colonel Muammar Qaddafi of Libya was the recipient of covert U.S. military assistance. During the early 1980s, Qaddafi was a fairly smalltime player in the world of terrorism. Amnesty International listed him as responsible in the killing of fourteen people (most of whom were Libyans), but U.S. government officials were calling Qaddafi "the king of international terrorism" and "the mad dog of the Middle East."[92] All the while, Edwin P. Wilson and others were funneling weapons to Qaddafi at the behest of the CIA.[93] Whatever intrigue was at work in the simultaneous denouncing and arming of a "mad dog" (and a number of plausible if paranoid scenarios have been proposed), a breaking point came with the 1986 U.S. bombing raid on Libya in which Qaddafi's infant daughter was one of the more than one hundred people who were killed.

Manuel Noriega of Panama was another leader who was demonized by the U.S. after he had received substantial American military and economic support. In "Operation Just Cause" in December 1989, U.S. troops invaded Panama for the express purpose of capturing Noriega and bringing him to the U.S. for trial on charges of violating U.S. law.[94] The official tally of casualties from the action was very precise regarding Americans (23 killed, 324 wounded), but less so for Panamanians (500 something); the later uncovering of mass graves dug by bulldozers suggests that thousands of Panamanians may have been killed. Some speculate that the U.S. disgruntlement with Noriega may have begun with his lagging support for the Nicaraguan Contras, but the charges lodged against him in the U.S. claimed that he was a kingpin of international terrorism and drug trade. If so, he was a U.S. kingpin, for all but one of the charges in the indictment against him related to activities performed while he was still receiving U.S. support. Indeed, in the Noriega trial, the prosecution conceded that Noriega had personally received at least $300,000 from the U.S. government to spy against his own government in Panama.[95]

In Operation Restore Hope in Somalia and again in Operation Restore Democracy in Haiti, American troops found themselves confronted by weapons that had been supplied by the U.S. In Somalia, so-called "warlords" had come into possession of the considerable cache of weapons the U.S. had given to the Somali dictator Siad Barre.[96] In Haiti in 1994, U.S. troops faced off against U.S.-trained General Raoul Cédras and a Haitian military armed by the U.S. The joint United Nations/United States occupation of Haiti was accompanied by increases in all of the following: privatization of industries, national debt, unemployment, inflation, hunger, and reports of police abuse. Restored to office to serve out the remaining months of his term, Haitian President Jean-Bertrand Aristide later stated that it was an error to have relied on U.S. forces for his restoration. Operation Restore Democracy kept U.S. troops occupied in Haiti for years with the task of "nation building," this despite a Haitian general strike calling for the removal of all foreign troops and a 1998 bill passed by the Haitian legislature outlawing the presence of foreign troops.[97]

One stark example of America reaping the terror it has sown emerges from the recent history of Afghanistan. Spanning more than a decade and involving decisions of both Republican and Democratic administrations ranging from Carter to Bush, Sr., the United States gave billions of dollars in covert and overt military assistance to rebels seeking to dislodge the Soviet-backed government in Kabul. The United States trained and sponsored "freedom fighters" from near (Pakistan) and far (Algeria and Egypt) to go to Afghanistan to oust the Soviet imperialists.[98] The unsavory methods of these freedom fighters included burning down schools and shooting down Afghan civilian airliners, but while they were opposing the Soviets, the Western media were not describing them as "terrorists."[99] Following the ouster of the Soviets, many of the non-Afghan freedom fighters went home, taking their newly acquired guerrilla tactics with them and discovering that there were freedom fights to be waged elsewhere. In both Algeria and Egypt, returning fighters engaged in violent campaigns in their own homelands as part of efforts to install Mujahedeen-style governments that would be free from the taint of Western influence.[100] And now that the Soviet imperialists had been driven out of Afghanistan, what about the American imperialists in the Middle East? When American troops preparing for the Gulf War arrived in Saudi Arabia on August 7, 1990, some Muslims considered it to be a sacrilege that armed nonbelievers would be allowed in such close proximity to the holiest sites of Islam. Among those who were outraged were some of the fighters whom the United States had trained and armed for warfare in Afghanistan. Those found guilty of the 1993 World Trade Center bombing in New York City included men who had received U.S. backing during the war to drive the Soviets from Afghanistan.[101] The U.S. embassies in Kenya and Tanzania were bombed eight years to the day after U.S. troops arrived in Saudi Arabia. When the U.S. retaliated against the suspected bombers by launching cruise missiles at "terrorist camps" in Afghanistan, the U.S. military had no difficulty in finding the location of the camps, for those very camps had been built by the CIA, albeit the camps had been built at a time when the "terrorists" were still known as "freedom fighters."[102]

And so in quite literal and astonishingly repetitious fashion, the United States has created its own terror. But the terror is not only that which threatens from foreign shores. Unwittingly, governments serve as powerful models for their own citizens regarding the efficacy and assorted justifications of violence. Cross-national studies have indicated that domestic homicide rates rise in nations that are at war, with the highest increases being in those nations that win wars, i.e., the nations for which the resort to violence is most efficacious.[103] In *Civilization and Its Discontents*, Sigmund Freud hypothesized that warfare serves to maintain social harmony by projecting aggression outward onto a foreign enemy.[104] Empirically, however, Freud was mistaken insofar as those who are most zealous in projecting aggression outward also experience increased domestic hostilities. Indeed, the connection between domestic and international violence is likely symbiotic. There is something horribly unsettling about the fact that, in the nation with the world's largest military budget, there are more gun dealers than gas stations.[105] Following a spate of high school shootings, the most notorious of which was at Columbine High School in Littleton, Colorado, politicos dashed about the country proffering cures for the violence of our children. Perhaps our schools should have dress codes and metal detectors. Maybe we ought to censor video games and Internet sites. The suggestion that we might be able to beat the violence out of them was implicit in the Oklahoma state legislature's resolution reminding parents that corporal punishment was still legal in that state. Or, suggested some in Congress, perhaps we should tack the Ten Commandments on every schoolhouse wall as a type of Heimlich maneuver for the conscience. But few political leaders suggested a need to examine the manner in which American military exploits were modeling violence as honorable. Following the terror in Littleton, as leaders were somberly warning that "We've just got to stop having this violence in America," America was spending millions of dollars an hour bombing Serbs.

The prophet puts it best: We are becoming a terror to ourselves (Jeremiah

20:4). And ominously, another prophet adds: "For they sow the wind, and they shall reap the whirlwind" (Hosea 8:7).

*   *   *

The Rev. Benjamin M. Weir was held hostage by guerrillas in Lebanon for fourteen months. He was subjected to harsh conditions and occasional brutality from his captors, yet upon his release, he was notably free of acrimony and free of the ethical dualism to which he easily might have fallen prey. Weir said, "I shy away from the word 'terrorist,' a loaded term that tends to set up opposites. Actions of governments, including my own, can sometimes be classified as terrorism as terrible as that of individuals."[106]

While ethical dualism would seem to heighten the sense of evil in the world by clearly demarcating the soldiers of righteousness from the forces of the damned, in fact, such dualism blinds us to the presence of evil by evoking flimsy, cartoon caricatures. On August 20, 1998, as President Clinton announced cruise missile attacks in retaliation for the embassy bombings in Africa, he stated that America was acting against groups that "share a hatred for democracy, a fanatical glorification of violence." His was an effort to breathe life into a comic strip of turbaned figures huddled in the desert and reaching demonic consensus: We hate freedom. We hate justice. Therefore, let us be terrorists and attack the good America.

Such ethical dualism is accompanied by alarmingly simple solutions. Eliminate terrorism by eliminating terrorists. End evil by killing evil people. But just as ethical dualism is too bold at identifying the evil without, it is too meek at discerning the evil within. The zeal of the battle against terrorists abroad blinds us to the manner in which terrorism is winning a spiritual victory in our midst. The terrorist idea that meaningful change can be wrought by inflicting sufficient quantities of violence is overtaking us just as surely as it has overtaken the bombers of embassies. Whether the violence to be employed is by means of a cruise missile or an explosives-laden truck matters far less than the shared terrorist conviction that justice or freedom or peace can be precipitated by inflicting death. Nothing that terrorists can do to the body is as frightening as a terrorist victory in the soul. Terrorism is winning — not militarily abroad, but spiritually within.

Yet, in this focus on the manner in which America creates its own terror, is there not danger of another form of demonization — a demonization of America itself? After all, the U.S. is not alone in this practice of creating and precipitating terror in the name of renouncing terror.[107] Moreover, America is not the Great Satan. Like all nations, the United States is a fallen principality. As with any mortals who hold political office (and who are held by it), U.S. political leaders may act out of motivations which are self-serving or suspect, but it is equally true that great harm may be inflicted as the result of *good* intentions. The words of Paul are applicable to citizens, political leaders, and fallen principalities and powers of all stripes: "I do not understand my own actions. For I do not do what I want, but I do the very thing I hate" (Romans 7:15).

In an essay in *Time* magazine, journalist Lance Morrow commented on the "surreal confusion" that surrounded the U.S. decision to send troops to Somalia in 1992. Following upon wrenching televised images of mass starvation in the horn of Africa, it was initially announced that U.S. troops would facilitate the distribution of food to the neediest areas, but the troops soon became mired in the much different task of seeking to disarm an assortment of "warlords" (many of whom possessed weapons originally supplied to the Somali government by the U.S.) as a prelude to "nation building." Morrow observed that America found itself "first impersonating Mother Teresa and now John Wayne."[108] Neither of the impersonations is without some degree of sincerity. To portray the actions of the United States as motivated only by capitalist greed or schemes for world domination is to engage in the same dualistic thinking that portrays "terrorists" as merely intentional choosers of evil. All wars are based on blatant lies and brutal terror, but they are also based on assumptions that these unsavory means can be harnessed in the pursuit of good ends that will someday be evident to all.[109] Part of the pathos of war lies in the repeated recourse to this illusion that good will come of it. During America's War in Vietnam, some of America's "best and brightest" undoubtedly believed that the Vietnamese were being "saved" as they were being bombarded by rarely paralleled devastation.[110] Despite lurking suspicions that the war against Yugoslavia was about saving NATO by showing what an important role NATO could play in the post-Soviet world, some participants undoubtedly believed that they were saving Kosovo, and the possibility that saving Kosovo would require reducing Kosovo to rubble was no deterrent. Destruction will serve to hasten the day when reconstruction is possible. Devastation is the prelude to salvation. In war, the saved and the damned are identical.[111]

So the terror that is perpetrated by both mighty states and guerrilla bands is not only motivated by the quest for material gain and political domination; terror may come on the heels of good intentions and in pursuit of lofty goals. And the victims of terror are not only those who are bombed and bludgeoned; terror consumes the terrorist as well. Even if the terrorist claims that violence has been efficacious in achieving the sought-for goal, that achievement must be defended against opponents who have now learned the power of terror. It is a perpetual quest to defend oneself against the fear that one seeks to instill in the other. The national security state and the terrorist organization are engaged in a horrible dance with one another in which places and partners are exchanged, and the dance goes on. It is captivity. As described by José Comblin, it is "the slavery of fear, the slavery of the need for security. A person entirely committed to security loses all freedom."[112] And much else is lost as well. Ramsey Clark notes that the continuous effort to combat violence and fear by instilling fear "is destroying all of our institutions."[113] While a few may grow rich at the international arms bazaar, shopping for security is an act of self-ravagement, a devouring of wealth and planet and therefore a devouring of self.

A view of the world that is based on ethical dualism fails to comprehend the manner in which "righteous empires" and "Third World Hitlers" and "evil terrorists" are all held captive in a system of militarism — all held captive by notions that they are using violence and fear in the pursuit of noble ends, when in fact these assorted principalities are merely being manipulated by both violence and fear. As Marx noted in *Capital*, the systems designed by humans to harness productivity and creativity have spun out of control and threaten to control us. As Mary Wollstonecraft Shelley noted in *Frankenstein*, the technologies that humans have created and mastered have taken on a life of their own and threaten to become our master.[114] And as noted by Jacques Ellul and Barbara Ehrenreich and a host of others, violence has also spun out of control. If it was ever possible to manipulate fears or effectuate domination or achieve security through resort to violence, it is no longer so. Violence has spun out of control, not because of the evil designs of American politicos or terrorist chieftains, but because of the autonomy of the war system itself. Violence is not put to use by people; it uses people and it uses them up. The centrifugal momentum of militarism is wielded by neither emperors nor thugs; it wields *them*. No matter if the people with the guns are seeking revolution or security or both or neither, the violence itself has a life of its own. Whether fought by mighty armies or mere militias, the institution of war has become self-replicating and independent of human governance.

Whatever the technological developments that have contributed to the autonomy of the war system, violence itself has always functioned in a way that ensnares and captivates people. There is a grinding inevitability to its functioning which Jacques Ellul explicated as "the laws of violence." Ellul's laws seem based on both insightful reading of history and prescience, and they are worth the summary: (1) Reliance on violence entails continuity, i.e., once one resorts to violence, there is no getting away from it. (2) Violence elicits reciprocal violence. (3) The law of "sameness" suggests that all kinds of violence are tediously alike, with no way to distinguish between a violence that liberates and a violence that enslaves.[115] (4) Violence has the power to produce nothing but violence; it is not able to produce peace or justice or anything except for more violence. (5) Violence is always based in hatred, but those who resort to violence will always seek to justify its use.[116]

Captivity entails spiritual crisis, not only for the pharaohs who are beset by hardness of heart, but also for the common folks whose yearning to worship God is hindered by the geography of enslavement — by the strangeness of the land (Psalm 137:4), by the lack of wilderness in which to celebrate the festival of God (Exodus 5:1). Captivity to violence is sustained through strange mythologies that proffer salvation. The mythologies of liberalism speak of "making the world safe for democracy." The mythologies of reactionaries speak of "a Reich to last a thousand years." And the mythologies of revolutionaries assert that "It is to violence that Socialism owes those high ethical values by means of which it brings *salvation* to the modern world."[117]

Since captivity to violence has a spiritual dimension, it cannot be opposed by political tools alone. There is a need for demythologizing, a need for unmasking the mere terrorism inherent to all violence.[118] Where shall we place our feet, where shall we aim our weapons that is not holy? The myths of violence stand in the way of our seeing the world as the creation, the holy turf of God. The myths of terrorism hinder that flash of recognition by which we see the holy image of God in our sisters and our brothers.

Crusades

Demonization evokes counter-demonization. Holy war elicits holy war. The phenomenon can be seen at work in both ancient and recent history. In its more recent manifestation, Edward W. Said notes the demonizing role that is played by code words like "terrorism" and "Islamic fundamentalism." Not infrequently, the use of the terms entails self-aggrandizement. In contrast to terrorists, the West is moderate and civilized. In contrast to fundamentalists, the West is rational and reasonable. Of course, those who have been designated as immoderate, irrational, and uncivilized respond with demonizations of their own, which pay "little more attention to detail, critical differentiation, discrimination, and distinction than has been lavished on them by the West. . . . This is an ultimately senseless dynamic."[119] It is also a deadly dynamic.

The theme of ethical dualism in which the armies of "light" oppose the armies of "darkness" emerges with alarming frequency from church history. One obvious example of the resultant terror is the crusades of the 11th through the 13th centuries (with reverberations far beyond). This section will not presume to offer a complete history of the crusades. Rather, the focus will be on providing illustrations of two phenomena: (1) Demonization and holy war evoke the same in response. In this regard, it is instructive to survey the perspectives of the Muslim defenders of the "holy lands." (2) When the crusading spirit is unleashed, the circle of those who are targeted is ever-expanding. In the crusades of the 11th to the 13th centuries, the infidels grew to include not only Muslims but Jews and Byzantines and heretics and those who condoned heresy and those who were insufficiently zealous in their repression of heresy. When there is a conviction that evil can be suppressed by terror and a suspicion that evil is contagious, the consequences are nihilistic.

The crusades were not a product of historical inevitability. Jerusalem first came under Muslim rule when the Caliph Omar took the city in 638 C.E. Religious tolerance was extended to Christians from the very day that Omar rode his white camel into the city. Legend has it (and perhaps history has it as well) that Omar was received by the Christian Patriarch Sophronius, who invited the Caliph to visit the Church of the Holy Sepulcher. The Islamic hour for prayer arrived while Omar was at the Church, and he asked Sophronius where he might spread his prayer-rug. The Patriarch invited the Caliph to pray inside the Church, but fearing that his followers would claim the site of his prayers for Islam, Omar chose to offer his prayers outside on the porch of the Martyrium. In fact, the porch became a site of significance for Muslims, while the Church remained a locale for Christian worship.[120]

Under a succession of Ommayad, Abbasid, and Fatimid Islamic rulers, religious tolerance was extended to Jews, Christians, and usually Zoroastrians. These "People of the Book" were required to pay special taxes and were prohibited from carrying weapons, but their religious observances and places of worship were protected. The exception to prove the rule was the decade from 1004 to 1014 when the unpredictable Fatimid Caliph Hakim unleashed a period of persecution against Christians, forcing conversions and destroying churches, including the Church of the Holy Sepulcher. Before his eventual disappearance, Hakim proclaimed himself to be an incarnation of Allah and he turned his attention to the persecution of other Muslims.[121] The Muslim rulers who replaced Hakim restored protection for Christians and granted permission to the Byzantine emperor to rebuild the Church of the Holy Sepulcher. In the 1040s, Jerusalem was astir with church builders and Byzantine officials.

The relative tolerance experienced by the Christians of Jerusalem was also extended to Christian pilgrims from the West. Within the first millennium of the church, the idea that pilgrimage to Jerusalem, Bethlehem, and other biblical cities was meritorious gained momentum only slowly. Augustine viewed such journeys as dangerous and wasteful. Jerome lived in Jerusalem, and while he denied that pilgrimage earned spiritual merit, he did allow that such journeys might be an expression of faith. Some of the earliest pilgrims returned with souvenirs of a rather macabre nature in the form of relics that were asserted to be the bones, fingers, hair, blood, thumbs, or other bodily remnants of an assortment of saints. Such finds served to nurture European interest in pilgrimage and interest in the other forms of commerce the Levant might have to offer. Although the journey to Jerusalem was never easy during the first millennium, travelers were assisted by a growing number of monasteries that provided accommodations for pilgrims.

The physical and financial burdens of the journey to Jerusalem were lent theological significance by the medieval church's emphasis on the sacrament of penance. A sacrament, said Augustine, was a visible form of an invisible grace, and medieval theological manuals in the West devoted considerable attention to the modes by which penance might be made visible. Bernard of Clairvaux was not alone in assigning a role to "works" and "mortification of the flesh" as means by which believers could make visible repentance for post-baptismal sins.[122] In some areas of medieval Europe, church courts and civil courts were barely distinguished from one another, and the same might be said of "sins" and "crimes." By sending outlaws on pilgrimage to Jerusalem, there were the multiple advantages of imposing punishment, providing for the physical discomfort by which penance became visible, and ridding the community of unwanted persons for extended periods of time.[123] Even killings that were committed in the context of warfare required penance, so common folks and noblemen alike embarked on penitential pilgrimages. Later, some Muslims would remark on the irony that the Islamic presence in Jerusalem was considered a desecration of the "holy land," but there was no defilement at all when Christendom sent outlaws and murderers on pilgrimage there.

If pilgrimage secured spiritual merit for lawbreakers and war fighters, more was the merit that might be secured by common folks or clergy whose sins were less ostentatious. The flow of pilgrims opened renewed ecclesiastical contacts between the alienated churches of West and East. In the closing decades of the 11th century, however, pilgrimage was disrupted by the outbreak of warfare in the region. Relations between Byzantium and Fatimid Egypt had been good, but the Byzantine Emperor Alexius Comnenus was alarmed by the rise of the Turks who, under Sultan Suleiman ibn Kutulmish, had established a capital at Nicaea, less than a hundred miles from Constantinople.[124]

The disruption of pilgrimage provided the pretext for Pope Urban II to preach the first crusade in 1095, but he may have been influenced by a host of motivations. Urban II had cause to take bold initiatives that might bolster the status of his own papacy in view of the fact that Clement III, a rival pope supported by Emperor Henry IV, was firmly entrenched in Rome. Urban II was sensitive to the concerns of the merchants of northern Italy that the advance of the Turks had disrupted not only the journeys of pilgrims but also the flow of commerce. In addition, Urban had been pursuing a policy of *rapprochement* with Byzantium in hopes of assuming leadership of a unified church, a turn of events that would certainly undermine the position of the "antipope" in Rome.[125] By sending forces to assist in the battle against the Turks, Urban might expect that he would be ingratiating himself to the Byzantine emperor.

To muster support for a crusade, Urban would have been able to draw upon large pockets of anti-Islamic sentiment in the West. As historian Steven Runciman observes, the Byzantines had arrived at an accommodation with Islamic culture and most Muslim rulers. Indeed, it is likely that most residents of Constantinople "would have felt far more at home in Cairo or Baghdad than in Paris or Aachen or Rome. But to the Western world the Moslems were strange and terrible."[126] In the West, Muslims were known as Saracens (*Sarra geniti,* i.e., those who claim descent from Abraham's first wife, Sarah).[127] Westerners knew much less about the faith of the Saracens than about the military threat they posed, with Saracen incursions across the Mediterranean, including southern Italy and Spain.[128] The common misconception in the West was that Mohammed was a demon or a false god to whom the Saracens prayed.[129] It was not until the 12th century that Peter the Venerable translated the Koran into Latin, but his efforts were hardly in the interest of improved understanding. Peter identified Islam as "the dregs of all heresies," worse than all of the others that had been "aroused by the diabolical spirit in the 1,100 years since the time of Christ."[130] This demonization persisted well after the Koran translation, with William the Bishop of Tyre identifying Mohammed as "the firstborn of Satan."[131]

When he preached the first crusade at the Council of Clermont on November 27, 1095, Pope Urban II both drew from and contributed to this tradition of viewing Saracens as allies of Satan. Several reports of Urban's speech survive, but the report by Robert the Monk is the only eyewitness account. In Robert's rendition, Urban offered a remarkable piece of oratory, alternating between appeals to the listeners' selflessness and to their greed, to their faith and to their prejudices, to their yearning for peace and to their hankering for war. While Urban addresses his audience of mostly Franks as a "race beloved and chosen by God," he informs them that the East has been invaded by "an accursed race, a race wholly alienated from God." According to Urban, the invaders were routinely destroying churches and torturing Christians, with the dismemberment of individual believers being mirrored in the dismemberment of the kingdom of the Byzantines. You Franks of "great courage," you who "have extended the sway of the holy church over the lands of the pagans," will you not intervene? "Let the holy sepulchre of our Lord and Saviour, which is possessed by the unclean nations, especially incite you, and the holy places which are now treated with ignominy and irreverently polluted with the filth of the unclean." If you are hindered by attachment to property or by love of family, then remember the words of the Lord: "Everyone that hath forsaken houses, or brethren, or sisters, or father, or mother, or wife, or children, or lands for my name's sake shall receive an hundred-fold and shall inherit everlasting life." The biblical admonition coincides with pragmatic consideration:

> . . . this land which you inhabit, shut in on all sides by the seas and surrounded by mountain peaks, is too narrow for your large population. Hence it is that you murder and devour one another, that you wage war. . . .
>
> Let therefore hatred depart from among you, let your quarrels end, let wars cease, and let all dissensions and controversies slumber. Enter upon the road to the Holy Sepulchre; wrest that land from the wicked race, and subject it to yourselves.

And when Pope Urban II finished speaking, the people chanted "God wills it."[132]

In this initial crusading impulse as expressed by Urban II, the earthly and heavenly Jerusalem were merged.[133] There was more than the hint of a suggestion that the fate of the eschatological Zion hinged on militarily wresting control of the temporal city from the hands of those who were "wholly alienated from God." As historian Zoé Oldenbourg notes, there was also a sense in which crusaders "confused Christ and the place where Christ lived on earth to such an extent that they saw him banished, driven out of his birthplace, or a prisoner, tortured by his enemies in his own lands."[134] For Jesus, taking up the cross meant suffering death at the hands of those who wielded the sword. For the crusaders, taking up the cross meant taking up the sword. Cross insignia were sown onto the outer garments of the crusaders as they set off to rescue Jesus by conquering the precincts where he had trod.

Despite the pandering to Frankish pride, Urban's speech revealed an awareness that all was not well among Franks and others in the West. Internal strife and wars amongst assortments of lords and nobles were brutalizing people and land. The cult of knighthood was in full flourish. Dating from the same era as Pope Urban II, *The Song of Roland* tells the story of the knight Roland and his relationship with no one so much as his sword, which he names Durandal; the sword's handle is gilt with holy relics to increase its murderous potential. So widespread was warfare in the West that the church promoted proposals for "the Peace of God" and "the Truce of God" which sought to limit fighting to certain seasons of the year or days of the week. There is something disturbingly modern about Urban's proposal for attaining domestic "peace" by launching a war against a foreign enemy who had been thoroughly demonized. "Let therefore hatred depart from among you . . ." by embarking on war. War is peace.

It was simply impossible to reconcile the pacifist tradition of the early church with the medieval ideal of knighthood, but some had tried. Early in the 10th century, Odo the Abbott of Cluny had written the *Life of St. Gerald of Aurillac,* the purported story of a saint who somehow managed to combine the fighting life of a knight with the monastic prohibitions against bloodshed. Gerald always approached his enemies with an eye to reconciliation, but if he was forced to fight to defend the lives of the poor, he did so with the back of his sword and with his spear reversed to the blunt end so that he never wounded an opponent.[135]

Such a model would be viewed as absurd by the crusaders of the 11th century. When Jerusalem fell to crusaders in 1099, rather than avoiding the shedding of blood, several crusading eyewitnesses appear to revel in it. Fulcher of Chartres, a chaplain to Baldwin of Flanders, reported that many of the Saracens attempted to flee into Solomon's Temple, but no men, women, or children were allowed to survive: "Within this Temple about ten thousand were beheaded. If you had been there, your feet would have been stained up to the ankles with the blood of the slain."[136] In reporting to the Pope on the victory at Jerusalem, Raymond of St. Giles told of a similar outcome, but the blood was deeper: "And if you desire to know what was done with the enemy who were found there, know that in Solomon's Porch and in his temple our men rode in the blood of the Saracens up to the knees of their horses."[137] Other contemporaries were less sanguine in their evaluations of the crusaders. As the crusaders passed by and through Constantinople, Anna Comnena, the daughter of the Byzantine emperor, expressed perplexity and alarm that among "the Latin barbarians" even the priests were permitted to shed blood. Indeed, as Bainton observed, the crusades marked the total collapse of even clerical and monastic pacifism.[138]

But if the crusades marked the death of clerical pacifism, ecclesiastical prohibitions against the shedding of blood by laypeople had been on the deathbed for centuries. Contrary to the long tradition that there must be repentance for blood shed in any war (even those of the "just" variety), as early as the middle of the 9th century, there was the suggestion that some carefully circumscribed forms of military engagement might actually serve as a vehicle of grace. Pope Leo IV (847-55) was extremely concerned that Rome itself had been sacked by Saracen raiders during the reign of his predecessor, Sergius II.[139] This concern was doubtless motivation for Leo's proclamation that anyone who was killed while battling for the church would receive heavenly rewards. Only a few years later, Pope John VIII declared that soldiers dying in the church's defense were martyrs with all of their sins forgiven. In 1064, Pope Alexander II removed the martyrdom requirement, extending indulgences to anyone who joined the military campaign against the Saracens in Spain.[140] And so Urban II had precedent when he declared that those who embarked on the holy war to Jerusalem would be granted remission of all their sins. For centuries, pilgrims had wended their way to Jerusalem as an act of penance for bloodshed. Now, crusaders headed for Jerusalem to earn their penance *through* bloodshed. It was a quite astounding reversal. Gone was the finicky Augustinian concern about killing without passion. Jeremiah 48:10 became the biblical text most frequently quoted by crusaders,[141] becoming a type of battle cry: "Accursed is the one who is slack in doing the work of the Lord; and accursed is the one who keeps back the sword from bloodshed." Not even martyrdom was required. As Bernard of Clairvaux preached the second crusade, he spoke of the glory and the blessings that would be attained by those who returned from battle as well as those who did not.[142]

Bernard of Clairvaux was a dominant influence in the history of the crusading movement. In 1146, Bernard's efforts to muster crusaders was as effective as had been Urban's preaching fifty years earlier.[143] But even more influential than his preaching of the crusade was his role in the establishment of the Order of the Knights Templar. The very notion of "fighting monks" would have been an outrage at earlier points in church history, but at Bernard's urging, the Council of Troyes in 1128 officially recognized the Templars and commissioned them to assure the safety of pilgrims *en route* to the "holy lands." In 1139, Pope Innocent II approved the commissioning of the Templars with the stunning commendation that they had "consecrated their hands to God in the blood of the unbelievers."[144] Other orders of military monks followed, including the Order of the Hospital, originally founded for charitable work but assigned military functions in the 12th century.

The concept of a fighting monk was sufficiently novel that one of the Templars, Hugh of Payens, asked Bernard to write a tract in their defense. Bernard's tract defended not only the Templars but the morality of violence itself. "If the cause of the fighting is good," he wrote, "the consequence of the fighting cannot be evil. . . ."[145] At another point in his writings, it became clear that ensuring the safety of pilgrims was no longer the issue, if that actually ever had been the primary concern for any of the leaders of the crusades. For Bernard of Clairvaux, the issue was combating evil and the primary manifestation of evil was Islam:

> The soldier of Christ kills safely; he dies the more safely. He serves his own
> interests in dying, and Christ's interests in killing. . . . He is the instrument

of God for the punishment of malefactors and for the defence of the just. Indeed, when he kills a malefactor this is not homicide, but malicide, and he is accounted Christ's legal executioner against evildoers.[146]

If Bernard provided a type of theological justification for crusade, others sorted out the legal justifications. Such was the work of Huguccio, a proponent of Gratian's doctrine of just war. In general, Huguccio maintained, only defensive wars were just, but since heretics and infidels were defying the laws of God, they must be denied protection under the laws that should ordinarily govern warfare. As John Ferguson remarks, "It was an all-too-convenient doctrine in the age of Crusades."[147]

But it was far from certain that either theological or legal justifications mattered much to many of the crusaders. Although crusading proved financially ruinous to some of the barons and knights, for others among the nobility, crusades presented the opportunity for possible expansion of power and wealth; there developed among them family traditions of crusading through several generations.[148] For common people, the crusade might offer an opportunity to escape appalling conditions of servitude and poverty.[149] Even when the personal motivations loomed large, however, there was a prevailing sense among both lords and serfs that the cause was righteous because the adversaries were unrighteous. Implicit in the demonization of enemies is the sanctification of oneself and of one's purpose. If God wills it, then God will help. Indeed, all of the gods will help, for during the crusading era, a whole pantheon of warrior saints acquired the virtual status of minor deities.[150] Primary among them was Saint George, the slayer of dragons. "Saint George, be with us now," crusaders prayed, and by fighting at their side, the warrior saint both quelled the terror of the righteous and instilled terror into the ranks of the infidels.

Malcolm Lambert was certainly correct in observing that "Crusade was a blunt instrument."[151] Once unleashed, crusades and holy wars have no masters and acquire a momentum of their own. Even Urban II experienced consternation at how quickly people and events veered out of control at the very origins of the first crusade. Urban had envisioned an orderly procession of crusaders, with military leadership provided by a collective of barons and knights but with overall ecclesiastical control established through the leader picked by Urban, Adhemar the Bishop of Le Puy. Once the crusading spirit was loose, however, other skilled preachers were able to assemble thousands of Frank and German crusaders who demonstrated their zeal to battle the infidels by setting off for the Levant before the forces under Adhemar had been gathered. The most prominent contingent of these ad hoc crusaders was the force assembled by Peter the Hermit. Poorly provisioned, these crusaders relied on food and other supplies that were volunteered or, more often, seized from towns and villages along the way.[152] Even before they met any Muslims, Peter's crusaders sacked and burned a number of towns, including Belgrade.[153] Within weeks of the departure of the forces led by Peter the Hermit, another ad hoc group of crusaders set out from Germany. Inflamed by visions of infidels ruling the homeland of Jesus, these crusaders proceeded to attack others whom they also held responsible for the betrayal of the Lord. Scores of Jews were killed in massacres and their communities were plundered.[154] When the main force of crusaders led by the barons and knights finally took Jerusalem in 1099, the Jews there fared no better. After many of the Jerusalem Jews had gathered inside the synagogue for prayers, the crusaders barred the doors and windows and torched the building.[155]

In subsequent crusades to the Levant and elsewhere, Jews and other minorities continued to be targets of the crusaders. In 1320 in Spain, for example, a young man was said to have had a vision in which a dove appeared to him and declared that he would be a shepherd in leading others to battle against the Moors. The ensuing Shepherds' Crusade spread through several regions of Spain and France. When a supposed plot was uncovered in which the Muslim king of Granada enlisted the complicity of Jews and lepers in a plan to poison the wells of Christians, Jews and lepers became the primary victims of the Shepherds' Crusade.[156] Already in 12th-century Spain, the Jewish philosopher and theologian Yehuda Halevi wrote, "Christian and Muslim share the whole world between them" but "they wage their wars and drag us down in their fall."[157] Of course, the Christian treatment of Jews was not lost on Muslim polemicists, some of whom depicted the annual Holy Week attacks on Jews as indicative of the contrast between Christian barbarity and Islamic tolerance.[158]

Initial Muslim response to the crusaders in the Levant was ineffective in large part due to disunity among assorted leaders. As with Christianity, Islam is not monolithic. As the first crusaders approached Jerusalem, a major rift existed between the Sunnite Turks and the Shi'ite Egyptians, neither of whom would have been distraught at seeing the other defeated by crusaders.[159] But the blatant terrorism of the crusaders would play a role in eventually eliciting an effective military response. In 1098 at the town of Maarat an-Numan, the crusaders promised safety to the residents if the town surrendered, but once inside the walls, the crusaders engaged in slaughter. They also engaged in cannibalism. The Frankish chronicler Radulph of Caen acknowledged, "In Ma'arra our troops boiled pagan adults in cooking pots; they impaled children on spits and devoured them grilled." In written explanations to the pope, commanders asserted that it was a "terrible famine" that forced upon the army "the cruel necessity of feeding itself upon the bodies of the Saracens."[160] In subsequent

Arabic literature, including the stories and fables collected in the *Arabian Nights,* Westerners were often depicted as anthropophagi.

As word began to spread of an invasion by cannibals, Jerusalem fell in 1099. While the medieval world (like the modern world) was no stranger to atrocity, Steven Runciman comments that the slaughter at Jerusalem had a lasting impact:

> The massacre at Jerusalem profoundly impressed all the world. No one can say how many victims it involved; but it emptied Jerusalem of its Moslem and Jewish inhabitants. Many even of the Christians were horrified by what had been done; and amongst the Moslems, who had been ready hitherto to accept the Franks as another factor in the tangled politics of the time, there was henceforward a clear determination that the Franks must be driven out. It was this bloodthirsty proof of Christian fanaticism that recreated the fanaticism of Islam. When, later, wiser Latins in the East sought to find some basis on which Christian and Moslem could work together, the memory of the massacre stood always in their way.[161]

Few Muslims escaped the devastation in Jerusalem, but one small group of refugees led by Abu Sa'ad al-Harawi managed to reach Baghdad. On August 19, 1099, during Ramadan, the month of obligatory fasting, al-Harawi entered the great mosque of Baghdad and began eating in full view of the faithful. When he was surrounded by an angry crowd, he asked them how they could be so infuriated in response to the food that passed his lips but passive in response to the Westerners who had invaded their land, destroyed their holy places, and slaughtered their brothers and sisters.[162]

But the atrocities at Jerusalem did not evoke an immediate holy war response. The *jihad* came decades later after a greater degree of Arabic unity had been achieved under Saladin. In the meantime, many of the crusaders from the West and many of the Franks who ruled the Kingdom of Jerusalem continued to shape their own bad reputation. Truces and treaties were routinely made and broken by the crusaders in the belief that one did not owe truthfulness to the enemies of God.[163] Lies could be utilized freely against adversaries of bad character and they reflected not at all on the character of the liars.

It was a broken truce that provided Saladin with justification for launching a holy war of his own that culminated in the capture of Jerusalem in 1187. In the words of one commentator, it was as if the "spirit of holy war animating the Christian camp seems now to have departed and lodged in the Moslem camp."[164] Saladin ordered the beheading of all Templars and Hospitalers who were taken captive. While Saladin himself was an advocate of tolerance for Christians outside of the military orders, there was a general deterioration in the status of Christians living in areas ruled by Muslims.[165] Terror elicited a backlash of terror.[166] And demonization elicited counter-demonization. Muslims were declared martyrs if they died while battling the "polytheists," the designation given to Christian trinitarians. Even in the generally restrained writings of Saladin's secretary, the Franks were "worshippers of Satan; blasphemers against nature human and divine."[167]

In Islam, once declared, a holy war was *fard 'ayn,* a collective responsibility that entailed obligations for each individual believer. Pope Innocent III (1198-1217) announced a similar obligation for Christians as he assembled still another crusade to attempt the capture of Jerusalem once again. Peter Partner notes that Innocent III "has been identified as marking the culmination of a process by which all barriers between religion and war in Latin Catholicism were removed." Urging a type of "sacred violence," Innocent depicted Christ himself as calling for war. "Pope Innocent said that refusal to serve in the holy war amounted in itself to infidelity to Christ. The parallel with Muslim doctrine is striking."[168]

But the crusade launched by Innocent III was no exception to the rule that holy wars have no masters. Setting out to battle the infidels, the crusaders paused along the way to attack and conquer Constantinople. With crosses still sewn to their garments and flags, the crusaders engaged in "plundering convents, churches, and palaces, and raping Greek women by the thousands."[169] It will be recalled that some of the motivation of Urban II in preaching the first crusade had been to provide assistance for the Byzantines in their battle against the Turks. Historian Edward Gibbon observed that Byzantium had prayed for rain and had been inundated by a flood.[170]

While it was only belatedly that Innocent III gave his blessing to the sacking of Constantinople, he was zealous in urging a crusade against another group of Christians, the Cathars of southern France. He offered the same indulgences to those who went on crusade against the Cathar heretics as were offered to those who battled the Muslim infidels.[171] It might be counted strange that a crusade was launched against a dualistic "heresy" when the crusade itself was such an enterprise of dualism. But Innocent perceived his as an era in which evil had to be rooted out. The crusade against the Albigensians was accompanied by the establishment of ecclesiastical inquisitions. How often it is that wars are accompanied by and followed by repression.[172] It is as if the enemy without had come nearer. Demons are omnipotent, and once challenged on the battlefield, they assume a different guise and infiltrate into the hearts and minds of our neighbors. For Muslim holy warriors as well, the *jihad* was an instrument that could

110

be turned against Islamic "heretics" and dissenters.[173] In the West as well as the East, once the concept of holy war gained currency, it was invoked for a wide-ranging assortment of political struggles both trivial and profound.[174]

Did it never occur to medieval men and women that this was an inherently senseless process, with holy war evoking holy war and demonization eliciting demonization? Did it never occur to them that this was a trap in which they were condemned, like Sisyphus, to repeat perpetually the same actions and experience the same unsurprising outcome? Did it never occur to them that they were sowing and reaping terror and ultimately becoming a terror to themselves? In fact, questions and challenges to the very idea of holy war were raised by more than a few medieval Muslims and Christians. Of course, most who raised the challenges were not writing the history of the time, but one who was writing the history was the remarkable 13th-century historian Ibn al-Athir, one of the first Muslims to draw comparisons between crusade and *jihad*.[175] In the West, challenging the moral legitimacy of the crusades figured prominently in having one's views declared heretical. For the Cathars, for the Waldensians, and later for John Wyclif, wars were sinful, and crusades more so because they wreaked carnage under pretense of holy cause. Opposition to holy war became such a hallmark of heresy that inquisitors took to asking suspects about their attitudes toward the crusades.[176]

One wonders at the questions such inquisitors might have asked. What do you think of our wars? Is our cause not just? Is our enemy not evil? And our terror, is it not holy?

Sowing and Reaping: Terror and the Prophetic Tradition

In Galatians 6:7, Paul writes, "Do not be deceived; God is not mocked, for you reap whatever you sow."

The biblical theme of reaping what one sows has been subject to no small abuse. At times, the theme is impressed into the service of the blatantly commercial manipulations of religionists: Send your seed money now and you will reap a hundredfold as God prospers you. At other times, the assertion that we reap what we sow is interpreted as synonymous with the trite claim (and a false claim) that people get what they deserve. Such a claim is a transparent endorsement of the status quo. The poor are poor because (whether through indolence or lack of cleverness or genetic defect or past sins) they deserve to be poor. On the other hand, if you live right, work hard, and have a modicum of intelligence, you too could be filthy rich. In this view, the presence or absence of moral rectitude contributes to whether one avoids or suffers poverty, violence, disease, and a host of other misfortunes. This is essentially a Western, trivialized version of the Eastern doctrine of the universal law of moral causation, or *karma*. In more profound renditions that do not serve as simplistic endorsements of the status quo, the doctrine of karma is a significant element of faith in several of the great Eastern religions, including Buddhism, Hinduism, Sikhism, and Jainism. But whether in trivial or profound version, the doctrine of karma is alien to the biblical theme of sowing and reaping.[177]

In Paul's brief comment in Galatians 6:7, it is clear that the sowing and reaping of which he writes is neither an endorsement of "what is" nor a claim of moral causation. Implicit in his introductory phrase, "Do not be deceived," is the possibility or even the likelihood that the empirical world of the status quo presents a deceptive picture regarding both sowers and reapers. Mighty empires prosper as they continue to slaughter the innocent. Like Job, the righteous suffer oppression and humiliation. The capitalist illusion that poverty is alleviated by hard work and free enterprise is as anti-biblical as the communist illusion that poverty is mitigated by revolution. The agricultural basis of the sowing and reaping metaphor is itself testament to the fact that those who work hard at planting and harvesting a good crop cannot necessarily expect to benefit from their efforts. In ancient Israel as well as in Paul's Hellenistic milieu (as well as in our own time), "aliens" and other agricultural workers who were toiling on land that did not belong to them could expect little more than gleanings. So, do not be deceived. The assorted fortunes of those who surround us (and of us as well) are not necessarily indicative of the sowing they have done — any more than they are indicative of divine blessings or curses. For the "harvest-time" is not yet (Galatians 6:9).[178]

But in addition to warning us not to be deceived by appearances, Paul introduces another reality that is totally contrary to any mechanistic laws of moral causation. He introduces the free and sovereign God, the God who is not mocked. Among his many great contributions, Karl Barth emphasized the *freedom* of God, and it is God's freedom that is especially pertinent here. In freedom, God judges that which is sown and sets the "harvest-time." In freedom, God chooses to bind the sower to moral causation or to set the sower free to reap an unmerited harvest of goodness. But God's freedom should not be confused with neutrality, as in the stoic notion of "freedom from attachment." As biblically portrayed, God's freedom is always freedom *for* the covenanted community and, through them, freedom *for* humanity. Rather than being neutral or detached, this is a free God of radical passion who stands *with* humanity. And it is precisely as an expression of this stand *for* and *with* humanity that God also stands *against* an assortment of human actions and institutions, human oppression and carnage. God's freedom, God's lack of neutrality, God's standing *for* humanity by standing *against* inhumanity — these all emerge with particular clarity in the prophetic tradition.[179] Also emerging from the prophetic tradition is a free-wheeling but partisan application of the sowing and reaping theme. God calls upon the prophets to intervene on behalf of the poor who are reaping only injustice. But with regard to the mighty, the empires, the godlets with bloodied swords, God calls upon the prophets to announce that these mighty ones will reap the full measure of the blood they have shed. And the prophets not only announce, they appear to taunt. You lords and princes who protest the terror that has come to your door, what else could you expect when terror is all that you have sown? The prophets do not speak of karmic fate. They speak the words of a passionate God who is filled with wrath at the empires filled with blood.

The prophetic applications of the sowing and reaping metaphor might be illustrated by a brief survey of some of the writings associated with the prophets Jeremiah and Ezekiel. Both prophets focused on the meaning of the Babylonian captivity, with Jeremiah speaking and writing from within Jerusalem and Judah while Ezekiel worked among the community of exiles in Babylon. In the early 6th century B.C.E., there is chronological overlap between the end of Jeremiah's work and the beginning of the prophesying by Ezekiel. And there is another type of overlap as well. Like all of the prophets of the Hebrew Bible, Jeremiah and Ezekiel are both anguished and emboldened, seized and set free, condemned and saved by the fiery word of God. God *spoke* to them, not in a way that was literally real, but in a way that was much more than literally real. And the prophets were able to understand that which God spoke not through a mere literal hearing but through responding to that word which overwhelmed them, indeed, compelled them.[180] It is only after protest that Jeremiah receives the word (Jeremiah 1:6), while Ezekiel seems to have an instinctive appetite for the word (Ezekiel 3:3). In both cases, however, the word of God is placed into the mouth of the prophet and becomes a veritable part of who the prophet is. For both Ezekiel and Jeremiah, abandonment of the word could only be effectuated as an abandonment of self.[181] But this is not to imply that the prophetic mission was an existential quest for self-fulfillment or that it was a mission undertaken with self-confidence. Inevitably, the prophet moves against the current of popular sentiment and suffers for it. In the case of Jeremiah in particular, the one whom the prophet blames for his suffering is none other than God. As in many human relationships, the most intense disputes erupt between those who are closest, and so it is also between Jeremiah and God. As Jeremiah travels about at God's behest warning the people of the violence and desolation to come, warning of the terror that is all around, he is greeted with mockery. He is dubbed "Terror is all around," a nickname that is whispered as he passes by as if he were some clownish Chicken Little (Jeremiah 20:10). Jeremiah is wounded by the mockery and he lashes out, not at those who belittle him, but at God. In fact, Jeremiah pushes the limits of the Hebrew tradition of arguing with God to the point of near-blasphemy, charging that God has engaged in seduction and virtual rape: "O LORD, you have enticed me, and I was enticed; you have overpowered me, and you have prevailed. I have become a laughingstock all day long; everyone mocks me" (Jeremiah 20:7).[182] One might imagine Jeremiah wishing that he were in possession of the pyrotechnics of a powerful prophet like Elijah so that he too could deal with his detractors by calling down a terrifying rain of fire from the heavens (1 Kings 18:17-40). But in comparison to the dazzling displays of Elijah, Jeremiah's initial response to the false prophet Hananiah seems tepid (Jeremiah 28:1-9).[183] Jeremiah is an anguished soul. With no rain of fire to provide vindication, the only fire for Jeremiah is that which burns in his bones if he tries to refrain from speaking God's word which has been placed in his mouth, stuck in his craw (Jeremiah 20:9).

Writing from within exile, Ezekiel expressed less of his personal anguish than did Jeremiah, although he was no less burdened. Indeed, at a point of immense personal anguish, the death of his wife, Ezekiel is instructed by God to refrain from any show of mourning as a sign to the people that they will experience numbing, inexpressible grief (Ezekiel 24:15-27). It was a fate that Jeremiah was spared because he heeded the admonition not to marry (Jeremiah 16:1-9). On the face of it, these divine instructions to the prophets seem harsh indeed. To these prophets, God offers fewer reassurances of prophetic power than reminders of human frailty, with God persistently addressing Ezekiel as "Mortal." Gone is any sense of the prophetic triumphalism with which Elijah disposed of the prophets of Baal. Instead, one is left to wonder at what a dreadful thing it is to love and be loved by this God whose word is so powerfully indifferent to public humiliation and public opinion. Ezekiel was even denied the satisfaction of being a minority of one who at least had "the truth" on his side, for he was simply wrong and mistaken on several points, and perhaps God was mistaken as well. In an amazing verse, Ezekiel 20:25, the prophet cites God's own judgment on the laws that were given to the Hebrew community of the exodus: "Moreover I gave them statutes that were not good and ordinances by which they could not live."[184] If Ezekiel portrays God as repenting of certain laws, the errors of the prophet are clearer still. It restores one's confidence in the assorted redactors and copyists of the biblical text as well as one's confidence in the writing of the prophet himself to see that Ezekiel's mistakes were left intact. In Ezekiel 26:1-14, a text dating from 586 B.C.E., the prophet foretells the destruction of Tyre by the Babylonian, Nebuchadrezzar. In Ezekiel 29:17-20, written in 570 B.C.E., the prophet concedes that Tyre did not fall to Nebuchadrezzar, so instead, Ezekiel predicts that the Babylonian leader will capture Egypt. Again, historical events were to prove Ezekiel's forecast mistaken.[185] But such errors in prediction do nothing to detract from the stature of Ezekiel in his truly prophetic role, a role that does not involve "fortune telling" in any penultimate sense. Rather, the prophet is one who sees God's action in the heart of things, not in a way which claims that all that happens is the will of God, but rather in a way which recognizes that, whatever happens, God's will is ultimate. For both Ezekiel and Jeremiah, this meant that nothing — not even conquest and exile — could separate people from the love of God. And as we will see, in both Ezekiel and Jeremiah this also meant that, unless there is intervention by God, those who sow terror are absolutely powerless to reap anything but terror. As presented biblically, the prophetic role has to do with seeing into the very crux of history and discerning there that God's will is ultimate, not only in the sense of chronological finality, but also in the sense of that ultimate meaning upon which we may now stake our lives.

But whatever the role of the prophets in discerning that the will of God will prevail, should we not be able to expect a certain degree of prophetic accuracy in the more mundane forecasting of historical events? Is it not fair to expect that, at some point, the utility of the prophet is dependent upon getting predictions right? Quite to the contrary, the surest sign that the community has allowed the prophetic message to be of utility to them is if the historical events foreseen by the prophet do *not* come to pass. This was the paradoxical dilemma of the sulking Jonah; insofar as the people of Nineveh heeded the truth he spoke, Jonah was proven wrong (Jonah 3:4-5). A similar paradox is evident in Ezekiel's role as sentinel for the house of Israel (Ezekiel 33:7-9); a catastrophe is looming, and it will not occur only if the people heed the sentinel's warning that it *will* occur.[186] Indeed, this paradoxical dilemma is inherent to the prophetic mission itself. Elie Wiesel perceives the dilemma at work as an anguishing Jeremiah announces doom on Jerusalem:

> In the cosmic catastrophe that Jerusalem's destruction represents, there is no winner.
>
> The prophet knows it; he alone knows it. Therein lies his insoluble dilemma: if tragedy strikes, is it not because of his foreknowledge of that tragedy? What is he supposed to do with his knowledge? If he reveals it, the dreaded event may not come to pass. In other words: only if he tells the truth about what may and will happen is there a chance for it not to happen; only if he tells the truth can it prove to be false![187]

In the face of such dilemmas, in the face of personal anguish and public humiliation, is it any wonder that the persona of the prophet is marked by a certain wildness? Gottwald observes that the demeanor and thought of Ezekiel in particular is "a compressed distillation of that agony of renunciation and rebirth through which the deported Judahites passed. . . ."[188] Daniel Berrigan notes that Ezekiel's humiliation continues to this day with a number of psychoanalysts joining in the judgment of Ezekiel's contemporaries that he was a madman — psychotic and paranoid, with alternating delusions of persecution and grandeur.[189] Some scholars have even claimed that the etymology of the Hebrew *nabi* (prophet) can be traced to a stem word that refers to gushing speech, deep breaths, and madness.[190] While there can be no doubt that the Hebrew prophets were maladjusted, it is an evasion to try to trace the prophetic abnormality to pathology of the psyche. Rather, the prophets were maladjusted to the mainstream spirituality and the official religiosity of their age. They were maladjusted to the quiescence and obedience that passed for good social order, an order of mass impoverishment and copious bloodshed. They were abnormal in their refusal to join in the endless rounds of compromise of spirit and conscience. In short, as Abraham Heschel described it, the maladjustments and abnormalities that beset the prophets were actually a form of "moral madness."[191]

Yet, in view of the prophetic revulsion at the clamor and swagger of empires, why would Jeremiah and Ezekiel counsel nonresistance to invasion and exile at the hands of the Babylonians? Babylon was, after all, a veritable model of all that was wrong with empire. Even if the moral sensitivities of the prophets ran towards pacifism (as was certainly the case with Jeremiah),[192] could they not at least have advocated a campaign of nonviolent resistance to the Babylonian interlopers? In fact, the position that emerges from the writings of both Jeremiah and Ezekiel was less pro-Babylonian than a principled stand against the ruling elite of Judah. By examining the considerable sociological and political information contained in the book of Jeremiah, Norman Gottwald perceives the presence of two opposing parties within Judah in the period of 609-586 B.C.E.[193] The party that was comprised of the kings and the majority of bureaucrats, priests, and court prophets like Hananiah maintained that Judah, with the assistance of Egypt, needed to assert its autonomy from Babylon. The future of the state, and therefore the survival of the people as well, hinged on political independence, even if that independence was purchased at the price of indebtedness to Egypt. Opposing this party were prophets such as Jeremiah, Habakkuk (Habakkuk 1:6), and Uriah of Kiriath-jearim (Jeremiah 26:20-23). They maintained that the ruling class was not the guarantor of justice or of the people's welfare, and that the state was not the guarantor of communal identity and faith. This was their claim because these prophets and their God were "seeing from below," whereas the royal consciousness of the powerful and the wealthy only allowed for "seeing from above."[194] From below, from among those who had been marginalized, it was possible to see that the skirts of the powerful had been washed in "the life-blood of the innocent poor" (Jeremiah 2:34), that the guilt of the nation of Judah and the city of Jerusalem exceeded that of Sodom, which "did not aid the poor and needy" (Ezekiel 16:49). The whole nation bears responsibility, but special culpability attaches to the shepherds who have ill-served the flock (Jeremiah 10:21; Ezekiel 34:10).[195] And now, with Babylon at the gates, should the poor and the faithful expect that these shepherds have mended their ways? Indeed, should God expect that the nation has been converted to righteousness and justice and peace? No, let Babylon come. Let the nation fall. What of value would be spared by preserving this ruling class, this state, these political configurations and national boundaries? Nothing depends on it — not peace, not the well-being of the poor, and certainly not God. O yes, with Babylon at the gates, the leaders call on the God whom they had long forgotten (Jeremiah 2:26-28; Ezekiel 7:18-20). O yes, with conquest looming, the allies of the powerful suddenly develop an uncharacteristic hankering for peace (Jeremiah 6:14; 8:11; Ezekiel 7:23-25; 13:10, 16). But before, when they were safely ensconced behind throne and sword and wealth, God counted for nothing and their only mention of "peace" was in their support for the endless wars that would ensure the "peace," the wars that passed for "peace" (Jeremiah 22:17; Ezekiel 22:6). You for whom bloodshed was justice and terror was peace now reap the terror you have sown.

This harsh judgment on the nation is reflected in the individual encounter between Jeremiah and Pashhur, the priest who was the chief officer in charge of the maintenance of order in the temple precinct in Jerusalem. The encounter occurred soon after Jeremiah had performed a sign-act in full view of elders and priests in the valley of Ben-Hinnom, also known as Topheth (Jeremiah 19:1-13). On instructions from God, Jeremiah had purchased an earthenware jug, which he took to Topheth near the Potsherd Gate, a spot that was littered with pottery rejects.[196] So too, the plans of Judah and Jerusalem were being rejected by God. Such was the pronouncement of the prophet as he smashed the earthenware jug. The location was not without significance. It was here in the valley of Topheth, Jeremiah reminded (7:30-32; 19:4-5), that the people had offered the innocent blood of their own children as sacrifice to Baal. And now this horror that had been sown would be reaped. But rather than serving as food for some god, the bodies of the people would be food for wild animals (19:7). Rather than serving as an offering to Baal, the bodies of the children would be cannibalized by their own parents (19:9). Like Ezekiel's valley of the dry bones (Ezekiel 37:1-2), the valley of Topheth would be strewn with corpses, a scene of utter devastation, a valley of death victorious. When he smashes the earthenware jug, Jeremiah smashes all illusions that lives can be sacrificed with impunity, that bloodthirsty gods can be served with no consequence. Jeremiah carries his somber vision to the doorstep of the temple itself (19:14-15) and it is there that he is met by Pashhur.

What was it that Pashhur found objectionable in the words and deeds of Jeremiah? Was Pashhur not a priest himself, and a defender of the holy of holies? Like Jeremiah, he certainly would have taken his stand with Yahweh and not with Baal. Like Jeremiah, he certainly would have been repulsed by child sacrifice; indeed, serving as an officer of the temple, Pashhur was likely more meticulous than Jeremiah in denouncing any practices that departed from the officially prescribed rituals of worship. What outraged Pashhur was not Jeremiah's call for allegiance to Yahweh, but Jeremiah's claim that Yahweh was somehow independent of temple and city and nation. Allegiance to God and allegiance to country, are these not two sides of one coin? Or, in a metaphor less mercantile, is God not woven into the very fabric of the present order? To tear this fabric is to rip away at holiness itself. Or, to pile on another metaphor still, is God not in the very clay that powerfully binds this order together as a world without end, amen? No, says Jeremiah, God is the potter and not the clay, and after repeated efforts at gently molding and shaping, the potter may decide to smash her creation if it fails to reflect the utility or beauty intended. The potter had never intended that this creation should become a vessel for sacrificing children, neglecting the poor, sowing terror. To Pashhur, that must have sounded like blasphemy, for how can one judge this order that has been created without also passing judgment on the creator? But Jeremiah's bold assertion is that it is none other than the Creator who is passing judgment. God is not a part of your temple, your city, your bloody system. God never intended that the clay should take this shape (19:5), and if the reputation of the potter is assailed in the smashing of the pottery, so be it. This hollow configuration of religion, violence, and power — let it be smashed.

Pashhur is overseer of the temple (20:1), but God has appointed Jeremiah as overseer of nations and kingdoms (1:10).[197] Pashhur is vested with office and status by a religious hierarchy grateful for the armed security that he and his temple police provide. In contrast, Jeremiah is devoid of office and status among the kingdoms, which claim above all else that they will be subject to no oversight, that they are authorities unto themselves.[198] Jeremiah is interfering in matters in which he has no status, no business, no concern save the concern of God.[199] In the sacred precincts of the temple, Pashhur welcomes interference neither from Jeremiah nor from God. Indeed, it is precisely the essence of Pashhur's job description to prevent such irruptions and disruptions from without the temple. If God has a word to offer, Pashhur is certain that God will offer it from within the temple and not from without. Pashhur's task is to defend the domesticated deity who speaks only from within the nexus of the alliance of religion and state, who speaks only from within the heart of current power arrangements.[200] Pashhur has Jeremiah arrested, beaten, and locked up in the stocks of the prison at the Upper Gate of Benjamin. Jeremiah's offense was that he had dared to pronounce a judgment on the current order and that he had dared to represent the judgment as a word from God. The maintenance of public order required that Jeremiah be locked up in the stocks, just as God was locked up in the temple. But when Jeremiah was released the next day, both prophet and God were unrehabilitated. Jeremiah boldly approached Pashhur and pronounced, "The LORD has named you not Pashhur but 'Terror-all-around.' For thus says the LORD: I am making you a terror to yourself and to all your friends . . ." (Jeremiah 20:3-4).[201] Pashhur and his family, the kings and their treasure, Judah and its cities will be overthrown by Babylon (20:4-6). The veil will be lifted from the current order of things which seemed so solid, and this order will be shown to have been nothing but disorder. The plunder that passed for national treasure will be plundered. The terror that passed for security and defense and strength will be reaped as terror-all-around.

But we must not imagine Jeremiah as happy or self-satisfied with the judgment he has to announce. While Jeremiah seems to taunt the powerful and the complacent, while he seems to extend a virtual invitation for the Babylonian disaster to strike, he did not gloat and he did not relish the consequences of the terror that was returning to its source. Instead, Jeremiah and Ezekiel and all of the prophetic harbingers of pending disaster grieve at that which they foresee.[202] The grief over the approaching terror is too powerful for words, and so Ezekiel is alternately instructed to let the moaning of his broken heart[203] be heard in public (21:6) and to stand as mute testimony to inexpressible grief (24:15-17).

These are two sides of the prophetic mission: to announce judgment on the present order and to weep at the consequences the judgment portends. This biblical pattern is so pronounced that it seems fair to suggest that if either side of the mission is lacking, then the word that is being offered is not prophetic. Zealously advocating overthrow of the current system with little thought to the violence and suffering of the past and of the future *might* make for victorious revolutions and *might* entail prescient social and political analysis, but it is not prophetic. On the other hand, only to weep, only to commiserate over the condition of the hungry and the homeless *might* be an expression of compassion. To attempt to gather contributions for the poor in an age of "compassion fatigue" *might* make for good social work and effective charity. But if there is only charity and not also a judgment on the current order that creates such poverty and suffering, then it is not a prophetic word that is being offered. The prophet announces a judgment from God. The prophet weeps at the judgment that has been announced.

Ezekiel loves and rebukes Jerusalem. Ezekiel cries for and is silent for Jerusalem. Ezekiel trembles at the terror of that which has been sown and that which will be reaped by Jerusalem. In Ezekiel 24, the stage is set for a horrible fall as siege is laid to the city on January 15, 588 B.C.E.[204] But then, we are left on the brink of disaster. Just as the prophet's mouth is closed, we do not learn of the fate of the city until much later (Ezekiel 33:21). Instead, there is a remarkable excursus — a series of oracles against the nations.

There at the walls of a doomed Jerusalem, our attention is suddenly transported to other nations. What accounts for this sudden shift in the text of Ezekiel? While Ezekiel is certainly not alone in this prophetic habit of addressing foreign nations (see Isaiah 13–23; Jeremiah 46–51; Amos 1–2; Zephaniah 2), why now when he has brought us to the outskirts of a Jerusalem on the outskirts of disaster? Were these oracles inserted into the text at this point due to the whim of some heavy-handed interpolator among Ezekiel's disciples?[205] In fact, the message that is communicated by interrupting the terror of Jerusalem with the oracles against the nations is hardly whimsical. On the one hand, the oracles have the impact of furthering the word of judgment against Judah and Jerusalem. These people who were chosen and set aside by God, see how much they have come to resemble the other nations. In turning from God, they have sought to establish their security through wealth and armies. In surrendering their distinctiveness, Judah and Jerusalem have surrendered themselves to the power of terror. But on the other hand, let no nation gloat at the crumbling walls of Jerusalem. Like the prophets, you nations should be weeping over Jerusalem, for the fate of that city is your fate as well. You who are haughty and powerful, you will reap the terror that you have sown.

In all of prophetic literature, the oracles against the nations take the form of lawsuits, with charges brought, testimony gathered, and judgments announced.[206] Since the nations did not have the same type of covenantal relationship with Yahweh as did Israel, the typical charges against the nations did not focus on faithlessness to Yahweh nor on failure to adhere to covenantal laws. Rather, the charges against the nations focus on the arrogance of accumulating wealth while ignoring the poor.[207] The nations, it is charged, are proud of violence and of wars fought and won. To Edom: "The terror you inspire and the pride of your heart have deceived you, you who live in the clefts of the rock, who hold the height of the hill. Although you make your nest as high as the eagle's, from there I will bring you down, says the LORD" (Jeremiah 49:16). To Tyre: "How you have vanished from the seas, O city renowned, once mighty on the sea, you and your inhabitants, who imposed your terror on all the mainland!" (Ezekiel 26:17) To all of the mighty nations who thunder and roar: "At evening time, lo, terror! Before morning, they are no more. This is the fate of those who despoil us, and the lot of those who plunder us" (Isaiah 17:14). But these prophetic oracles against the nations cannot be reduced to a simple formula of pronouncing vengeance on those who have terrorized Israel. Indeed, Jeremiah's version of the oracles included nations with which Israel had never had dealings. Rather than being an expression of parochial pique, such oracles constitute a universal judgment on the terror inflicted by the proud and the mighty.[208]

Including Babylon? Especially Babylon. It is clear in Jeremiah 42:7-12 that Babylon was to be an instrument of God, an expression of both judgment *and* *mercy*.[209] But it is precisely *mercy* which Babylon was unwilling to sow. Babylon is the sower (Jeremiah 50:16), but all that has been sown is terror, a horrible harvest to be reaped. Who can Babylon blame? Are there terrorists arrayed against the empire? Are there demons gnawing from without and from within? When Jerusalem faced collapse, the prophet did not allow the city to blame its plight on demonized enemies; much less will the prophet countenance Babylonian claims of blamelessness. "You set a snare for yourself and you were caught, O Babylon . . ." (50:24). Indeed, it is not claiming too much to assert that such is the biblical fate of all empires. They will fall and they will fall hard, all of these great ones who live by the power of the sword. Babylon is taken up into biblical literature as a paradigm of empire and of rebellious principalities and powers.[210] Do not think that your life (your life in body or spirit) can be saved by standing behind the military shield of empire. Hope goes with those who depart reliance on such power (Jeremiah 51:45).

*   *   *

Hope? How is it possible to speak of any hope in the face of these prophetic portraits of utter devastation? Jerusalem: fallen. The nations: fallen. Terror sown and terror reaped. The prophets have made their point too well. When violence threatens and the powerful issue pleas of innocence, we know now that their pleas are just more arrogance. As the mighty seek to demonize their enemies, we know now of the kinship they share. We know now that the prophets see the very judgment of God in league with Babylon, the most demonic of all enemies. And we know too that Babylon will fall. We know that the poor suffer, not only in the ascendancy of the mighty, but also in their fall. Where is the hope in this?

It is the mighty who desire a quick, cheap rush to hope with their restoration to power assured, as if the judgment of God was just a bump in the road. The great ones urge that we rush down that road leading to the bright future (which resembles nothing so much as the bleak past). "Let bygones be bygones" is the rule of the rulers. Let the terror of the past remain interred with the victims. Like the judgment of God, it is over and done with. In the future, the poor will be afforded better treatment, violence will be used for only the best of reasons and only ever as a last resort, and so on and so on.

The prophets are too acquainted with grief to allow for any cheap rush to hope. The prophets are too acquainted with terror to allow for any distance to be placed between the perpetrators of violence and the harvest of death. When we most long for hope, the prophets offer a tour of death instead. In a manner more somber than Dante, they guide us through the underworld. Isaiah (chapter 14) and Ezekiel (chapter 32) serve as guides on this tour.

In cosmology common to the ancient Near East, waters run through Sheol.[211] Not unlike the River Styx, it is by means of these waters that the dead are transported to the underworld. But the waters can be like a torrent (Psalm 18:4), ensnaring victims in a one-way journey, for the exit from Sheol is blocked by bars and gates that do not open out (Jonah 2:6). While the inhabitants of the underworld cannot break free, the waters can. When human destructiveness reaches the point at which death has dominion, then "hell on earth" is realized in a mythological and a literal sense. Then the waters of the deep surge forward to meet a humanity surging toward death. This is Ezekiel's portrayal of God's judgment on Tyre (26:19-21). The violence that Tyre has sown is so great that the city will reap the waters of the underworld, the very waters of death.[212] Terror brings hell on earth.

And what of the fate of the mighty ones, the ones who sat atop this deluge? Not unpredictably, the powerful reckoned that they would maintain their stature in Sheol, and they bolstered their view with a wealth of mythology. Sheol, it was held, had its own form of hierarchy with the most contemptible regions being reserved for those who lacked ritual purity — for those whose corpses lay unburied or (in Hebrew thought) for the uncircumcised. In contrast, the lords and princes expected a place of distinction, a comfortable perch on which they might lounge henceforth (Isaiah 14:18). Isaiah and Ezekiel, our tour guides to the underworld, subvert in toto the illusions of the mighty. To the mightiest of the mighty, the king of Babylon, Isaiah proclaims that he will join the unburied, his corpse cast from its tomb (14:19). "You will not be joined with them in burial, because you have destroyed your land, you have killed your people" (14:20). Ezekiel addresses the mighty with a virtual dance of death (Ezekiel 32:17-32).[213] Will the lords and princes and the powerful nations be granted the choicest morsels in the Pit? Our guide Ezekiel tells us to look. There are the mighty ones "in the uttermost parts of the Pit" (32:23) among the impure, the uncircumcised. In describing the powerful in Sheol, Ezekiel invokes a refrain more ominous than monotonous: there is Assyria "who spread terror in the land of the living" (v. 23); and Elam "who spread terror in the land of the living" (v. 24), "for terror of them was spread in the land of the living" (v. 25); and "Meshech and Tubal are there . . . for they spread terror in the land of the living" (v. 26), "for the terror of the warriors was in the land of the living" (v. 27); and the princes of the north and the Sidonians "for all the terror that they caused by their might" (v. 30); and the Egyptian Pharaoh as well, for "he spread terror in the land of the living" (v. 32). The land of the living is not made for terror. Make hell on earth and only hell can be reaped. It is a horrible calculus which the powerful hope to ignore, but the prophets do not allow for escape, not even escape in death. The terror that is sown is reaped even in the underworld.

Dead, gone, unburied, confined to the uttermost regions of the Pit. An unenviable position indeed, but the mighty ones have yet to face their greatest terror, for there in Sheol alongside them are none other than those who are "killed by the sword" (Ezekiel 32:21). In still another refrain, Ezekiel tells repeatedly of the powerful nations and kings who "are placed among the slain" (32:26). In other words, the powerful are placed among the victims of power. There is no longer any distance between the perpetrators and the victims of violence. There is no longer any question of "putting the past behind us." The powerful are now face to face with their own victims, face to face with a nightmare of their own making. It is a moment of high drama, a moment of terror perhaps, but Ezekiel and Isaiah tell us very little of that moment. We know enough to avoid turning that moment into a tawdry tale of horror in which the victims now violently pursue the mighty in fits of vengeance. In this Sheol, after all, the dead cannot be rendered deader. The moment is far more poignant than anything vengeance could provide. To face the violence we have inflicted or sanctioned. To face the worst within ourselves. To look into the eyes of those whom we have wronged, of those whom we most wish to leave behind, forgotten. To face them, to speak with them, to sit at table and break bread with them, to *be* with them from now until forever. In some sense, each moment of our lives contributes to this deathless moment, this moment beyond death when we stand face to face with those whom we have hurt, with those whom we have healed, with those whom we have loved, and with those whom we have hated. Before he speaks of hope, the prophet takes us to the Pit. Beware of the hope that is peddled hastily and cheaply.

There is one more tour to take before the prophet points to hope, and once again, it is a tour among the dead. This time, it is God who takes Ezekiel on a tour to the valley of the dry bones (37:1-14). The valley appears to be a forgotten battlefield, an unclean place strewn with the decayed corpses of the unburied dead. Like the valley of child sacrifice, the valley of Topheth where Jeremiah smashed the earthenware jug, Ezekiel's valley of the dry bones is the scene of death victorious. Yet it is precisely here that God chooses to offer hope. What terror condemns to the Pit, God's Spirit can bring to life. The effort to forget the battlefield, the terror, and the victims is a path of no hope. If death is no longer to have dominion, it is our own victims we must most remember. The dry bones must take on flesh and breathe and speak. It is the anthropology of hope that the victims of terror will be re-membered.[214] In the valley of the dry bones, God remembers. If the mighty ones in Sheol (Ezekiel 32) perform a dance of death, then in the valley (Ezekiel 37), the dry bones arise to perform a dance of death defeated.

Of course, Ezekiel's prophecy is specifically a vision of restoration for Israel (37:11), but it is no less hopeful for its specificity. While Israel could only hope to reap the violence and the faithlessness that had been sown, a faithful God intervenes with a new hope. Incredibly, exile becomes the site of God's presence and of God's promise for restoration and redemption.[215] It is clear that Yahweh is God of all the nations because the words of promise and reassurance are given in a foreign land and because the bloody schemes of kings and empires are thwarted. But what of those other nations? Is there hope for them as well? With the promise of Israel's restoration at hand, Ezekiel tells us little about hope for the nations beyond the fact that God's holiness has now been displayed "in the sight of many nations" (39:27). Instead of fretting about the nations, Ezekiel's love of Israel and his joy at the promised restoration cause him to leap into that future and to see how it might be shaped in righteousness and harmony. Ezekiel the architect, planning the design of the new temple down to the last cubit (40:1–43:17). Ezekiel the surveyor, setting the boundaries and apportioning the land for all the tribes of Israel (47:13–48:29). Ezekiel the merchant, assuring that the weights and measures will be honest (45:10-12). Ezekiel the landscaper, observing how the waters will flow, the waters for fishing and swimming, the sacred waters of life (47:1-12). Ezekiel the lover of Israel, the lover of the God who restores.

It is left for other prophets to tell us more about the hope for other nations. Isaiah is certainly one prophet who does so. It is as if Isaiah's hope for Israel cannot be contained, and so it overflows the banks to encompass others. It is an unruly hope that surges forth until the promise to Abram is fulfilled, that "in you all the families of the earth shall be blessed" (Genesis 12:3). And astonishingly, one expression of Isaiah's hope *for* the nations (Isaiah 19:19-25) comes at the very core of Isaiah's oracles *against* the nations. This hope of Isaiah is nothing other than the hope of God. The kings and mighty nations wish to rush past judgment in search of hope found cheaply, but the hope of God lies at the very heart of the judgment of God. Hope for Egypt, for Assyria, for the nations is found only by hearing the judgment, by living in it, by passing through it rather than around it. Then, at the heart of judgment, the nations can hear the word of hope: "On that day Israel will be the third with Egypt and Assyria, a blessing in the midst of the earth, whom the LORD of hosts has blessed, saying, 'Blessed be Egypt my people, and Assyria the work of my hands, and Israel my heritage'" (Isaiah 19:24-25).

Remarkably, Isaiah has gone much further than merely to announce hope for the nations. In prophesying that "Israel will be the third," has he not forthrightly bound the hope of Israel with the hope of the nations? In biblical literature, it is not surprising to find the hope of the nations dependent on hope for Israel. But is it also possible that Israel's hope is dependent on hope for the nations?

Certainly for Israel and Assyria and Egypt alike, the source of hope is God. To deny the hope of one is to deny the hope of all. Therein lies a conundrum for both ancient folks and modern. What I most wish to deny to my demonized adversary is the possibility of hope, but when I do so, I deny that possibility for myself as well. It is a maddening link, forged by a God who is not, after all, incapable of taking sides. This is a God who takes the side of the poor, the exiled, the powerless, the victims. So why will God not take my side as I set about to battle evil? Why will the hope of God not depart the enemy camp?

Heschel observed that the ultimate problem of humanity is not the problem of evil but the problem of our relationship with God:

> The Biblical answer to evil is not the good but the *holy*. It is an attempt to raise man to a higher level of existence, where man is not alone when confronted with evil. Living in "the light of the face of God" bestows upon man a power of love that enables him to overcome the powers of evil. . . .
>
> We do not wage war with evil in the name of an abstract concept of duty. We do the good not because it is a value or because of expediency, but because we owe it to God.[216]

Though it is maddening, what I owe to God is intertwined with what I owe to my enemy. And the hope too is intertwined. Hope is not possible for me unless it is also possible for the most demonic of my adversaries.

       *   *   *

Why do the prophets weep? From the beginning, do they not already know that all will be all right? Have they not already ingested a hopeful word from the God of hope? How can one hold together this mourning and this hope? As the prophets perform their signs, their pottery smashing (Jeremiah 19:1-13), their baggage packing and their hole digging (Ezekiel 12:1-16), do they not already know in their hearts that Jerusalem will be redeemed? Why then the broken hearts? These prophets who see from below, who see from the midst of the wreckage left behind by the destitution and brutalities of the great society, why would they weep as the mighty are toppled? Should they not instead rejoice as the terror of the powerful comes home to roost? Why do the prophets weep?

God knows that Ezekiel may be asked to explain why he weeps (Ezekiel 21:6-7). Tell them, says God to Ezekiel, that you weep because of the sword: "Cry and wail, O mortal, for it is against my people; it is against all Israel's princes; they are thrown to the sword, together with my people" (21:12). It is not only the princes who reap the terror, but all of the house of Israel (Ezekiel 12:10). Even if one were to maintain a callous stance of indifference regarding the fate of the powerful (which the prophets do not), those who suffer most include the powerless. Often, those who had precious little to do with sowing seeds of violence are the ones who are brutalized in the wars fought back and forth, and in the ethnic cleansings, and in the terrorist attacks and retaliations, whereas the wealthy and the powerful sit safely ensconced behind layers of "security."[217] But even more than the human rulers, the institutions, thrones, principalities, bureaucracies, states, and all of the assorted inhuman powers that take on a life of their own and govern human existence — these are all untouched by the terror suffered by mere mortals. "Mortal," God repeatedly calls Ezekiel. It is for these *mortals* that the prophets weep, for the powerless people, and also for the powerful people who one day might be rendered powerless by terror. Neither the prophets nor their God seek the senseless murder of mortals. The sowing and reaping of that terror is not the work of God. The prophetic vision is filled with more wrath, more hope, and more meaning than could ever be contained in random brutalities. It is not mortal terror that will bring down principalities. It is the God of the prophets who brings down the thrones, who overthrows the institutions, who announces doom on principalities and states and powers. For the terror they have sown, every kingdom and guerrilla band, every mighty government and terrorist cell is judged, is fallen, is doomed. *This* is the intervention of God.

There is no news to the sowing and reaping of terror. History has a belly full of it. One might call it karma. Sow bloodshed and reap bloodshed, although the bloodied are often not sowers. What is new is the intervention of God to pronounce judgment on the whole system of terror. God is no respecter of dualities; God does not will the death of mortals, whether wicked or righteous (Ezekiel 33:10-20). Rather, God pronounces doom on all power that is based on violence and terror.

For those who share the faith of the prophets, it is no mere anachronism to sense that somehow the prophets weep for us as well. "Terror all around" is our plight too. The principalities and powers have been heedless of the prophets' words and of God's judgment. The prophetic drama unfolds still, awaiting resolution. Insofar as Ezekiel the sentinel is faithful to the word of God which is offered for his time, his place, and his people, that word transcends the history of that time to become a word of God for our time too. The sentinel is on the wall. We heed the warning, or not.

And it is not just warnings, it is also visions that await fulfillment. Jeremiah had a vision of a new covenant with God, a covenant that would be written on the human heart. "I will make an everlasting covenant with them, never to draw back from doing good to them; and I will put the fear of me in their hearts, so that they may not turn from me" (Jeremiah 32:40). For Jeremiah, "terror all around" was the surest sign that the fear of God (which is also the love of God) was not in the human heart. Actions are but a pale reflection of what is in the heart.[218] Jeremiah's vision waits.

Perhaps it is not strange that prophetic visions of hope for the nations come in the very midst of prophetic oracles against the nations. The hope of the nations does not lie in the restoration, the reformation, or the fine-tuning of thrones, political institutions, and apparatus of power. The hope of the nations lies in really *hearing* the judgment of God — *hearing* in the same way that the prophets heard, which also necessarily means *responding* and turning around. Karl Barth saw an intimate connection between God's "No" and God's "Yes." He explored the manner in which God's judgment is persistently an expression of God's mercy. As Krister Stendahl described it, "Judgment and mercy are not balanced over against each other in a scheme in which a last judgment is tempered and adjusted by God's grace, or Christ, or the blood, or the cross, or the intercession of the saints. That is not the way it is. Mercy, salvation, liberation are all part of God's judgment."[219] Mercy is a gift that is only experienced by passing through God's judgment and not around it.

Ezekiel the sentinel gives forth a warning. Jeremiah the anguished finds terror all around. The prophetic moments of warning and judgment are also moments of mercy in which we may choose to turn around — moments in which we may renounce the sowing and reaping of terror. Until we do, the prophets weep.

CHAPTER IV

The Terror of God

From the days of John the Baptist until now the kingdom of heaven has suffered violence, and the violent take it by force.

MATTHEW 11:12

Storming the Kingdom of God

Some say that human and divine terror meet in the End, and there are some who yearn for this meeting, who pursue it and even seek to force it. Judaism gave birth to the phrase "forcing the end"[1] to describe the apocalyptic activism of those who tire of waiting for God to establish the New Jerusalem or, more ominously, who tire of waiting for the cataclysmic destruction of the world. While the Lord's Prayer urges the coming of God's kingdom (Matthew 6:10; Luke 11:2), others beckon the onset of Armageddon.

If visions of the terminus of human history seem obscure, so too is the terminology that has been applied to these visions. Scholars debate the basis for (or even the need for) distinctions among various descriptive terms such as "eschatological" and "apocalyptic" and "millenarian" and "chiliastic." Most scholars agree in treating as synonymous the terms "chiliasm" and "millenarianism," deriving respectively from Greek and Latin words for "thousand." Millenarians/chiliasts assert the imminence of the thousand-year period of harmony, the reign of the saints that figures in some Jewish and Christian versions of endtime history. Beyond that, agreement among the millenarians themselves fades. Will there be an ultimate showdown with evil, and if so, will it precede or follow the millennium? Do the saints play a role in inaugurating the millennium, or is

it fully an intervention by God? Is humanity on the right track, easing, progressing, evolving our way into this new and saintly era, or instead have we been
tediously mired in a fallen state, perhaps even regressing and devolving so that
only a radical disruption of the current state of the world can offer any hope? It
depends. As we shall see, the contours of the millennial vision depend not only
on variations in readings of Scripture but also on variations in relationships to
power and social change.

If "millenarianism" and "chiliasm" may be treated as synonyms, the comparing and contrasting of "eschatology" and "apocalypticism" is a topic of greater
debate. While the Greek roots of "eschatology" would seem to offer a straightforward definition of "discourse on last things," it is not always clear whether
eschatos refers to a chronological "end" point to human history or to the "ultimate" concern of human history (e.g., Revelation 1:17). In biblical texts, the
term is even used in an inversive fashion so that the "last" (i.e., the least) become
the first (e.g., Mark 9:35; 10:31; Matthew 20:16).[2] Likewise, questions arise regarding the word "apocalypse," derived from the Greek *kalupto* ("covering" or
"veil"), with "apocalypse," thus meaning an "unveiling" or (as translated in Revelation 1:1) a "revelation." But what is it that is being "unveiled"? Is this an unveiling of the end of human history, or of the true meaning of our current condition, or of the will of God, or of all of these? And if it is an unveiling that is
intended, why does apocalyptic literature seem so obscure to so many readers?

These questions will reemerge, but since the purpose here is to glimpse the
confluence of terror and some versions of endism, brief and tenuous definitions of "eschatology" and "apocalypticism" must suffice. Of the many books
and articles written on the subject, there seems to be a growing consensus that
apocalypticism is a specific manifestation of eschatology. Eschatology explores
the manner in which history is teleological, i.e., the manner in which there is an
"end" that gives structure and meaning to the whole of history. Apocalypticism
asserts more specifically that this "end" has come near and that its proximity
has an impact, not only on human history, but on the cosmos.[3] Whatever the
merit of these tenuous differentiations, it is clear that the biblical texts of Judaism and Christianity include perspectives that are eschatological as well as
those that are apocalyptic. When doing theology, it is a questionable enterprise
to appeal to biblical eschatology for the purpose of excising the "more radical"
apocalypticism.[4] Both are present in the biblical story, and they merge in the
radical eschatology and apocalyptic expectancy that surround the biblical portrayal of the teaching and ministry of Jesus.[5]

Precision of definition is rendered more elusive by the fact that there is a
plethora of variegated manifestations of both "apocalyptic" as literary genre
and "apocalypticism" as social movement. Not infrequently, visions of the end

are consonant with visions of the beginning so that the redeemed of the end time actually find themselves returning to Eden, returning to that primordial time "when there was no fear, no terror."[6] The question of special pertinence here is, does the path to the restoration of "no terror" necessarily pass through an apocalyptic escalation of terror? To this question too, apocalypticism offers no uniform response, with some apocalypticists choosing to withdraw from the world and others seeking to transform it through reliance on methods ranging from utopianism to terrorism. Terror could be (and has been) utilized either by apocalyptic movements that view the world as progressing towards the dawn of a new, millennial age, or by movements that perceive the world as in a precipitous decline, teetering on the edge of the abyss.[7] If the world is progressing, a dose of terror might serve to finish off the remaining forces of malignity; if in decline, a dose of terror might serve to finish off the world itself. In either event, terror might somehow become holy. Rather than being a sign of the world's corruption, terror might become the means by which corruption may be hastened towards its ultimate demise.

If the versions of apocalypticism are many and varied, so too are those social and cultural environments in which apocalypticism might flourish. Gone are the days when it could be claimed with assurance that apocalypticism is "the community response of the oppressed and afflicted to a world" that offered scant hope.[8] In the millennia since biblical apocalypses first appeared, apocalypticism has emerged in movements both revolutionary and reactionary, enlisting support from the impoverished or the wealthy or both. Bernard McGinn observes that apocalypticism may serve either a "confirmatory function" or a "revolutionary function."[9] If, for example, one's ruler happens to be the righteous "Last Emperor" whose reign is viewed as ushering in the messianic age, then one must confirm or support that reign by resisting the final onslaught of the forces of evil. In contrast, if governance is under the sway of satanic forces, apocalypticism may serve a decidedly revolutionary function. In this latter case, as J. F. C. Harrison notes, "Political radicalism and religious millenarianism were not alternatives so much as different aspects of the same phenomenon."[10] But if not all apocalypticism is revolutionary, neither are all revolutions apocalyptic. Millenarianism and apocalypticism are more apt to arise in situations in which the revolutionary fervor is a reaction against the undermining of traditional cultures and established worldviews.[11] And so there are innumerable choices in apocalypticism: salvation of the world or salvation from the world, a millennium within history or a paradise outside of history, the reign of God as imminent or immanent, destruction or redemption or both, the dreams of the dispossessed or the designs of the potentates, the visions that reinforce or reform or remove the current order, the nonviolent activism of those who hope for a decisive intervention by God, or "the inevitable violence of any millennial sect hell-bent on infinite happiness."[12]

No single theory can explain what might make an environment fertile for apocalypticism and millenarianism. A sense of "relative deprivation"? While that may certainly play a role, not all poor people are millenarians and some of the well-heeled are. A clash of cultures? That would certainly account for the Native American Ghost Dance religion, but not for the outburst of apocalypticism that followed the Tokyo earthquake of 1923. The rapid onset of a major disaster? Such a thesis might explain the flagellant response to waves of plagues in medieval Europe, but it fails to account for the paucity of apocalyptic speculation in the midst of the devastation of the Irish potato famine.[13] But what's more, is humanity not always beset by deprivations and disorientations and clashing cultures and major disasters? Is there some sense in which endism may be woven into the very fabric of humanity, not least because we are mortal creatures, each of us facing our personal encounters with ends?[14]

All eras present environments that are rich with possibilities for the production and consumption of apocalyptic visions, but not all eras indulge these possibilities to the same degree. Our own era seems especially indulgent in this regard, what with the word "apocalypse" entering the popular vocabulary and the adjective "apocalyptic" being applied to ephemera ranging from snowstorms to glitches on Wall Street. This expansive use of "the apocalypse" may be an understandable reaction in an era that has devised the terror of world-ending weapons and ecological collapse, but unlike those apocalyptic movements that offer either warning or hope, contemporary manifestations of pop apocalypticism are merely maudlin versions of fatalism. Rather than urging engagement with the world (as some forms of apocalypticism certainly do), the doomsday scenarios of Hollywood counsel passivity and escapism as we watch our superheroes save us from the latest inferno or meteor or alien invasion.[15] As the end of history has moved from being a prerogative of God alone to being an option for humanity, doomsday anxiety has been matched by lethargic denial, as if the fate of the world is safer in the hands of a resigned humanity than of an angry God.[16] This strange mixture of anxiety and denial may partially account for the current popularity of the horror genre in novels, television, and film. The horror is sufficiently paranoid to appeal to the quest for thrills, but the anxiety is safe and is designed to inspire people to nothing beyond indulgence in the most banal "entertainment." As the saying goes, the world doesn't end in a bang or a whimper; it ends in kitsch.

Indeed, according to some raconteurs in the "poststructuralist" school of philosophy, we have already passed through the kitschy end of the world. French academic Jean Baudrillard paints a vision of the "post-apocalyptic" world currently in the making: a world cleansed of viruses (except for the "virus" of sadness), a veritable rule of the Beast in the guise of a global Disney World.[17] If the world has already ended, how can one respond but in resignation? Of this school of thought, Robert Jay Lifton writes,

> . . . we speak of living in an age that is not only post-modern but also post-Freudian, post-Marxist, post-Communist, postideological, post-revolutionary, postcolonial, postwar (whatever the war), post–Cold War, posthistoric, postnarrative (in terms of literature), and postfigurative (in terms of art). Within the realm of the postmodern there is talk of what could be called the "postauthor" and the "postself." Although these "post"s are often meant to serve as springboards for renewals of one sort or another, the terminology nonetheless leaves us in a kind of nothingness, in a more or less permanent postmortem. The world is frequently experienced as already dead, requiring only the clearing of debris.[18]

But if the world has already ended in the minds of the poststructuralists, many of the people who witnessed the arrival of the year 2000 begged to differ. It was a remarkable (if only calendrical) point at which anxieties and denials met with hopes of new beginnings and fears of apocalyptic terror.

*   *   *

Millennium fever was in the air for months and years preceding December 31, 1999. Leaving aside the arcane question of whether the new millennium started with the year 2000 or 2001, round numbers on our humanly concocted calendars have the power to evoke wonderings about whether God might judge it a propitious time to intervene in human affairs in a truly millennial fashion.[19] The State of Israel took the preventive measure of expelling members of several Christian "sects" who apparently held the notion that assaults on key religious sites might clear the way for messianic visitation.

But for some people standing at the edge of the year 2000, the terror had more to do with web sites than with religious sites. The "Y2K computer bug" attracted worldwide attention and billions of dollars in an effort to squelch potentially apocalyptic scenarios that included disruption of food and water supplies and medical services, meltdown of nuclear plants and military security, and loss of "power" (in more senses than one). While the potential for widespread suffering was apparently real, it can be observed in retrospect that a certain poetic justice was at work — the hubris of technological achievement being terrorized by the technology itself.

On the eve of the year 2000, other forms of terror also filled the airwaves and the millennial consciousness. In Chechnya, under the pretext of battling Chechen "terrorists," Russian troops were terrorizing the people of Grozny with air and ground bombardment. Along the U.S. border with Canada, there were several arrests of people seeking to enter the United States with the alleged intent of launching terrorist attacks on New Year revelers, a threat given sufficient credence to cancel the revelry at Seattle's Space Needle. After Kashmiri separatists with suspected links to Pakistan hijacked an Indian passenger jet and held it for days in Afghanistan, Indian Prime Minister Vajpayee announced that "the battle against terrorism" would be at the top of India's agenda for the new millennium. No small feat that, setting the agenda for the next thousand years, with top billing going to the war on terror.

In addition to their coincidence on the eve of the year 2000, there was another element of commonality to all of these stories of terror and counterterror, i.e., the Islamic identity of those who were charged with plotting or precipitating terrorism. The Kashmiri separatist hijackers were Muslim, and the Chechen rebels were predominantly Muslim, and it was claimed that the suspects arrested at the U.S. border had ties to "Islamic fundamentalists" in Algeria. No few media commentators have portrayed these events as part of a larger phenomenon they call "Islamic terrorism," a phrase that is in itself highly offensive to Muslims. The view of Islam as monolithic and as singularly preoccupied with holy war has even led some pundits to assert that, with the Pakistani nuclear weapons program, "Islam now has the bomb." For these same commentators, any reference to Timothy McVeigh as a "Christian terrorist" or U.S. weapons as "Christian bombs" would be unthinkable. In fact, terrorist organizations have been founded by people claiming association with virtually every one of the world's major religions, and the very names of these organizations are often suggestive of divine sanction. Yes, there are the well-known Hezbollah ("Party of God") and Mujahedeen ("those who engage in struggle for the sake of God"). But there is also Dal Khalsa ("Army of the Pure"), a group that has been implicated in hijackings and bombings and that draws its membership from among Sikhs.[20] And with primarily Jewish membership is Mivtzan Elohim ("Wrath of God"), a group said to have been formed by Mossad (the Israeli intelligence agency) to engage in "counterterrorist" violence; in July 1973, members of this group murdered Moroccan waiter Ahmed Bouchiki in the mistaken belief that he was the head of the Black September organization.[21] And there are violent groups galore claiming Christian inspiration. To cite but a few examples in which the names convey the faith claim, in Spain, the fascist group Guerrilleros Del Cristo Rey ("Warriors of Christ the King") once enjoyed considerable support among Spain's army and police forces, while the United

States has seen the likes of the "Christian-Patriots Defense League" and "Covenant, the Sword, and the Arm of the Lord."

Some "terrorism experts" present a balanced view and acknowledge that, in the words of one, "none of the world's major religions" can claim immunity to the "volatile mixture of faith, fanaticism and violence."[22] But other experts, along with some reporters in the U.S. news media, focus on the violence of Muslims (and not of Christians) in a manner evocative of the spirit of medieval crusades. For example, in one of his more recent books, Walter Laqueur writes, "The current resurgence of religious terrorism is largely identified with trends in the Muslim and the Arab world, much to the chagrin of the defenders of Islam and Islamists in the West and East." Fearless to cause chagrin, Laqueur adds that "those emphasizing the essentially peaceful character of radical Islam find it difficult to account for the fact that in the contemporary world most of the violent conflicts, internal and external, happened and continue to happen in Muslim countries or in those with active Muslim minorities."[23] Actually, with Islam being the second largest and the fastest growing religion in the world, the greater difficulty might be in finding countries without "active Muslim minorities." Laqueur's argument is flawed in its failure to cite recent conflicts (often between professing Christians) in Central America and Northern Ireland and Rwanda and South Africa, and his argument is disingenuous if he seeks to blame the presence of Muslims for the genocidal policies that targeted Muslims in Bosnia and Kosovo. In a move that is highly suspect for someone writing from outside the faith, Laqueur proceeds towards a refutation of Islam based on an appeal to the Koran: "In Sura 2, verse 256, it says that there should be no religious compulsion, but adherence to this rule is a rare exception in Islam. On the whole, violence is sanctified in Islam if it is carried out against infidels or heretics 'in the path of Allah.'"[24]

Judging from such comments by experts, one might be led to ask why Islam generates so much terrorism. The question itself is revealing. Shoot-outs at Waco and Ruby Ridge and elsewhere and the bombing in Oklahoma City were not followed by inquiries into why Christians are such killers. Neither was there widespread wondering about why Judaism is so generative of assassins following Dr. Baruch Goldstein's murder of 29 Muslims at the Ibrahim Mosque in 1994 or following the killing of Yitzhak Rabin by Yigal Amir ("I acted alone and on orders from God").[25] There is an awareness in the West that "Judaism" and "Christianity" are not monolithic realities. On some level, there is an awareness that the Amish farmers of Lancaster County are set apart (both technologically and ethically) from the satellite feeds of the Christian Broadcasting Network, that a Friends meeting and a Pentecostal revival are likely to differ in ways other than just the auditory, that Roman Catholic convents and monasteries are not populated by those who are likely to drink strychnine or handle vipers in the quest for sanctification.[26] Many of us who are not Muslims may have a vague sense that there are Shi'ite and Sunni expressions of Islam. There may also be some level of popular awareness that the casual mingling of Islam with elements of older (and frankly animistic) religions in some sections of Indonesia would not be acceptable to many Muslims in Saudi Arabia, just as the dominant Saudi understanding of Islamic jurisprudence would meet with objections from some American Muslims. Yet, even this degree of differentiation is lacking in Laqueur's observations about the violence that "is sanctified in Islam."[27] The more revealing question may have to do not with why Islam generates so much terrorism, but with why such an antagonistic view of Islam has developed in the West.

The rise of "Islamic fundamentalism" has been viewed by the terrorism experts as an especially threatening phenomenon. In the strictest sense, this application of the term "fundamentalism" is a misnomer. The term "fundamentalist" was first coined in 1920 to describe proponents of *The Fundamentals,* a version of essential Christian beliefs published and distributed by California oil millionaires, Lyman and Milton Stewart.[28] But the term has found a broader application, due in part to the work of Martin Marty and R. Scott Appleby, founders of the "Fundamentalism Project" of the American Academy of Arts and Sciences. In this broader application, whether in Islam or Hinduism or Christianity, "fundamentalism" is "a strategy . . . by which beleaguered believers attempt to preserve their distinctive identity as a people or group" through "selective retrieval of doctrines, beliefs, and practices from a sacred past."[29] The strategy might entail an effort to make such doctrines, beliefs and practices normative for the larger, pluralistic society in which the "fundamentalists" find themselves. Like the 20th-century Christians who gave birth to the name, "fundamentalists" of other religions are portrayed as anti-modernist, viewing innovations in technology and economics and social organization as symptoms of decline rather than progress.[30]

It is this anti-modernism (and not terrorist attacks) that poses the more persistent challenge by Islamic "fundamentalists" to Western visions of the ascendancy of global capitalism. The opposition to what capitalists and Marxists have called "development" is based not in an anxiety to preserve primitivism but in a desire to avoid the cultural disruptions and growing gaps between the rich and the poor that often come in the wake of the application of development models of technological and economic change. Concern for the poor can be a liberationist facet of fundamentalist opposition to so-called "progress," and it was an important facet of the Iranian revolution.[31]

Yet clearly, not all of Islam is opposed to modernism, but the view that it is finds expression in a school of thought known as "Orientalism." Emerging in Britain as justification for colonial rule, Orientalism maintained that the people of the East are mired in a type of perennial childhood, gifted in forms of superstitious spirituality but lacking in the modernization that the West would be able to offer.[32] To no small degree, the United States has assumed the hegemonic role once held by Britain and France in areas of the world where Muslims constitute a majority, and to no small degree as well, the U.S. has inherited Orientalist attitudes. In Orientalist fashion, Americans are especially prone to viewing all struggles emanating from these areas of the world as "Islamic" and superstitiously religious, even when the struggles are clearly generated by political or economic or human rights concerns.[33] As in the war against the Soviet presence in Afghanistan, the United States has been willing to support those "Islamic freedom fighters" whose purposes happen to coincide with continued U.S. hegemony in the region because, after all, "'Islam' is . . . what holds the West's oil reserves. . . ."[34] But when it is the U.S. presence that is opposed, the specter of "Islamic terrorism" is raised. An unholy warrior, the "Islamic terrorist" is motivated by primitive, religious impulses to oppose the inevitability of enlightenment and progress. His religious motivation makes him especially lethal and especially immune to reasoned appeals for compromise and negotiation.[35] His tenacious adherence to a narrow view of orthodoxy renders both foreign infidels and co-religionists vulnerable to his attacks. He loves *jihad* because his faith demands it. This is the "Islamic terrorist," a creation not of Islam but of Western, Orientalist thinking.[36]

To assert the need to abandon this construct of "Islamic terrorism" is not to deny that the history of Islam (like the history of Christianity) has seen its share of violence. Indeed, following the death of the Prophet Mohammed, violence attended the struggle over the line of succession to leadership of the community. The Shi'ites or Shia (*Shi'at Ali,* or "followers of Ali") asserted that leadership belonged to the family of the Prophet and not to an elected caliphate as the Sunnis asserted. Thus for the Shia, the first Imam was Ali, cousin and son-in-law of the Prophet. When Ali was murdered, the line of succession went to his two sons, Hasan, who was apparently poisoned following his abdication, and Husayn, who was killed by Ummayed government troops at Karbala in Iraq in 680. The martyrdom of Husayn is remembered to this day with Shi'ite mourning during Muharram, the month of Husayn's death. Special significance also surrounds the person of the Twelfth Imam (or the Seventh Imam for the Ismaili Shia) who disappeared and who is currently hidden in "occultation" but who will reappear in the final days as the *Mahdi* (the Rightly Guided Imam).

Among the several schools of Islam, the belief is prevalent that history is teleological and that both believers and nonbelievers will stand before the judgment of God in the last days. As with Jewish and Christian apocalypticism, there have been movements within Islam that have proclaimed the arrival of the end time, and some "Mahdists" have even been violent in their efforts to force the end.[37] Some Islamic versions of the final days are filled with terror in which a prominent role is played by the figure of Dajjal, a type of anti-Mahdi who is not found in the Koran but in the *Hadith,* the body of traditions and commentaries written in the first centuries following the Prophet.[38] Just as church history has witnessed the activities of those who have not been loath to label their adversaries as "Antichrist," some Muslims have wielded "Dajjal" in a similar fashion. If the United States is "the Great Satan," the hegemonic efforts of earlier imperial powers met with similar designations. In racist and condescending fashion, a 1927 British government report fretted that the Muslim identification of European colonizers with Dajjal was "potentially the most important factor in arousing the ignorant and credulous African Mohammedan to fanaticism and unrest."[39]

With Islam, no less than with Judaism or Christianity, end-time speculation can be inducted into the service of a wide range of causes, some of them violent, some of them not. In times of war, apocalypticism might function as little more than a form of hyper-patriotism that seeks to incite the troops to "apocalyptic" levels of savagery. During the war between Iran and Iraq, for example, one member of the Iranian Parliament proclaimed that the victory of Iran was imperative as a prelude to the march on Jerusalem "in order to acclaim the reappearance of the Hidden Imam as the Mahdi, and to witness the reappearance of Jesus Christ and his final conversion to Islam."[40] But for other Muslims, end-time visions function as a summons to peace, such as in the thoroughly orthodox Islamic vision of ultimate reconciliation amongst Muslims and Jews and Christians.

There is a multilayered complexity in the relationships between Muslims and Christians (as, indeed, there is in the dialogue between any faith groups).[41] Relationships are shaped not only according to that which is in the heart of the Muslim believer, but also according to that which is in the eye of the Christian beholder, and vice versa. The eyes of Christians have been clouded by the political allegiances and Orientalist attitudes of the West. When an unarmed opponent of autocratic rule was filmed as he stood alone before the awesome size and power of a Chinese tank in Tiananmen Square, his act was justifiably lauded by Westerners as a singularly courageous expression of love of freedom. In contrast, during the Iranian revolution, when unarmed Muslim protesters assembled in the face of the automatic weapons and tanks of the Shah's troops, the Western news media gave voice to characterizations of "Muslim fanatics" who were filled with "lust for martyrdom."[42]

The Orientalist thinking that has facilitated the characterization of the "Muslim terrorist" has also obscured the recognition of the pervasive theme of compassion in the Islamic faith. In the Koran, every sura but one begins with the words, "In the Name of God, the Compassionate, the Merciful." Mohandas Gandhi, who suffered the Orientalism directed against Hindus, looked for inspiration to the martyred Imam Husayn, and the inspiration he found was not a "lust for martyrdom" but a commitment to nonviolent struggle: "From Husayn I learned how to be downtrodden and oppressed — how to rise up and be victorious."[43] Those who emphasize the holy war tradition in the history of Islam often ignore the manner in which that tradition has been transformed through a process of interpretation that may have begun with the Prophet Mohammed himself. According to the *Hadith,* Mohammed once proclaimed after he had returned from battle, "Now we turn from the lesser jihad to the greater jihad," namely, the struggle against the sin and faithlessness within the self.[44] Indeed, Islamic history offers several examples of Muslim pacifism. Abdul Ghaffir Khan is remembered as "the Gandhi of the frontier provinces" for his leadership in organizing nonviolent resistance to British rule among the Pathans in northern India; the nonviolent resistance was sustained in the face of military repression and executions.[45] Furthermore, terror is not inherent to Islamic depictions of the final days or of the judgment of God. One teaching tells the story of a man who, while walking through the wilderness, removed a thorny branch from across the path so that other travelers would not become ensnared in it, and for that act alone, he was given Paradise.[46]

In addition to its disparagement of Islam, Orientalism serves to feed the millennial pretensions of the West and of the United States in particular. Since the dismantling of the former Soviet Union, there are fears that a united "Islamic fundamentalism" may pose one of the few lingering threats to the U.S. role as the sole superpower. In U.S. history, a claim has repeatedly emerged that the United States has been divinely chosen to serve as "the city on the hill," the millennial beacon for humanity.[47] It is a potent claim that manages to combine both patriotic and religious fervor. It is also a claim that would take a dim view of any contrary assertions from those areas of the world that are currently welcoming a revival of Islam.[48]

When conflicts turn violent, few national or subnational groups have resisted the temptation to claim religious sanction for their cause. This has proven to be neither more nor less likely among Muslims. Indeed, during the Persian Gulf War, there was a strange resonance between the religious appeals of Iraqi President Saddam Hussein and those of U.S. President George Bush, Sr. President Hussein told his people that God was "the great divine reinforcement" by which Iraq would prove victorious. Iraq had been blessed by God as

139

the "cradle of divine messages and prophecy throughout the ages," and in response, the people of Iraq would "fight in his cause. . . . And who is more faithful to his covenant than God?"[49] President Bush reminded his people that the United States is "a nation founded under God and that from our very beginning we have relied upon His strength and guidance in war and in peace."[50] Following the military victory, Bush spoke before the National Religious Broadcasters and thanked them for "helping America, as Christ ordained, to be a light unto the world." Bush declared that the teachings of Jesus had been the moral force behind the victory. When he ordered bombing in the "no fly zone" of southern Iraq in the week before he left office, Bush stated that the bomber pilots had done the work of the Lord.[51]

If the remarks of President Bush sound zealous, they were not altogether creative. There are many historical precedents for his identification of the United States as an instrument in building the kingdom of God — and as an instrument in inflicting the terror of God.

*   *   *

Gold and conquest are tools of the eschaton, or at least such was the belief of Christopher Columbus whose millennial preoccupations have been underappreciated. Columbus revealed in a letter that God had made him "the messenger of the new heaven and the new earth" promised in the book of Revelation. He reckoned that the old earth had "about 155 years" left, which added urgency to the need for Spanish conquest and governance of Jerusalem and for gold to subsidize the discovery of a new route to Asia. The shortcut to Asia would certainly be a trade route, with all of the material benefits that that implied, but Columbus professed even greater concern for the missionary obligation to preach the true faith throughout the world before the end of time.[52] The shortcut for trade would also be a shortcut for salvation for the many in the East who were yet untouched by the missionary efforts of Columbus's Italy and Spain. It was why he named his "Asian" landfall "San Salvador." Vested with his millennial vision, Columbus would even be willing to engage in slaughter of native people in his quest to save them.

Thus, even before the Europeans knew that they were encountering a "new" world, their journeys were filled with millennial expectancy and a sense of divine purpose, sentiments that were magnified with European settlement. From the very first day, "the kingdom of God had indeed been the dominant idea in American Christianity. . . ."[53] It was John Winthrop, the first governor of the Massachusetts Bay Colony, who originally declared that the task of New England Puritans was to build the shining "city on a hill" that would serve as a model for all humanity, a veritable New Jerusalem. But first Winthrop had to address the fact that "the hill" on which the city was to be built did not belong to the settlers. Like many who propose to commit thievery on a large scale, Winthrop spun a web of self-serving legalisms to justify assuming "ownership" of land inhabited by indigenous people. His arguments were similar to those that would be put forward by advocates of the movement to enclose common-use land in England. Winthrop declared that the "new" world was legally a "vacuum." Since the native people had not "subdued" the land, their only claim to it would be based on a "natural right" that lacked the legal standing of a "civil right." The very fact that Winthrop found it necessary to advance such a strange argument betrays an interesting element of self-doubt about the rightness of the actions of those who proposed to set the millennial standard for humanity. Self-doubts were covered by biblical texts. Ownership of the land by the chosen people was guaranteed by none other than God: "Ask of me, and I will make the nations your heritage, and the ends of the earth your possession" (Psalm 2:8). And if force was needed to take possession of the land, then Winthrop understood Romans 13 as justifying that as well.[54]

But if "possession" of the earth was guaranteed to God's chosen people, how did the New England Puritans know that they were in fact the chosen ones? Again, biblical themes were used to allay the doubts that arose. There was a clear "analogy" (Jonathan Edwards used that specific word) between the settlers of New England and the Hebrew people who had been called out of Egypt to wander in the wilderness towards the promised land. New England certainly qualified as wilderness, "till of late, wholly the possession of Satan," wrote Edwards. Yet, if Satan could be banished, it might be in this new world, this New England, that God would find the proper setting "when he creates the *new heavens* and *new earth*."[55] The word "new" was not insignificant. To a considerable extent, the sense of having been elected for a unique covenant with God was dependent upon the sense of newness. Thomas Paine, though lacking the theology, was the faithful inheritor of the spirit of these New England Puritans when he later wrote, "we have it in our power to begin the world over again. A situation similar to the present has not happened since the days of Noah until now. The birthday of a new world is at hand."[56] Some thought Paine too modest in only going back to Noah. Why not Adam? The theme of "the American Adam," of primordial innocence redivivus, would find repeated expression in American literature, a prime example being the character of Natty Bumppo in James Fenimore Cooper's *The Deerslayer*.[57] Or why not the Second Adam — the Savior Nation? Whether as new Israel or first or second Adam, the sense of election was eventually enunciated in the great seal of the United States: NOVUS ORDO SECLORUM, the new order of the ages. For his work in leading the New Israel out of British captivity, George Washington became an icon. Shortly after his death, there were several overtly religious paintings of the "Apotheosis of George Washington." In the painting by John James Barralet, Washington is transfigured by light and, as he ascends towards the heavens, he is attended by angels — as if he were a holy man, a prophet, a god.[58]

Such a triumphant picture of the new order and its icons is only made possible by skipping lightly over the first two centuries of European settlement in North America. Truth be told, there were doubts aplenty about whether the colonists had been specially chosen by God, and the doubts were prevalent not only among indigenous people and African slaves but among the colonists themselves. Additional insecurity surrounded the question of whether the saints were in fact on the cusp of millennial dawn, or was it apocalyptic dusk? In either event, whether that which approached was a new beginning or a terrifying end, increased activity might be expected from the "Satan" whose prior possession of the wilderness was so powerfully apprehended by Edwards and others. Cotton Mather was not surprised when he learned from the 17-year-old servant, Mercy Short, that the devil who possessed her was "a short and black man . . . not a Negro but of a Tawney or an Indian colour. . . ."[59] Nor was it surprising that it was a young woman who was vulnerable to the wiles of Satan. If Satan was to be denied access to the community of saints, then the weaker gender required the guidance and governance of men.[60] The governance could be brutal. While the witch hunts in New England never reached the scale of the terror in medieval Europe, it was still a deadly business. One's sense of being chosen is enhanced if there is clarity about who is not chosen and if pains are taken to separate them from the community. Such an understanding was implicit in the title "Puritan," originating in the call "to purify."[61] Assurance of being chosen was melded with the need to expose and reject the evil in others. Millennial hopes seesawed with apocalyptic terror. Damian Thompson observes, "Fear of witches is above all evidence of End-time anxiety, since it was believed that the Last Days would see a terrible loosing of the powers of darkness. But if the New Englanders could keep their 'city on the hill' undefiled by evil, then this could be a sign of the coming of the Millennium."[62]

These quandaries pervade the history of religion in America: How do we know that we are chosen? Is it the Beginning or the End? Claims for the new Beginning were put forward by scores of utopian communities in U.S. history. For many of the participants, these communities represented no mere experiments; claims were made for this or that community that it was the very seedbed of Zion, the incarnation of God's kingdom, or, in the words of New Harmony's Robert Owen, the "Millennium in practice."[63] How did they know that this was their role? Some communities sought assurance in Calvinist doctrines of election, while others (notably, John Humphrey Noyes and the Oneida Community) espoused doctrines of Perfectionism well beyond anything envisioned by John Wesley.[64] Some of these communities withdrew into preserves of piety from which they issued harsh denunciations of the dominant culture. The Shakers, for example, offered exemplary witness to abolitionism, feminism, and pacifism, but their odd fate was described by Eugen Weber: "Conscientious isolation from society made Shakers better citizens of the society they renounced; market economy proved harder to resist than persecution. . . ."[65] As the old saying has it, they sought to do good and they ended up doing quite well. The Mormons constituted another group whose millennial vision was not dimmed by the fierce persecution they met. Joseph Smith and Brigham Young did not so much choose isolation from the dominant society as they were driven into it, but they were nonetheless able to draw upon the ready "analogy" of the chosen people fleeing Egypt into the desert. In the literal desert at the western edge of U.S. expansion, the Latter-Day Saints set for themselves that task which is "American to the core," the task of building Zion.[66] Though the U.S. had faltered, the Mormons affirmed through "an eschatology that was explicitly American" that the kingdom of God might yet begin in the U.S.[67] Religiously oriented, this perennial (if not tedious) sense of new beginnings has become a prerequisite for involvement in U.S. politics. The Reagan campaign of 1984 gave best expression to the theme, simple but pregnant: "It's morning in America."

Well, maybe not. A contrary proclamation has also been prominent in U.S. history, stated with equal simplicity but less pregnancy: "Prepare for the End." Garry Wills is certainly correct in observing that, "when the followers of Elizabeth Clare Prophet gathered in 1990 to go underground at the world's rending, they were as American as apple pie — or as violence."[68] With Campbellites and Millerites and Russellites and others, there has been an American cacophony of endism. The end was sometimes near because of social decadence, at other times because of apocalyptic mathematics.[69] Even some groups that were founded in millennial hope for a new beginning became convinced of the approach of apocalyptic terror; the People's Temple, for example, was born in the dream of a socialist order in which justice and racial harmony would prevail, but it died in a nightmare involving paranoid visions of the Beast and nuclear Armageddon.[70] But beliefs about the proximity of Armageddon did not preclude the hopes for new beginnings. Perhaps on the other side of destruction, construction might begin. Such formulas, however, are conducive to terrorism. As one author put it, "It is only one short step from the belief that destruction must precede construction to the belief that destruction in itself is valuable. . . ."[71]

It is perplexing, this question of whether we stand at the beginning or the end, and the perplexity was not even avoided by those who proclaimed that "It's morning in America." Of course, it is obligatory that the electorate should be greeted with feel-good mornings and millennial dawns. Even Walter Mondale, Reagan's 1984 opponent, declared in fine millennial (if not idolatrous) fashion that "America is forever."[72] But no matter the new beginning that was hyped by the Reagan campaign, the President himself repeatedly voiced his conviction that the end was near. "This could be the generation that sees Armageddon," he said, and according to Jerry Falwell, Reagan told him, "Jerry, I sometimes believe we're heading very fast for Armageddon right now."[73] If someone with a finger on the nuclear button believes that God wills cataclysmic destruction, would pushing the button constitute doing the will of God? President Reagan never revealed whether his thoughts turned to such matters, but in other respects, the policies of his Administration were clearly influenced by notions that the earth itself would not be needed much longer. In testifying before a committee of Congress in 1981, Secretary of the Interior James Watt said that the need for environmental protection and "resource" preservation must be put into perspective: "I don't know how many future generations we can count on until the Lord returns."[74] It's evening in America.

Serious consequences are attached to the sense of either beginning or ending, but profound repercussions are also implicit in the quandary over election. The Puritans, the founding "fathers," the prophets of utopia or of doom, or indeed, any of us — how do we know for what we are chosen or even if we are chosen? The simplest answer of Calvinism is that we don't know, that we can't know. Whether an individual or a community are among the elect is fully a matter of God's deciding and, as if to foreclose any further wondering, the doctrine of predestination suggests that the decision has always already been made. There should be no illusions of coaxing God into redeciding based on the righteousness of one's works or based on anything else for that matter. In a classic study of special pertinence to the manner in which the quandary over election was worked out sociologically and historically, Max Weber noted that Calvin "rejects in principle the assumption that one can learn from the conduct of others whether they are chosen or damned. It is an unjustifiable attempt to force God's secrets. The elect differ externally in this life in no way from the damned. . . ."[75] Clear enough, but the reason Weber had something to study was because Calvin had only the first word in Calvinism and not the last. Weber traces the incremental steps by which English Puritans came to see signs of election where Calvin saw none. Certainly Calvin would have had no objection to the understanding that all of the resources which sustain life are gifts from God, and that thanksgiving was the proper response from humanity. Nor could he have had much objection to the thoroughly biblical idea that the servants must act responsibly with the talents the master entrusts to them. Are these talents not entrusted to them as a blessing from God? (The slope gets slipperier.) Is it possible that an increase in the talents is a sign that the servant has been faithful to his or her calling? While avoiding any Arminian notion that the servant's work is productive of salvation, is it not possible to see the servant's prosperity as a sign of *God's* blessing on this faithful one? It is doubtful that Calvin would have slid down that slope, but many Puritans did.[76] Through prosperity, the election that had been invisible became "the city on the hill" for all to see.

Jonathan Edwards was not one who believed that the End was imminent, although he was not beyond suggesting otherwise if he judged that the unrepentant might be moved by a dose of fear. But Edwards's apocalyptic mathematics were quite specific in projecting that Antichrist and papacy would end in 1866 and that Satan would finally be defeated in the year 2000.[77] And so there was time, grace-filled time in which the city could be built and prepared to fulfill its millennial role, but also dangerous time in which the elect would be exposed to temptations that might lead them away from their calling — dangerous time in which the city might fall into the hands of those who were not chosen. In fact, even before the foundations of the city had been properly laid, before the new establishment was firmly in charge, and long before the U.S. War of Independence, the new order was already being denounced with apocalyptic zeal. Already, there was a need for a new New Israel.

Part of the problem with "the city on the hill" was that it was a city. As political, economic, and ecclesiastical power became concentrated in cities such as Boston, Philadelphia, and Charleston, Euro-American settlers on the frontier to the west became convinced that the urban civilization of the new world resembled that of the old. Millennial possibilities could only be discovered and nurtured away from the centers of power. In the wilderness, the chosen people battled demons; in the cities, power brokers reached accommodation with them. Historian Catherine McNicol Stock observes that the term "frontier" has often been used for the dubious purpose of narrating the "advance" of white civilization. Nonetheless, Stock finds that "frontier" can still be employed fairly to describe that space in which cultures met and often clashed. From the 17th through the 19th centuries in North America, the frontier was that space in which Euro-Americans met Native Americans, Hispanics, and Asians.[78] Woven into the very fabric of U.S. origins, terrorism emerged in two forms: (a) in the violent confrontations between cultures on the frontier, and (b) in violent confrontations between the growing consciousness of rural interests and the power elites of the cities. This is not to suggest in either case that all such encounters were violent, but when they were, these confrontations met even the classical definitions of terrorism, with non-state groups seeking to further their causes by instilling fear through random violence.

The treatment of indigenous people as "devils" may have influenced the Delaware prophet, Neolin, when he had a vision that the real devils were white people. The Ohio River nations responded to Neolin's call for unity, and under the leadership of Ottawa chief Pontiac in 1763, forts and settlements from Pennsylvania to Wisconsin came under attack. Pennsylvania Quakers persisted in a policy of seeking nonviolent engagement with Native people, and that drew the ire of settlers near Paxton, Pennsylvania. Organized by a Presbyterian minister, a group that became known as the "Paxton Boys" believed that all Natives constituted a threat and they proceeded to attack a group of Susquehannocks who were living peacefully as Christian converts in Conestoga, Pennsylvania. Before the Susquehannocks could be rescued, the Paxton Boys hatcheted and scalped six people, including two women and a boy. For safety, the survivors were moved to Lancaster, but there they were murdered in another attack two days after Christmas in 1763. Emboldened by this "success" and irate at the colonial government's failure to understand the predicament of settlers on the frontier, a large group of armed settlers assembled in February 1764 and prepared to march on Philadelphia. Civil war was averted when none other than Benjamin Franklin agreed to meet the group in Germantown to hear their concerns. Placated by vague promises from Franklin, the group dispersed as planting season approached.[79]

In the late 18th century, both before and after the War of Independence, western Massachusetts and the eastern regions of upstate New York were swept by land riots and terrorist activism. The owners of massive estates employed private armies to conduct midnight raids on the homes and fields of squatters and tenant farmers whose payments were in arrears. In response, rural rebels targeted landowners, bankers, and the governing authorities. In Massachusetts, the most sustained rural insurgency was led by Revolutionary War veteran Daniel Shays in 1786. Some of the same leaders who had organized rebel units and encouraged mob actions before and during the War now found themselves in the position of suppressing rebellions and mobs. Massachusetts Governor James Bowdoin called on local militias to protect courthouses and banks from attacks by forces loyal to Shays, but a number of militia units refused. Bowdoin then relied on the donations of fearful, wealthy contributors to fund a personal army. The Governor's army had no more legal standing than did Shays's rebels, but Bowdoin subdued the rebellion by wielding his private army, restricting the right to assembly, and suspending the writ of habeas corpus. When the U.S. Constitutional Convention met in 1787, provisions for a standing army were incorporated into the Constitution as much due to concerns over domestic turmoil as due to concerns over foreign invasions.[80]

Rather than taking up the debate over who had been chosen by God to fulfill a millennial role, many rural rebels of the 18th century focused on more prosaic issues like survival. But the New Jerusalem was not forgotten. With the ratification of the U.S. Constitution, radical preachers like Herman Husband of Pennsylvania denounced the centralized government of the new nation as "a beast's head." While Husband had previously believed that all American states would share equally in the incarnation of God's kingdom, he came to believe that the eastern regions were God-forsaken. The chosen people now resided in the mountains of western Pennsylvania which were, said Husband, the "everlasting hills" promised to the descendants of Abraham (Genesis 49:26).[81]

Throughout U.S. history, the rural struggle for survival has taken a rich variety of populist forms that have defied the mundane political characterizations of "left-wing" and "right-wing."[82] Many of these struggles have been profoundly anti-authoritarian, opposing the power of both centralized government and big business. In rural environments that have been stereotyped as "masculinist," support for women's rights flourished, with the Grange being an early and active proponent of women's suffrage. In rural environments that have been stereotyped as conservative and unsophisticated, there have been creative and sustained efforts at seeking justice through such techniques as unionization of mineworkers and noncooperation by farmers. In the 1930s, for example, the Farmers' Holiday Association sought to combat rural poverty and bank foreclosures by encouraging farmers to withhold products from the market so that prices might rise to meet the cost of production. As one leader of the movement put it, "We'll eat our wheat and ham and eggs and let them eat their gold."[83] In actions that have been emulated since, Holiday Association members responded to bank foreclosures by blocking access to auctions, acquiring foreclosed properties at extremely low prices, and giving the properties back to the prior owners.

Not all rural activists were nonviolent, however, and neither were the political leaders and wealthy business owners who opposed them. When a strike was organized in 1913 at the Ludlow, Colorado coal mine owned by John D. Rockefeller, terrorist tactics were employed by both sides, but Rockefeller had more resources to inflict greater terror. When the Colorado governor called up the National Guard, Rockefeller paid for their wages. On the morning of April 20, 1914, the Guard used machine guns to attack a strikers' tent colony sheltering over a thousand children, men, and women, and then they set fire to the tents. In that attack alone, thirteen people were killed by gunfire and eleven children and two women were burned to death.[84]

The powerful were well served, however, whenever country folks became convinced that the threats to rural survival were coming not from the political and financial interests of the establishment but from "aliens" who were competing for scarce jobs and resources. Racist vigilantism has been one of the primary forms of American terrorism. The Texas Rangers were initially established by the Republic of Texas in the 1840s to "defend" white settlers against Native Americans and Hispanics, but when Texas became a state, the Rangers continued on as a voluntary and self-supporting army; American folklore has depicted the Texas Rangers as a heroic band defending freedom rather than a racist group spreading terror. Farther to the west and to the north, Asian immigrants became targets for vigilante violence, with the Union Pacific coal fields of Wyoming becoming a Chinese killing zone during the 1880s. Lynching was the major terrorism directed against African Americans in the South and elsewhere. Between 1889 and 1893, almost seven hundred people died at the hands of lynch mobs. In 1892 alone, twice as many people were lynched as were legally executed in the United States, with the "legal" executions also disproportionately targeting African Americans.[85]

In more recent versions of racist terrorism in the U.S., the theme of the "chosen people" has reemerged in a distinctive form known as "Identity Christianity." Identity Christian doctrines have been endorsed by a number of groups whose members have been involved in terrorist actions, including the Aryan Nations, the Order, the Christian-Patriots Defense League, and Covenant, the Sword, and the Arm of the Lord. While Identity Christianity has kinship with the idea of America as New Israel, its roots can be traced back further still to theories about "Anglo-Israelism," which circulated in 16th-century England and gained prominence in several 19th-century writings. The theories purport to address the lack of definitive historical record regarding the fate of the "lost tribes" of the kingdom of northern Israel following Assyrian exile. In his 1841 book, *Our Israelitish Origins,* John Wilson claimed that the lost tribes had settled in Europe after having migrated across the Caucasus Mountains (hence the name "Caucasian").[86] Wilson argued that northern Europeans were the descendants of these lost tribes. Later, Edward Hines (1825-1891) gained popularity in England by arguing that Wilson had been a bit too expansive in his identification of the descendants of the tribes, and that in fact, it was only the British who were the lost Israelites.[87] When Anglo-Israelism was conjoined with 20th-century antisemitic conspiracy theories, it assumed a form more pernicious than that envisioned by the simple chauvinism of Edward Hines.

The premier document for anti-Jewish conspiracy theorists is *The Protocols of the Learned Elders of Zion,* first published in Russia in the early 20th century. The work purports to be a verbatim transcript of 24 secret meetings of Jewish leaders plotting to establish a worldwide Jewish empire. Already in 1921, *London Times* journalist Philip Graves showed the work to be fraudulent. Graves discovered that large sections of the *Protocols* had been plagiarized from an

1864 book by French attorney Maurice Joly, *Dialogues in Hell Between Machiavelli and Montesquieu.* Joly's work was not anti-Jewish; it was a satire aimed at Napoleon III who, being unamused, sent Joly to prison.[88] Nonetheless, in *Mein Kampf* (1924), Hitler cited the *Protocols* as a major influence on his thinking. The *Protocols* has been reprinted and circulated by Henry Ford, Father Charles Coughlin, and contemporary Identity Christians. Convinced of a Jewish conspiracy for world domination, antisemites found in Anglo-Israelism a convenient vehicle for demonstrating that contemporary Jews are not the descendants of the chosen people. For some Identity Christians, not even all Anglo-Saxons are included among the elect. Richard Butler, a founder of the Church of Jesus Christ Christian (better known by its other name, the Aryan Nations), claims to have discovered the identity of the elect by examining the word "America" linguistically. "Ameri," says Butler, means "heavenly" and "rica" means "reich." Thus, Amerigo Vespucci notwithstanding, "America" means "God's heavenly reich on earth."[89]

This reich of God will not be established without violence, say many of the leaders of Identity Christianity. In fact, through reliance on a "two seed" theory of creation, Identity preachers assert that race war and ethnic conflict are woven into the very fabric of creation. In the Identity version, Adam and Eve were the first white people, with all non-Aryans being descendants of the pre-Adamic races, which constitute a different species than white people.[90] Abel was the legitimate offspring of Adam and Eve, but in the Fall, Eve had sex with the serpent (Satan) and gave birth to the Jew, Cain. Race war originated in the killing of Abel by Cain, after which Cain went on to have non-Aryan offspring with the pre-Adamic races, known as "mud people" or "beasts of the fields." It was no surprise when the Jews crucified the Aryan Jesus, since the murderous character of Jews has been evident since the dawn of time. The race war of the beginning is reflected in Identity visions of the end. Armageddon will be a race war and it is fast approaching. In fact, as the Aryan Nations Creed asserts, the battle has already been joined: "*WE BELIEVE* there is a battle being fought this day between the children of darkness (today known as Jews) and the children of light (God), the Aryan race, the true Israel of the Bible. . . . The usurper will be thrown out by the terrible might of Yahweh's people. . . ."[91]

Among Identity Christians and their allies in the militia movement, there are plentiful preparations for the apocalyptic battle against ZOG (the Zionist Occupational Government). Survivalist literature and weapons manuals are much in evidence at Identity gatherings such as the 1991 "Scriptures for America Bible Camp." Some of the booklets are just repackaged versions of U.S. military training manuals. Indeed, former U.S. military personnel are prominent in the leadership positions among both Identity Christians and militia groups.[92]

At the camp in Mountain Home, Arkansas, that housed about one hundred members of Covenant, the Sword and the Arm of the Lord, food, weapons, and even cyanide were stockpiled with the self-described purpose being "to build an Ark for God's people during the coming tribulations on the earth."[93] But this post-tribulationist tendency to withdraw into survivalist communities is more than balanced by the influence of "dominion theology" among Identity believers. The more mainstream versions of dominion theology are associated with the Christian Reconstructionist followers of Rousas John Rushdoony. The key texts for dominionists are Genesis 1:26-28 and Genesis 2:19, texts in which humanity is given the right to "name" and to "have dominion over" other creatures, or in the parlance of dominion theology, "name it and claim it for the Lord."[94] Those who might be tempted into survivalist retreat are admonished with texts such as Jude 3-4: "contend for the faith" because (rendered more ominous with an Identity reading) "certain intruders have stolen in among you. . . ." And if the contending is to be violent, that too is given a gloss of theological respectability by means of biblical eisegesis. Though rebuked by Jesus, Peter's action in John 18:10 is commended by Harold Stockburger, founder of the American Patriot Federation of Tennessee: "It says he drew his sword. This group of men who were traveling across the countryside were armed to the teeth. . . . Peter's sword was probably the equivalent of a .357 magnum today."[95] According to one recruit, weapons figured prominently in his initiation into a militia group in a ceremony at a rural Missouri church building. Armed men lined the aisles as the new recruits were told that they were now "God's soldiers" in a "holy war." Then a militia organizer proclaimed from the pulpit, "Soon we will be asked to kill, but we will kill with love in our hearts because God is with us."[96]

It must be emphasized that, while they are certainly not pacifists, most militia members and most Identity Christians do not endorse or engage in criminal activity. Even when there is reliance on a rhetoric of hyper-violence, it would be incorrect to assume that Identity Christians or militia groups account for a large share of the violence in America.[97] While it does not render the violence less outrageous or tragic, rarely have killings or bombings been linked conclusively to these groups. Of course, what constitutes the "link"? There is no evidence, for example, that Timothy McVeigh received any material support or cooperation from militia groups in his bombing of the Murrah Building. But what of the moral culpability for the inspiration he found in the violent rhetoric of the militia groups he visited? And, to expand the circle still further, what of the moral culpability for the brutalizing effect of McVeigh's experience in the Persian Gulf War, a war supported by 90 percent of U.S. citizens? McVeigh was assigned as a Bradley gunner, and his Army buddies report that he was "just thrilled" when he blew up his first Iraqi vehicle. McVeigh's friend Kerry Kling reports, "He said when they were invading Iraq he saw an Iraqi soldier coming out of a bunker and that when the first round hit his head, it exploded. He was proud of that one shot. It was over eleven hundred meters, and shooting a guy in the head from that distance is impressive."[98] McVeigh's mother reported that he was "totally changed" by his experience in the war, and that when he came home, "It was like he traded one Army for another."[99] Or, it might be added, it was like he failed to respect the carefully nurtured differentiation between "heroic" and "terrorist" violence.

How can citizens respond to the militia movement and how can people of faith respond to Identity Christians? The response of labeling these people as members of "a lunatic fringe" or "right-wing hate groups" is not a form of helpful engagement but a form of hatred itself. Certainly the response must entail discussion of how all of us are called to deal responsibly with basic facts and with historical documents and with biblical text. Clearly and demonstrably, the Jews constitute a religious group and (to some extent) an ethnic group, but not a racial group. Clearly and demonstrably, *The Protocols of Zion* is a fraudulent work. Clearly and demonstrably, there is nothing intrinsic to the text of Genesis that lends credence to a "two seed" theory of creation, but it is revealing that Identity believers have found it necessary to address the biblical accounts of creation. As much as any other biblical texts, the creation accounts bear witness to our common origin and to the primordial reality that we are all sisters and brothers, all Cain and all Abel, all shaped from the same dust (Genesis 2:7). In short, we are all "mud people." But while responsibility to the biblical text is important, there can be no illusions that swapping biblical texts will sway most Identity believers or militia members, for in fact, these movements are less motivated by biblical inspiration than by raw pain and by no small number of *legitimate* contemporary grievances. The best model for response is the biblical reconciliation preached and practiced by Will Campbell and others in their relationships with both civil rights workers and members of the Ku Klux Klan. While Campbell repeatedly risked life and limb in his advocacy of justice for African Americans, he nonetheless maintained friendships with members of the Klan, even visiting an imprisoned Grand Dragon. Campbell pointed to the hypocrisy of white Christians who denounce the racism of "rednecks" and "hillbillies" while those same respectable Christians prosper in a society built by slavery, a society in which the gap between white and black income is growing, in which rates of black imprisonment are obscene. Before engaging in vitriolic and easy denunciations of the Klan, Campbell advised, undertake the more costly examination of the racism closer to home.[100]

And before engaging in easy denunciations of "right-wing hate groups," there should first be a recognition and advocacy on behalf of the legitimate grievances of militias and Identity Christian groups. In recent years, a primary focus of militia protest has been the federal government assaults on the home of Randy Weaver in Ruby Ridge, Idaho and on the community of Branch Davidians in Waco, Texas. At the very least, the government's actions in both of these cases must be characterized as inept, showing little regard for the lives of people on either side of the standoffs. Moreover, in both of these cases, it is more than a right-wing love of conspiracy theories which suggests that federal officials were involved in entrapment and cover-up. Randy Weaver's illegal action of sawing off the barrels of a shotgun was at the behest of an FBI informant posing as a gun dealer.[101] The subsequent standoff led to the killing of Weaver's son and wife and a U.S. Marshall. And in Waco, it not only fueled conspiracy theories, it *was* a conspiracy of silence and cover-up when federal agents concealed the nature of the incendiary gas canisters they fired into the home of the Davidians, no matter the ultimate findings about how the deadly fire started. David Koresh and other Branch Davidians were less influenced by Identity beliefs than by a tradition that has a long history in America, Adventism. An even longer tradition dating back through Münster to Masada and before clearly demonstrates that there is nothing like a siege to provoke impulsivity and self-destructiveness in apocalyptic groups. The federal government knew that, and yet government agents persisted in bizarre behaviors like blaring rock music and the sound of rabbits being slaughtered into the Davidian home. The federal government knew that the siege could have no good end. People of faith warned them of that, including a letter from James Dunn of the Baptist Joint Committee and Dean Kelley of the National Council of Churches to President Clinton begging him to lift the siege in Waco:

> Threats of vengeance and the mustering of troops and tanks are but proof to the "faithful" that the powers of the world are arrayed against them, evidence of their importance in the cosmic struggle — confirmation of their worst fears and validation of their fondest prophecies. Their level of commitment to their faith is higher than most people give to anything and is therefore very threatening to others. To invade a center of energy of that kind is like sticking a finger in a dynamo. *Whether it explodes or implodes, the result will be tragic for all.*[102]

The Davidian community at Mount Carmel was part of a host of millennial communities in American history who understood their lives to be precursors of the kingdom of God. While it was not typical of Adventism, David Koresh's preoccupation with guns was also a thoroughly American phenomenon. What was unique was that this was the first time that the weight of the federal government was brought to bear in the largely successful eradication of a millennial community.[103] Militia members are correct in observing that the outrage of most Americans has been quite muted regarding the actions of government agents at both Ruby Ridge and Waco. One need not endorse the bombing of federal buildings to renounce the government's treatment of the Weavers and the Davidians. One might pray that a lesson has been learned for the future that sieges should be lifted and negotiations pursued, even if the dialogue takes years. The preservation of even one life is worth far more than a millennium of negotiations. And who knows? In the process of talking, people may begin to care for each other's fate.

There are a number of other areas in which the causes of militia and Christian Identity groups need to be the causes of the larger faith community. The tradition of rural radicalism has offered hope for dispossessed people who have otherwise been forgotten. Despite the numerous biblical admonitions against driving widows from their homes (e.g., Mark 12:40; Luke 20:47), rural bank foreclosures have been doing precisely that. In Boundary County, Idaho, the county in which Randy Weaver lived, 80 percent of the land is government-owned. While ecological preservation deserves support, when the government holds land for the sake of leasing it to timbering and mining corporations, it is a situation akin to exploitative colonialism, with local residents and local ecology being the losers. When rural people feel a way of life slipping away, the response of faith is not repression but compassion and community. Where others have failed to respond, militia groups and Identity Christians have done so. At times, they have responded with language that is strongly biblical, calling on people to "come out of Babylon," to surrender earthly citizenship so as to become citizens of the kingdom of God. Colonel Bo Gritz asked, "Do you see the sign, scent, stain and mark of the beast on America today?"[104] Some of these "right-wing" groups have even employed techniques of *non*violence such as tax resistance, and, contrary to the stereotypes of militias, they have often opposed military exploits such as the invasion of Haiti.[105]

So, the contemporary expressions of rural radicalism found among some militia groups and Identity Christians cannot be dismissed in a cavalier fashion, any more than the people themselves can be dismissed as "lunatics" or "hate mongers" or "white trash." The larger faith community should respond supportively whenever these groups provide advocacy for vulnerable people or whenever they face violent siege by government authorities. Some survivalists and Identity Christians and militia members do in fact represent a form of "radicalism" in the sense of *radix*, returning to earlier roots and traditions that are endangered. And for that reason, the critique of these contemporary expressions of rural radicalism must focus on the ways in which *they are not radical enough.*

These radicals are not radical enough in total commitment to God. To be sure, the willingness to risk one's life is indicative of a level of commitment that would shame most "mainstream" Christians. But the nature of commitment to God is summarized in the admonition, "you shall have no other gods before me" (Exodus 20:3). Idolatry is sometimes plain for all to see. The Aryan Nations chapel at Hayden Lake, Idaho was once adorned by a portrait of Hitler with a caption that read, "When I Come Back, No More Mr. Nice Guy."[106] Such idolatrous messianism is palpable. Less evident (and therefore more dangerous) are the idols to which we sacrifice our lives, the idols of success and wealth and power. Rural radicalism has become infested with an idolatry of race and ethnicity. It is an idolatry that (like all idolatry) perverts and obscures and ultimately kills. At times, the idolatrous commitment is to "Aryanism" and at other times it is to the "Militia" itself. Samuel Sherwood, head of the United States Militia Association, was fond of asking his audience, "Do you know why Jesus was killed? There was no militia. Think of that for a moment."[107] Mr. Sherwood's perception is obscured. A militia was in fact present. It was the well-armed Aryan militia of Roman soldiers who killed the Jew, Jesus.

These radicals are not radical enough in their rejection of the control that the powerful wield over vulnerable people. Militia members often claim, "Gun control is for one thing only, people control." But in fact, far more than any legislation that has ever been devised, the gun itself is an instrument of people control. If we must seek to be sensitive to the paranoia that circulates among militia groups, we must also be sensitive to the paranoia of government agents who suspect militias of scheming to take control rather than resist control. A stance consistently opposed to the authoritarian control of people would call for government agents and private citizens alike to *dis*arm rather than featuring the "right" to bear arms as a premiere cause on the agenda. Violence is a downward spiral. It is certainly true that government sieges and "counterterrorist" assaults encourage increased levels of armament and violence by insurgent groups. But it is also true that insurgent violence provides a pretext for increased levels of governmental authoritarianism and militarization.[108]

These radicals are not radical enough in their millennial hopes or in their discernment of the nature of Babylon. Contemporaries need to be reminded of how quickly the rural radicals of an earlier era were able to perceive that the "New Israel" offered nothing new at all. There is nothing new in any of this: the murder of Weaver family members *or* the murder of federal agents, the slaughter of innocents in the Davidian community *or* the slaughter of innocents in federal buildings, bank foreclosures *or* bank robberies, contempt for rural white people *or* contempt for blacks and Jews. When there is nothing new, a lofty call to "come out of Babylon" is merely a call to change the mask of the Beast. There can be no faithful apocalyptic visions of the people of God gathered into survivalist arks. God has decreed that there will be no more arks, no more escapes. Whether we count it as a blessing or a curse, we are all in this together. God's covenant was extended to Noah and to "every living creature of all flesh" (Genesis 9:15, 16). One could not imagine a more inclusive formula than that. It is as if God was aware of the human enmity that would label other people as "beasts of the field." God's covenant is with "every living creature of all flesh."

These radicals are not radical enough in their understanding of "dominion" and "possession." Richard Butler of the Church of Jesus Christ Christian calls for a "cleansing" in the United States of the "aliens" who are flooding into "our ancestral lands, threatening dispossession. . . ."[109] In addition to the fact that people other than Butler may have a better claim to calling North America "ancestral land," this understanding of possession and dispossession ignores the manner in which the earth itself is a gift from God and ultimately belongs to God alone. We are all aliens, sojourners, stewards for only a season.

These radicals are not radical enough in their critique of tolerance. Mark Reynolds, Christian Identity adherent and militia member, hosts a radio program called "Love of Truth" on which he stated, "So-called tolerance is anti-Christian and lukewarm." Perhaps so, but then Reynolds proceeded to advocate laws "to execute sodomites" and warned that government officials could "end up hanging from telephone poles or trees."[110] In other words, Reynolds opted for something even worse than tolerance. That which is biblically rejected as lukewarm is not rejected for the sake of a passionate brutality but for the sake of a compassionate love. It is precisely this love which is the identifying characteristic of discipleship. It is not left-wing or right-wing politics. It is not membership in this or that racial group or militia group or anti-militia group. It is love. "I give you a new commandment, that you love one another. Just as I have loved you, you also should love one another. By this everyone will know that you are my disciples, if you have love for one another" (John 13:34-35).

There was a loving response from the community several years ago when the home of a Jewish family was attacked in Billings, Montana. Organized by the local police chief, Wayne Inman, and the publisher of the *Billings Gazette,* Wayne Schile, the good people of Billings responded to the attack by displaying paper menorahs in their windows.[111] For those Christians in Billings who displayed the menorah, this is a wonderful sign of faithfulness to Jesus. In times of persecution, for Christians to put on the badges of Jews or of Muslims or even of atheists, or to put on the badges of other Christians who happen to be gay or who have been labeled as heretical or unholy on any number of scores, these are signs of faithfulness to Jesus. Such small signs offer more salt and light than do millennial pretenses to building the "city on the hill."

An awareness of the violent forms in which millennialism has sometimes found expression in American history might well engender hesitation in characterizing the actions of other groups, nations, and faiths. Those who speak of "Islamic terrorism" need to check for the log in the American eye. Likewise, those who set about to build the New Jerusalem need the reminder offered by William Stringfellow:

> Blasphemy occurs in the existence and conduct of a nation whenever there is such profound and sustained confusion as to the nation's character, place, capability, and destiny that the vocation of the Word of God is preempted or usurped. Thus the very presumption of the righteousness of the American cause as a nation *is* blasphemy.[112]

Currently, the kingdom of God is not among us as a mighty nation but as a mustard seed.

*   *   *

Eschatology can be dangerous stuff, a point not lost on some of the greatest theologians of the West. The very notion of an End deprives all human power arrangements of ultimacy, and apocalypticism suggests that these arrangements should be scuttled sooner rather than later. Is there not something that needs to be tamed in the very wildness of apocalyptic language, in the symbols that can be harnessed for God-knows-what purposes, in the beasts and dragons that lend themselves too readily to association with the lords and masters of this or any time or place? Luther and Calvin thought so. While Luther believed that the last days were near and while he was promiscuous in his references to the papal "Antichrist," he was nonetheless aware of the threat that millenarians posed to the princes with whom he was allied. Luther called the book of Revelation "neither apostolic nor prophetic" and he relegated it to the status of an appendix in his German Bible.[113] Given Calvin's extensive commentaries on so much of the biblical text, the meagerness of his comments regarding Revelation said much.

The theological efforts to quell the dangers associated with apocalypticism can be traced to origins in the Constantinian accommodation between church and state. Such an accommodation was clearly impossible if communities of believers persisted in identifying the empire as "beast." Instead, one of the earliest proposals for an empire-friendly "imperialist eschatology" was put forward by Eusebius, "Constantine's court theologian."[114] While he was more circumspect than Eusebius, Jerome also proposed an eschatology in which empire's role was positive. Jerome differed with those who perceived the presence of empire in the identity of the "lawless one" described in 2 Thessalonians 2:4: "He opposes and exalts himself above every so-called god or object of worship, so that he takes his seat in the temple of God, declaring himself to be God." Instead, Jerome asserted, the empire was actually the power "restraining" the lawless one until the time of Jesus' coming (2 Thessalonians 2:6-8). Augustine followed with his own version of toned-down eschatology, identifying the kingdom of God with the church. The impact was to tame the visions of the redemption of all creation and to shift the focus from the cosmic struggle over the fate of the world to the privatized struggle over the fate of individual souls. The year after Augustine's death, the Council of Ephesus put the stamp of orthodoxy on his view that eschatology need pose no threat to empire.

Definitions of orthodoxy notwithstanding, popular speculation persisted that perhaps the powers of state and church would not pass through apocalypse unscathed. In medieval Europe, these speculations were influenced most by the work of the Cistercian abbot, Joachim of Fiore (1135-1202). Mystical and complex, the writings of Joachim defy simple summary, but a central feature of his thought was the trinitarian division of human history into overlapping eras or states *(status)*. The first era of God the Father, beginning with Adam and lasting until Christ, was typified by the state of order and marriage. The second era of Christ, the time of clerics and church, began with King Josiah and extended through Joachim's own time. The third era of the Holy Spirit would be the time of monastic order and, Joachim thought, it may have been dawning with Saint Benedict. So where is the revolutionary appeal in that? In fact, Joachim of Fiore was no revolutionary. Whatever his originality, he conformed carefully to orthodoxy in a time that was becoming more insistent on sniffing out the heterodox. His overlapping eras defied the zeal of those who would seek to attach specific dates to world-shaking transformations or apocalyptic interventions. He advocated no overthrow of institutions and he warned of no pending bloodshed beyond the warnings that were already plentiful among ecclesiastics about the divine terror that would be poured out "upon all the wickedness and injustice of men who are unwilling to do penance for their sins."[115] Joachim seemed so benign to the social order of his day that the kings and princes, the popes and bishops who sat atop that order sought his counsel.

What eventually proved so subversive about Joachim's thought was simply his orientation towards the future. Augustine's association of eschatology and ecclesiology necessarily focused on the past and on the present, but in his reflections on historical eras, Joachim introduced expectancy and possibilities for change and transformation.[116] Today's givens need not be those of tomorrow. In hands less orthodox and more revolutionary than Joachim's, such ideas were sparks in dry tinder.[117]

The Apostolic Brethren, organized around 1260, have been described as "the first group in European history to take the fatal step from preaching apocalyptic ideas to armed resistance to the forces of Church and state."[118] Led by Fra Dolcino, the Apostolic Brethren believed that the age of the Spirit would be ushered in by the extermination of church leaders and their political allies, but instead the Brethren themselves were eradicated in a battle at Monte Rebello in 1307. If the Apostolic Brethren were the first to combine Joachite ideas with armed insurrection, they were very soon joined by others. Between 1320 and 1380, the weavers of Ghent, Bruges, and Ypres rose repeatedly in insurrectionary movements that employed terrorist attacks against landowners, clerics, tax collectors, and Jews.[119] As always, the terror of repression more than matched the terror of insurrection.[120] Scores of cloth workers at Ypres were hanged as rebels, but some were sentenced by the inquisition to be burned as heretics. While economics doubtless played a role in the motivations of these Flemish insurrectionists, economics and apocalyptics were not so easily divorced. Even the "Church Fathers" had taught that the Edenic state of nature had been egalitarian; would it not be so again in the Millennium? So, thought some, let us hasten God's rule by forcibly instituting that egalitarianism for which we are destined in any event.[121] The conjoining of egalitarianism and apocalypticism also figured in the English Peasants' Revolt of 1381. A leader in the revolt was a priest named John Ball, probably a real person, but one around whom considerable legend has accumulated. The state of primordial equality was emphasized by Ball's preaching on the traditional saying:

> When Adam delved and Eve span,
> Who then was the gentleman?[122]

According to the monk and chronicler Thomas Walsingham, Ball advised that the old order could be overthrown quite simply by first "killing the great lords of the realm, then slaying the lawyers, justices and jurors."[123] Of course, peasants were not the only ones covering their violence with apocalyptic righteousness. During the same period and before and since, imperial propagandists were busily declaring that this or that French or German prince was actually the "Angelic Emperor" whose reign would be of millennial import.[124]

In the 15th and 16th centuries, waves of peasant revolts and millenarian terror swept through eastern and northern Europe. In Bohemia, extremists among the Taborites were recommending that the Millennium be ushered in with tactics reminiscent of those espoused by John Ball: "All lords, nobles and knights shall be cut down and exterminated in the forests like outlaws."[125] The center of political and religious power was Prague, which the Taborites identified as Babylon while declaring that their own fortress at Tabor would come to be recognized as the City of God.[126] Taborite apocalypticism played an influential role elsewhere in Europe, in part because Taborite armies advanced as far as Leipzig and Nuremberg, but also because the agitation in Bohemia attracted visits from apocalyptically minded preachers near and far. One of these was Niklas Storch, a weaver and teacher who imparted his end-time doctrines to one of history's most renowned proponents of millenarian terror, Thomas Müntzer.

Friedrich Engels was certainly correct when he observed how much Thomas Müntzer differed from "those dreamy chiliastic sects . . . hiding behind an appearance of humility and detachment. . . ."[127] What is far less certain is Engels's portrayal of Müntzer as a heroic proletarian struggling for equality. In fact, most of Müntzer's statements advocating egalitarianism can be traced to the final weeks of his life, when he was fully dependent on armed peasants for his own protection. Less than a year earlier when he preached a sermon before Duke John of Saxony in July 1524, the role that Müntzer seemed to relish most was not that of proletarian revolutionary but that of court prophet or palace priest. Drawing on the book of Daniel for his text, Müntzer preached that the last days had arrived for the old world which had fallen totally under the reign of Satan. A righteous ruler must arise to defeat the papacy and all of the other unrighteous religious and political leaders who constituted the forces of Antichrist. And of course, preached Müntzer to Duke John, the righteous ruler would need the guidance of a righteous prophet, much as Daniel had served to interpret visions at the court of Nebuchadnezzar. One element of Müntzer's thought that also figured prominently in the perspectives of other violent millenarians was the belief that somehow God *needed* people to take the lead and to act decisively in effectuating the divine plan. Müntzer was quite blatant in voicing the conviction that God's plan would fail if people declined the opportunity to exterminate the unrighteous. Before Duke John he preached:

> Drive Christ's enemies out from among the Elect, for you are the instruments for that purpose. Dearly beloved brethren, don't put up any shallow pretence that God's might will do it without your laying on with the sword, otherwise your sword might rust in its scabbard. . . . Christ is your master. So don't let them live any longer, the evil-doers who turn us away from God. For a godless man has no right to live if he hinders the godly. . . . The sword is necessary to exterminate them.[128]

159

When John of Saxony seemed no readier than other rulers to lead the forces of righteousness, Müntzer decided to do it himself. "Harvest-time is here, so God himself has hired me for his harvest. I have sharpened my scythe. . . ."[129] In May 1525, Müntzer was beheaded following a battle near Mühlhausen between peasants and an alliance of princes. Also slaughtered were thousands of peasants, some of whom actually may have believed Müntzer's claim that he would protect them by catching enemy cannon balls in the sleeves of his cloak.

In 1534-1535, millenarians gained control of the town of Münster in northwest Germany near Holland. The ascendancy of millenarianism in Münster received its initial support less from rural peasants than from guilds, but invitations were soon extended for all who shared in the hopes of building New Jerusalem to come to Münster, and ominously, newcomers were encouraged to bring along whatever knives or bows or guns they had at their disposal.[130] The chiliasts at Münster were known as "Melchiorites" because of the inspiration they received from the teachings of Melchior Hoffman. Like Thomas Müntzer, Hoffman was quite inclusive in identifying the forces of Antichrist with popes, princes, priests, Lutherans, and others, but unlike Müntzer, Hoffman was not an advocate of violence. Despite his violent rhetoric, Hoffman had been influenced by Anabaptism and he espoused no violent opposition to the forces of Antichrist. Not so with the Melchiorites at Münster. Under the rule of John Matthys and then of John of Leyden, a reign of terror was established in Münster, a situation greatly exacerbated when the local bishop with the support of secular rulers laid siege to the city. Inside the city, hundreds of people were executed on charges ranging from heresy to hoarding food. At first, some were executed for marital infidelity, but when John of Leyden decided to introduce polygamy, some were executed for monogamy. Outside the city, a different reign of terror was begun. Due to the perception that events at Münster were inspired by Anabaptism, neighboring principalities declared Anabaptism a capital offense. Irenic people who were already being persecuted by both Lutherans and Catholics faced still harsher measures as patrols scoured the countryside to apprehend Anabaptists for execution.[131] As the siege was tightened around Münster, the city's inhabitants were reduced to eating grass and whitewash from walls. When the city's fortifications were breached on the night of June 24, 1535, the bishop offered safe-conduct to the residents if they laid down their arms and returned to their homes. The bishop lied. Troops went door to door during several days of methodical slaughter.

On some fundamental ideas, the revolutionary millenarians did not much differ from the Lutherans and Catholics who enjoyed official sanction. All seemed to share a belief that the last days were approaching and, while not agreeing on his identity, all sensed the presence of the Antichrist. There was a shared conviction that the will of God was eminently discernible and that political and juridical means could be utilized to force whole societies into compliance with that will. And if all else failed to bend the people to God's will, neither Catholic princes nor chiliastic leaders of Münster nor Luther himself would stop short of terror. Martin Luther wrote,

> A rebel is not worth rational arguments, for he does not accept them. You have to answer people like that with a fist, until the sweat drips off their noses. The peasants would not listen; they would not let anyone tell them anything, so their ears must now be unbuttoned with musket balls till their heads jump off their shoulders. Such pupils need such a rod. He who will not hear God's word when it is spoken with kindness, must listen to the headsman, when he comes with his axe. If anyone says that I am being uncharitable and unmerciful about this, my reply is: This is not a question of mercy; we are talking of God's word. It is God's will that the king be honored and the rebels destroyed; and he is as merciful as we are.[132]

Of course, millenarians were also "talking of God's word" when they identified their own revolutionary efforts with the final revolution that would overthrow all kings who were allied with the tyrannical Beast. It was precisely the conviction that they were doing God's will that made them so immune to all of Luther's "rational arguments." Were their motivations not political and economic? Probably not to a greater or lesser extent than were the motivations of Lutheran or Catholic princes and ecclesiastical leaders. With varying degrees of sincerity, all understood their own motives as based in the will of God. Rosemary Radford Ruether describes the process by which the ephemeral struggles of revolutionaries become identified with God's ultimate goal for history:

> Their effort to rise up and throw off the shackles of oppression is given a transcendent motive power by . . . fusion of the particular revolution with the final revolution. The little band of insurrectionists, often setting out with a ragged force against great odds . . . become, in their own imaginations, the right arm of God's wrath. The flash of their pitchforks in the moonlight becomes the lightning of the Coming of the Lord. The trampling of their boots is the thunder of the messianic horseman. . . . Such a fusion of the momentary with the final revolution is both transcendently heroic and transcendently self-deluding. The result of such a projection was often the pathetic slaughter of men whose visions far exceeded their practical capacities, but at the same time, these visions . . . enabled a tiny band to astonish and terrorize those in power.[133]

161

It was evident in 17th-century England that millenarian terror could be wielded by either potentates or insurrectionists. On the eve of the 17th-century revolution, England was so awash with discourse on the "Beast" of Revelation that the noun "animal" emerged in the common vocabulary in order to clarify those instances in which the reference was to creatures of a non-satanic sort.[134] While there are but a few biblical references to Antichrist, all of them in the epistles of John, the popular Geneva translation of the Bible was not so restrictive in its use of the term. In marginal notes, the Geneva Bible identified "Antichrist" as a virtual synonym for the papacy.[135] With the identity of Antichrist so clearly established, even kings could engage in chiliastic speculation, as in fact James I did when he wrote an exposition of several verses of Revelation 20 while he was still James VI of Scotland.[136] When the Reverend Edmund Calamy preached before the House of Commons and prayed, "arise oh Lord and confound Antichrist,"[137] those he wished to see confounded were not monarchists but Irish rebels who, being both seditious and Catholic, bore a dual mark of perdition. But the apocalyptic language of the Bible is sufficiently unfriendly to earthly powers and sufficiently unrestricted in the depiction of how those powers might be manifested that the king could not hope to perpetually avoid his own candidacy for Antichrist. It was quite gingerly that Puritans and Parliament set out upon the path that would end in the identification of King Charles I as enemy of God and country. Even when armed hostilities first occurred, ministers like Herbert Palmer insisted that the struggle with the king was not an attack "against the king's person" but was actually an effort to save the king from the "malignants" who surrounded the throne.[138] Chiliastic enthusiasm does not long countenance such fine distinctions. By 1645, the preacher Thomas Coleman was telling the members of the House of Commons that they had been anointed to do battle against "the militia of hell and the trained bands of Satan."[139] What was initially presented as a movement to defend the king's person led to his execution in 1649, with Puritans and Parliament offering plentiful biblical precedents for the daring act of regicide.[140] But that was hardly the end of Antichrist or Beast. While Cromwell's tenure was quite moderate in comparison to other post-revolutionary reigns of terror, there was still a need for repressive vigilance because, as the Puritans were fond of reminding, *Satan never turns Christian.*[141] Quite predictably, following the king's execution, there were some who identified the new regime as Antichrist. A millenarian group known as the Fifth Monarchists advocated the overthrow of all earthly rulers so that the way might be cleared for the reign of "King Jesus." The Fifth Monarchists took their name from Daniel's interpretation of the dream of Nebuchadnezzar; there would be four temporal kingdoms that would be overthrown, but the one that followed would last forever (Daniel 2:36-45).

While Cromwell had initially been favored by some Fifth Monarchists, he too came to be identified as Antichrist. Thomas Venner led a group of Fifth Monarchists in brief but bloody insurrection in 1657. What with regicide and insurrection and the End perpetually looming and Antichrists galore, it was all too much. No wonder that, with the restoration of monarchy in 1660, speculation about the timing of apocalypse was made a criminal offense.[142]

*　　　*　　　*

Contemporary expressions of apocalypticism have not been immunized against taking on the terrorist guise of those who seek to force the End. We meet these guerrillas of Armageddon not in the pre-industrial reaches of the Amazon River basin or the Borneo highlands (although they may be there as well) but in the very heart of "post"-industrial, high-tech civilization. They provoke anxieties not with the glint of pitchforks in moonlight but with potential acquisition of world-rending nuclear, chemical, and biological weapons. You will be met by scorn if you tell them that these weapons belong only in the hands of responsible governing authorities. History has amply shown that one person's responsible authority is another's Antichrist. They will tell you that these weapons are least safe in the hands of those who are prone to fits of nationalistic pique. If these weapons are to be held by anyone, are they not safest in the possession of those who have received a revelation of the divine plan for human history? On the contrary, you might protest, most dangerous of all are those religious zealots who believe that their every action is sanctioned by God's plan. Well then, they ask you, is it religious or secular zealotry that motivates the "responsible" actions of governing authorities? The Americans over Hiroshima, the Khmer Rouge in Cambodia, the Hutus in Rwanda, the Stalinists, the Nazis, the Leopolds, the Idi Amins, governing authorities all, all hearing voices and receiving revelations from devils or angels or bureaucratic planners who have devised the latest scheme to win the war to end all wars. You judge that the weapons of mass destruction are safest in these hands? The guerrillas of Armageddon have a valid point, do they not? They unmask the hypocrisy of the superpower preachments on nonproliferation, the hypocrisy of the claim that only certain leaders are moral enough to stockpile weapons of utter immorality.

Of the recent groups that have formulated plans on how to begin the End, the greatest notoriety has gone to Aum Shinrikyō, one of the hundreds of new religions to have emerged in Japan since the end of World War II.[143] The apocalypticism at loose in the larger culture can fuel and shape the apocalypticism of smaller groups. The Japanese have had to contend with the doomsday scenarios to which we all are heir, including the specter of global warming and

163

ecological collapse, but Japanese apocalypticism has also been influenced by a history of devastating earthquakes and, not least, by an attack with doomsday weapons that left two of Japan's cities incinerated. Also leaving a deep impression on Aum's leader, Shōkō Asahara, was the Gulf War with all of its focus on nuclear, chemical, and biological weapons of mass destruction.[144] While many of Japan's new religions are marked by eclecticism, Asahara went well beyond most of them in drawing together a stew of beliefs and doctrines from a wide range of religious and secular sources. On the timing and circumstances of apocalypse, he referred to the texts of Daniel and Revelation, and most of all to the writings of Nostradamus. From Hinduism, Asahara claimed that his "guru" was Shiva, the deity whose dance destroys the world and calls it into being. From Tibetan Buddhism, he emphasized the "gods of terror." "Our time is the era when salvation is done by gods of terror." The gods of terror force us to recognize our accumulation of bad karma and evil, and in so doing, "their severe, wrathful judgment is actually a manifestation of love."[145] Asahara also made idiosyncratic use of the Tibetan Buddhist concept of *poa*, a spiritual exercise intended to assist a dying person in attaining a favorable rebirth. In Asahara's teachings, *"poa"* became a verb synonymous with "kill," but the killing was actually a service insofar as it prevented the victim from committing further sin and amassing more bad karma. Prior to the sarin nerve gas attack in Tokyo's subways in 1995, Asahara had already instructed followers to *"poa"* several of Aum's opponents. Aum built laboratories to work on the development of chemical and biological weapons and covertly sent representatives to states of the former Soviet Union in hopes of acquiring nuclear weapons. The plan was to *poa* the world in an act that Robert Jay Lifton dubbed "altruistic genocide."[146] A U.S. Senate committee held hearings on Aum Shinrikyō and declared that a threshold had been crossed, the threshold separating the potential from the actual "specter of terrorist groups using weapons of mass destruction."[147] The Senate committee did not note that the significance of the threshold had long since been diminished by the numerous governments (and therefore, presumably, non-terrorists) that had already crossed it. But the Aum phenomenon does point to a challenging (though not new) complication for those who believe that the way to combat terror is with terror. How does one mount a credible military deterrent against nations or groups who are convinced that the world is slated for destruction in any event? Violence from all sides is welcomed by those who believe that salvation lies on the other side of global extermination.

Of course, this is not the belief that most of us hold. For many believers, eschatology (if it matters at all) has become a far more sedate affair. One prevalent version of "post-millennialism" asserts no need for cataclysmic disruptions in order for humanity to embark upon the millennial period of harmony and righteousness; the second coming is scheduled for the far side of the millennium after the nations, unhindered by a chained Satan, have already evolved their way into the thousand-year reign of righteousness.[148] This potential for the progressive betterment of humanity was already implicit in Joachim's theorizing about relatively smooth transitions between the ages. Perhaps there is no need for the chiliasm of despair and suffering, terror and revolution. As a less gloomy alternative, "evolutionary progress is the religion of possession, power and confidence."[149] Does this progressive view of history manage to avoid the terror associated with some other versions of eschatology?

As with all eschatology, the evolutionary view of history is metahistorical, which is to say, it is a view that arises less from exploration of history itself than from *a priori* philosophical or faith commitments. After all, when two readers approach the same accounts of history, where one might read of the glorious advance of civilization, the other might read of mere changes in the configuration of the clubs with which people bludgeon one another. G. W. F. Hegel read of the advance of civilization. Through his virtual identification of the "Universal Spirit" with the historical process itself, Hegel sought to overcome what Mircea Eliade and others have called "the terror of history" — the threats of absolute freedom, of cosmic solitude, of meaninglessness. Hegel read teleological meaning into the historical process and even into current events to the extent that he considered "reading the morning papers a sort of realistic benediction of the morning."[150]

Carl Braaten uses Latin terms to illustrate the divergence of two major branches of eschatology. "There are two Latin words for future: *futurum* and *adventus*. *Futurum* . . . is the future actualization of potentialities within things. *Adventus* is the appearance of something new that is not yet within things, not even as potentiality."[151] *Futurum* most closely captures the spirit of evolutionary eschatology. Utopian potential is already present within things. Within what "things"? Is this potential present within people as well? Many early advocates of evolutionary eschatology laid the groundwork for Hegel's later assessment that it was the historical process itself that bore the progressive potentiality. The 17th-century naturalist, Robert Boyle, likened creation to a clock in which there is evidence of a divine clockmaker. Thomas Burnet, 17th-century theologian and scientist, took Boyle's image one step further to an analogy that has been favored by deists ever since. God made the clock, said Burnet, with the built-in potential for progressive changes even in the absence of divine intervention.[152] Though Burnet viewed it otherwise, this amounted to a virtual deification of the historical process. The complementary view that it was people who bore the evolutionary potential was fostered by the work of naturalist Jean

Baptiste Lamarck (1744-1829). The later work of Darwin risked detracting from the glory of humanity through too-facile associations of human evolution with that of other species, but with Lamarck, there was a clearer sense that the human species itself was embarked upon a course of steady improvement. It was as if the wound-up clock of historical progress had also been implanted into the very soul of humanity.[153]

There is no denying that some have been enlisted into worthy causes by this faith that humanity is evolving towards millennial righteousness. Influenced by faith in progress, the French priest Henri Grégoire (1750-1831) was an early proponent of equal rights for black people and Jews.[154] In the 19th century, the abolitionism and social activism of New England Unitarians were spurred by confidence that their involvements were allied with the progress to which humanity was fated. The prolific Boston minister James Freeman Clarke wrote, "The progress of the human race is fixed by laws immutable as the nature of God. The fidelity of man may hasten it; the wilfullness of man may retard it, but Divine Providence has decreed its certain issue."[155] The degree of Clarke's confidence in progress was evident in his straightforward prediction that all human vices would be eradicated by the year 2000. Faith in progress was also a central component of the Social Gospel movement of the early 20th century in the U.S. Walter Rauschenbusch wrote, "The swiftness of evolution in our own country proves the immense latent perfectability in human nature."[156] The evolution that Rauschenbusch cited as proof of perfectability may have been an indication instead that those imbued with faith in progress "looked for and found evidences of improvement as determinedly as sixteenth-century Protestants had sought examples of decline."[157] But the belief in progress did not entail inevitable support for Social Gospel visions of justice and equality. Some who subscribed to faith in progress believed that the evolutionary potential was inherent to "civilization," not to people, and certainly not to all people equally.[158] Progress required the spread of "civilization" and not merely the inevitability of historical process.

Adam Smith became even more specific about what it was that carried the germ of progress, namely, human desire. Smith came from a time and place (18th-century Scotland) that were flush with both ideas of progress and rising economic expectations. In a startling reversal of Joachim's vision of the new age as being an era of "Spirit" and of monastic poverty, Smith envisioned an era in which progress was assured by indefinite economic expansion based on the insatiable desire for material acquisition. Smith's work involved nothing short of "the moral rehabilitation of desire," as Christopher Lasch called it. Since Smith recognized the insatiable quality of greed, he also asserted the need for desires to be disciplined and, said Smith, discipline is best inculcated in those societies that teach the military virtues and maintain large standing armies. Lasch quite credibly contends that modern ideas of progress are less secularizations of Christian eschatology than restatements of Adam Smith's confidence in economic expansion disciplined by military virtues.[159]

If modern ideas of progress are owing to visions of an expanding economy, credit must also be given to the related phenomenon of faith in scientific and technological development. One of the most prominent of the theological proponents of evolution in the 20th century was Teilhard de Chardin, who asserted that religion and science are two faces of one knowledge. "Scientifically," Teilhard wrote, "we can envisage an almost indefinite improvement in the human organism and human society."[160] The indefinite improvement would lead humanity towards the "Omega Point" of eventual union with God. In Teilhard, one can sense the overweening presence of Darwinian biology and the physics of the big bang, but true to his era, there was little hint of chaos theory. For Teilhard (and for many since), little attention was paid to the manner in which the illusion of steady "scientific progress" is maintained only by ignoring the repeated crises and paradigm shifts in the history of science.[161] For Teilhard (and for many since), little attention was paid to the manner in which "technological progress" is actually a system of enslavement to the need for technological solutions to the problems created by technology itself.[162] One example of an acute problem created by technological developments in weaponry is the threat of nuclear annihilation. What to do? Metanoia? Disarm the weapons, turn around, and set out on a different path? Impossible, we are told, because "the genie is out of the bottle," which is another way of saying that humanity is controlled by technological developments that cannot be undone. And so the solutions that are offered in response to the nuclear threat are the technological fixes of sophisticated laser gizmos and missile defense shields. Teilhard de Chardin was no advocate of nuclear weapons, but he needed to somehow account for their annoying appearance on the evolutionary path towards the Omega Point. Hiroshima and Nagasaki, he said, were examples of the growing pains through which humanity needed to pass. Thomas Merton noted the irony in this. Just at the point that the potential for nuclear extermination emerged, ". . . just at the point where eschatology in the old sense seems more credible than ever, Christians are turning to the hope of a technological golden age!"[163]

Terror is not absent from the evolutionary views of eschatology; rather, it is reinterpreted as something other than terror. Terror as growing pain. Terror as the necessary (if regrettable) medium through which humanity will ingest the requisite wisdom to embark upon the next step of betterment. And where is God? One possibility is that God is complicit in the terror itself, that God is the author of these "growing pains" as the necessary instrumentalities by which humanity would be perfected. Another possibility is that God is at a faraway distance, not in the sense of divine transcendence but in the sense of remote aloofness. God is as remote as the primeval clockwinder, as remote as the Omega Point of our final destination. In the meantime (which is our time), we are left alone either to endure or endorse the growing pains.

Teilhard de Chardin was exemplary of a Catholic version of evolutionary eschatology, but there were also influential Protestant versions deriving from the 19th-century liberal theology of Albrecht Ritschl. According to Ritschl and his disciples, humanity has been assigned the task of perfecting the social and moral order. Jesus provided the example in this confident quest for perfected order, but beyond that, little could be known of transcendence. These were the teachers of whom Karl Barth wrote:

> One day in early August 1914 stands out in my personal memory as a black day. Ninety-three German intellectuals impressed public opinion by their proclamation in support of the war policy of Wilhelm II and his counselors. Among these intellectuals I discovered to my horror almost all of my theological teachers whom I had greatly venerated. In despair over what this indicated about the signs of the time I suddenly realized that I could not any longer follow either their ethics and dogmatics or their understanding of the Bible and of history.[164]

If one believes that humanity is engaged in steady progress toward perfection, all sorts of terror can be rationalized. Barth came to understand that redemption was not the logical outcome of the historical process; redemption is only possible as a radical disruption of that process, the disruption brought by Jesus as the living Word of God. Barth came to understand that christology was of far greater centrality than a mere "Jesus as example" motif. And he came to understand that, without the transcendent judgment of God, that which was triumphant was not human progress but human terror.

While Barth had some theological impact, it is still secularized faith in progress that remains the dominant version of eschatology today. Theology matters little for many of these visions of progress, but there are still occasional efforts to graft the eschatology of Teilhard de Chardin or of Wolfhart Pannenberg onto accolades for technological development. One recent example is the popular book by Frank Tipler, *The Physics of Immortality*. Tipler presents a number of perspectives that are reductionistic in the extreme. He begins with a view of a human being as "a purely physical object, a biochemical machine completely and exhaustively described by the known laws of physics."[165]

Progress is dependent on the "invasion" and "conquest" of other disciplines by physics (p. 8). Even morality can be reduced to questions of fact. "*All* disputed issues are disputes over matters of fact."[166] But out of such reductionism, Tipler proposes an expansionist vision of the descendants of humanity reaching out "to engulf the entire universe and gain control of it" (p. 19). The amazing amount of energy required for such a venture will be provided by literally disassembling the earth and much beyond. "In the very long run, first the entire solar system, then the entire Galaxy, then the entire Virgo Cluster of galaxies, and finally the entire universe of matter will be taken apart and converted into habitat for the expanding biosphere."[167] The "Omega Point" of all this expansion is the computers of the far distant future which, as part of the quest for total knowledge, will resurrect a conscious "emulation" of every person who has ever lived. Since erasing such subprograms would be a waste of energy, "Once resurrected, cheap altruism will probably keep them alive forever" (p. 246). It is this "cheap altruism" that passes for the love of God. Yet, it is the call of the future Omega Point that will "assure our civilization of ever growing total wealth, continually increasing knowledge, and quite literal eternal progress" (p. 217).

One is left with the sense that there is something more dystopian than utopian in such visions of technological paradise. In all evolutionary eschatology, the Millennium is not derived from radical disruption but from history and therefore necessarily from the present. What is dystopian about visions of technological paradise is the presumption that we can smooth off the rough edges of the present and call it Zion. We already know about expanding out to engulf the universe because, writ small, it is precisely such imperialism that characterizes our current age. We know about disassembling planets because already we can barely hear the screams of vanishing species above the crash of rainforests being felled. It is this which already fuels the "ever growing total wealth" of the few. In short, we already know of our capacity to create hell in the quest for heaven. If revelation and apocalypse constitute an "unveiling," then the vision of technological paradise is a type of anti-apocalypse, taking that which surrounds us now and covering it with the veil called "Millennium." Faith in progress is not an eschatological vision devoid of terror. It merely takes the terror of our present era and calls it human destiny.

*　　　*　　　*

Jonathan Edwards was anxious to find the proper way to destroy the world. He was an intellectual living in an age that was flush with the newness of Newtonian science. The laws that God had built into the very foundation of the world were being discovered and there was a conviction that not even God would violate these laws. The natural laws that had governed the world from the beginning would also bring the world to its fiery end. But how? Some believed that geothermal power would be the mechanism of the doomsday conflagration, and some Protestants believed it was more than coincidence that papal regions of Italy were areas of volcanic instability.[168] And then there were comets. Through much of human history both before and since Newton, comets have been feared as either harbingers or instruments of the end. Increase Mather had said that a comet is a "warning piece" fired by God "before his Murdering pieces go off."[169] William Whiston, a contemporary of Newton who was influenced by his work, wrote *A New Theory of the Earth* (1696), a book that attracted wide attention for its speculations on the mechanisms by which a comet would usher in doomsday. The flooding that would be precipitated by a comet passing too close to earth was precluded by the covenant with Noah, but if the comet first became superheated by a close encounter with the sun and then approached the earth — voilà, the fire to end all.

And then what? That is the question that troubled Jonathan Edwards. Destruction ensured nothing beyond destruction. Edwards read Whiston, but he was not satisfied that any of the speculations on the laws of nature could account for anything beyond conflagration. There was no redemption in it. If confident visions of human progress offered redemption without judgment, then the theories of cataclysm offered only a wrathful judgment with no redemption. In this sense, Jonathan Edwards was posing the questions that must be posed to all terrorists. After you have caused the explosion, then what? After you have spilled the blood upon the ground, then what? You are really quite powerless to determine anything that follows your explosions. There is no redemption in any of it. Destruction has no power to commence the kingdom of God. It is a point lost on terrorists of all stripes.

But Jonathan Edwards did not neglect the earth's destruction. He eventually adopted the position that the reign of the saints would precede the cataclysm, but when human depravity inevitably reasserted itself, the saints would ascend to heaven before the earth was consumed by flames. Contemptuous of the laws-of-nature crowd, Edwards cared little for how the fire would start.[170]

Nor did Jonathan Edwards renounce terror. Indeed, as much as any cleric in all of church history, he made an art form out of conjuring the terror of God to scare the devil out of believers and to scare the virtue into them. Best known is his 1741 sermon, "Sinners in the Hands of an Angry God." The means that Edwards utilized was a blatant effort to instill terror into his congregation, but the end he sought was nothing less than the conversion and eternal salvation of many. He preached, "The God that holds you over the pit of hell, much as one holds a spider, or some loathsome insect over the fire, abhors you, and is dreadfully provoked. . . ." The preaching betrays a certain conviction that people are more motivated by the avoidance of hell than by the yearning for heaven, that the power of terror is greater than the power of love. It was such convictions and such preaching that led Perry Miller, the premier intellectual historian of Puritanism, to label Edwards a "terrorist."[171]

If Jonathan Edwards's efforts to evoke images of the terror of God qualify him as a terrorist, he was a terrorist of philosophical bent. He was the inheritor of the Puritan tradition in which election and regeneration were a matter of God's deciding, but the human soil could be prepared for God's planting by appeal to both mind and will, intellect and passions. The Puritans sought to shape a path between the Anglican emphasis on ritual, intellect, and tradition and the "antinomianism" of Anne Hutchinson or the Quakers whose appeals to the heart were resistant to the guidance of clerics. But insofar as the Puritans were not prepared to abandon a role for the passions, fear was fair game, and it was most effectively instilled through the medium of the sermon.[172] In his sermons, Edwards mercilessly exploited that fear, but there is a markedly contrasting tenor to his philosophical writings. In *The Nature of True Virtue,* it is not terror but "benevolence to being in general" arising from a "benevolence" towards God which is the basis of all true virtue. Edwards even offers an incisive critique of the strikingly modern notion that "all love arises from self-love."[173] Yet, terror still lurks in the corners of Edwards's essay. If all else fails, then let the self-interest of avoiding punishment serve to instill a modicum of virtue. "It is proper for a judge when he condemns a criminal, to endeavour so to set his guilt before him as to convince his conscience of the justice of the sentence. This the Almighty will do effectually, and do to perfection. . . ." Wicked people "will be sent away as cursed into everlasting fire prepared for the devil and his angels."[174] Virtue born of benevolence was best, but virtue born of terror was better than wickedness. And if even fear failed to deter the wicked, then their terrifying fate in the everlasting fire might still serve a purpose, namely, to lighten the hearts of the saints. In his preaching, Edwards reveals his saints to be a self-righteous and vengeful lot: "The sight of hell's torments will exalt the happiness of the saints forever." The terror of God was a multifaceted blessing; the fear of it could serve to convert the wicked, the horror of it could serve to punish the unconverted, the sight of it could serve to increase the joy of salvation.

Edwards was not alone in suggesting that the terror of God was a joy for those who were properly situated. As early as the 4th century, Lactantius, the tutor of Constantine's son, wrote with satisfaction of the approaching time when "all that multitude of the godless shall be annihilated, and torrents of blood shall flow." If people of other faiths are spared, it will be only so that

Christ can "hand over all heathen peoples to servitude under the righteous who are alive. . . ."[175] As we have already seen, whenever kings or revolutionaries reckoned that they were instruments of the divine terror, blood flowed indeed. Along with Eugen Weber, one senses of these assorted millenarians that they "were less interested in the Millennium per se than in the extermination that would precede it. . . ."[176]

But what of the other use of divine terror, the (loosely understood) "pastoral" application of terror to coax people into proper action or proper belief? In *The Confessions,* Augustine cited the role that terror played in his own conversion, and his use of the theme has undoubtedly influenced many preachers since. Augustine wrote of the untimely death of a young friend at which "my heart was utterly darkened; and whatever I beheld was death."[177] The mediating and moderating presence of fear was all that prevented Augustine from falling totally away from the possibility for salvation.

> I was becoming more miserable, and Thou nearer. Thy right hand was continually ready to pluck me out of the mire, and to wash me thoroughly, and I knew it not; nor did anything call me back from a yet deeper gulf of carnal pleasures, but the fear of death, and of Thy judgement to come; which amid all my changes, never departed from my breast.[178]

Clearly, Augustine's view of the role that fear might play in conversion is at considerable remove from that of Jonathan Edwards. For Augustine, God is "continually ready to pluck me out of the mire," while for Edwards, God is continually ready to drop sinners into the fire. While Edwards harnesses fear in an assault on the insecurities of others, in *The Confessions* (though less elsewhere), Augustine writes of the role of fear in self-reflection, indeed, the role of fear in offering him freedom from the inevitability of the path on which he had previously embarked. As the French historian Jean Delumeau observes at the conclusion of his massive study of fear and guilt in Western culture, fear has two sides.[179] The assertions of some modern psychotherapists notwithstanding, neither fear nor guilt are alien intruders that need to be banished from human consciousness. Like the human awareness of mortality, fear or guilt can become blessings in disguise, spurs to creativity and love and *metanoia,* or alternately, they can become part of "the mire" itself, ensnaring people into preoccupation with self or with death. So when the theologians and preachers nurture fears, questions must be raised regarding the fruits of their preachments. Are we left with an image of God drawing "nearer" or an image of God who "abhors" us? Are we encouraged in the love of others or in *contemptus mundi?* Are we moved towards choosing life (Deuteronomy 30:19) or towards a preoccupation with death? Are we left with an assurance of the eschatological victory of God or are we left with the certainty that there is a hell and with a fair certainty of who will be there?

The theme of harnessing fear for salvific purposes antedates Augustine. Early hermitic and cenobitic movements emphasized the sanctifying effect of meditating on death. Among others, Basil, Macarius the Elder, and Pachomius all recommended continual reflection on one's own death as the necessary preparation for judgment and eternity. Evagrius (d. 400) suggested that reflection on death be combined with consideration of the contrasting fates that awaited the sinners and the righteous:

> Remember the day of your death. . . . Imagine the fearful and terrible judgement. Consider the fate kept for sinners, their shame before the face of God and the angels and archangels and all men, that is to say, the punishments, the eternal fire, worms that rest not, the darkness, gnashing of teeth, fear and supplications. Consider also the good things in store for the righteous: confidence in the face of God . . . the kingdom of heaven, and the gifts of that realm, joy and beatitude.[180]

The combination of fear of God, reflection on death, and *contemptus mundi* is explicit in the sayings of Anthony the Great: "Always have the fear of God before your eyes. Remember him who gives death and life. Hate the world and all that is in it. Hate all peace that comes from the flesh. Renounce this life, so that you may be alive to God."[181]

Throughout church history, there have been efforts to harness these themes of terror and death for catechetical and missionary purposes. In *Le Pédagogue chrétien*, the Jesuit Philippe d'Outreman wrote, "O! What dreadful terror. . . . If the righteous man will be saved by the skin of his teeth, what will become of a sinner?"[182] Yet, if the terror of God had a salutary effect on the obdurate, perhaps it was not altogether "dreadful." A Catholic missionary manual of the early modern period contains a hymn that is sung not so much to God or to other believers as to the terror itself, urging it on: "Blaze, fires, rage on you deadly storms/ To serve the wrath of God/ Take what remains of guilty human forms/ For none can hide from His fierce rod."[183] If the terror itself was sometimes praised, there was similar potential in the focus on death. No clear line divided the edifying awareness of mortality from morbid preoccupations. Before making major decisions, Pope Innocent IX stared at a painting of himself lying on a deathbed. Alexander VII kept a coffin under his bed and ate from plates embossed with images of skulls.[184]

For a time and to a degree, the Protestant Reformation reacted against the ecclesiastical peddling of terror. With Luther and with Calvin, words like "reassurance" and "comfort" and "consolation" reappeared in the theological vocabulary. But if too much terror could be the cause of despair, Luther and Calvin were also aware that too much reassurance could be the cause of sinning. In the *Institutes,* Calvin invokes both misery and comfort, both contempt for the world and thanksgiving for it. Calvin writes of the soul that "seeks its happiness on earth. To counter this evil the Lord instructs his followers in the vanity of the present life by continual proof of its miseries. Therefore, that they may not promise themselves a deep and secure peace in it, he permits them often to be troubled and plagued either with wars or tumults, or robberies, or other injuries."[185] By granting such permission, is God then in league with the miseries and terrors that plague us? Walking a fine line, Calvin ushers us past the question with a call for gratitude and a distinction between contempt and hatred. "But let believers accustom themselves to a contempt of the present life that engenders no hatred of it or ingratitude against God. Indeed, this life, however crammed with infinite miseries it may be, is still rightly to be counted among those blessings of God which are not to be spurned."[186] Perhaps Calvin was alluding to the biblical themes of resisting conformity to the world (Romans 12:2) and of being in the world but not of it (John 17:14-18), but the distinction between "contempt" and "hatred" sounds strained to the modern ear.

The subtlety of Calvin's distinction was also lost on some of his Puritan descendants, with *contemptus mundi* giving way to terroristic discourse that verged on the misanthropic. If humanity was too depraved to respond to the love of God, then why not try to elicit response with the terror of God? Indeed, preachers could seek to shake their congregations from lethargy by means of a dual dose of terror, what with the end-time scheming of Satan to the one side and the wrath of God to the other. The English Puritan Christopher Love explained that "sermons of terrour have done more good upon unconverted souls, then [*sic*] sermons of comfort ever have done. Sermons of hell may keep many out of hell. . . ."[187]

But not all were exposed equally to such homiletical terrorism. It would take a bold preacher indeed to threaten lords and princes with damnation. Delumeau notes, "There undoubtedly existed a temptation to preach a sugar-coated religion to the great and wealthy. . . ."[188] While the powerful were often spared the preaching of hellfire, they were nonetheless concerned that hell not be abolished or diminished. The 1552 Articles of the Church of England specifically condemned belief in universal salvation, and in 1585, Queen Elizabeth herself issued a statement denouncing those who lacked belief in hell. The defense of hell by the ruling class may have had less to do with a concern for orthodoxy than with a conviction that hell was "necessary . . . to keep the lower orders in due subordination."[189] In other words, a strong and healthy hell kept the rabble in line.

Among both Lutherans and Calvinists, some thought it expedient to instill an awareness of the terror of God at an early age. Lest the spirituality of young-sters be warped by a sense that death is far off, an early awareness of terror might assist in shaping habits of piety. In the 1530s in Saxony, a Lutheran su-perintendent required the children in his care to memorize the following dia-logue and recite it during worship:

> The child: Tell me what Scripture says will happen to ingrates who scorn the word of God.
>
> Another child answers: God will scorn and mock such a man, even if he will suffer intolerable anguish (Prov. 3). He will not hear him, but terri-bly punish him with numerous torments and disasters (Lev. 26), fevers, consumption, boils, plagues, swellings, war, fire, destruction, hail storms, epidemics, and utter ruin. In short, God will pour on him so many terrors, miseries, sufferings, failures, and misfortunes that he will sink to the bot-tom of despair.[190]

I have been unable to learn the age of the children who recited this litany of horrors. It would have taken a fairly erudite bunch of children even to under-stand what they were reciting. What was the impact on the children? Did such a ponderous proclamation induce nightmares or self-righteousness? Or was it fun? A work that similarly peddled terror in 17th-century New England was Michael Wigglesworth's *The Day of Doom*. It was a book of verse that was read by both adults and children in the majority of Christian households in New En-gland. Perry Miller noted that several modern commentators likened the book to child abuse and asserted that it "drove Puritan children crazy, but it did nothing of the sort: they loved it."[191] Perhaps so. It may be that the assorted ter-rors functioned as a type of 17th-century cartoon. But the children may have given a less cavalier reception to the harping of clerics on the theme of death at an early age. In 1653, Thomas Shepard preached a warning to the children of Cambridge Church that their conversion was required long before they reached the age of twenty: "I tell you young persons that have passed your 20 years and slept out your opportunities tis a wonder of wonders if ever God show you mercy."[192] When two undergraduates broke through the ice while skating on Fresh Pond and drowned, Increase Mather used the incident to warn other stu-dents at Harvard College that it was the hand of God which brought untimely deaths: "If you slight and make light of this hand of the Lord, or do not make a due improvement of it, you may fear, that God has not done with you, but that he has more arrows to shoot amongst you, that shall suddenly strike some of you ere long."[193]

While the ministerial appeal to terror boomed from the pulpit, it also reached a wider audience in early New England through the inexpensive and widely circulated publications known as "penny godlies." A pervasive theme of the penny godlies was that of terror striking when it was least expected, but another theme focused on a form of terror that was precisely timed and calculated, namely, the execution of criminals. Execution sermons and gallows confessions were published together with vivid eyewitness accounts of the suffering of the condemned. In 1717, the gallows speeches of a group of pirates executed in Rhode Island were published overnight by a Boston printer, no small feat for that or any age.[194] Thomas Shepard warned that the fate of such outlaws is the fate of all unrepentant sinners. "Thou art condemned," wrote Shepard, "and the muffler is before thine eyes, God knowes how soon the ladder may bee turned, thou hangest but by one rotten twined thread of thy life over the flames of hell every houre."[195]

Such use of terror appeals to nothing so much as the self-interest and "self-love" that Jonathan Edwards renounced in his writings on true virtue, but as we have seen, Edwards himself was not averse to engaging in the homiletics of terror. While Edwards helped to spark the Great Awakening of the 1740s, the revival followed a path that turned away from the Calvinism Edwards valued. Puritanism gave way to enthusiasm.[196] Predestination gave way to the efficacious power of individual conversion, and if the love of God failed to win such conversion, then terror might be the tool of salvation. The theme was revisited in the revival of 1831 with Charles Grandison Finney seeking to win a congregation in Troy, New York with visions of hell: "Look! Look! See the millions of wretches, biting and gnawing their tongues, as they lift their scalding heads from the burning lake! See! See! how they are tossed, and how they howl. . . . Hear them groan, midst the fiery billows."[197]

At about the same time that Finney was evoking fearsome images to instill righteousness in America, John Nelson Darby was busy in England devising a novel approach to eschatology and to biblical interpretation that would dramatically separate the righteous from the damned. In a system that became known as "premillennial dispensationalism," Darby superimposed the seventy weeks of Daniel 9 onto a schematic version of history. Unique to his system is the manner in which Darby "stopped the clock," as it were, at the end of week sixty-nine. He maintained that the entirety of "the present dispensation of the church" falls between week sixty-nine and the beginning of the end-time in week seventy. By asserting that no one knows when the seventieth week will begin, Darby sought to defuse rampant speculations on the timing of apocalypse.[198] And in another unique aspect of his system, Darby also sought to defuse the anxieties of believers regarding the terrors of the end time. Darby made short shrift of the diversity in biblical literary forms and theologies as he wove together assorted texts to create a smoothly coherent account of end-time events. The rule of the saints in the Millennium (Revelation 20) will be preceded by the "great tribulation" (Matthew 24), a time of anguish and suffering in which the forces of Antichrist will be given free reign to do their worst. But the faithful need not fear this suffering because they will have been taken from the earth before the tribulation begins. Darby called this pre-tribulation rescue "the rapture." He derived his idea of the event chiefly from the text of 1 Thessalonians 4:16-17: "For the Lord himself, with a cry of command, with the archangel's call and with the sound of God's trumpet, will descend from heaven, and the dead in Christ will rise first. Then we who are alive, who are left, will be caught up in the clouds together with them to meet the Lord in the air; and so we will be with the Lord forever."

The manner in which Darby was able to convey a sense of enveloping disparate biblical texts within a unified system held special appeal for those who subscribed to ideas of biblical inerrancy. Premillennial dispensationalism only began to win significant numbers of adherents in the United States with late 19th-century evangelicalism and early 20th-century fundamentalism.[199] These were the movements that alarmed and angered the already ill-tempered social critic, H. L. Mencken. He lumped together fundamentalists, evangelicals, and millenarians as "Christian bumpkins" who threatened civilization itself. "Civilization will gradually become felonious everywhere in the Republic, as it already is in Arkansas."[200] Mencken expressed disdain for most things rural, but he feared that fundamentalist bumpkins were also invading the city. "Heave an egg out of a Pullman window and you will hit a fundamentalist almost anywhere in the US today. They swarm in the country towns. . . . They are thick in the mean streets behind the gasworks. They are everywhere learning is too heavy a burden. . . . They march with the Klan, with the Christian Endeavor Society. . . ."[201] But contrary to Mencken's characterization, belief in biblical inerrancy did not necessarily indicate opposition to learning. Instead, some proponents of inerrancy were advocating a form of democratization of access to the biblical text, an access they believed had become blocked by esoteric doctrines and dogmas. Such fundamentalists traced their roots to the "Scottish Common Sense Realism" of Francis Bacon and Thomas Reid. They understood their mission as identical to that of the Reformation, making the Bible available to all believers and thus encouraging study and learning.[202] Also unfair was Mencken's characterization of fundamentalists as mean-spirited. Many proponents of inerrancy were encouraging believers to act on the "plain sense" of the biblical text by feeding the hungry and clothing the naked. No matter one's evaluation of the cogency of fundamentalism, meanness is not inherent to the movement. On the other hand, with the notion of "the rapture," meanness of spirit and vengeance hold sway.

In fairness, it must be noted that there are several versions of the rapture and not all of them envision the saints observing from midair as the sinners suffer the terrors of tribulation down below. Groups of dispensationalists have differed on whether the rapture will occur before, during or after the seven-year period of tribulation. Such differences were and are vested with great significance by some evangelicals, with quarreling among pre-, mid-, and post-tribulationists resulting in the demise of evangelical consensus at the important Niagara Bible Conference in 1901.[203] Contemporary post-tribulationists include some Identity Christians and survivalists who have armed themselves in the expectation that they will not be raptured before the terror begins. But it is Darby's pre-tribulation version of the rapture that has won the most adherents. This is the rapture of the bumper sticker slogans: WARNING, IN CASE OF RAPTURE THIS CAR WILL BE UNMANNED, and GET RIGHT OR GET LEFT.[204] This is the rapture that emboldens the breezy self-confidence of pop-apocalypticist Hal Lindsey who, when asked if the tribulation would take the form of a nuclear war, smiled and replied that he did not worry about that because, "I ain't gonna be here."[205] This is the rapture in which the saints are akin to an audience at a horror movie, floating at a safe distance while being thrilled by scenes of the terror suffered by others. Both military superpowers and the raptured righteous claim the right to float unscathed above a world of suffering humanity.

Assorted versions of the idea of "rapture" have proliferated among new religious groups, some of them self-identified as "Christian" and others not. The leaders of Uganda's Movement for the Restoration of the Ten Commandments believed that they had been chosen by the Virgin Mary to survive the terror of the last days; it was a terror that some in the Movement proceeded to precipitate through a series of mass murders that were uncovered in 2000. In Japan, members of Aum Shinrikyō experimented with technologies that would enable them to survive the nuclear and chemical devastation of the planet. Some Aum members likened their status to that of Jonathan Livingston Seagull, the spiritually superior bird who soared to great heights to escape the mundane fate of the rest of the flock.[206] The Order of the Solar Temple, based in Switzerland and Canada, maintained that its members would escape the destruction of "the whole wicked world" by being ferried across space to the star Sirius and being transformed there into angelic beings. The Solar Temple gained notoriety in 1994 when dozens of its members died in coordinated murders and suicides.[207]

In the United States, Heaven's Gate also drew upon the idea of "exiting" earth through space in order to advance to the "next level." While the external appearance of the group was quite benign, the leader of Heaven's Gate, Marshall Applewhite, expressed no small contempt for most of the world's occupants. After the group's members exited, the earth would have to be "spaded under" because, said Applewhite, "The weeds have taken over the garden and disturbed its usefulness beyond repair." The "weeds" to which he referred are human beings. "The weeds are now getting rid of weeds — from gangwars to nations involved in ethnic cleansing. This is simply a part of the natural recycling process. . . ."[208] Lifton remarks, "What made Heaven's Gate so deceptive a phenomenon was the way it combined a soft external patina with an intense expression of the violent urges of our historical moment."[209]

Clearly, neither murder nor suicide are intrinsic to the idea of rapture, but what is intrinsic is a perspective on both God and humanity that is irreconcilable with the Sermon on the Mount and with the proclamation of the Gospel as good news rather than bad. With the rapture, gone is the faith in the God who wants none to perish (2 Peter 3:9); gone is the faith in God's announcement of universal restoration (Acts 3:19-21). In its place is universal devastation for all except the righteous. This constitutes a blatant evasion of the way of the cross.[210] Significantly, the "first resurrection" in the millennial vision of Revelation 20 is of "those who had been beheaded for their testimony to Jesus and for the word of God" (20:4). The saints who reign are not those who have escaped the tribulation but those who have suffered its full fury. The evidence of their faithfulness did not lie in their assent to a set of doctrinal beliefs but in their sufferings and deaths as criminals.[211]

The resurrection has little to do with life extension or with the vindication of certain righteous individuals. The resurrection is the vindication of God and the proclamation of the victory of God's justice. Resurrection is the ultimate answer to the question of theodicy.[212] The emphasis is quite wrongly placed whenever individual believers focus on their own certainty of resurrection or rapture as a form of self-vindication. The role for believers is not to escape the tribulations of the current age, but to share fully in the suffering, to give prayerful voice to the groans of the creation yearning for redemption (Romans 8:18-27). The suffering of the last days, which is the culmination of the terror of history, is shared by all of creation so that the rejoicing in the new heaven and the new earth may also be shared.[213]

Terrorists wage war on the world, or on specific portions of it. Theological terrorists claim that the war is at the behest of God and that God will rescue them from this world on which they war. This is precisely contrary to the discipleship stance recommended by Karl Barth, the stance of seeking to represent God's cause in the world yet not wage war on the world, love the world and yet be completely faithful to God, suffer with the world and speak a frank word about its need and at the same time go beyond this to speak the redeeming word about the help it waits for, carry the world up to God and bring God into the world, and be an advocate for men before God and a messenger of God bringing peace to men, pleading unceasingly and unswervingly before God and to God "Thy Kingdom Come!" and waiting and hastening with men toward this coming. Is that not the highest and most promising thing a man can do at this moment — if he can?[214]

*   *   *

I have a friend named Fran who delights in tooling down the highway in her rusty station wagon, her tape deck blaring Pearl Jam. On her car's back bumper is a sticker proclaiming, "I'd rather be in Gehenna." Fran is a secular humanist and proud of it. She puts no stock in "myths" (a word she uses as a synonym for "lies") about heaven or hell. She sports the bumper sticker in hopes of eliciting comments like, "Gehenna? Isn't that somewhere in Ohio?" The bumper sticker seems to aim for humor based on the casual stating of a shocking preference. I'd rather be camping? Perhaps. I'd rather be in Vermont? Perhaps. But, I'd rather be in hell?

In both academic and popular circles, we are seeing a resurgence of interest in hell. It is as if the minions of the demonic, seeing the trendy and generally vacuous attention currently being heaped on angels, have risen up to demand equal time. While a 1965 Gallup poll showed that 54 percent of Americans believed in the existence of hell, by 2000 the number had risen to 73 percent believing in hell (but only 6 percent believing that they would personally end up there).[215] Books proliferate on the origins of hell, its history, and the various distinctions among Gehenna and the Pit and Hades and Sheol. Some volumes are notable mostly for their colorful illustrations with fiery splashes of yellow, orange, and red. Others trace a careful history of hell from Zoroastrian dualism to the apocalyptic yearnings of first-century Palestine.

Fran's bumper sticker aside, the idea of *deciding* to go to hell is a matter more substantial than it may at first appear. Is it ever possible that damnation might be the cost of discipleship? It is a question that occurred to Dietrich Bonhoeffer as he was deciding to cooperate with people who were plotting the assassination of Hitler. It is a question that occurred to Simone Weil: "If it were conceivable that in obeying God one should bring about one's own damnation while in disobeying him one could be saved, I should still choose the way of obedience."[216] The urgency of the question was quite different for Bonhoeffer

180

than for Weil. With Weil, the question occurs as a type of spiritual riddle to which she already knows the answer that she will give. In a sense, she is restating the assertion from Spinoza's *Ethics* that one who truly loves God will do so without expecting any love in return. But with Bonhoeffer, we witness the full urgency and anguish of one who was convinced that the historical moment in which God had placed him required him to act in a way that was utterly condemned by God. Could he choose hell in the name of God? In fact, Bonhoeffer's role in the resistance entailed laying plans for the German church after Hitler's demise rather than actually planning the attempt on Hitler's life.[217] Still, he did not seek to evade the moral guilt for his complicity with those who were plotting a horrible deed, namely, killing a child of God, which is who Hitler was — a twisted, pathetic child of God.

In a much different time and circumstance, the possibility of deciding to go to hell was also posed by Niccolò Machiavelli. Certainly Bonhoeffer is a much more sympathetic figure than Machiavelli, but Machiavelli is making a comeback of sorts. His resuscitation is reflected in Sebastian de Grazia's Pulitzer Prize–winning biography, *Machiavelli in Hell*. While scholars once speculated that *The Prince* counseled such a degree of brutality that it had to be a satire, Henry Kissinger appeared on the 1999 CNN segment "Voices of the Millennium" to praise the political realism of Machiavelli.

Machiavelli contends that the most successful prince is the one who is prepared to consciously choose evil actions when the "necessity" arises. De Grazia writes that these evil choices are in the name of love of country, which he likens to love for a woman:

> And in one of the last letters, Niccolò exclaims to his old friend Vettori: "I love my country more than my soul." Certainly this declaration can and does mean willingness to suffer anything for one's country — shame, torture, mistreatment, dishonor, exile. It can and does mean willingness to lie, cheat, and kill, to do evil for one's country, thereby forfeiting one's soul. It can and does mean dying for one's country and — if necessary — going to hell for her.
>
> The code of love rests intact: the lover bound to his lady's service, to suffer her whims, her rejections, bound to champion her honor, to save her from dragons, bound to go to hell for her.[218]

But to state the matter thus is to risk misleading us on Machiavelli's understanding of both "country" and "lady." Some women would not choose to be loved by the one who writes ". . . fortune is a woman and whoever wishes to win her must importune and beat her. . . ."[219] And the residents of some countries would not choose to be loved by the one who writes ". . . the nature of people is fickle, and it is easy to persuade them of something but difficult to keep them in that persuasion. And so it is best to have matters ordered in such a way that when people no longer believe in the innovation they can be compelled to believe by force."[220] In *The Prince* especially, Machiavelli is not writing about "the country" as a collectivity of people he loves; he is writing about "the state" as an apparatus and about how to maintain the prince's position in it. Contra de Grazia, the prince is choosing hell not to secure the welfare of his people, but to secure his own status and legacy. The prince is less a martyr than a Faust.

Terror is the primary tool of the prince, with fear of force and of pain as the primary motivators in politics. The prince must study war incessantly, and he must never be reluctant to engage in it, for "a war is never avoided but merely postponed to your own disadvantage."[221] Whether it is against foreign or domestic adversaries, "injury" must be inflicted in a manner that renders retaliation impossible. For the prince, "cruelty is used well" if it is severe and used all at once rather than relying on the "timidity" of a less severe cruelty that would have to be applied repeatedly.[222] It is an effective tactic, this "cruelty all at once." When lesser terrorists strike randomly, sporadically, repeatedly, their cruelty seems unremitting. But by inflicting large-scale cruelty all at once, the prince seems like no terrorist at all.

Into this unlikely mix of Bonhoeffer, Weil, and Machiavelli, let us add one final example of deciding to go to hell. The setting is the Mississippi River where Huck Finn is floating with his friend Jim, a runaway slave. Reared in a culture that preached that helping a runaway slave was tantamount to spitting in the eye of God, Huck faced the choice of betraying his friend or suffering eternal damnation. In what is arguably one of the greatest lines in Western literature, Huck decides: "All right, then, I'll *go* to hell."[223]

On the face of it, Huckleberry Finn's decision is more laudable than that of Machiavelli's prince. Huck simply acts to help a friend, and while his action might deprive Miss Watson of some supposed "property," he leaves no princely carnage in his wake. But there is also a certain moral integrity to Machiavelli's position. Although Machiavelli maintained that the good of the polis and the security of the prince's position in it were worthy ends, he did not deny the moral culpability of those who used evil means in pursuit of those ends. It was as if Machiavelli believed that a good goal justified evil means politically, but not morally. For the sake of his state, the prince decides to go to hell. Machiavelli knew that the price for making a holocaust of others is not paid simply with the bodies of those who are victimized; such actions also burn the perpetrator's own spirit and humanity. One cannot intentionally kill others without inflicting another kind of death on oneself, a spiritual death.

In the frankness with which Machiavelli wrote about choosing "evil" and assigning culpability for such a choice, his reflections had a moral integrity that is lacking in modern bloodletting. Military "missions" are no longer evil; they are humanitarian. Decisions to embark on such missions are less cause for damnation than cause for palace priests to extol the justness of it all. And if the killing becomes excessive, culpability is not borne, it is shuffled, either up the chain of command to the Führer or down the chain of command to a platoon at My Lai. One could do worse than to share Machiavelli's candor in naming evil and in assigning culpability for it. Of course, Machiavelli's prince had a freer hand. In the modern setting, culpability is less of a premium commodity. Behind the executioner are judge and jury and legislators and governor and the rest of us paying the bill for the executioner to act.

In one fundamental way, however, Machiavelli does allow his prince to evade responsibility. The prince escapes; he escapes to hell. This postmortem hell has often been viewed as an essential element in the terror of God, and yet, there is a sense in which the very concept distances us from moral responsibility. It functions like a credit card — or (more accurately) a discredit card — which allows us to commit or endorse horrendous actions now in the belief that their consequences will be reaped only at some later date. Act now, pay later. But the biblical proclamation has little to say about where we are after we are dead and much to say about where God is now. In the incarnation of Jesus, God has invaded our world. God's love and God's judgment are much nearer than either heaven or hell. Likewise, the consequences of our actions are immanent. We may choose now to share in the joy of God's reign, to love and serve sisters and brothers, to nurture our spiritual life through worship and prayer — or we may choose to suffer the spiritual death that inevitably precedes, surrounds, and follows violence and injustice. We will be known not by a postmortem destination but by the immanent fruits of our actions. Consequence and judgment are no farther away than God, and as Clarence Jordan observed, God is not in heaven, with all well on the earth. God is on earth and all hell's breaking loose.[224]

A few years ago while I was working as a campus minister at a small New York college, a certain student of fundamentalist persuasion frequented the ministry office in an effort to convince me of my apostasy. Our conversations were generally good-humored, although I sensed his occasional exasperation. One day he sought to convince me that I was in error to believe that the Pauline phrase "justification by faith" could refer to God's faithfulness towards humanity. "No," he corrected me, "Paul is talking about the faith of each individual believer." He then said that it sometimes appeared as if I didn't even believe that hell existed, and that such a lapse in belief would be a serious matter. "Do you believe there is a hell?" he asked. My request for clarification made it clear that he was speaking of hell as a literal locale prepared for those who had "died in sin." "I don't know," I responded. "But let's make a pact. If you and I get to the Pearly Gates and we discover that some people have been sent to hell, let's picket the gates of heaven until those in hell are freed." He sat in stunned silence and stared at me for what must have been a full minute. Then he suddenly became animated and his voice boomed: "Are you crazy?"

Perhaps so. First, it is a crazy presumption to think that I might see the Pearly Gates. Are the goats not separated from the sheep (Matthew 25)? (And how keenly aware am I of my goatish ways.) Is the rich man not separated from Lazarus (Luke 16)? (And compared to most people on the planet, I am very rich indeed.) But even for those more worthy than I, to picket the gates of heaven would be to toss themselves rather flippantly upon the mercy of God. After all, few possess the credentials that allowed Abraham to argue with God in Genesis 18. My fundamentalist friend would have me remind you that a great chasm is fixed between the elect and the damned, a chasm over which none can cross (Luke 16:26). He would want me to tell you that this clearly biblical teaching refutes all notions of universal salvation, whether in the version first taught by Origen or in any of the versions since.[225] The terror of God is not to be denied. Humanity is divided. The chasm can be crossed by no one.

By no one, that is, except God.

In September 1996, the news media were quick to treat the nation to the courtroom drama of a sentencing hearing in which the anguished father of a murdered child spoke to the man who had been convicted of the murder. "When you get to where you're going," he said, "say hello to Hitler, Dahmer, and Bundy." This unholy trinity represents the commonest conception of hell. A place full of evil people and evil deeds. A place devoid of God. No one can deny this father his grief for his daughter or his rage at the one who could commit so hate-filled an act as killing a child. God grieves with him. God rages with him.

But God does much more. It is precisely when grief or rage or bitterness overwhelms our capacity to love or to forgive that God steps in to love and to forgive on our behalf. There is guilt so great that it can *never* be avenged, guilt so great that it can only be forgiven.[226] It is upon the least lovable people that God heaps the burning coals of love (Romans 12:20-21). This is the terror of God. This is the fire of hell, the eternal torment. Those who would reject all love are forced to endure it.[227]

Transmitted from Zoroastrian dualism, the Jewish and Christian hell was born in the apocalyptic experience of oppressed people who faced privation and extinction. Theirs was an understandable yearning for ultimate vindication. But beneath the dominant theme that the oppressor would be damned lies a contrary, non-dualistic idea that liberation is made of sterner stuff — perhaps even the possibility that, once deprived of power, the powerful themselves might be liberated. As Karl Barth notes, God's wrath, God's judgment, God's "No" is spoken only for the sake of God's "Yes." It is God who crosses the chasm. It is God who decides to go to hell armed with the burning coals of love.

So what can we say, then, to Huck Finn and to Niccolò Machiavelli's prince? Huck's is the easier case. He has been sold a bill of goods. Many before and since him have been encouraged to believe that social standards are God's standards, that fear of the state is fear of the Lord. It ain't so, Huck. God is with Jim and with you there on the river. God is the current that carries you to freedom.

And to the prince? Without obsequious bowing, let us approach him and say this: It is true that there is much that you can do. If you wish, you can lie and steal. You can inflict terror and death. You can implicate us all in your decisions. And you can make of earth a hellish place for many. But there is a limit to your power. That limit is God. And one of the things you cannot decide to do is to escape by going to hell. Because God will pursue you there. And God will find you there. And, to your horror, God will love you there. You will be made to sit at table with your victims and to suffer their love as well. You will be *burned* by love. And you will be redeemed.

But insofar as there is corporate responsibility for the actions of the prince, we also share his fate. We are forewarned. We cannot distance ourselves from our victims through technology or geography or politics. We will sit at table with them and look into their eyes. And we cannot distance ourselves from God by deciding to go to hell. The Pit itself is filled with the presence of God (Psalm 139:7-8). Jesus is already there preaching to the unreachable and loving the unlovable (1 Peter 3:19; Ephesians 4:9-10). This is the terror of God from which we cannot hide because, in Jesus, God invades not only the earth but hell itself. God is the one who decides to go to hell. Hallelujah and amen.

The Abolitionists and the Judgment of God

As John Nelson Darby was in England in the 1830s expounding upon his version of the rapture, his ideas would have seemed quite odd to black Christians who were enslaved in the United States. Being carried away before the tribulation arrives? They were living in the very *midst* of tribulation and terror, a terror concocted by neither God nor Antichrist but by pious, white Christians. Indeed, slaveholders have always openly acknowledged that they needed to instill terror in the enslaved people. The preferred tool of terror for the Romans was the cross; Americans preferred the tools of whips and nooses. A group of South

Carolina slaveholders in the 1840s encouraged their peers to embrace the fact that the "principle of fear" was the only principle upon which slavery could be maintained.[228] As Darby speculated on the avoidance of end-time terror, slaveholders speculated on the current need to instill it.

Equally foreign to the concerns of enslaved Christians were any doctrines of biblical inerrancy. How would such a concern even make sense for a group to whom literacy was denied? It was the slaveholder who was concerned to defend the inerrancy of the Bible, especially on points like Abraham's ownership of slaves, and Paul's return of Onesimus to Philemon, and Paul's apparent failure to renounce slavery in 1 Corinthians 7:21.[229] It was the slaveholder who would teach the slave all that he or she needed to know about the Bible, even if some of the teachings were blatant lies. One catechism designed for teaching slaves recommended that "Thou shalt not commit adultery" should be interpreted as a commandment "to serve our heavenly Father, and our earthly master, obey our overseer, and not steal anything."[230] It was the slaveholder who became quite proficient at quoting Scripture. Frederick Douglass cites one biblical passage of which his master was especially fond: "I have said my master found religious sanction for his cruelty. . . . I have seen him tie up a lame young woman, and whip her with a heavy cowskin upon her naked shoulders, causing the warm red blood to drip; and, in justification of the bloody deed, he would quote this passage of Scripture — 'He that knoweth his master's will, and doeth it not, shall be beaten with many stripes.'"[231]

But this is not to suggest that either the rapture or the Bible were unimportant for black Christians who were enslaved. More immediate and concrete than anything Darby envisioned, the "rapture" was escape from the tribulation of slavery. Douglass used that precise word to describe his first experience of freedom: "I was now my own master. It was a happy moment, the rapture of which can be understood only by those who have been slaves."[232] Spirituals were often sung, not with a hope for eventual redemption from "sin," but with a faith in God's help towards imminent freedom from slavery. Thus, "Steal Away" is suggestive of going to the woods for a secret meeting of slaves, and "Follow the Drinking Gourd" contains a rather thinly veiled suggestion to follow the big dipper constellation north to freedom in Canada. In "Swing Low Sweet Chariot," looking over "Jordan" meant, for some, looking over the Ohio River, and the "band of angels" included Harriet Tubman and her coworkers.[233] Tubman was the courageous woman who, having escaped from slavery herself, returned South on nineteen dangerous journeys to lead over 300 people out of slavery.

If the escape from tribulation had a sense of immediate relevance among black Christians, there was a similar relevance to the Bible stories they heard. In many traditional African religions, life was not separated into the "secular" and the "sacred," the "here" and the "hereafter."[234] If freedom and joy were valid experiences in "heaven," then they were valid now as well.[235] Try as the slaveholder might to conceal the subversive elements of the biblical story, the master could not prevent the slave from knowing that Moses led the Hebrew people out of captivity, that Jesus had been scourged and whipped, that God's people survived lions and fiery furnaces, that God would "make a way out of no way." Such stories did not indicate that the Bible was an inerrant book; much more, they indicated that the Bible was a survival manual, a reliable testimony to God's faithfulness in the midst of oppression. Some slaves became involved in millenarianism, one prominent example being Nat Turner who viewed his own slave rebellion as a precursor to the battle of Armageddon. More common than such millenarianism, however, was the sense of God as a present help in the midst of troubles. Harriet Tubman saw visions and spoke with God and asked for concrete assistance from God in the midst of danger. At times the communication was intimate, requiring not even words. A narrator relates the following story of Tubman:

> One of her most characteristic prayers was when on board a steamboat with a party of fugitives. The clerk of the boat declined to give her tickets, and told her to wait. She thought he suspected her, and was at a loss how to save herself and her charge, if he did; so she went alone into the bow of the boat, and she says, "I drew in my breath and I sent it out to the Lord, but that was all I could say; and then again the third time, and just then I felt a touch on my shoulder, and looked round, and the clerk said, 'Here's your tickets.'"[236]

Black Americans were active in the movement to abolish slavery long before the cause became prominent on the agenda of the white, Christian reformers of the 19th century. Even before 1800, Richard Allen, Benjamin Banneker, and Absalom Jones were all issuing strong denunciations of slavery. By the time William Lloyd Garrison began publishing *The Liberator* in 1831, fifty black-organized abolitionist groups were already active in major cities like Boston, New York, and Philadelphia.[237] Many of the pre-Garrisonian, white abolitionists did not view slavery as indicative of an evil system; America was still the "New Israel," with slavery being a mere aberration that had been inherited from the old world. Some white Christians believed that the 1808 congressional ban on the importation of slaves took care of the "problem," and that slavery could be left alone to gradually fade from the American scene. In fact, the number of people enslaved continued to grow dramatically following the 1808 ban, in part due to surreptitious slave trading and in part due to the automatic enslavement of babies born to slaves. Prior to the 1830s, the most influential "antislavery" organization founded by white Christians was the American Colonization Society, a group that campaigned to send freed blacks to Africa. While the Society was ostensibly an "antislavery" group, its membership actually included some slaveholders who believed that ridding the country of all blacks who were not in bondage was a worthy goal.[238]

In contrast to the earlier and feebler efforts of white Christians, the activists of the New England Anti-Slavery Society (founded in 1832) and the American Anti-Slavery Society (1833) were abolitionists worthy of the name. The rise of this later wave of abolitionism coincided with the evangelical revival that was sweeping the northern U.S. and the western frontier. Theodore Weld (1803-1895) was one of several abolitionist leaders who had experienced conversion at a revival meeting organized by Charles Finney. Finney, an opponent of slavery, later served as professor of theology at Oberlin College, an important Ohio stop on the underground railroad.[239] The perfectionism that pervaded the evangelical revival was also an important feature of abolitionist thought in the 1830s and 1840s. Abolitionists were often proponents of temperance as well. The hope was for repentant slaveholders to abandon their sins much as reformed drunkards renounced their attachment to alcohol.[240] Theodore Weld wrote that the slaveholder and the drunkard were similarly incapacitated: "Arbitrary power is to the mind what alcohol is to the body; it intoxicates."[241] Arthur Tappan, the first president of the American Anti-Slavery Society, had abandoned his earlier affiliation with the American Colonization Society when he learned of Liberia's involvement in the rum trade.

The perfectionist theme in abolitionism was not an unmixed blessing. On the one hand, the perfectionism sometimes served as a spur to greater commitment and creativity among abolitionists. In an effort to end the taint of any personal complicity with the slave system, some northern abolitionists adopted the position of "come-outers," abandoning affiliation with any churches or social institutions that were insufficiently resolute in their condemnation of slavery. Feminist abolitionists were the earliest advocates of boycotts of merchandise produced by slave labor. In Philadelphia, Lucretia and James Mott ran a store selling only free-labor products, including wool garments rather than cotton and maple sugar rather than cane sugar.[242] But alongside such creativity and commitment, the perfectionist desire to be free of complicity with slavery also gave rise to some proposals that conveyed the strange sense that the purity of the abolitionist was of greater import than the fate of the slave. "Disunionism," for example, was a proposal that was at one time supported by both Frederick Douglass and William Lloyd Garrison. In order to avoid any association with slavery, disunionism proposed that the North should secede from the South.

The New England Non-Resistance Society, founded by Garrison and others in 1838, gave what was called "ultraist" expression to both abolitionism and perfectionism. Non-Resistance Society members were known as pacifists and as "no-government people." While members of the Society were proponents of "anarchy," the word itself was renounced for all of its negative connotations. Indeed, debates about what constituted "anarchy" figured prominently in the espousal of both pro- and anti-slavery positions. John C. Calhoun and other advocates of slavery argued that chaos and evil were omnipresent, that civilization itself was dependent upon the coercion which all governments utilized, and that the ideology of slavery was therefore a necessary element in the effort to forestall mere anarchy. In contrast, Garrison and other non-resistants argued that the "government of God" alone had the power to hold back chaos and "anarchy" and that all coercive institutions represented a usurpation of the moral accountability that the individual owed to God alone. As Garrison put it, "Non-resistance makes men self-governed. The kingdom of God is within them. Some speak of anarchy in connection with non-resistance. But this principle teaches those who receive it to be just, and upright, and kind, and true, in all the relations of life. It is the men of violence who furnish anarchists."[243] Slavery was the ultimate expression of the effort to hold people accountable to human masters rather than to God alone.

While some perfectionists were communitarians (e.g., John Humphrey Noyes), there was an individualistic emphasis in Garrison's portrayal of moral accountability. What enabled people to be "self-governed" was the kingdom of God "within" each individual rather than "among" or "in the midst of" the human community. Due to this emphasis on individual moral accountability, the Non-Resistance Society never developed unified or consistent positions on a number of pressing issues. Individual conscience held sway. Regarding tax payments, for example, there was an uneasy awareness of the manner in which government revenues were used to enforce the system of slavery, but only a minority of abolitionists protested payment of taxes. While non-resistants clearly opposed the system of military conscription, Garrison nonetheless advised that young men cooperate with the system by paying a fine to avoid enlistment rather than going to jail. Most non-resistants refused to vote and believed that slavery had to be abolished by moral persuasion rather than legislation since government constituted just another form of coercive "mastery." Still, non-resistants were clearly not disinterested in the results of elections and of the legislative process, and some actually joined the abolitionist Liberty Party. Consistency and unity were not strong suits with the non-resistants. But if perfectionistic individualism contributed to inconsistencies in the non-resistant movement, it was also perfectionism that led Henry Wright and others to pursue consistency to the point of legalism and rigidity. In an article in *The Liberator,* Wright pondered the question of whether he would vote if he knew that his single ballot would make the difference in achieving the abolition of slavery. He arrived at the conclusion that he would not cast the ballot since voting itself constituted support for a system of oppression.[244]

For abolitionists, the term "non-resistance" did not imply passivity and submission to tyrannical power but rather the effort to oppose evil with good and violence with nonviolence. These non-resistants were pacifists rather than passivists, but theirs was a pacifism with a strongly pragmatic orientation. Nonviolence "works." The pages of *The Liberator* were filled with stories of the efficacious nature of nonviolence — how nonviolence turned back assaults from brutal attackers, how nonviolence was more effective than legal action in collecting debts, how nonviolence was a path of great "safety."[245] While there are plentiful historical examples of those who chose nonviolence even to the point of martyrdom, some non-resistants argued that nonviolence was a technique for the avoidance of martyrdom. Such pragmatic pacifists face some obvious dilemmas. What if nonviolence does not "work"? What if nonviolence is ineffective in providing for personal safety or in achieving the goal of the abolition of slavery?

The question of personal safety and nonviolence came to the fore dramatically with the 1837 murder of the abolitionist editor, the Reverend Elijah P. Lovejoy. While this was the first killing of a white abolitionist to gain national attention, it was certainly not the first encounter with danger. Two years before Lovejoy's death, Garrison had barely escaped lynching at the hands of an angry mob in Boston. Throughout the incident, Garrison had called on his followers to remain nonviolent. Lovejoy was also a proponent of nonviolence, even in the face of a mob that destroyed his printing presses in Missouri. Following that attack, Lovejoy moved to what he thought might be the greater safety of Alton, Illinois. It was there that he was killed by a pro-slavery mob in November 1837. For many abolitionists, the tragedy was exacerbated by the startling revelation that Lovejoy had died with a gun in his hand. Since nonviolence had not been effective in curbing the attacks against him and his family, Lovejoy had opted for violence. The case became a pretext for further derision from those who already doubted the sincerity of the followers of "non-resistance." For Garrison and others who had known Lovejoy, the incident provoked anguish on a number of levels. Garrison mourned his friend while refusing to embrace his actions. He declared that, while Lovejoy "was certainly a martyr — strictly speaking — he was not . . . a Christian martyr."[246]

Slave revolts gave a sharp focus and an urgency to the question of how nonviolence could be effective in pursuing the goal of abolition. While there had been a number of slave rebellions and conspiracies (e.g., the Gabriel Conspiracy in Virginia in 1800 and Denmark Vesey's conspiracy in South Carolina in 1822), it was Nat Turner's rebellion that provoked the greatest alarm and resulted in the greatest bloodshed. While the rebellion lasted only two days in August 1831, over fifty white people were killed in Southampton County, Virginia in what Turner believed to be the beginning of the end-time battle between the dark Children of Light and the white Children of Darkness.[247] Turner's slaughter of whites was not indiscriminate; he spared the lives of several poor whites who held no slaves and who expressed no attitudes of superiority to blacks. While Turner himself avoided apprehension and the noose for several months, reprisals against others were swift and furious. Over a hundred black slaves and freedmen were killed by vigilante attacks and judicial executions. In the view of most slaveholders, the rebellions were simple acts of terrorism that confirmed the suspicion that blacks were too innately barbaric to merit emancipation.[248] Yet, the slave rebellions served to highlight the hypocrisy of the slaveholders. While the slaveholders were denouncing the abolitionism of northerners who claimed to value "non-resistance" and "nonviolence," was it not precisely the qualities of patient suffering and nonviolence that the slaveholder demanded of the slave? And for that matter, what did the non-resistance movement expect of the slave? Some white abolitionists became involved in the underground railroad efforts to offer assistance to escaping slaves, but the message of the non-resistance movement was addressed primarily to whites and not to blacks who remained enslaved. Even if there had been a medium through which non-resistants could have communicated with slaves, it is not clear what the content of the communication would have been. Would there have been encouragement for blacks to nonviolently refuse cooperation with enslavement? But non-cooperation in any form elicited brutal reprisals from slaveholders. How could northern abolitionists encourage non-cooperation by slaves when they were not even offering consistent encouragement for white non-cooperation with conscription and tax payments? If there was to be a nonviolent end to the violence of slavery, it was not clear how it would happen beyond the hope for mass conversion. Garrison renounced the violence of Nat Turner's rebellion, but he also asked Americans to forswear hypocrisy by acknowledging that Turner's methods differed little from those of the rebels of 1776. Years later, while the Non-Resistance Society continued to extol the pragmatic value of nonviolence, there was still no coherent vision of how nonviolence could be a tool of liberation. In response to Harriet Beecher Stowe's novel, Garrison praised the patient suffering of Uncle Tom as an exemplary expression of "Christian non-resistance."[249]

Frederick Douglass was no Uncle Tom. His escape from slavery alone indicated that Douglass thought that the times demanded something more than

patient suffering. In the North, Douglass began his career of abolitionist agitation as an ally of Garrison, subscribing fully to the principles of non-resistance.
In 1846, in the face of growing sentiments that abolition could only be won
through violence, Douglass boldly declared, "Were I asked the question
whether I would have my emancipation by the shedding of one single drop of
blood, my answer would be in the negative."[250] Yet, within only a few years of
that statement, Douglass became an advocate of armed resistance to slavery.
What happened?

One happening with widespread repercussions was congressional passage
of the Fugitive Slave Law of 1850, a law that criminalized any rendering of assistance to blacks who escaped slavery and declared that escapees who reached
states where slavery had been abolished must nonetheless be returned to their
"owners." The Fugitive Slave Law was the result of a political compromise in
which California was admitted as a free state but slaveholders were given a
tighter rein on their "property." It was a law that was widely unpopular in the
North, with some clerics who had not even been particularly outspoken abolitionists declaring that the Fugitive Slave Law criminalized basic Christian charity. The statute seemed designed to make violence inevitable. One of the first violent encounters related to its enforcement came in the small village of
Christiana in Lancaster County, Pennsylvania where a Maryland slaveholder in
pursuit of four escapees was killed by a mob.[251] In a case that provoked the ire
of many, Virginia slave hunters captured fugitive Anthony Burns in Boston in
1854. A courthouse guard was killed as abolitionists attempted to rescue Burns
from captivity. As a thousand angry protesters rallied to demand the release of
Burns, the Massachusetts militia was called up and President Franklin Pierce
sent in federal troops. With sabers drawn, guns at ready, and artillery pieces in
tow, a massive contingent of troops marched Burns to Boston Harbor and
loaded him onto a steamer for return to slavery. A *Richmond Enquirer* editorial
reflected an awareness that the Fugitive Slave Law was doomed if it needed persistently to rely on such a show of force; while celebrating Burns's capture, the
Enquirer observed that "a few more such victories and the South is undone."[252]

Garrison struggled to devise a means of opposing the Fugitive Slave Law that
would be both nonviolent and effective. He proposed that non-resistants should
identify slave hunters and follow them wherever they went in order to warn potential victims of their presence. But Douglass was done with such methods. The
Fugitive Slave Law was the last straw on the back of his nonviolence. Writing
soon after the capture of Burns, Douglass asserted that it was time for black people to refute the stereotype of black passivity and patience: "This reproach must
be wiped out, and nothing short of resistance on the part of colored men, can
wipe it out. Every Slave-hunter who meets a bloody death in his infernal busi-

ness, is an argument in favor of the manhood of our race."[253] The emphasis on "manhood" was not gratuitous. If slaveholders had portrayed black men as savages, abolitionists had overcompensated with a stereotype of meekness. Douglass came to believe that the best way to rebuke both stereotypes was to call black men to respond to the provocation of slavery with righteous violence.

As Frederick Douglass proceeded to preach his new message of violent resistance and black manhood, a revealing encounter took place when he was confronted by a black woman who was also a former slave, Sojourner Truth. Sojourner was in the front row at a crowded public meeting in Faneuil Hall in Boston at which Douglass was the featured speaker. Douglass called on black people to stop placing their hopes in the ultimate conversion of white people to the cause of justice. Emancipation would not come without bloodshed, said Douglass, and black men must be prepared to fight to redeem themselves. The audience responded with hushed awe, but as Douglass finished speaking and sat down, Sojourner Truth broke the silence with a question spoken loudly enough for all to hear: "Frederick, *is God dead?*"[254]

Questions regarding the identity of God and the nature of God's actions in the world became crucial in shaping the direction of abolitionism. Sojourner Truth's question to Douglass was a pithy statement of her own faith in a God who is not dependent on human violence, a God who actively intervenes in human history to "make a way out of no way." With the hope of God and the redemption of Jesus, Sojourner wondered how Douglass could possibly believe that there was no hope for white people or that there was no redemption for black people except in the force of arms. Her understanding of God was similar to that of Harriet Tubman — God as a present help for those who are downtrodden. Sojourner once attended an adventist camp meeting, and she confronted the doctrine of the rapture and the image of the God of terror that she heard being preached there:

> You seem to be expecting to go to some parlor *away up* somewhere, and when the wicked have been burnt, you are coming back to walk in triumph over their ashes — this is to be your New Jerusalem!! Now *I* can't see any thing so very *nice* in that, coming back to such a *muss* as that will be, a world covered with the ashes of the wicked! Besides, if the Lord comes and burns — as you say he will — I am not going away; *I* am going to stay here and *stand the fire,* like Shadrach, Meshach, and Abednego! And Jesus will walk with me through the fire, and keep me from harm. Nothing belonging to God can burn, any more than God himself; such shall have no need to go away to escape the fire! No, *I* shall remain. Do you tell me that God's children *can't stand fire?*[255]

For Garrison, Douglass, and some of the other abolitionists, the portrayal of how God intervenes in history was quite different from the picture presented by Sojourner Truth. Even after Douglass parted company with the non-resistants, Garrison continued in his advocacy of nonviolence. But all the while that he was a proponent of non-resistance, Garrison expressed a view of God as one who, while slow to anger, was capable of horrendous violence. There was something of Jonathan Edwards in Garrison's warning that an angry God was growing impatient with slavery and that, if hearts were not converted soon, it was God who would unleash the cataclysmic destruction that would effectuate change. This view of the terror of God as arrayed against the terror of slavery was not original with Garrison. The slaveholder Thomas Jefferson had already pondered the possibility when he wrote, "I tremble for my country when I reflect that God is just: that his justice cannot sleep forever: that . . . a revolution of the wheel of fortune, an exchange of situation is among possible events, that it may become probable by supernatural interference! The Almighty has no attribute which can take side with us in such a contest."[256] It was certainly fair to portray the God of Exodus as taking the side of the slave, but what became less tenable — especially for those in the non-resistance movement — was the image of a God who wins justice through the infliction of terror and violence. Was it not a backhanded exaltation of violence to claim that humans were not allowed to wield it but that the violent wrath of God was the ultimate and most effective tool for the accomplishment of the divine will? And in the meantime, did the absence of violence indicate that God was temporarily condoning slavery? All of the emphasis on God's "patience" and God's justice, which "cannot sleep forever," was that not a fairly blatant insult against God? Was there not more than the hint of a suggestion that slavery persisted because God had not yet become sufficiently riled at this crudest expression of injustice? And for non-resistants who based their nonviolence on the example of Jesus as the Prince of Peace, how could they simultaneously issue threats from the God of terror? Is Jesus a revelation from God, a revelation of the very nature of God, or is there another God, a God of terror who is somehow separate from Jesus of Nazareth? If there is any concern for coherent monotheism, how can one claim that Jesus is "non-resistant" but God is not? And finally, when the wrath of God finds expression in human history, is it not people who serve as instruments of God's terror? If the wrath of God is to come in the form of violence, how is it possible to condemn the violence of those who are, after all, only doing the will of God? It was on the shoals of such questions that the nonviolent movement for the abolition of slavery foundered and ultimately sank.

As early as 1829, William Lloyd Garrison was warning that, due to the persistence of slavery, "The terrible judgments of an incensed God will complete the catastrophe of republican America."[257] Garrison's statement expressed a theological viewpoint that was fairly prevalent among abolitionists, but one that is problematic in at least two respects. First, the emphasis is on the future ("will complete") wrath and judgment of God, thus striking an apocalyptic note. It is a statement that adds to the sense of the future inevitability of violence. Is there not a way to speak about the *present* wrath and judgment of God? Like Sojourner Truth and Harriet Tubman, many have recognized God's help and God's love as *present* realities. Likewise, there is no need to give only a future orientation to divine anger, as if God first had to store up a mighty reservoir of fury. Second, Garrison's statement and similar statements by others suggest a link between God's anger and violent "catastrophe." Who or what requires that link between God's anger and violence? Does the Bible require it?[258] People who are unable to express anger without resorting to violence are judged to be troubled, scarred, and scared. Is God scared (which would certainly give an unexpected meaning to the references to "the terror of God")? While God is clearly transcendent to all of humanity and to all such questions and judgments, it is nonetheless possible to speak of (in the phrase of Karl Barth) "the humanity of God" in Jesus; the incarnation is anthropomorphism that comes from God's side. The Gospels portray Jesus at a number of points (e.g., in his relationship to the "scribes and Pharisees") as expressing a stern yet nonviolent anger. The revelation of God in Jesus is a refutation of any link between God's wrath and violence. The statements by Garrison and others linking God's wrath to pending cataclysm serve as pretext for viewing any war that might come as the action of God rather than viewing war as a failure of humanity. Rather than affirming God's judgment of slavery, such a stance denies God's judgment of war.

Garrison read the signs of his time as a fulfillment of his own prophecy that God was preparing to go to war. He understood Nat Turner's rebellion as an apocalyptic warning issued by God.[259] The content of the warning, he wrote, was that only immediate emancipation could save America "from the vengeance of Heaven." The "bloody vengeance" of God for the sin of slavery was a repetitious theme in the writings of other abolitionists as well, including those of Henry C. Wright, Stephen S. Foster, and Parker Pillsbury.[260] The emphasis on "vengeance" suggested that, beyond the goal of ending slavery, the terror of God would exact quid pro quo retribution for all of the sufferings that slavery had entailed.[261] It was a juridical view of God that was punitive rather than restorative; the scales of justice would be balanced only when one side "paid" in suffering an amount commensurate with the suffering the other side had already paid. The perspective that pervaded many of the black spirituals and the extemporaneous speeches of Sojourner Truth also posited a view of God as Judge, but with a starkly different emphasis; the scales of justice would be balanced, not by additional suffering, but by the God who bestows restorative and reparative blessings on those who have suffered great harm.

The actions and the very persona of John Brown provided some abolitionists with further evidence of the imminence of God's vengeance. Indeed, Brown was prepared to proclaim himself an instrument of that vengeance. He declared that "the crimes of this *guilty land* will never be purged away but with *blood*."[262] Harpers Ferry was not Brown's first experience with bloodshed. The Kansas-Nebraska Act of 1854 had provided for "popular sovereignty" in the new territories so that settlers could decide whether slavery would be allowed or prohibited. The result was "Bloody Kansas," with pro- and anti-slavery forces fighting to gain dominance in the territory. John Brown was in the thick of it, organizing the flow of weapons to opponents of slavery in Kansas and leading an ad hoc band of fighters. At Pottawatamie, Brown's men used their swords to hack to death five unarmed people; the victims were not slaveholders, but they held political opinions in support of slavery. It was on October 16, 1859 that Brown and eighteen followers captured the federal arsenal at Harpers Ferry, Virginia. Brown's band of fighters included some of his sons, some fugitive slaves, and several college students from Oberlin. Brown was hoping that his raid would spark major slave insurrections and armed assistance from northern abolitionists, but the arsenal was retaken within two days. Among the seventeen people who were killed in the raid were ten of Brown's own men (including two of his sons), two slaves, one free black person who was an uninvolved bystander, and a local mayor who had drawn up a will providing for the emancipation of his slaves. If Brown's idea had been to strike a blow at the very foundation of slavery, the identity of his victims represented nothing of the sort. Nonetheless, between his arrest on October 18 and his execution on December 2, 1859, the vast majority of northern abolitionists spoke out in Brown's defense, hailing him as a prophet and a martyr. The contrasting evaluation of John Brown by slaveholders in the South was unequivocal: Brown was a blatant terrorist, aided and abetted by the whole abolitionist movement. Just a few months after Brown's raid, a book on American slavery by William Lloyd Garrison was published under the title *Reign of Terror*. Reflective of the other divisions in the U.S. was this polarity in the identification of who the terrorists were — slaveholders or John Brown and his raiders?[263]

For abolitionists who were not committed to non-resistance, the endorsement of John Brown was uncomplicated to the point of enthusiasm. Elizabeth Cady Stanton declared that she would not hesitate to offer the lives of her sons in so holy a cause: "I would consecrate them all to martyrdom, to die, if need be, bravely, like a John Brown, on the accursed soil of Southern despotism, boldly declaring that Jesus died to give to the nations of the earth a blood bought liberty."[264] But for Garrison and other representatives of non-resistance, the response to John Brown's raid was waffling to the point of incoherence. Since Garrison was influenced by both individualism and perfectionism, he thought that it might be possible to maintain personal purity by refusing to participate in violence while simultaneously expressing support for the actions of abolitionists who were persuaded in conscience that violence was not sinful. Garrison had applied an earlier version of that standard in his reaction to Nat Turner's rebellion. While he would personally refuse to use the carnal tools of violence, Garrison asserted that anyone who admired the rebels of 1776 had no grounds to "deny the right of the slaves to imitate the example of our fathers."[265] But John Brown was no Nat Turner. Brown was not a slave who was organizing for violent self-defense against his own oppressors. For a brief time following the Harpers Ferry raid, that distinction was very important as "Some abolitionists, Garrison included, hurried to separate their beliefs in the slave's inherent right to rebel from their genuine abhorrence of Brown's terrorism."[266] But that fine distinction did not hold beyond a few days. Incoherence crept in as Garrison described Brown's raid as "wild, misguided, and apparently insane . . . though disinterested and well-intended." To an abolitionist gathering in Worcester, Garrison urged that "no apologies" be made for Brown's raid since it too shared in the spirit of slave insurrections and the 1776 rebellion, but just a few days later, Garrison wrote in *The Liberator,* "We do not and cannot approve any indulgence of the war spirit." At a speech on the occasion of Brown's execution, Garrison urged "Success to every slave insurrection . . ." and he celebrated the fact that those who believed in the use of carnal weapons had decided to take those weapons out of "the scale of despotism, and throw them in the scale of freedom."[267] Garrison was not alone in the waffling. The abolitionist George Cheever wrote that the Harpers Ferry raid had convinced him that "The storm of God's wrath was thickening over us. Already the big drops began to fall." William Goodell wrote that, while he was personally opposed to all use of violence, Harpers Ferry had indicated that violence was "the providential remedy: the permitted remedy, the retributive remedy, when the divine warnings are unheeded."[268] As the stage was set for the Civil War, it was also set for the collapse of non-resistance. The way was cleared for pacifists and anarchists to endorse a government at war.

The collapse of non-resistance was in part due to a particular view of millennialism and of the terror of God. Abolitionists and non-resistants specifically could claim that their support was not for the Union Army but for the efficacy of God's wrath. When Garrison was asked to choose biblical texts for a worship service on the Sunday after Fort Sumter was attacked, he chose assorted texts from Jeremiah 50 and 51, texts that tell of God assembling a mighty force from the north to smite a sinful Babylon.[269] To this, Garrison added Jere-

miah 34:17: "Therefore, thus says the LORD: You have not obeyed me by granting a release to your neighbors and friends; I am going to grant a release to you,
says the LORD — a release to the sword, to pestilence, and to famine." It was the
millennial view of the North as an instrument for God's use in the chastisement
of sin that led Julia Ward Howe to pen the words for "The Battle Hymn of the
Republic" and set it to the tune of "John Brown's Body." Howe drew heavily
from the apocalyptic imagery of Revelation, including the text of 14:19-20: "So
the angel swung his sickle over the earth and gathered the vintage of the earth,
and he threw it into the great wine press of the wrath of God. And the wine
press was trodden outside the city, and the blood flowed from the wine press, as
high as a horse's bridle, for a distance of about two hundred miles." But it is
noteworthy that Howe was not particularly enamored of apocalypticism herself. She was a friend of Ralph Waldo Emerson, who had once said to a Miller-
ite, "The end of the world does not affect me; I can live without it." Howe's personal lack of apocalyptic conviction made her use of the imagery all the more
revealing. She was giving voice to the millennial fervor that was prevalent in the
culture at large.[270]

Also giving voice to the millennial fervor was President Lincoln. While history has generally treated him kindly as a "martyr" and as "the great emanci-
pator," some historians offer reminders that Lincoln's support for abolition
and equality was late and circumscribed. In his debates with Stephen Douglas,
Lincoln had announced his opposition to political and social equality for
black people. Prior to his presidency, he had supported most of the legislative
compromises that had left slavery intact. Even when the President finally issued his Emancipation Proclamation, it seemed to be motivated more by military strategy than by convictions about freedom; indeed, slaves held in areas
controlled by the North were specifically excluded from emancipation. Still,
Lincoln was too complex an individual to be reduced to a mere political or
military opportunist. History allows us to see flashes of his insight and of his
anguish. One cannot help but admire the humility and subtle irony of his reference to Americans as the "almost chosen people," a phrase we can scarcely
imagine on the lips of Puritan ancestors or in the pandering speeches of modern politicos. We catch glimpses of Lincoln's resistance to taking delight in
bloodshed; in commuting a death sentence, he wrote that he did so not because of any merits in the defendant's case "but because I am trying to evade
the butchering business lately." Garry Wills asserts that this refusal to delight
in butchery typified Lincoln's approach to the Civil War: "There is nothing
more astonishing in the history of war than this attempt to wage it without being partisan, to forgive while killing, and to ask forgiveness from those one
kills."[271] But in fact, there is nothing astonishing about that at all. With greater

or lesser sincerity, it is the norm of the history of war. It is precisely the pretense that it is possible "to forgive while killing" that has spurred the actions of crusaders ancient and modern. The image of an anguishing Lincoln is the one best loved by modern leaders when they are in the midst of deciding that the time for bloodshed has arrived.

Lincoln's appeal to the millennial fervor at loose in the land was most in evidence in his Second Inaugural Address. For all its rhetorical eloquence, it is a statement that virtually equates the will of God with whatever happens in history — slavery as well as the end of slavery, war as well as the end of war. While it is certainly true that Lincoln was more the subject than the director of the forces that swirled around him, there was something too clever in Lincoln's attributing to God the decision of whether the war would continue or not; as commander-in-chief, Lincoln had already decided that the war would only end in unconditional surrender. Also note the manner in which Lincoln deploys the image of the retribution of God, balancing bloodied lash with bloodied sword.

> The Almighty has His own purposes. "Woe unto the world because of offenses! for it must needs be that offenses come; but woe to that man by whom the offense cometh!" If we shall suppose that American Slavery is one of those offenses which, in the providence of God, must needs come, but which, having continued through His appointed time, He now wills to remove, and He gives to both North and South this terrible war, as the woe due to those by whom the offense came, shall we discern therein any departure from those divine attributes which the believers in a Living God always ascribe to Him? Fondly do we hope — fervently do we pray — that this mighty scourge of war may speedily pass away. Yet, if God wills that it continue, until all the wealth piled by the bondman's two hundred and fifty years of unrequited toil shall be sunk, and until every drop of blood drawn with the lash, shall be paid by another drawn with the sword, as was said three thousand years ago, so still it must be said "the judgments of the Lord are true and righteous altogether."[272]

Throughout the cataclysm, some few non-resistants remained faithful to both abolitionism and pacifism. Among them was the poet John Greenleaf Whittier, who viewed John Brown's raid, not as an insurrection of freedom, but as a "severe test" for "our non-resistance principles."[273] Adin Ballou, founder of the Hopedale Community, consistently asserted that slavery should be opposed, not because it might provoke future terror or violence from either God or warring states, but because slavery *is* terror and violence. Therefore, Ballou declared, to encourage violence in any form was to encourage the very spirit on which slavery feeds.[274] Throughout the war, the labor organizer Ezra H. Heywood remained an ardent advocate of abolitionism, anarchism, and pacifism.[275] Alfred H. Love, head of a Philadelphia clothing firm, refused to produce uniforms for the army, and, despite Garrison's advice to do so, he refused to pay the commutation fee when he was drafted since it would have given the state "the means with which to buy flesh and blood to take my place." Love would have been jailed had the draft board not found him ineligible for the military due to poor eyesight, a finding that he did not urge. After the Civil War, Love remained active in peace organizations.[276] Many members of the Church of the Brethren and the Mennonites remained true to their traditional peace position. The Church of the Brethren pastor, John Kline, was murdered in 1864 after he had spent years riding back and forth across battle lines to visit imprisoned pacifists and to encourage fidelity to the peace position among believers in both North and South.[277] Some feminists retained their commitment to nonviolence, and they creatively utilized methods of active non-resistance in the post-bellum struggle for women's rights.[278]

But Garrison surrendered to the spirit of war, even while his perfectionism led him to argue that the inconsistent was consistent: "Although Non-resistance holds human life in all cases absolutely inviolable by professed Non-resistants yet it is perfectly consistent for them to petition, advise, and strenuously urge a pro-war government to abolish slavery by the war power."[279] Some abolitionists had less difficulty in declaring forthrightly that it was God who waged the Civil War. In 1863, in a sermon preached as the war raged, the Rev. Gilbert Haven of Boston declared, "He is pushing us forward to His, not our, Millennium. He is using and blessing us if we choose to work with Him. If not, He is none the less using us, while also chastising, for the advancement of mankind to the same goal."[280] For some, the war that was raging was nothing less than the battle of the end time. "The great battle of Gog and Magog," declared the Rev. Rolla Chubb, "is being fought on the gory field of Armageddon, which is the American Republic. . . ."[281] For those of postmillennialist persuasion, the war was serving a salvific purpose in getting humanity back on track in progress towards the Millennium. To his book of Civil War poetry, Herman Melville appended a prayer that the "terror" through which the country was passing might serve to kindle "Progress and Humanity."[282] In either perspective, for premillennialists and postmillennialists alike, the Civil War was the terror of God and the terror of God was serving salvific purposes. The Rev. George Ide declared, "The cause of our country and the cause of religion, the cause of humanity, the cause of eternal Right and Justice, are so intimately blended in this crisis, that you cannot separate them. The triumph of the Government will be . . . the triumph of pure Gospel."[283]

In 1864, the pacifist "no-government man," William Lloyd Garrison, cast an election ballot for the first and only time in his life. He voted for Lincoln.

*   *   *

Sometimes we argue most with those whom we admire. I stand in admiration of the early witness of Frederick Douglass and William Lloyd Garrison. As abolitionists and pacifists and anarchists (though they did not use that name), they and a handful of others constituted for a time a faithful minority within a minority. But while they started out with a keen desire to avoid the compromises that most people make routinely, they ended up by making a major sacrifice of the spirit of nonviolence when they believed that abolitionism required it. The Civil War was never simply about slavery (or states' rights or economics or any other single issue), but Garrison and most other Americans came to believe that it was precisely that simple — either a continuation of slavery or a marching off to war. In the name of abolition, Garrison declared that it was "time to keep silent" on non-resistance.[284] It was what Staughton Lynd called "the most striking failure of nonviolence in American history to date."[285]

In retrospect, it can be observed that there were at least four factors at work in the collapse of pacific abolitionism:

1. The emphasis on individualism. In accentuating the moral accountability that the individual owed to God alone, the non-resistance movement opened what Lewis Perry called a "bewildering void between self-sovereignty and divine sovereignty."[286] Adin Ballou sought to fill the vastness of that void with a sense of Christian community (e.g., Hopedale), which is perhaps one of the reasons he retained his pacifism while all about were losing theirs. Individual conscience and actions do not occur in a vacuum devoid of corporate responsibility and consequences. In pretending that they could remain "non-resistants" while encouraging others to engage in abolitionist violence, the non-resistants were being insufficiently evangelical about their own faith.

2. The view of nonviolence as a pragmatic tool. Indeed, nonviolence was not only viewed as effective but also as safe and relatively painless. Ideas about tax resistance and other forms of civil disobedience were current among abolitionists, but such a path was viewed as crossing the line to "resistant" rather than "non-resistant" activism. Such a path would have also contradicted the notion that nonviolence is painless. And so, slave auctions were rarely disrupted and the jails were not filled in response to the Fugitive Slave Act. The understanding of nonviolence was so circumscribed by "non-resistance" and "safety" that, when all of the petitions and speeches and meetings of the abolitionists proved inadequate, they were less prepared to engage in nonviolent resistance

than to endorse the violent resistance of others. Those who emphasize the efficacious manner in which nonviolence "works" are likely to be discouraged when they encounter instances in which nonviolence "fails" by pragmatic standards — instances in which violence is deemed "necessary." One senses such discouragement in the waffling of Garrison and others. Instead, they could have been encouraged with an awareness that the biblical calls to turn the other cheek and to love enemies are calls to discipleship, not calls to effectiveness. In the pursuit of social or personal goals, nonviolence may be more or less effective than violence. Evidence that nonviolence is not always safe and that it does not always "work" is provided by the cross. Love and peace are not pragmatic tools; they are manifestations of the reign of God.

3. The emphasis on perfectionism. As with the emphasis on individualism, a major problem with perfectionism in the non-resistance movement was the pretense that one could maintain personal purity while encouraging others to engage in all manner of sin. But in a larger sense, why was it even deemed necessary to conjoin a commitment to nonviolence with notions about works righteousness and human perfectability? Pacifism may as easily (and more accurately) be conjoined with confessions of the *lack* of personal righteousness. Such a formulation would read something like this: I am aware of my own fallibility to the point that I am unwilling to take the life of another person, even if I hold the (possibly mistaken) belief that the goals which he or she is pursuing are less righteous than my own. I can still engage in a rich variety of legal or illegal activism in pursuit of my goal or in defense of a cause, but it is my own fallibility (rather than perfection) and my own sinfulness (rather than righteousness) that prohibit the finality of taking another life. Nonviolence need not (and should not) be based on any notions of works righteousness or perfectionism. It is the path onto which a faithful Christ calls his bumbling, fallible, and unfaithful disciples.

4. The identification of the terror of God with human violence. The model of God as presented by many non-resistants was incoherent and served to reinforce a view of war as both inevitable and justified: Jesus is non-resistant, but God is not; slavery is an offense against God, but due to divine patience, it is temporarily countenanced; violent insurrections and raids are "warnings" from God; and finally, while personally choosing to follow the Prince of Peace, the "non-resistant" supports the war as a blood-soaked intervention by an angry God. The few abolitionists who continued to espouse nonviolence recognized the human propensity to proclaim each and every act of violence as "the one exception" to the nonviolent rule. There is a corresponding human propensity to discern in each and every war the exceptional instance of divine intervention in history. There is no mystical insight at work in such discernment. One need only proclaim, as Urban II told the crusaders, "God wills it."

I do not know how Douglass responded to the question from Sojourner Truth, "Frederick, is God dead?" Any number of responses are possible. One could respond, as some did, that God lives and that the battlefields soon to be littered with corpses would provide evidence of the terror of the living God.

One could also respond that, without God, there is no limit to the ways in which human beings enslave and terrorize one another. Rather than being all-powerful and all-terrifying, God is the end of human power and terror. God lives. The evidence is in the living black women and men who made their way underground to freedom. The evidence is in the night that Garrison's neck escaped the noose. And above all, the evidence is in the bloody murder of Jesus denounced by resurrection. He lives.

The Terror of God in the Apocalypse

There is general agreement that the author of the book of Revelation was a criminal. Of course, criminality was not such a rare commodity in the Roman Empire. As laws proliferate, so do outlaws. When fears abound that things are falling apart, penology and punitive impulses are enlisted to hold things together. In Machiavellian parlance, if they cannot love the Empire, at least make sure they fear it. It was an awareness of penology as a tool for instilling fear in citizens that led Joseph Conrad to write in *The Secret Agent,* "The terrorist and the policeman both come from the same basket." If Conrad's remark seems unkind to policemen, it is nonetheless insightful on the "basket," i.e., on the sameness with which juridical systems and terrorists presume that fears can be generated and harnessed to good effect. It is a strand that runs through history, not so? Like furry creatures chasing but never quite catching their own tails, empires repeatedly return to the same vain hope that more laws and harsher penalties will lead to the fear of lawbreaking, which will lead to more order and security, which will lead to peace and harmony. Prisons bulge and executioners buzz. When in America, do as the Romans did. The Romans were in the business of pursuing peace through punishment. It was for punishment that John was sent to Patmos.

But if John was not well loved by the Roman Empire, John's writing indicates that the feeling was mutual. Moreover, his writing indicates that his punishment did not have the intended effect of instilling fear. While John writes with encouragement for those who "fear God" and the "name" of God (Revelation 11:18; 14:7; 15:4; 19:5), he writes nothing to encourage fear of Empire. In fact, John unleashes and unveils a withering portrait of Empire that is nothing short of subversive. It may have been a prior expression of such subversive visions that led to John's banishment on Patmos. The possibility casts a new light on the terror that the powerful seek to wield. The powerful seek to evoke fear of punishment in John and others of like spirit because, if truth be told, the powerful are afraid of John and the vision he brings. Terror is sometimes born of repressed fear and pain. In *King Lear,* Shakespeare points to this potential source of terror. In the face of a growing sense of betrayal by his daughters, the King vows that he would prefer to wreak havoc on the earth than to weep.

> And let not women's weapons, water-drops,
> Stain my man's cheeks! — No, you unnatural hags,
> I will have such revenges on you both,
> That all the world shall — I will do such things, —
> What they are, yet I know not; but they shall be
> The terrors of the earth. You think I'll weep;
> No, I'll not weep. . . .
>
> *(King Lear,* Act 2, Scene 4)

If you think that the king is weak or in pain, he will show you pain. If you think that the king is terrified, he will show you and the rest of the world what terror really is. The powerful were afraid of John because he had lifted up the veil named "the glory of Rome" and he had told of the horrendous things he had seen behind it. That was the crime for which he had to pay. You must never look too closely at the making of sausages or empires. You will be repulsed. John puts our face in it.

While there is general agreement that John had been sent to Patmos as punishment, there is some dispute on the nature of the legal sanction that he suffered. Earlier generations of scholars assumed that Patmos was a harsh penal colony with mines in which prisoners were forced to labor, but more recent scholars have speculated that Patmos may have simply been a site of banishment with no additional sufferings imposed beyond exile.[287] For the imposition of punishments in Roman jurisprudence, the nature of the crime was of lesser import than the status of the accused. Banishment was the preferred punishment for those who had some claim to social standing, whether due to citizenship or wealth or connections to some well-placed patron. Execution was ordinarily reserved for those of lesser status, with crucifixion being the favored mode of execution for slaves and others of low esteem. His presence on Patmos suggests that, like Paul, John was not totally bereft of legal standing or social status.[288] If John was entitled to some measure of privilege under the imperial system, it adds poignancy to his relentless unveiling of Rome. John was biting the hand of the Beast that was claiming to feed him, and the Beast was biting back.

If there is debate about the punishments John endured, there is no doubt about the torments that have been inflicted for centuries on his book. As we have seen, Revelation has served for some as a call to arms against demonic enemies. Is the Beast there in the papacy, or in the monarchy, or in the pitchfork-wielding peasants who threaten to undo all civilizing powers? Some have read it as a guidebook on how the world will end, and others as a manual on how to end the world. From Müntzer to Asahara, Revelation has been read as a literal call to arms, as an invitation to participate in the fury and terror of God. The book has been tormented. At the risk of adding to the torment, our investigation of terror leads us to the Revelation of John, not in the hope of offering detailed exegesis, but in an effort to discover the extent to which this book merits its reputation as a definitive depiction of an angry God who is on the verge of destroying the world, and who might invite us to join in the destruction.

It must immediately be noted that, although Revelation has acquired the reputation of being a book of considerable blood and terror, the reputation may not be so well deserved. Eugen Weber, who bothered to do the counting, reckons that "Ninety-eight verses (of over four hundred) in the Apocalypse of John speak of catastrophe, and 150 refer to joy, consolation, brightness, and hope. That Christian culture retained the former perspective and placed its hopes in terror, not in joy, should tell us something about human nature — or human experience."[289] The back of God's hand and the devastation of the planet somehow seem more credible than a consoling God who promises a new earth. Garry Wills also notes that "the plausibility of the supernatural is retained longer by hellish than by heavenly images."[290] Why is that? Is it because we are so keenly aware of the human proclivity for terror that we judge that it is terror we deserve? Thankfully, Revelation does not vest such human judgments with ultimacy. It is God who is Judge, and when we meet "fear" *(phobeo)* in Revelation, it is in the call to "fear the name" of God or in the words of consolation, "Do not be afraid" (1:17; 2:10). Revelation is more a book about terror defeated rather than terror inflicted, which is why worship and liturgy are such a central feature of the book. As Walter Wink observes, Revelation presents some surrealistic and unnerving scenes.

> But it contains not a single note of despair. Powerful as the Dragon of the abyss may appear, he has been stripped of real heavenly power. Those still in the clutches of the Enemy may not yet experience it, but the decisive battle has already been won. . . . This is the rock on which we stand: the absolute certainty of the triumph of God in the world.
>
> That is why the celebration of the divine victory does not take place at the end of the Book of Revelation, after the struggle is over. Rather, it

breaks out all along the way (1:4-8, 17-18; 4:8-11; 5:5, 9-14; 7:1-17; 11:15-19; 12:10-12; 14:1-8; 15:2-4; 16:5-7; 18; 19:1-9). We have here no sober pilgrims grimly ascending the mount of tears, but singers *enjoying* the struggle because it confirms their freedom. Even in the midst of conflict, suffering, or imprisonment, suddenly a hymn pierces the gloom, the heavenly hosts thunder in a mighty chorus, and our hearts grow lighter.[291]

Until recently, the dominant view among biblical scholars was that John wrote during a period of intense persecution, and that the "extreme" perspective of Revelation (in contrast to the "moderate" Paul, these scholars asserted) was a response to the reign of terror to which the Jewish Christian sect was being subjected. There is a growing consensus, however, that the persecutions under Domitian (81-96 C.E.) were no more severe than those under most Roman emperors, and that in comparison to a Nero, Domitian might have even passed for tolerant.[292] Rather than being a time of hot persecution, it was a time when the Empire experienced relative calm, when wealth abounded, when the terror of the powerful seemed like no terror — in short, a time like ours. And so, John depicted the Empire not only as a "Beast" with fangs bared in preparation for violence, but also as a "Whore" who seduced victims onto the path of imperial Rome with no need for violent persecutions. Her seductions were so successful that she had accumulated great wealth (Rev. 17), and this in turn added to her allure.[293] In addressing his message to "the angels" of seven faith communities, John encouraged them to resist the seductions of Empire with "patient endurance" (2:2; 2:19; 3:10). Do not abandon the love of God (2:4) for the love of the one who seduces.[294] Do not abandon wealth in spirit and life for mere material riches (2:9). John understood material wealth as a major component of the seductive "glory of Rome." In fact, the wealth of Rome was dependent upon the impoverishment of distant provinces. As many as six thousand ships arrived annually at ports near Rome bearing grain from Africa and Asia Minor where local populations went hungry.[295] Participation in the economic life of the Empire necessitated involvement with the state-sanctioned religions and imperial cults. The temple of Saturn in Rome served as headquarters of the state treasury, and the temple of Artemis in Ephesus served a similar function for the province of Asia. Local temples served as banks, holding mortgages and lending money at interest.[296] John revealed that seductive wealth ultimately led to the commodification of human life itself, with "human lives" among the cargoes bought and sold by Empire (Rev. 18:11-13).[297] John warned the congregation at Laodicea that they had been seduced by wealth: "For you say, 'I am rich, I have prospered, and I need nothing.' You do not realize that you are wretched, pitiable, poor, blind, and naked" (3:17). If believers could not withstand the se-

206

ductions of the Whore, how could they withstand the persecutions of the Beast? Thus, John's vision had as much to say about the nature of contemporary faith communities as it did about the culmination of history. As Wayne Meeks observes,

> What is more distinctive about the eschatology of the early Christians, as of other apocalyptic groups, is that expectation of a final judgment is at the same time expectation of the final definition and vindication of the community. When initiates into the Christian group are taught that those who do x, y, and z 'will not inherit the kingdom of God,' they are not merely being warned that if they revert to such vices they will someday be punished. They are being told something about the community to which they are now joined, something about the character of the people over whom God reigns in the new age.[298]

John was telling the faithful that their communities must never be defined by the wealth, power, and terror of Rome.

From the very first verse of his text, John describes his writing as a "revelation" *(apokalypsis)* of Jesus Christ which God had made known to him through an angel. It is the only use of the word "revelation" in the entire book, and the opening verses allow for several possibilities of who or what it is that is being revealed. Is this an unveiling of "Jesus Christ" or of "what must take place" (1:1) or of "the word of God" (1:2) or of all of these and more? Without using the precise word, "unveilings" aplenty take place in John's visions of the scroll sealed with seven seals (5:1), the seven bowls of God's wrath (16:1), and even the new heaven and new earth (21:1). But when we ask the book of Revelation to tell us who or what is "hiding" *(krypto)*, we are led to Revelation 6:15-17:

> Then the kings of the earth and the magnates and the generals and the rich and the powerful, and everyone, slave and free, hid in the caves and among the rocks of the mountains, calling to the mountains and rocks, "Fall on us and hide us from the face of the one seated on the throne and from the wrath of the Lamb; for the great day of their wrath has come, and who is able to stand?"

The book of Revelation unveils the hiding places of the powerful and of the rest of humanity as well. This is a book in which *we* are subjected to revelation — we humans who, despite our pretense to mighty enterprises, cannot stand the light of day, the light of God.

Who is it who is more veiled and elusive, more secretive and hidden — God or humanity? The revelations of God have been persistent, gracious, and transparent to the point of incarnation. People have the greater proclivity for hiding, the greater need for revelation. As with *apokalypsis,* the Greek word for truth, *aletheia,* begins with the negative particle suggesting that there is something that had previously been elusive that is now being uncovered.[299] "Truth" is the end of hiddenness. Much of Western pedagogy has been geared to the assumption that it is "truth" itself which is in hiding. In a too-facile association of "truth" with "facts," the student is taught to adopt an "objective" stance in relationship to the world. Elusive "truth" will be uncovered if the world is examined from an impersonal distance, if it is prodded and dissected.[300] In sharp contrast, the author of the Gospel of John (apparently unrelated to John of Patmos) depicts the truth as highly personal. In John 14, Jesus does not claim to *tell* the truth but to *be* the truth. Jesus tells the disciples that they already know the way, but when (doubting) Thomas questions how that could be, Jesus responds, "I am the way, and the truth, and the life" (John 14:4-6). Pilate notwithstanding (John 18:38), the truth is not elusive. We are the ones who are elusive of the truth who searches us out. In the light of Jesus, it is not God who stands in need of revelation or unveiling. The curtain that served to hide the Holy of Holies (Exodus 26:31-35) has been torn open (Luke 23:45; Mark 15:38; Matthew 27:51) and the way is clear to approach God with confidence and hope (Hebrews 10:19-25). The ways of humanity are more veiled and not nearly so hopeful. The curtain behind which humanity hides goes by many names — history, civilization, empire, superpower, enlightenment, progress, free enterprise. John of Patmos pulls aside the curtain on all of these.

Flannery O'Connor once wrote, "You shall know the truth and the truth shall make you odd."[301] Perhaps being "odd" is part of what it means to be "free" (John 8:32) in an age of uniformity and objectivity. Many count the book of Revelation as very odd indeed. If it is an odd book, it is because John of Patmos was passionate about his vision without the slightest hint of interest in objectivity. If it is an odd book, it is because John's vision was clearly at odds with the dominant visions of his day. Even if it was not a time of intense persecution, John's writing shares with other apocalyptic writings the quality of being "underground literature"[302] insofar as it saw underneath the calm exterior of things and took a stand alongside those who were being crushed under the glory of civilization. But whatever oddness there is in the book of Revelation, it is not attributable to some supposed cryptic code. While John utilized myths and symbols with which most modern readers are unfamiliar, it is unfair to charge him with cryptic intent. Revelation is not a Gnostic writing, and John was not offering a privatized, secret knowledge.[303] Nor was he writing in code so as to avoid additional legal prosecution from Rome; on the contrary, Revelation is dangerously transparent at any number of points, including its association of the kings with the seven hills of Rome on which the Whore is seated (17:9). What may at first appear to be obscurantism in the book of Revelation is not due to cryptic intent but to the visionary quality of John's perceptions. He is not only writing but also *seeing* in apocalyptic mode — *seeing* underneath, behind, and beyond the surface of things. In "A Vision of the Last Judgment," William Blake provided an illustration of this altered, visionary perception:

> "What," it will be Questioned, "When the sun rises, do you not see a round disk of fire somewhat like a Guinea?" "O no, no, I see an Innumerable company of Heavenly host crying, 'Holy, Holy, Holy is the Lord God Almighty.'"[304]

But John's visionary perceptions were not hallucinatory or free-floating. The visions of the book of Revelation were guided by and grounded in two primary commitments, neither of which implied a contradiction of the other: (1) John was a *Jewish* apocalyptic writer whose modes of perception and style of expression were shaped by the evolving tradition of *Jewish* apocalypticism and prophetic eschatology, and (2) John was thoroughly *christocentric* in a place and time when such implied no inherent critique or refutation of Judaism.

1. As much as any other text in the New Testament, Revelation draws upon and is grounded in the symbols, worldview, and narratives of the Hebrew Bible.[305] Although Revelation is liberally strewn with quotations from and allusions to texts ranging from Genesis through the prophets, attention is naturally drawn to the manner in which John employs the apocalyptic writings of Daniel. The scroll that is unsealed in Revelation draws directly from the account of the scroll that remains sealed in Daniel 12:4. Both John and Daniel use the archetype "Babylon" to identify oppressive powers — Rome in the case of Revelation and, almost three hundred years earlier, the Seleucid rule of Antiochus IV Epiphanes in the case of Daniel. It was the reign of Antiochus that sparked the violent resistance of the Maccabees, but many scholars have come to believe that the apocalyptic writings of Daniel did not arise from within the ranks of Maccabean revolutionaries but were instead composed from within the circle known as the Hasidim (the "Pious" or the "Just"). The Hasidim constituted a movement that, like the Maccabeans, was fully opposed to the tyrannical rule and Hellenistic culture of Antiochus, but the Hasidim were unwilling to sacrifice any of the precepts of their faith or the principles of their laws to the exigencies of revolution.[306] Daniel's accounts of the faithful enduring and surviving fiery furnaces and lions (Daniel 3 and 6) amounted to what Norman Cohn described as a call to "nonviolent resistance; by standing firm under persecu-

tion they will have undergone an inner refinement and purification. . . ."[307] But what about those who do not survive the fire of persecution? God's cause will still be vindicated, perhaps even by means of the resurrection of the dead (Daniel 12:2).[308] The oppression will come to an end, but not by means of Maccabean revolutionaries or military strength or foreign alliances. In Daniel 8:23-25, the prophet has a vision of an oppressive ruler who is "skilled in intrigue" and "strong in power," a ruler who "shall cause fearful destruction" and "shall make deceit prosper," but this ruler too "shall be broken, and not by human hands." Daniel's vision of remaining steadfast in the midst of oppression was fully in accord with the Hebrew Bible's portrayal of God as the one who remains faithful through times of persecution as well as peace, through times of disaster as well as assurance. For other nations, disaster meant that the god(s) had failed and that the rulers and the people had been deprived of their heavenly foundation. It was a literal "dis-aster," the fall of a heavenly power, and the old god would have to be traded for another. Terror had come upon the nation because the old god had proven to be less terrifying and powerful than other gods.[309] But the Hebrew Bible presents a demythologizing of terror and disaster. God remains faithful even as the people suffer the terror that has come (more often than not) as the result of the course that the nation itself has pursued. And when the blameless suffer (as they always do), God is still faithful in ways that are totally surprising to those who expect their only help to come from "human hands" and human arms. The faith of Daniel and of the other Hebrew prophets is also the faith of John of Patmos.

2. As with other New Testament authors, John of Patmos entered into disputation with other parties within Judaism (Rev. 2:9; 3:9), but it was in a time and place in which such disputes, though vociferous, were understood to be disagreements internal to a single faith community. Without making any claim to negating the prophetic vision of Judaism, the book of Revelation is thoroughly christocentric. Like Paul, the author of Revelation refers to Jesus of Nazareth in "shorthand," focusing attention on his death and resurrection.[310] The "slaughtered Lamb," John's favored image for Jesus, is fully grounded in the pivotal story of the Hebrew people. The slaughtered Lamb who is worthy (Rev. 5:9-10) is the Paschal Lamb whose blood compelled the destroyer to pass over as the slaves set out upon their exodus to freedom (Exodus 12:21-33).[311] But part of what makes Revelation seem so mysterious and fantastic is the extravagant liberty with which John deploys his images and metaphors. And so, the Lamb is also the shepherd (Rev. 7:17). And the powerful Lion of Judah (Genesis 49:9-10; 1 Maccabees 3:4), the symbol of royalty, is identified as Christ, the slaughtered Lamb (Rev. 5:5). It is a bold and intentional mixing of metaphors in which the Lion and the Lamb not only lie down together (Isaiah 11:6-9), but they become

one another. The royal strength of the Lion of Judah is derived not from its ability to slaughter but from its identity as the slaughtered Lamb. Similarly, John reinterprets those Psalms that have been understood traditionally as hymns to the victory of the divine warrior (e.g., Psalms 96, 97, 98) into a "new song" for the Lamb (Rev. 14:1-7).[312] And in what might be called an ultimate coupling of metaphors, John associates references to God and the Lamb (7:10; 14:4; 21:22) and is finally able to refer to "the throne of God and of the Lamb" (22:1, 3).[313]

The freedom with which John deploys and mixes metaphors prepares the reader of Revelation for the unexpected ways in which John appropriates the images of combat, wrath, and violence. G. B. Caird notes that "John . . . is fond of a resonant title for God, 'the Omnipotent,' which he uses nine times. But he repeatedly makes it clear that in using it he is recasting the concept of omnipotence, which he understands not as unlimited coercion but as unlimited persuasion."[314] And so when "war" is introduced in Revelation 12:7, it is not fought on earth with human armies arrayed against one another; it is a war in heaven in which the defeated forces of Satan the dragon are unmasked, cast down to earth, deprived of all pretense to holiness (12:8-9). If such heavenly warfare has its mirror image on the earth, it is significant that the forces of Satan are not defeated by the terror of violence and armaments but by "the blood of the slaughtered Lamb" and by the testimony of the martyrs who "did not cling to life even in the face of death" (12:11). Bloodshed is the means by which mighty empires and terrorists of all stripes seek to claim their victories, but Revelation unveils that it is precisely their own shedding of blood that is the means by which the powers are defeated. The shed blood of the Lamb and of the martyrs becomes the instrument of God's victory. Terrorists great and small believe that every drop of blood that is shed brings them closer to victory. The exact opposite is true. Every drop of blood that is shed confirms their ultimate defeat, confirms that their fate is already sealed.

How is it that the blood of Babylon's victims becomes the means by which Babylon falls? Typically, Revelation does not answer that question with logical analysis but with visionary images — specifically, with the gory image of the wine press which was hijacked into the service of "The Battle Hymn of the Republic." Although "the wine press of the wrath of God" (14:19-20) is often misunderstood as being an instrument for crushing the victims of some supposed slaughter by God, the text itself makes clear that such is not the case. The scene of the harvest that is thrown into the wine press is introduced with encouragement for endurance (14:12) and with a voice that proclaims from heaven, "Blessed are the dead who from now on die in the Lord" (14:13). While the pronouncement that harvest time is near can clearly serve as a warning of pending judgment (Jeremiah 51:33; Joel 3:9-14), John's terms for "harvest" (the noun

211

therismos and the verb *therizo*) are consistently used in the Septuagint and in the New Testament to refer to the ingathering of the faithful to the kingdom of God (e.g., Matthew 9:37; Mark 4:29; Luke 10:2; John 4:35-38).[315] When "the vintage of the earth" had been gathered (Rev. 14:19), "the wine press was trodden outside the city" (14:20). The locale is not without significance. It was "outside the city" that Jesus was crucified, and by association, his faithful disciples who are martyred also suffer there (Hebrews 13:12-13). And so, John of Patmos is depicting "the great wine press of the wrath of God" as gathering together, pressing down and transforming all of the violence, humiliation, injustice, and terror suffered by the Lamb and the other victims of Empire. What are the qualities and purposes of the copious "blood" that flows from the wine press? It depends. The manner in which the blood of the Lamb and of his martyrs is perceived and received depends upon whether one is celebrating the reign of God or the reign of Empire. Those who proclaim that "power and might" belong to God alone (Rev. 7:12) may wash their robes in the purifying blood of the Lamb (7:14). This is a remarkable inversion of the holy war tradition, which held that all whose bodies or garments are contaminated by the blood of victims (Isaiah 63:1-6) must undergo a process of ritual purification (Numbers 31:19-20). But in Revelation, the blood of the victim becomes the very medium of purification.[316] When Genesis 49:11 offers a vision of a time when Judah "washes his garments in wine and his robe in the blood of grapes," it is a promise of a time so fruitful that grapes will not have to be used sparingly. The blood of the Lamb and the blood of the martyrs will also be fruitful as it is put to use in the service of God's reign. No suffering for the love of God is ever forgotten, no sacrifice is ever without fruit.

But the blood of the victims becomes a very different matter for the Empire. Assumptions had abounded among the mighty and the wealthy that bloodshed would be the means by which the glory of Empire would be secured in perpetuity, but now instead, a "double draught" (Rev. 18:6) is prepared for the Empire as the blood of its own victims (16:6; 17:6) is mixed with the wrath of God. It is blood that is poured out of seven bowls (16:1) upon the Empire and upon all of the great cities of the nations (16:19). But when mixed with God's wrath, the blood of the victims does not purify; it produces the final intoxication that precedes and accompanies the fall of Babylon (17:2, 6; 18:3). Thus does Revelation unveil Empire. The glory, military might, and wealth of Empire are revealed as blood and death. As Jacques Ellul comments, "There is an auto-destruction of political forces at the interior of history. That which makes them live, that which gives them authority, that upon which they are based, is the very spirit that finally repudiates them. . . ."[317] Blood is the foundation, the sustenance, the glory, and the apotheosis of every superpower — and it is this same blood of the victims which the Empire had thought was gone forever that now comes back in mighty torrents to mark the fall of Babylon.

A violent image, yes, but it is essential to be clear about who is the perpetrator of violence. The book of Revelation offers an unflinching portrayal of God's wrath and judgment, but bloodshed is consistently attributed not to God, but to Babylon and the Beast and the dragon. The "sword" of God is not an instrument of bloodshed. In his vision of "one like the Son of Man" (Rev. 1:13), John observes that "from his mouth came a sharp, two-edged sword" (1:16).[318] The sword that comes from the mouth is the word of God (Hebrews 4:12), and it is the truth of God's word and the blood of the victims that are the sole weapons in the arsenal of the Lamb. John's references to the divine sword are persistently accompanied by qualifiers indicating that it is the sword of the mouth or the sword of truth (e.g., Rev. 1:16; 2:16; 19:15).[319] "The kings of the earth and their armies" (19:19) are "killed" (19:21) and defeated by the truth of God's word (19:11-13) rather than by carnal weapons, which is why they can appear again, deprived of earthly power and transformed in the light of New Jerusalem (21:24).[320] The gory scene of the flesh of the kings and their armies being consumed by birds (19:21) is John's incorporation of Ezekiel's vision of all earthly might and military power being consumed after the defeat of Gog and Magog (Ezekiel 39:9, 17-20). When the Hebrew prophets announced that the terror sown would soon be reaped, the judgment they announced was always accompanied by mourning for those who had already suffered and for the suffering still to come. But in Revelation, the faithful do not mourn (19:1-6) because the vision John sees is not that of a carnal battle or of terror soon to be reaped. John's is a vision of nothing less than the end of terror and of the vindication of all who have suffered it. And just in case we have missed the point that God is not calling the faithful to violence and bloodshed, John hits us over the head with it by drawing our attention to one of the heads of the Beast: "One of its heads seemed to have received a death-blow, but its mortal wound had been healed. In amazement, the whole world followed the beast" (13:3). Mark this down, all you who have secreted away the semi-automatics in preparation for Armageddon. *Nota bene,* all terrorists who assume that the Great Satan can be put to flight by the next round of well-placed bombs. America, write it down and refer to it next time you get the blasphemous notion that God is on the side of your swords of nuclear or other vintage. Commit it to memory, all nations of the earth who hold the arrogant and vain conviction that terror will be ended with one last spurt of terror. *The Beast cannot be killed with violence.* The mortal wound is healed. Like Hydra, the Beast is strengthened by all violent assaults.

The mortal wound of the Beast that is healed is not a sign of resurrection, of death defeated. Indeed, it is what Daniel Berrigan calls an "anti-resurrection."

"Again and again he is patched up. He still lurches about the world. . . . But what the beast cannot promise or confer, on himself or others, is new life — rebirth — moral change. He is always the beast, always the same, reappearing armed with new slogans, new credentials, new plausibility."[321] Rather than a sign of new life, the mortal wound that is healed is a sign of alliance between Beast and Death, a cozy arrangement in which all death inflicted merely serves to strengthen both Beast and Death.

But *genuine* resurrection makes its appearance in the book of Revelation. If Daniel merely hinted at it, John not only affirms resurrection, but he revels in it and he bases the cogency of his entire vision upon it. Indeed, it is resurrection that John identifies as the terror of God. The resurrection is depicted as the terror of God arrayed against Beast and Empire in no fewer than three concrete examples, two of which are tied to specific visions within the text and the third of which is a theme pervading the entire book. (1) In Revelation 11:3-11, John has a vision of two witnesses sent by a voice from heaven, but the Beast "will make war on them and conquer them and kill them . . ." (11:7). "But after the three and a half days, the breath of life from God entered them, and they stood on their feet, and those who saw them were terrified" (11:11). Resurrection deprives Empire of its only power, the power of death. Resurrection poses the terrifying possibility that people will give glory to God rather than to the Beast (11:13). (2) Resurrection is the terror of God insofar as the "great and small" alike awaken to judgment (20:11-15). The judgment of God is an undoing of the pretense that the judgments of the Empire are the only valid judgments. How could the judgment of God appear as anything but terror when it is pronounced against all that we hold dear? Our wealth, our government, our religion, our (for lack of a better word) civilization. (3) Resurrection as the terror of God pervades the book of Revelation in the figure of the slaughtered Lamb. It is the slaughtered Lamb who conquers. It is this resurrection terror of God that marks the imminent demise of earthly terror.

John's Revelation has never been a comfortable text. Whenever Empire and Church cavort, it can be an embarrassing text. Early on, Constantinian theologians sought to replace the expectation of God's imminent reign with privatized warnings to individual sinners. Johann Metz notes, "The questions that concern the apocalyptic vision most deeply — to whom does the world belong? to whom do its sufferings and its time belong? — have, it would seem, been more effectively suppressed in theology than anywhere else."[322] Today, the text is abused by terrorists who peruse it for encouragement or by more "moderate" Christians who see it as an esoteric text about the end of the world. The world is still here. We are too busy to be bothered by such ramblings. We are too busy with our jobs and with matters of social and political importance (Revelation 18:11-24).

Revelation is not a book about the end of the world. Its ultimate vision is not one of destruction but one of re-creation in the new heaven and new earth. Nor is it only a book about the future. While it is certainly that ("How long?" the martyrs ask from beneath the altar in 6:9-11), it is also a vision that gives meaning to the past and demythologizes the present. John writes of the God "who is and who was and who is to come" (Revelation 1:8). Insofar as we allow John's vision to pervade our own time, we are met by the sobering reality that the whole world followed the Beast (13:3). And it is also sobering to reflect on the fact that, as Caird reminds, "the locust plague that issues from the abyss is said to have human faces (ix.6); for though evil may assume a thousand disguises, in the final analysis it has a human face."[323] Perhaps, but that is saying too little. For evil is not merely the work of individual human beings or the sum total work of all humans together but *more* than the sum total. It is the cumulative spirit that is reflected in and reflective of the independent beings known as principalities and powers. That is why Paul offers the reminder that the battle of the faithful is not against flesh and blood (2 Corinthians 10:1-4). It is also why, in apocalyptic literature, the judgment of God is pronounced above all against the *nations* and against the powers that represent them.[324] And as Revelation makes clear, the judgment is pronounced against *all* nations. All nations bear the mark of the Beast. It is only the idolizing of the nation itself that could lead Americans or any other people to believe that their nation is exempt in this regard.

But just as Revelation is not about the destruction of the world, neither does judgment have the final word. The final word is given to a vision on which we wait — the new heaven and the new earth. And since it is this on which we wait, our waiting is not marked by passivity. We are instead engaged in the biblical struggle. "In the Bible, there is really only one story: that of a people struggling to leave empire behind and set out to follow God."[325] And the Lamb waits too. In the new earth, the Lamb has come down from heaven and waits for us. This Second Advent is fully in accord with the First Advent.[326] Revelation offers no more sanction for terrorism than does the angel in Luke 2:10: "Do not be afraid; for see — I am bringing you good news of great joy for all the people. . . ."

*   *   *

It was in 1975 that I heard the two best sermons I have ever heard preached on the book of Revelation. The first was a commencement address delivered before a solemn assembly of students, clerics, and academics. The second was the mere recitation of a text delivered in a ramshackle soup kitchen in Washington, D.C.

As I was preparing to graduate from Bethany Theological Seminary in 1975,

I went to hear the commencement address at neighboring Northern Baptist Seminary in Oak Brook, Illinois. Those assembled in caps and gowns were about to embark on careers of service to the church and, like all graduates, they were determined to change the world. The commencement speaker was William Stringfellow and the text he chose was the description of the Beast in Revelation 13:7: "Also it was allowed to make war on the saints and to conquer them. It was given authority over every tribe and people and language and nation. . . ." The homily was a powerful invocation of the word of God, and it was also the antithesis of what commencement speakers are supposed to do. Commencement is a time to point to successes achieved and offer assurances of successes still to come. Stringfellow spoke of the defeat of the saints. Already frail of health, Stringfellow spoke in monotone, which only added power to his homily. His meditation on the defeat of the saints was a renunciation of all triumphalism, be it academic, ecclesiastical, economic, political, or military. It was a reminder that the saints are not raptured out of terror and into victory. It was a reminder that Easter is preceded by the cross, that God's cause is not served by the righteous who are triumphant but by the faithful who are defeated.[327]

And then there was the word of God in the soup kitchen. Over the past years, I count myself as fortunate to have been able to volunteer from time to time in free kitchens in several cities. I never did much — just chopped some potatoes and washed some dishes — but I got much in return. I got to meet people and I grew to learn that folks on the bottom of the social ladder can be as happy or as sad, as friendly or as obnoxious as folks at the top. When I graduated from seminary in 1975, I joined Church of the Brethren Volunteer Service and I was sent to Washington, D.C. to work with the free kitchen run by the Community for Creative Nonviolence. I got to meet Margaret there. Winter and summer, Margaret wore a big, heavy coat, and each morning when she came into the kitchen, she would reach inside the coat and pull out a meat cleaver and wave it in the air and call out, "Good morning, everybody. How are you-all doing this morning?" And then she would put the meat cleaver back inside her coat, sit down, and calmly have some food. It was Margaret's way of saying, "Don't you try to jump me in the back alley." But Margaret was never known to hurt a single soul. And then there was North Carolina. He lived in a big cardboard box about two blocks from the kitchen. He once found a harmonica in the trash somewhere and he used it to provide music for the kitchen. North Carolina was also the kitchen philosopher. He would sit back and talk about how every time he wanted to go uptown, the bus was headed downtown, but it didn't really matter because who had money for the bus anyhow and life is like that, isn't it?

Well, in December 1975, I did have money for the bus and I went to Chicago for a few days to visit with some friends. It was there that I received news that North Carolina had died. On a colder than usual Washington, D.C. night, he had been killed by hypothermia in his cardboard home. I returned to D.C. for the funeral and the mourning and the guilt that we all felt at the Community. The Community hospitality house for homeless people was already filled to overflowing. What could be done to prevent more deaths? Scott Wright, one of our Community members, suggested that we should go down to the kitchen and keep it open all night. There weren't any beds, but people could share some warmth and some coffee and maybe some space to rest their heads on the tables.

It was already night when Scott and I arrived at the kitchen. I remember being tired and grouchy from the bus trip and the emotional intensity of the funeral, so I just vegetated in a corner while Scott set up all the chairs and turned on the coffee. There were no lights in the front of the building, so Scott put some candles out on the sidewalk to let our friends know that the kitchen was open. Slowly, the ragtag group started coming in from the cold.

We missed North Carolina's harmonica, so Scott asked, "Does anyone want to sing anything or does anyone want to recite some poems or hear some readings?" Well, who should speak up but a no-good old wino named Cool Breeze. Cool Breeze was trouble every time you saw him. He was always obnoxious and he was always trying to sneak his bottle of cheap wine into the kitchen so he could just drink away and start trouble. So Cool Breeze speaks up, half drunk already, slurring his words he says, "Yah, I wanna hear somethin' from the Bible." Sitting over in my grouchy corner, I thought, "Right — as if that wino knows anything about the Bible." Scott explained that there weren't any Bibles at the kitchen. We kept the Bibles back at the house because we didn't want folks to feel like they had to buy our faith in order to get free food. "No problem," said Cool Breeze, and he pulled a Bible out of his coat and handed it to Scott. Turns out that the Bible had been given to Cool Breeze by the Gideons during one of his many trips to jail on public intoxication charges. "What do you want to hear?" asked Scott. And just like he knew what he was talking about, that old wino Cool Breeze said, "The Revelation to Saint John, chapter twenty-one, verses one through seven."

Scott read, and right from the very first word, Cool Breeze recited along: "Then I saw a new heaven and a new earth. . . ." Cool Breeze — his words were slurred, but there was no mistaking it. It was Revelation 21, the word of God spoken in a way I had never quite heard before or since. ". . . and God himself will be with them; he will wipe every tear from their eyes. Death will be no more; mourning and crying and pain will be no more. . . . See, I am making all things new."

Well, for reasons I do not understand, that was one of several conversion experiences in my life. What was it? Was it those words of promise spoken in a ramshackle setting? Was it the conjoining of the voices? The voice of Scott, a man of gentle faith and nonviolence, with the rough and slurred voice of Cool Breeze, also a man of faith who had been brought low by the great society as surely as by his bottle? Or was it simply fatigue that left me open to hearing these verses of Scripture in my guts as well as in my ears? I do not know.

But this I do know. As day broke and Scott and I left the kitchen, I knew it to be absolutely true — there *will be* a new heaven and a new earth. And we are going to be there. Oh, we may be transformed. We may not have our finery and our fancy attitudes, but we're going to be there. And Margaret, she may not have her meat cleaver, but she's going to be there too. And North Carolina, he's going to be there too. And that no-good old wino Cool Breeze, he's going to be there too.

Maranatha. Come, Lord Jesus.

CHAPTER V

Beyond Terror and Counterterror

In that region there were shepherds living in the fields, keeping watch over their flock by night. Then an angel of the Lord stood before them, and the glory of the Lord shone around them, and they were terrified. But the angel said to them, "Do not be afraid; for see — I am bringing you good news of great joy for all the people: to you is born this day in the city of David a Savior, who is the Messiah, the Lord."

LUKE 2:8-11

After the sabbath, as the first day of the week was dawning, Mary Magdalene and the other Mary went to see the tomb. And suddenly there was a great earthquake; for an angel of the Lord, descending from heaven, came and rolled back the stone and sat on it. His appearance was like lightning, and his clothing white as snow. For fear of him the guards shook and became like dead men. But the angel said to the women, "Do not be afraid; I know that you are looking for Jesus who was crucified. He is not here; for he has been raised. . . ."

MATTHEW 28:1-6

219

On Not Making Concessions to Terrorism

The greatest concession to terrorism is mimesis, and it is also the most frequent concession. Insurgents and counterinsurgents, spies and counterspies, terrorists and counterterrorists — even the vocabulary suggests that these ostensible opponents are united by a fraternity of deadly and duplicitous tactics as well as by the shared conviction that horrible actions are sanctified by the noble goals in the minds of the perpetrators. The "war on terrorism" is violent and punitive. The war will be won by those who are able to exact the higher price in lives and resources, by those who are able to instill the greater fear. In short, the victor in a violent war on terrorism will be the party that is most adept at inflicting terror. The quest to win the war is ultimately nihilistic. If terrorism is to be defeated by exacting the higher price, utilizing the more efficacious violence and instilling the greater fear, then the war will be won by the party that is able to muster the will and the resources to commit the genocidal and suicidal act of destroying the planet. The only peace that can come from the effort to oppose terror with terror is the peace of the graveyard.

If mimesis is the most common concession to terrorism, the question of who is the imitated and who the imitator is really a chicken-or-egg quandary. No small number of insurgents and guerrillas who have been labeled terrorists have borrowed tactics, weapons, and personnel from the military establishment of the state itself, and terrorist campaigns are sometimes pursued with no higher goal than to *become* the state. In the words of an Albert Camus character, "One begins by wanting justice — and one ends by setting up a police force."[1] But the state is also quick to adopt tactical lessons from its would-be opponents. Terrorist tactics are nonpartisan. They can be utilized by all sides, as indicated in the recommendation of former CIA Director William Colby: "We probably cannot eliminate terrorism, but we can take steps to contain it. . . . The most successful tactic against the guerrilla or terrorist is to recruit him, not shoot him."[2] Colby was certainly correct in observing that terror is not contained by shooting people, but neither is it contained by recruitment. The nature of terroristic actions does not change with the shifting ideological allegiances of the actors. Colby's recommendation is less a prescription for containment than an acknowledgment of the kinship inherent to the terrorism of the power-brokers and the power-seekers.[3]

Of course, it is not mimesis that most world leaders have in mind when they stress the importance of making no concessions to terrorists. What "no concessions" means in the parlance of governments is that the governing authorities will not make deals with terrorists or pay ransoms to them or even confer legitimacy upon them by entering into negotiations.[4] Terry Anderson was held hostage by the Hezbollah in Lebanon from 1985 to 1991, and while he is certainly no supporter of meeting the demands of hostage-takers, he also notes that there is considerable danger to hostages *and others* when "A principled refusal to make concessions has translated into an enormous reluctance even to talk with anyone who might be involved."[5] When there is no talking, additional violence becomes likely. Yet, in his prescriptions for "fighting" terrorism, Benjamin Netanyahu warns that the dangers of talking exceed the dangers of force, "For in negotiating," Netanyahu writes, "the government issues an open invitation for more terror, an invitation which puts at risk the safety of every citizen in society."[6] And so in the name of making no concessions to terrorism, governments make the greatest concession of all, meeting terror with terror.

And there are additional concessions that governments have made in the name of fighting the war against terrorism, especially concessions that entail placing restrictions on the rights, freedoms, and privacy of citizens. After arguing that terrorists need "the permissiveness of liberal society" for survival, Walter Laqueur asserts that ". . . the basic question is not whether terrorism can be defeated; even third-rate dictatorships have shown that it can be put down with great ease. The real problem is the price that has to be paid by liberal societies valuing their democratic traditions."[7] A growing number of governments have agreed that "the price that has to be paid" entails sacrifices of rights and liberties.

The recommendations from Benjamin Netanyahu provide examples of the types of legislation that have been considered or adopted by many governments. Netanyahu proposes measures to allow for increased infiltration and surveillance of groups "inciting" to violence:

> . . . I propose that the laws of every free society must be such as to permit the security services to move against groups which incite to violence against the country's government or its citizens. The test is simple. If the law does not allow a government to sift through the extremist splinters advocating violence in order to identify which groups are actively *planning* terrorist actions and to shut them down *before* they strike, then the law is insufficient.[8]

Netanyahu's "simple" test is complicated by the subjectivity of phrases like "incite to violence" and "extremist splinters." In the 1940s in Palestine, for example, British rulers had the bodies of bombing victims to support their view that Menahem Begin, Netanyahu's Likud colleague, was an extremist who participated in and incited violence. Yet, in the 1940s in India, the British rulers believed that Mohandas Gandhi was also an "extremist," and while he personally disavowed bloodshed, the British believed that Gandhi was "inciting" others who were not similarly inclined towards nonviolence. The word "extremist" is sufficiently elastic to allow governments to use it as a label against any opposition, and the notion of "incitement" could be used to hold nonviolent activists responsible for the violence of others.[9] Nonetheless, Netanyahu recommends that detention, interrogation, and search and seizure be permitted without a warrant when there is "strong suspicion of terrorist activity."[10] Netanyahu acknowledges that "In some countries, these measures would necessarily mean shifting the legal balance between civil liberties and security."[11] But he contends that civil liberties can be safeguarded by requiring periodic review of anti-terrorist legislation and procedures; if any practices infringe upon "the rights of innocent citizens," then "the particular provisions in question can be jettisoned." Leaving aside the question of whether it is only the rights of "innocent citizens" that should not be infringed, one must wonder about Netanyahu's assumptions regarding the ease with which security measures can be "jettisoned." Judicially, security measures are quickly enshrined by the concept of legal precedent. Politically, security measures are unlikely to be "jettisoned" by politicos who stumble over one another in the competition not to appear "soft" on crime or terrorism.

In the name of combating terrorism, Argentina, Chile, Germany, Uruguay, and scores of other nations have passed legislation easing restrictions on search and seizure and lengthening the permissible period of detention without trial. In the wake of Red Brigade activism, Italy passed laws permitting wiretaps and searches without warrants and allowing detention of terrorist suspects for up to 12 years without trial.[12] In his battle against Shining Path guerrillas and the Tupac Amaru Revolutionary Movement, President Alberto Fujimori of Peru cracked down on terrorism by cracking down on civil rights. Since "terrorist groups" were "convinced they could take advantage of the Western legal tradition with its emphasis on due process and assumption of innocence until proven guilty," Fujimori introduced an "emergency legal framework" that included replacing civilian courts with military tribunals.[13] In 1986, France established a team of "anti-terrorist judges," and in 1998, some of these judges presided at an assembly-line style, mass trial of 138 Algerian terrorism suspects, some of whom had already spent four years in French prisons awaiting trial.[14] Following the August 15, 1998 bombing in Omagh by the group calling itself "the Real IRA," British Prime Minister Tony Blair and Irish Prime Minister Bertie Ahern were quick to agree to new security measures that included easing the burden for proving guilt in paramilitary cases. Such cases were already heard by judges alone without benefit of juries, but Blair and Ahern agreed to new provisions which stipulated that judges in paramilitary cases could arrive at a finding of guilt based only on the testimony of a senior police officer and that guilt could be inferred from the refusal of the accused to answer questions. The conservative newsmagazine *The Economist* editorialized, "Emergency legislation has a miserable history in Britain. It has not only failed to halt terrorism, it has often helped to fuel it by creating miscarriages of justice that have undermined rather than supported the rule of law."[15] In the United States, "anti-terrorist" legislation has expanded the federal government's reliance on the death penalty, has allowed for kidnapping of foreign suspects accused of violating U.S. laws even when the alleged violations occurred outside the United States, and has allowed prosecutors to use classified documents without giving defendants access to the material that is being used against them.[16] Michael Parenti observes, "Numerous crime bills have contained 'counterterrorist' measures that pose more dangers to our freedom and security than anything terrorists might do."[17]

In the name of fighting the war on terrorism, some governments have also moved to place restrictions on freedom of speech and freedom of press and broadcast media. The basis for such restrictions is the belief that terrorist acts are a type of theater designed to attract publicity to a cause. Terrorism expert Walter Laqueur writes that terrorists "are, in some respects, the super-entertainers of our time" and he asserts that "The real danger facing the terrorist is that of being ignored. . . ."[18] Israel's Benjamin Netanyahu maintained that "unreported, terrorist acts would be like the proverbial tree falling in the silent forest."[19] Britain's Margaret Thatcher declared, "We must try to find ways to starve the terrorist and the hijacker of the oxygen of publicity on which they depend."[20] Between 1988 and 1994, Britain attempted to effectuate such starvation by banning all broadcast interviews with "terrorists" and their supporters. The legislation was designed to deny access to the broadcast media by the IRA, Sinn Fein, and other paramilitary groups, but the ban became the subject of mockery when television and radio stations began using actors to read the scripts of interviews with paramilitary leaders.[21] Contrary to the assertions of would-be censors, there is little evidence that media coverage attracts converts to terrorism. If anything, media coverage of violent acts contributes to the demonization of whole groups of people as "terrorists." Terrorists are not in danger of being ignored because cameras love bomb blasts, but those things that *are* in danger of being ignored are the more fundamental questions of justice and reconciliation, which are lost in the rush to cover the violence. What is needed is not *less* but *more* media coverage in the form of information that facilitates engagement. Most Palestinian participants in the first Intifada were seeking to mount a *non*violent movement of noncooperation with Israeli governance, but the media focus turned to the minority of protesters who pelted vehicles with rocks. Justice concerns were obfuscated by both the rock throwers and the *limited* nature of the media coverage.[22]

There is something hypocritical in the fretting of governments over the "oxygen of publicity" afforded "terrorist" violence while governmental violence enjoys ready access to such oxygen. Moreover, governments are notorious for media manipulation on the subject of terrorism. In the United States, for example, the release of the FBI report, "Terrorism in the United States 1995," was greeted by banner headlines that dutifully reported the FBI findings of a dramatic increase in terrorist attacks inside the U.S. In contrast to "the relatively low 1994 levels," the FBI report found that "The number of people killed in terrorist attacks in the United States increased sharply. . . ."[23] One needed to read beyond the headlines to discover that the "relatively low" level of 1994 was zero terrorist attacks and that the dramatic increase in 1995 was due to one attack, the Oklahoma City bombing. Certainly, the Oklahoma City attack should not be counted as insignificant, but neither should it be used so crassly as a ploy for increased FBI funding. Likewise, the media dutifully reported the Secretary of State's findings in "Patterns of Global Terrorism: 1998" that there were seven "state sponsors of terrorism" — Cuba, Iran, Iraq, Libya, North Korea, Sudan, and Syria. But the media paid far less attention to other statements within the report. After applying the "sponsors of terrorism" label, the report went on to acknowledge that "Cuba no longer supports armed struggle in Latin America or elsewhere." And "There is no evidence of Libyan involvement in recent acts of international terrorism, however." And, while North Korea continued to provide safe haven for a 1970 hijacking suspect, ". . . North Korea has not been linked definitively to any act of international terrorism since 1987. . . ." And "There is no evidence of direct Syrian involvement in acts of international terrorism since 1986. . . ."[24] It seems fair to wonder, then, if the U.S. designation of certain nations as "state sponsors of terrorism" is based on anything other than the druthers of political leaders. At the very least, U.S. government officials should be more circumspect before accusing terrorists of media manipulation.

In addition to issuing misleading information on terrorism, the U.S. government has also blocked public access to information, most notoriously through covert operations and national security classifications, but also by bringing direct pressure to bear on journalists and reporters. From a source affiliated with a Lebanese newspaper, journalist Dale Van Atta learned of the Iran-Contra arms for hostages scheme a year before it became public, but he was convinced of the need to suppress the story by Noel C. Koch, head of the counterterrorism office in the Pentagon. By being a good, investigative reporter, Van Atta was placed in an anguishing position. Koch successfully convinced Van Atta that release of the story would endanger the lives of hostages, but Van Atta also knew that withholding the story would allow the U.S. to continue in its deception and its arms deals which would also take a toll in lives.[25] Ominously, censorship need not be legislatively mandated when significant segments of the news media become convinced of the need to exercise self-censorship in the name of national security. Speaking at the CIA's Langley, Virginia headquarters in 1988, *Washington Post* publisher Katherine Graham was preaching to the choir when she said, "We live in a dirty and dangerous world. There are some things the general public does not need to know and shouldn't. I believe democracy flourishes when the government can take legitimate steps to keep its secrets and when the press can decide whether to print what it knows."[26] When the government utilizes the resources provided by the public to inflict violence, the public needs to know.

Along with the concerns raised above, the violent "war against terrorism" must be rejected on three additional counts: (1) violent and punitive responses have not curtailed terrorism, nor is there a reasonable prospect that they will do so in the future; (2) the actual harm done by counterterrorism often exceeds the harm done by the terrorism it is intended to combat; (3) the perspectives on security, freedom, and humanity that are intrinsic to the war on terrorism are untenable from the vantage point of both human dignity and biblical faith.

1. Violent and punitive responses have not curtailed terrorism, nor is there a reasonable prospect that they will do so in the future.

The claim that violence can be ended with violence is often proffered along with the clichéd advice to "Fight fire with fire." Actually, the fire cliché has greater cogency than the claim about fighting violence with violence insofar as some wilderness fires can in fact be fought by starting backfires to deprive the primary conflagration of fuel. Of course, if the fire happens to be in one's own home, starting another fire merely hastens the rate of destruction. Violence is a fire in our home.

When states employ repression and violence in their fight against "terrorism," some revolutionary groups and guerrilla separatist movements have actually won adherents as a result. It is as if the state becomes the monster the revolutionaries knew it was all along. Under the repressive regime of Francisco Franco in Spain, support for the ETA Basque separatist movement grew, and the group's violent activism persists to this day. Intentionally eliciting violent response becomes part of the strategizing of guerrilla groups. Bruce Hoffman recounts how, in a manner akin to the calculations of Menahem Begin in Palestine, George Grivas of the Cypriot EOKA "calculated that the unrelenting terrorist onslaught would sap the morale of British forces and compel them to over-react with counterproductive, self-defeating measures directed against the law-abiding Greek-Cypriot community."[27] Harsh criminal penalties against individuals charged with terrorism are similarly ineffective. Liberal use of the death penalty has been part of the effort to instill terror in those who instill terror, but the executed are hailed as martyrs who inspire renewed zeal for the struggle. In 1956, the Algerian FLN's campaign of terror only escalated after France executed by guillotine two FLN fighters. The FLN announced that, for every guerrilla who was executed, one hundred French citizens would be killed, and within three days, 49 French civilians were gunned down. Elsewhere and since then, other disasters have resulted from the effort to combat terrorism with exemplary punishments.[28]

Modern terrorists are likely to subscribe to the slogan of those 18th-century Americans who were also denounced for their terrorism: "Live free or die." People who fully expect to be met by violence will not find the threat of force to be very meaningful. The threat will be less meaningful still to apocalyptic activists for whom violent opposition is merely further confirmation of the need to assist the world towards its imminent demise. Will the threats of violent counterterrorism and harsh criminal penalties send the terrorists scrambling for cover? When a bomb ripped through the Naples to Milan express train in 1985 killing fifteen people and injuring over a hundred, a wide assortment of groups were sent scrambling to take credit. Everyone from the neo-fascist Black Order to the neo-communist Red Brigade claimed responsibility, come what counterterror may.[29]

2. The actual harm done by counterterrorism often exceeds the harm done by the terrorism it is intended to combat.

The biblical prophets did not do ethics by body count. The fate of the entire nation may depend on whether the cause of a single widow is met with justice (Isaiah 1:21-23; Jeremiah 7:5-7; Zechariah 7:8-14; Malachi 3:5), and the fate of the entire creation may depend on whether a single murder is met by endless cycles of revenge or whether it is met instead by intervention that says "no more" (Genesis 4:8-16). From a biblical perspective, violence and brutality cannot be divided into categories such as bad, worse, and worst. But for the nations, such categorizations of violence are standard fare. Since the nations claim that their assorted wars on terrorism are designed to protect human lives, it is fair to evaluate the claim.

In April 1986, a bomb was set off in a West Berlin discotheque. A Turkish woman and an American GI were killed in the blast, and another GI died of injuries several weeks later. It was a horrible act with a horrible toll in human life. In a finding based on scant evidence that remains suspect to this day, U.S. President Reagan announced that Libya was responsible for the terrorist attack in Berlin, and to counter such terrorism, Reagan ordered a nighttime aerial assault on the cities of Tripoli and Benghazi. The surprise attack was in violation of international laws agreed upon after the surprise attack on Pearl Harbor in 1941. Over one hundred civilians of nine different nationalities were killed in the U.S. bombardment of Libya. France had angered the U.S. by denying overflight permission for the bombers, but the United States assured France that it was an accident when one of the U.S. bombs destroyed the French embassy in Tripoli. Though less severe, damage was also sustained by four other embassies. Like the disco bombing, the U.S. bombing of Libya was a horrible act with a horrible toll in human life. It was terror disguised as a war on terror. In terms of lives lost, it was terror that put to shame the pretenses to terror of the disco bombers.[30]

After the military regime was ousted from power in Argentina in 1983, President Raul Alfonsin appointed a commission of inquiry to investigate the anguishing history of torture, death squads, and disappearances in Argentina under military rule. The commission concluded that the "terrorism" of the military regime was "infinitely worse" than the terrorism it was claiming to combat.[31] Such findings point to a phenomenon not unique to Argentina. In many settings, the state's counterterrorism is more deadly than that which it allegedly combats. In Turkey, for example, a 1999 report by Human Rights Watch found that extra-judicial killings by police at demonstrations and during house raids increased significantly after Turkey's "Anti-Terror Law" went into effect in 1991.[32] And in El Salvador, Guatemala, and Honduras, hundreds of thousands have been killed in governmental onslaughts of counterterrorism that has been encouraged and sponsored by the United States.

In Guatemala, the bloody history of U.S.-sponsored counterterrorism extends back for decades. Frequently, what fell under the rubric of "counterterrorism" was a full-scale assault against the lives and land claims of Guatemala's aboriginal people. Already in 1968, a U.S. State Department memorandum acknowledged the following:

> The Guatemalan Government's use of "counter-terror" to combat insurgency . . . is indiscriminate, and we cannot rationalize that fact away . . . people are killed or disappear on the basis of simple accusations. . . . The official squads are guilty of atrocities. Interrogations are brutal, torture is used and bodies are mutilated. . . . We *have* condoned counter-terror; we may even in effect have encouraged or blessed it. . . . We will stand before history unable to answer the accusations that we encouraged the Guatemalan Army to do these things.[33]

With U.S. assistance, the Guatemalan regime was still continuing its "war on terrorism" in 1980 when Amnesty International issued its report, *Guatemala: Government by Political Murder*. In October 1982, Amnesty issued another report detailing the murders of 2,600 Guatemalan civilians, but two months later, President Reagan was in Guatemala to praise its government's dual efforts to institute democracy and to fight terrorism.[34] In 1987, Guatemala's Defense

Minister argued that the still-rising death toll could not be blamed on the military since they had only "reacted against the terrorists," while President Cerezo maintained that many of the "disappeared" were not people who had been abducted by death squads but people who had merely decided to travel abroad.[35] After it became public that several U.S. citizens had been brutalized by the military while working in Guatemala, the Clinton White House was finally forced to order an investigation of the U.S. role in Guatemala's campaign of counterterror. Sister Diana Ortiz, a U.S. Ursuline nun who worked in a literacy program for Mayan children, contributed to evoking public scrutiny of the U.S. role in "counterterror" when she told of her own survival of abduction, rape, and torture by Guatemalan security forces. The 1996 report of the U.S. Intelligence Oversight Board was a tepid understatement of the U.S. role in training Guatemalan security forces in the use of torture:

> . . . the School of the Americas and Southern Command had used improper instruction materials in training Latin American officers, including Guatemalans, from 1982 to 1991. The materials had never received proper DOD [Department of Defense] review, and certain passages appeared to condone (or could have been interpreted to condone) practices such as executions of guerrillas, extortion, physical abuse, coercion, and false imprisonment.[36]

When the Pentagon was eventually forced to declassify the instruction manuals in question, what was revealed was blatant advocacy of murder ("neutralization"), torture, censorship, blackmail, false arrest, and abuse of the relatives of suspects in detention. In one manual titled "Terrorism and the Urban Guerrilla," blatant violations of human rights were taught in the name of fighting terrorism.[37]

Military officers from most Latin American countries have been trained at the School of the Americas (recently renamed the Western Hemisphere Institute for Security Cooperation) at Fort Benning, Georgia, and at similar U.S.-sponsored military training schools. These schools specialize in the teaching of counterinsurgency and counterterrorism. The list of atrocities associated with the graduates of these schools defies classification as merely coincidental. Often, the atrocities are committed with the use of weapons supplied by the United States. Members of the Honduran "Battalion 316" death squad were graduates of the School of the Americas, as were two of three officers cited in the assassination of Archbishop Romero, three of five officers cited in El Salvador for the rape and murder of four U.S. church women, and nineteen of twenty-six Salvadoran officers cited for the 1989 murder of six Jesuit priests, their housekeeper, and her daughter. The School of the Americas is "a school of terrorists," says Roy Bourgeois, a priest who was exiled from Bolivia during the dictatorship of one of the school's graduates, Hugo Banzer Suárez. In urging that the school be closed, a 1995 *Los Angeles Times* editorial observed that "it is hard to think of a coup or human rights outrage that has occurred in [Latin America] in the past 40 years in which alumni of the School of the Americas were *not* involved."[38]

It is possible to grant, of course, that some who have been guilty of atrocities might have engaged in violence with the sincere conviction that they were merely faithful workers in the cause of "counterterrorism." If they subscribed to the view that ethics can be done by body count, it is certainly possible that the instructors at the schools and the authors of the training manuals and even the death squad members themselves may have believed and may continue to believe in all sincerity that they are killing for the sake of preventing terror. It is more difficult, however, to attribute even such misguided sincerity to the U.S. efforts to train and supply the Nicaraguan Contras. With the Contras in the 1980s, covert U.S. training manuals contained blatant espousal of "terrorism" without even bothering to call it by another name. *Psychological Operations in Guerrilla Warfare* was one of the manuals prepared by the CIA for the Contras, and it included a section with instructions on "Implicit and Explicit Terror." The manual is frightening and refreshing in its candor. Gone is the obfuscating terminology of "counterterrorism." At the time, U.S. leaders were publicly supporting "the Contra freedom fighters," but at the same time in secret, U.S. officials were knowingly recruiting, training, and paying for terrorism.

It is sometimes possible to measure and compare the harm that is done by deeds that wear the labels of "terrorism" and "counterterrorism," and by such measurements, "counterterrorism" has claimed the higher toll in human lives. But we risk becoming callous if we allow our conscience to be swayed by mere national identity or religious affiliation or ideological allegiance or body count or terminological distinctions. We must allow ourselves to feel outrage and pain whether the victims are the Protestants of Northern Ireland or the Catholics, whether they are Israelis or Palestinians, whether they are among the hundreds of people who suffered from terrorist assault in Oklahoma City or the hundreds of thousands who suffered from U.S.-sponsored counterterrorist assault in Latin America.

3. The perspectives on security, freedom, and humanity that are intrinsic to the war on terrorism are untenable from the vantage point of both human dignity and biblical faith.

Human security is severely threatened by malnutrition and infant mortality, by global epidemics of AIDS and other life-threatening illnesses, by greenhouse gases and poisoned waters that respect no national boundaries. But in the militarized consciousness of counterterrorism, security has nothing to do with feeding hungry people, or treating the sick, or caring for the environment. In counterterrorism, security has to do with the perpetual quest to acquire the sufficient level of armed force to deter potential attack from armed force.

American freedom is severely threatened by conformity, by "mass" media and consumer culture, and by the alarming fact that there is so little alarm over U.S. rates of incarceration. Today, nearly one percent of the entire population of the United States is caged in federal, state, or local "correctional" facilities. But in the counterterrorist zeal to thwart potential adversaries, the danger is not from too little freedom but from too much. Through reliance on perpetual vigilance, surveillance, detention, and interrogation, the counterterrorist hopes to eradicate those realms of privacy from which conspiracy and terrorism spring.

In its 1981 ruling in *Haig v. Agee,* the U.S. Supreme Court found that "it is 'obvious and unarguable' that no governmental interest is more compelling than the security of the Nation."[39] It was clear from the ruling that the Court understood "security" as having to do with military preparedness and "intelligence" capabilities. Yet even for governments, the view that such security is the most compelling interest is not at all "obvious and unarguable." The view of security as the highest value of government is based on a specific version of political philosophy associated with the writings of Thomas Hobbes, a philosophy that is quite arguable.[40] Hobbesian anthropology maintains that the natural human condition is fraught with insecurity and with the antagonism and competitiveness innate to the human struggle for survival. It is only the state, said Hobbes, which is able to offer a modicum of security. By surrendering their natural state of freedom, humans are able to enjoy a higher level of security. For Hobbes, the value of security trumps the value of freedom.

Hobbesian philosophy is flawed on several counts, one example being its estimation of the state as the only potential guarantor of military or paramilitary security. Hobbes lived in an age that was not so richly populated by global corporations and wealthy individuals capable of purchasing a wide array of paramilitary security services. For those with sufficient resources, the sacrifices offered to the god "security" are measured in dollars rather than freedom. A dramatic increase in the number of companies offering weapons and the personnel to use them, security training, surveillance equipment, detection devices, bulletproof vests, and bombproof buildings has turned "private security into a growth industry *par excellence* worldwide."[41] Typically, the employees of the private security industry are former military or police personnel who offer their government-subsidized training and experience to private employers;

these employers are not beholden to make their profits in a manner that co-incides with the interests of the governments that trained their employees. Guns and gunners can be hired by governments as well as by their opponents. Liberia, New Guinea, and Sierra Leone are among the nations in which merce-naries have played a dominant role in coups and countercoups. Not given to hyperbole, military historian Martin van Creveld describes an ominous trend:

> . . . the reemergence of mercenaries — soldiers of fortune, as they prefer to call themselves — in the service of both governments and their oppo-nents is one of the outstanding developments of the last quarter of the twentieth century. To put it in a different way, terrorists, members of the security industry, and the state's security establishment appear to be growing interchangeable in theory and, in at least some cases, in practice as well.[42]

No irony was intended when the United Nations' 1999 "Human Development Report" cited mercenary armies, military hardware companies, and other ele-ments of the private security industry as "a severe threat to human security."[43] Coups and countercoups aside, there are questions about the degree to which the security industry can advance the more prosaic "security" of deterring ter-rorist attacks. At the 1996 Atlanta Olympic Games, a bomb attack was not pre-vented even though security officers outnumbered athletes two to one, and for a time, there was even speculation that security personnel might be implicated in the attack. There are always chinks in the armor. Security is elusive and the quest for it perpetual. A growth industry indeed.

The problem with Hobbes's philosophy, however, does not have to do merely with the question of whether the state or any other entity can be the guarantor of security. The more fundamental question is whether "security" it-self merits the position of being considered a preeminent value in life. It strains coherence and credulity to argue that "freedom" (the freedom of privacy and the freedom of individual rights) must be sacrificed to security while simulta-neously claiming that the goal of security is "freedom" (the independence of the nation state and "freedom from fear"). In fact, the quest for security is a sign of enslavement to fear and not freedom from it.

The cross is a reminder that those who most valued security were the crucifiers and not the Crucified. When Jesus' followers offered the security of their swords, Jesus responded, "No more of this!" (Luke 22:49-51). The Hebrew prophets were equally contemptuous of the perpetual quest for armed security (Jeremiah 9:23-24; Hosea 10:13-14). "Not by might, nor by power, but by my spirit, says the LORD of hosts" (Zechariah 4:6). If one sought to assemble a list of "the important values in life" from a biblical perspective, one might find ample biblical support for including values such as love of God and love of humanity, values such as servanthood and discipleship. But one would find scant support for the value of security.

Armed security functions by creating insecurity for all potential adversaries. In its quest for security, the war on terrorism spreads insecurity. Salvadoran security forces were pursuing their "war on terrorism" when they entered the village of El Mozote in 1981. Within hours, 767 people had been killed — every resident of the town except for one. The sole survivor was Rufina Amaya, a woman who witnessed brutality on a scale that most of us cannot imagine. To this day, Amaya is haunted by her inability to save her nine-year-old son as she heard him calling, "Mama, they are killing us."[44]

Ten of the twelve officers cited as responsible for the El Mozote massacre were trained in counterterrorism at Fort Benning's School of the Americas. Many of the weapons they used had been acquired through military assistance from the United States.

*   *   *

Violence is rarely judged to be "good" in and of itself. It is always the worthiness of the intended goal of the violence that is supposed to slosh back over the violence itself and render it "justified" or at least "necessary." Except for impulsive crimes of passion, violence is always attached to an end that is theoretically pure and noble. Neither terror nor counterterror are passionate forms of violence but rather calculating forms of violence designed to instill fear in pursuit of goals which, it is claimed, will someday be unveiled as the essence of justice. According to John of Patmos, the unveiling has already occurred and we find not justice and nobility but a beast.

Few in history have embraced the label of "terrorist." Most "terrorists" understand themselves as counterterrorists, fighting to end injustices and insecurities. And most "counterterrorists" would deny that they are engaged in any actions approximating terrorism, a phenomenon they are fighting to end. But truth be told, the only way to move beyond terror and counterterror is to stop the fighting, to surrender the pretense that justice is won through terror, or security through counterterror.

Based on the history and perspectives explored throughout this study, I have assembled several proposals on how to set about the effort of ending the violence and moving beyond the perpetual cycles of terror and counterterror. I have no illusions that these proposals offer "the answer" to violence on our planet or in our neighborhoods, but rather I offer them as potentially fruitful starting points. They are arranged as two groups of four proposals. The first group is addressed to the principalities and powers — to the governments and agencies and corporations that are too often heedless of the deadly consequences of their actions. The second group is addressed to individuals and communities — to us people who are too often resigned, too often heedless of the fact that our individual and communal actions can have good consequences.

1. As a necessary step towards the curtailment of terror and counterterror, the United States, Britain, France, and other major weapons suppliers need to stop the international selling, trading, and gifting of arms. Export licenses for weapons and weapons components should be denied to corporations, and if the World Trade Organization rules that such denials are a restriction on "free trade," then there is one more reason for abolishing the WTO.[45] In the corporate and governmental protests that "If we don't sell them, somebody else will," there is an echo of the complaints of drug pushers. In order to counter such fretting, the United States, Britain, and other nations heavily involved in the arms trade should lead the way in the United Nations in proposing a ban on the international trade in weapons. Moreover, the United Nations is well positioned to formulate a program for an international "arms buy-back" akin to the model of the "gun buy-back" program currently offered in some (too few) U.S. towns and cities. The weapons coming to the UN through the program could be delivered to an agreed-upon, neutral site for dismantling and recycling. Payments for the weapons could be offered in the form of food, medical, or educational assistance programs, or cash, with financial backing for the program coming from contributions from member nations, savings from an end to costly UN military interventions, and private donations from individuals who would like to see a world less armed to the teeth.

What does the weapons trade have to do with terrorism? Everything. Terrorists are the Afghan "freedom fighters" who were lavished with U.S. weapons and training before the days of the World Trade Center and Nairobi and Dar es Salaam. Terrorists are Savak and the Shah who assembled a sparkling array of Western armaments before the days when the hostage-takers of Tehran inherited those arms. Terrorists are the Baath rulers of Iraq who savaged the Kurds while receiving Western nuclear technology before the days of Kuwait. Terrorists are Manuel Noriega and his colleagues who were literally on the U.S. payroll and receiving U.S. weapons in the days before they turned into thugs and Hitlers and used their U.S. weapons to oppose a U.S. invasion. Terrorists are the United States and Russia and other nuclear powers who used their weapons to sustain a "balance of terror" in the days before the Soviet Union collapsed — and, it is argued, the balance of terror is needed still to thwart attacks from rogue nations and (for lack of a better word) terrorists.

International arms dealers generate their own markets because with weapons, as with other addictive substances, the acquisition of them generates additional acquisition in the future, not only by the original buyer but also by all potential adversaries. Some terrorism experts claim that, as a revolutionary tactic, terrorist violence is a doomed enterprise if the state is able to maintain a totalistic monopoly on the instruments of violence. But the terrorist need not fear. The terrorist's best ally is the militarism of the state and the greed of the state. The likelihood of the state being able to maintain a monopoly over sophisticated weapons technology decreases as the sheer quantity of weaponry approaches a level that defies effective monitoring. And the terrorist is assisted by the greed of the state and of corporate interests who understand the immense profits to be realized in the development and sale of weapons systems — and of the systems to defend against the systems — and of the surveillance equipment to oversee it all. With the world awash in lethal hardware and software, access to weapons is assured for all terrorists in the guise of mighty lords and princes, or terrorists in the guise of the liberation armies of any and every backwater precinct, or terrorists in the guise of individuals with visions of how to save the world or end it.

Engels once wrote, "Violence is the accelerator of economic development."[46] The opposite has proven true in the Third World, where violence is the major contributor to economic instability. Engels's claim finds greater support among the capitalist arms dealers of the United States who have realized huge profits from violence and the threat of it. The United States bears special responsibility for ending the international weapons trade since the U.S. accounts for fully two-thirds of all worldwide arms exports. In citing U.S. weapons exports as a major threat to global health, the *British Medical Journal* noted in 1995 that a large portion of the U.S. arms were going to fragile, autocratic regimes and subsequently ending up in the hands of who-knows-who.[47] Latin American regimes have used U.S. "war on drugs" assistance to battle guerrillas based on the flimsy assertion that the guerrillas were "high on drugs." In Afghanistan, U.S. weapons supplied for the guerrilla war against the Soviets were skimmed off and used by rebel factions to fight one another.[48] Neither Ethiopia nor Eritrea have democratic forms of governance, but both states were supplied with U.S. weapons and both states used those weapons against one another in a war that lasted for years; the war only added to the crisis in the horn of Africa, already suffering from widespread drought and starvation. Of the eleven nations intervening in the 1998 Congolese civil war, nine had received U.S. weapons and military training in 1997. The last five times U.S. troops went into combat, they faced opponents who had recently received U.S. weapons and/or U.S. military training.[49] Indeed, the fact that the world is awash in sophisticated weapons technology, much of it supplied by the United States, is used as evidence of the need for the U.S. to spend more on its own military budget. There can be no "peace dividend," say military contractors, because we live in a dangerous world — a world made all the more dangerous by the weapons sales and exports of the military contractors themselves.[50]

An end to the international arms trade is only the first step in a process that must include superpower disarmament as well. As the most heavily armed nation on the planet, the U.S. must lead in *dis*armament. It is not viable for the U.S. to continue claiming the right to nuclear deterrence while simultaneously preaching nuclear nonproliferation. If a nuclear balance of terror is ethically defensible and effective as a peacekeeping tool, then the U.S. should be preaching the spread of nuclear weapons. But since no peace has been kept and since weapons of mass destruction are opposed to all morality save nihilism, then the U.S. needs to practice what it preaches to the non-nuclear nations of the world. As with other highly militarized nations, in the U.S., science, technology, and culture have been perverted by a myopic focus on weaponry.[51] By reordering national priorities, disarmament can serve the present generation.

But consideration must also be given to the generations still to come and the terrors they will face. Nation states are mortal creatures. Just as with other endeavors like building the tower of Babel, or having children, or writing books, the building and nurturing of the state can be a manifestation of the human striving after immortality. The striving is in vain. Life and the renunciation of death are gifts, not human productions or reproductions. Like the Soviet Union, the United States is doomed. Whether the United States falls tomorrow or after a million tomorrows, this power will fall and all of the weapons of terror in its possession will fall into the hands of others, perhaps into the hands of "mere terrorists."[52] In the treasonous words of John of Patmos, Babylon is fallen.[53] Disarmament now is a strong measure that can be taken against the terrorism of the present and of the future.

2. In addition to working for an end to the trade and acquisition of arms, the effort to move beyond terror and counterterror must entail a disarmament of spirit so that international relations can be freed from the constant threat of military interventions and military adventurism. In the United States, the willingness of political leaders to launch military interventions more quickly and with slighter public support has become a virtual hallmark of "strong leadership."[54] There is a fine line, however, between the perception of the U.S. as resolute and always ready to protect its interests and the perception of the U.S. as unpredictable and always ready to lash out when it finds new interests to protect. The lethal strike that comes without warning is the modus operandi of terrorists great and small.[55] If the period without violence is too prolonged, then

the fear that has been instilled in potential adversaries begins to wane. The occasional bombing maintains the fearsome image.[56]

Military intervention is a form of terrorism that is especially generative of new manifestations of terrorism. The U.S. arming and training of rebels in Afghanistan is just one recent example of such sowing and reaping of terror. As one author describes it, "It is curious — to say the least — that the United States in this way enabled Afghanistan to become the largest and most effective training ground for what has subsequently been described in the US and elsewhere as international . . . terrorism."[57] The untoward consequences of the U.S. military adventure in Afghanistan will continue for generations, not only because of the continued activism of the Afghan freedom-fighters-turned-terrorists, but also because of what the intervention has meant for neighboring states. With Pakistan, for example, there had been a ban on U.S. aid due to the Pakistani nuclear weapons program. But when the U.S. sought to use Pakistan as a transshipment point for weapons and mercenaries destined for Afghanistan, the ban was suddenly lifted, and Pakistan became the third largest recipient of U.S. aid even while the Pakistani nuclear program was accelerated.[58]

More recently, military interventions have assumed the guise of "humanitarian" missions designed to bring an end to "ethnic cleansing" and genocide. Historical experience indicates, however, that warfare merely exacerbates intra- and inter-communal hostilities and creates an environment fertile for genocide as foreign observers are expelled and wartime paranoia increases. In Kosovo, violence against Kosovar Albanians increased dramatically after the NATO airstrikes began and violence against Kosovar Serbs increased in the aftermath of the NATO occupation. NATO pronouncements notwithstanding, there was nothing humanitarian about the methods that were used in the 1999 war against Yugoslavia. While the U.S. and its NATO allies denounced the use of chemical weapons, NATO forces released tons of toxic chemicals into the environment by repeatedly bombing the petrochemical complex near the Serb city of Pancevo.[59] While the U.S. denounced the Iraqi nuclear weapons program, tons of U.S. nuclear waste were dumped on both Iraq and Yugoslavia in the form of "depleted uranium" shells. Biologists interviewed by BBC News estimated that more than 10,000 fatal cancer cases will result from the depleted uranium dumped on Kosovo and Yugoslavia.[60] This is terrorist warfare under the guise of humanitarian intervention.

The call to move beyond terror and counterterror by ending the international arms trade and ending reliance on military interventions does not constitute a call for isolationism. Those who fear that ending the arms trade would contribute to massive unemployment have failed to consider how many people could be gainfully employed in seeking to address the *global* need for medical researchers and health care practitioners, farmers who can grow an earth-friendly crop and transportation personnel who can deliver the food to areas of drought and famine, workers who can plant trees and dig wells for safe drinking water, emergency personnel who can respond to natural disasters, artists who can give voice to the spirit of their own culture and reach across cultural divides, mediators and negotiators who can search for resolution to potential conflicts and who can nurture reconciliation, educators, unarmed observers, and witnesses for peace. Isolationism? Many things besides weapons can move across national borders.

Will a reorientation of national priorities away from militarism spell an end to all terrorism? Edward Herman comments:

> It is, of course, impossible to eliminate entirely individual acts of terror — they are inescapable in a complex, dynamic world in which means of destruction are readily available to the alienated and oppressed. But a substantial fraction of *real* acts of retail terror arise out of world failures to alleviate widespread misery and injustice and to deal intelligently and humanely with local and regional grievances (Northern Ireland, Israel-Palestine).[61]

While we should avoid suggesting that poor people are somehow more apt to engage in violence, Herman is certainly correct that grievances and potential conflicts have not been addressed humanely. "Peace" cannot be a matter of merely negotiating treaties and adjusting institutional structures and national boundaries. If there is no focus on reconciliation and justice, then what passes for "peacekeeping" is the military task of keeping apart the warriors and preventing violent contact rather than seeking the nonviolent engagement of the populace.[62] Peace agreements require not only the involvement of power brokers and warlords, but also and especially the involvement of the disempowered so that trusting relationships among individuals and communities can foster reconciliation in ways that institutions and constitutions can never achieve. Reconciliation is thwarted whenever peace agreements are sealed with promises of military assistance, and reconciliation is not furthered by World Bank loans of millions or billions designed to create an environment friendly to no one but multinational corporations. Reconciliation could be better fostered by drawing on the success of the "micro loan" and "micro grant" movement, which provides resources (often $100 or less) to individuals who are engaged in traditional enterprises. In settings ranging from Kosovo to Kashmir to the U.S., such micro investment could be used to foster productive and reconciling interaction across cultural, religious, ethnic, and racial lines. The important goal is to restore the trusting communities that existed prior to the peddling of hate and the influx of weapons.[63] When what passes for peace is imposed through armaments and military interventions, grievances are only compounded by the physical, emotional, and economic harm inflicted by the "humanitarian" violence itself. In the former Yugoslavia, people suffered less from "age-old hatreds" between religious and ethnic groups and more from the horrible legacy of World War II violence among Croats, Serbs, Bosnians, and others. And people of the next generation will find that their grievances have less to do with whether one prays in a Serbian Orthodox Church or a mosque and more to do with the horrible legacy of violence left by both Slobodan Milosevic and NATO.[64]

3. In order to move beyond terror and counterterror, it is closing time. It is time to close down the operations of the CIA and other agencies which, in the name of "intelligence," have woven webs of secrecy to deprive the public of knowledge about actions perpetrated in our name. It is also time to close down the operations of the Western Hemisphere Institute for Security Cooperation and the more than 150 similar training schools which, in the name of counterterrorism, train international military personnel in the use of terror.[65]

There is nothing particularly novel or extreme in the proposals to close these institutions. With the end of the Cold War, Senator Daniel Patrick Moynihan introduced a bill in 1991 to abolish the CIA.[66] While Moynihan's bill never had much chance of passage, CIA officials were sufficiently alarmed at the prospect of budget cuts following the disintegration of the Soviet Union that they went scrambling after new definitions of the Agency's purpose. After all, both the Central Intelligence Agency and the National Security Council were created by the National Security Act of 1947, a piece of legislation designed to address post–World War II preoccupations with an alleged Soviet threat. With the loss of communism as a *raison d'être*, the CIA needed new justifications for its budget (the amount of which, incidentally, is secret).[67] At the Agency's fiftieth anniversary in 1997, CIA officials announced that the war on drugs and the war on terrorism would top the CIA's agenda in the post–Cold War world.[68] In fact, as the public is only beginning to learn, the CIA knows a great deal about both drug smuggling and terrorism.

The U.S. war in Southeast Asia and the surrogate wars through the Contras in Nicaragua and the rebels in Afghanistan were all surrounded by accusations of CIA involvement with drug traffickers.[69] At worst, some of these accusations claimed that CIA personnel and other U.S. government officials were directly involved in approving plans for drug smuggling and money laundering.[70] At minimum, as CIA Inspector General Frederick Hitz acknowledged in 1998 congressional testimony, the Agency knowingly worked with "dozens of people and a number of companies who were involved in the drug trade."[71]

If the CIA has unexpected forms of familiarity with the drug trade, it has an even longer history of familiarity with terrorism and surreptitious forms of violence that are perpetrated with full "deniability" and with public accountability to no one. Democracy is merely a pretense if the people have no way of knowing the uses to which their leaders are putting their tax dollars. The people did not know about CIA sponsorship of several military incursions into Communist China in the 1950s. The people did not know about the CIA planes that bombed Guatemala in 1960. The people did not know about the CIA supplying weapons to Iraqi Kurds in 1973, but then abandoning the Kurds to bloody massacre since the CIA purpose was to use the Kurds to destabilize the government of Iraq but not to overthrow it.[72] The people did not know about the CIA involvement in creating "Operation Gladio" in post–World War II Europe. Operation Gladio successfully established secretive, paramilitary units with stockpiles of weapons in virtually every nation of Western Europe (even in neutral Switzerland) with the avowed intent of conducting guerrilla warfare in the event of a successful Soviet invasion. The invasion never came, but Gladio units have been active nonetheless. Gladio paramilitary forces have been implicated in a score or more of terrorist bombings in the 1970s and 80s in Germany and Italy. As late as 1990, Italian Prime Minister Giulio Andreotti revealed that over 600 people were still on the Gladio payroll in Italy.[73]

Inscribed on the walls of the old CIA headquarters were words from Jesus: "You shall know the truth and the truth shall set you free" (from John 8:32).[74] Besides being an example of the biblical illiteracy and perversion of faith that typifies all government intrusions into the realm of "religion," the use of the engraving to adorn a CIA building is blatant deception and *un*truth. Whatever the intelligence role of the CIA may be in accumulating facts, the Agency has as part of its very purpose the withholding of both facts and truth from the public. At times, the facts are not withheld but manufactured. Historian Roger Morris, a member of the National Security Council in both the Johnson and Nixon Administrations, reported that the CIA consistently issued a "systematic overstatement" of Soviet military strength.[75] The CIA numbers have been grist for public fears and political debates over spending gaps and bomber gaps and missile gaps and antiballistic missile gaps. The CIA campaign of "disinformation" aimed at other countries has made its way back into the United States in the form of CIA-subsidized news services to which U.S. media have unwittingly subscribed.[76]

As the cult of secrecy expands, the future will have fewer Roger Morrises and Daniel Ellsbergs to tell what they know about CIA deceptions and covert military actions. What was once a requirement that intelligence personnel take a secrecy oath covering a specified period of time after they left government employment has now turned into a lifetime secrecy contract for over a million employees of the federal government and government contractors. Secrecy oaths are now required of members of House and Senate intelligence committees, and the packet of rules issued by the House Conference of the Majority in 1995 required the oath for every member of the House.[77] The frequency with which Congress and congressional committees meet in closed session has been increasing. Representative democracy becomes a sham when representatives are required to keep secrets from the people they represent, and there can be little doubt that the current cult of secrecy is designed as much to protect the government from public scrutiny as from the scrutiny of "foreign enemies." Noam Chomsky writes, "It is important to bear in mind that the reliance on clandestine terrorism and proxy forces was undertaken to evade public opinion. . . . Clandestine operations are not a secret to their victims, or, generally, to foreign powers. . . ."[78]

If it is the truth which sets one free, then intelligence agencies have denied freedom to many. Intelligence agencies are at the core of a system in which there is gnosis for the few and an enforced "not knowing" for the public. The evasion of public knowledge is also an essential component in the counterterrorism and "low-intensity conflict" that are taught at military training centers like the Institute for Security Cooperation at Fort Benning, Georgia. The most effective warfare is that which does not provide grisly scenes for viewing on the evening news. Killing priests and nuns attracts negative attention, so one training exercise at the Institute actually involved taking control of a mock village while managing to avoid killing the village priest. It became a bit of a joke that the priest was killed or injured in 75 percent of these exercises.[79]

In order to move beyond terror and counterterror, intelligence agencies like the CIA and military training centers like that at Fort Benning must be shut down along with the entire cult of secrecy. The secrecy must be ended, not because intelligence agencies hire evil people, but because military assignments pursued in an atmosphere of concealment allow even decent people with multibillion-dollar budgets to convince themselves that their actions are not evil. With reference to the Revelation of John, Daniel Berrigan wrote, "Unsealing, unmasking, revealing, these are offices of the truth, of God. Need one add, of ourselves? Evil is most itself, most entrenched and confident, when it is concealed."[80] As Dale Aukerman observed, what lies at the very core of military concealment is not hatred or greed or arrogance but a "brazen denial" of the God who sees.[81] However effective concealment might be at avoiding public scrutiny, it is only illusion when we convince ourselves that we avoid the eyes of God (Proverbs 15:3; Hebrews 4:13), the seeing of God (Isaiah 47:10; John 3:20), the judgment of God (Psalm 33:13-19).

4. In order to move beyond the "home-grown" manifestations of domestic terror and counterterror, there must be an end to governmental reliance on entrapment and informers and covert "sting" operations, all of which serve only to exacerbate suspicions and mistrust. In standoffs, there must be a willingness to rely on mediators and to negotiate for as long as it takes to avoid the loss of life. Claims of injustice that are brought to the fore deserve careful investigation, full disclosure, and reconciling response, even if the claims are put forth by groups that have been labeled "extremist." There must be movement away from the military model of law enforcement that now pervades federal, state, and local police forces. And we must work for a society in which the gun and the bomb are not idolized as instruments of freedom. If gun control is people control, the gun itself is an instrument of even greater people control, whether wielded by terrorist or counterterrorist.

When governments respond to domestic dissent and political unrest with spying, entrapment, and a show of force, governments risk initiating a spiral of violence and counter-violence.[82] Yet, it is precisely these types of activities that have typified domestic counterterrorism programs in the U.S. since the 1980s. A turning point came with the 1986 *Public Report of the Vice President's Task Force on Combating Terrorism.* The Task Force proposed decreasing public access to information because, they worried, the Freedom of Information Act might be abused by terrorists. At the same time, the Task Force proposed increased governmental access to information through "conventional human and technical intelligence capabilities that penetrate terrorist groups and their support systems." In 1986 alone, the FBI conducted 8,450 domestic terrorism investigations. In 1987, there were the first documented cases of FBI agents refusing to follow orders as it became clear that the "terrorism" investigations were being ordered on groups ranging from Physicians for Social Responsibility (winner of the 1985 Nobel Peace Prize) to Christian pacifists who opposed U.S. foreign policy.[83]

Concurrent with an increase in domestic spying, the 1980s and 1990s were marked by encouragement for localities across the U.S. to strive for a high level of military preparedness as part of the war on terrorism. The SWAT team (Special Weapons and Tactics) became a common feature of big cities and small towns alike, a legacy that remains with us to this day. James William Gibson describes how

> Even small towns had squads equipped with M16s and H&K 9mm submachine guns fitted with noise suppressors, along with sniper rifles and other military hardware. . . .
>
> Moreover, many local police units had been integrated into state, regional, and national command-and-control "counterterror" networks.

For example, in the 1980s the Federal Emergency Management Agency (FEMA) . . . became an intelligence organization that coordinated local police departments in war games which involved sweeping arrests, mass imprisonment, and/or combat against political dissidents, potential terrorists (such as environmentalists), and illegal aliens.[84]

Yet, even while preparations were being laid to spy upon terrorists and to meet them with SWAT teams, American popular culture was busily extolling the virtues of lone warriors and small groups of fighters who fit the description of no one so much as terrorists. For those who believed that the War in Vietnam was lost when Washington bureaucrats prevented our troops from achieving victory, there was a growing sense that the defense of the American dream had to be pursued outside the constraints of polite society. For those of like mind in an earlier generation, the hero was Douglas MacArthur, who was ready to move from Korea to China until the bureaucrats stopped him. In post–Vietnam War popular culture, a whole slate of fictional heroes was introduced in films like *Rambo, Road Warrior, Death Wish, Lethal Weapon,* and *Red Dawn.* In such films, the "good guys" won for a change, it was claimed, because their violence was not constrained by the rules of bureaucrats or by the legal niceties that protected the criminal class. Outside of Hollywood, similar sentiments attracted a growing readership to *Soldier of Fortune* magazine and increased enrollment at freelance schools that offered training for mercenaries. Occasional murders were committed by some who offered their services through *Soldier of Fortune* classified ads. And occasional acts of terrorism were committed by those who attended mercenary schools, including men who happened to be Sikhs who were trained at a mercenary school run by Frank Camper near Birmingham, Alabama; the graduates went on to blow up an Air India flight in 1985, killing all 329 people aboard.[85] If the paramilitary movement has been embarrassed by such incidents, it has not been deterred.

It is terrifying, this assortment of counterterror networks and SWAT teams and militia groups and mercenaries-in-training, all armed to the teeth and all ready to generate terror in their struggles against their assorted versions of terrorists. At the center of it all is a preoccupation with lethal hardware, with the "special weapons" as the SWAT teams call them. But lest we think that such preoccupations are limited to the SWAT teams and the militia groups and the sweaty warriors of Hollywood, gun manufacturers have taken to advertising in venues such as the *Ladies Home Journal* with the reminder that guns are necessary to the safety of a household. David Kairys, professor at Temple University Law School, argues that such advertising is fraudulent. Bringing a gun into the home makes it several times more likely that someone in the household will die by gunshot, says Kairys, including a tenfold increase in the risk of suicide for any teenagers in the home.[86]

One cannot help but wonder, too, if our global household was not safer before so many counterterrorists rushed to our defense.

*   *   *

One of Gandhi's many profound insights was that the state cannot govern without some degree of cooperation from the governed. Likewise, the violence of both terrorists and counterterrorists cannot grind on if common folks resist. The second section of this chapter offers brief sketches of three individuals who resisted terror with nonviolence. However, to hold up individuals who have given exemplary witness is to risk having them dismissed as "saints." Even if we view ourselves as people of slighter virtue, individuals and communities can make important contributions towards moving beyond terror and counterterror. Indeed, the stance that offers the *least* hope is the one that claims terrorism and the war on terrorism involve issues that can only be resolved by the principalities and powers. While the powers offer only more of the same, individuals and communities can act in ways that interrupt the perpetual sowing and reaping of terror.

1. We can act to resist the temptation to terror in our own lives. Terror can enter our lives in ways that are obvious (such as physical abuse in relationships) but also in ways that are more subtle (such as the attempts to instill fear and establish control in relationships through anger, lies, or manipulation). The terror generated by bigotry is sometimes clearly visible in the murder of black people or gay men; but the subtler expressions of racism, sexism, homophobia, and other bigotries also have the effect of undermining communities. The dualistic view of the world as populated by good people (counterterrorists) and bad (terrorists) is sometimes denoted by the presence of the gun in the nightstand drawer. But in subtler fashion, the daily choices we make ranging from the television we watch (or not) to the books we read (or not) can serve to engender or resist the dualistic consciousness on which terror and counterterror thrive. Clichéd as it may sound, the most important place to begin moving beyond terror and counterterror is in our own homes. As Ramsey Clark put it, "If we want to end all terrorism, we have to stop practicing terrorism in our lives, in our families, in everything we do. And then we can live in a world without fear of others."[87]

2. We can act to withhold our consent — indeed, we can act to express vociferously our dissent the next time and every time politicos tell us there is one last manifestation of evil in the world that needs to be met with military force.

When they tell us so tediously that justice, freedom, and the fate of the planet require that we march to war, let us march for peace instead. The perfect formula for generating international terrorism is to keep the war machine well honed, to spread about liberally armaments and training in techniques of guerrilla warfare to all of the "freedom fighters" who are arrayed around the globe, and to let cruise with frequency the missiles aimed at the heart of evil. Let us dissent from all that.

Currently, public support for military actions is virtually instinctive, especially so if troops have already been placed in harm's way. It is claimed that, to question the endeavor, to express less than enthusiastic support is to show callous disregard for the lives of the young women and men who face enemy bullets on our behalf. As if by magic, the charge of disregard for life is leveled against those who oppose placing troops on the battlefield while the potentates who placed them there are held immune. Speaking at his Nuremberg trial, Hermann Goering explained the process: ". . . the people can always be brought to the bidding of the leaders. That is easy. All you have to do is to tell them they are being attacked, and denounce the pacifists for lack of patriotism and exposing the country to danger." And already in 1957, a figure no less than General Douglas MacArthur (no pacifist he) observed the process at work in the United States: "Our government has kept us in a perpetual state of fear — kept us in a continuous stampede of patriotic fervor — with the cry of grave national emergency. Always there has been some terrible evil at home or some monstrous foreign power that was going to gobble us up if we did not blindly rally behind it. . . ."[88]

We can refuse to be terrified upon command. When Franklin Roosevelt said in his First Inaugural Address in 1933 that "the only thing we have to fear is fear itself," he was probably not thinking of the fears that governments generate as justification for military interventions, but the consequences of such fears are in fact fearful. If we can resist the appeals to fear that are presented as justification for the next war and for the one after that, then perhaps we can eventually find ourselves in the happy circumstance in which there is habitual opposition rather than instinctive support for military adventures.

Currently, of course, leaders know about the massive (albeit ephemeral) public support that comes their way when a military venture is launched. Some commentators have wondered about the degree to which this phenomenon might subtly influence (if not determine, as Goering asserted) leaders' decisions regarding the "necessity" or timing of military attacks. Some wondered about whether it was entirely coincidental that President Reagan ordered the invasion of Grenada on October 25, 1983, only two days after a truck-bomb attack left 241 U.S. Marines dead in Lebanon; although Grenada was certainly small pickings, within hours, the U.S. was "coming back strong" from its "defeat" in Lebanon.[89] Likewise, Senator Arlen Specter of Pennsylvania wondered aloud in front of the press about the degree to which the timing of President Clinton's decision to launch cruise missiles against Sudan and "terrorist camps" in Afghanistan may have been influenced by a desire to remove the public focus from the White House sex scandal. But whether the decisions of Reagan, Clinton, and other leaders have been self-serving or selfless or (as is often the case for most people) some mixture, there is no doubt that the use of force elicits public support.

The phenomenon is disturbingly predictable. While there may be vigorous debate and lack of consensus before hostilities begin (as during the period before the Gulf War), once the attack is launched, "support" for the troops is manifested as support for the war, and typically, the support is alarming in its mass. In the United States, the effect of relegating the declaration of war to the status of constitutional artifact has been to give the president a freer hand in shortening or even eliminating the period of public discussion and disagreement and moving directly to the period of public support that materializes when military action is a *fait accompli*. One need not attribute evil motivations to presidents or other leaders to be disturbed by this trend towards precluding debates on military actions. Among social scientists, Irving Janis has done pioneering studies of the manner in which "groupthink" asserts itself when policymaking groups remain small and insulated. When military actions are planned without public debate or even public cognizance, the secretive nature of the undertaking requires that the group advising the commander-in-chief will be small and insular. Janis describes some of the dangers that arise as groupthink emerges:

> In dealing with a rival nation, policy-makers comprising an amiable group find it relatively easy to authorize dehumanizing solutions such as large-scale bombings. An affable group of government officials is unlikely to pursue the difficult and controversial issues that arise when alternatives to a harsh military solution come up for discussion. Nor are the members inclined to raise ethical issues that imply that this "fine group of ours, with its humanitarianism and its high-minded principles, might be capable of adopting a course of action that is inhumane and immoral."[90]

Among the symptoms of groupthink that Janis cites are "Stereotyped views of enemy leaders as too evil to warrant genuine attempts to negotiate. . . ."[91]

In addition to *being* a form of terrorism, each military attack feeds weapons, training, and/or hatred to the terrorists of tomorrow. To change that, individuals, faith communities, all people who are interested in ending the cycles of terror and counterterror are already in possession of a potent tool — the ability to withhold consent and to express dissent. Lives would be saved if every decision for the use of force was met with opposition rather than predictable consent. Blood would be spilt less readily if people who are not even of pacifist persuasion were to insist that killing is sufficiently serious as to require a full disclosure and discussion of the issues *before* any use of force. For the U.S., while a nuclear conflict requiring decisions within minutes is a possibility in a well-armed world, such a scenario cannot be used as an excuse for the lack of a war declaration in Vietnam, Grenada, Nicaragua, Panama, Haiti, Iraq, Yugoslavia, Sudan, Afghanistan, and the plethora of other nations in which the U.S. has intervened militarily in recent years. Full disclosure and discussion *before* the use of force would require granting substantial access to the media by governmental representatives and common citizens of the nation or nations that are potential military targets. If leaders cannot meet across negotiating tables, perhaps both leaders and common folks can meet across the airwaves. Would this mean giving media access to the next "Hitler" we encounter? One important way in which we can refuse to give consent to hasty and frequent military interventions is to refuse to participate in the demonization of adversaries. The Hitler analogy is an incitement to violence. If Hitler analogies there must be, then let us use them only as indicators of the authoritarianism, militarism, and ethnocentrism that *we* must avoid.

Nonviolent dissent and noncooperation are the antithesis of both terror and counterterror. Both terrorists and counterterrorists assert that *others* must pay the price for the "just cause" that is being pursued, whereas nonviolent dissent and civil disobedience insist that the sacrifice should not be borne by others but by the dissenters themselves. The sacrifices that dissidents have borne range from commitment of time and energy to incarceration to injury and death. The one "rule" on which nonviolent activists agree is also the feature that most clearly marks such activism as the antithesis of terror and counterterror — i.e., no action should be undertaken in which there is any foreseeable risk of physical injury or death to any adversaries or any bystanders or any other people outside of the group of activists themselves.[92]

Terrorism has been described as a tool that is most likely to be used by the poor and the weak who lack the resources to engage in more conventional forms of conflict. In addition to being a slander on the poor, this description ignores the immense capacities that all people have to effectuate change through nonviolent dissent and noncooperation.[93] Gandhi and others have demonstrated that such nonviolence can be a highly effective form of activism for the dispossessed. But equally as slanderous as the association of the poor with terrorism is the association of nonviolent resistance with terrorism. Robin Morgan notes that this smear has been used against many of the activist women she met in the Third World:

> For the record, then. Women taking to the streets banging pots and pans during food-shortage riots are not engaged in terrorist activity. Women marching in a public demonstration against a colonial government are not engaged in terrorist activity. Peasant women agitating for land rights, squatting on their small sharecropped farms, are not engaged in terrorist activity.[94]

And, it might be added, those who offer nonviolent resistance to the next U.S. military intervention will not be engaging in terrorist activity. They will be opposing it.

3. Here is another recipe for making a locality ripe for terror: undermine traditional culture(s), pour in plenty of weapons, and introduce competition for economic survival.[95] All of these ingredients accompany the global spread of corporate capitalism in the so-called "New World Order." In the economic choices we make, individuals and communities can have an impact in fostering or resisting the destruction of communities half a world away. Our economic choices have the power to shape our own lives for better or worse ("We are what we eat"), but in an era of enforced global economic integration, our choices also impact the lives of people we will never meet. We may sometimes find that the best choice we can make is not the choice to be an "educated consumer" but to be an educated non-consumer. Indeed, in a world of limited "resources" and of stark economic disparities, one choice that has been offered as good news (though it be heard as bad) is the decision to climb down the social ladder (e.g., Matthew 6:24; Mark 10:17-22; Luke 8:14).[96]

Glaring economic disparities create environments that generate violence, not only among the poor (as if the poor were somehow more susceptible to violent impulses), but among members of all economic groups. It is certainly true that disparity heightens the appeal of those who are organizing for violent rebellion by the poor or (even more likely) by the "near-poor" and middle-class groups beset by rising expectations. But it is no less true that disparity contributes to violence by the wealthy. Those who benefit from inequities might understandably experience their position as highly vulnerable to attack since the ecology of the planet cannot sustain a wealthy lifestyle for more than a small percentage of humanity. Therefore, the beneficiaries of disparity may feel a need to maintain the disparity by force.[97]

Although it is rarely acknowledged that military might is assembled for the maintenance of inequity, a few leaders have been remarkably candid in commenting on this aspect of U.S. military and foreign policy. In 1948, George Kennan, then head of the State Department's policy planning staff, issued a study in which he wrote:

> We have about 50 percent of the world's wealth, but only 6.3 percent of its population. . . . Our real task in the coming period is to devise a pattern of relationships which will permit us to maintain this position of disparity without positive detriment to our national security. To do so we have to dispense with all sentimentality and day-dreaming. . . . We should cease to talk about vague and . . . unreal objectives such as human rights, the raising of living standards and democratization. The day is not far off when we are going to have to deal in straight power concepts. The less we are hampered by idealistic slogans, the better.[98]

More recently, after the fall of the Berlin Wall, General A. M. Gray, Commandant of the U.S. Marine Corps, argued against cuts in military spending because "The underdeveloped world's growing dissatisfaction over the gap between rich and poor nations will create a fertile breeding ground for insurgencies. These insurgencies have the potential to jeopardize regional stability and our access to vital economic and military resources."[99] Of course, depending on one's perspective, the "underdeveloped world" is also known as the exploited world, a world whose vital resources are not necessarily ours for the accessing. Whatever one calls these "worlds," there is no doubt that the planetary gap between the rich and the poor has been expanding dramatically. When applied to economics, the cliché that "A rising tide lifts all boats" may be balm for the conscience of the wealthy, but it is an irredeemable falsehood. According to the 1999 United Nations Human Development Report, the income ratio between the fifth of the world's people living in the richest countries and the fifth in the poorest countries was 30 to 1 in 1960, 60 to 1 in 1990, and 74 to 1 in 1997.[100]

But why, then, the proposals to be "non-consumers" and to "climb down the social ladder"? Why not a proposal to decrease the disparity by hastening the pace of Western investment in the Third World? In fact, as the UN statistics indicate, the Western investment of the past 40 years has *increased* the gap between rich and poor. Even if there were illusions that such investment could be crafted in a way that would give all six billion residents of the planet a lifestyle comparable to middle-class Americans or Europeans, can a viable claim be made that the planet could sustain such added ecological onslaught? But more directly to the point of terror and counterterror, there is growing evidence that corporate investments and global economic *integration* contribute to local *frag-*

mentation. Communal disintegration is engendered as outside investments tend to favor those who already have status and resources in local communities. As social stratification becomes more rigid, the environment is ripe for economic and political power brokers to play out competition along the lines of supposed "age-old ethnic hatreds."[101] Illustration of the process at work is provided in the writings of Swedish-born Helena Norberg-Hodge, a philosopher and teacher who has lived for over three decades in the Himalayan province of Ladakh in Kashmir. When Norberg-Hodge was first welcomed as a resident of the province, there were no roads connecting Ladakh to the outside world, but with the roads came tourists, then an infrastructure to support the tourist industry, then outside investment and Western-style media and education. While Ladakh was once agriculturally self-sufficient, food is now imported. Cooperative farming has given way to competition for jobs. Concomitant with all of this, religious divisions have arisen in Ladakh. Ironically, Norberg-Hodge notes, as divisions have solidified along Muslim and Buddhist lines, religious devotion actually has been declining. In 1986, for the first time, Norberg-Hodge heard her friends beginning to define one another according to whether they were Buddhist or Muslim. Since then, several people have been killed in violence between Muslims and Buddhists.[102] Ladakh is certainly not alone in experiencing the communal fragmentation that accompanies global economic integration.

To emphasize the importance for the "First World" of non-consumption and decisions to climb down the social ladder is not to deny the need for information and self-education regarding purchasing decisions. Boycotts and economic sanctions have been tools for nonviolent change in efforts ranging from the organizing of migrant farm workers in the United States to the ending of apartheid in South Africa. There are manufacturers of consumer products that make profits from child labor and sweatshops and the slave labor of prisoners, mega-stores that wreck local environments both ecologically and economically, oil companies that have been implicated in the killing of civilian protesters in Nigeria and in the violent crushing of dissent in Aceh province in Indonesia.[103] Is it not fair that consumers should be allowed to boycott corporations that engage in such practices? Not according to big businesses and the World Trade Organization and U.S. federal courts. The State of Massachusetts passed a "selective purchasing law" aimed at curtailing business with Burma (Myanmar), where a military junta had annulled the election to the presidency of Nobel Peace Prize laureate Aung San Suu Kyi. A consortium of corporations successfully sued to have the law overturned by federal courts.[104] But even when the courts decide that states may not engage in selective purchasing, it is still possible for individuals to be informed and to make those purchasing decisions that do not support reigns of terror.[105]

A change of attitude in the First World can be a major first step towards curtailing the economic globalism that fragments communities and sows terror in the Third World. We must surrender the illusion that people with cultures and technologies different from our own are "underdeveloped." We must surrender the illusion that people in the Third World are waiting with bated breath to have what we have and to be who we are. Several years ago, Martin Khor, president of the Third World Network, was asked about his opposition to global trade agreements. Was he not concerned about people in the Third World who would be deprived of Western standards of living? Jerry Mander paraphrases the response he heard from Martin Khor:

> I think you have it backward. Those who most depend on an expanding economy are not Malaysians or other Third Worlders, but you in the First World. In your world, you no longer have contact with the land, and you don't know how to get along without luxuries. For us, if the whole global trade system collapsed, we might be better off. . . . We wouldn't mind having some of the new technologies you offer, and some kinds of trade are very useful, but if the Western colonial powers and transnational corporations would simply leave us alone, stop exploiting our resources and land so we could again retain their use, we could probably survive quite well. But what would you do?[106]

4. Though it may sound trivial, it is nonetheless true that a small pebble tossed into a lake can produce ripples that travel from shore to shore. It is in the simple acts of kindness and life-affirmation that terror is renounced. We are not called to world-transforming actions but to live humanly and faithfully, even in the midst of apocalyptic terror. *Barefoot Gen* and *Maus* are two novels which, despite their comic strip format, offer stark portrayals of two horrible acts of terrorism — the atomic bombing of Hiroshima *(Barefoot Gen)* and the persecution of the Jews in Nazi Europe *(Maus)*.[107] Yet even in the midst of terror, say these two novels, the survivors were able to show compassion, bind wounds, share food, comfort children. In such actions, terror is denied the total power towards which it aims. The defeat of terror lies in actions such as these.[108]

Where fear has reigned, it is possible to create zones that are free from terror — beachheads that witness to the reign of God. In Tacoma, Washington, the Catholic Worker community's hospitality house for homeless people is located in a section of the city that was once beset by vacant lots full of broken glass and used syringes and rusty, abandoned cars. Several years ago, members of the Worker community came up with the idea of turning one of the lots into an urban, organic garden. They approached an elderly widow who rarely left her house due to fear of violence on the streets. They proposed that, in return for garden water from her hose, they would clear the lot next to her home, bring in topsoil, and plant and help to tend a garden. The woman agreed, and the garden became the first of a series established on once-vacant lots. Today in Tacoma, there is a working, urban farm that is able to provide food for hungry people and, by selling food to local businesses, provide employment for homeless people. Where people were once afraid to leave their homes, progress has been made towards establishing a terror-free zone.[109]

In order to witness to the defeat of terror, churches and other faith communities must also be zones that are free from terror. Rather than peddling fears and threats of damnation, the church is called to witness to the one and only sufficient antidote to terror — the resurrection of Jesus. All of the principalities and powers experience this resurrection as "the terror of God" insofar as it unveils the defeat of death, and it is the sting of death (1 Corinthians 15:54-55) that has served as the foundation of both terrorism and the war on terrorism. But now all things are new, and the ministry of the church is not to preach and practice fear, but to preach and practice the defeat of death — indeed, to preach and practice the reconciliation that has already been accomplished by God.

> So if anyone is in Christ, there is a new creation: everything old has passed away; see, everything has become new! All this is from God, who reconciled us to himself through Christ, and has given us the ministry of reconciliation; that is, in Christ God was reconciling the world to himself, not counting their trespasses against them, and entrusting the message of reconciliation to us. So we are ambassadors for Christ, since God is making his appeal through us; we entreat you on behalf of Christ, be reconciled to God. (2 Corinthians 5:17-20)

Paths of Nonviolence: Tolstoy, Day, Tutu

Throughout church history, there have been faithful witnesses to the Gospel renunciation of violence and the defeat of death in the resurrection of Jesus. It is nonviolence that interrupts the cycle of terror and counterterror. This is not to suggest that nonviolence is an especially effective instrument in the pursuit of political, social, or economic goals; indeed, nonviolence is not an "instrument" and it is rarely judged to be effective by the common standards of power politics. But nonviolence is a *way of being in the world* that interrupts the cycle of terror and counterterror by exercising control over the one and only person

251

who any of us can ever hope to control or should ever desire to control, i.e., oneself. Rather than seeking to coerce the actions of others, the nonviolent witness says in effect, "The terror stops with me. I will seek to return love for hate. I will seek to refuse all cooperation with violence. I will seek reconciliation rather than retribution." This emphasis on oneself, however, is only a way of speaking about the one and only person over whom control can or should be exercised. This is not to suggest that nonviolence is egocentric or individualistic. In fact, nonviolence is nurtured and sustained in the context of community and, as suggested by the theme of reconciliation, nonviolence entails a radically communitarian vision for humanity.

What follows are brief introductions to some of the thoughts and actions of three major proponents of nonviolence within the last century. In very different settings, each responded to terrorism. The following individuals have been chosen in part because of the power of their witness, the cultural diversity they represent, and the fact that they emerge from three different Christian traditions — Russian Orthodox, Roman Catholic, and Protestant. While a different aspect of nonviolence is emphasized with each individual — love, nonviolent resistance, reconciliation — these are not conflicting but mutually supportive aspects of the way of peace. Regarding each of these individuals and the many other witnesses (famous or not) who might have been chosen, it should be noted that we dishonor them when we regard these people as exceptional "saints" who were superhuman in their capacity for spirituality or love. Saints do not witness to the potential for transcending our own humanity, but rather they witness to the gift of God's image, which has been bestowed upon all humanity, no matter how fallen and broken we may be. We do these witnesses honor by thanking God for using them to point to the paths of discipleship on which we too may walk.

Leo Tolstoy: Love as the Path Beyond Terror

Leo Tolstoy is remembered as a great novelist and as an advocate of nonviolence whose writings had substantial influence on the thought and work of Mohandas Gandhi. But it would not be wrong to remember Tolstoy also as a man of mighty contradictions. Tolstoy's biographer records the "horror" that Tolstoy himself must have experienced when surveying the inconsistencies between his family life and the principles he espoused:

> He preached universal love — and made his wife miserable; poverty — and lived in luxury; forgetfulness of self — and recorded his every twinge;

fusion with God — and wasted his life in domestic bickering; contempt for fame — and curried his celebrity with correspondence, receptions, photographs; the worship of truth — and was driven every single day to the shabbiest dissimulation.[110]

Nor do the contradictions end there. The poet Kenneth Rexroth adds, "A hero of the siege of Sebastopol who became a pacifist, a passionate gambler who freed his serfs before the Emancipation, a young rake who in later life denounced the music of Beethoven, women's sweaters and unchaperoned canoe trips. . . ."[111] Nor do the contradictions end there. His writings contained occasional flashes of misogyny and antisemitism even as he expressed his allegiance to equality. He welcomed excommunication by the Russian Orthodox Church even as he gave profound expression to some of the enduring insights of Eastern Christianity. And he was *Count* Leo Tolstoy, a Russian prince who proposed the abolition of all governments. The contradictions are so raw and obvious that some historians have chosen to dismiss Tolstoy as a utopian thinker whose dangerous ideas were refuted by his own life. Others have contended that the contradictions indicate that Tolstoy, while a great novelist, was an insincere and windy moralist; such is the suggestion in historian Paul Johnson's unkindly titled chapter, "Tolstoy: God's Elder Brother."[112]

There is no need to "explain away" the inconsistencies in Tolstoy's thought and life; indeed, such efforts risk detracting from who he was. It is fair to observe, however, that many of the inconsistencies and contradictions have to do with the contrast between two distinct periods in his life. It was only after Tolstoy had been born into nobility, joined the army, and realized considerable success as a novelist that he experienced a crisis that caused him to reflect anew on questions concerning God, love, community, and nonviolence. Tolstoy's crisis of despair did not come *despite* his success but *because of* success. As early as 1863, soon after his marriage to Sofya, there were hints that Tolstoy saw something illusory in the worldly standards of happiness and success. He wrote in his diary, "Just lately, we felt that there was something terrifying in our happiness. . . . We started to pray." And later that same year he wrote, "It is appalling, dreadful, insane, to allow one's happiness to depend upon purely material things. . . ."[113] What started as terror at the thought of losing happiness turned into despair in the midst of success. Feeling his suicidal potential, Tolstoy gave up hunting trips so as not to be near guns. He wrote in his *Confession,* "All this was happening to me at a time when I was surrounded on all sides by what is considered complete happiness: I was not yet fifty, I had a kind, loving and beloved wife, lovely children, and a large estate that was growing and expanding with no effort on my part."[114] One of several turning points for Tolstoy came during a family stay in Moscow in December 1881. He spent a portion of one day in a poor section of the city, handing out money to people on the street, and then he returned to his Moscow residence to be served a five-course dinner by footmen dressed in white. In the middle of the meal, he rose from the table and exclaimed to Sofya, "One cannot live so! It is impossible!"[115] He spent the remainder of his life trying to live otherwise, dispossessing himself of his considerable wealth (some of it going to his wife and children), freeing his serfs, working in the fields, responding to the needs of the poor, and renouncing terror in all its forms.

And what is the source of terror? Another great Russian novelist, Fyodor Dostoyevsky, searched for the source of terror in the recesses of the hearts of revolutionists. In *The Possessed*, Dostoyevsky offered a glimpse of the destructive impulses that emerge when revolutionary zeal for righteousness is divorced from allegiance to church and country. When the French playwright Albert Camus produced a stage adaptation of *The Possessed*, he retained Dostoyevsky's sense of terror as arising from the violent and misguided quest for "justice," although Camus was more willing than Dostoyevsky to name church and state along with revolutionaries as actors in the misguided quest. But those were not the sources of terror that most interested Tolstoy. Certainly his novels were set against the backdrop of the maneuvering and clashing of principalities and powers, a primary example being Napoleon's invasion of Russia as the context for *War and Peace*. But what most interested Tolstoy was the way in which the conventional lives of conventional people could serve as a source of terror. In characters such as Anna Sherer and Prince Vasily in *War and Peace* and in a character such as Anna Karenina, Tolstoy sees conventional people moving through life in pursuit of self-fulfillment and happiness with little reflection on the consequences of the pursuit. Such consequences include the elevation of self and disregard of others, the very essence of conflict and hostility. If Tolstoy's view of conventional life sounds harsh, it was to a considerable degree a self-judgment since the pursuit of happiness had been his own preoccupation too. In his insightful study of the theology in Tolstoy's writings, Richard Gustafson discerns how the theme emerges from *Anna Karenina*:

> Tolstoy considers Anna's final vision of life the inevitable conclusion to be drawn from life understood as individual self-fulfillment. The pursuit of happiness for yourself alone, regardless of others, which in the end is what the fantasy of romance entails, inexorably leads to a world of struggle and strife. Individualism inevitably turns into a Hobbesian war of each against each and a Darwinian struggle for existence.[116]

For Tolstoy, terror is not the product of evil scheming but the byproduct of conventional living. Again, the insights of Gustafson:

> What is done in the salon is done throughout society. Conventional people can coerce, connive, and condone their own self-interest, not knowing they are coercing, conniving, and condoning. Conventional people make possible the inhumanities of governed society, its wars, its penal colonies, its mass poverty, its abject slavery. Conventional consciousness leads to the circle of violence.[117]

If one is engaged in a search for terrorist and malefactor, one must search within. Tolstoy thus renounces the ethical dualism and demonizing of others which is itself a powerful contributor to violence. Even if one believes that some people are essentially evil (which Tolstoy did not), and even if one believes that the Gospel allows for violence in response to evil (which Tolstoy did not), ". . . it is absolutely impossible to find that safe and indubitable sign by which a malefactor may be unerringly told from one who is not. . . ."[118]

Tolstoy perceived the path of love as the one hope by which individuals and the human community could be freed from the violence associated with the self-interested pursuit of happiness. He did not mean, of course, the path of romantic love nor love alone for one's own family or circle of friends. So anxious was he to distinguish "real love" from romantic love that he wrote in his diary that "the only real love is the one whose object is unattractive" and that "divine love, love for God is known only through love for our enemies." In the presence of the enemy, of the one who hates you, love can sometimes take the form of non-action or "non-resistance" in which you "concentrate all your energy on not not loving, on not allowing into your soul any hostile feeling."[119] In the Gospels, love can be "commanded" in precisely this sense of the double negative, i.e., we are commanded to refuse to not love, or stated differently, when we are unable to love, we are commanded to move our inability aside so that the God who is able to love on our behalf may be made manifest. Tolstoy did not shy away from the implication that such love was a "work" of righteousness, but in its larger meaning, wherever it is present, love is not a testimony to human righteousness but to the activity of the God who is love. In *War and Peace*, the deathbed discoveries of Prince Andrew impart the mystical wisdom of Eastern Christianity. God is love and love is the source of all life. Each person is an image, a particle of that love. It is love which defeats death, for in dying, each particle returns to the eternal source of love. Tolstoy's doctrine of God was not that of the Unmoved Mover but of the Love who is the Force of Life. He saw Darwinian and Hobbesian notions of life forms struggling against one another as no more plausible than notions of God at war with God. Instead, all of creation is caught up in the process of returning to the source who is Love, the process of being adopted as children of God (Romans 8:14-23). As Gustafson notes, Tolstoy's vision, like that of many within Eastern Christianity, is not pantheistic (all is God) but panentheistic (all in God).[120]

While Tolstoy was fond of the word "non-resistance," it is clear that he did not view the concept as fostering passivity. Indeed, movement and engagement are central features of Tolstoy's ethics. Virtue cannot be accumulated and stored, but it is only realized in the movement towards Love. If the Pharisee is static in righteousness, but the harlot, the terrorist, the thief are moving towards Love, then the greater virtue is in the movement.[121] This movement is a spiritual quest in which all people ultimately find that their vocation is the vocation of love. But as Tolstoy makes clear in his story of *Father Sergius,* though the movement is spiritual, we can only ever pursue it in the carnal world. Thus Tolstoy renounced all dualism that would claim we can love in spirit while killing in body. Since the spiritual cannot be divorced from the carnal, neither can love be expressed through violence — not love of country, nor love of justice, nor love of enemies, nor love of future generations, nor any love at all. Likewise, the virtue of love can never be harnessed to utility. We must only consider the movement of love in which we are now engaged (or not) and not some theoretical goals to be served by our current actions. To inquire into the utility of love is akin to profane wonderings about what purpose God serves. Devoid of utility, love is the antithesis of power. This view was central to Tolstoy's anarchism. He believed that neither power nor the refusal of power guaranteed freedom from being coerced, but a refusal of power did guarantee freedom from coercing others.[122]

Tolstoy spent the last thirty years of his life seeking to live by these principles and discovering that he was not alone in the effort. Tolstoy began his book, *The Kingdom of God Is Within You* (1893), with expression of amazement at the number of people who had contacted him to let him know of earlier or recent versions of "non-resistance." Tolstoy already had vague familiarity with some of these, but he devoted the opening pages of *Kingdom* to reviewing what he had learned about groups ranging from the Mennonites to the Quakers, and individuals ranging from the 15th-century Bohemian reformer, Peter Chelčický, to William Lloyd Garrison and Adin Ballou.[123] In his own pursuit of nonviolence, Tolstoy sometimes seemed optimistic about the potential of the world to move beyond militarism; he denounced the U.S. war in the Philippines and the British war against the Boers with the observation that a day was dawning in which "even schoolchildren condemn war!" But then his thoughts turned gloomy and pessimistic when he saw how quickly people rallied to battle in the Russo-Japanese War, and how he even felt twinges within himself of desire for Russian victory.[124] In the chaotic Russian environment during and after that war, Tolstoy consistently denounced the methods of both the terrorist revolutionaries and the counterterrorists set loose by the Tsar. In a risky and audacious letter, Tolstoy wrote Tsar Alexander III asking him to spare the lives of the terrorists who had assassinated his father. Tolstoy urged the Tsar to "forgive, return good for evil. . . . Then, as wax melts in the fire, the revolutionaries' opposition will melt in the deed of their emperor. . . ." The Procurator of the Russian Orthodox Holy Synod told the Tsar that Tolstoy's proposal was a "mental aberration" and a "monstrous scheme," and the Tsar showed his agreement by hanging the assassins.[125]

There were others for whom Tolstoy was able to intervene with greater effect. When famine and mass starvation threatened Russian peasants in 1897, Tolstoy organized material relief, though not without some pangs of conscience at begging money from wealthy donors whom he believed responsible for the plight of the peasants he sought to assist.[126] And in the case of the Doukhobors, Tolstoy intervened in remarkable fashion. The Doukhobors, or "Spirit Wrestlers," a group of Christians originating in Russia, came gradually to a stance of total pacifism. In 1895, under the influence of a leader named Verigin, the Doukhobors even surrendered their hunting rifles in a huge bonfire known as "The Burning of Arms." The government reaction was swift and violent when the Doukhobors also announced that they would henceforth refuse to be conscripted into the army. Doukhobors were driven from their homes and their leaders were arrested and threatened with execution. In response, Tolstoy, Peter Kropotkin, and Canadian Quakers were among those who organized and funded the emigration of the Doukhobor community from Russia to Canada with the understanding that they would be exempted from military obligations in their new homeland.[127]

In the Doukhobors and others of like spirit, Tolstoy saw something remarkable at work. Love expressed as a simple refusal to kill caused massive consternation and brutal response from the powers that be. It is as if the whole system felt itself in danger of unraveling in the face of a simple act of nonviolence.[128] It remained for others like Gandhi, Day, King, and Tutu to further explore the path of love in the unraveling of power. But Tolstoy had made an important contribution in detailing how the pursuit of individual happiness and security was not a path beyond terror but one of the foundations of it.

Some libertarian proponents of individualism have laid hold of the title "anarchism," by which they mean that nothing should be denied to the sovereignty of the individual. Since the brandished gun is the guarantor of such sovereignty, the right to bear arms is a fundamental concern of libertarians. The tradition from which Tolstoy drew and that which he expressed recognized that such individualism was in fact slavery — slavery to fear in the quest for security and sovereignty. Tolstoy recognized that something more communal was required if humanity was to move beyond power and terror, if humanity was to experience freedom. Such was also the position of another anarchist from the Russian Orthodox tradition, Nikolai Berdyaev. Berdyaev wrote, "Slavery to self and slavery to the objective world are one and the same slavery. The pursuit of mastery, power, success, glory, the enjoyment of life, is always slavery. . . . The lust for power is a slavish instinct."[129]

The pursuit of success, power, and security only has the potential to divide humanity into opposing forces, nation states, terrorists and counterterrorists, and, at the extreme, individuals segregated one from another, loudly proclaiming with gun in hand that they are free. Tolstoy taught that the opposing forces are fated to be together, united not by some powerful emperor, but by the renunciation of power. It is the will of God, the will of Love, that "we cannot be saved separately, we must be saved all together."[130]

Dorothy Day: Nonviolent Resistance as the Path Beyond Terror

Nonresistance. Nonviolent resistance. The words themselves suggest that these two positions might be antagonistic one to another, and at times, activists have indicated that the differences are more than linguistic. Recall the abolitionists in the U.S., some of whom believed that a refusal of payment of the taxes that supported the slave system would amount to a violation of their nonresistant principles. Of course, the state seeks obedience in all things. Does "nonresistance" mean that, short of picking up a gun, such obedience must be given? After all, offering hospitality to an escaped slave constituted a form of "resistance" to the Fugitive Slave Law. Yet, some proponents of nonresistance busily aided and abetted escaped slaves based on their conviction that the essence of nonresistance was not obedience but nonviolence. Although the vocabulary suggests otherwise, history points to a commonality of spirit among proponents of nonresistance and noncooperation and nonviolent resistance.

The common ground for nonresistance and nonviolent resistance is already hinted at in the biblical text. Without denying that there is a rich diversity in biblical theology and ethics, it is nonetheless possible to discern a common spirit in all of the following biblical texts on resistance and nonresistance:

"You have heard that it was said, 'An eye for an eye and a tooth for a tooth.' But I say to you, Do not resist an evildoer. But if anyone strikes you on the right cheek, turn the other also; and if anyone wants to sue you and take your coat, give your cloak as well; and if anyone forces you to go one mile, go also the second mile." (Matthew 5:38-41)

When they had brought them, they had them stand before the council. The high priest questioned them, saying, "We gave you strict orders not to teach in this name, yet here you have filled Jerusalem with your teaching and you are determined to bring this man's blood on us." But Peter and the apostles answered, "We must obey God rather than any human authority." (Acts 5:27-29)

Submit yourselves therefore to God. Resist the devil, and he will flee from you. (James 4:7)

Discipline yourselves, keep alert. Like a roaring lion your adversary the devil prowls around, looking for someone to devour. Resist him, steadfast in your faith, for you know that your brothers and sisters in all the world are undergoing the same kinds of suffering. (1 Peter 5:8-9)

The "evildoer" who must not be resisted in Matthew 5 is another human being. Do not strike back. Do not seek retribution. Do not rely on the tools of the "evildoer." In contrast, the "devil" who must be resisted is not a human being but a power who represents the malignant spirit of the age. The mode of resistance includes the willingness to bear suffering rather than to inflict it. All of these texts are in accord with the observations of the Pauline writer of Ephesians. "For our struggle is not against enemies of blood and flesh, but against the rulers, against the authorities, against the cosmic powers of this present darkness, against the spiritual forces of evil in the heavenly places" (Ephesians 6:12).

Dorothy Day embraced the term "nonviolent resistance" and she understood it as an expression of discipleship. It was simultaneously a refusal to do injury to any other person while actively resisting all the terrors engendered by the principalities and powers, by what Day in her plainspoken way called "this filthy, rotten system." She did not view herself as naturally predisposed to acts of resistance. She hated jails, but she found herself jailed on numerous occasions. She hated guns and violence, but she was not dissuaded by threats of violence or even by gunfire. Day came under literal fire during a visit to the Koinonia Community in Americus, Georgia in 1957. Clarence Jordan joined with others in founding Koinonia as a farming community that sought to live by biblical principles of nonviolence and equality. Some citizens in the vicinity of Americus did not take kindly to what they saw as Koinonia's espousal of "race mixing." Shots were fired into community buildings, and Koinonia's produce stand was firebombed more than once. As part of the nonviolent effort to deter such attacks, Day volunteered to help keep nighttime watch during her visit. One night as she held vigil in a station wagon parked at the gate to the farm, another car sped by and a shotgun blast sent pellets ripping into the station wagon. Day narrowly escaped injury or death.[131] She acknowledged the fear she experienced in the midst of the attack, but she always viewed her own fear not as a deterrent to action but as encouragement to greater faithfulness. On the topic of fear, she frequently offered reminders to herself and to others of the words from the Johannine epistle:

> There is no fear in love, but perfect love casts out fear; for fear has to do with punishment, and whoever fears has not reached perfection in love. We love because he first loved us. Those who say, "I love God," and hate their brothers or sisters, are liars; for those who do not love a brother or sister whom they have seen, cannot love God whom they have not seen. The commandment we have from him is this: those who love God must love their brothers and sisters also. (1 John 4:18-21)

Dorothy Day is remembered as the founder of both the paper and the communities that go by the name of "Catholic Worker," but she herself renounced the claim to being the founder of anything. Insofar as anyone could be called the originator of the Catholic Worker movement, Day attributed significance to the teachings of Peter Maurin, an itinerant philosopher of peasant background from France. Many of Maurin's teachings reflected the post–World War I "Christian personalism" of French philosophers such as Emmanuel Mounier and Jacques Maritain. Like other personalist philosophers, Maurin rejected the notion of "progress" in human history, and he also disavowed an approach to change that "objectivized" human needs as social problems requiring institutional solutions. The future will be different, Maurin believed, only if we begin living differently in the present, and that requires not an institutional solution but a personal commitment. The first concern of the personalist is not what "they" ought to do about problems, but what "I" and "we" can do in community. Maurin said, "Be what you want the other fellow to be." And again, "We should be announcers, not denouncers." And again, "Don't criticize what is not being done. Find the work you can perform, fit yourself to perform it, and then do it."[132]

The works which Day and Maurin saw that needed to be done were works of justice and works of mercy. With the initial support of a small community, hospitality houses and free kitchens were started in response to the needs of the homeless and the hungry. To spread the message of justice, the *Catholic Worker* paper was first published in 1933. Day observed that it all happened without much forethought. The pot of soup that she always kept on her stove for hungry guests turned into a food line for hundreds of people by 1936, and as more space was required for those in need of shelter, another apartment was rented and then another and then a house.[133] In the years since, Catholic Worker communities have been started in cities throughout the U.S. and in several other countries.

Neither Day nor Maurin viewed the Catholic Worker as being engaged in generosity or charity, and they were certainly not offering food and shelter as tools for proselytism.[134] The bread that was being given to the poor already belonged to them, not by virtue of legal possession but by virtue of the more important reality that bread is a gift from God for the sustenance of all life. To encounter the needy is to encounter the opportunity to serve God, and therefore, it is the beggar and not the giver who must be thanked. Peter Maurin wrote, "People who are in need and are not afraid to beg give to people not in need the occasion to do good for goodness' sake. . . . Although you may be called bums and panhandlers you are in fact Ambassadors of God."[135] The Catholic Worker view of poverty involved a dialectic. While voluntary poverty was part of the path of discipleship, involuntary poverty was a sign of a culture in rebellion against God. As described by Leon Bloy, another personalist philosopher from France, involuntary poverty could only be experienced as a source of "terror" and "despair," whereas voluntary poverty was a path of freedom that left one dependent on nothing and no one save God.[136] Or as Peter Maurin put it, voluntary poverty freed one to be interested in standards of loving rather than standards of living.

From the leadership circles of the Catholic Church and from elsewhere, there was widespread admiration for the Catholic Worker kitchens and hospitality houses, and there was equally widespread condemnation of Catholic Worker pacifism. When Day rejected the violence from all sides in the Spanish Civil War and then again in "the Good War," World War II, subscriptions to the paper and contributions to the community fell dramatically. Many wrote to warn Day that her "pacifist harangues" were endangering the "wonderful work" she was doing with the poor. Just as Martin Luther King, Jr. was later told that he should stop commenting on the War in Vietnam and stick to his area of civil rights expertise, Day was told that she should stick to serving the poor and let the politicians and theologians worry about issues of war and peace.[137] Her concern, however, was not with "issues" but with the Gospel, and the Gospel had as much to say about loving enemies as it did about feeding the hungry. Indeed, resisting violence and feeding the hungry were only two faces of one reality — the biblical call to show love for God by loving the least of our sisters and brothers (Matthew 25:31-46), no matter if they are considered "least" in terms of wealth or righteousness or lovability.

For Dorothy Day and for others in the Catholic Worker movement, the meaning of nonviolent resistance was clarified as they sought to resist the nuclear balance of terror. Following the atomic bombings of Japan, the Workers sent a telegram to President Truman expressing horror at his decision to use the bomb and urging him to abandon this new weapon. "Far better to be destroyed ourselves than to destroy others with such fiendish and inhuman ingenuity. . . . When St. John and James suggested that Jesus call down fire from heaven on a hostile people, he said, 'You know not of what spirit you are. The Son of man came not to destroy souls but to save.'"[138] Nuclear weapons served to reinforce Day's belief in resistance to all federal tax payments. While she probably earned below the taxable income level in most years, she received frequent threats from the IRS regarding her failure to cooperate with the tax system. Once, after she had treated an IRS auditor to lessons on the Gospel and nonviolence, she told the exasperated man, "I'll tell you what. You estimate my income for the past ten years, and you estimate what I owe you, and I won't pay it! How's that?"[139]

In 1955, Day and a number of other Workers were jailed in an act of resistance to nuclear weapons. It was in that year that New York City instituted air raid drills. At the blare of sirens, citizens were to head for underground shelters, but a contingent of Catholic Workers chose instead to sit on park benches, posters in hand. To head for shelter would be to surrender to the terror that the weapons were intended to instill. To head for shelter would be to cooperate with the illusion that nuclear wars can be survived and even won, with the illusion that the possession and use of such weapons could be rational or moral. The Workers who refused to seek shelter passed out leaflets before the drill, leaflets that read in part, "In the name of Jesus who is God, who is Love, we will not obey this order to pretend, to evacuate, to hide . . . we will not be drilled into fear. . . . We do not have faith in God if we depend upon the Atom Bomb."[140] But what if the U.S. were to surrender these weapons and suffer invasion from a hostile power? Day wrote, "There are all manner of ways of resisting the enemy in an occupied country, and I am not talking about sabotage and destruction either. I am talking about the resistance the Christian ought to give, to be trained to give, with nonviolence, with Christian love."[141]

For years, Day continued to be arrested as she refused to go to the underground shelter. And for years too, she continued to work to offer shelter to the homeless. These she understood as two sides of the witness to one Lord. Nor was she alone in the effort. Members and supporters of Catholic Worker communities have continued in the service and the resistance. Several generations of resisters who have gone to prison for resisting conscription, taxes, and weapons are indebted to the thought and work of Dorothy Day.

The principles of nonviolent resistance maintain that evil and terror can never be defeated once and for all in "a war to end all wars" or in a decisive "war on terrorism." What is required instead are daily acts of resistance, beginning first with resistance to the terror and lack of love within oneself. In offering resistance to the actions of others, Sister Char Madigan of the Catholic Worker observes that the point is "Not to win out over them, but to win them over."[142] And what if they are not amenable to being won over? What if they are a Hitler or a Stalin? Dorothy Day quoted her friend, Father John Hugo, that "we loved God as much as the one we loved the least." And then she added, "What a hard and painful thing it is to love the exploiter. When I was interviewed by Mike Wallace on television, and he asked me, 'Do you think God loves a Hitler and a Stalin?' I could only quote, 'God loves all men. God wills that all men be saved.'"[143]

A hard saying indeed. What would this mean if it were true that we love God only as much as the person we love least? Would it not mean that, when we have finally won the victory in our war on terrorism, when we have finally managed to exterminate all the thugs and Hitlers and terrorists, we will have expressed nothing so much as our total confidence in the death of God?

Desmond Tutu: Reconciliation as the Path Beyond Terror

We should allow the record of apartheid in South Africa to show us just how dangerous it is when the powerful decide to conduct a "war on terrorism," how deftly security concerns are harnessed as the pretext for repression, how quickly the identification of "terrorists" expands to include all rebels and all rebel sympathizers and all dissidents and all people of a certain skin pigmentation without exemption for children, how easily bigotry is given free reign to define other human beings as evil and then to brutalize them, how predictably what falls under the rubric of "counterterrorism" is unveiled to be the very essence of terrorism itself.

Prominent events in the apartheid government's "war on terrorism" included the Sharpeville massacre of 1960 in which security forces shot to death 69 people during a peaceful demonstration against the Pass Law. It was following this massacre that the African National Congress (ANC) and the Pan African Congress (PAC) departed from their policies of nonviolent opposition to apartheid to allow for the use of violence. It was another of the many tragic examples of the downward spiral of violence in which the state's use of force in the name of opposing "terrorism" actually served to shape and elicit the violent opposition the state had claimed to be battling. The repressive laws followed. The 90 Day Detention Act of 1963 was followed by the 180 Day Detention Law of 1965 and then the Terrorism Act of 1967, which allowed security forces to hold suspects for an unlimited period of time without legal counsel or court hearings. A 1974 change in the Riotous Assemblies Act allowed the Minister of Justice to outlaw political gatherings and to determine what was and was not "political." It was designated a "political" gathering when thousands of schoolchildren marched in Soweto in 1976 to protest the mandated teaching of the Afrikaans language in schools; a melee erupted after a 13-year-old child was shot in the back by police, and the security forces went on to kill over 500 young black people. The unwanted media attention was suppressed by the 1976 Internal Security Act, which provided for censorship of newspapers and the silencing of a wide array of organizations and individuals. And each successive measure since then was more draconian, betraying the apartheid government's belief that "terrorism" could be ended if a little more control could be established, if a little more fear could be instilled. The state of emergency was the everyday state of affairs.[144]

But draconian as it was, all of the legislation and all of the highly visible omnipresence of the security forces was only one aspect of the apartheid government's war on "terrorism." For years, what went on in secret was more brutal still, with kidnappings, beatings, torture, and killings especially designed to see that death was accompanied by the greatest possible pain and horror. Incidents of covert brutality were only acknowledged years later in testimony heard by the post-apartheid Truth and Reconciliation Commission.

> . . . former policemen Hennie Gerber and Johan van Eyk told how they abducted, blindfolded, tortured, and murdered a suspected PAC member, Samuel Kganaka. They took him to an isolated rural setting, kicked and beat him, tied him up and hung his body upside down . . . and applied electric shocks to his private parts. Later they built a fire under his head to "dry him out." While Kganaka's fat splattered and sizzled over the fire, Jack Mkoma, a private guard and police accomplice was sent out to fetch brandy. . . .[145]

When the chairman of the Commission, Desmond Tutu, heard such testimony, he wept, not only for the victims who had been subjected to such horrors, but also for the perpetrators who had allowed themselves to become such cold killing machines. The dehumanization of the terror cut both ways. After hearing testimony of how the police abducted Sizwe Kondile and held a barbecue as they watched Kondile's body burn, Tutu wrote,

> What had happened to their humanity that they could do this? How were they literally able to stomach it? Burning human flesh has a odor which is stomach-turning for most normal people. Is it that they had to split themselves into two different personalities to be able to go on living? How was it possible for them to return from such an outing to their homes, embrace their wives, and enjoy, say, their child's birthday party?[146]

Desmond Tutu had always been one of the greatest threats to apartheid in South Africa because it was simply impossible for the regime to dismiss him as a "terrorist." Certainly, the government made him suffer for his faith and his actions. Along with the other indignities that all black men and women suffered in the old South Africa, Tutu was also subjected to numerous arrests and death threats and repeated suspensions of his passport. But as he acquired international reputation and prominent standing in the church, the South African regime recognized that they could not make him "disappear" with impunity. Tutu served as Anglican Bishop of Lesotho, and then General Secretary of the South African Council of Churches, and then Bishop of Johannesburg, and then Archbishop of Cape Town. But it was not only his official status in the church that gave the government pause. It was also the fact that he clearly had been a person of goodwill and transcendent joy even in the midst of pain, a person of prayer in circumstances that seemed to renounce the reality of God, a person of intervention who was willing to risk his own life in nonviolent defense of the lives of adversaries as well as allies. In apartheid South Africa, he stood before the guns of white security forces to defend the lives of black protesters, and he stood before angry mobs to defend the lives of outnumbered white policemen and suspected black informers who were in danger of "necklace" murder.[147] Indeed, like Tolstoy, Gandhi, Day, and other proponents of nonviolence, Tutu saw the need for total consistency between means and ends. If the goal is an end to terror, then terror cannot be the means by which one arrives there. If the goal is the "beloved community," as Martin Luther King, Jr. called it, then the path leading towards the goal must somehow embody that community as already present.[148] Such a view of the consonance of means and ends is fully in accord with Jesus' proclamation of the presence of the Kingdom of God.

For Desmond Tutu, faith has never been a facet of life that is somehow separable from politics or the struggle for freedom. When Jim Wallis interviewed him in 1988, Tutu was asked to comment on how he could remain a person of hope in the midst of horrendous suffering and pain. He replied,

> Wouldn't you be? Nothing can be more hopeless than Good Friday; but then Sunday happens. You can't but be a prisoner of hope.
>
> And you also meet so many wonderful people, people who have suffered and remained faithful. One such person is a man I met when I was praying with the people in Mogopa one night. Now this is someone whose house was going to be demolished the next day. Clinics, churches, and shops had been demolished already. And people were going to be moved at the point of a gun. And he got up, and he prayed, in the middle of the night, "God, thank you for loving us."
>
> You couldn't have heard a more nonsensical prayer in the middle of that kind of situation. And yet, here was a man who didn't seem to know any theology but who could offer a prayer of thanksgiving.[149]

Tutu is himself a person of unrelenting prayer. Journalist Antjie Krog recalls her first interview with him. Soon after Krog and another interviewer arrived at the Archbishop's residence, Tutu appeared, dressed in khaki shorts, socks and a T-shirt with the printed slogan, "I love to read." Immediately following introductions, the journalists started to launch into questions, but, "He held up his hand. Let us pray. And to our utter astonishment, he mumbled a kind of prayer, clearly not intended for our ears. What kind of intimidation was this?"[150] As Krog came to learn, it was not intimidation; it was Tutu. As another journalist, Pippa Green, told Krog, "Yes, on the way to a march or a struggle funeral, in the back of the car, he usually sits bowed and praying all the way. . . . Just a mumbling human bundle. But when the door opens and he gets out among the masses of people, he is at once extraordinary and exceptional — larger, stronger than all of us."[151] As a person of strong faith, Tutu's anguish over apartheid was only compounded by the fact that the men who sat atop the system of oppression were not people who had proclaimed themselves to be opponents of God but people who claimed to rule in the name of God.[152]

One of the charges that has been leveled against Tutu is that he has been "too Christian" in the spirit and the language with which he has fulfilled his responsibilities as chairman of the South African Truth and Reconciliation Commission. In the formal sense, of course, the Commission was a fully secular undertaking. In order to achieve a negotiated end to the apartheid regime, in order to avoid the predicted "bloodbath," how does one deal with the legacy of atrocities? What could be done to address all of the suffering that had come as the result of the reign of terror, the terrorism, and the counterterrorism? Apartheid government officials were demanding an outcome similar to that reached in Chile by which the Pinochet regime agreed to step aside in return for guarantees of blanket amnesty and "truth commission" proceedings that would only be conducted in secret. Some rebels were demanding instead a "Nuremberg solution" in which apartheid government officials would face criminal trial and punishment.[153] What was agreed upon was neither the amnesia of Chile's agreement nor the hangings of Nuremberg. The suffering in South Africa (and in Chile and Germany as well) had been too great to be dealt with by simple forgetting or simple hangings. It was agreed that amnesty would be granted to all former officials and operatives of the apartheid government and to all former opponents of the government who had been guilty of atrocities *if* they appeared before the Truth and Reconciliation Commission and publicly acknowledged what they had done.[154]

Was Tutu "too Christian" as head of the Truth and Reconciliation Commission? He can only be who he is. He has never been an advocate of theocracy. He has never advocated that government positions should be held by people of a certain faith affiliation, but neither has he advocated that people should surrender faith when performing public functions. It was not preachiness on Tutu's part but an aspect of the very nature of the Commission itself which meant that "confession," a traditional sacrament of the church, was suddenly presented in a national arena as a possible instrument in the first steps towards healing.

And did it "work" as part of the path leading away from terror? For every "yes" there is a "no." Yes, the worst predictions of bloodbath have not come to pass, but no, the people of South Africa are still suffering multifarious forms of violence as part of the legacy of apartheid. Yes, because there are some profound stories of reconciliation and caring relationships being developed between victims and perpetrators,[155] but no, because some pain is too deep, some "confessions" too grudging, some rage too raw to engender much beyond coexistence. Yes, because the truth "came out" and some survivors learned the painful facts they wanted to know about the fate of loved ones, but no, because some facts are forever buried and the facts are only ever a poor substitute for the truth.

Cynthia Ngewu's son, Christopher Piet, was murdered in apartheid South Africa. How is it possible even to ask her to consider something called "reconciliation"? Yet, she considered it as a possible path beyond both her own sorrowful rage and the brutality of the perpetrator. Cynthia Ngewu said, "This thing called reconciliation . . . if I am understanding it correctly . . . if it means this perpetrator, this man who has killed Christopher Piet, if it means he becomes human again, this man, so that I, so that all of us, get our humanity back . . . then I agree, then I support it all."[156] Desmond Tutu maintains that the story of the Bible is the story of the divine and human struggle for precisely this type of reconciliation.[157] Cynthia Ngewu understands well. The biblical story is her story.

The Terror of the Cross and the Hope of the Resurrection

Long before Machiavelli committed the notion to writing, the first-century Roman occupiers of Palestine understood the maxim that, if rulers are not loved, at least they should be feared. Of necessity, fear was a pervasive feature of an imperial society in which slaves outnumbered "masters." The terror that came in the form of banditry, slave revolts, and popular rebellions was matched and surpassed by the terrorism of the imperial regime. In this environment, Jesus of Nazareth announced the reign of God. He summoned disciples into the presence of a Kingdom which is not shaped by imperial forces nor by armed revolts. Although there is undeniable diversity in the various Gospel portrayals of Jesus, there is marked consistency in several themes pertinent to our topic: (1) Jesus renounced the dehumanization on which terrorism thrives. Where exclusion was the rule, Jesus violated it. He expended himself in ministry to the expendable — lepers, demoniacs, prostitutes, Samaritans, tax collectors, zealots. (2) The "politics of Jesus" was not based on any illusion that evil means might be utilized in the pursuit of good ends. The end to which Jesus pointed was the reign of God, but proleptically, that end is already present in the life of Jesus and in his call to "follow me." Therefore, disciples are not called to devise means for building the Kingdom of God. Rather, disciples are called to live in the "end time," i.e., in the presence of God's reign, which already offers the freedom to love enemies and to do justice. (3) In the cross, Jesus suffered the full terror the world has to offer, and in the resurrection, this terror was defeated. Whether it is in the name of liberation and revolution or in the name of security and order, every act of terror is a reenactment of the crucifixion. When we remember the crucifixion, must we not seek to serve the victims of terror? When we preach the resurrection, must we not seek to end the terror that is precipitated in our names? As Clarence Jordan observed, the evidence that Jesus lives "is not a vacant grave, but a spirit-filled fellowship. Not a rolled-away stone, but a carried-away church."[158]

On first glance, it seems exceedingly strange that the pronouncement of the two most joy-filled events in the Gospels were accompanied and surrounded by fear, but such was in fact the case — with the heralding of the birth of Jesus and with the witness to his resurrection. When the birth of Jesus was announced to the shepherds in the fields, they were "terrified" (Luke 2:9), and there was a need for reminders to all who received news of the birth: "Do not be afraid" (Matthew 1:20); "Do not be afraid" (Luke 1:30; 2:10). And among the witnesses to the empty tomb, the guards were stunned with fear (Matthew 28:4), and the women experienced "terror and amazement" (Mark 16:8; Luke 24:5), "fear and great joy" (Matthew 28:8), and the other disciples were "startled and terrified" (Luke 24:37). For them too, "Do not be afraid" (Matthew 28:5, 10; Mark 16:6). All of the fears that surrounded these events were not only attributable to the shock the witnesses experienced when they were met by strangers who appeared as "an angel of the Lord" (Luke 2:9; Matthew 28:2-5) or as "two men in dazzling clothes" (Luke 24:4) or "a young man, dressed in a white robe" (Mark 16:5). The terror was more profound and more pervasive than that. The lives of these witnesses were pervaded by the terrors of their time. How could the witnesses to the birth of Jesus experience only joy when they knew that they lived in a time and place in which bad news followed good, in which the powers marked the birth of Jesus with the slaughter of the innocents (Matthew 2:16-18)?[159] And how could the witnesses to resurrection experience only joy when they had so recently witnessed the terror of crucifixion?

But the witnesses were not the only ones who were afraid. For very different reasons, the governing authorities were terrified as well. They sensed that something was afoot, abirth, astir, alive, that represented a supreme threat to their power. Following the crucifixion of Jesus, it is more than a little ironic that the governing authorities remembered the promises of Jesus better than the disciples did. As the disciples were fearing, grieving, and hiding, the powers were conspiring to prevent their own worst fear, namely, that their own judgment would be rendered null and void, that their own terror would not be efficacious, that death would not have the final word. They rolled the stone into place. They declared resurrection illegal.[160] They waited in fear. Their worst fear was realized. Resurrection.

Writing from exile on Patmos, John was perfectly situated to recognize the resurrection as the terror of God (Revelation 11:3-11), as the wrath of the Lamb (Revelation 6:15-17) that deprives the violent of their power. In effect, the resurrection is God's war on the terrorism of both guerrilla bands and nation states. Where terrorism fosters and reflects the disintegration of community, resurrection marks the inauguration of community. Where terrorism reflects the dualism that identifies some people as evil and as fair targets, the bodily resurrection is an affirmation of the love that is due all people in spirit *and body*.[161] Where terrorism reflects a messianism that announces and encourages the violent conflagration of the world, the resurrection is God's incarnation in the world. Where terrorism assembles sufficient quantities of weapons to assure victory, the resurrection is embodied in the one who suffers defeat. Where terrorism sows and reaps death, resurrection is God's reaping of life from the grave.

Christoph Blumhardt observed that while the warring nations may experience the judgment of God as terror, it is actually the coming of summer.[162] God's judgment is summer for those who have little power to defend and no weapons with which to defend it. For the shepherds on the hillside, for the women at the tomb, summer comes. For them, fear does not have the final word. For them, "Do not be afraid."

September 11, 2001:
The Terror and the Hope

On September 11, 2001, the United States was struck by the worst terrorism ever to be visited on this country in a single day to this point. Each life which was lost was of inestimable value, and there were many lives lost on that day. The horrible grief suffered by so many will remain as an ache for the rest of our lives. The visual images of terror are permanent, as are the remembrances of where we were when the planes hit the towers, when the section of the Pentagon collapsed, when the plane fell from the sky near Pittsburgh. Media commentators and political leaders were of one accord in insisting that our world had changed forever.

And yet, the sadness of September 11 is only exacerbated by the growing awareness of how very little has changed. There has been no change in the fact that, when terrorists and counterterrorists exchange brutalities, it is primarily the innocent who suffer and die. The people in the passenger jets and in the World Trade Center, the people beneath the U.S. cruise missiles and smart bombs — many of these people were bystanders, and many of them had little connection to or interest in whatever grievances motivated the violence. Even at the Pentagon and at Afghan government offices, those who suffered and died were not primarily policy makers and event shapers but functionaries and office workers.

But there has also been no change in the dualistic presumption that it is a simple matter to sort out the innocent and the good from the guilty and the evil. There has been no change whatsoever in the governing illusion that the problem in the world is evil people and that the answer is to eliminate them. On September 14 at a prayer gathering at the Washington National Cathedral, Pres-

271

ident Bush asserted, "Just three days removed from these events, Americans do not yet have the distance of history, but our responsibility to history is already clear to answer these attacks and rid the world of evil." Many Americans did not have any sense either of what factors could have motivated the suicidal violence of the attackers — factors which might have included the perception of the U.S. and Israel as condoning and precipitating all sorts of terrorism as long as the victims are Arab, and the perception of the hegemonic military and economic presence of the U.S. in southwest Asia as an insult to Islam. Certainly, these have been among the factors which have allowed some to engage in dualistic denunciations of the U.S. as a "Great Satan." Meanwhile, on September 12, President Bush maintained, "This will be a monumental struggle of good versus evil. Good will prevail." On September 15, the President opined that the U.S. would be opposing "a group of barbarians" and "people who hate freedom." These Manichaean views entailed some of the same characterizations utilized by Clinton and his predecessors Bush and Reagan as they all battled assorted "Hitlers" — Qaddafi, Noriega, Hussein, Milosevic.

There was no change in the rapidity with which grief and fear turned to rage and counterterror. Even though the attacks in the U.S. were not by military means but by means of passenger jets, there was no change in the belief that security can be won militarily, and little attention was paid to the manner in which such security is illusory and the quest for it self-generating and perpetual. There was no change in the notion that a superpower should be able to float unscathed and invulnerable above the terror suffered by the rest of the world. In a manner akin to John Nelson Darby's raptured Christians floating triumphant above a world in tribulation, America too should be able to escape the suffering of lesser mortals.

And so there was no change as the United States joined once again in the downward spiral of violence — which may have been precisely the response for which the September 11 attackers wished. The attackers doubtless knew that the chances for increased anti-American sentiments were enhanced if they could provoke a fit of U.S. violence. An NBC poll released on September 13 showed that 83 percent of Americans believed that the U.S. should take military action. The poll findings were both frightening and sad insofar as the urging of military action came at a time when the perpetrators had barely been identified by informed speculation, let alone by evidence. Americans wanted to lash out by means of that asset which has been identified as the greatest power available — the U.S. military. But lash out how and against whom? There was little doubt that the U.S. war machine could be militarily successful in an encounter with any other nation-state on the planet, but how could that war machine be utilized against scattered groups and individuals who urged and welcomed the superpower's violent lashing out? While most Americans called for military action, the military by which the war on terrorism would be fought appeared muscle-bound — appeared powerless to do anything but inflict still more terror on still more innocent victims. Very little has changed.

There was no change in the processes by which terror has been sown and reaped. The primary suspects in the World Trade Center attacks were associated with the groups of "freedom fighters" originally organized as part of the U.S.-sponsored effort in the 1980s to drive the Soviet military from Afghanistan. As if such history mattered not at all, in the weeks following September 11, the initial U.S. response was to provide increased military support for the Northern Alliance forces seeking to drive the Taliban from power. In the newest superpower definitions and manipulations, the Northern Alliance freedom fighters were opposing the Taliban, who were once anti-Soviet freedom fighters but who had now turned into anti-U.S. terrorists. The immediate exigencies of the need to fight the war on terrorism precluded consideration of whatever the military support of the Northern Alliance was sowing for the future. The historical amnesia also entailed the intentional forgetting that Pakistan was being denied U.S. military and economic assistance because of its nuclear weapons program. Because Pakistan's turf was now needed as the front line in the war against terrorism, the significance of nuclear nonproliferation paled — even as there was renewed fretting over the potential for terrorist attack with nuclear, biological, or chemical weapons.

There was no change in the U.S. practice of assembling "coalitions" of nations with promises of military training and weapons sales and gifts. Indeed, the promise of military assistance has also been the U.S. approach to securing "peace" treaties (e.g., the treaty between Egypt and Israel). Earlier in the Gulf War and now again in the "coalition against terrorism," the alliances are cemented with promises of weapons. Such military generosity will haunt the planet for years to come.

There was no change in the ease with which pressing social needs — Social Security, health care for children and the elderly, access to prescription medications — were given a back seat to whatever additional spending was requested by military and intelligence-gathering agencies. Some elected representatives who had been miserly in appropriating money for food programs became liberal in their willingness to fund the war on terrorism. When it came to funding that war, a President and a Congress who had preached the virtues of fiscal discipline became suddenly and predictably prodigal.

There was no change in the manner in which many political leaders posited security and freedom as values which are antagonistic one to another. On September 13, only two days after the attack, wiretap provisions were appended to a Senate appropriations bill in what one sponsor called "the first legislative strike against terrorism." The measure, which expanded the government's wiretapping authority and provided for increased surveillance of Internet communications, was passed on a voice vote with little discussion. It was an early indicator that the speed of airline check-in was not the only freedom endangered in the renewed quest for security against terrorism.

There was no change in the reality that terrorists and counterterrorists learn from one another, emulate one another, and ultimately become one another. On September 16 on CNN Late Edition with Wolf Blitzer, several members of the Senate Intelligence Committee and the Senate Armed Services Committee openly discussed the possibility of recruiting members of "terrorist organizations" to assist in the effort to combat terrorist organizations. There were also numerous calls to repeal regulations forbidding U.S. involvement in the assassination of foreign leaders. If all is fair in war, then when one declares a war on terrorism, all is fair.

There was not the slightest change to the reality that there is nothing on the planet — absolutely nothing — which does more to create refugees and to spread hunger, starvation, and disease than war or the threat of war. As the saber-rattling of the U.S., Britain, and others sparked the mass movement of people away from Afghanistan's cities and toward the Afghan frontiers, the increased paranoia of the already-oppressive Taliban government led to the expulsion of several international aid organizations. The mass movement of terrified people always constitutes a humanitarian crisis of huge proportion. Eventually, it mattered little that the U.S. military promised (as always) to minimize the "collateral damage" suffered by innocent civilians. The innocent were already dying in large numbers of hunger and hypothermia and disease along the dirt paths and in the refugee camps of Afghanistan and its neighbors. There was something cynical in Osama bin Laden's profession of concern for the suffering of the people of Afghanistan when he himself had apparently helped to plan violent actions with callous indifference toward the retaliation which he knew would come. But there was also something cynical in the simultaneous dropping of bombs and food packages by U.S. and British forces. The U.S. and British governments noisily proclaimed to the world (especially to the Muslim world) that they were concerned for the fate of Afghan refugees who were being driven from their homes by U.S. and British military action. If it was cynical, it was not new — this effort to give warfare a humanitarian veneer.

Meanwhile, in the United States, there was no change in the encouragement for Americans to buy and to consume. Some of the very same leaders who had asserted that the events of September 11 had changed our world forever urged a quick return to normal for American consumerism. If Americans paused too

274

long to mourn or to reflect, the loss of dollars which could be spent on travel or on consumer goods would harm an already shaky economy. The quick resumption of consumption was urged by both the mayor and the governor of New York as well as the President. One must assume that there was a purpose in the President's choice of words when he stated on the evening of September 11, "Tomorrow morning, the government will be open for business," and when he repeated in the following weeks, "America is back in business." It was as if we were being encouraged to guzzle gasoline on our way to the mall without pausing to reflect on how our consumption of the planet's wealth might be contributing to suffering or resentment abroad. In the call to consume, citizens were being told in effect that they could contribute to victory in the war on terrorism not through self-sacrifice but through self-indulgence.

There was no change in the American proclivity toward conformity, which is especially evident during times of crisis. The call of "united we stand" quickly deteriorates into a dim view of any dissenting voices. For a time at least, the need for unity cannot abide the bipartisan, let alone any broader range of opinion. Following the President's address to a joint session of Congress on September 20, Senate Minority Leader Trent Lott said, "Tonight, there is no opposition party." In the zeal of an unguarded moment, the senator failed to remember that such lack of opposition is the fondest wish of tyrants everywhere. When Congress was asked to grant sweeping special powers to the President to conduct the war on terrorism, Congresswoman Barbara Lee cast the only dissenting vote — a vote of no small courage. Nonetheless, we are assured by pundits that it is patriotism and not conformity that is back in vogue. And so in shop windows and on front porches and radio antennae of SUVs and pickup trucks, flags appeared again and again and again.

When conformity is heightened and the range of acceptable opinion is narrowed, those of minority race, religion, or culture face increased danger. There was no change in the tendency of both politicos and common folks in the U.S. to speak of "Islamic terrorism" and "Muslim terrorists," but now such words had additional potential for incitement to violence. In the U.S., there were violent attacks against Muslims and Arab Americans and even Sikhs, the latter because the mere presence of the turban led attackers mistakenly to associate Sikhism with Islam. President Bush sent the correct message when he visited the Islamic Center in Washington and announced that Muslims were not the enemies, although part of his motivation may have been to enhance the potential for recruiting nations with Muslim majorities into the coalition for the war on terrorism. The President showed less sensitivity when he described the war as a "crusade." (Dredging up the memories of a millennium, Osama bin Laden and his allies were already busily denouncing Westerners as "Christian crusaders.") And the President showed less sensitivity too in calling for new powers for the Immigration and Naturalization Service — powers to detain and deport certain categories of both "legal" and "illegal" aliens. Since the days of the Hebrew prophets, aliens have been identified as among the most vulnerable of people, and they have just been rendered more vulnerable still. While both Republicans and Democrats in the 2000 campaign denounced the use of racial or ethnic profiling in law enforcement, it is precisely such profiling of Arab Americans and Muslims which has figured prominently in the terrorism investigations by the FBI and other agencies.

And of course, there was no change in the views expressed by some that the terror inflicted by one side or another was somehow a manifestation of the terror of God. On September 14 from a mosque in Islamabad, prayer leader Maulana Abdul Aziz declared that the World Trade Center towers had fallen because "Allah intensified the fire and destruction of those planes." Osama bin Laden himself proclaimed that God was "giving Americans what they deserve." There was an odd similarity in the view expressed by some Christians that, since God is omnipotent, whatever happens must somehow represent the will of God. But why would the terror of God take this form at this time? According to the Reverends Jerry Falwell and Pat Robertson, God had lifted a curtain of protection from around the United States because of the divine wrath against secularists and gay men and lesbians. The statement was later recanted; the sting remains, as does the wondering at the theology that could generate such an insult against God.

Nonetheless, even if it was not possible to so readily discern the purposes of God in the terrorism of the moment, was it possible now to call upon God's aid in the pursuit of justice? The Taliban leader, Mullah Muhammed Omar, believed so. He proclaimed, "Believe in God, for with the grace of God the American rockets will go astray and we will be saved." And U.S. patriots believed so too. To the point of tedium, "God bless America" was the slogan proclaimed by every car wash and burger joint across the country. I saw not a single sign on a commercial enterprise beseeching God to watch over the people of Afghanistan. There has been no change in the view of some that God is a tribal deity attended by court prophets and palace priests.

And so the anguish of September 11 is only compounded by this realization of how very little has changed. Despair attends the awareness that we are confronted not by a new story but by a story which is very old — as old as the slaughter of the innocents, as old as the senseless murder of Abel. All killing is fratricide, is sororicide. Cain kills Abel. There is nothing new.

It is God who brings the only surprise into this story. It is a surprise which is new and hopeful but also maddening as God spares Cain. The guilt of Cain is palpable, but God spares him with a mark of protection and a place of refuge (Genesis 4:1-16). What would the alternative be? It could only be the endless cycles of revenge and brutality which would call into question creation itself. Cain has already proven himself to be quite acquainted with such brutality. Now he is made to face a much harder reality — the burning coals of God's love (Romans 12:20-21). Cain is a marked man. We would mark him for death. God marks him for life. That is the only surprise in the story of Cain and Abel, and it is the only hope.

Faithful action must witness to such hope and must be grounded in it. How easy it would be instead to allow our actions to be governed by fear or anger or the despairing awareness of how little has changed. Such fear, anger, and despair were factors in the collapse of nonviolent movements in the past. Recall the opposition to the War in Vietnam and the birth of the Weather Underground. Recall the nonviolent abolitionists who, in despair, endorsed a Union Army in the Civil War. We must move beyond bemoaning how little has changed. We must move beyond denouncing political leaders. We must move into hope.

Hope in a time such as this? Be prepared to give an accounting of the hope that is in you (1 Peter 3:15). Let us give the accounting, then, and let us take hope.

Take hope in the witness of those who have been willing to risk their lives in the service of others (John 15:12-13). If times of violence and suffering remind us of the human capacity for sin, they also remind us that such sin can never obliterate the image of God in which we have been created. We have such reminders in the actions of firefighters and rescue workers in New York and Washington and in the actions of relief and rescue workers in Afghanistan and Pakistan. We are reminded that such witness may be offered not only in the heroic acts by which lives are risked and saved, but also in the small acts of kindness which turn aside hate and fear.

Take hope in the fall of Babylon (Revelation 18:1-3). In a time when some are zealous to draw distinctions between the purportedly legal and moral violence of the state and the illegal and immoral violence of non-state groups, we may offer reminders that the judgment of God is arrayed against all of the rebellious principalities and powers. Our allegiance is to God and not the state (Acts 5:29). Our struggle is against "the cosmic powers of the present darkness" and not against flesh and blood (Ephesians 6:10-17).

Take hope in the witness of the remnant who speak for peace (Zechariah 8:4-12) — that ragtag assortment of the faithful who believe that peace is possible when all about proclaim that it is not. It is time to acknowledge that the "just war" doctrine is one of the greatest sins that Christendom has visited upon humanity. Once one allows that "only this time" the war is just, one should not be surprised by how often history offers up the need for just such just wars. It is time to take hope and to thank God for the witness of those who have remained constant in their calls for peace — for the Mennonites and the Quakers and the Church of the Brethren, for the ten thousand who marched on Washington on September 29, and for the thousands more who will still come to speak a precious word of peace.

Take hope that the prayers and lamentations of September 11 might yet turn to repentance and *metanoia* — hope that the guerrilla bands and the superpowers alike might cease from spreading their "terror in the land of the living" (Ezekiel 32:22-32). Take hope in the witness of Nineveh (Jonah 3:6-10), in the witness of the sulking Jonah (Jonah 4).

And above all, take hope in Christ crucified and resurrected. It is the resurrection which is the terror of God to all who believe that death should have the final word. It is the promise of the resurrection which renders null and void the victories of all who shed blood.

Terror surrounded the life of Jesus like great parentheses. At his birth, Herod pursued him with slaughter, and in his crucifixion, he shared the fate of condemned slaves and others of low esteem. But Jesus was not contained by the terror, for at his birth and at his resurrection, messengers from God proclaimed to all who would hear: "Do not be afraid" (Matthew 1:20; Luke 1:30; 2:10); "Do not be afraid" (Matthew 28:5, 10; Mark 16:6). It is with those words of reassurance that we might be empowered to live our lives in witness to the love of God. Take hope.

Endnotes

NOTES TO CHAPTER I

1. As Sallie McFague observes, conflicting images of God are not merely a product of post-biblical theologizing; they are integral to the biblical text. See McFague, *Models of God: Theology for an Ecological, Nuclear Age* (Philadelphia: Fortress Press, 1987).

2. The point here has to do with Job's identity as patriarch, not with his historicity. But Robert Gordis notes that "the patriarchal setting in the prologue" to Job led some rabbinic commentators to assert that Job was a real historical figure of the patriarchal era, perhaps an associate of Abraham. Gordis, *The Book of God and Man: A Study of Job* (Chicago: University of Chicago Press, 1965), p. 225.

3. The case that the book of Job is in part a refutation of patriarchal assumptions about justice is well made by Carol A. Newsom in her brief commentary on "Job" in *The Women's Bible Commentary*, edited by Carol A. Newsom and Sharon H. Ringe (Louisville: Westminster/John Knox Press, 1992), pp. 130-36.

4. The argument is traced from Abraham to Elie Wiesel in Anton Laytner, *Arguing with God: A Jewish Tradition* (Northvale, N.J.: Jason Aronson, Inc., 1990). Laytner notes (p. 34) that, in his arguments with God, Job "is Israel personified as an individual. Job symbolizes Israel in exile."

5. In grappling with the dilemma posed by theodicy, a recent, helpful direction has entailed challenging and reworking the traditional language of God's "omnipotence." For such a challenge from a more philosophical, process theology point of view, see Charles Hartshorne, *Omnipotence and Other Theological Mistakes* (Albany: State University of New York Press, 1984). A critique with more immediate social implications is offered by feminist theologians. See, for example, Dorothee Soelle, *The Strength of the Weak: Toward a Christian Feminist Identity*, trans. Robert and Rita Kimber (Philadelphia: Westminster Press, 1984).

6. This version of Isaiah 40:3-4 is offered in King's "I Have a Dream" speech, *A Testament of Hope: The Essential Writings and Speeches of Martin Luther King, Jr.*, ed. James M. Washington (New York: HarperCollins, 1991), p. 219.

7. An alternate spelling is "Falange." Summary information on Amal, Phalange, Hezbollah, and other Lebanese groups can be found in Sean Anderson and Stephen Sloan, *Historical Dictionary of Terrorism,* Historical Dictionaries of Religions, Philosophies, and Movements, No. 4 (Metuchen, N.J.: Scarecrow Press, 1995).

8. Cited by Eqbal Ahmad, "Just What in the World Makes Terrorism Tick?" *Los Angeles Times,* July 8, 1985, reprinted in *Terrorism: Opposing Viewpoints,* ed. Bonnie Szumski, Opposing Viewpoints Series (St. Paul, Minn.: Green Haven Press, 1986), p. 59.

9. Dom Helder Camara, *Spiral of Violence,* trans. Della Couling (Denville, N.J.: Dimension Books, 1971).

10. In times of wars of independence and civil wars, the categories of "civilian" and "noncombatant" are blurred to near-extinction. Who are the governing authorities to whom one should be subject (Romans 13)? Paying (or withholding) taxes will leave one side or the other claiming that it is aid and comfort to the enemy. One of George Washington's southern commanders, Nathanael Greene, advised his troops that "to strike terror into our enemies" was the proper way to deal with Loyalist sympathizers. In a letter to Thomas Jefferson, Greene described the impact of one raid by his troops on a Loyalist community: "They made a dreadful carnage of them, upwards of one hundred were killed and most of the rest cut to pieces. It has had a very happy effect on those disaffected persons of which there were too many in this country." Cited by Howard Zinn, *A People's History of the United States* (New York: HarperPerennial, 1990), p. 82.

11. Robin Morgan, *The Demon Lover: On the Sexuality of Terrorism* (New York: W. W. Norton, 1989), p. 285.

12. Moshe Greenberg notes the manner in which the poetry of Job utilizes a rich variety of dialectical pairings, one example being the terrifying nightmares (7:14) and the oracular dreams (33:15). Greenberg, "Job," in *The Literary Guide to the Bible,* ed. Robert Alter and Frank Kermode (Cambridge, Mass.: Harvard University Press, 1990), p. 302.

13. See Edward Herman and Gerry O'Sullivan, *The Terrorism Industry: The Experts and Institutions That Shape Our View of Terror* (New York: Pantheon, 1990).

14. Edward S. Herman, "Terrorism: Misrepresentations of Power," in *Violent Persuasions: The Politics and Imagery of Terrorism,* ed. David J. Brown and Robert Merrill (Seattle: Bay Press, 1993), p. 59.

15. Herman, "Terrorism: Misrepresentations of Power," p. 61. In a chart, Herman reports the results of his survey of four seminal books by terrorism experts. In the four books combined, Herman found that there were 733 identifications of "Non-Western/left-wing" groups as terrorist organizations, but only two such identifications of "Western/right-wing" groups. The experts and their books are: Christopher Dobson and Robert Payne, *The Terrorists: Their Weapons, Leaders, and Tactics* (New York: Facts on File, 1982); Walter Laqueur, *The Age of Terrorism* (Boston: Little, Brown, 1987); Claire Sterling, *The Terror Network* (New York: Holt, Rinehart, Winston/Reader's Digest, 1981); Paul Wilkinson, *Terrorism and the Liberal State* (New York: New York University Press, 1986).

16. The survey appears in Alex P. Schmid, Albert J. Jongman, et al., *Political Terrorism: A New Guide to Actors, Authors, Concepts, Data Bases, Theories, and Literature* (New Brunswick, N.J.: Transaction Books, 1988), pp. 5-6.

17. Bruce Hoffman, *Inside Terrorism* (New York: Columbia University Press, 1998), p. 43.

18. Hoffman, *Inside Terrorism*, pp. 88-89; Anderson and Sloan, *Historical Dictionary of Terrorism*, pp. 371-73. The books by Hoffman and by Anderson and Sloan both inaccurately conflate the Sacarii with the Zealots. While neither group was fond of the Roman occupiers, the Sacarii antedated the Zealots by a decade or more. Josephus records Sacarii attacks on the high priest and on Roman-allied religious officials, but none on the Romans themselves. See Richard A. Horsley, with John S. Hanson, *Bandits, Prophets, and Messiahs: Popular Movements at the Time of Jesus*, New Voices in Biblical Studies (New York: Harper & Row, 1985), pp. 200-216. Horsley and Hanson join in labeling Sacarii tactics as "terrorism" and they draw analogies to more modern, anti-colonial movements that were denied access to participation in the political process.

19. Anderson and Sloan, *Historical Dictionary of Terrorism*, pp. 8-9.

20. When exploring association between religion and terrorism, it bears mentioning that, just as the Sacarii are not typical of Judaism and assassins are not typical of Islam, so too, the Thugs are not representative of Hinduism nor even of the devotees of Kali. Granted, the goddess presents a fearful visage, her teeth dripping with blood and her necklace adorned with human skulls. Granted too, the name of the goddess was repeatedly invoked in what has been described as "a terrorist campaign" against the British partition of Bengal in 1908. See Richard G. Fox, *Gandhian Utopia: Experiments with Culture* (Boston: Beacon Press, 1989), pp. 118-19. Gandhi himself was repulsed by the animal sacrifices he witnessed at a Kali temple. Mohandas K. Gandhi, *An Autobiography: The Story of My Experiments with Truth*, trans. Mahadev Desai (Boston: Beacon Press, 1957), pp. 234-36. For Ramakrishna, however, Mother Kali served as the inspiration for mystical visions of universal love. Inspired by Kali, Ramakrishna and his disciple, Vivekananda, preached the presence of truth in all religions and the presence of God in the villain as well as the saint. R. C. Zaehner, *Hinduism* (New York: Oxford University Press, 1966), pp. 161-69.

21. This argument is made by David C. Rapoport, "Fear and Trembling: Terrorism in Three Religious Traditions," *American Political Science Review* 78, no. 3 (September 1984): 659.

22. Both the Jenkins quotation and the Hoffman observation appear in Hoffman, *Inside Terrorism*, p. 31.

23. Laqueur, *Age of Terrorism*, pp. 142-56.

24. Cited by Annie Goldson in "Terrorism and the Role of the Media: A Symposium," in *Violent Persuasions*, p. 179.

25. Laqueur, *Age of Terrorism*, p. 11. Anderson and Sloan state the matter rather boldly: "The genesis of modern terrorism took place during the French Revolution and the reaction that followed it." Anderson and Sloan, *Historical Dictionary of Terrorism*, p. 9. Hoffman's observation is a bit more cautious: "The word 'terrorism' was first popularized during the French Revolution." Hoffman, *Inside Terrorism*, p. 15.

26. Crane Brinton, *The Anatomy of Revolution* (New York: Vintage Books, 1956), p. 186.

27. Brinton, *Anatomy of Revolution*, p. 208.

28. In the Moscow Trials that constituted part of Stalin's Terror, Bukharin was among the accused who were charged with "terrorist activities." Maurice Merleau-Ponty, *Humanism and Terror: An Essay on the Communist Problem*, trans. John O'Neill (Boston: Beacon Press, 1969), pp. 44-45. Merleau-Ponty was one of the founders of a school of philosophy

known as "existential phenomenology." His book, *Humanism and Terror,* was originally published in 1947 in France and was a response to virulent anti-communism. With justification, Merleau-Ponty warned about the violence that is hidden in Western, democratic institutions and penal codes. At points, however, his book reads like an apologia for Stalinism. If Merleau-Ponty was somewhat optimistic about the beneficent potential of the Terror in Russia, he was outrageously so about the potential of violence to eradicate itself (p. 34): ". . . if one gives violence its name and if one uses it, as the revolutionaries always did, without pleasure, there remains a chance of driving it out of history."

29. Jacques Ellul, *Autopsy of Revolution,* trans. Patricia Wolf (New York: Alfred A. Knopf, 1971), p. 81.

30. Simon Schama, *Citizens: A Chronicle of the French Revolution* (New York: Alfred A. Knopf, 1989), p. 578.

31. The personal piety or even asceticism of prominent revolutionaries is noted by Brinton, *Anatomy of Revolution,* p. 190.

32. This image of bloodshed winning and nurturing freedom is exploited by many governments, revolutionary or not. The prominence which the French revolutionaries gave to the association between blood and freedom, and even between blood and bread, is noted by Schama, *Citizens,* p. 447. At times, the imagery of blood merged with the messianic notion that France had a special role to perform in the salvation of humanity. J. L. Talmon, *Political Messianism: The Romantic Phase* (London: Secker & Warburg, 1960), pp. 252-53.

33. Cited and translated by Crane Brinton, John B. Christopher, and Robert Lee Wolff, *A History of Civilization,* vol. 2: *1715 to the Present,* 2nd ed. (Englewood Cliffs, N.J.: Prentice-Hall, 1960), p. 115.

34. Cited by Schama, *Citizens,* p. 707.

35. Olivier Bernier cites the very precise figure of 2,585 deaths attributable to the Revolutionary Tribunal. Bernier, *Words of Fire, Deeds of Blood: The Mob, the Monarchy, and the French Revolution* (New York: Anchor Books, 1990), p. 413. Others assert that, during the brief period between May 1793 and July 1794, the Terror as a whole resulted in the deaths of 20,000 French women and men. Brinton, Christopher, and Wolff, *History of Civilization,* vol. 2, p. 116.

36. These and other examples of the centralization of political power are noted by Murray Bookchin, *The Third Revolution: Popular Movements in the Revolutionary Era,* vol. 1 (New York: Cassell, 1996), pp. 358-60.

37. Cited by Olivier Blanc, *Last Letters: Prisons and Prisoners of the French Revolution, 1793-1794,* trans. Alan Sheridan (New York: Farrar, Straus and Giroux, 1989), p. 142.

38. Bernier, *Words of Fire, Deeds of Blood,* p. 413.

39. Cited by Hoffman, *Inside Terrorism,* p. 17. It is the *Oxford English Dictionary* which attributes the popularization of the term "terrorist" to Burke.

40. A summary of Burke's positive evaluation of the state and negative evaluation of egalitarianism is offered by Francis Canavan, S.J., "Edmund Burke," in *History of Political Philosophy,* ed. Leo Strauss and Leo Cropsey, Rand McNally Political Science Series (Chicago: Rand McNally, 1972), pp. 659-78.

41. Cited by Walter Laqueur, *Terrorism: A Study of National and International Political Violence* (Boston: Little, Brown and Company, 1977), p. 4.

42. These comments by Burke, appearing in his *Thoughts and Details on Scarcity,* are discussed by Stephen Charles Mott, *A Christian Perspective on Political Thought* (New York: Oxford University Press, 1993), p. 129.

43. Cited by E. P. Thompson, *The Making of the English Working Class* (New York: Vintage Books, 1966), p. 90.

44. Kirkpatrick Sale, *Rebels Against the Future: The Luddites and Their War on the Industrial Revolution, Lessons for the Computer Age* (New York: Addison-Wesley, 1995), p. 79. This is not to imply that most Luddites were pacifists, but at the time the magistrates denounced the "terror," John Wesley had been the only person killed.

45. Hobsbawm, *Primitive Rebels: Studies in Archaic Forms of Social Movement in the 19th and 20th Centuries* (New York: W. W. Norton, 1965), pp. 58-59. Hobsbawm's account of the Lazzarettiani movement appears on pp. 65-73. See Chapter 4 below for accounts of some millenarians who are in fact schooled in militarism, but Hobsbawm's remarks are certainly applicable to the Lazzarettiani.

46. George Woodcock, *Anarchism: A History of Libertarian Ideas and Movements,* 2nd ed. (New York: Penguin Books, 1986), p. 275.

47. These events are described by James Joll, *The Anarchists* (New York: Grosset & Dunlap, 1966), pp. 117-24.

48. Garrison will figure in the second section of Chapter 4 below. Consideration will be given to the work of Day and Tolstoy in the second section of Chapter 5. Least known of those mentioned is Gustav Landauer. Among the few works available in English, Landauer's story is best told by Eugene Lunn, *Prophet of Community: The Romantic Socialism of Gustav Landauer* (Berkeley: University of California Press, 1973). A friend of Martin Buber, Landauer was clearly influenced in his anarchism by the prophetic tradition of the Hebrew Bible. He believed that the state could be destroyed only by obviating it through the establishment of communities and mutual aid cooperatives. Through such communities, one could seek to live out the vision of the new within the shell of the old world that was passing away. Of state violence, Landauer wrote, "War is an act of power, of murder, of robbery; . . . it is the sharpest and clearest life expression of the state." Cited by Lunn, p. 242. Although he opposed revolutionary violence as well, Landauer was murdered by German troops as they suppressed the Munich revolution of 1919. In one of his writings on "utopian socialism," Martin Buber includes a chapter on Landauer and Buber himself displays some empathy for the anarchist position. Buber, *Paths in Utopia,* The Martin Buber Library (Syracuse, N.Y.: Syracuse University Press, 1996).

49. These phases are noted by Adrian Guelke, "Wars of Fear: Coming to Grips with Terrorism," *Harvard International Review* 20, no. 4 (Fall 1998): 44. Also referring to terrorism as having various eras is Hoffman, *Inside Terrorism,* p. 17.

50. Laqueur, *Terrorism,* p. 14.

51. For an account of Bakunin's struggles with Marx, see Paul Thomas, *Karl Marx and the Anarchists* (London: Routledge & Kegan Paul, 1980), pp. 249-340. It should be noted that Marx himself endorsed the slogan "revolutionary terrorism" during a brief period in 1848. James H. Billington, *Fire in the Minds of Men: Origins of the Revolutionary Faith* (New York: Basic Books, 1980), p. 409.

52. Michael Bakunin, *God and the State* (New York: Dover Publications, 1970), p. 3.

53. Cited by Paul Avrich in his introduction to *The Anarchists in the Russian Revolu-*

tion, ed. Paul Avrich, Documents of Revolution (Ithaca, N.Y.: Cornell University Press, 1973), p. 9.

54. Cited by Paul Avrich, *Anarchist Portraits* (Princeton, N.J.: Princeton University Press, 1988), p. 39.

55. Quoted by Avrich, *Anarchist Portraits,* p. 38.

56. Billington, *Fire in the Minds,* pp. 409-10.

57. Billington, *Fire in the Minds,* p. 478. Of course, apocalyptic scenarios can cut both ways. Billington notes in another book that, soon after the revolution of 1917, some who had supported the revolution began to characterize the new regime as the Antichrist. James H. Billington, *The Icon and the Axe: An Interpretive History of Russian Culture* (New York: Vintage Books, 1970), pp. 506-7.

58. Billington, *Fire in the Minds,* p. 412.

59. Avrich, *Anarchist Portraits,* p. 73.

60. Laqueur, *Terrorism,* pp. 71-72, 100, 107-8.

61. In his later book, Laqueur presents the case that Germans and much of the rest of the world knew about the genocide as it was occurring. Laqueur, *The Terrible Secret: Suppression of the Truth About Hitler's "Final Solution"* (New York: Henry Holt and Company, 1998).

62. Hoffman, *Inside Terrorism,* p. 25.

63. Quoted by Laqueur, *Terrorism,* p. 71.

64. A similar sleight of hand is detectable in those definitions of terrorism that utilize the category of "unlawfulness." The February 1986 Public Report of the Vice President's Task Force on Combatting Terrorism defines terrorism as ". . . the unlawful use or threat of violence against persons or property to further political or social objectives." This emphasis on "unlawful" violence was subsequently utilized in the definitions proffered by the FBI and the U.S. Department of Defense. (These subsequent definitions are quoted by Hoffman, *Inside Terrorism,* p. 38.) If illegality is a decisive criterion for discerning terrorism, then *ipso facto* again, those who make the laws can define themselves as non-terrorists, even if their actions are genocidal. An unwitting side effect of this approach to definition is that it makes terrorists of George Washington, Thomas Jefferson, and others of their ilk.

65. Jean-Paul Sartre, "Preface," in Frantz Fanon, *The Wretched of the Earth,* trans. Constance Farrington (New York: Grove Press, 1963), p. 17.

66. Sartre, "Preface," p. 30.

67. Fanon, *Wretched of the Earth,* p. 94.

68. Quoted by Laqueur, *Terrorism,* p. 206.

69. Billington, *Fire in the Minds,* p. 509.

70. Morgan, *The Demon Lover,* p. 162.

71. Fanon, *Wretched of the Earth,* p. 61.

72. The study by Gene Sharp remains the best source for providing historical illustrations of the power of nonviolent action. See Sharp, *The Politics of Nonviolent Action,* 3 volumes (Boston: Porter Sargent Publishers, 1973).

73. Fanon, *Wretched of the Earth,* p. 67.

74. Fanon, *Wretched of the Earth,* p. 42. Although Fanon's book was written in an era of anti-colonial struggles, his reminders have pertinence for post-colonial and neo-colonial eras as well. The manner in which some contemporary Christian missionary efforts are also

evangelizing on behalf of capitalism and consumerism is explored by Steve Brouwer, Paul Gifford, and Susan D. Rose, *Exporting the American Gospel: Global Christian Fundamentalism* (New York: Routledge, 1996).

75. Friends Committee on National Legislation, *Washington Newsletter*, May 1986, appearing in *Terrorism: Opposing Viewpoints*, p. 18.

76. While the powerful may have greater resources at their disposal, the dissemination of propaganda is utilized by both the state and opponents of the state. In his classic study, Jacques Ellul differentiated between "the propaganda of agitation and the propaganda of integration." Ellul, *Propaganda: The Formation of Men's Attitudes*, trans. Konrad Kellen and Jean Lerner (New York: Vintage Books, 1973), pp. 70-79. Special problems arise when revolutionaries who had previously advocated violence suddenly find themselves in leadership positions in a newly created state and now need to denounce "terrorism." The leaders of both the State of Israel and the Palestinian Authority have faced these problems of reversal when moving from the propaganda of agitation to integration, from the espousal of the supposed violence of liberation to the combating of terrorism.

77. The clearest articulation of the network thesis was Claire Sterling's *The Terror Network*, a book that came highly recommended by Reagan Administration officials. Bruce Hoffman is among recent writers who classify the global network idea as "conspiracy theory." Hoffman, *Inside Terrorism*, p. 27. Edward Said observes that the positing of KGB links for all acts of terror in the 1980s was based on the same bifurcations by which U.N. Ambassador Jeane Kirkpatrick drew distinctions between the Western allies who happened to be "authoritarian" and the opponents of the West who were "totalitarian." Edward W. Said, *Culture and Imperialism* (London: Chatto & Windus, 1993), p. 30.

78. These designations are used throughout the book, but see especially Morgan, *The Demon Lover*, p. 145.

79. Eugene Victor Walter, *Terror and Resistance: A Study of Political Violence with Case Studies of Some Primitive African Communities* (New York: Oxford University Press, 1972), p. vii.

80. Walter, *Terror and Resistance*, p. 3.

81. St. Augustine, *Concerning the City of God Against the Pagans*, trans. Henry Bettenson (New York: Penguin Books, 1984), IV, 4, p. 139.

82. A recent example is the manner in which the Rev. Billy Graham pronounced the cause "just" when he was summoned to the White House by George Bush on the eve of the Persian Gulf War.

83. The notion is not altogether absurd. Piracy has persisted throughout the history of human seafaring, but especially in 17th- and 18th-century Europe, some segments of the populace were heartened by portrayals of pirates as countercultural figures who resisted the political establishment. Pirates were said to have seized slave ships and to have freed the human cargo. Stories were told of equality between women and men, and of the democracy that reigned on board pirate ships and in the pirate colonies of Madagascar. David Cordingly, *Under the Black Flag: The Romance and the Reality of Life Among the Pirates* (New York: Harcourt Brace & Company, 1995), pp. 12, 146-47, 192. Cordingly argues that most of these portrayals were fabrications.

84. In a recent article, Walter Laqueur briefly traces the history of "restraint in warfare," and then he notes, "Although 'just war' doctrine has never engendered a 'just terror-

ism' counterpart, at least some past terrorist campaigns have been fought for a just cause, against oppressors and tyrants. For this reason, apprehended terrorists are not treated like common criminals . . ." — a fact that Laqueur laments. Laqueur, "Terror's New Face: The Radicalization and Escalation of Modern Terrorism," *Harvard International Review* 20, no. 4 (Fall 1998): 51.

85. This observation by Charles Villa-Vincencio appears in his introduction to *Theology & Violence: The South African Debate*, ed. Charles Villa-Vincencio (Grand Rapids: Eerdmans, 1988), p. 1. As in Germany under Nazism, South Africa under apartheid presented a special challenge to the dominant church tradition, which held that the government alone had a monopoly on "legitimate" violence. George Edwards recounts the horror within the British Council of Churches in 1970 when one of its own committees issued a report sanctioning the use of violence as a last resort to end white supremacy in South Africa. The report asserted that "there can be a just rebellion as well as a just war. . . ." Firmly rejecting the report, the majority of the British Council seemed driven to pacifism, albeit fleetingly. George R. Edwards, *Jesus and the Politics of Violence* (New York: Harper & Row, 1972), pp. 128-30.

86. Klaus Wengst, *Pax Romana and the Peace of Jesus Christ*, trans. John Bowden (Philadelphia: Fortress Press, 1987), pp. 11-12.

87. The chapter headings in *City of God* were likely written by Augustine himself, and chapter 17 of book V is titled, "The profit the Romans gained from their wars and the benefits they conferred on the vanquished." Augustine, *City of God*, p. 205.

88. The account from Plutarch is cited by Wengst, *Pax Romana*, p. 39.

89. Cited by Wengst, *Pax Romana*, p. 13. Slavery was probably not among the "enticements" that Agricola paraded, but such was in fact the fate of many who were defeated by Rome. The price of slaves would rise and fall with Rome's changing fortunes in battle. See Karl Kautsky, *Foundations of Christianity*, trans. Henry F. Mins (New York: Russell & Russell, 1953), p. 32.

90. Quoted by Wengst, *Pax Romana*, p. 16.

91. Cited by Harold Mattingly, *Christianity in the Roman Empire* (New York: W. W. Norton, 1967), p. 77.

92. "A Commentary on Habakkuk," in *The Dead Sea Scrolls: A New Translation*, trans. Michael Wise, Martin Abegg, Jr., and Edward Cook (New York: HarperCollins, 1996), p. 117. It has been noted that both the Qumran community and early Christians exhibited a tendency to read biblical texts with an eschatological consciousness, and this is clearly evident in the Habakkuk commentary. See James C. VanderKam, "The Dead Sea Scrolls and Christianity," in *Understanding the Dead Sea Scrolls: A Reader from the Biblical Archaeology Review*, ed. Hershel Shanks (New York: Random House, 1992), p. 197. There is a broad consensus among scholars that the Kittim of the Habakkuk commentary are the Romans. Elsewhere in biblical and deuterocanonical literature, the translation of the "Westerners" is influenced by context. 1 Maccabees 1:1 refers to Macedonians and Greeks; Daniel 11:30 could refer to a large swath of Mediterranean coastline, while Jeremiah 2:10 is ordinarily translated as "Cyprus." Jonathan A. Goldstein notes that the word "Kittim" probably originated with Kitian on Cyprus. Goldstein, *1 Maccabees*, Anchor Bible, vol. 41 (Garden City, N.Y.: Doubleday, 1976), pp. 191-92.

93. "Commentary on Habakkuk," *Dead Sea Scrolls*, p. 118.

94. "The Fourth Book of Ezra," trans. B. M. Metzger, in *The Old Testament Pseudepigrapha*, vol. 1, ed. James H. Charlesworth (Garden City, N.Y.: Doubleday, 1983), p. 549.

95. Goldstein points out that, in order to avoid the impression that Torah was being violated, the author of 1 Maccabees emphasizes that the Romans were not neighbors, that they were "far distant from them" (8:4, 19). Goldstein, *I Maccabees*, pp. 346-47.

96. On the nonviolent victory of God in the crucifixion and resurrection of Jesus, see the last section of Chapter 5 below.

97. It is fair to say that Jesus was surrounded by some who wished for and perhaps even plotted the violent toppling of the Roman occupiers, but the additional claim that Jesus himself was a "Zealot" has not been sustained. The most prominent advocate of the "Jesus as Zealot" position was S. G. F. Brandon, *Jesus and the Zealots: A Study of the Political Factor in Primitive Christianity* (New York: Charles Scribner's Sons, 1967). In *Bandits, Prophets, and Messiahs*, Horsley and Hanson provide evidence that the organized movement identified as "Zealots" did not arise until 67-68 C.E., and that prior to that time, "zealot" was a fairly generic term referring to the anti-Roman sentiments that manifested as social banditry and scarcely organized agitation. Any association of Jesus' disciples with zealotry could have been only of this earlier variety. In this regard, Oscar Cullmann makes the shocking (and improbable) suggestion that in referring to Peter "Bar Jona," Matthew 16:17 cannot with certainty be translated as "son of John" (or "son of Jonah") but may in fact be a borrowing from the Akkadian "barjona," meaning "terrorist." Cullmann, *The State in the New Testament* (New York: Charles Scribner's Sons, 1956), pp. 16-17. George Edwards notes that, in seeking to establish the link between Jesus and the Zealots, Brandon utilizes arguments of silence, e.g., while Jesus was critical of the Pharisees, the Herodians, and the Sadducees, he fails to mention the "Zealots." A similar argument from silence could be (and has been) used to make Jesus an Essene. Edwards, *Jesus and the Politics of Violence*, pp. 15-16.

98. See the comments by Abraham J. Malherbe, *Social Aspects of Early Christianity*, 2nd ed. (Philadelphia: Fortress Press, 1983), pp. 20-21.

99. Cited by Wayne Meeks, *The Moral World of the First Christians*, Library of Early Christianity, no. 6 (Philadelphia: Westminster Press, 1986), p. 152. Meeks observes that this concession to being something less than "perfect" was "an interpretation which would become very popular in modern times."

100. Wengst, *Pax Romana*, pp. 105-18.

101. Jean-Michel Hornus, *It Is Not Lawful for Me to Fight: Early Christian Attitudes Toward War, Violence, and the State*, rev. ed., trans. Alan Kreider and Oliver Coburn (Scottdale, Pa.: Herald Press, 1980), pp. 46-47, 80.

102. The quotation, with italics, appears in Jaroslav Pelikan, *Jesus Through the Centuries: His Place in the History of Culture* (New Haven: Yale University Press, 1985), pp. 49-50.

103. In Eberhard Arnold, *The Early Christians after the Death of the Apostles*, trans. the Hutterian Society of Brothers (Rifton, N.Y.: Plough Publishing House, 1972), pp. 108-9.

104. In Arnold, *The Early Christians*, p. 97.

105. With hesitance, I use the word "pagan" to refer to the adherents of the traditional gods of the Romans. The word carries considerable baggage today, but it did as well earlier in the history of its use. Originally, the Latin *paganus* seems to have meant "rustic country

person" or "peasant," but it evolved to acquire the additional meaning of civilian as distinguished from a soldier. Why, then, was the term "pagan" not applied to the Christians who were far more likely to be civilians than were others? Hornus notes that the word became entangled in the zeal with which the early Christians used military imagery to portray themselves as soldiers of Christ in contrast to the "pagans" who were not such soldiers. Hornus, *It Is Not Lawful for Me to Fight*, p. 71. On the Christian use of military imagery, see below.

106. Robert L. Wilken, *The Christians as the Romans Saw Them* (New Haven: Yale University Press, 1984), p. 118. Wilken observes that, unlike some other pagan critics, Celsus' criticisms of the Christians were based on considerable knowledge of their movement.

107. Cited by Roland H. Bainton, *Christian Attitudes Toward War and Peace: A Historical Survey and Critical Re-evaluation* (Nashville: Abingdon Press, 1960), p. 68.

108. The passage from Tertullian's *Apology* appears in Hornus, *It Is Not Lawful for Me to Fight*, p. 215.

109. "Ignatius to the Romans," in Herbert A. Musurillo, *The Fathers of the Primitive Church* (New York: New American Library, 1966), p. 76.

110. Cited by Elaine Pagels, *The Gnostic Gospels* (New York: Vintage Books, 1981), pp. 103, 106. Pagels notes that some Gnostic believers were also martyred. Those who were most likely to refuse any compromise with the persecutors were the Gnostics who believed that Jesus actually suffered and died in more than apparitional form.

111. "The Martyrdom of Polycarp," in Musurillo, *Fathers*, pp. 83-84.

112. From Clement of Alexandria's "Exhortation," cited by Hornus, *It Is Not Lawful for Me to Fight*, p. 72.

113. Bainton, *Christian Attitudes*, pp. 70-71.

114. See Williston Walker, Richard A. Norris, David W. Lotz, and Robert T. Handy, *A History of the Christian Church*, 4th ed. (New York: Charles Scribner's Sons, 1985), p. 123.

115. Roland Bainton, an author not given to hyperbole, writes that "The accession of Constantine terminated the pacifist period in church history." Bainton, *Christian Attitudes*, p. 85.

116. Michael Grant, *Constantine the Great: The Man and His Times* (New York: Charles Scribner's Sons, 1994), p. 131.

117. Bainton, *Christian Attitudes*, p. 86.

118. A. H. M. Jones, *Constantine and the Conversion of Europe*, rev. ed. (New York: Collier Books, 1962), p. 169.

119. See Ramsay MacMullen, *Christianizing the Roman Empire (A.D. 100-400)* (New Haven: Yale University Press, 1984), pp. 44-47. Robin Lane Fox notes that Constantine offered no objections when his troops greeted him with the words, "Constantine, may the immortal gods preserve you for us." Fox, *Pagans and Christians* (New York: Alfred A. Knopf, 1987), p. 622.

120. Neil B. McLynn, *Ambrose of Milan: Church and Court in a Christian Capital* (Berkeley: University of California Press, 1994), p. 45. McLynn doubts the traditional view that Ambrose ordered the tortures to show that he was unfit for the bishopric. Ordering tortures and executions was just part of the standard operating procedure for governors.

121. See McLynn, *Ambrose*, pp. 254-55.

122. Cited by Bainton, *Christian Attitudes*, p. 90.

123. McLynn, *Ambrose*, p. 104.

124. Cited by Bainton, *Christian Attitudes*, p. 90.

125. McLynn writes, "There was no precedent for this incorporation of imperial victory in the Eucharist." *Ambrose*, p. 354. While history remembers Ambrose as the one who extracted penance from Theodosius following the slaughter of several thousand Thessalonicans, pacifism was certainly not the issue. In another incident in which a local bishop led a gang in the destruction of a synagogue at Callinicum on the Euphrates, Ambrose objected to the plans of Theodosius to punish those responsible. Ambrose asked of the emperor, "Will you give the Jews this triumph over the church of God?" Events surrounding the incident are described in McLynn, *Ambrose*, pp. 298-309.

126. The reappearance of the goddess is described by Mattingly, *Christianity in the Roman Empire*, p. 72.

127. *City of God*, V, 26, p. 223.

128. The issue posed by the varying identities are explored by Thomas S. Burns, *Barbarians Within the Gates of Rome: A Study of Roman Military Policy and the Barbarians, ca. 375-425 A.D.* (Bloomington: Indiana University Press, 1994), pp. 221-23, 230-32.

129. *City of God*, I, 7, pp. 12-13.

130. Hermann Dörries writes, "Augustine was enough of a Roman to think of the enemy in terms only of the invading barbarians, the lawless rebels." Dörries, *Constantine the Great*, trans. Roland H. Bainton (New York: Harper & Row, Publishers, 1972), p. 115.

131. In an interesting sideline to his study, Solomon Katz notes the degree to which Edward Gibbon, the renowned historian of the decline of Rome, actually agreed with those who held Christianity responsible for the fall of the empire. Katz, *The Decline of Rome and the Rise of Mediaeval Europe* (Ithaca, N.Y.: Cornell University Press, 1955), pp. 71, 82-83.

132. *City of God*, IV, 33, p. 176.

133. *City of God*, V, 25, p. 220.

134. *City of God*, XIX, 15, pp. 874-75.

135. Cited by Hornus, *It Is Not Lawful for Me to Fight*, pp. 64-65. This prevalent association of military defeat with divine judgment earned Attila the Hun the name, "Scourge of God." Coincidentally, it was also a total inversion of the tradition of the martyrs that suffering could be part of a more profound victory.

136. *City of God*, I, 11, p. 20.

137. In Augustine's letters, cited by Clyde L. Manschreck, *A History of Christianity in the World: From Persecution to Uncertainty* (Englewood Cliffs, N.J.: Prentice-Hall, 1974), p. 86.

138. Cited by Herbert A. Deane, *The Political and Social Ideas of St. Augustine* (New York: Columbia University Press, 1963), p. 161. Note that for Augustine, as for modern commentators, the command of "lawful authority" is a significant element in distinguishing the just use of violence from mere terrorism.

139. From a letter by Augustine, cited by Deane, *Political and Social Ideas*, p. 312n.28.

140. Cited by Hornus, *It Is Not Lawful for Me to Fight*, p. 301n.68.

141. The story of Clovis and the contrast with the saying to Peter is recounted by John Ferguson, *War and Peace in the World's Religions* (New York: Oxford University Press, 1978), p. 106.

142. Norman Cohn is not alone in theorizing Zoroastrian influence in the development of Jewish and Christian apocalypticism. He notes ample opportunities for contact between Zoroastrians and Jews of the Diaspora, along with the influence that may have been brought during the occupation of Judea under the Achaemenian empire. Cohn, *Cosmos, Chaos, and the World to Come: The Ancient Roots of Apocalyptic Faith* (New Haven: Yale University Press, 1993), pp. 220-26. In a more circumspect fashion, Jeffrey Burton Russell allows for the possibility of cross-fertilization between Zoroastrianism and Judaism in the apocalyptic development of the idea of Satan. Russell, *The Devil: Perceptions of Evil from Antiquity to Primitive Christianity* (New York: New American Library, 1979), pp. 217-20.

143. The trickster can appear in divine, human, or animal form. The animal version is captured in delightful and insightful form in the Native American coyote trickster tales, especially those of the Jicarilla Apache. Regarding human tricksters in biblical traditions, see Susan Niditch, *Underdogs and Tricksters: A Prelude to Biblical Folklore* (New York: Harper & Row, Publishers, 1987).

144. While the concept of religion as projection has had some prominent exponents of late, the idea itself is not new. Augustine mentions the Roman god Panic, along with Victory, Felicitas, Fortuna, and a host of others, and while he does not use the word, his clear suggestion is that such gods are projections. Augustine, *City of God*, IV, 9-24, pp. 145-66.

145. "Protagoras," 358d, trans. W. K. C. Guthrie, in *Plato: The Collected Dialogues*, ed. Edith Hamilton and Huntington Cairns, Bollingen Series LXXI (New York: Pantheon, 1961), p. 349.

146. A. Baumann, *"charadh,"* in *Theological Dictionary of the Old Testament*, vol. 5, ed. G. Johannes Botterweck and Helmer Ringgren, trans. David E. Green (Grand Rapids: Eerdmans, 1986), p. 166.

147. Horst Balz and Günther Wanke, *"phobeo, phobos,"* in *Theological Dictionary of the New Testament*, vol. 9, ed. Gerhard Friedrich, trans. Geoffrey W. Bromiley (Grand Rapids: Eerdmans, 1974), pp. 191-92.

148. With specific reference to truth and falsity, Plato has Socrates discussing this dual nature of Pan in "Cratylus," 408b-d, trans. Benjamin Jowett, in *Plato: Collected Dialogues*, pp. 444-45.

149. *Mythologies of the World: A Concise Encyclopedia*, ed. Rhoda A. Hendricks and Max S. Shapiro (Garden City, N.Y.: Doubleday, 1979), p. 148.

150. A. Baumann notes the association of fear, trembling, and birth pangs implicit in the Hebrew *chyl*, with later application to the birth of the messianic age. In Isaiah 66, the rebirth of Jerusalem is without labor (v. 7), but the word of God causes trembling (vv. 2, 5). Baumann, *"chyl,"* in *Theological Dictionary of the Old Testament*, vol. 4, ed. G. Johannes Botterweck and Helmer Ringgren, trans. David E. Green (Grand Rapids: Eerdmans, 1980), pp. 344-47.

151. The association with dance of *chyl* and *yare'* and other Hebrew words for "terror" is noted by H. F. Fuhs, *"yare'"* in *Theological Dictionary of the Old Testament*, vol. 6, ed. G. Johannes Botterweck and Helmer Ringgren, trans. David E. Green (Grand Rapids: Eerdmans, 1990), pp. 293-95.

152. On the link between swooning in terror and ritualized proskynesis, see Othmar Keel, *The Symbolism of the Biblical World: Ancient Near Eastern Iconography and the Book*

of Psalms, trans. Timothy J. Hallett (New York: Seabury Press, 1978), pp. 308-10. Such trembling and swooning may also be evoked by beauty, hence the odd phrase in Song of Solomon 6:4,10 in which the beloved is described as "terrible as the army with banners." See Marvin H. Pope, *Song of Songs*, Anchor Bible, vol. 7C (New York: Doubleday, 1977), pp. 560-63.

153. One classic description of the *mysterium tremendum* in the encounter with the holy is the book by Rudolf Otto, *The Idea of the Holy*, trans. John W. Harvey (New York: Oxford University Press, 1958).

154. The "German Christian" movement was notorious for its appeal to Romans 13 as a basis for strict obedience to Hitler. A church struggle ensued when the "Confessing Church" movement resisted such an idolatrous understanding of the state. See Arthur C. Cochrane, *The Church's Confession under Hitler* (Philadelphia: Westminster Press, 1962). Although it bears no references to "terror," another text that has been misused in similar fashion is the synoptic Gospel account of the attempt by some Herodians and Pharisees to entrap Jesus with the question of whether taxes should be paid to the emperor (Matthew 22:15-22; Mark 12:13-17; Luke 20:20-26). An answer of "yes" would have earned the contempt of most Jews who wished to be rid of the Roman occupiers; an answer of "no" would have been seditious. Jesus gave neither answer, although there have been many in the history of biblical interpretation who have read the phrase "Render unto Caesar" as a simple "yes." Jesus escaped the trap by asking to see a coin that bore the image of the emperor, a coin that many faithful Jews would have considered to be a graven image in violation of the second commandment. By producing the coin, Jesus' interrogators were indicting themselves. The discernment of what belongs to the emperor and what belongs to God who is the Creator of all is a responsibility that is given to the faithful who seek to understand God's will rather than to the emperor who wills total obedience to his own rule. As John Howard Yoder notes, this text (and Romans 13 as well) deals with *competing* loyalties and the matter cannot be sorted out by merely assigning "spiritual things" to God and everything else to Caesar. Yoder, *The Politics of Jesus* (Grand Rapids: Eerdmans, 1972), p. 53. Regarding the graven image on the coin, see Donald D. Kaufman, *What Belongs to Caesar? A Discussion on the Christian's Response to Payment of War Taxes* (Scottdale, Pa.: Herald Press, 1969).

155. It is partly Paul's unfavorable view of incumbent political authority that leads Mark Nanos to hypothesize that Romans 13:1-7 is actually an admonition to the Gentile converts in Rome to be subject to the governing authorities of the synagogue, not the state. In this reading, reference to the "sword" (v. 4) is a figurative way of referring to the disciplinary powers of synagogue leaders, similar to the figurative "armor of light" in Romans 13:12. It is a unique argument, but one that merits consideration. Nanos, *The Mystery of Romans: The Jewish Context of Paul's Letter* (Minneapolis: Fortress Press, 1996), pp. 289-336. Less appealing is the argument of Horsley and Silberman that Paul's admonition in Romans 13:1-7 constituted a "huge gamble" that the *parousia* was imminent and that the governing authorities should be placated so that Paul's mission could proceed. Such an argument attributes to Paul an unlikely "ends justifies the means" approach to ethics. Richard A. Horsley and Neil Asher Silberman, *The Message and the Kingdom: How Jesus and Paul Ignited a Revolution and Transformed the Ancient World* (New York: Grosset/Putnam, 1997), p. 191.

156. Stringfellow, *Conscience and Obedience: The Politics of Romans 13 and Revelation 13 in Light of the Second Coming* (Waco, Tex.: Word Books, 1978), pp. 46-48. Helpful reflection on Romans 13 as well as other biblical views of the state can be found in Jacques Ellul, *Anarchy and Christianity*, trans. Geoffrey W. Bromiley (Grand Rapids: Eerdmans, 1991). The current context does not permit an exploration of the language of "power" that Paul uses in Romans 13, including *exousia* and *archon*. The classic study of this is Clinton Morrison, *The Powers That Be: Earthly Rulers and Demonic Powers in Romans 13:1-7*, Studies in Biblical Theology, no. 29 (Naperville, Ill.: Alec R. Allenson, 1960). An excellent treatment is also provided in a more recent work, *The Powers*, a three-volume set by Walter Wink. See especially vol. 1, Wink, *Naming the Powers: The Language of Power in the New Testament* (Philadelphia: Fortress Press, 1984).

157. Yoder, *Politics of Jesus*, p. 211n.18.

158. See the comments of Fuhs, *"yare',"* *Theological Dictionary of the Old Testament*, vol. 6, p. 310.

159. A. Baumann notes the reactive nature of this fear. This, combined with other considerations, leads to "some doubt on the question of whether divine terror is as well-defined a phenomenon as is often assumed." Baumann, *"charadh,"* *Theological Dictionary of the Old Testament*, vol. 5, p. 169.

160. Hans-Jürgen Zobel, *"'emah,"* in *Theological Dictionary of the Old Testament*, vol. 1, rev. ed., ed. G. Johannes Botterweck and Helmer Ringgren, trans. John T. Willis (Grand Rapids: Eerdmans, 1977), p. 220.

161. The eschatological nature of the formula is noted by Baumann, *"charadh,"* *Theological Dictionary of the Old Testament*, vol. 5, p. 170.

162. Further attention will be devoted to the eschatological "terror of God" in the third section of Chapter 4, and to the eschatological "Fear not" in the third section of Chapter 5 below.

163. Fuhs, *"yare',"* *Theological Dictionary of the Old Testament*, vol. 6, p. 299.

164. With acknowledgment to the work of Paul Ricoeur, Walter Wink explores the connection between creation out of terror and the "myth of redemptive violence." Wink, *The Powers*, vol. 3: *Engaging the Powers: Discernment and Resistance in a World of Domination* (Minneapolis: Fortress Press, 1992), pp. 13-17.

NOTES TO CHAPTER II

1. Annamarie Oliverio contrasts the ready depiction of the victims of "terrorist attack" with the effort to suppress any depiction of the victims of U.S. military violence. Such contrast points to a larger struggle for control of historical narration and "the production of meaning." Oliverio, *The State of Terror*, SUNY Series in Deviance and Social Control (Albany: State University of New York Press, 1998), pp. 5-8.

2. In recovery from traumas ranging from domestic abuse to political terror, the importance of providing a safe environment for both remembrance and mourning is emphasized by Judith Lewis Herman, M.D., *Trauma and Recovery* (New York: Basic Books, 1992).

3. Forgiveness that does not pass through the fire of memory bears some kinship to what Dietrich Bonhoeffer called "cheap grace." Susan Jacoby writes, "Remembrance is un-

questionably a form of revenge, but, in one of the great paradoxes of civilized life, it is equally indispensable to the attainment of true forgiveness." Jacoby, *Wild Justice: The Evolution of Revenge* (New York: Harper & Row, 1983), p. 1.

4. Milan Kundera, *The Book of Laughter and Forgetting,* trans. Michael Henry Heim (New York: Penguin Books, 1981), p. 3.

5. Kundera, *Book of Laughter and Forgetting,* p. 7.

6. Kundera's comments are from an interview with Philip Roth which appears as a postscript to *Book of Laughter and Forgetting,* pp. 234-35.

7. The active sense of the word is emphasized by Johannes Behm, *"anamnesis,"* in *Theological Dictionary of the New Testament,* vol. 1, ed. Gerhard Kittel, trans. Geoffrey W. Bromiley (Grand Rapids: Eerdmans, 1964), pp. 348-49.

8. Wayne A. Meeks, *The Origins of Christian Morality: The First Two Centuries* (New Haven: Yale University Press, 1993), p. 33. Elsewhere (p. 5), Meeks observes that "Making morals means making community."

9. This triumphalist (even eschatological) characterization is that of Francis Fukuyama, *The End of History and the Last Man* (New York: Avon Books, 1993).

10. Although it has been on the wane since the collapse of the Soviet Union, there was a similar optimism in the Marxist doctrine that nationalist and ethnic rivalries would be subsumed by class solidarity. See the comments of David Callahan, *Unwinnable Wars: American Power and Ethnic Conflict,* A Twentieth Century Fund Book (New York: Hill and Wang, 1997), pp. 11-13.

11. Du Bois, "The Souls of White Folk," in *The Selected Writings of W. E. B. Du Bois,* ed. Walter Wilson (New York: New American Library, 1970), pp. 89-90.

12. The story of the conversion is recounted by Adam Hochschild, *King Leopold's Ghost: A Story of Greed, Terror, and Heroism in Colonial Africa* (Boston: Houghton Mifflin, 1998), p. 50.

13. It is a horrifying history brilliantly told by Hochschild, *King Leopold's Ghost.* Another "rubber terror" during the same period in the British-Peruvian plantations of southwestern Colombia is described by Michael Taussig, *Shamanism, Colonialism, and the Wild Man: A Study of Terror and Healing* (Chicago: University of Chicago Press, 1987).

14. Philip Gourevitch, *We Wish to Inform You That Tomorrow We Will Be Killed with Our Families: Stories from Rwanda* (New York: Farrar, Straus and Giroux, 1998), p. 48.

15. Human Rights Watch, *Slaughter Among Neighbors: The Political Origins of Communal Violence* (New Haven: Yale University Press and Human Rights Watch Books, 1995), p. 14.

16. Gourevitch, *We Wish to Inform You,* pp. 56-57.

17. Gourevitch quotes a story from the front page of *The New York Times* in October 1997, which reported on "the age-old animosity between the Tutsi and Hutu ethnic groups." The groups are not ethnic and the animosity is not age-old. Gourevitch, *We Wish to Inform You,* p. 59.

18. Robert Melson notes that it was no coincidence that both Armenian and Jewish genocides were perpetrated in situations of general warfare. "Wartime conditions heighten feelings of threat, permit administrative measures that would not be tolerated otherwise, and provide a cover from external interference and condemnation." Melson, "Provocation or Nationalism? A Critical Inquiry into the Armenian Genocide of 1915," in

Frank Chalk and Kurt Jonassohn, *The History and Sociology of Genocide: Analyses and Case Studies,* published in cooperation with the Montreal Institute of Genocide Studies (New Haven: Yale University Press, 1990), p. 285. It might be added that a major Iraqi terror campaign against the Kurds was launched in the midst of the Iran-Iraq war and that "ethnic cleansing" in the Balkans has been perpetrated in the context of more generalized warfare. Indeed, the initial impact of NATO air attacks on Yugoslavia in March 1999 was an expulsion of European observers from Kosovo and an intensification of the slaughter of Kosovar Albanians. It was further confirmation of Melson's claim that war provides a fertile environment for genocide.

19. Human Rights Watch, *Slaughter Among Neighbors,* p. 19.

20. Cited by Gourevitch, *We Wish to Inform You,* p. 325.

21. "Decimation" means the death of one out of every ten people. Out of an original population of seven and one-half million Rwandans, over eight hundred thousand people were killed within a few months in 1994. Gourevitch calls it "the most efficient mass killing since the atomic bombings of Hiroshima and Nagasaki." Gourevitch, *We Wish to Inform You,* p. 3.

22. In addition to refusing to join in the killing (which was itself a grave offense), some Hutu actively rescued and hid intended Tutsi victims from Hutu death squads. Human Rights Watch, *Slaughter Among Neighbors,* p. 32.

23. Cited by Gourevitch, *We Wish to Inform You,* p. 28. Gourevitch takes the title of his book from the letter written by the refugees at Mugonero to their pastor: "We wish to inform you that we have heard that tomorrow we will be killed with our families."

24. For more on Desmond Tutu, see Chapter 5 below. On the stand taken by Father Dhelo and the unhappy ending in the massacre at Mokoto, see Gourevitch, *We Wish to Inform You,* pp. 277-79.

25. In continuing to defend the Salvadoran regime after the murders, then–U.N. Ambassador-designate Jeanne Kirkpatrick stated, "The nuns were not just nuns. The nuns were also political activists. We ought to be a little more clear about this than we actually are." The comment is cited by Melinda Roper, "'Do This in Remembrance of Me': Discipleship in the Face of Evil," *Sojourners* 19, no. 10 (December 1990): 17. For a firsthand description of creative nonviolence in the midst of the violence in El Salvador, see the book by my friend Scott Wright, *Promised Land: Death and Life in El Salvador* (Maryknoll, N.Y.: Orbis Books, 1994).

26. Jack Nelson-Pallmeyer observes that the work of groups like the Fellowship of Reconciliation and Witness for Peace are examples of "the seed of what is needed" to provide nonviolent intervention in areas like the Balkans. Nelson-Pallmeyer, "Wise as Serpents, Gentle as Doves? The Challenge to Nonviolence in the Face of Pleas for Intervention," *Sojourners* 22, no. 3 (April 1993): 13.

27. Chalk and Jonassohn, *History and Sociology of Genocide,* p. 409.

28. Callahan, *Unwinnable Wars,* p. 16.

29. Carolyn Nordstrom, "The Backyard Front," in *The Paths to Domination, Resistance, and Terror,* ed. Carolyn Nordstrom and JoAnn Martin (Berkeley: University of California Press, 1992), p. 271n.1. In noting this trend, Nordstrom adds, "It may safely be said that the least dangerous place to be in a war today is the military."

30. Human Rights Watch, *Slaughter Among Neighbors,* pp. 114-25. None of this is to

deny the bloodshed in Balkan history, but atrocities were most often sparked by participation in general warfare or intentional governmental policy of communal disruption; both were the case with the Croatian Nazi puppet state during World War II, a state under which Serbs, Jews, and others suffered horribly. The 1389 battle of Kosovo between Serbs and Turks was accorded prominence by Slobodan Milosevic in his plan for a "Greater Serbia," but in fact, Kosovo has been under Serb governance for only 60 of the 600 years since the battle. Those who trace the "age-old hatreds" to 1389 and before are inadvertently endorsing Milosevic's reading of history. See Marlene Nadle, "The Myth and Milosevic," *The Nation* 268, no. 14 (April 19, 1999): 5-6.

31. Elizabeth Holler, "Grief Upon the Earth: Faces of War in the Former Yugoslavia," *Sojourners* 22, no. 3 (April 1993): 22.

32. The cutting off of hands was a widely used technique to attempt to terrify village communities into compliance with colonial rule in the Congo. More recently in Mozambique, the RENAMO guerrillas, who received support from the U.S., white-ruled Rhodesia, and white-ruled South Africa, used dismemberment to communicate messages about village and communal destruction. See Nordstrom, "Backyard Front," pp. 262-71.

33. Elie Wiesel and Philippe de Saint-Cheron, *Evil and Exile,* trans. Jon Rothschild (Notre Dame: University of Notre Dame Press, 1990), p. 156.

34. Quoted by Daniela Gioseffi, "Introduction," in *On Prejudice: A Global Perspective,* ed. Daniela Gioseffi (New York: Anchor Books, 1993), p. xlv.

35. Hochschild, *King Leopold's Ghost,* p. 250.

36. Quoted by Marcelo Suárez-Orozco, "A Grammar of Terror: Psychocultural Responses to State Terrorism in Dirty War and Post–Dirty War Argentina," in *Paths to Domination, Resistance, and Terror,* p. 235.

37. Rosemary Radford Ruether, *Gaia and God: An Ecofeminist Theology of Earth Healing* (New York: HarperCollins, 1992), p. 254.

38. Berry, *Sex, Economy, Freedom, and Community: Eight Essays* (New York: Pantheon, 1993), p. 23.

39. For example, see Michel Foucault, *Power/Knowledge: Selected Interviews and Other Writings, 1972-1977,* ed. Colin Gordon (New York: Pantheon, 1980), pp. 55-62.

40. For examples of such a trend in penology, see Michel Foucault, *Discipline and Punish: The Birth of the Prison,* trans. Alan Sheridan (New York: Vintage Books, 1979), pp. 10-16.

41. Edward M. Opton, Jr., "It Never Happened and Besides They Deserved It," in Nevitt Sanford, Craig Comstock, and associates, *Sanctions for Evil: Sources of Social Destructiveness,* The Jossey-Bass Behavioral Science Series (San Francisco: Jossey-Bass, 1971), p. 54.

42. Konrad Lorenz, *On Aggression,* trans. Marjorie Kerr Wilson (New York: Harcourt Brace & Company, 1974), p. 237.

43. Lorenz, *On Aggression,* pp. 242-43.

44. Arendt, *Eichmann in Jerusalem: A Report on the Banality of Evil,* rev. ed. (New York: Penguin Books, 1977), pp. 25-26.

45. A tape transcript of police interrogation of Eichmann, appearing in *"The Good Old Days": The Holocaust as Seen by Its Perpetrators and Bystanders,* ed. Ernst Klee, Willi

Dressen, and Volker Riess, trans. Deborah Burnstone (New York: The Free Press, 1991), pp. 221-22.

46. Hochschild, *King Leopold's Ghost*, p. 4.

47. Cited in *"The Good Old Days,"* p. 252.

48. Arendt, *Eichmann in Jerusalem*, p. 289.

49. The psychological research of Stanley Milgram and others has shown a human proclivity to obey authority, especially if reassurance is given that those in authority will assume ethical and legal responsibility for the consequences of obedience. See Milgram, *Obedience to Authority: An Experimental View* (New York: Harper Torchbooks, 1975).

50. This creation of a second self is called "schizoid" by Charles Drekmeier, "Knowledge as Virtue, Knowledge as Power," in *Sanctions for Evil*, p. 217. The experience of this "second self" is described by Susanna Ronconi who was once a member of the Red Brigade, the group responsible for the kidnapping and subsequent murder of former Italian Premier Aldo Moro. "In a sense committing violence is a violence against yourself because it is not something you would naturally wish to do. Because you have to put something of yourself to one side when you do it, you are forcing out the desire to preserve life. It is one of the reasons it is impossible to go on doing it for a long time." Ronconi goes on to speak of the use of violence as entailing the suspension of emotion and of time, with everything moving in slow motion as if "crossing a threshold." Ronconi's statement is reported by Eileen MacDonald, *Shoot the Women First* (New York: Random House, 1991), p. 187.

51. Quoted by Drekmeier, "Knowledge as Virtue," p. 212.

52. Hochschild, *King Leopold's Ghost*, p. 220. Hochschild explains that Caudron was one of the few white people in Leopold's Congo to be charged with the murder of Africans. The charges may have been brought because Caudron's brutality was so profuse as to actually interfere with rubber collection.

53. The story of this anti-Japanese racism and of the corresponding propaganda campaign by the Japanese government to demonize the Americans and the British is told by John W. Dower, *War Without Mercy: Race and Power in the Pacific War* (New York: Pantheon, 1986).

54. MacDonald, *Shoot the Women First*, p. 221.

55. Cited by Bruce Hoffman, *Inside Terrorism* (New York: Columbia University Press, 1998), p. 159.

56. Jackson's experience is recounted by Richard Clutterbuck, *Protest and the Urban Guerrilla* (New York: Abelard-Schuman, 1974), pp. 301-2. Not all glimmers of human understanding in situations of terror are attributable to the so-called "Stockholm Syndrome" by which traumatized victims begin to identify with their captors. When TWA Flight 847 was hijacked and held for seventeen days in Beirut in 1985, Allyn Conwell was chosen as spokesman for the captives and he gave repeated live, broadcast interviews while under captivity. When Conwell exhibited some knowledge of the situation in Lebanon and expressed support for his captors' demand that Israel withdraw from southern Lebanon, Reagan Administration officials chalked it up to the "Stockholm Syndrome" and Reagan himself characterized the hijackers as "misfits, looney tunes." See the comments by Robert Merrill, "Case Studies in Terrorism: A Symposium," in *Violent Persuasions: The Politics and Imagery of Terrorism*, ed. David J. Brown and Robert Merrill (Seattle: Bay Press, 1993), pp. 121-23.

57. Ahmad, "Just What in the World Makes Terrorism Tick?" *Los Angeles Times,* July 8, 1985, reprinted in *Terrorism: Opposing Viewpoints,* ed. Bonnie Szumski, Opposing Viewpoints Series (St. Paul, Minn.: Green Haven Press, 1986), pp. 59-60. It can seem contrived, of course, if a defendant appeals to prior exposure to violence as an excuse for terrorist acts, as when, for example, Timothy McVeigh's defense on charges of bombing the Oklahoma City Federal Building cited his outrage at the injustices committed against Randy Weaver's family and against the Branch Davidians in Waco, injustices of which McVeigh was not the immediate victim. McVeigh's reaction to these injustices is discussed by David Hoffman, *The Oklahoma City Bombing and the Politics of Terror* (Venice, Calif.: Feral House, 1998), pp. 73-76. In his study of what he called "the terrorist mind," Gerald McKnight cites several instances of individuals within guerrilla groups who had previously witnessed violence, one example being a Uruguayan who joined the Tupamaros after witnessing the police open fire on unarmed students. But a more typical example, McKnight asserts, was the FLQ guerrilla group in Quebec which drew most of its members not from among "the oppressed classes" but from among students with middle-class or wealthy backgrounds. McKnight, *The Terrorist Mind* (Indianapolis: Bobbs-Merrill, 1974), pp. 95, 149.

58. The quotations and studies are cited in an article by Michael Kramer, "Why Guns Share the Blame," *Time,* May 8, 1995, p. 48.

59. Lochte's quotation appears in MacDonald, *Shoot the Women First,* p. xiv.

60. Quoted in MacDonald, *Shoot the Women First,* p. 240.

61. MacDonald, *Shoot the Women First,* p. xviii.

62. Proll quoted by MacDonald, *Shoot the Women First,* p. 204.

63. Proll quoted by MacDonald, *Shoot the Women First,* p. xix.

64. Quoted by McKnight, *The Terrorist Mind,* p. 26.

65. Quoted by McKnight, *The Terrorist Mind,* p. 29.

66. In chapter one above, it was noted that a similar dispassionate approach to violence was recommended by none other than Augustine of Hippo in his defense of the "just war."

67. O'Bradaigh quoted by McKnight, *The Terrorist Mind,* p. 60.

68. McKnight calls Herron a "terrorist against terror." See McKnight, *The Terrorist Mind,* pp. 65-68.

69. Cited by McKnight, *The Terrorist Mind,* p. 114.

70. As portrayed in the 1998 film *Life Is Beautiful,* when reality itself is circumscribed by terror, the desire to protect children can take the form of using imagination to transport them to an alternative reality. Is this transcendence or deception? Is this a great refusal to allow terror to define reality or is it an escape into fantasy?

71. Quoted by MacDonald, *Shoot the Women First,* p. 104.

72. Albert Camus, *The Just Assassins,* in *Caligula and Three Other Plays,* trans. Stuart Gilbert (New York: Vintage Books, 1958), Act I, p. 245.

73. Camus, *Just Assassins,* Act I, pp. 248-49.

74. Camus, *Just Assassins,* Act II, p. 258.

75. While the "innocent" have always suffered in warfare, it is primarily civilians who are being killed in today's wars. In noting the charge that terrorists target innocent bystanders, Robin Morgan observes, "I think it is not coincidental that random murder of

average citizens, including those in no way connected to power, emerged as a strategy of insurgent struggle *after* the random murder of average citizens had become a 'legitimate' military tactic in conventional warfare. The London blitz. The bombing of Cologne and Dresden. Hiroshima. Nagasaki." Morgan, *The Demon Lover: On the Sexuality of Terrorism* (New York: W. W. Norton, 1989), pp. 44-45.

76. Sontag, *Illness as Metaphor* (New York: Farrar, Straus and Giroux, 1988), p. 83.

77. In *Terrorism: Opposing Viewpoints*, p. 94.

78. Cited by Martin Dillon and Denis Lehane, *Political Murder in Northern Ireland* (Baltimore: Penguin Books, 1973), p. 286.

79. Hoffman, *Inside Terrorism*, p. 7.

80. MacDonald, *Shoot the Women First*, p. xiii.

81. King's view is summarized by John J. Ansbro, *Martin Luther King, Jr.: The Making of a Mind* (Maryknoll, N.Y.: Orbis Books, 1982), pp. 87-90.

82. Quoted by Vamberto Morais, *A Short History of Anti-Semitism* (New York: W. W. Norton, 1976), p. 116.

83. See David Nirenberg, *Communities of Violence: Persecution of Minorities in the Middle Ages* (Princeton, N.J.: Princeton University Press, 1996), pp. 7, 14.

84. John Ferguson, *War and Peace in the World's Religions* (New York: Oxford University Press, 1978), pp. 32-34.

85. While Christopher Hitchens betrays a lack of sensitivity to Eastern spiritual concepts such as the transmigration of souls, legitimate questions about the opinions and activities of the Dalai Lama of Tibet are raised by Hitchens, "The Divine One," *The Nation* 267, no. 4 (July 27/August 3, 1998): 8.

86. In his study of antisemitism, John G. Gager cites the proposition from Lewis Coser's *The Functions of Social Conflict:* "The closer the relationship, the more intense the conflict." See Gager, *The Origins of Anti-Semitism: Attitudes Toward Judaism in Pagan and Christian Antiquity* (New York: Oxford University Press, 1985), p. 11.

87. On conflict over symbols and the importance of symbols in community life, see Peter Berger and Thomas Luckmann, *The Social Construction of Reality* (Garden City, N.Y.: Doubleday, 1967).

88. Anyone who doubts the power of the "merely" symbolic to generate controversy and even violence is referred to two essays by Peter Brown, "Relics and Social Status in the Age of Gregory of Tours" and "A Dark Age Crisis: Aspects of the Iconoclastic Controversy," both appearing in Brown, *Society and the Holy in Late Antiquity* (Berkeley: University of California Press, 1989). Nor is the phenomenon of reverence for the symbolic confined to a bygone age. As Wayne A. Meeks observes concerning myth, "It is not the case, as the famous demythologizer Rudolf Bultmann believed, that modern people cannot think in mythic terms; our common problem is rather that we believe too many myths, and most of them too cheap and sordid. . . ." Meeks, *Origins of Christian Morality*, pp. 1-2. Likewise, even apart from traditions of Eastern Orthodoxy, we modern folks are not lacking in relics and icons; they are plenteous and, unlike the Orthodox variety, most are tawdry.

89. Ruether, *Faith and Fratricide: The Theological Roots of Anti-Semitism* (Minneapolis: Seabury Press, 1974), p. 30.

90. J. N. Sevenster is among recent scholars who posit a "pagan" origin for antisemitism. Hannah Arendt is among those who assert that modern antisemitism is a

unique phenomenon which is disconnected from Christianity. For comments on each, see Gager, *Origins of Anti-Semitism,* pp. 31, 267. The use of the term "antisemitism" is not without problems. A Semite (a descendant of Noah's son, Shem) is one who speaks a Semitic language, which includes not only Hebrew but also Arabic. While there is certainly prejudice and violence against Arabs, the term "antisemitism" has been commonly used to refer to anti-Jewish thought and action. The term was coined in 1879, so reference to antisemitism in antiquity is formally anomalous, but common usage ignores that particular as well. Some authors rely on the spelling of "antisemitism" without hyphen or capitalization to convey that they are using the term in its common sense and not as a reference to hatred of all Semites.

91. Rosemary Radford Ruether subtitles one of her chapters "The Rejection of the Jews in the New Testament," and she writes in her concluding chapter, "The foundations of anti-Judaic thought were laid in the New Testament." *Faith and Fratricide,* p. 226.

92. It is certainly not Ruether's intent to provide such exoneration. As we will see below, among her suggestions for countering antisemitism, Ruether provides some helpful reflections on christology.

93. Franklin H. Littell, *The Crucifixion of the Jews: The Failure of Christians to Understand the Jewish Experience* (New York: Harper & Row, 1975), p. 24.

94. Mark D. Nanos, *The Mystery of Romans: The Jewish Context of Paul's Letter* (Minneapolis: Fortress Press, 1996), p. 4. It will be recalled from Chapter 1 that Nanos understands Romans as Paul's appeal for continued unity between the early Christian movement and the larger Jewish community, and that he understands Romans 13 as an admonition to be subject to the governing authorities of the synagogue.

95. The phrase "intra-Jewish polemic" is favored by Gager, *Origins of Anti-Semitism,* p. 9.

96. Paul Johnson, *A History of the Jews* (New York: Harper & Row, 1988), pp. 145-46.

97. Many are familiar with the contrast that Luther posited between "justification by faith" (good, Pauline Christian) and "works righteousness" (bad, Jewish). Regarding a similar tendency among some liberation theologians to posit Judaism as the oppressive background against which Paul struggled, see Elisabeth Schüssler Fiorenza, *In Memory of Her: A Feminist Theological Reconstruction of Christian Origins* (New York: Crossroad, 1988), pp. 105-10.

98. E. P. Sanders, *Paul, the Law, and the Jewish People* (Minneapolis: Fortress Press, 1983), p. 207.

99. On this point, the scholarly work of Paula Fredriksen and others is summarized by Neil Elliott, *Liberating Paul: The Justice of God and the Politics of the Apostle,* The Bible & Liberation Series (Maryknoll, N.Y.: Orbis Books, 1994), pp. 146-47.

100. See Elliott, *Liberating Paul,* p. 140. Elliott acknowledges the contribution of Krister Stendahl in applying the concept of "call" rather than "conversion" to Paul's experience on the Damascus road.

101. Elliott, *Liberating Paul,* p. 179.

102. For an overview of the hospitality provided for messianic movements in both Judaism and Christianity, see Jack Gratus, *The False Messiahs* (New York: Taplinger, 1976).

103. With this, Horsley and Silberman comment, "The question reportedly posed to Jesus in Jerusalem some forty years earlier had been decisively answered: tribute must now

be rendered only to Caesar." Richard A. Horsley and Neil Asher Silberman, *The Message and the Kingdom: How Jesus and Paul Ignited a Revolution and Transformed the Ancient World* (New York: Grosset/Putnam, 1997), p. 213.

104. Gavin I. Langmuir, *History, Religion, and Antisemitism* (London: I. B. Tauris, 1990), p. 279. N. T. Wright effectively disputes the claim that the Jesus sect was driven out of Judaism following the destruction of the Temple in 70. See Wright, *Christian Origins and the Question of God*, vol. 1: *The New Testament and the People of God* (Minneapolis: Fortress Press, 1992), pp. 161-66.

105. Paul Johnson notes an increase in anti-Christian polemic in the Jewish Bible commentaries following the war of 133-36. Johnson, *History of the Jews*, p. 147. As Langmuir observes, however, the anti-Christian writings were few and brief, with Talmudic Judaism more often opting to ignore the Christian movement. Langmuir, *Antisemitism*, p. 282. In contrast, the *adversus Judaeos* tradition of the Patristic period in the church was extensive and virulent. See the review by Ruether, *Faith and Fratricide*, pp. 117-82.

106. Jules Isaac, *Has Anti-Semitism Roots in Christianity?* (New York: National Conference of Christians and Jews, 1961), p. 45. Following the murder of his wife, his daughter, and other members of his family by the Nazis in 1943, Isaac devoted the rest of his life to the study of the relationship between Christianity and antisemitism. His most influential book was *Jesus and Israel*, published in 1948.

107. Ruether, *Faith and Fratricide*, p. 180.

108. St. Augustine, *Concerning the City of God Against the Pagans*, trans. Henry Bettenson (New York: Penguin Books, 1984), XVIII, 46, pp. 827-28.

109. See Ruether, *Faith and Fratricide*, pp. 209-10.

110. The phrase comes from Paul Lawrence Rose, *Revolutionary Antisemitism in Germany from Kant to Wagner* (Princeton, N.J.: Princeton University Press, 1990), p. 53.

111. René Girard has accorded the scapegoat a prominent place in the history of religions. For a good (albeit laudatory) summary of Girard's views on the scapegoat, see Raymund Schwager, S.J., *Must There Be Scapegoats? Violence and Redemption in the Bible*, trans. Maria L. Assad (New York: Harper & Row, 1987), pp. 1-25. Questions on the utility of the scapegoating paradigm are raised by Nirenberg, *Communities of Violence*, pp. 241-43.

112. Langmuir, *Antisemitism*, p. 284.

113. This version of projection is cited by Rose, *Revolutionary Antisemitism*, pp. 53-54.

114. Cited by Rose, *Revolutionary Antisemitism*, p. 6. Rose notes that intentional ambiguity is a common feature of antisemitic writings, including the writings of Hitler.

115. See Rose, *Revolutionary Antisemitism*, pp. 38-39.

116. Messianism is a common element in various manifestations of revolutionary nationalism. On the redemption theme in the French Revolution, see note 32 in the first chapter above. Jonathan Edwards was a proponent of the view that America was the "New Israel." Edwards preached that the mission of redemption had been forfeited by both the Jews (who "have been guilty of crucifying" Jesus) and the "old continent" (Europe), but his confidence in the destiny of the New Israel was such that Edwards was not an advocate of antisemitic terror. Jonathan Edwards, "The Latter-Day Glory Is Probably to Begin in America," in *God's New Israel: Religious Interpretation of American Destiny*, ed. Conrad Cherry (Englewood Cliffs, N.J.: Prentice-Hall, 1971), pp. 55-59.

117. Gager cites the study by Uriel Tal of the Second Reich period in Germany, which "demonstrated the co-existence and mutual impact" of Christian and anti-Christian varieties of antisemitism. Gager, *Origins of Anti-Semitism,* p. 267.

118. Quoted by Merle Hoffman, "I Am a Child of the Holocaust," in *On Prejudice,* p. 79.

119. Richard Wolin, *The Politics of Being: The Political Thought of Martin Heidegger* (New York: Columbia University Press, 1990), pp. 89-90, 126.

120. In describing gangs, police, and Marines as examples of communities that are bonded by the resort to violence, Gil Bailie uses the phrase "pathological *Gemeinschaft,*" a phrase he attributes to Mike Davis. While the reference to pathology falls into the trap of the illness metaphor, Bailie offers some helpful reflections on communities bonded by violence in *Violence Unveiled: Humanity at the Crossroads* (New York: Crossroad, 1995), pp. 60-64.

121. Alexander Donat, "The Holocaust Kingdom," in Albert H. Friedlander, *Out of the Whirlwind: A Reader of Holocaust Literature* (New York: Schocken Books, 1976), p. 180. As Donat notes, it is not accurate to portray Jews as passively watching as the slaughter unfolded. While we read too little of the nonviolent Jewish resistance to the Nazis, an overview of the armed resistance is provided in *They Fought Back: The Story of Jewish Resistance in Nazi Europe,* ed. and trans. Yuri Suht (New York: Schocken Books, 1975).

122. Rosemary Ruether identifies this theme of waiting for the Second Coming as a key to the formulation of a christology that avoids antisemitism. See Ruether, *Faith and Fratricide,* pp. 246-51.

123. "Kingdom" language is used in no small number of biblical texts, but it is not language that is free from problems. It needs to be noted that the language itself occasionally stands in tension with the image it strives to evoke. While kingdoms might commonly be perceived as oppressive political entities, God's reign is biblically portrayed as bringing reconciliation to humanity and to the rest of nature as well (Isaiah 11:6-9). While the king is a male autocrat, God is not only Father but also Mother (Isaiah 66:13). While the king is lion, God is hen longing to gather her endangered offspring under her wing (Ruth 2:12; Matthew 23:37; Luke 13:34). While the king can afford to waste both wealth and subjects, God is the Woman searching for the lost coin (Luke 15:8-10).

124. Andre Schwarz-Bart, *The Last of the Just,* trans. Stephen Becker (New York: Atheneum, 1960), pp. 365-66.

125. Elie Wiesel, *Night,* trans. Stella Rodway, in *Night/Dawn/Day* (Northvale, N.J.: Jason Aronson, Inc., 1985), p. 72.

126. Wiesel, *Night,* p. 43.

127. Wiesel, *Night,* p. 76.

128. Wiesel, *Night,* p. 97.

129. Monteilhet, cited by Jacques Ellul, *Hope in Time of Abandonment,* trans. C. Edward Hopkin (New York: Seabury Press, 1973), p. 191.

130. See Kevin Wright, *The Great American Crime Myth* (New York: Praeger, 1987), p. 24.

131. In one of his typically insightful books about children, Robert Coles conducted a series of interviews regarding faith with Christian, Jewish, and Muslim children. One image of the devil that emerged from the interviews was that of a character who is lurking

and waiting to grab the unsuspecting victim. One girl reported that a nun told her that the devil "gets you and he'll never let go of you." The girl "felt terror (but also a thrill) at the thought of such lasting possessiveness." Coles, *The Spiritual Life of Children* (Boston: Houghton Mifflin, 1990), p. 17.

132. See Diether Kellermann, *"gur, ger,"* in *Theological Dictionary of the Old Testament,* vol. 2, rev. ed., ed. G. Johannes Botterweck and Helmer Ringgren, trans. John T. Willis (Grand Rapids: Eerdmans, 1977), pp. 439-40. The linguistic association is also noted in Brown, Driver, and Briggs, with additional evidence that the Hebrew root *magor* is associated with words meaning "sojourning place" (e.g., Genesis 37:1) as well as "fear, terror" (e.g., Isaiah 31:9; Jeremiah 6:25; 20:4). Francis Brown, S. R. Driver, and Charles A. Briggs, *A Hebrew and English Lexicon of the Old Testament* (Oxford: Clarendon Press, 1972), pp. 157-59.

133. Roland de Vaux notes an association between the laws of hospitality and the laws of asylum. If implicated in a crime, the *ger* was to be received into the cities of refuge (Numbers 35:15; Joshua 20:9). Roland de Vaux, *Ancient Israel,* vol. 1: *Social Institutions* (New York: McGraw-Hill, 1965), p. 10. Contrary to the laws of Hammurabi, biblical law also offered asylum to runaway slaves, although these fugitive slaves were not confined to cities of refuge (Deuteronomy 23:15-16). Such runaways were accorded the status of *ger.* See Ian Cairns, *Word and Presence: A Commentary on the Book of Deuteronomy,* International Theological Commentary (Grand Rapids: Eerdmans and Edinburgh: The Handsel Press Ltd., 1992), pp. 205-6.

134. Christiana van Houten, *The Alien in Israelite Law,* Journal for the Study of the Old Testament Supplement Series 107 (Sheffield, U.K.: Sheffield Academic Press, 1991), p. 54. Childs also notes the precarious position of the *ger* who is separated from the protection of the clan. Brevard S. Childs, *The Book of Exodus: A Critical, Theological Commentary,* The Old Testament Library (Philadelphia: Westminster Press, 1974), p. 478. This basic vulnerability is not contradicted by the fact that an occasional resident alien could prosper, as indicated by Leviticus 25:47.

135. On God as the protector of the *ger,* see Cairns, *Word and Presence,* p. 34.

136. On the incorporation of the themes of *go'el* and Jubilee Year in New Testament theology, see Robert B. Sloan, Jr., *The Favorable Year of the Lord: A Study of Jubilary Theology in the Gospel of Luke* (Austin: Schola Press, 1977). André Trocmé noted that there is an association between redemption and vengeance in that the *go'el* is also the one who seeks retribution when a kinsperson has suffered violence. Here, God's role as *Go'el* is in part a plea for an end to human retaliation ("Vengeance is mine," Deuteronomy 32:35; Romans 12:19). Eventually, in the Suffering Servant theme of Deutero-Isaiah, God is also identified as the one who, through the Servant, suffers retaliation on behalf of others. See André Trocmé, *Jesus and the Nonviolent Revolution,* trans. Michael H. Shank and Marlin E. Miller (Scottdale, Pa.: Herald Press, 1973), pp. 25-26.

137. Van Houten, *Alien in Israelite Law,* p. 50.

138. Van Houten, *Alien in Israelite Law,* p. 67.

139. Two seminal works on the "revolt model" are George E. Mendenhall, *The Tenth Generation: The Origins of the Biblical Tradition* (Baltimore: Johns Hopkins Press, 1973), and Norman K. Gottwald, *The Tribes of Yahweh: A Sociology of the Religion of Liberated Israel, 1250-1050 B.C.E.* (Maryknoll, N.Y.: Orbis Books, 1979).

140. Mendenhall, *Tenth Generation,* p. 162.

141. Gottwald, *Tribes of Yahweh,* pp. 4-5. Gottwald assembles a compendium of pre-monarchic narratives extant within the Hebrew Bible (*Tribes of Yahweh,* pp. 45-59). Contrary to the Deuteronomistic portrayal of the extermination of populations, the pre-monarchic annals (e.g., Joshua 11:1-9) state only that the kings were "struck down," chariots were burnt, and horses that served as tools of war were hamstrung (*Tribes of Yahweh,* p. 543). Mendenhall also questions the historicity of any portrayal that depicts a campaign of terror. Mendenhall writes of the social and political "withdrawal" of the proto-Israelites from the repressive city-states of Canaan. He sees important clues to the origins of Israel in the Genesis 1 creation account in which all of humanity is created in the image of God. Unlike Babylonian and other Near Eastern creation myths, Genesis does not portray the power of kingship and the state as grounded in creation. See Mendenhall, *Tenth Generation,* p. 211.

142. Gottwald, *Tribes of Yahweh,* p. 214.

143. Mendenhall, *Tenth Generation,* pp. 135-38. Gottwald, *Tribes of Yahweh,* p. 213.

144. Mendenhall, *Tenth Generation,* p. 224. Gottwald, *Tribes of Yahweh,* pp. 490-91.

145. Gottwald, *Tribes of Yahweh,* p. 253.

146. Gottwald, *Tribes of Yahweh,* pp. 216-17.

147. Gottwald, *Tribes of Yahweh,* p. 410.

148. In this brief outline of the revolt model, Gottwald and Mendenhall have been treated as one, but it must be observed that there are some sharp differences between the two. Gottwald asserts that the Israelite confederacy did in fact exercise power through social structures and institutions (*Tribes of Yahweh,* p. 600) and he charges that Mendenhall's insufficient appreciation of that power constitutes "a form of unclarified anarchism" (*Tribes of Yahweh,* p. 914n.4). Of course, whether clarified or not, anarchistic strains in biblical faith have been identified by scholars in addition to Mendenhall. (See, for example, Jacques Ellul, *Anarchy and Christianity,* trans. Geoffrey W. Bromiley [Grand Rapids: Eerdmans, 1991], pp. 45-85.) Gottwald's critique of Mendenhall is shaped by Gottwald's own allegiance to sociological methodology, an allegiance that at times seems to slip into sociological determinism. He writes that "neither deities nor philosophic first principles viewed as uncaused causes, rather than as the ideas of human beings, have any place in the historical dialectic of social evolution" (*Tribes of Yahweh,* p. 602). And later he writes that "the entire biblical theological abstract superstructure" must be overturned so that "the religion of Israel is seen as an intelligible social product . . ." (*Tribes of Yahweh,* p. 912). In viewing the covenant and the confederacy as a free choice of the proto-Israelites, Gottwald gives short shrift to the fact that those people themselves viewed the covenant as the free choice of Yahweh. For insightful critique of Gottwald from one who nonetheless appreciates elements of the revolt model, see Walter Brueggemann, *Theology of the Old Testament: Testimony, Dispute, Advocacy* (Minneapolis: Fortress Press, 1997), pp. 50-53.

149. The contrast with charity is noted by Bruce Vawter and Leslie J. Hoppe, *A New Heart: A Commentary on the Book of Ezekiel,* International Theological Commentary (Grand Rapids: Eerdmans and Edinburgh: The Handsel Press Ltd., 1991), pp. 208-9.

150. Karl Georg Kuhn, *"proselytos,"* in *Theological Dictionary of the New Testament,* vol. 6, ed. Gerhard Friedrich, trans. Geoffrey W. Bromiley (Grand Rapids: Eerdmans, 1968), p. 731.

151. Norwood begins his monumental history of religious refugees with reflections on these biblical texts. See Frederick A. Norwood, *Strangers and Exiles: A History of Religious Refugees,* vol. 1 (New York: Abingdon Press, 1969), pp. 21-22.

152. For reflections on a contemporary theology of exile, see the concluding chapter of Daniel L. Smith, *The Religion of the Landless: The Social Context of the Babylonian Exile* (Bloomington, Ind.: Meyer-Stone Books, 1989), pp. 201-16.

NOTES TO CHAPTER III

1. This version of the story appears in David Edwards, *Burning All Illusions: A Guide to Personal and Political Freedom* (Boston: South End Press, 1996), p. 65.

2. A helpful overview of Buddhist monism is provided by D. T. Suzuki, "General Characteristics of Buddhism," in *Readings in Eastern Religious Thought,* vol. 2: *Buddhism,* ed. Allie M. Frazier (Philadelphia: Westminster Press, 1969), pp. 70-89.

3. The same cannot be said of noncanonical Gospels. Among the writings associated with Gnosticism, for example, "The Gospel of Truth" identifies "terror and disturbance and instability and doubt and division" with mere "disturbing dreams" and "illusions at work." As one of the "empty fictions" that "come into being like the shadows and phantoms of the night," terror will be exposed to the light and then we will know "that it is nothing." "The Gospel of Truth," trans. Harold W. Attridge and George W. MacRae, in *The Nag Hammadi Library,* ed. James M. Robinson, 3rd ed. (New York: Harper & Row, 1988), p. 45.

4. During the Reagan administration, Abu Nidal had been designated "public enemy number one." Robert Fisk, "Talks with Osama bin Laden," *The Nation* 267, no. 8 (September 21, 1998): 25.

5. Robert Merrill, "Simulations and Terrors of Our Time," in *Violent Persuasions: The Politics and Imagery of Terrorism,* ed. David J. Brown and Robert Merrill (Seattle: Bay Press, 1993), p. 33. While the hostage-taking in Iran had galvanized American attention on the phenomenon of terrorism, Merrill notes that there was also a campaign by the Reagan administration to depict terrorism (supposedly funded and directed from Moscow) as the premier threat to national security and to the personal security of Americans. Thus, Merrill observes, "the first item on the agenda" of the new Reagan policy "was to terrorize the imaginations of Americans" regarding the threat of terrorism.

6. From a purely statistical vantage point, much else produces a higher body count as well. Robin Morgan cites the fact that, in 1985, when 23 U.S. citizens were killed in terrorist attacks around the world, one hundred were killed by lightning. Morgan, *The Demon Lover: On the Sexuality of Terrorism* (New York: W. W. Norton, 1989), p. 30. Yet by 1986, due in part to the Reagan administration focus, "terrorism" ranked number one in polls inquiring about the major concerns of Americans. Terrorism far outranked other concerns like homelessness, pollution, racism, or even the perennial American concern over pocketbook economic issues. In 1986, fewer than thirty U.S. citizens were killed in what were described as "terrorist attacks," but, as former Attorney General Ramsey Clark notes, about 12,000 citizens died as the result of accidental falls during that same year. Yet there was no "war on accidents." Clark, "Beyond Terrorism," in *Violent Persuasions,* p. 72. It is

testimony to the fear that can be evoked by the very concept of "terrorism." As Richard Clutterbuck observed, violence by subnational groups in the name of a political cause garners greater attention but produces fewer deaths than the more mundane forms of violence in typical American cities. In Northern Ireland, for example, 1973 was a particularly violent year, but while 259 people were killed that year among the 1.5 million residents of Northern Ireland, three times as many people were murdered among the 1.5 million residents of Detroit. Clutterbuck, *Protest and the Urban Guerrilla* (New York: Abelard-Schuman, 1974), p. 4. While these assorted statistics may serve to add perspective to our perceptions of the magnitude of the terrorist threat, mere numbers should never lead us to dismiss the anguish and horror that are left in the wake of terrorist attacks. If the death toll is low in some attacks, it is not for lack of trying. As Timothy McVeigh reportedly told his attorney in the Oklahoma City bombing case, "We needed a body count to make our point." Tragically, the bomber of the Murrah Federal Building got his body count. McVeigh's reported comment is cited by Bruce Hoffman, *Inside Terrorism* (New York: Columbia University Press, 1998), p. 177.

7. A similar question is posed by Edward S. Herman, *Beyond Hypocrisy: Decoding the News in an Age of Propaganda* (Boston: South End Press, 1992), pp. 28-29. In the film documentary, *Hearts and Minds,* the recorded comments of American generals on the low Vietnamese valuation of life are juxtaposed with wrenching scenes of an outpouring of grief at a funeral in Vietnam.

8. Shea made the statement during a NATO briefing broadcast on CNN Morning Edition on Wednesday, April 28, 1999.

9. See the comments by Howard Zinn, "Their Atrocities — and Ours," *The Progressive* 63, no. 7 (July 1999): 20-21.

10. Andrew Bard Schmookler notes the sense of violated dignity and "sustained insult" that surrounded the reaction to the holding of American hostages in Iran. It did not diminish the insult as it became clear that the Iranian government was complicit with the "student" hostage-takers. Schmookler, *The Parable of the Tribes: The Problem of Power in Social Evolution* (Boston: Houghton Mifflin, 1984), pp. 165-66. Concern and compassion should not be governed by numbers, so concern for the fate of these hostages was to be expected and encouraged (even though, as Schmookler wrote, they constituted "less than .00000025 percent of our citizens"). But concern over the fate of the hostages seemed somehow disconnected from the sense of national indignation at this insult from mere terrorists. No similar sense of either insult or shame accompanies the fact that well over a million Americans sit captive in our own penal institutions.

11. Pierre Clastres offers an insightful exploration of the contrasts between "archaic" societies in the Americas (e.g., the Guayaki, the Mandan) and the "complex" societies of the Incas and the Aztecs. While the latter, hierarchical societies are marked by a centralized monopoly on violence, the archaic societies are egalitarian "societies without a state" in which chiefs served the primary function of peacefully resolving intra-communal conflicts. Clastres, *Society Against the State: Essays in Political Anthropology,* trans. Robert Hurley with Abe Stein (New York: Zone Books, 1989).

12. Sagan, *At the Dawn of Tyranny: The Origins of Individualism, Political Oppression, and the State* (New York: Alfred A. Knopf, 1985), p. 321.

13. In this regard, Barbara Ehrenreich cites "eerie parallels between feudal Japan and

305

feudal Europe." Ehrenreich, *Blood Rites: Origins and History of the Passions of War* (New York: Henry Holt and Company, 1997), p. 144.

14. Ehrenreich, *Blood Rites*, pp. 146-48.

15. Ehrenreich, *Blood Rites*, p. 179.

16. For a contemporary overview of the manner in which technologically sophisticated weaponry is no longer under the sole purview of the nation state, see Martin van Creveld, *The Transformation of War* (New York: The Free Press, 1991), pp. 192-227.

17. Georges Sorel, *Reflections on Violence*, trans. T. E. Hulme (New York: Peter Smith, 1941), p. 68. Emphasis in the original.

18. Chief Blackbird of the Ottawa Nation, "Germ Warfare Against the Indians," in *On Prejudice: A Global Perspective*, ed. Daniela Gioseffi (New York: Anchor Books, 1993), pp. 43-44.

19. Edward Zuckerman, *The Day after World War III* (New York: Avon Books, 1984), p. 83.

20. Gregg Herken, *Counsels of War* (New York: Alfred A. Knopf, 1985), p. 179. In the 1950s, Herken notes, the devices "detected only one supposed nuclear terrorist — a hapless woman attempting to smuggle a hundred radium-dial watches in her corset."

21. Herken, *Counsels of War*, p. 53.

22. Already in 1978, Sidney Lens reported on serious U.S. consideration of nuclear attacks in six separate post–World War II crises. Among these were the crises over Korea, Berlin, Vietnam, and Cuba. Lens, *The Day Before Doomsday: An Anatomy of the Nuclear Arms Race* (Boston: Beacon Press, 1978), pp. 119-23.

23. Schaap, "Case Studies in Terrorism: A Symposium," in *Violent Persuasions*, p. 94.

24. Examples abound of the intentional employment of "madman" strategies in both nuclear and non-nuclear scenarios. H. R. Haldeman reports that President Nixon's decision to bomb Hanoi and Haiphong on Christmas Eve 1972 was part of an effort to convince the Vietnamese that he was mad and would stop at nothing. Herken, *Counsels of War*, p. 368n.9. President Reagan's decision to bomb Libya in April 1986 was part of a campaign to convince allies that they could reign in American impulsivity by imposing sanctions on Libya. As one U.S. official said at the time, "We've got the madman factor going for us. You know, 'Keep me from killing again.'" Cited by Noam Chomsky, *The Culture of Terrorism* (Boston: South End Press, 1988), p. 51.

25. Herken, *Counsels of War*, p. 208.

26. The desire to retain "the madman factor" may be one of the influences in the continuing U.S. refusal to renounce both first use of nuclear weapons and nuclear attack on non-nuclear states. See Ira Shorr, "Nuclear Insecurity," *In These Times* 23, no. 16 (July 11, 1999): 10-12.

27. Michael Walzer, *Just and Unjust Wars: A Moral Argument with Historical Illustrations* (New York: Basic Books, 1977), p. 255.

28. Walzer, *Just and Unjust Wars*, p. 267.

29. Walzer, *Just and Unjust Wars*, p. 272.

30. Walzer, *Just and Unjust Wars*, p. 282.

31. Benjamin Netanyahu, *Fighting Terrorism: How Democracies Can Defeat Domestic and International Terrorists* (New York: Farrar, Straus and Giroux, 1995), pp. 124-25. It must be noted that Netanyahu's unfortunate "Islamic terrorism" phrase is no fairer than

characterizing the actions of the state of Israel as "Jewish imperialism" or dubbing the numerous bombing decisions of President Clinton as "Baptist militarism."

32. Netanyahu, *Fighting Terrorism*, pp. 132-33.

33. Netanyahu, *Fighting Terrorism*, pp. 121-22.

34. In his study of nationalism, Eric Hobsbawm reflects on the potential disintegration of "some of the most ancient states" as well as the possible creation of new nations like Scotland and Quebec, which "can today be discussed as a realistic possibility, which it was not twenty-five years ago." Likewise, the disintegration of the Soviet Union could hardly have been predicted five years in advance. E. J. Hobsbawm, *Nations and Nationalism since 1780: Programme, Myth, Reality,* 2nd ed. (Cambridge: Cambridge University Press, 1992), pp. 168-69.

35. Van Creveld, *Transformation of War,* p. 166.

36. Barbara Ehrenreich cites the routinely waged wars of ants in *Blood Rites,* p. 232.

37. As Maurice Berger writes, ". . . terrorism, whether it is perpetrated by or against the state, abhors neutrality. . . ." Berger, "Visual Terrorism," in *Violent Persuasions,* p. 20.

38. In his study of foreign policy, Richard J. Payne cites a number of instances in which political leaders have invoked the specter of Munich, but their renunciations of appeasement have been in situations that were in no way similar to that of Chamberlain. Payne, *The Clash with Distant Cultures: Values, Interests, and Force in American Foreign Policy* (Albany: State University of New York Press, 1995), pp. 68-70, 104-6.

39. Jacques Ellul, *Violence: Reflections from a Christian Perspective,* trans. Cecelia Gaul Kings (New York: Seabury Press, 1969), p. 29.

40. Michael Parenti, *Against Empire* (San Francisco: City Lights Books, 1995), pp. 91-92.

41. Netanyahu, *Fighting Terrorism,* pp. 5-6, 22. At another point (p. 68), Netanyahu approvingly cites the comment made by George Shultz while he was Secretary of State: "These terrorists aren't human beings. They're animals."

42. Regarding all of these demons, Michael Parenti poses the rhetorical question, "Why do they stalk us instead of, say, Denmark or Brazil?" Then he cites the Roman and the British as examples of empires that were similarly stalked. "And if enemies were not to be found, they were invented." Parenti, *Against Empire,* p. 46. In fact, there does appear to be a chicken-and-egg, symbiotic relationship between the militarized quest for security and the attraction of and/or perception of terrorist threat.

43. For reflections on the convergence of wartime and peacetime in the perpetual state of emergency of the "adrenalin society," see Schmookler, *Parable of the Tribes,* pp. 111-14.

44. Parenti, *Against Empire,* p. 63.

45. William D. Hartung, "Gold-Plating the Pentagon," *The Nation* 268, no. 8 (March 1, 1999): 6.

46. Parenti, *Against Empire,* p. 63.

47. Payne, *Clash with Distant Cultures,* p. 115.

48. See the comments of David Callahan, *Unwinnable Wars: American Power and Ethnic Conflict,* A Twentieth Century Fund Book (New York: Hill and Wang, 1997), pp. 213-14. While Callahan advocates "efforts to reduce the flow of light weapons into ethnically volatile regions," he gives inadequate attention to the manner in which today's peaceful re-

gion is tomorrow's volatile one, and to the manner in which weapons themselves may contribute to the volatility.

49. Payne, *Clash with Distant Cultures*, p. 65. Edward Herman notes that a single post–Gulf War trip by then–Defense Secretary Cheney netted $2.1 billion in arms sales. Herman, *Beyond Hypocrisy*, p. 206n.17.

50. Parenti notes that the U.S. military is the single largest consumer of nonrenewable energy resources as well as the single greatest polluter with toxins including PCBs, plutonium, and "spent uranium" shell casings. Parenti, *Against Empire*, pp. 59-60.

51. Similar questions about the meaning of national security when the planet itself is terrorized are posed by Morgan, *Demon Lover*, p. 152.

52. Drawing on the works of Dom Helder Camara and Emmanuel Mounier, there are helpful reflections on violence as both "act" and "state" in Robert McAfee Brown, *Religion and Violence: A Primer for White Americans* (Philadelphia: Westminster Press, 1973), pp. 34-38.

53. The figures are based on a UNESCO study and are cited by Jeffrey A. Sluka, "The Anthropology of Conflict," in *The Paths to Domination, Resistance, and Terror*, ed. Carolyn Nordstrom and JoAnn Martin (Berkeley: University of California Press, 1992), p. 19.

54. Recall that President Carter dismissed UN Ambassador Andrew Young after Young had "informal" contacts with PLO representatives.

55. While governments have always engaged in subterfuge, state secrecy and espionage have reached their cultish dimensions only in very recent years. Richard J. Barnet reminds that it was as recent as the Hoover administration that Secretary of War Henry Stimson dismissed a proposal for a national intelligence agency because "Gentlemen do not read each other's mail." Barnet adds that this was the same "prehistoric era" in which a general vetoed plans for a new bomber because it was immoral to plot the killing of civilians. Barnet, *Roots of War* (Baltimore: Penguin Books, 1972), p. 31. Not infrequently today, information that is already possessed by foreign adversaries is classified as secret by the U.S. government in order to keep it out of the hands of the American public. In one example cited by former Attorney General Ramsey Clark, "Our government didn't keep the bombing of Cambodia secret so the Cambodians wouldn't discover it. They had a pretty good idea it was happening every time the ground shook. The secrecy was to deceive the American people. . . ." Clark, "Beyond Terrorism," in *Violent Persuasions*, p. 82.

56. Janis, "Groupthink among Policy Makers," in Nevitt Sanford, Craig Comstock, and associates, *Sanctions for Evil: Sources of Social Destructiveness*, The Jossey-Bass Behavioral Science Series (San Francisco: Jossey-Bass, 1971), p. 79.

57. Cited by Payne, *Clash with Distant Cultures*, p. 15.

58. John Pilger, *Distant Voices* (New York: Vintage Books, 1994), p. 13.

59. Cited by Eric Alterman, "Speaking Truth to Power," *The Nation* 266, no. 9 (March 16, 1998): 6. The notion that it is somehow disastrous when citizens express dissenting views in the presence of public servants might well be accompanied by a sense of foreboding. As Archibald MacLeish warned, while freedom was once understood as something that one used, it is increasingly viewed as a possession that one puts away and saves, like a deed or a stock or a bond. Such freedom has little utility or meaning. Commentary on the MacLeish quotation is offered by Charles Drekmeier, "Knowledge as Virtue, Knowledge as Power," in Sanford, Comstock, and associates, *Sanctions for Evil*, p. 233.

60. On attempts to justify violence as either permissible or obligatory and the tendency of the former to become the latter, see Timothy Binkley, "Consensus and the Justification of Force," in *Reason and Violence: Philosophical Investigations,* ed. Sherman M. Stanage (Totowa, N.J.: Littlefield, Adams & Co., 1974), pp. 123-41. It should be noted that there is a corresponding effort to portray the violence of the adversary as mere "terrorism," i.e., as neither obligatory nor ethically/legally permissible.

61. An example of a fumbling attempt at deception was a 1981 story floated by the White House that Libya was sponsoring a group of terrorists to assassinate President Reagan. It is unclear whether there was ever any kernel of truth to the story, but administration officials tried to keep it newsworthy for weeks with suggestions that there was one team and then two of five terrorists and then twelve coming from Canada and then Mexico and including Iranians and then Syrians. The story eventually turned to vapor, but "Never had a team of assassins received such advanced billing," notes Parenti, *Against Empire,* p. 93. An example of a lie that received more sophisticated treatment was the 1990 story that Iraqi forces in occupied Kuwait were entering hospitals and throwing Kuwaiti babies out of their incubators. The horrifying story received prominent play in the media and it was only a year later that the investigations of Alexander Cockburn proved it to be a lie. The story had been totally fabricated by the public relations firm of Hill and Knowlton, which had been hired by the Kuwaiti ambassador to the U.S. to bolster pro war sentiment. Robert Merrill, "Terrorism and the Role of the Media: A Symposium," in *Violent Persuasions,* p. 228.

62. Along with a few Lenin tidbits on lying, the Trotsky quotation was approvingly cited by Maurice Merleau-Ponty, *Humanism and Terror: An Essay on the Communist Problem,* trans. John O'Neill (Boston: Beacon Press, 1969), p. 103. Merleau-Ponty went on to denounce the "Quaker hypocrisy" with which some ethically fastidious people stood aloof from the struggle of the workers. "To tell the truth and to act out of conscience are nothing but alibis of a false morality. . . ."

63. Protecting the lives of U.S. citizens had also been used as rationale by President Johnson in the invasion of the Dominican Republic. Coincidentally, the rationale of protecting Soviet citizens had been used in the Soviet invasions of Czechoslovakia and Hungary. Reagan's decision to invade Grenada to protect U.S. medical students there came after assurances from the government of Grenada that the students were in no danger and that they would be given safe passage if they wished to leave. In fact, Canadian medical students had already been safely evacuated shortly before the invasion. U.S. "rescue" forces relied on tourist maps of Grenada and it took them thirty-six hours to reach the students after the initial landing, but no students were harmed. Payne, *Clash with Distant Cultures,* pp. 206-7.

64. The attack was so hastily arranged that four of the five members of the Joint Chiefs of Staff were excluded from the decision to bomb. Christopher Hitchens, "The Clinton-Douglas Debates," *The Nation* 267, no. 16 (November 16, 1998): 8. The Pentagon never produced convincing evidence that the Al-Shifa plant in Sudan made chemical weapons materials, but as Hitchens observes, "a very large number of people are going to die . . . as a direct result of the destruction of a poor nation's chief producer of medicines. . . ."

65. Military response sows the seeds of more terrorism. Bruce Hoffman cites evidence that the 1986 U.S. air strikes against Libya for supposed Libyan involvement in interna-

tional terrorism were actually followed by *increased* Libyan state-sponsorship of terrorist attacks. Hoffman, *Inside Terrorism*, p. 192.

66. Stephen E. Atkins, *Terrorism: A Reference Handbook*, Contemporary World Issues Series (Santa Barbara, Calif.: ABC-CLIO, Inc., 1992), p. 22. Atkins notes that this Directive provided legal pretext for the 1986 air strikes against Libya. Unfortunately, Atkins was not correct in his speculation that "World opinion was so hostile to the destruction and the civilian deaths from that attack that it is unlikely that this type of action will be used again."

67. Walzer, *Just and Unjust Wars*, p. 207.

68. Albert Camus, *The Rebel: An Essay on Man in Revolt*, trans. Anthony Bower (New York: Vintage Books, 1956), p. 241.

69. In fact, Iraq had legitimate grievances over Kuwaiti extraction of oil from the Ramaila field, but the U.S. never allowed consideration of these grievances as a possible path towards negotiated withdrawal of Iraqi forces from Kuwait. Payne, *Clash with Distant Cultures*, p. 109.

70. Tony Auth of the *Philadelphia Inquirer* lampooned the jobs argument in a cartoon of troops on Iwo Jima raising a flag which read "Help Wanted." Herman, *Beyond Hypocrisy*, p. 54.

71. Payne, *Clash with Distant Cultures*, p. 117. Prior to the congressional vote, President Bush, Sr. argued that he did not need authorization in any event, and that he would be willing to commit troops without a single member of Congress voting in favor. Parenti, *Against Empire*, p. 152. A similar "last best hope for peace" vote by Congress in 1986 authorized funding for the Contras as a way of forcing the Sandinista government of Nicaragua into negotiations. The congressional vote came five days after Nicaragua had already accepted the Contadora Treaty which had been negotiated with regional governments but elements of which were unacceptable to the U.S. Chomsky, *Culture of Terrorism*, pp. 11-12.

72. The whole process is actually well depicted in Dr. Seuss's story of the attempts by the Yooks and the Zooks to outdo one another. See Dr. Seuss, *The Butter Battle Book* (New York: Random House, 1984).

73. Atkins, *Terrorism: Reference Handbook*, p. 24.

74. An extradition treaty between the U.S. and Cuba was not signed until 1973. Atkins, *Terrorism: Reference Handbook*, p. 89.

75. Laura Flanders, "Chemical Arms Scam," *The Nation* 265, no. 21 (December 22, 1997): 5.

76. Herman, *Beyond Hypocrisy*, pp. 30-32.

77. Kissinger quoted by Parenti, *Against Empire*, p. 143. Allende was replaced by Augusto Pinochet, whose state terror spilled over onto U.S. soil in the 1976 Washington, D.C. car bombing that killed former Chilean diplomat Orlando Letelier and his assistant Roni Moffitt. See Edward S. Herman, *The Real Terror Network: Terrorism in Fact and Propaganda* (Boston: South End Press, 1982), p. 66. Some documents on the U.S. involvement with Pinochet were recently declassified, but documents pertaining to the murders of Letelier and Moffitt were not among them. Peter Kornbluh, "Chile Declassified," *The Nation* 269, no. 5 (August 9/16, 1999): 21-24.

78. William Blum, "A Brief History of U.S. Interventions: 1945 to the Present," *Z Magazine* 12, no. 6 (June 1999): 25-30.

79. Barnet, *Roots of War*, p. 156.

80. Turner quoted by Chomsky, *Culture of Terrorism,* p. 27. Chomsky also describes (p. 208) how the Baptist Convention of Nicaragua, a church group with few sympathies for the Sandinista government, denounced the U.S. intervention and the Contra attacks on schools, medical clinics, and cooperative farms.

81. Parenti, *Against Empire,* p. 24.

82. Herman, *Beyond Hypocrisy,* p. 36.

83. Evidence of the CIA involvement was uncovered by Bob Woodward's investigative reporting on CIA Director William Casey and is cited by Noam Chomsky, *Necessary Illusions: Thought Control in Democratic Societies* (Boston: South End Press, 1989), p. 271.

84. "As it turns out, the two terrors needed one another to feed their own perverse aims," writes Marcelo Suárez-Orozco, "A Grammar of Terror: Psychocultural Responses to State Terrorism in Dirty War and Post–Dirty War Argentina," in *Paths to Domination, Resistance, and Terror,* p. 232.

85. This example of the "symbiosis" which occurs with terrorist methodology is cited by James H. Billington, *Fire in the Minds of Men: Origins of the Revolutionary Faith* (New York: Basic Books, 1980), p. 508.

86. Van Creveld, *Transformation of War,* p. 174.

87. Cited by Blum, "Brief History of U.S. Interventions," p. 26.

88. Herman, *Beyond Hypocrisy,* p. 50.

89. Payne, *Clash with Distant Cultures,* pp. 101-3, 128-29.

90. Netanyahu, *Fighting Terrorism,* pp. 72-73.

91. Morgan, *Demon Lover,* p. 47.

92. Edwards, *Burning All Illusions,* p. 19.

93. Wilson's later report on his own activities is cited by Morgan, *Demon Lover,* pp. 134-35.

94. The whole incident sets an odd and frightening legal precedent. If citizens of other countries can be arrested for actions performed outside the U.S. that happen to violate U.S. law, the notion of "policing the world" becomes absurdly literal. Why should other countries refrain from this same style of law enforcement? Most Americans today (including the president and first lady) are in violation of the understanding of Islamic law enforced by the Taliban government of Afghanistan. Is our immunity from Taliban arrest based only on the lack of Taliban military power to enforce their understanding of justice? In such an international law of the jungle, might does make right.

95. See Edwards, *Burning All Illusions,* pp. 17-18, and Herman, *Beyond Hypocrisy,* pp. 36, 50.

96. Payne, *Clash with Distant Cultures,* pp. 65-66.

97. Parenti, *Against Empire,* pp. 129-31. See also Dan Coughlin, "Haitian Lament: Killing Me Softly," *The Nation* 268, no. 8 (March 1, 1999): 20-23.

98. Netanyahu, *Fighting Terrorism,* pp. 80-81; Parenti, *Against Empire,* p. 122.

99. Fisk, "Talks with Osama bin Laden," pp. 25-26.

100. Parenti notes that the earliest attacks by returning Algerian fighters were against women's rights groups. Parenti, *Against Empire,* p. 122.

101. Payne, *Clash with Distant Cultures,* p. 66; Netanyahu, *Fighting Terrorism,* pp. 81, 96-97.

102. Fisk, "Talk with Osama bin Laden," p. 25.

103. See Dane Archer and Rosemary Gartner, *Violence and Crime in Cross-National Perspective* (New Haven: Yale University Press, 1984). The association between wartime and increased violent crime is also noted by Daniela Gioseffi, "Introduction," in *On Prejudice,* p. xxxvii. Increases in U.S. rates of crime and domestic violence during World War II are noted by Bruce D. Porter, *War and the Rise of the State: The Military Foundations of Modern Politics* (New York: The Free Press, 1994), p. 284. After years of decline, U.S. murder rates rose sharply during the years of the American War in Vietnam, and in 1991, the year of the Gulf War, violent crime rose 8 percent in the U.S.

104. See the comments of Sagan, *Dawn of Tyranny,* pp. 248-51.

105. Payne, *Clash with Distant Cultures,* pp. 58-59. Regarding the claim that gun ownership is a legitimate form of self-defense, Payne cites the fact that American gun owners are forty-three times more likely to use their guns to kill themselves or family members than to kill criminal intruders in their homes. Avoidance of gun ownership is clearly the more effective approach to self-defense.

106. Weir quoted by Robin Wright, "Address the Causes, Not Just the Effects," *Los Angeles Times,* October 20, 1985, reprinted in *Terrorism: Opposing Viewpoints,* ed. Bonnie Szumski, Opposing Viewpoints Series (St. Paul, Minn.: Green Haven Press, 1986), p. 48.

107. In one of the more notorious cases of state-sponsored terrorism performed at the behest of a Western democracy, France arranged for the bombing of the Greenpeace ship *Rainbow Warrior* while it was docked in Auckland, New Zealand. One crew member was killed in the bombing. As part of an anti-nuclear protest, the *Rainbow Warrior* had been preparing for nonviolent intrusion into the French nuclear testing zone in the Pacific. Morgan, *Demon Lover,* p. 149.

108. For the Morrow quotation along with commentary, see Gil Bailie, *Violence Unveiled: Humanity at the Crossroads* (New York: Crossroad, 1995), p. 19.

109. It seems to be mere ideological pretense when Merleau-Ponty asserts that proletarian revolutionaries are engaged only in *"praxis"* and that "the categories of 'ends' and 'means' are entirely alien to Marxism." Merleau-Ponty, *Humanism and Terror,* p. 126.

110. Richard Barnet observes that "major decisions are the products of bureaucratic coalitions. It is impossible to ascribe them to any single cause and the attempt is often ludicrous." Economic determinists had a difficult time explaining "the seemingly irrational persistence of the United States in Vietnam. . . ." There was a sense of relief when they finally discovered that some U.S. oil companies had invested in exploration in Vietnam. Barnet, *Roots of War,* p. 159. Potential oil wells notwithstanding, the whole war *was* irrational, driven by captivity to the belief that the next round of violence against the Vietnamese would precipitate their salvation and our vindication.

111. The nation state is not alone in this practice of destroying those who are to be saved. For some who have been in full rebellion against political authority, as Albert Camus observed, "the revolution, in itself, was more important than the people it wanted to save. . . ." Camus noted the strange additions and subtractions of the revolution: "As for the oppressed, since they were going to be saved once and for all, they could be oppressed still more. What they would lose, the oppressed of the future would gain." Camus, *The Rebel,* pp. 161-62.

112. José Comblin, *The Church and the National Security State* (Maryknoll, N.Y.: Orbis Books, 1979), p. 93.

113. Clark, "Beyond Terrorism," p. 84.

114. The examples of autonomous social phenomena in the writings of Marx and Shelley are cited by Ehrenreich, who offers insightful comments on the autonomy of the institution of war in *Blood Rites,* pp. 231-38. Ehrenreich calls this section of her book, "The Beast in Modern Form."

115. Many are those who would wish to define their own violence as a uniquely justifiable variety of bloodletting. Merleau-Ponty wrote, "We do not have a choice between purity and violence but between different kinds of violence." Merleau-Ponty, *Humanism and Terror,* p. 109. He was doubtless correct in describing it as "violence" when people are held in subjugation and poverty, and he was correct in observing that no humans can claim "purity," but he was mistaken in claiming that revolutionaries use a "different kind of violence." Likewise, Americans were correct in viewing the bombings of U.S. embassies in Africa as terrorism, but mistaken in thinking that the American retaliatory strikes were something other than terrorism.

116. With helpful commentary, these laws of violence appear in Ellul, *Violence,* pp. 93-108.

117. With emphasis in the original, the comment is from Georges Sorel, *Reflections on Violence,* p. 295.

118. A helpful exploration of the task of demythologizing is that of Walter Wink, *The Powers,* vol. 2: *Unmasking the Powers: The Invisible Forces That Determine Human Existence* (Philadelphia: Fortress Press, 1986).

119. Edward W. Said, *Culture and Imperialism* (London: Chatto & Windus, 1993), p. 376.

120. Steven Runciman, *The First Crusade* (Cambridge: Cambridge University Press, 1992), p. 1.

121. Runciman, *First Crusade,* pp. 11-12. The fate of Hakim is unknown. One of his associates, Darazi, fled to Lebanon and founded an Islamic sect. The Druze of Lebanon still await the return of Hakim.

122. Jaroslav Pelikan, *The Christian Tradition: A History of the Development of Doctrine,* vol. 3: *The Growth of Medieval Theology (600-1300)* (Chicago: University of Chicago Press, 1978), pp. 208-10.

123. Richard A. Newhall, *The Crusades,* rev. ed., Berkshire Studies in European History (New York: Holt, Rinehart and Winston, 1963), p. 25.

124. Runciman, *First Crusade,* pp. 23-32.

125. J. N. D. Kelly, *The Oxford Dictionary of Popes* (New York: Oxford University Press, 1988), pp. 159-60.

126. Runciman, *First Crusade,* p. 35.

127. William A. Clebsch, *Christianity in European History* (New York: Oxford University Press, 1979), p. 140.

128. Even in this atmosphere of perceived threat, not all were convinced that Saracen rule was a fate worse than the governance Christendom had to offer. In Spain, some Christians fought as allies of the Muslims in the various wars of conquest and *reconquista.* In fact, the famed El Cid (Rodrigo Díaz) was a mercenary who alternately fought on behalf of both Christian and Muslim rulers. Peter Partner, *God of Battles: Holy Wars of Christianity and Islam* (Princeton, N.J.: Princeton University Press, 1997), pp. 99, 102.

129. Gustave E. von Grunebaum, *Medieval Islam: A Study in Cultural Orientation,* 2nd ed. (Chicago: University of Chicago Press, 1961), p. 48.

130. Cited by Pelikan, *Growth of Medieval Theology,* p. 242. Partner is overly kind in his assessment of Peter the Venerable as "the enlightened Abbot of Cluny" who sponsored translation of the Koran "in the belief that it would lead to reasoned missionary argument." Partner, *God of Battles,* p. 88.

131. Cited by Partner, *God of Battles,* p. 89.

132. Robert the Monk, "Speech of Pope Urban II at the Council of Clermont 1095," trans. D. C. Munro, in *The Medieval World: 300-1300,* ed. Norman F. Cantor (New York: Macmillan, 1963), pp. 200-202. The version of the biblical text (Matthew 19:29) is that given in the translation of Robert the Monk's account.

133. See Zoé Oldenbourg, *The Crusades,* trans. Anne Carter (London: Weidenfeld & Nicolson, 1998), p. 584.

134. Oldenbourg, *Crusades,* p. 593.

135. Rosalind and Christopher Brooke, *Popular Religion in the Middle Ages: Western Europe 1000-1300* (London: Thames and Hudson, 1984), pp. 56-57.

136. Fulcher of Chartres, cited in *History: The End of the World,* ed. Lewis H. Lapham with Peter T. Struck (New York: History Book Club, 1997), p. 54.

137. Raymond of St. Giles, Count of Toulouse, "The Capture of Jerusalem by the Crusaders," trans. D. C. Munro, in *Medieval World,* p. 206.

138. Roland H. Bainton, *Christian Attitudes Toward War and Peace: A Historical Survey and Critical Re-evaluation* (Nashville: Abingdon Press, 1960), p. 114.

139. Nicolas Cheetham, *Keepers of the Keys: A History of the Popes from St. Peter to John Paul II* (New York: Charles Scribner's Sons, 1982), pp. 68-69.

140. Runciman, *First Crusade,* pp. 34, 36. As if concerned that the less palpable forgiveness of sins would be insufficient motivation for the campaign against the Saracens, Pope Gregory VII granted to campaigners the right of possession to any lands they conquered, subject only to the ultimate governance of the papacy. The popularity of several of the crusades to the Levant was of such magnitude that there were concerns that the battle against the Saracens in Spain would be neglected. There were repeated papal assurances that indulgences applied to the Spanish crusaders as well, and there were even papal prohibitions against crusaders leaving Spain to fight elsewhere. Carolly Erickson, *The Medieval Vision: Essays in History and Perception* (New York: Oxford University Press, 1976), p. 68.

141. Bainton, *Christian Attitudes,* p. 112.

142. Rosalind and Christopher Brooke, *Popular Religion,* p. 60.

143. Cheetham, *Keepers of the Keys,* p. 111.

144. Cited by Partner, *God of Battles,* p. 104. The brief phrase from Innocent II stuns on a number of accounts. In an earlier era of church history, some soldiers who were baptized by immersion held their right hands above the water in the rather superstitious belief that they could thereby continue to wield the sword in their unbaptized hands. For Innocent II, wielding the sword actually consecrates the hands. Another remarkable inversion is evident in Innocent's coupling of consecration with the blood of murdered "unbelievers" rather than with the blood of the slaughtered Lamb; the former is an encouragement to slaughter while the latter is a judgment on slaughter.

314

145. Cited by Malcolm Barber, *The Trial of the Templars* (Cambridge: Cambridge University Press, 1980), p. 7.

146. Bernard of Clairvaux, quoted by Partner, *God of Battles*, p. 105.

147. Ferguson, *War and Peace in the World's Religions* (New York: Oxford University Press, 1978), p. 109.

148. Jonathan Riley-Smith, *The Crusades: A Short History* (New Haven: Yale University Press, 1987), p. 108.

149. An indication of the cruelty of servitude in the period was the fact that the church at one point found it necessary to issue a reminder that to beat a servant to death was a sin for which penance would have to be paid. Oldenbourg, *Crusades*, p. 17.

150. Oldenbourg, *Crusades*, pp. 34-35.

151. Malcolm Lambert, *Medieval Heresy: Popular Movements from the Gregorian Reform to the Reformation*, 2nd ed. (Oxford: Blackwell, 1992), p. 98.

152. Newhall, *Crusades*, p. 43.

153. Runciman, *First Crusade*, p. 55.

154. Partner, *God of Battles*, p. 79.

155. Oldenbourg, *Crusades*, p. 137.

156. David Nirenberg, *Communities of Violence: Persecution of Minorities in the Middle Ages* (Princeton, N.J.: Princeton University Press, 1996), pp. 43-68. Nirenberg perceives a challenge to the authority of the French monarchy as an additional factor at work in the intricacies of the history of the crusades of the pastoureaux, the Shepherds' Crusade of 1320 and the Cowherds' Crusade of the following year.

157. Cited by Erwin I. J. Rosenthal, *Judaism and Islam* (London: Thomas Yoseloff, 1961), p. 136.

158. Nirenberg, *Communities of Violence*, p. 200.

159. Newhall, *Crusades*, pp. 44-45. Runciman also attributes the military success of the first crusade to the assistance provided by Byzantium and to "the disunity of the Moslem world." Runciman, *First Crusade*, p. 192.

160. Cited by Amin Maalouf, *The Crusades Through Arab Eyes*, trans. Jon Rothschild (New York: Schocken Books, 1984), p. 39. In his notes (p. 270), Maalouf wonders whether the lack of reference to the well-documented cannibalism at Maarat in most modern accounts of the crusades is due to a desire to depict Western incursions as "civilizing" missions.

161. Runciman, *First Crusade*, p. 188.

162. Maalouf, *Crusades Through Arab Eyes*, pp. 52-53.

163. Newhall, *Crusades*, pp. 63-64. For one account by a contemporary of crusaders breaking agreements, see Behâ-ed-Din, "Richard I Massacres Prisoners after Taking Acre, 2-20 August 1191: A Saracen View of the Crusades," in *Eyewitness to History*, ed. John Carey (New York: Avon Books, 1987), pp. 35-37.

164. Philip K. Hitti, *Islam and the West: A Historical Cultural Survey* (Princeton, N.J.: D. Van Nostrand, 1962), p. 80. Oldenbourg also remarks on the contagious quality of holy war, noting that the "warlike piety" of the Franks "seems to have penetrated Islam in some underground way. The holy war had changed sides." Oldenbourg, *Crusades*, p. 418.

165. Von Grunebaum, *Medieval Islam*, p. 181.

166. Von Grunebaum notes, however, that most orthodox Muslims denounced the

more extreme "terrorist methods" adopted by the Neo-Ismaelite group that became known as the "Assassins." Von Grunebaum, *Medieval Islam,* p. 198n.64.

167. Cited by Oldenbourg, *Crusades,* p. 419.

168. Partner, *God of Battles,* p. 112.

169. Oldenbourg, *Crusades,* p. 580.

170. Gibbon's remark is cited by Newhall, *Crusades,* p. 37.

171. Steven Runciman, *The Medieval Manichee: A Study of the Christian Dualist Heresy* (Cambridge: Cambridge University Press, 1982), p. 139.

172. Modern examples abound. In the U.S., World War I was marked by persecution of pacifists and followed by repression of labor unions. World War II saw the persecution of Americans of Asiatic ancestry and was followed by the McCarthy era.

173. Partner, *God of Battles,* p. 103. Partner notes that the impact of the internal holy wars proclaimed by various Muslim leaders was mitigated by the fact that the caliphate never attained a centralized authority similar to the papacy.

174. For a brief account of the "crusades" proclaimed by various popes against the Hohenstaufen, see Joseph R. Strayer, *Western Europe in the Middle Ages: A Short History* (New York: Appleton-Century-Crofts, 1955), pp. 157-63. The crusade motif was even utilized by revolutionaries. In 17th-century England, prior to their conversion to biblical pacifism, William Dewsbury and other early Quakers understood their struggle against the king as a "crusade." Ferguson, *War and Peace in World's Religions,* p. 114.

175. Partner, *God of Battles,* p. 96.

176. Partner, *God of Battles,* pp. 156-58.

177. Without specific reference to the sowing and reaping theme, the "profound contrast" between the doctrine of karma and prophetic thinking is noted by Abraham J. Heschel, *The Prophets,* vol. 2 (New York: Harper Torchbooks, 1975), pp. 16-17.

178. It should be noted that Paul is not alone in refuting a simplistic formula of moral causation. In Matthew 13:1-32, 36-43, Jesus is presented as offering a collection of parables on the sowing and reaping theme. There are partial parallels in Mark 4:1-34 and Luke 8:4-18; 13:18-21. In each of the parables, human agency is not the decisive factor in determining what will be reaped. Indeed, the parabolic imagery shifts in the various redactions. While the identity of the "sower" remains vague in the versions of Mark and Luke, Matthew's eschatological framework is expansive in identifying two sowers, "the Son of Man" (13:37) and "the devil" (13:39), and in naming "angels" as the reapers (13:41). Likewise, Matthew identifies the "seed" as the "children" of the kingdom or of the evil one (13:38), while Luke identifies the seed as the word (8:14) and Mark seems to present the seed as a conflation of hearer and word (4:14-20). In all cases, the mustard seed is likened to the kingdom of God. The point is not that the Gospel writers are confused, but rather that the sowing and reaping metaphor is rich with possibilities of both transcendent and human sowers and reapers. There is no simple formula of karma or moral causation behind the metaphor. Note that the sowing and reaping metaphor is inverted in the parable of responsibility in Matthew 25:14-30 (Luke 19:11-27). It is not insignificant that it is the "wicked and lazy slave" who identifies the "master" as "a harsh man, reaping where you did not sow, and gathering where you did not scatter seed" (Matthew 25:24). But this parable in its entirety is less related to the sowing and reaping theme than to the claim that, as Schweizer puts it, people "must not seek anxiously for security, but venture themselves for

God." Eduard Schweizer, *The Good News According to Matthew,* trans. David E. Green (Atlanta: John Knox Press, 1975), p. 473.

179. Walter Brueggemann sees a sharp contrast between the God of the prophets and "the comfortable god of the empire, so fat and well fed as to be neutral and inattentive. . . . It is the way of the unifying gods of the empire not to take sides and by being tolerant to cast eternal votes for the way things are." Brueggemann, *The Prophetic Imagination* (Philadelphia: Fortress Press, 1978), p. 24.

180. For reflections on God's spoken word as more than literally real, and on responding as a mode of hearing, see Abraham Joshua Heschel, *God in Search of Man: A Philosophy of Judaism* (Northvale, N.J.: Jason Aronson Inc., 1987), pp. 178-83.

181. Regarding this "ingestion" of the word, see Karl Barth's description of the vocations to which Jeremiah and Ezekiel were called in *The Doctrine of Reconciliation,* vol. 4, part 3, second half, of *Church Dogmatics,* trans. G. W. Bromiley (Edinburgh: T. & T. Clark, 1962), pp. 581-83.

182. Elmer A. Martens notes that the Hebrew word *(patah)* here translated as "enticed" is used in several texts to refer to sexual seduction (e.g., Exodus 22:16; Judges 14:15), but, writes Martens, to translate the Jeremiah text with the bald statement "You have raped me" is an act of "over-translation." Nonetheless, it is clear that there is a very sharp edge to Jeremiah's complaint. Martens, *Jeremiah,* Believers Church Bible Commentary (Scottdale, Pa.: Herald Press, 1986), p. 136.

183. In response to Hananiah, "Jeremiah's arguments are almost groping," writes Gerhard von Rad, *The Message of the Prophets,* trans. D. M. G. Stalker (New York: Harper & Row, 1967), p. 179.

184. The following verse, Ezekiel 20:26, suggests that one of the laws that the prophet had in mind was a law regarding sacrifice of the firstborn. See Numbers 3:11-13; 8:16. Nonetheless, in verse 25, Ezekiel is making reference to several laws that were clearly of divine origin. Gerhard von Rad observes that, in Ezekiel 20:25, "prophetic interpretation reaches its boldest limits." Von Rad, *Message of the Prophets,* p. 195.

185. For comments on these mistaken predictions, see Norman K. Gottwald, *The Hebrew Bible: A Socio-Literary Introduction* (Philadelphia: Fortress Press, 1987), p. 488.

186. The paradox in Ezekiel's role of sentinel is noted by von Rad, *Message of the Prophets,* pp. 198-99.

187. Wiesel, *Five Biblical Portraits* (Notre Dame: University of Notre Dame Press, 1981), p. 114.

188. Gottwald, *Hebrew Bible: Introduction,* p. 491.

189. Berrigan, *Ezekiel: Vision in the Dust,* with art by Tom Lewis-Borbely (Maryknoll, N.Y.: Orbis Books, 1997), p. xiii.

190. H.-P. Müller cites the various arguments by which *nabi* is linked to Akkadian words for "gushing," ecstatic speech, or even Egyptian medical terms for "rave" and "to be excited," but Müller effectively raises doubts about each of these. Nonetheless, apart from linguistic questions, Müller writes that Ezekiel's trance (4:7f.) and rapture (37:1) "have something of an archaic and shamanistic air that does not eschew the pathological." H.-P. Müller, *"nabi,"* in *Theological Dictionary of the Old Testament,* vol. 9, ed. G. Johannes Botterweck, Helmer Ringgren, and Heinz-Josef Fabry, trans. David E. Green (Grand Rapids: Eerdmans, 1998), pp. 132-35, 148.

191. Heschel, *Prophets*, vol. 2, p. 188.

192. Elie Wiesel expresses the annoyance that must have been felt by the prophet's contemporaries at the "pacifism" of Jeremiah: "What he demands is surrender to the enemy, without a fight, without any attempt to resist. He advocates total, unconditional surrender, abdication of all that bears the mark of Jewish sovereignty, capitulation of all the fighting forces. Humiliation on a national scale — that is what the prophet suggests and indeed demands. Even if one understands his courageous speeches before the war, one must resent them during the war. They surely contributed to the defeat." Wiesel, *Biblical Portraits*, p. 115.

193. Gottwald describes what he calls the "autonomy" party and the "coexistence" party in *Hebrew Bible: Introduction*, pp. 402-4.

194. This contrast between the vantage points from which one "sees" is noted by Brueggemann, *Prophetic Imagination*, p. 116n.16.

195. On the conflation of collective and individual guilt in the theology of Ezekiel, see Norman K. Gottwald, *All the Kingdoms of the Earth: Prophecy and International Relations in the Ancient Near East* (New York: Harper & Row, 1964), p. 309.

196. Martens, *Jeremiah*, p. 130.

197. Bright offers the translation of "overseer" in both 1:10 and 20:1, and he notes the sharp contrast between the oversight provided by Jeremiah and the policing duties of Pashhur. While Pashhur seeks to maintain order, Jeremiah brings a word that threatens to overturn that order. John Bright, *Jeremiah*, Anchor Bible, vol. 21 (Garden City, N.Y.: Doubleday, 1965), p. 132.

198. On Jeremiah's authority over the nations that recognize no authority save their own, see Daniel Berrigan, *Jeremiah: The World, the Wound of God* (Minneapolis: Fortress Press, 1999), pp. 5-8.

199. "Indeed, the major activity of the prophets was *interference*, remonstrating about wrongs inflicted on other people, meddling in affairs which were seemingly neither their concern nor their responsibility." Abraham J. Heschel, *The Prophets*, vol. 1 (New York: Harper & Row, 1962), p. 205.

200. Berrigan bluntly notes that "the temple coterie must be accounted a sedulous ape of the state potentates." Berrigan, *Jeremiah*, p. 85.

201. Scholars differ as to whether Jeremiah may have been attempting a reversal of meaning of the name "Pashhur." While it is an Egyptian name, "Pashhur" could be confused with an Aramaic term meaning "fruitful on every side." Martens, *Jeremiah*, p. 134.

202. A possible exception to prove the rule of prophetic grief can be found in the book of Obadiah, a work too brief (and perhaps too bitter) to express much of mourning for an Edom slated for destruction; Edom had its chance to gloat (Obadiah 12, 13) but, in Obadiah's pared-down version of sowing and reaping (v. 15), what goes around comes around. Daniel Berrigan writes, "The bitterness of the prophet is off-putting. Until perhaps we are led to reflect that we too live in a time when bitterness of heart is the commonest of ills. . . . How easy . . . to identify our own 'Edomite,' personally demonized — as does our prophet here — once and for all tag the adversary, curse the unchosen one out of existence!" Berrigan, *Minor Prophets, Major Themes* (Marion, S.D.: Fortkamp Publishing/Rose Hill Books, 1995), p. 157. More prevalent among the prophets and much closer to the

spirit of Jeremiah and Ezekiel is Joel's outpouring of grief, the rending not of clothing but of hearts (Joel 2:13).

203. The Hebrew text in Ezekiel 21:6 literally refers to broken "loins." "Broken heart" is a fair translation insofar as modern expression tends to portray the heart as the seat of emotion. It is clearer in the Hebrew original, however, that Ezekiel experiences a mixture of grief *and* terror. As the catastrophe approaches, his "loins" are broken, i.e., he has lost emotional strength and is overcome by great sadness *and* great fear. See Bruce Vawter and Leslie J. Hoppe, *A New Heart: A Commentary on the Book of Ezekiel*, International Theological Commentary (Grand Rapids: Eerdmans and Edinburgh: The Handsel Press Ltd., 1991), p. 105.

204. Based on information supplied by Ezekiel 24:1, the date is calculated by Gottwald, *Hebrew Bible: Introduction*, p. 485. Among the more mundane contributions by Ezekiel is the great precision in dating that he utilized throughout his text.

205. Without denying the role of disciples and others in bringing the text of Ezekiel to its present form, considerations of theology, vocabulary, and style (including the presence of precision in dating) suggest that the oracles against the nations were based on prophecies by Ezekiel himself. Such is the position of a number of scholars, including Walther Eichrodt, *Ezekiel: A Commentary*, trans. Cosslett Quinn, The Old Testament Library (Philadelphia: Westminster Press, 1970), p. 351.

206. See Walter Brueggemann, *Theology of the Old Testament: Testimony, Dispute, Advocacy* (Minneapolis: Fortress Press, 1997), pp. 502-4.

207. It is noteworthy that, in unified literary form, Amos actually includes Judah and Israel in his oracles against the nations. Israel is charged with selling the poor into slavery and trampling "the head of the poor into the dust of the earth" (Amos 2:6-7).

208. The universality of Jeremiah's oracles against the nations is noted by von Rad, *Message of the Prophets*, p. 169.

209. It is clear that several hands were at work in the composition of the book of Jeremiah, including Jeremiah's biographer, Baruch. It entails unnecessary bifurcation, however, to claim (as some scholars do) that Baruch is "pro-Babylonian" (e.g., Jeremiah 42) while the author of the oracles against the nations is "anti-Babylonian." As the compiler(s) of the book in its present form discerned, questions of political allegiance or alliance are subverted by God's judgment on all nations.

210. In Isaiah's oracles against the nations, Babylon is charged with showing no mercy (Isaiah 47:6). Some commentators have noted that Babylon is absent from the oracles against the nations in Ezekiel. Eichrodt observes that Ezekiel's oracles seem to follow the pattern of the oracles in Jeremiah and, where we might expect to find the judgment on Babylon, we find instead Ezekiel's pronouncement against "Gog" (Ezekiel 38–39). While Eichrodt does not find it likely, he cites the possibility that Ezekiel, writing from exile in Babylon, may have used "Gog" as a cipher for Babylon. Eichrodt, *Ezekiel*, p. 523. By the time of the much later writings in Daniel and Revelation, the image of Babylon was in full flower as a biblical paradigm of empire. For insightful consideration of how Babylon came to enter Israel's discourse on empire, see the essay, "At the Mercy of Babylon: A Subversive Rereading of the Empire," in Walter Brueggemann, *A Social Reading of the Old Testament: Prophetic Approaches to Israel's Communal Life*, ed. Patrick D. Miller (Minneapolis: Fortress Press, 1994), pp. 111-33.

211. A summary of the view of Sheol common to several Near Eastern cultures is provided by Eichrodt, *Ezekiel,* pp. 373-77. In Babylonian creation mythology, Marduk defeats the sea monster Tiamat, and the body of Tiamat is used to hold back the watery chaos of the underworld. See Vawter and Hoppe, *New Heart,* pp. 143-44.

212. Tyre and Egypt were the two powers that managed to withstand Babylonian expansion. Such strength made them eligible for special attention from Ezekiel. Vawter and Hoppe, *New Heart,* p. 125.

213. "A dance of death" is the title that Eichrodt gives to his commentary on this section of the text. Eichrodt, *Ezekiel,* p. 436.

214. On this "anthropology of hope," see Berrigan, *Ezekiel,* pp. 95-96.

215. On the importance of exile as the arena for the promises of Yahweh, see Brueggemann, *Theology of the Old Testament,* pp. 171-73.

216. Heschel, *God in Search of Man,* p. 376.

217. A single modern example: few if any of the people killed and maimed in the bombings of the World Trade Center in 1993 or the U.S. embassies in Kenya and Tanzania in 1998 had any involvement in the decision to arm and train Afghan "freedom fighters," or in the decision to station U.S. troops in Saudi Arabia as prelude to war against Iraq. The U.S. played a role in sowing this terror, but the victims of this senseless violence were innocent. In Afghanistan, in New York City, in Kenya, in Tanzania, in Iraq, the innocent died while the powerful remained secure.

218. Heschel perceived that the visions of the prophets did not focus on new actions or new laws or new rules and regulations. Instead, they had visions of new heart and new being. "The fault is in the hearts, not alone in the deeds." Heschel, *Prophets,* vol. 1, p. 208.

219. Krister Stendahl, *Paul Among Jews and Gentiles and Other Essays* (Philadelphia: Fortress Press, 1976), p. 100.

NOTES TO CHAPTER IV

1. The etymology of the phrase as well as the reaction against those who showed "impatience" in waiting for the Messiah are explored by Gershom Scholem, *The Messianic Idea in Judaism* (New York: Schocken Books, 1971), pp. 56-57.

2. Gerhard Kittel, *"eschatos,"* in *Theological Dictionary of the New Testament,* vol. 2, ed. Gerhard Kittel, trans. Geoffrey W. Bromiley (Grand Rapids: Eerdmans, 1964), pp. 697-98.

3. Bernard McGinn illustrates these distinctions with the example of Augustine's virtual identification of the church with the kingdom of God. While this was certainly an eschatological perspective, it was "antiapocalyptic" in its impact of quelling any millennial hopes or other forms of expectancy. McGinn's remarks appear in his introduction to *Apocalyptic Spirituality,* trans. Bernard McGinn, The Classics of Western Spirituality Series (New York: Paulist Press, 1979), p. 5. Paul D. Hanson asserts that the literary genre "apocalyptic" derives from Hebrew "prophetic eschatology" (such as that of Ezekiel, Isaiah, and others). Hanson defines the terms and offers an overview of his position in *The Dawn of Apocalyptic: The Historical and Sociological Roots of Jewish Apocalyptic Eschatology,* rev. ed. (Philadelphia: Fortress Press, 1979), pp. 427-44. Not all scholars have endorsed Hanson's

thesis regarding the origins of the apocalyptic genre. Alternative positions are outlined by Leon Morris, *Apocalyptic* (Grand Rapids: Eerdmans, 1972), pp. 25-33.

4. A critique of the view that apocalyptic is a degenerate version of eschatology is presented by Carl E. Braaten, *Christ and Counter-Christ: Apocalyptic Themes in Theology and Culture* (Philadelphia: Fortress Press, 1972), pp. 2-23.

5. The emergent, contemporary view of the significance of apocalypticism for understanding "the historical Jesus" is, of course, traceable to Albert Schweitzer, *The Quest of the Historical Jesus: A Critical Study of Its Progress from Reimarus to Wrede,* trans. W. Montgomery (1910; reprint, New York: Macmillan, 1968).

6. This phrase described the Sumerian paradise of Dilmun in accounts dated as early as 4000 B.C.E. Cited by Damian Thompson, *The End of Time: Faith and Fear in the Shadow of the Millennium* (Hanover, N.H.: University Press of New England, 1996), p. 10. It should be noted, however, that not all myths related to creation and the primordial condition are devoid of terror. Idyllic visions are hardly evoked by the Babylonian combat between Tiamat and Marduk, or by the "Big Bang," or by the mortal combat between life forms in the "giant organic soup" of evolution's first light.

7. As if in mirror image, apocalyptic notions of decadence and progress are correlated. See the comments of Eugen Weber, *Apocalypses: Prophesies, Cults, and Millennial Beliefs Through the Ages* (Cambridge, Mass.: Harvard University Press, 1999), pp. 19-20.

8. The quotation is from Hanson, *Dawn of Apocalyptic,* p. 443. Hanson understands socio-political oppression to be the milieu that gave birth to biblical apocalypticism. While it seems reasonable to posit such a setting for the book of Daniel, it is less certain for the book of Revelation (as will be discussed in the third section of this chapter). Post-biblical apocalypticism cannot be identified so easily with any particular class or social setting.

9. Bernard McGinn, *Antichrist: Two Thousand Years of the Human Fascination with Evil* (New York: HarperCollins, 1994), p. 16.

10. J. F. C. Harrison, *The Second Coming: Popular Millenarianism, 1780-1850* (New Brunswick, N.J.: Rutgers University Press, 1979), p. 79.

11. In examining an early-20th-century millenarian movement in Brazil, Todd A. Diacon finds that a milieu is especially ripe for millenarianism if the crisis of values is internal to a community rather than simply being imposed by an outside invasion. Diacon, *Millenarian Vision, Capitalist Reality: Brazil's Contestado Rebellion, 1912-1916* (Durham, N.C.: Duke University Press, 1991), pp. 131-32, 143-45. The region that Diacon examined was also the locale of the earlier and equally millenarian Canudos rebellion, the subject of the acclaimed novel by Mario Vargas Llosa, *The War of the End of the World,* trans. Helen R. Lane (New York: Viking Penguin, 1997).

12. The latter phrase is from Francine du Plessix Gray, *Adam & Eve and the City: Selected Nonfiction* (New York: Simon & Schuster, 1987), p. 94.

13. Some of these examples along with brief reviews of the theories are offered by Thompson, *End of Time,* pp. xi-xv. Later (p. 323), Thompson concludes, "Disorientation is a necessary but not sufficient condition for the spread of apocalyptic belief. . . ."

14. Some believers in the imminence of apocalypse correlate (in an apparently unconscious fashion) their expectations about the timing of that event with an approximation of the length of their own life expectancy. This was one of the findings of a study of several New York City church groups by Charles B. Strozier, *Apocalypse: On the Psychology of Fun-*

damentalism in America (Boston: Beacon Press, 1994), pp. 116-19. Thompson also notes the manner in which "prophecies of the End resonate with the human consciousness of death." Thompson, *End of Time,* p. 332.

15. The passivity engendered by the "substitute hero" is noted by Hans Küng, *Eternal Life? Life After Death as a Medical, Philosophical, and Theological Problem,* trans. Edward Quinn (New York: Doubleday, 1985), pp. 204-6.

16. Lee Quinby notes the simultaneous presence of anxiety and denial in the contemporary "ironic stance in regard to human self-annihilation," a point she illustrates by observing that the 1989 Grammy awards ceremony honored the work of both Tracy Chapman ("Talkin' 'bout a Revolution") and Bobby McFerrin ("Don't Worry, Be Happy"). Quinby, *Anti-Apocalypse: Exercises in Genealogical Criticism* (Minneapolis: University of Minnesota Press, 1994), pp. xx, 48. Quinby offers a feminist critique of "apocalyptic discourse," but in the process she overloads the term "apocalyptic" to include such "categories" as "fixed hierarchy, absolute truth, and universal morality" (p. 55). In fact, some apocalyptic movements have been anarchist and, as Quinby acknowledges (p. 36), feminist liberation struggles are also inspired by eschatological visions. At times, Quinby's argument seems to be leveled more against the idea of a transcendent God than against "apocalyptic" per se, yet one could also argue that it is the renunciation of any sense of transcendence which has left humanity standing on the apocalyptic brink of self-annihilation. Nonetheless, Quinby's book offers powerful insight on the need for activist engagement. It also offers a good, quirky read of the end-time themes lurking in everything from contemporary fashion to genetic engineering.

17. Baudrillard, *Looking Back on the End of the World* (New York: Semiotext(e), 1989).

18. Robert Jay Lifton, *Destroying the World to Save It: Aum Shinrikyō, Apocalyptic Violence, and the New Global Terrorism* (New York: Metropolitan Books, 1999), pp. 272-73.

19. The depictions of some historians notwithstanding, a "panic terror" did not accompany the approach of the year 1000, partly due to the fact that most people were not familiar with calendrical formulations of time. For these people, apocalyptic anxiety was more likely to be evoked by the appearance of a comet than by the appearance of a date. For those scholarly monks and others who were familiar with calendars, round numbers held less apocalyptic interest than other dates that might be deduced from numerical symbols in Daniel and Revelation. Hillel Schwartz, *Century's End: A Cultural History of the Fin de Siècle from the 990s through the 1990s* (New York: Doubleday, 1990), pp. 6-7.

20. Sean Anderson and Stephen Sloan, *Historical Dictionary of Terrorism,* Historical Dictionaries of Religions, Philosophies, and Movements, No. 4 (Metuchen, N.J.: Scarecrow Press, 1995), pp. 78-81.

21. Stephen E. Atkins, *Terrorism: A Reference Handbook,* Contemporary World Issues Series (Santa Barbara, Calif.: ABC-CLIO, Inc., 1992), p. 134.

22. Bruce Hoffman, *Inside Terrorism* (New York: Columbia University Press, 1998), p. 90.

23. Walter Laqueur, *The New Terrorism: Fanaticism and the Arms of Mass Destruction* (New York: Oxford University Press, 1999), pp. 127-28.

24. Laqueur, *New Terrorism,* p. 129.

25. The statement by Rabin's assassin is cited by Hoffman, *Inside Terrorism,* p. 87.

26. The point here has to do with the diversity of expressions of Christianity, not with

an evaluation of the cogency of the various expressions. Of course, such evaluations would also differ. Of the examples cited, I must confess to feeling least enamored of the Christian Broadcasters, but others might have more questions about the serpent handlers. For these questioners, I recommend the revealing and sensitive book by Dennis Covington, *Salvation on Sand Mountain: Snake Handling and Redemption in Southern Appalachia* (New York: Penguin Books, 1995).

27. Laqueur is clearly not alone in this view that there is a near-causal association between Islam and violence. It is the same prejudice that sent counterterrorism investigators searching for "Muslim terrorists" in the hours following the attack on the Federal Building in Oklahoma City.

28. George M. Marsden, *Fundamentalism and American Culture: The Shaping of Twentieth Century Evangelicalism, 1870-1925,* (New York: Oxford University Press, 1980), pp. 118-19.

29. "Introduction" to Marty and Appleby, eds., *Fundamentalisms and the State* (Chicago: University of Chicago Press, 1993), p. 3.

30. Marsden notes that it was precisely militant opposition to modernism which most clearly distinguished the original Christian fundamentalists from the related traditions of evangelicalism, pietism, and millenarianism. Marsden, *Fundamentalism and American Culture,* p. 4.

31. *Zakat,* giving alms for the needy, is the third pillar of Islam. Its significance can be traced to the fact that, apart from Mohammed's family, the earliest converts to Islam were poor people and slaves. Geoffrey Parrinder, ed., *World Religions: From Ancient History to the Present* (New York: Facts on File Publications, 1971), pp. 467, 504. While the plea of justice for the poor is pervasive in Islam, for Shi'ites in particular, there is strong resistance to social structures that allow "some to pursue economic fortune at the expense of others." Steve Brouwer, Paul Gifford, and Susan D. Rose, *Exporting the American Gospel: Global Christian Fundamentalism* (New York: Routledge, 1996), p. 210. It should be noted that the intent here is not to portray all aspects of the Iranian revolution as liberating. Indeed, it could be argued that women in Iran have fared little better than women in countries that have adopted the capitalist model of development.

32. In the view of some Orientalists, the obverse was also true, i.e., that the West, in its rush towards modernization, had lost touch with spirituality. If the West could offer economic and technological development, perhaps the East could offer a rebirth of spirituality. Perhaps "the passage to India" was also somehow the passage to God. This concession to the potential merits of colonized people has been called "condescending veneration." For an overview of this aspect of Orientalism, see Richard G. Fox, *Gandhian Utopia: Experiments with Culture* (Boston: Beacon Press, 1989), pp. 105-11.

33. Edward W. Said, *Covering Islam: How the Media and the Experts Determine How We See the Rest of the World* (New York: Pantheon, 1981), p. 38.

34. Said, *Covering Islam,* p. xv.

35. Among those stressing the especially lethal nature of "terrorism motivated in whole or in part by religious imperatives" is Hoffman, *Inside Terrorism,* p. 93. While Hoffman avoids any unfair focus on Islam, the facts he cites in support of his findings are skewed in part by the subjectivity of determining what constitutes "religious imperatives."

Further influencing his findings is his exemption of the highly lethal nation state from his definition of "terrorism."

36. Even while writing about violence by Muslims, Robin Wright acknowledges that "Islam does not promote terrorism. Indeed, in its doctrines, Islam is the most tolerant of the world's monotheistic religions. It accepts Christians and Jews as 'people of the book,' and their leaders as men of the same God. Nor is there any quality inherent to the Shia, or any other sect of Islam, that promotes terrorism." With such a view, the title of her book is unfortunate. Wright, *Sacred Rage: The Crusade of Modern Islam* (New York: Linden Press/ Simon & Schuster, 1985), p. 20.

37. As Edward Said reminds, even Mahdism does not find singular expression. The ideological and violent Mahdism of 19th-century Sudan is far different than contemporary Sudanese Mahdism. Said, *Covering Islam*, p. 54. The Mahdi is not inherently a fearsome figure, but rather one who is sent by God to institute justice and equity. Bernard Lewis, *The Political Language of Islam* (Chicago: University of Chicago Press, 1991), p. 19.

38. McGinn offers a brief sketch of the history of Dajjal in *Antichrist*, pp. 111-13.

39. In an appendix titled "Other Antichrists," the British government report is quoted by Christopher Hill, *Antichrist in Seventeenth-Century England*, rev. ed. (New York: Verso, 1990), p. 182. Jesus is regarded as an important prophet in the Koran and he figures prominently in the end-time speculations of some Muslims. Certain of these versions of the apocalypse are pervaded by terror, including a Nation of Islam version in which, as described colloquially by Minister Louis Farrakhan, Jesus "has got a sword, and it's dripping with blood. No come back to teach nobody. He comes back to judge the wicked." Cited by Weber, *Apocalypses*, p. 213. It is notable that Minister Farrakhan's view of terror as innate to the apocalypse is one that might find agreement among certain millenialist Christians, though differences would doubtless emerge over his portrayal of a specifically Black Jesus whose sword was especially zealous in shedding the blood of white oppressors.

40. Quoted by Schwartz, *Century's End*, p. 208. In the origins of the Iranian revolution, Ayatollah Ruhollah Khomeini did not encourage his followers to associate their movement with Mahdism. The emphasis was on the struggle for justice now, in the absence of the Mahdi. Article five of Iran's Constitution asserts that it will be valid "as long as the Twelfth Imam is absent." Emmanuel Sivan, *Radical Islam: Medieval Theology and Modern Politics*, enlarged ed. (New Haven: Yale University Press, 1990), p. 194.

41. Of course, relationships can be viewed as quite simplistic if the goal is not to establish dialogue but to win "converts" by merely attacking other religions. In Nigeria, for example, certain groups of proselytizing Christians assisted with wide circulation of a book by G. Moshay, *Who Is This Allah?* The answer: Satan. Brouwer, Gifford, and Rose, *Exporting American Gospel*, pp. 173-74. Such an approach to evangelism betrays not only a profound lack of understanding of Islamic faith but also a cheapening of the Gospel, as if the living Word of God could be reduced to doctrinal assent.

42. Several examples of these characterizations of the unarmed Iranian protesters are cited by Said, *Covering Islam*, pp. 106-15.

43. Quoted by Sivan, *Radical Islam*, p. 203.

44. Cited by Peter Occhiogrosso, *Through the Labyrinth: Stories of the Search for Spiritual Transformation in Everyday Life* (New York: Viking, 1991), p. 304.

45. John Ferguson, *War and Peace in the World's Religions* (New York: Oxford University Press, 1978), p. 137.

46. Occhiogrosso, *Through the Labyrinth,* p. 295.

47. This is not to imply that the United States is the only nation with a history of millennial self-identification. Secularized versions of millenarianism fueled the regimes of Stalin in the Soviet Union and Hitler in Germany, with each claiming that the sacrifices of the moment would give birth to either a Workers' Paradise or a Reich to last a thousand years. The founding of the State of Israel in 1948 gave rise to millennial (and even apocalyptic) expectations, though often less markedly for Jews than for some Christians who maintain that a regathering of Israel will precede the second coming of Jesus. Poland's national messianism arose, not in the context of the exercise of political power, but in the context of rule by other nations. Thus 19th-century Polish nationalists emphasized the redemptive nature of the suffering of Poland, which they identified as "the Christ of nations." Weber, *Apocalypses,* pp. 128-29. Millenarianism and national messianism in the United States have less in common with the Polish theme of redemptive suffering than with the assertion of God-given dominion, which was also a prominent feature of the Calvinism of the Dutch settlers in South Africa. The similarities between the U.S. and Boer versions of national messianism are noted by Mark A. Noll, *One Nation under God? Christian Faith and Political Action in America* (New York: Harper & Row, 1988), pp. 188-92. Noll is not totally negative in his evaluations of the U.S. or Boer expressions of national messianism, noting that each encouraged a high valuation of "self-discipline, hard work, and purposeful energy." But in both the U.S. and South Africa, as Noll observes, the energy was often directed towards racist subjugation of native peoples and "specious moral posturing" in foreign policy and military exploits.

48. In 1993, Dee Dee Risher spoke with a delegation of Christians from Egypt, Israel, Jordan, and Lebanon. Among other topics, the delegation explored the manner in which "projection" may be a powerful factor in shaping the view of Islam held by many Christians in the West. Risher, "The Log in Our Eye: Is 'Islamic Fundamentalism' a Projection of Ourselves?" *The Other Side* 29, no. 3 (May-June 1993): 50-51.

49. Hussein's statements are quoted by Richard J. Payne, *The Clash with Distant Cultures: Values, Interests, and Force in American Foreign Policy* (Albany: State University of New York Press, 1995), pp. 120-21.

50. Quoted by Payne, *Clash with Distant Cultures,* p. 120.

51. Payne, *Clash with Distant Cultures,* pp. 30-31.

52. Weber, *Apocalypses,* pp. 167-68.

53. This observation is the premise of the classic analysis by H. Richard Niebuhr, *The Kingdom of God in America* (New York: Harper & Row, 1959), p. xii.

54. Winthrop's "legal" arguments and the centrality of these specific biblical texts are noted by Howard Zinn, *A People's History of the United States* (New York: HarperPerennial, 1990), pp. 13-14. Again, the use and abuse of Romans 13 is telling. How were Winthrop and his colleagues qualified to be the "governing authorities" (Romans 13:1) simply by making an appearance in New England? An alternative view, bizarre only in retrospect, might have held that the settlers were more akin to state-sponsored terrorists and that the native nations constituted the true "governing authorities." Of course, the argument could not be advanced by the native people who were not armed with Romans 13. Later, how-

ever, both sides were so armed when disputes arose between loyalists and revolutionaries over who had the legitimate claim to governing authority: the King of England or loose confederations of revolutionaries?

55. The quotations are from Jonathan Edwards, "The Latter-Day Glory Is Probably to Begin in America," in Conrad Cherry, ed., *God's New Israel: Religious Interpretations of American Destiny* (Englewood Cliffs, N.J.: Prentice-Hall, 1971), pp. 56-57. Emphasis in original.

56. Thomas Paine, *Common Sense and Other Political Writings,* ed. Nelson F. Adkins (Indianapolis: Bobbs-Merrill, 1953), p. 51.

57. See R. W. B. Lewis, *The American Adam: Innocence, Tragedy, and Tradition in the Nineteenth Century* (Chicago: University of Chicago Press, 1955), pp. 98-105. It might be noted in passing that, while the Puritan and utopian themes in early New England are both suggestive of communitarianism, the "Adam" theme (with its rejection of traditions) and the frontier motif in early U.S. experience are both evocative of individualism. In various guises, American individualism and communitarianism compete to this day.

58. Illustrations of several of these paintings along with commentary appear in Edwin S. Gaustad, *Faith of Our Fathers: Religion and the New Nation* (New York: Harper & Row, 1987), pp. 80-83.

59. Mather's recounting of the description is cited by Marion L. Starkey, *The Devil in Massachusetts: A Modern Enquiry into the Salem Witch Trials* (Garden City, N.Y.: Doubleday, 1969), p. 240.

60. It is significant that one of the earliest theological controversies in New England focused on a woman, Anne Hutchinson, who differed with the doctrines of the male ecclesiastical hierarchy. There were strong insinuations that Hutchinson and her associate, a healer named Jane Hawkins, were in league with Satan. Hutchinson was suspect for her prophesying and for her antinomianism, but above all for her knowledge of Scripture and her skills in theological discussion which stood as challenges to male authority. A good compilation of primary sources is *The Antinomian Controversy, 1636-1638: A Documentary History,* 2nd ed., David D. Hall, ed. (Durham, N.C.: Duke University Press, 1990). During the examination of Hutchinson before Governor Winthrop in Newtown court in 1637, the role of women in teaching emerged as central, with Hutchinson citing Titus 2:3-5 in which older women have a teaching role and Winthrop citing 1 Corinthians 14:34-35 in which women were to be silent in the assembly. Hutchinson was not intimidated by her powerful inquisitors. Some of her responses were boldly witty: "Do you think it not lawful for me to teach women and why do you call me to teach the court?" (p. 315). Remarkable language was used in the decree excommunicating Hutchinson from Boston Church: "*I doe cast you out* and in the name of Christ *I doe deliver you up to Sathan.* . . . And I doe account you from this time forth to be a Hethen and a Publican. . . . Therfor *I command you* in the name of Christ Jesus and of this Church *as a Leper to withdraw your selfe out of the Congregation . . .*" (p. 388, emphasis in original). Did it not occur to the good people of Boston Church that it was precisely with the outcasts and publicans and lepers that Jesus most associated?

61. McGinn notes the origins of the title in the zeal of Calvinist reformers "to purify" English churches of the last vestiges of the papal Antichrist. McGinn, *Antichrist,* p. 219.

62. Thompson, *End of Time,* p. 96.

63. Weber, *Apocalypses,* p. 168.

64. Spencer Klaw, *Without Sin: The Life and Death of the Oneida Community* (New York: Allen Lane/The Penguin Press, 1993), pp. 24-26.

65. Weber, *Apocalypses,* p. 174. The nonviolent and liberationist aspects of Shaker communities are highlighted by Ruby Rohrlich, "The Shakers: Gender Equality in Hierarchy," in *Women in Search of Utopia: Mavericks and Mythmakers,* ed. Ruby Rohrlich and Elaine Hoffman Baruch (New York: Schocken Books, 1984), pp. 54-61.

66. "American to the core" is the description of the Mormons (and, interestingly, of the Southern Baptists) offered by Harold Bloom, *The American Religion: The Emergence of the Post-Christian Nation* (New York: Simon & Schuster, 1993), p. 81.

67. Nathan O. Hatch, *The Democratization of American Christianity* (New Haven: Yale University Press, 1989), p. 187.

68. Garry Wills, *Under God: Religion and American Politics* (New York: Simon & Schuster, 1990), p. 20.

69. William Miller, for example, was less a raging prophet than a logician. The Adventists of 1844 were not embroiled in "forcing" the end nor in revolutionary zeal so much as in a logical, mathematical version of biblical inerrancy. They were not especially poor nor especially rich nor especially crazy. They perpetrated no violence, but they suffered both ridicule and violence when nothing of note happened on October 22, 1844. See Whitney R. Cross, *The Burned-Over District: The Social and Intellectual History of Enthusiastic Religion in Western New York, 1800-1850* (Ithaca, N.Y.: Cornell University Press, 1950), pp. 291-308. The Millerites were not the first or last group to survive mistaken predictions of the world's demise. One classic study found that such failed predictions might actually convince the group that its own actions or prayers had served to avert apocalyptic catastrophe. It is not unusual for failed predictions to be followed by increased confidence and proselytism. Leon Festinger, Henry W. Riecken, and Stanley Schachter, *When Prophecy Fails: A Social and Psychological Study of a Modern Group That Predicted the Destruction of the World* (New York: Harper Torchbooks, 1964). It should be added, of course, that this phenomenon is not common among groups whose predictions are accompanied by violent efforts to "force the end" since these groups often face violent extinction themselves in the backlash their actions elicit.

70. This is not to suggest that alarm over nuclearism or the identification of destructive power with "the Beast" of Revelation are without merit. The best essay I have read on the People's Temple is by Stanley Hauerwas, "On Taking Religion Seriously: The Challenge of Jonestown," in *Against the Nations: War and Survival in a Liberal Society* (New York: Winston Press, 1985), pp. 91-106. Hauerwas's insight on what was *not* wrong with the People's Temple could be applied with equal cogency to other groups such as the Branch Davidians. The problem with these groups was *not* that they took their faith seriously, nor that they were apocalyptic in orientation, nor that they were communitarian, nor that they were self-sacrificial, nor that they challenged society's understandings of power and wealth and family. Of those gathered at Jonestown, Hauerwas writes that "their mistake was not that they were willing to give their lives for what they believed but that what they believed was so wrong" (p. 102). What was so wrong was their belief that they were in ownership of their lives and could therefore take them rather than understanding their lives as belonging to God. What was so wrong was their belief that they could set aside the word of God

in deference to the words of Jim Jones. Hauerwas says that the most disturbing reaction to the tragedy at Jonestown suggests that it was caused by the gullibility of the community members who were predominately poor and black. The implication is that others of different race or class "would not have fallen for this kind of cheap and trashy religion" (p. 106n.12). Instead, Jonestown is a judgment on the American church, which has failed to teach believers about the discernment of idolatry and heresy (p. 99).

71. Bernard Levin, *A World Elsewhere* (London: Sceptre, 1995), p. 200.

72. Cited by Dale Aukerman, *Reckoning with Apocalypse: Terminal Politics and Christian Hope* (New York: Crossroad, 1993), p. 55.

73. Quoted by Aukerman, *Reckoning with Apocalypse*, p. 162.

74. Cited by Eugen Weber, *Apocalypses*, p. 202.

75. Max Weber, *The Protestant Ethic and the Spirit of Capitalism*, trans. Talcott Parsons (New York: Charles Scribner's Sons, 1958), p. 110.

76. Max Weber, *Protestant Ethic*, pp. 162-70.

77. Eugen Weber, *Apocalypses*, p. 171.

78. Catherine McNicol Stock, *Rural Radicals: Righteous Rage in the American Grain* (Ithaca, N.Y.: Cornell University Press, 1996), p. 7.

79. Stock, *Rural Radicals*, pp. 116-17.

80. Stock, *Rural Radicals*, pp. 39-43. It is noteworthy that some opponents of gun control base their arguments on the need for the citizenry to be well armed so as to be able to oppose the tyrannical pretensions of governing officials. The Second Amendment to the Constitution states, "A well-regulated militia, being necessary to the security of a free State, the right of the people to keep and bear arms, shall not be infringed." Written as it was in the immediate aftermath of Shays's rebellion and other mob actions, the Second Amendment's "well-regulated militia" was intended for the suppression of domestic rebellion, not the encouragement of it. A stance that would be consistently opposed to centralized authority would not call for the arming of the citizenry but for the *dis*arming of state and federal governments.

81. Hatch, *Democratization of American Christianity*, p. 32.

82. Political allegiance is better portrayed not as a point along a straight line from left to right but as positioning around a near-circular, curved line on which the extreme points almost meet. This accounts for any number of "strange bedfellow" arrangements. Both "right-wing" isolationists and "left-wing" pacifists and anti-imperialists oppose U.S. engagement in assorted wars. The World Trade Organization faces resistance from both "leftists" and "rightists" based on concerns ranging from the environment to human rights to national sovereignty to wariness about "one world government." Both "right-wing" libertarians and "left-wing" anarchists favor the dismantling of the power of centralized government.

83. Cited by Stock, *Rural Radicals*, p. 82.

84. Zinn, *People's History of United States*, pp. 346-49.

85. Stock, *Rural Radicals*, p. 125.

86. Eugen Weber cites Anglo-Israelite theories as probable source of "Caucasian," which he calls "a term dear to the United States Immigration Service. . . ." Weber, *Apocalypses*, p. 130.

87. The British are in proud company. Also tracing their lineage back to the lost Israel-

ites are the Lembas of southern Africa, the Jewish communities of the Caucasus, the Pathans of Afghanistan, the Ben Menashe of India, the Chiang-Min of the Tibetan-Chinese border region, and some Japanese, among others. Richard Abanes, *American Militias: Rebellion, Racism, and Religion* (Downers Grove, Ill.: InterVarsity Press, 1996), p. 260n.12.

88. Abanes, *American Militias*, pp. 137-38.

89. Abanes, *American Militias*, p. 262n.81.

90. Tortured linguistics also play a role with this theory. Militia leader Bo Gritz claims that "Adam" translated as "Au-dawn," meaning "blushing face." Abanes, *American Militias*, p. 184.

91. Cited by Hoffman, *Inside Terrorism*, p. 113.

92. Hoffman, *Inside Terrorism*, p. 111. Also see Kenneth S. Stern, *A Force upon the Plain: The American Militia Movement and the Politics of Hate* (New York: Simon & Schuster, 1996), pp. 155-59. Stern notes that in Canada and Australia as well as in the United States, there are links between some military and law enforcement personnel and militia movements.

93. Quoted by Hoffman, *Inside Terrorism*, p. 116.

94. Wills, *Under God*, p. 174.

95. The Stockburger quote and a critique of the Identity reading of key biblical texts appear in Abanes, *American Militias*, pp. 209-12.

96. In 1995, Flo Conway and Jim Siegelman conducted interviews with militia recruits for an article in the *Arkansas Democrat-Gazette*. Cited by Hoffman, *Inside Terrorism*, p. 111.

97. At times, accountability for violence is lost in the shadowy appearance and disappearance of terrorist groups. It is not even clear, for example, if the "Phineas Priesthood" is an organized group or merely a cover name used by individuals engaging in violence. The name is derived from the story of Phineas in Numbers 25 and the interpretation of that text as a supposed warning against "race mixing." The "Phineas Priesthood" name has been associated with bombings at Planned Parenthood clinics, murders at a gay bookstore in North Carolina, and bank robberies in Spokane, Washington. At some of the crime scenes, documents were left behind proclaiming that "the end of Babylon is come. Praise Yahweh!" Hoffman, *Inside Terrorism*, pp. 119-20.

98. Quoted by Stern, *Force upon the Plain*, p. 189.

99. Quoted by Stern, *Force upon the Plain*, p. 194.

100. An excellent critique of the classic CBS film documentary, "The Ku Klux Klan: An Invisible Empire," appears in Will D. Campbell and James Y. Holloway, *Up to Our Steeples in Politics* (New York: Paulist Press, 1970), pp. 142-46. For more on Campbell's story, I heartily recommend Will D. Campbell, *Brother to a Dragonfly* (New York: Seabury Press, 1977).

101. Stern, *Force upon the Plain*, p. 23.

102. Quoted by Thompson, *End of Time*, p. 297, with italics added by Thompson. Among armed apocalyptic movements, violence can be spurred on by martyrology, and the federal government has been only too obliging in expanding the ranks of the martyrs. See Lifton, *Destroying the World to Save It*, pp. 329-30.

103. Thompson writes, "The almost total destruction of a religious community by federal forces is without precedent in American history." Thompson, *End of Time*, p. 285.

In fact, federal forces played a powerful role in almost destroying the Ghost Dance religion and other forms of Native spirituality. Mount Carmel was the first millennial Christian community to meet that fate.

104. Quoted by Stern, *Force upon the Plain*, p. 30.

105. Stern, *Force upon the Plain*, p. 99. The opposition, of course, is based more on a repudiation of globalism than on a renunciation of militarism. Regarding the opposition to "one world government," much is made of the "paranoid" conspiracy theories circulating among militia groups, what with black helicopters and such. But even some conspiracy theories are not plucked totally from thin air. Foreign troops and police are in fact being trained in the United States, including those being trained in "counterterrorist" techniques at the notorious School of the Americas (recently renamed "Western Hemisphere Institute for Security Cooperation"). And with the United States building more prisons than any other nation on the planet, it is more than paranoia that might prompt dissenters of the right or the left to worry about loss of freedom and to speculate about the potential to incarcerate masses of people in "concentration camps." Indeed, as I observe below, the problem with the critique of America proffered by rural radicalism is that it is not radical enough. My analysis is informed by the similar analysis of my friend Dale Brown, who contrasted the biblical vision of Anabaptism with the insufficient radicalism of the counterculture of the 1960s and 70s. Brown, *The Christian Revolutionary* (Grand Rapids: Eerdmans, 1971).

106. Stern, *Force upon the Plain*, p. 20.

107. Cited by Stern, *Force upon the Plain*, p. 165.

108. As just one example, Diacon discovered this phenomenon of mutually reinforcing violence at work in the Contestado rebellion in Brazil. Government massacres sparked the transition from nonviolent to violent struggle by millenarian rebels. In turn, violence by the rebels served to provide the rationale for increased military spending and concentration of power in the central government. Diacon, *Millenarian Vision, Capitalist Reality*, pp. 122-24, 149-50.

109. Quoted by Hoffman, *Inside Terrorism*, p. 114.

110. Cited by Stern, *Force upon the Plain*, p. 223.

111. The story is told by Stern, *Force upon the Plain*, p. 248.

112. Stringfellow, *The Politics of Spirituality* (Philadelphia: Westminster Press, 1984), p. 63.

113. Weber, *Apocalypses*, p. 68.

114. These characterizations of Eusebius and his eschatology are from McGinn, *Antichrist*, p. 88.

115. Joachim of Fiore, "Letter to All the Faithful," in McGinn, *Apocalyptic Spirituality*, p. 113.

116. The "anti-Augustinian" nature of Joachim's view of change and meaning in history is emphasized in the study by Bernard McGinn, *The Calabrian Abbot: Joachim of Fiore in the History of Western Thought* (New York: Macmillan, 1985), p. 2.

117. It should be noted that some of the earliest movements to exhibit the influence of Joachim's writings were nonviolent and were revolutionary only in the teachings and practices that were declared heretical at a later date. One example is the Spiritual Franciscan movement and their fascinating leader, Peter John Olivi. Olivi opposed the subterfuges by

which those in religious orders could maintain vows of poverty by not owning but none-theless having use of material luxuries. In addition to poverty in ownership, Olivi favored poverty in "use." While such an idea hardly seems heretical, Norman Cohn is certainly cor-rect that many of the medieval movements that came to be declared heretical must be un-derstood within the context of what he calls "the cult of voluntary poverty." Cohn, *The Pursuit of the Millennium: Revolutionary Millenarians and Mystical Anarchists of the Middle Ages*, rev. ed. (New York: Oxford University Press, 1970), pp. 156-57. While some libertine heresies were unconcerned for piety in relationship to material wealth (e.g., the Adamites), the declaration that "All things are lawful for me" (1 Corinthians 6:12) was always the pre-rogative of the rich more than the poor. See Wayne A. Meeks, *The Origins of Christian Mo-rality: The First Two Centuries* (New Haven: Yale University Press, 1993), p. 132. Heresy hunters always kept a careful eye on movements of voluntary poverty because of the short-ness of the leap between renunciation of wealth and renunciation of the wealthy. If Olivi's emphasis on poverty was suspect, his eschatology was more so. Olivi's teaching that there were two Antichrists, the Mystical and the Great Antichrist, left the door open for his fol-lowers to denounce the demonic power pretensions of both church and state. But Olivi and his followers were no terrorists. Olivi's strongly kenotic theology emphasized that God had "emptied himself and took the form of a servant, suffering the death of the cross for the just at the hands of the unjust." Olivi, "Letter to the Sons of Charles II," in McGinn, *Apocalyptic Spirituality*, p. 173. The means by which the Antichrists would be overthrown, said Olivi, would entail no weapons beyond the teachings of a small band of Spiritual Franciscans. *Heresies of the High Middle Ages*, trans. Walter L. Wakefield and Austin P. Ev-ans, Records of Western Civilization Series (New York: Columbia University Press, 1991), p. 763n.25. Another of the earliest movements to be influenced by Joachim's ideas adhered to principles equally unacceptable as voluntary poverty, namely feminism. A group near Milan held that a woman named Guglielma was ushering in the third era of the Spirit. In this era, the "angelic pope" and all of the cardinals would be women. Such ideas were clearly unacceptable to the male ecclesiastical hierarchy, and in 1300, inquisitors ordered that the remains of Guglielma (d. 1281) be disinterred and burned. Malcolm Lambert, *Medieval Heresy: Popular Movements from the Gregorian Reform to the Reformation*, 2nd ed. (Cambridge, Mass.: Blackwell, 1992), pp. 199-202.

118. Thompson, *End of Time*, p. 67. Anachronistically, Thompson also dubs the Apos-tolic Brethren "one of the first 'doomsday cults.'"

119. Cohn, *Pursuit of the Millennium*, pp. 104-5.

120. Lambert notes the role played by fear in leading ecclesiastical and civil authorities to reliance on torture and other brutal tactics in their responses to *both* rebellion and her-esy. "Fear was part of the impulse to violence. Authority assumed that heresy and rebellion went together. There was a fear of the laity *en masse*, the *rustici* . . . and what they might do under a leadership hostile to churchmen." Lambert, *Medieval Heresy*, p. 27.

121. See Cohn, *Pursuit of the Millennium*, pp. 191-97.

122. Cited by Cohn, *Pursuit of the Millennium*, p. 199.

123. Quoted by Rodney Hilton, *Bond Men Made Free: Medieval Peasant Movements and the English Rising of 1381* (New York: Methuen, 1973), p. 222.

124. Hilton, *Bond Men Made Free*, p. 106.

125. The statement by Taborite Jan Přibam is cited by Cohn, *Pursuit of the Millennium,* p. 215.

126. Michael A. Mullett, *Radical Religious Movements in Early Modern Europe,* Early Modern Europe Today Series (London: George Allen & Unwin, 1980), pp. 20-21.

127. It was in 1850 that Engels wrote his Marxist analysis of Müntzer and the peasants' revolt. Engels, *The Peasant War in Germany,* trans. Moissaye J. Olgin (New York: International Publishers, 1966), p. 63.

128. Quoted by Cohn, *Pursuit of the Millennium,* p. 239.

129. Müntzer, quoted by Cohn, *Pursuit of the Millennium,* p. 237.

130. E. R. Chamberlin, *Antichrist and the Millennium* (New York: Saturday Review Press/E. P. Dutton, 1975), pp. 70-71.

131. Cohn, *Pursuit of the Millennium,* p. 267. Events at Münster have had a continuing impact even into modern times with misperceptions that Anabaptism is associated with extremist millenarianism and/or violence. One historian who has played an important role in countering this misperception is Donald F. Durnbaugh. Comments on Münster can be found in Durnbaugh, *The Believers' Church: The History and Character of Radical Protestantism* (New York: Macmillan, 1968), pp. 77-79.

132. Luther, "An Open Letter on the Harsh Book Against the Peasants," trans. Charles M. Jacobs, in *Luther: Selected Political Writings,* ed. J. M. Porter (Philadelphia: Fortress Press, 1974), p. 91.

133. Rosemary Radford Ruether, *The Radical Kingdom: The Western Experience of Messianic Hope* (New York: Harper & Row, 1970), pp. 29-30.

134. Hill, *Antichrist in Seventeenth-Century England,* p. 40. Hill also notes (p. 25) that as soon as John Napier had invented logarithms, he put his new system to use in speeding his calculations pertaining to the number of the Beast. A bizarre use of science, one might think, but it was actually more benign than our contemporary harnessing of science in the service of militarism.

135. Hill, *Antichrist in Seventeenth-Century England,* pp. 3-4.

136. Ernest Lee Tuveson, *Millennium and Utopia: A Study in the Background of the Idea of Progress* (New York: Harper & Row, 1964), pp. 52-54.

137. Calamy, quoted by Hill, *Antichrist in Seventeenth-Century England,* p. 78.

138. Cited by Michael Walzer, *The Revolution of the Saints: A Study in the Origins of Radical Politics* (Cambridge, Mass.: Harvard University Press, 1965), p. 293. When Palmer and others employed these meticulous distinctions in claiming that they were not attacking "the king's person," they were drawing on a long English tradition of near-metaphysical speculation on the relationship between crown and realm, between the king's body and the body politic. See Ernst H. Kantorowicz, *The King's Two Bodies: A Study in Medieval Political Theology* (Princeton: Princeton University Press, 1957).

139. Cited by Walzer, *Revolution of the Saints,* p. 295.

140. Favored biblical texts included the accounts of the slaying of the usurper Athaliah (2 Kings 11:1-16; 2 Chronicles 22:10–23:21), Samuel's killing of King Agag of the Amalekites (1 Samuel 15:32-33), and the slaying of King Amaziah who had "turned away from the LORD" (2 Chronicles 25:27). The regicidal use of these and other biblical texts is noted by Christopher Hill, *The English Bible and the Seventeenth-Century Revolution* (New York: Penguin Books, 1994), p. 247.

141. With emphasis in the original, the saying is cited by Walzer, *Revolution of the Saints*, p. 298.

142. Weber, *Apocalypses*, p. 74. Throughout this period, however, many radical Levellers and Diggers held millenarian views that were not at all conducive to terrorism. Gerard Winstanley, for example, did not identify the Beast as any individual or group but rather as "the spirit of monarchy" and "the spirit of subtlety and covetousness, filling the heart of mankind with enmity and ignorance, pride and vainglory, because the strong destroys the weak." The implication was that one could kill king or pope or hoards of rebels and the spirit of Antichrist would only be strengthened as a result. "If you would find true majesty indeed, go among the poor and despised ones of the earth," wrote Winstanley, "for there Christ dwells." Quoted by Hill, *Antichrist in Seventeenth-Century England*, pp. 116-17.

143. "New religions" is preferable to the more commonly used "sects" and "cults" when referring to these groups. In their popular use, "sect" and "cult" carry a pejorative sense that is not intended by the sociological use of the terms. Most religions have manifestations that are cultic and, as Ernst Troeltsch demonstrated, sect is a phase through which all religions pass prior to heightened institutionalization. Troeltsch, *The Social Teaching of the Christian Churches*, vol. 2, trans. Olive Wyon (New York: Harper & Row, 1960), p. 933.

144. Thompson, *End of Time*, p. 264.

145. The quotations are from Asahara's character in the Aum publication, *The Day of Perishing*. Cited by Lifton, *Destroying the World to Save It*, p. 48.

146. Lifton, *Destroying the World to Save It*, p. 88.

147. Senate report, quoted by Lifton, *Destroying the World to Save It*, p. 273.

148. The categories of pre- and post-millennialism are derived from wide-ranging speculations on a single biblical text — Revelation 20:1-7. Adherence to the categories is not always rigid or tidy. Historical events (e.g., the election of Ronald Reagan) have been known to turn "pre-mils" into "post-mils." See Wills, *Under God*, pp. 167-68.

149. Ruether, *Radical Kingdom*, p. 14.

150. Cited by Mircea Eliade, *Cosmos and History: The Myth of the Eternal Return*, trans. Willard R. Trask (New York: Harper & Row, 1959), p. 148. In the fourth chapter of this classic work, Eliade focuses on "the terror of history."

151. Braaten, *Christ and Counter-Christ*, p. 11.

152. Tuveson, *Millennium and Utopia*, p. 119.

153. R. W. B. Lewis points to an interesting quandary. In the United States, a strong tradition of faith in progress has abided side by side with faith in America as New Adam. From a state of primordial sinlessness, how does one progress to a state of being more sinless still? Lewis writes, "Both ideas were current, and they overlapped and intertwined." He advises that we must "settle for the paradox that the more intense the belief in progress, the more it stimulated a belief in a present primal perfection." Lewis, *American Adam*, p. 5n.5.

154. Weber, *Apocalypses*, p. 110.

155. Quoted by W. Warren Wagar, *Good Tidings: The Belief in Progress from Darwin to Marcuse* (Bloomington: Indiana University Press, 1972), p. 96.

156. Rauschenbusch, *Christianity and the Social Crisis*, ed. Robert D. Cross (New York: Harper & Row, 1964), p. 422. It should be noted that, while they both sought to address the

needs of impoverished people, the Social Gospel movement and the Salvation Army held quite contrasting perspectives on eschatology. In England in 1879, the renaming of William and Catherine Booth's "Christian Mission" as "Salvation Army" was not without significance. Contrary to any notions of evolution, the Booths believed that the world was approaching cataclysmic destruction and they incorporated themes of apocalyptic terror into the motto emblazoned on the Army's flag, "Blood and Fire!" While the Social Gospel sought to include the poor in the confident progress towards the millennium, the Salvation Army sought to convert the poor prior to the terror of Armageddon. See Roy Hattersley, *Blood and Fire: William and Catherine Booth and Their Salvation Army* (New York: Doubleday, 1999).

157. Tuveson, *Millennium and Utopia*, p. 143.

158. Tuveson, *Millennium and Utopia*, p. 188.

159. Christopher Lasch, *The True and Only Heaven: Progress and Its Critics* (New York: W. W. Norton, 1991), pp. 52-56.

160. Teilhard de Chardin, *The Phenomenon of Man*, trans. Bernard Wall (New York: Harper & Row, 1965), p. 284.

161. See Thomas S. Kuhn, *The Structure of Scientific Revolutions*, 2nd ed. (Chicago: University of Chicago Press, 1970).

162. Jacques Ellul, *The Technological Society*, trans. John Wilkinson (New York: Vintage Books, 1964), p. 429.

163. Thomas Merton, *Conjectures of a Guilty Bystander* (Garden City, N.Y.: Doubleday, 1968), p. 52.

164. Karl Barth, *The Humanity of God*, trans. John Newton Thomas and Thomas Wieser (Richmond, Va.: John Knox Press, 1960), p. 14. The nature and ramifications of Barth's turn away from liberalism are explored in several of the essays in *Karl Barth and Radical Politics*, ed. and trans. George Hunsinger (Philadelphia: Westminster Press, 1976).

165. Frank J. Tipler, *The Physics of Immortality: Modern Cosmology, God, and the Resurrection of the Dead* (New York: Doubleday, 1994), p. 1.

166. Tipler, *Physics of Immortality*, p. 331. Tipler makes short shrift of presenting the facts that might serve as the basis of love. Even more so, what "facts" could serve as the basis of love of enemies or as the basis of a decision to die rather than to kill? Love is not pursuant to a consideration of all the facts. Love is active *in spite of* all the facts.

167. Tipler, *Physics of Immortality*, p. 57. While the term "biosphere" sounds green-friendly, how can one maintain an ecological consciousness while disassembling the universe? Since the earth is slated for destruction by an expanding sun in seven billion years, Tipler observes, the "unintelligent" animal and plant life on earth is doomed anyhow. Disassembling these can serve our descendants as they set out to conquer galaxies. Such a utilitarian view of non-human aspects of the creation is reminiscent of Thomas Aquinas's claim that there will be no animals or plants in the Millennium because people will no longer have need of them. Tuveson, *Millennium and Utopia*, p. 18.

168. Perry Miller, *Errand into the Wilderness* (New York: Harper & Row, 1964), p. 224.

169. Quoted by Miller, *Errand into Wilderness*, p. 229.

170. Miller, *Errand into Wilderness*, p. 235.

171. Miller, *Errand into Wilderness*, p. 239.

172. Perry Miller, *The New England Mind: The Seventeenth Century* (Cambridge, Mass.: Harvard University Press, 1982), pp. 280-99.

173. Jonathan Edwards, *The Nature of True Virtue* (Ann Arbor: University of Michigan Press, 1960), p. 42.

174. Edwards, *True Virtue,* p. 73.

175. Lactantius, quoted by Cohn, *Pursuit of the Millennium,* p. 28.

176. Weber, *Apocalypses,* p. 151.

177. *The Confessions of Saint Augustine,* trans. Edward B. Pusey, The Modern Library (New York: Random House, 1949), p. 58.

178. *Confessions,* pp. 116-17.

179. Delumeau, *Sin and Fear: The Emergence of a Western Guilt Culture, 13th-18th Centuries,* trans. Eric Nicholson (New York: St. Martin's Press, 1990), p. 555.

180. Evagrius, from Benedicta Ward, ed. and trans., *The Desert Christian: The Sayings of the Desert Fathers* (New York: Macmillan, 1975), p. 63.

181. Anthony the Great, from Ward, *Desert Christian,* p. 8.

182. Cited by Delumeau, *Sin and Fear,* p. 330.

183. Cited by Delumeau, *Sin and Fear,* p. 407.

184. Are such actions inculcating an edifying sense of transitoriness, or are they indulging a morbid fascination with death? The question can also be put to spiritual traditions other than Christianity. I have a friend named Jimmy whose spiritual practice tends towards an eclectic, Westernized version of Buddhism. Several years ago, Jimmy returned from a trip to Nepal with a gift that had been given to him by a Buddhist monk. It was the upper portion of the skull of a monk who had died years before. Jimmy used the skull as he had been advised, as a bowl for his food, a persistent mealtime reminder of the transitory quality of life. Jimmy is a gentle and nonviolent soul, but he outdid Pope Alexander VII in bringing an awareness of death to the dining room. While I was fascinated by Jimmy's story of how he came into possession of the skull and how he got the relic past customs, I must admit to being somewhat repulsed by the thing itself. My preference is for repast as a time of thanksgiving and communion rather than a time for reflection on the illusory or transitory quality of life, though I confess to sometimes eating dinner while watching television newscasts, which is also a focus on the grotesque and illusory qualities in life.

185. John Calvin, *Institutes of the Christian Religion,* ed. John T. McNeill, trans. Ford Lewis Battles, The Library of Christian Classics, vol. 20 (Philadelphia: Westminster Press, 1960), pp. 712-13.

186. Calvin, *Institutes,* p. 714.

187. Cited by Delumeau, *Sin and Fear,* p. 501.

188. Delumeau, *Sin and Fear,* p. 331.

189. Christopher Hill, *The World Turned Upside Down: Radical Ideas During the English Revolution* (New York: Penguin Books, 1975), p. 178.

190. Quoted by Delumeau, *Sin and Fear,* pp. 512-13.

191. Miller, *Errand into Wilderness,* p. 218.

192. Rev. Thomas Shepard, quoted by David D. Hall, *Worlds of Wonder, Days of Judgment: Popular Religious Belief in Early New England* (New York: Alfred A. Knopf, 1989), p. 135.

193. Increase Mather, "Man Knows Not His Time," in Perry Miller and Timothy H. Johnson, eds., *The Puritans: A Sourcebook of Their Writings,* vol. 1, rev. ed. (New York: Harper & Row, 1963), pp. 347-48.

194. Hall, *Worlds of Wonder,* p. 182.

195. Quoted by Hall, *Worlds of Wonder,* p. 134.

196. Harold Bloom is among those who maintain that contemporary religion in America has been shaped less by Puritanism than by enthusiasm. He calls such religion "Gnostic" in its emphasis on personal experience and its devaluing of community. Bloom, *The American Religion,* pp. 22-27, 54. Randall Balmer also explores the manner in which Calvinism was surpassed in American Protestantism by a strain of evangelicalism that viewed "salvation as a matter of volition — we must *choose* to forsake our sinfulness and follow Christ." Balmer, *Mine Eyes Have Seen the Glory: A Journey into the Evangelical Subculture in America* (New York: Oxford University Press, 1989), p. 203.

197. Finney, quoted by Klaw, *Without Sin,* p. 21.

198. Marsden, *Fundamentalism and American Culture,* pp. 51-55.

199. Strozier, *Apocalypse,* pp. 182-84.

200. H. L. Mencken, *Prejudices: A Selection,* ed. James T. Farrell (New York: Vintage Books, 1958), p. 168.

201. Mencken, quoted by Weber, *Apocalypses,* p. 190.

202. Wills, *Under God,* pp. 131-32.

203. Marsden, *Fundamentalism and American Culture,* p. 93.

204. Slogans cited by Balmer, *Mine Eyes Have Seen the Glory,* p. 165.

205. Cited by Wills, *Under God,* p. 147. Hal Lindsey and Charles Swindoll are among the evangelical authors who have been influenced in their approach to biblical studies by the teachings of "Colonel" Robert Thieme of Houston's Berachah Church. Thieme contends that the relationship of the various "persons" of the Trinity is such that one may substitute the name "Jesus" for all appearances of the name "Jehovah" in the Hebrew Bible. Thus, says Thieme, it is Jesus who leads holy warriors into battle. "The Lord Jesus Christ holds the record for slaughtering the enemy." But that is nothing compared to the scene that will greet raptured Christians hovering above the carnage of the tribulation. Jesus "will break His own record in this application of righteous violence at the close of the Tribulation." Thieme, quoted by Wills, *Under God,* p. 402n.18. Dr. David Yonggi Cho also promises that the righteous will have a safe perch from which to witness the terror of the tribulation. Cho has been head pastor of South Korea's Yoido Full Gospel Church which, with over 700,000 members, is billed by the Guinness Book of Records as the world's largest church. In a Korean society coping with a persistent threat of war, Dr. Cho asserts that the tribulation will be quite bloody, killing a major segment of the world's population. Is there a symbiotic relationship between contemporary militarism and end-time visions of violence? Lydia Swaine, Dr. Cho's assistant for foreign affairs, acknowledged that the church's growth has been spurred in part by anxieties regarding the future. "The threat of war always prepares the heart for Jesus," she said. Thompson, *End of Time,* p. 242.

206. Lifton, *Destroying the World to Save It,* pp. 123-24.

207. Thompson, *End of Time,* pp. 218-21.

208. Applewhite, quoted by Lifton, *Destroying the World to Save It,* p. 314.

209. Lifton, *Destroying the World to Save It,* p. 305.

210. Aukerman, *Reckoning with Apocalypse,* pp. 63-64.

211. In another key text for proponents of the rapture, Paul also asserts that "the dead in Christ will rise first" (1 Thessalonians 4:16). Paul is less clear than Revelation about whether he is referring specifically to martyrs, but in his admonitions to perseverance, he is not propounding a view of discipleship as avoidance of suffering, let alone satisfaction in the suffering of others.

212. See Hans Küng, *Eternal Life?,* p. 88, and Ernst Bloch, *Man on His Own,* trans. E. B. Ashton (New York: Herder and Herder, 1971), p. 94. The theme will be revisited in Chapter 5 below.

213. Jürgen Moltmann observes that, in apocalyptic, "The whole world is now involved in God's eschatological process of history, not only the world of men and nations. The conversion of man in the prophetic message then finds its correlate in the conversion of the whole cosmos, of which apocalyptic speaks." Moltmann, *Theology of Hope: On the Ground and the Implications of a Christian Eschatology,* trans. James W. Leitch (New York: Harper & Row, 1967), p. 137.

214. An appreciation for the work of Christoph Blumhardt was the context for Barth's comments. Karl Barth, *Action in Waiting for the Kingdom of God,* trans. Hutterian Society of Brothers (Rifton, N.Y.: Plough Publishing House, 1979), pp. 22-23.

215. Gerald L. Zelizer, "Churches Give Hell a Makeover," *USA Today,* February 21, 2000, p. 15A.

216. Simone Weil, *Waiting for God,* trans. Emma Craufurd (New York: Harper & Row, 1973), p. 47.

217. Jørgen Glenthøj, "Dietrich Bonhoeffer's Way Between Resistance and Submission," in *A Bonhoeffer Legacy: Essays in Understanding,* ed. A. J. Klassen (Grand Rapids: Eerdmans, 1981), pp. 170-77.

218. Sebastian de Grazia, *Machiavelli in Hell* (Princeton, N.J.: Princeton University Press, 1989), p. 156.

219. Niccolò Machiavelli, *The Prince,* trans. Thomas G. Bergin (New York: Appleton-Century-Crofts, 1947), (Ch. XXV) p. 75.

220. Machiavelli, *Prince,* (VI) p. 15.

221. Machiavelli, *Prince,* (III) p. 8.

222. Machiavelli, *Prince,* (VIII) pp. 25-26.

223. Mark Twain, *The Adventures of Huckleberry Finn* (New York: Washington Square Press, 1950), p. 273.

224. Clarence Jordan, *The Substance of Faith and Other Cotton Patch Sermons,* ed. Dallas Lee (New York: Association Press, 1972), p. 24.

225. The most cogent defense of universalism I have encountered is that offered by Jacques Ellul, a theologian who was not easily dismissed as a mere liberal. See Ellul, *What I Believe,* trans. Geoffrey W. Bromiley (Grand Rapids: Eerdmans and London: Marshall Morgan and Scott, 1989), pp. 188-213. Surprisingly, the pacifist scholar John Howard Yoder defends the doctrine of hell as a necessary component of free will. Yoder writes that "any universalism which would seek, in the intention of magnifying redemption, to deny to the unrepentant sinner the liberty to refuse God's grace would in reality deny that human choice has any real meaning at all." Yoder, *The Original Revolution: Essays on Christian Pacifism* (Scottdale, Pa.: Herald Press, 1971), p. 65. Yet, for better or for worse, it is pre-

cisely human will that has had a fairly free reign in history. The eschatological judgment of God is not about the vindication of human free will but about the revelation of God's reign and the vindication of God's cause.

226. See Hans Küng, *Eternal Life?*, p. 62.

227. "Fiery love" was the primary experience of God for the 17th-century German mystic, Jacob Boehme. There was alchemical power in the Fire's ability to transform people. Boehme prayed, "O fiery Love of God, You have broken death in our humanity, and destroyed hell. . . ." Boehme, *The Way to Christ,* trans. Peter Erb, The Classics of Western Spirituality (New York: Paulist Press, 1978), p. 86.

228. Kenneth M. Stampp, *The Peculiar Institution: Slavery in the Ante-Bellum South* (New York: Vintage Books, 1956), p. 146.

229. These and other texts which were dear to the slaveholders are listed by Noll, *One Nation under God?*, pp. 116-19. The biblical debate over slavery was a powerful factor in the North-South divisions of Presbyterians, Baptists, and Methodists in the 1830s and 1840s.

230. The catechism is quoted by James H. Cone, *The Spirituals and the Blues: An Interpretation* (Maryknoll, N.Y.: Orbis Books, 1992), p. 23. It was no accident that the definition of adultery was avoided. The slave system itself thrived on coerced adultery. Rape of black women by slaveholders was not uncommon, but even more routine were the decisions of the slaveholders about who should have children with whom and about which families should be separated at the auction block.

231. Frederick Douglass, *Narrative of the Life of Frederick Douglass, an American Slave,* ed. Houston A. Baker, Jr. (New York: Penguin Books, 1982), pp. 98-99. The slaveholder was apparently quoting a version of Luke 12:47, a line from one of Jesus' parables of the kingdom. At the time the *Narrative* was published (1845), Douglass added an appendix affirming his own faith while denouncing American Christianity. He wrote, "I love the pure, peaceable and impartial Christianity of Christ; I therefore hate the corrupt, slaveholding, women-whipping, cradle-plundering, partial and hypocritical Christianity of this land. . . . We have men sold to build churches, women sold to support the gospel, and babes sold to purchase Bibles for the *poor heathen! all for the glory of God and the good of souls!* The slave auctioneer's bell and the church-going bell chime in with each other, and the bitter cries of the heart-broken slave are drowned in the religious shouts of his pious master. Revivals of religion and revivals in the slave-trade go hand in hand together." Douglass, *Narrative,* pp. 153-54, emphasis in the original. His keen insights on the hypocrisy of Christians probably contributed to his later decision, described in a letter, to "cut loose from the church." William S. McFeely, *Frederick Douglass* (New York: W. W. Norton, 1991), p. 85.

232. Douglass, *Narrative,* p. 150.

233. Cone, *Spirituals and Blues,* pp. 80-81.

234. Cone, *Spirituals and Blues,* p. 39.

235. The ecstatic quality that was often present in the worship services of slaves was unnerving to white preachers, even to those who were acquainted with white enthusiasts. The ecstatic spirituality of blacks was suggestive of something dangerous, something that defied control. See Christine Leigh Heyrman, *Southern Cross: The Beginnings of the Bible Belt* (New York: Alfred A. Knopf, 1997), pp. 49-52.

236. From the "Narrative of Harriet Tubman," in Charles L. Blockson, *The Underground Railroad* (New York: Prentice-Hall, 1987), p. 122.

237. John Hope Franklin, *From Slavery to Freedom: A History of Negro Americans,* 3rd ed. (New York: Vintage Books, 1969), p. 250.

238. Noll, *One Nation under God?*, p. 108.

239. Finney's formative influence on the radical abolitionist movement is a matter of some dispute. Mark Noll credits Finney with "a strong stand against slavery. . . ." Noll, *One Nation under God?*, p. 112. But Nat Brandt notes that "Finney was no saint on the issue of racial equality; he was against slavery . . . but acknowledged having a 'constitutional' dislike of blacks. . . ." In his younger days, Finney had once declared that slavery was a "dispensation of providence," a statement that was remembered unkindly by some of the abolitionist students at Oberlin. Nat Brandt, *The Town That Started the Civil War* (Syracuse, N.Y.: Syracuse University Press, 1990), pp. 37, 261.

240. Cushing Strout, *The New Heavens and New Earth: Political Religion in America* (New York: Harper & Row, 1975), pp. 160-61.

241. Quoted by Franklin, *From Slavery to Freedom,* p. 245.

242. Margaret Hope Bacon, "By Moral Force Alone: The Antislavery Women and Nonresistance," in *The Abolitionist Sisterhood: Women's Political Culture in Antebellum America,* ed. Jean Fagan Yellin and John C. Van Horne (Ithaca, N.Y.: Cornell University Press, 1994), pp. 277-79. With honey and maple sugar made expensive by short supply, abolitionists conducted some of the earliest U.S. experiments in the production of beet sugar as an alternative sweetener. Of course, the use of the boycott is not restricted to causes of liberation. As abolitionist agitation increased, resolutions were passed in Virginia and elsewhere to use no products from north of the Mason-Dixon line. Peter Wallenstein, "Incendiaries All: Southern Politics and the Harpers Ferry Raid," in *His Soul Goes Marching On: Responses to John Brown and the Harpers Ferry Raid,* ed. Paul Finkelman (Charlottesville: University Press of Virginia, 1995), p. 157.

243. Quoted by Lewis Perry, *Radical Abolitionism: Anarchy and the Government of God in Antislavery Thought* (Knoxville: University of Tennessee Press, 1995), p. 53.

244. Perry, *Radical Abolitionism,* p. 89. While I cite Wright's position as an example of legalism, I must admit to finding some merit in his conclusion. He posed an extreme version of the question of means and ends. If one believes that slaveholding is sinful *and* that participation in an oppressive political system is sinful, is it possible to choose sin in the name of curtailing sin? Perhaps the problem with Wright's position is his inadequate appreciation for the presumptuous nature of the pursuit of sinlessness and works righteousness. Our task is not to abolish sin but to nurture an awareness of the manner in which the Fall pervades all of our decisions and actions — voting *as well as* not voting. But Wright was certainly correct that the choice of a supposed "lesser evil" is still a choice of evil.

245. See Peter Brock, *Freedom from War: Nonsectarian Pacifism, 1814-1914* (Toronto: University of Toronto Press, 1991), p. 98.

246. Cited by Henry Mayer, *All on Fire: William Lloyd Garrison and the Abolition of Slavery* (New York: St. Martin's Press, 1998), p. 237.

247. Strout, *New Heavens and New Earth,* pp. 175-76. In the various sources I have consulted, figures on the numbers of whites killed range from fifty to seventy people.

248. Mayer, *All on Fire,* p. 121.

249. Perry, *Radical Abolitionism,* pp. 233-34.

250. Douglass, in *The Power of the People: Active Nonviolence in the United States,* ed. Robert Cooney and Helen Michalowski, from an original text by Marty Jezer (Philadelphia: New Society Publishers, 1987), p. 30.

251. Most of the prominent politicians of the day became embroiled in the aftermath of the events in little Christiana. There were trials for treason in Pennsylvania and threats of secession by the State of Maryland. The violence and its aftermath are the topics of the article by Fawn M. Brodie, "Born out of Violence," in *Violence in America: A Historical and Contemporary Reader,* ed. Thomas Rose (New York: Vintage Books, 1970), pp. 122-39.

252. Cited by Brandt, *Town That Started Civil War,* p. 22.

253. Cited by Brandt, *Town That Started Civil War,* p. 22.

254. *Narrative of Sojourner Truth: A Bondswoman of Olden Time, with a History of Her Labors and Correspondence Drawn from Her "Book of Life,"* The Schomburg Library of Nineteenth-Century Black Women Writers (New York: Oxford University Press, 1991), p. 168.

255. *Narrative of Sojourner Truth,* pp. 111-12. All contemporary reports indicate that Sojourner Truth was a powerful presence at public gatherings. Her sharp mind and keen insights made her especially skilled at extemporaneous speaking. Without detracting from these qualities, it must be observed that the considerable attention paid to her was also partly due to the fact that she was often the only black woman in attendance at feminist, abolitionist, or evangelical gatherings organized by whites. Other black women were certainly involved in reform efforts, but movements and organizations were often racially segregated. See Nell Irvin Painter, "Difference, Slavery, and Memory: Sojourner Truth in Feminist Abolitionism," in *Abolitionist Sisterhood,* pp. 139-58. There was also segregation based on gender. Lucretia Mott was denied a seat at the World Anti-Slavery Convention in London in 1840. Indeed, the sexism prevalent among male abolitionists may have been a factor in convincing some women of the need to participate in the women's rights movement. Bacon, "By Moral Force Alone," *Abolitionist Sisterhood,* p. 293. It was at the 1851 Woman Rights Convention in Akron, Ohio that Sojourner Truth delivered her famous "Ar'n't I a Woman" speech, but the well-known version of this speech was based on a transcription first published in 1878 by Frances Gage, the organizer of the Ohio convention. An earlier version which appeared in the *Anti-Slavery Bugle* only a few weeks after the convention was bereft of the "Ar'n't I a woman" refrain and of the tortured southern dialect of the Gage version, which included such lines as this: "I think that b'twixt de niggers of de Souf and de women of de Norf all a talkin' about rights, de white man will be in a fix pretty soon." Sojourner Truth was born in New York and she was bilingual in English and Dutch, the language of her "owner." While her speeches were clearly powerful, they were just as clearly *not* spoken in southern dialect. See Jeffrey C. Stewart, "Introduction," in *Narrative of Sojourner Truth,* pp. xxxiii-xxxv.

256. Thomas Jefferson, *Notes on the State of Virginia,* ed. William Peden (New York: W. W. Norton, 1972), p. 163.

257. Garrison, quoted by Strout, *New Heavens and New Earth,* p. 163.

258. The nature of the terror of God in the book of Revelation will be explored in the third section of this chapter.

259. Mayer, *All on Fire,* p. 121.

260. James Brewer Stewart, *Holy Warriors: The Abolitionists and American Slavery* (New York: Hill and Wang, 1976), p. 152. Nathaniel P. Rogers was one of the few non-resistants to suggest that it was wrong for abolitionists to appeal to God's "vengeance." He posed quandaries like the following: If capital punishment is a sin (as Rogers believed it to be), then how can one go on to suggest that capital punishment provokes a death penalty from God? Inspired by anarchism, Rogers suggested that it was better to view God as the *Abba* who instructs rather than as the Master who compels. Perry, *Radical Abolitionism*, pp. 117-23.

261. See Mayer, *All on Fire*, p. 490.

262. John Brown, quoted by Strout, *New Heavens and New Earth*, p. 187, emphasis in original.

263. See Wallenstein, "Incendiaries All," pp. 152-53.

264. Stanton, quoted by Wendy Hamand Venet, "'Cry Aloud and Spare Not': Northern Antislavery Women and John Brown's Raid," in *His Soul Goes Marching On*, p. 112. In her time, Stanton was certainly not alone in the dangerous failure to distinguish between the bloodshed of war and the sacrifice of the blood of Jesus. Her equation of the mission of Jesus with an Americanized version of "liberty" was also not unique.

265. Garrison, cited by Mayer, *All on Fire*, p. 494.

266. Stewart, *Holy Warriors*, p. 174.

267. Garrison quotations from Mayer, *All on Fire*, pp. 494, 498, 502-3.

268. Cheever and Goodell, cited by Perry, *Radical Abolitionism*, p. 270.

269. Mayer, *All on Fire*, p. 519.

270. Weber, *Apocalypses*, p. 178.

271. Wills, *Under God*, p. 214.

272. Lincoln's Second Inaugural Address, as cited in Strout, *New Heavens and New Earth*, p. 199.

273. See Mayer, *All on Fire*, p. 498.

274. Perry, *Radical Abolitionism*, pp. 260-63.

275. Heywood's pacifism was severely criticized by fellow abolitionist George Stacy. While Stacy acknowledged that non-resistance was correct in the abstract, he asked, "if man in an unregenerate state will fight, can we refrain from the desire that they will fight on the side of freedom?" Cited by Perry, *Radical Abolitionism*, p. 287. A desire analogous to Stacy's might be the hope that slave traders will at least use their proceeds to buy Bibles — the very type of hypocrisy that Douglass denounced in his *Narrative*.

276. Brock, *Freedom from War*, p. 123.

277. *Power of the People*, pp. 19-20.

278. Bacon, "By Moral Force Alone," pp. 294-97.

279. Garrison, quoted by Perry, *Radical Abolitionism*, pp. 266-67.

280. Haven, "The War and the Millennium," in *Slavery Attacked: The Abolitionist Crusade*, ed. John L. Thomas (Englewood Cliffs, N.J.: Prentice-Hall, 1965), p. 173.

281. Cited by Strozier, *Apocalypse*, p. 177.

282. Melville, quoted by Strout, *New Heavens and New Earth*, p. 203.

283. Ide, quoted by Strozier, *Apocalypse*, p. 172.

284. Perry, *Radical Abolitionism*, p. 287.

285. Staughton Lynd, ed., *Nonviolence in America: A Documentary History* (Indianapolis: Bobbs-Merrill, 1966), p. xviii.

286. Perry, *Radical Abolitionism*, p. 301.

287. For a brief description of the distinctions between *relegatio in insulam* and the harsher *deportatio in insulam*, see G. B. Caird, *The Revelation of Saint John*, Black's New Testament Commentaries (Peabody, Mass.: Hendrickson Publishers, 1966), pp. 21-22.

288. Wes Howard-Brook and Anthony Gwyther, *Unveiling Empire: Reading Revelation Then and Now*, The Bible and Liberation Series (Maryknoll, N.Y.: Orbis Books, 1999), p. xxvii.

289. Weber, *Apocalypses*, p. 230.

290. Wills, *Under God*, p. 75.

291. Walter Wink, *The Powers*, vol. 3: *Engaging the Powers: Discernment and Resistance in a World of Domination* (Minneapolis: Fortress Press, 1992), p. 321.

292. Howard-Brook and Gwyther, *Unveiling Empire*, pp. xxi-xxiii. See also Norman Cohn, *Cosmos, Chaos, and the World to Come: The Ancient Roots of Apocalyptic Faith* (New Haven: Yale University Press, 1993), pp. 215-16. While John cites the killing of Antipas in Rev. 2:13, he does not provide the lists of contemporary martyrs that one might expect in a time of heavy persecution. Cohn goes even further to express doubt that John was on Patmos as the result of banishment. Contra Cohn, there is ample evidence that Patmos was part of a group of islands that were routinely used as sites of exile, so it is a fair assumption that banishment was the "persecution" that John endured "because of the word of God" (Rev. 1:9). The tradition that such was the case appears in the writings of Irenaeus and Eusebius (no detractor of Empire he) and Jerome.

293. John did not manage to escape the stereotyping of women that was prevalent in his patriarchal culture. In addition to the "whore," John deploys female imagery in his presentation of the New Jerusalem as a virginal bride (21:2) and in his description of the woman "clothed with the sun" giving birth to a messiah (Rev. 12). Taken together, these female images fit too neatly into the caricatures of women as virgins, whores, or mothers. See Susan R. Garrett, "Revelation," in *The Women's Bible Commentary*, ed. Carol A. Newsom and Sharon H. Ringe (Louisville: Westminster/John Knox Press, 1992), p. 377.

294. In the teachings on the end of the age, Matthew portrays Jesus as also calling for endurance as the disciples face the hatred of "all nations." Jesus warns that "the love of many will grow cold." See Matthew 24:9-13.

295. Howard-Brook and Gwyther, *Unveiling Empire*, p. 99.

296. Howard-Brook and Gwyther, *Unveiling Empire*, pp. 103-4.

297. Jacques Ellul made the case that John's apparently repetitious citation of "slaves — and human lives" (18:13) was an intentional reference to the reality that the interior "souls" of people were being bought and sold, including the interior lives of those who were not necessarily in physical bondage. We become such cargo whenever our lives are "bound in a completely clear fashion to economic activity, to commerce and enrichment. . . ." Ellul, *Apocalypse: The Book of Revelation* (New York: Seabury Press, 1977), p. 195. While it may be intended as merely a clever saying, the corruption of the Cartesian axiom into the modern slogan, "I shop, therefore I am," is actually quite revealing of the manner in which Western "consumers" become enslaved to economic activity.

298. Meeks, *Origins of Christian Morality*, p. 179.

299. Northrop Frye, *The Great Code: The Bible and Literature* (New York: Harcourt, Brace Jovanovich, 1982), p. 135.

300. For an insightful critique of these dominant strains in Western pedagogy, see Parker J. Palmer, *To Know As We Are Known: A Spirituality of Education* (New York: Harper & Row, 1983). There are, of course, consequences to our style of education. Palmer cites (p. 4) a Carnegie Commission survey of American undergraduates. The students were asked if they were optimistic or pessimistic about their own personal futures. By a vast majority, the students responded that they were optimistic, what with the prospect of a degree and a strong job market and a good economy. When they were asked whether they were optimistic or pessimistic about the future of the planet, the students responded that they were pessimistic, what with the threat of environmental collapse and terrorist attacks and nuclear holocaust. The students were being "objective," as if their own personal futures were somehow independent of a world in imminent danger. To hold the world at a distance is to deny that the terror my brothers and sisters experience has any meaning for me.

301. O'Connor, quoted by Howard-Brook and Gwyther, *Unveiling Empire*, p. 272.

302. Thompson, *End of Time*, p. 14.

303. While John's writing begins with a reference to "revelation," the Gnostic Gospel of Thomas begins with a reference to "secret sayings." The Gospel of Thomas repeatedly offers encouragement to rid oneself of the world as if undressing (sayings 21, 37, 56). "The Gospel of Thomas," trans. Thomas O. Lambdin, in *The Nag Hammadi Library*, 3rd ed., edited by James M. Robinson (New York: Harper & Row, 1988), pp. 124-38. In contrast to the vision of Revelation, the ideal held out by the Gospel of Thomas is to become solitary and detached. As Wayne Meeks notes, "For Thomas as for John, the economic order is dangerous, but not because it involves compromise with the order dominated by the whore Rome-Babylon. Rather, trade entangles us with the world as such — but so does family life, so does sexuality, a settled living, indeed everything that connects 'a body to a body.'" Meeks, *Origins of Christian Morality*, p. 184. Where John encourages coming out of Babylon, Thomas encourages departure from the world.

304. Blake, "A Vision of the Last Judgment," cited by Harrison, *The Second Coming*, p. 216.

305. Indeed, the "Jewish" character of Revelation is of such strength that some authors have been led to question whether there was anything specifically "Christian" in the original text. J. Massyngberde Ford argues that Rev. 4–11 was authored by someone from within the circle around John the Baptist, Rev. 12–22 was composed by a later disciple of the Baptist, and Rev. 1–3 and assorted other interpolations that refer to Jesus were inserted by a later Jewish Christian redactor. See Ford, *Revelation*, Anchor Bible, no. 38 (Garden City, N.Y.: Doubleday, 1975), pp. 3-4, 50-56. While the argument is creative, simpler explanations are available for the "Jewish" character of Revelation if one accepts the thoroughly Jewish identity of the first-century followers of Jesus.

306. One pertinent example is the question of Sabbath observance raised in 1 Maccabees 2:29-41. On the relationship between the Hasidim and the Maccabeans, see Otto Plöger, *Theocracy and Eschatology*, trans. S. Rudman (Richmond, Va.: John Knox Press, 1968), pp. 7-10; and Martin Hengel, *Judaism and Hellenism: Studies in Their Encounter in Palestine During the Early Hellenistic Period*, trans. John Bowden (Philadelphia: Fortress Press, 1981), pp. 175-80.

307. Cohn, *Cosmos, Chaos, and World to Come,* p. 173.

308. Norman W. Porteous describes Daniel 12:2 as indicative of "at least a modified belief in resurrection. . . ." Porteous, *Daniel: A Commentary,* The Old Testament Library (Philadelphia: Westminster Press, 1965), p. 20. Robert A. Anderson writes that whether Daniel provides "the first clear reference to resurrection in the Hebrew Scriptures" depends on one's understanding of Isaiah 26:19. Is Isaiah alluding to a belief in resurrection or not? Anderson notes that some scholars read both Daniel 12:2 and Isaiah 26:19 as saying less about individual resurrection than about the restoration of the people of God, as in the vision of the valley of the dry bones in Ezekiel 37:1-14. Anderson, *Signs and Wonders: A Commentary on the Book of Daniel,* International Theological Commentary (Grand Rapids: Eerdmans and Edinburgh: The Handsel Press Ltd., 1984), p. 147. In either event, resurrection or restoration, it is God's cause that is vindicated. If Daniel 12:2 does point to a belief in resurrection, it is notable that the persecutors and the faithless do not awaken to fiery punishments but to "shame" and to "contempt," that is, to a harsh recognition of the consequences of their own deeds.

309. Howard-Brook and Gwyther, *Unveiling Empire,* p. 132. See also Cohn, *Cosmos, Chaos, and World to Come,* p. 143.

310. Elisabeth Schüssler Fiorenza, *The Book of Revelation: Justice and Judgment* (Philadelphia: Fortress Press, 1985), pp. 120-25. Fiorenza notes that Paul and John of Patmos also have a similar style of posing alternatives regarding "lordship." While Paul poses the eschatological alternatives as either the lordship of Christ or the lordship of rebellious cosmic powers, John poses the alternatives as either the rule of God and the Lamb or the rule of Rome.

311. Fiorenza, *Book of Revelation,* pp. 73-74. In these verses, Fiorenza also observes a link between the "saints" who are ransomed by the blood of the Lamb "from every tribe and language and people and nation" (Rev. 5:9) and the 144,000 who are "redeemed from humankind as first fruits" (Rev. 14:1-5). Fiorenza writes (p. 74) that the reference to "first fruits" indicates that the 144,000 are not some righteous elite for whom salvation is reserved but "the sign of the universal eschatological salvation of all people and nations."

312. The reworking of the themes from Psalms is traced by Howard-Brook and Gwyther, *Unveiling Empire,* pp. 198-202.

313. See Caird, *Revelation,* p. 290.

314. G. B. Caird, *The Language and Imagery of the Bible* (Philadelphia: Westminster Press, 1980), pp. 51-52.

315. Caird notes that "Matt. xiii.24-43 might seem to be a partial exception, since the weeds are reaped along with the wheat. . . . But even here the object of the reaping is the storing of the crop, not the bonfire." Caird, *Revelation,* p. 190.

316. See Howard-Brook and Gwyther, *Unveiling Empire,* pp. 210-11.

317. Ellul, *Apocalypse,* p. 193.

318. Note that the "lawless one" in 2 Thessalonians 2:8 is also destroyed by the "mouth" of Jesus. Whether 2 Thessalonians is authentically Pauline or not, Paul's view of the end of domination by the powers is complementary to Revelation's view of the fall of Babylon. See Hendrik Berkhof, *Christ and the Powers,* trans. John H. Yoder (Scottdale, Pa.: Herald Press, 1977), p. 36.

319. In Revelation 6, while the Lamb opens the seals to unveil the contents of the

scroll, the creatures who are revealed do not represent the will of the Lamb. Indeed, one rider is named "Death, and Hades followed with him" (6:8), and it is precisely these two who are thrown into the lake of fire by the judgment of God (20:14). Likewise, the sword of war and bloodshed (6:4) does not represent the will of the Lamb.

320. Walter Wink notes that the theme of "cosmic restitution" in the book of Revelation prevents any demonizing of the kings or other people who have been in complicity with the Beast. Wink, *The Powers,* vol. 1: *Naming the Powers: The Language of Power in the New Testament* (Philadelphia: Fortress Press, 1984), pp. 52-54.

321. Daniel Berrigan, *The Nightmare of God,* with photo etchings by Tom Lewis (Portland, Ore.: Sunburst Press, 1983), p. 79.

322. Johann Baptist Metz, *Faith in History and Society: Toward a Practical Fundamental Theology,* trans. David Smith (New York: Seabury Press, 1980), p. 178.

323. Caird, *Revelation,* p. 293.

324. D. S. Russell, *The Method and Message of Jewish Apocalyptic,* The Old Testament Library (Philadelphia: Westminster Press, 1964), pp. 379-85.

325. Howard-Brook and Gwyther, *Unveiling Empire,* p. 183.

326. An awareness of the manner in which First and Second Advents must be understood together pervaded the theology of William Stringfellow. On Stringfellow's approach of permitting Revelation to demythologize the present, see Stanley Hauerwas and Jeff Powell, "Creation as Apocalyptic: A Homage to William Stringfellow," in *Radical Christian and Exemplary Lawyer: Honoring William Stringfellow,* ed. Andrew W. McThenia, Jr. (Grand Rapids: Eerdmans, 1995), pp. 31-40.

327. A version of the sermon that he preached in 1975 appears in Stringfellow, *Conscience and Obedience: The Politics of Romans 13 and Revelation 13 in Light of the Second Coming* (Waco: Word Books, 1978), pp. 109-12. It also appears in the excellent anthology compiled by my friend Bill Wylie Kellermann, ed., *A Keeper of the Word: Selected Writings of William Stringfellow* (Grand Rapids: Eerdmans, 1994), pp. 348-51.

NOTES TO CHAPTER V

1. The line appears in Act IV of *The Just Assassins,* in Albert Camus, *Caligula and Three Other Plays,* trans. Stuart Gilbert (New York: Vintage Books, 1958), p. 281.

2. Colby, cited by Robin Wright, *Sacred Rage: The Crusade of Modern Islam* (New York: Simon & Schuster, 1985), p. 265.

3. William Perdue makes the case that "state terrorism" is characterized by any of the following actions: (1) a state's attempt to dominate its own people through surveillance, mass arrests, or capital punishment; (2) military actions that put the lives of civilians at risk; (3) assassination attempts against the leaders of other nations; and (4) covert operations to destabilize another state. See William D. Perdue, *Terrorism and the State: A Critique of Domination Through Fear* (New York: Praeger, 1989). The United States is not alone among nations that have employed such techniques of state terrorism, often in the name of fighting a "war against terrorism." Edward S. Herman observes that "Since 1959 Cuba has been subjected to many more terrorist acts than any western democracy, very possibly more than all of them put together. . . ." These acts have included attacks on

power plants, hotels, sugar refineries, and civilian airliners, as well as eight *admitted* U.S.-sponsored attempts to murder Fidel Castro. It is not the nature of the actions but the identities of the target and the perpetrator that account for the failure of most U.S. media to report these events as acts of terrorism. Herman asks, "If Colonel Kaddafi had admitted to eight attempts on the life of the President of the United States, what would be the world reaction?" Herman, *The Real Terror Network: Terrorism in Fact and Propaganda* (Boston: South End Press, 1982), p. 64.

4. While most governments of the world have publicly adopted a "no concessions to terrorists" position, what goes on beyond the view of the public may be at considerable variance from this stance. The protestations of Oliver North notwithstanding, the Iran-Contra affair was a blatant agreement to sell weapons in exchange for hostages; it was revelatory of the interests of both parties to the agreement that what was being sold was not food or medicines but weapons. Whether governments are willing to confer legitimacy on terrorists by meeting with them is highly dependent on *whose* "terrorists" they are. In the 1980s, Soviet leaders were unwilling to meet with the "Afghan terrorists" who were being dined (but not wined) in Washington, D.C. and other Western capitals. William Blum recalls, "In 1986, British Prime Minister Margaret Thatcher, whose emotional invectives against 'terrorists' were second to none, welcomed Abdul Haq, an Afghan rebel leader who admitted that he had ordered the planting of a bomb at Kabul airport in 1984 which killed at least 28 people." Blum, *Killing Hope: U.S. Military and CIA Interventions since World War II* (Monroe, Maine: Common Courage Press, 1995), p. 345. Once the Soviets were driven from Afghanistan and the Afghan fighters turned their attention to other would-be imperialists, they quickly became persona non grata in Western capitals.

5. Terry Anderson, "Painful Lessons: Hostage-taking and US Foreign Policy," *Harvard International Review* 20, no. 4 (Fall 1998): 64.

6. Benjamin Netanyahu, *Fighting Terrorism: How Democracies Can Defeat Domestic and International Terrorists* (New York: Farrar, Straus and Giroux, 1995), p. 146.

7. Walter Laqueur, *Terrorism: A Study of National and International Political Violence* (Boston: Little, Brown and Company, 1977), p. 221.

8. Netanyahu, *Fighting Terrorism*, p. 139, emphasis in the original.

9. The recommendation for increased surveillance of "extremist" groups would entail the use of paid government infiltrators and informers. In the United States, the histories of the antiwar movement, the Black Panther Party, and the American Indian Movement have provided evidence of a number of instances in which government plants actually proposed and encouraged violence on the part of the opposition groups.

10. Netanyahu, *Fighting Terrorism*, p. 141.

11. Netanyahu, *Fighting Terrorism*, p. 143.

12. Stephen E. Atkins, *Terrorism: A Reference Handbook*, Contemporary World Issues Series (Santa Barbara, Calif.: ABC-CLIO, Inc., 1992), p. 28.

13. Alberto Fujimori, "Terror, Society, and Law: Peru's Struggle Against Violent Insurgency," *Harvard International Review* 20, no. 4 (Fall 1998): 60.

14. "Assembly-Line Justice," from *Le Monde*, September 3, 1998, translated and reprinted in *World Press Review* 45, no. 11 (November 1998): 12.

15. "Victory for the Real IRA," from *The Economist*, August 29, 1998, reprinted in *World Press Review* 45, no. 11 (November 1998): 12.

16. The provisions for the prosecutorial use of classified documents have been applied in immigration and deportation cases, but the provisions may have applicability in other cases as well. In 1976, I left a "Pentagon Bicentennial Tour" group and entered the office of the Undersecretary of the Navy for Research and Development, an office that was heavily involved in the development and deployment of the Trident nuclear submarine. I was arrested and charged with pouring blood on classified government files, a felony count of destruction of government property. In civil disobedience cases, my friends and I have ordinarily approached courts with full acknowledgment of what we have done and why we have done it. But in 1976, friends urged me to file a "motion for discovery" asking the prosecution to produce the evidence, i.e., to permit me to examine the bloodied, classified files. A federal magistrate in Alexandria, Virginia granted my motion over government objections that they should not be required to bring classified materials into an open courtroom. The felony count was dropped and I was sentenced to ten days in jail on a misdemeanor charge. Today, the outcome might be different due to changes in provisions that protected not only the guilty (me) but the innocent as well.

17. Parenti, *Against Empire* (San Francisco: City Lights Books, 1995), p. 153.

18. Laqueur, *Terrorism,* p. 223.

19. Netanyahu, quoted by Bruce Hoffman, *Inside Terrorism* (New York: Columbia University Press, 1998), p. 143. Netanyahu's statement comes close to suggesting that the problem with terrorism is the reporting of it. Reported or not, the survivors of violence and the family members of the victims of violence are not unaffected by "the proverbial tree falling." Whatever the strategic or political merits of ignoring acts of terrorism, violence is not primarily a strategic or political problem but a crisis of spirit and humanity.

20. Thatcher, quoted by Dale Van Atta, "Carbombs and Cameras: The Need for Responsible Media Coverage of Terrorism," *Harvard International Review* 20, no. 4 (Fall 1998): 70.

21. Hoffman, *Inside Terrorism,* pp. 235-36n.50.

22. Regarding similar problems with the media coverage of the troubles in Northern Ireland, see Brian Hamilton-Tweedale, "Reporting 'Terrorism': The Experience of Northern Ireland," in *On Prejudice: A Global Perspective,* ed. Daniela Gioseffi (New York: Anchor Books, 1993), pp. 404-9.

23. FBI report, cited by David McGowan, *Derailing Democracy: The America the Media Don't Want You to See* (Monroe, Maine: Common Courage Press, 2000), pp. 62-63.

24. Quotations from the State Department report appear in McGowan, *Derailing Democracy,* p. 64.

25. See Van Atta, "Carbombs and Cameras," p. 68.

26. Katherine Graham, cited by McGowan, *Derailing Democracy,* p. 109. In fairness to Graham, it should be noted that many of her statements were more supportive of the need to know rather than the need not to know. In less secretive environs than the CIA, Graham once stated, "Publicity may be the oxygen of terrorists. But I say this: News is the lifeblood of liberty. If the terrorists succeed in depriving us of freedom, their victory will be far greater than they ever hoped and far worse than we ever feared." Quoted by Van Atta, "Carbombs and Cameras," p. 70.

27. Hoffman, *Inside Terrorism,* p. 59.

28. Several of these are cited by Hoffman, *Inside Terrorism,* pp. 61-62. Susan Jacoby

also notes the persistence with which exemplary execution "inspires rather than deters acts of violent fanaticism." Nonetheless, even in nations that have abolished capital punishment, "terrorism" is most frequently cited in opinion polls as a crime deserving of the death penalty. Jacoby, *Wild Justice: The Evolution of Revenge* (New York: Harper & Row, 1983), pp. 246-47.

29. The event is recalled by Robin Morgan, *The Demon Lover: On the Sexuality of Terrorism* (New York: W. W. Norton, 1989), p. 170.

30. The attack on Libya and the events that preceded it are described by Ramsey Clark, "Beyond Terrorism," in *Violent Persuasions: The Politics and Imagery of Terrorism,* ed. David J. Brown and Robert Merrill (Seattle: Bay Press, 1993), p. 72.

31. The commission findings are reported by Edward S. Herman, "Terrorism: Misrepresentations of Power," in *Violent Persuasions,* p. 49.

32. The Human Rights Watch report is quoted by McGowan, *Derailing Democracy,* p. 32.

33. State Department memorandum of March 29, 1968, quoted by McGowan, *Derailing Democracy,* p. 80, emphasis in original.

34. Herman, "Terrorism: Misrepresentations of Power," in *Violent Persuasions,* p. 49.

35. See Noam Chomsky, *The Culture of Terrorism* (Boston: South End Press, 1988), p. 235.

36. Intelligence Oversight Board report cited by Jack Nelson-Pallmeyer, *School of Assassins: The Case for Closing the School of the Americas and for Fundamentally Changing U.S. Foreign Policy* (Maryknoll, N.Y.: Orbis Books, 1997), p. 51.

37. Nelson-Pallmeyer, *School of Assassins,* pp. 51-52.

38. Editorial quoted by Nelson-Pallmeyer, *School of Assassins,* p. xii. The School remains open despite a 2001 name change to the "Western Hemisphere Institute of Security Cooperation."

39. The statement of the Court is cited with approval by Netanyahu, *Fighting Terrorism,* p. 148.

40. The work of Hobbes as the philosophical basis for governmental reification of security is explored by José Comblin, *The Church and the National Security State* (Maryknoll, N.Y.: Orbis Books, 1979), pp. 89-95.

41. Martin van Creveld, *The Rise and Decline of the State* (Cambridge: Cambridge University Press, 1999), p. 404.

42. Van Creveld, *Rise and Decline of the State,* p. 406.

43. See McGowan, *Derailing Democracy,* pp. 93-94.

44. Amaya's story is retold by Nelson-Pallmeyer, *School of Assassins,* p. 98.

45. While WTO authority does not currently extend to all weapons and weapons systems, it could be understood as applying to some weapons components. There is already a powerful case for the abolition of the WTO based on human rights and environmental concerns. See *The Case Against the Global Economy: And for a Turn Toward the Local,* ed. Jerry Mander and Edward Goldsmith (San Francisco: Sierra Club Books, 1996).

46. Engels, quoted by Morgan, *Demon Lover,* p. 46.

47. The *British Medical Journal* article is cited by McGowan, *Derailing Democracy,* p. 95. The U.S. is also a world leader in the export of leg-irons, handcuffs, electroshock batons, and cattle prods, many of those items going to countries with horrid human rights

records. With the U.S. a close second, Britain leads the world in the export of surveillance technology.

48. Blum, *Killing Hope,* pp. 204, 350-51.

49. McGowan, *Derailing Democracy,* pp. 97-99.

50. For specific examples of the hypocritical nature of the weapons suppliers' "dangerous world" argument, see Blum, *Killing Hope,* p. 2.

51. There are analogies to the terrorism of Aum Shinrikyō. Shōkō Asahara invested considerable financial resources into the recruitment of scientists and the building of sophisticated laboratories. As part of an effort to understand meditation techniques, Aum scientists actually embarked on some potentially fruitful research into human brain waves and brain physiology. But the more benign research of the Aum scientists was persistently undermined by the greater priority that was given to uncovering the destructive potential of assorted chemical and biological agents. Robert Jay Lifton, *Destroying the World to Save It: Aum Shinrikyō, Apocalyptic Violence, and the New Global Terrorism* (New York: Metropolitan Books, 1999), pp. 116-17.

52. We may not know for some time how we have fared following the collapse of the Soviet Union. Overnight, several new nations joined the nuclear club, with Kazakhstan possessing the world's third largest nuclear arsenal. Russia went scrambling to negotiate acquisition of some of the weapons while Western nations went scrambling to pay for dismantling of others. Russian General Lebed has revealed that, of 100 suitcase-sized nuclear weapons once in the possession of the Soviet special forces, two-thirds can no longer be accounted for. Van Creveld, *Rise and Decline of the State,* p. 419n.6.

53. On the refutation of the imperial myth of eternity in the Revelation of John, see Wes Howard-Brook and Anthony Gwyther, *Unveiling Empire: Reading Revelation Then and Now,* The Bible and Liberation Series (Maryknoll, N.Y.: Orbis Books, 1999), pp. 233-35.

54. Presidents count on the historical pattern in which, even if the public is not supportive of military intervention beforehand, once hostilities have begun, citizens rally to the cause under the "support our troops" banner. There is also a tendency for people to want to share in the credit once the achievement of a military objective is a *fait accompli.* Since the declaration of war is a constitutional fossil, presidents have been allowed to act as if they were in possession of a private army. Regarding his military intervention in Panama, Theodore Roosevelt correctly observed, "I took the Canal Zone and let Congress debate." On the eve of the Gulf War, President Bush, Sr. stated that he was willing to commit troops to combat without a single supporting vote in Congress. See Parenti, *Against Empire,* p. 152.

55. Edward Herman distinguishes between the "wholesale terror" of the state and the "retail terror" of small groups and individuals. He notes the manner in which the state uses retail terror as an excuse in the "engineering of consent" for wholesale terror. Herman, *Real Terror Network,* p. 212.

56. As noted earlier in this book, the maintenance of an image of unpredictability has become an intentional part of military strategizing. "Essentials of Post–Cold War Deterrence," the 1995 report from the U.S. Strategic Command, states, "The fact that some elements [of the U.S. government] may appear to be potentially 'out of control' can be beneficial to creating and reinforcing fears and doubts within the minds of an adversary's decision makers. . . . That the U.S. may become irrational and vindictive if its vital interests

are attacked should be a part of the national persona we project to all adversaries. . . . It hurts to portray ourselves as too fully rational and cool-headed. . . ." STRATCOM report, cited by McGowan, *Derailing Democracy,* p. 162.

57. Peter Partner, *God of Battles: Holy Wars of Christianity and Islam* (Princeton: Princeton University Press, 1997), p. 304.

58. Alexander Cockburn and Jeffrey St. Clair, *Whiteout: The CIA, Drugs and the Press* (New York: Verso, 1999), p. 263; Blum, *Killing Hope,* p. 345.

59. McGowan, *Derailing Democracy,* pp. 183-87.

60. McGowan, *Derailing Democracy,* pp. 188-92. Estimates for the number of cancer cases that will result from the depleted uranium shells used in Iraq range up to half a million. Despite U.S. assurances that care was being exercised during the Gulf War to protect Iraqi civilians, U.S. bombers intentionally targeted two Iraqi nuclear reactors. It was a dangerous precedent, the first time in history that operational nuclear reactors came under military attack. The attacks violated UN mandates despite General Schwarzkopf's assurances that the bombings had been carefully calibrated to avoid nuclear meltdown. Blum, *Killing Hope,* p. 334.

61. Herman, *Real Terror Network,* p. 212.

62. See Ronnie D. Lipschutz, "Beyond the Neoliberal Peace: From Conflict Resolution to Social Reconciliation," *Social Justice: A Journal of Crime, Conflict, and World Order* 25, no. 4 (Winter 1998): 5-19.

63. In Northern Ireland, decommissioning negotiations would have been unthinkable without years of micro-level efforts by common folks in community relations programs, educational projects, and sponsorship of integrated activities for Catholics and Protestants. See Elizabeth H. Crighton, "Beyond Neoliberalism: Peacemaking in Northern Ireland," *Social Justice: A Journal of Crime, Conflict, and World Order* 25, no. 4 (Winter 1998): 75-89. In the same issue of *Social Justice,* Joel Beinin writes of the potentially reconciling impact of non-governmental projects such as the shared exhibits by Israeli and Palestinian artists organized by Israeli artist David Reeb. Beinin, "Palestine and Israel: Perils of a Neoliberal, Repressive *Pax Americana*": 25.

64. See Franke Wilmer, "The Social Construction of Conflict and Reconciliation in the Former Yugoslavia," *Social Justice: A Journal of Crime, Conflict, and World Order* 25, no. 4 (Winter 1998): 90-113.

65. The figure of more than 150 U.S. training centers for foreign military officers (located in the U.S. and abroad) is from an Amnesty International report cited by McGowan, *Derailing Democracy,* pp. 91-92.

66. The Senator's bill is described by Angus Mackenzie, *Secrets: The CIA's War at Home* (Berkeley: University of California Press, 1997), p. 183.

67. While secret, current estimates are that CIA funding ranges from $35 billion to $50 billion hidden away in several categories of the federal budget. Michael Parenti notes that the secrecy of CIA appropriations is in direct violation of Article I, Section 9 of the U.S. Constitution which states in part, ". . . a regular statement and account of the receipts and expenditures of all public money shall be published from time to time." Parenti, *Against Empire,* p. 152.

68. Cockburn and St. Clair, *Whiteout,* p. 392.

69. The accusations are reviewed and their merits are evaluated by Cockburn and St.

Clair, *Whiteout*. See also McGowan, *Derailing Democracy*, pp. 104-13, and Blum, *Killing Hope*, pp. 350-51.

70. Evidence pointing to a CIA-Contra drug connection was presented most prominently by investigative reporter Gary Webb in a series of articles appearing in the *San Jose Mercury News*. Webb was not alone in finding the evidence disturbing. In Central America, it may be Costa Rica that has the strongest claim to stable, democratic governance. On July 22, 1989, the government of Costa Rica announced that it considered several high-level U.S. officials to be drug traffickers and that they would be barred from entering the country. Included on the list were Lt. Col. Oliver North, John Poindexter, and Major General Richard Secord. See McGowan, *Derailing Democracy*, p. 106. Charges of drug money support for the Contras date from the period when Congress voted an end to U.S. funding for the Contra war in Nicaragua. Contra supporters in the U.S. government then arranged for private funding of the war. The Sultan of Brunei gave $10 million and Saudi Prince Bandar gave a few million. Readers of *Soldier of Fortune* magazine sent in checks for five, ten, a hundred dollars. "Lady Ellen" was the name given to the helicopter that was funded in part by $65,000 from Texas donor Mary Ellen Garwood. On the privately funded phase of the Contra war, see James William Gibson, *Warrior Dreams: Violence and Manhood in Post-Vietnam America* (New York: Hill and Wang, 1994), pp. 278-80.

71. In his congressional testimony, Inspector General Hitz also revealed that, in 1982, a memorandum of understanding had been signed between the CIA and Attorney General William French Smith freeing the Agency from responsibility to report allegations and suspicions of drug trafficking by paid and non-paid "assets, pilots who ferried supplies to the Contras as well as Contra officials and others." Cockburn and St. Clair, *Whiteout*, pp. 391-92.

72. Blum, *Killing Hope*, pp. 17, 242-44.

73. Blum, *Killing Hope*, pp. 106-8. Human Rights Watch was among the organizations protesting the recommendations issued in June 2000 by the U.S. National Commission on Terrorism. Among other proposals, the Commission recommended lifting all restrictions on the CIA's ability to recruit foreign informers and operatives who have had a record of involvement in murder, torture, and other human rights abuses. While the objections of Human Rights Watch are certainly well founded, there is little in its history to indicate that the CIA has respected restrictions on recruitment in any event. The experience with Operation Gladio suggests that the Agency may already be following William Colby's advice to recruit rather than shoot terrorists.

74. Nelson-Pallmeyer, *School of Assassins*, p. 1.

75. Morris is quoted by Blum, *Killing Hope*, p. 6.

76. Blum cites the example of the CIA-subsidized Forum World Features which, at its peak in the 1960s, regularly provided news articles for publication in 140 newspapers around the world, including 30 papers in the U.S. Blum, *Killing Hope*, pp. 104-5. On the continuing rebound of CIA disinformation into the U.S., see Parenti, *Against Empire*, p. 153. Even the CIA has experienced rebound from its own disinformation. Lincoln Gordan, past president of Johns Hopkins University, was hired by the CIA as an outside consultant to check on the accuracy of the thesis put forward by Claire Sterling in her book, *The Terror Network*. Gordan discovered that a portion of Sterling's thesis relied on

false stories the CIA had planted in the Italian news media. Gibson, *Warrior Dreams*, pp. 271-73.

77. Mackenzie, *Secrets*, pp. 199-200. When House Intelligence Committee member Robert Torricelli revealed that a Guatemalan officer who was on the CIA payroll was responsible for the murder of a U.S. citizen who ran a hotel in Guatemala and a rebel leader who was married to a U.S. citizen, then-Speaker Newt Gingrich expressed outrage and demanded punishment — not punishment of the officer responsible for the killings but of Torricelli who had revealed the secret. Nelson-Pallmeyer, *School of Assassins*, p. 48.

Upon occasion, secret information will be exposed inadvertently in congressional hearings. Michael Parenti recounts one chilling example:

"During the Iran-Contra hearings, Representative Jack Brooks (D-Tex.), taking his investigative functions seriously, asked Lieutenant Colonel Oliver North if there was any truth to the story that he had helped to draft a secret plan, code-named Rex Alpha 84, to suspend the Constitution and impose martial law in the USA. A stunned expression appeared on North's face and the committee chair, Senator Daniel Inouye, stopped Brooks from pursuing the question, declaring in stern tones 'I believe the question touches upon a highly sensitive and classified area. So may I request that you not touch upon that, sir.'

"Brooks responded that he had read in several newspapers that the National Security Council had developed 'a contingency plan in the event of emergency that would suspend the American Constitution and I was deeply concerned about it.' Inouye again cut him off. It was a tense moment."

Parenti, *Against Empire*, pp. 150-51.

78. Chomsky, *Culture of Terrorism*, p. 41. Angus Mackenzie also notes that secrecy was once understood by its practitioners and enforcers as a hedge against military threats, and "Only recently in the history of the world's oldest republic has secrecy functioned principally to keep the American people in the dark about the nefarious activities of their government." Mackenzie, *Secrets*, p. 202.

79. Nelson-Pallmeyer, *School of Assassins*, pp. 26-27, 66.

80. Berrigan, *The Nightmare of God*, with photo etchings by Tom Lewis (Portland Ore.: Sunburst Press, 1983), p. 48.

81. Dale Aukerman, *Reckoning with Apocalypse: Terminal Politics and Christian Hope* (New York: Crossroad, 1993), p. 111.

82. In Brazil's Contestado Rebellion (cited earlier in this book), a rural peasants' movement turned to violence only after a show of military force by the government. In turn, the violence of the peasants contributed to increased Brazilian militarism and authoritarianism. Todd A. Diacon, *Millenarian Vision, Capitalist Reality: Brazil's Contestado Rebellion, 1912-1916* (Durham, N.C.: Duke University Press, 1991), pp. 122-24, 149-50.

83. The targets of the investigations were not surprising in view of the Task Force's definition of "terrorism" as including "political theater designed to undermine or alter governmental authority or behavior." Under such a definition, electoral campaigns might qualify as terrorism, and as Angus Mackenzie notes, the Boston Tea Party would certainly qualify. The first agents who refused to follow orders were from the Buffalo, New York office of the FBI. In Peoria, Illinois, Special Agent John C. Ryan, a 21-year veteran of the FBI, was fired for refusing to conduct a terrorism investigation on anti-Contra protesters whom he knew to be Christian pacifists. Mackenzie, *Secrets*, pp. 147-49.

84. Gibson, *Warrior Dreams,* p. 286. Gibson notes that this mobilization and massive expenditure of funds took place at a time when the warrant for it was not self-evident. "It should be stressed that the number of terrorist incidents on American soil in the early and mid 1980s was *tiny.* A citizen was 124 times more likely to choke to death while eating than to be killed in a terrorist attack — a mere sandwich was a far more perilous foe than the evil one" (p. 287).

85. On the *Soldier of Fortune* ads and the Air India bombing, see Gibson, *Warrior Dreams,* pp. 195-204.

86. The comments by David Kairys are cited by Russell Mokhiber and Robert Weissman, *Corporate Predators: The Hunt for Mega-Profits and the Attack on Democracy* (Monroe, Maine: Common Courage Press, 1999), pp. 190-92.

87. Clark, "Beyond Terrorism," in *Violent Persuasions,* p. 86.

88. The quotations from both Goering and McArthur are cited by McGowan, *Derailing Democracy,* p. 59.

89. Gibson, *Warrior Dreams,* p. 277.

90. Irving L. Janis, *Groupthink: Psychological Studies of Policy Decisions and Fiascoes,* 2nd ed. (Boston: Houghton Mifflin, 1983), p. 12. The phenomenon of a small, amiable group more readily approving violent solutions is not limited to the inner circles of political power. As Sanford and Comstock note, the sanctioning process that could lead to police brutality or a plane hijacking is the same process. Sanford and Comstock, "Sanctions for Evil," in Nevitt H. Sanford, Craig Comstock, and associates, *Sanctions for Evil: Sources of Social Destructiveness,* The Jossey-Bass Behavioral Science Series (San Francisco: Jossey-Bass, 1971), p. 4. Robert Jay Lifton observed how the violence of Aum Shinrikyō depended on the mutual assent that flowed between the guru and his inner circle of disciples. Lifton, *Destroying the World to Save It,* p. 112. Former Secretary of Defense Robert McNamara has recently expressed regret regarding some of his actions during the U.S. War in Vietnam. Yet, even during his tenure as president of the World Bank, McNamara continued to express confidence in the style of decision-making that contributed to atrocities in Vietnam. "I have always believed," he wrote, "that the more important the issue the fewer people should be involved in the decision." McNamara, quoted by Jerry Mander, "Facing the Rising Tide," in *Case Against the Global Economy,* p. 14.

91. Janis, *Groupthink,* p. 174. The credibility of Janis's analysis is only enhanced by the fact that he wrote years before U.S. military showdowns with multiple "Hitlers" — Noriega, Hussein, Milosevic.

92. Beyond this basic "rule," activists have differed on whether property damage (e.g., the destruction of draft files) is allowable as *nonviolent* civil disobedience. I agree with those who maintain that carefully considered and circumscribed property damage (e.g., damage to instruments of violence) may qualify as *nonviolent* protest, but to engage in actions that involve the foreseeable risk of physical injury to other people is not nonviolent. An example of dissident violence — indeed, terrorism — in the U.S. was the wave of "antiwar" bombings around the country in the late 1960s and early 1970s. Targets included ROTC buildings, Selective Service offices, National Guard armories, police stations, and offices of IBM, Standard Oil, GTE, and other corporations. Telephoned warnings received before the bombs exploded enabled remarkably effective evacuations of buildings, but the bombers were clearly risking the lives of others and exacting high financial sacrifices from

their adversaries. If such bombers assumed that they were not targeting human lives, that pretense was laid to rest on August 23, 1970 when an explosion at the University of Wisconsin Army Mathematics Research Center killed one student and injured four others who happened to be working late in a building that was thought to be vacant. Alphonso Pinkney, *The American Way of Violence* (New York: Vintage Books, 1972), pp. 195-97, 201.

93. Thomas C. Schelling did not escape the prejudice that recourse to terrorism was especially appealing to the poor, but he did recognize nonviolent resistance as a competing model of activism. He wrote, ". . . non-violence has to compete with terrorism; I wish it competed better." Schelling, "Some Questions on Civilian Defence," in *Civilian Resistance as a National Defence: Non-violent Action Against Aggression,* ed. Adam Roberts (Baltimore: Penguin Books, 1969), p. 355.

94. Morgan, *Demon Lover,* p. 191.

95. Todd Diacon cites the introduction of economic competition and the fracturing of traditional cultures as two of the ingredients that are important to the emergence of violent millenarianism. See Diacon, *Millenarian Vision, Capitalist Reality,* pp. 145-48.

96. Thomas E. Schmidt notes that the pervasive Gospel tradition of "hostility to wealth" did not emerge as hostility to the wealthy. Schmidt argues that, as a "religious-ethical tenet," the hostility to wealth proclamations could in fact be received as good news across various socio-economic groups. To the poor, it was a sorely needed affirmation of their inherent worth and dignity. To the middle class, it was encouragement for solidarity against the dominant values of Hellenistic culture. And to the rich, it was a reminder that they were not powerless to effectuate spiritual change. Within this latter group, the message may have held special appeal for some of those with whom Paul had dealings, such as the wealthy women and the upwardly mobile freedmen who were experiencing "status inconsistency." Schmidt, *Hostility to Wealth in the Synoptic Gospels,* Journal for the Study of the New Testament Supplement Series 15 (Sheffield, U.K.: Sheffield Academic Press, 1987), pp. 164-65, 226n.1.

97. On some of the mechanisms by which "significant disparities between social groups in access to life chances" contribute to the generation of terror and counterterror, see Jeffrey A. Sluka, "The Anthropology of Conflict," in *The Paths to Domination, Resistance, and Terror,* ed. Carolyn Nordstrom and JoAnn Martin (Berkeley: University of California Press, 1992), pp. 18-36. These remarks about disparity contributing to terror and counterterror are not intended to imply that inequity is not in itself a form of violence. It is. As Alexander Cockburn observes, "When the International Monetary Fund (IMF) imposes an austerity policy on a country in order to ensure that the country's debts to the developed world can continue to be repaid, they don't proceed to the armory, remove the guns, and fire on people. Sometimes the program has to be enforced by guardsmen and soldiers who do use guns to quell the protests of the people. But more often, the program simply removes more and more wealth from the people and ships it north to the United States, Europe, or Japan. . . . We are looking at huge terror." Cockburn's remarks are from "Terrorism and the Role of the Media: A Symposium," in *Violent Persuasions,* p. 234.

98. Quoted by Michael T. Klare and Peter Kornbluh, eds., *Low Intensity Warfare: Counterinsurgency, Proinsurgency, and Antiterrorism in the Eighties* (New York: Pantheon, 1988), p. 48.

99. Gray, cited by Nelson-Pallmeyer, *School of Assassins,* p. 94.

100. See McGowan, *Derailing Democracy,* pp. 38-39.

101. Lipschutz observes that "markets tend to provide greater and more remunerative opportunities to those who are already well-off. . . . With a global economy that reaches into more and more corners of the world, and players who regard questions of distribution as anathema, we are faced with dialectically linked integration *and* fragmentation." Lipschutz, "Beyond the Neoliberal Peace," *Social Justice:* 14.

102. Helena Norberg-Hodge, "The Pressure to Modernize and Globalize," in *Case Against the Global Economy,* pp. 33-46.

103. See Mokhiber and Weissman, *Corporate Predators,* pp. 116-17.

104. Mokhiber and Weissman, *Corporate Predators,* pp. 55-57, 65-67.

105. One may justifiably wonder why the State of Massachusetts is denied the ability to engage in selective purchasing while the government of the U.S. has had a free hand in imposing sanctions on Iraq for years, sanctions that have been binding on Massachusetts and every other state. Of course, the courts explain it as part of the federal prerogative to set foreign policy. The U.S. policy towards Iraq is a reminder that not all boycotts and sanctions are benign. It is possible to organize economic boycotts in a manner designed to influence the policies and practices of an adversary without undermining the health and well-being of the population. Such has not been the case with U.S. sanctions against Iraq. The punitive sanctions against the people of Iraq have been denounced by groups like the U.S. Catholic Bishops (1998) and by editorials in publications like *The New England Journal of Medicine* (1997). Already in 1995, the United Nations' Food and Agriculture Organization announced, "More than one million Iraqis have died — 567,000 of them children — as a direct consequence of economic sanctions. . . ." Quoted by McGowan, *Derailing Democracy,* p. 180.

106. Martin Khor, as paraphrased by Jerry Mander, "Facing the Rising Tide," in *Case Against the Global Economy,* p. 18.

107. Keiji Nakazawa, *Barefoot Gen,* trans. Project Gen (Tokyo: Project Gen, 1978); Art Spiegelman, *Maus,* 2 vols. (New York: Random House, 1993).

108. In writing of "doomsday cults," Robert Jay Lifton observes, "When we consider further the social and psychological roots of the collective urge to kill the world, we are likely to see more of ourselves in it and to begin to think of such groups as something of a dark underside or 'cultural underground' of our own society. We are also likely to discover that whatever renders our society more decent and more inclusive in its benefits is likely to undermine the totalistic impulse to destroy everything." Lifton, *Destroying the World to Save It,* p. 340.

109. The story of the Catholic Worker efforts in Tacoma is told by Howard-Brook and Gwyther, *Unveiling Empire,* pp. 266-67.

110. Henri Troyat, *Tolstoy,* trans. Nancy Amphoux (Garden City, N.Y.: Doubleday, 1967), p. 668.

111. Rexroth's observations appear in his introduction to Leo Tolstoy, *The Kingdom of God Is Within You,* trans. Leo Wiener (New York: Farrar, Straus and Giroux, 1961), p. vii.

112. Paul Johnson, *Intellectuals* (London: Weidenfeld and Nicolson, 1989), pp. 107-37.

113. Tolstoy's diary, quoted by Troyat, *Tolstoy,* pp. 260, 265.

114. Cited by David Edwards, *Burning All Illusions: A Guide to Personal and Political Freedom* (Boston: South End Press, 1996), p. 130. Edwards emphasizes that Tolstoy himself

came to the view that his despair was rooted in his success, a success that separated him from working people, from the earth, and from the ability to express love in a way that was not egocentric.

115. The incident is retold by Johnson, *Intellectuals*, pp. 124-25.

116. Richard F. Gustafson, *Leo Tolstoy, Resident and Stranger: A Study in Fiction and Theology* (Princeton: Princeton University Press, 1986), p. 130.

117. Gustafson, *Tolstoy, Resident and Stranger*, p. 410.

118. Tolstoy, *Kingdom of God*, p. 37.

119. The quotations from Tolstoy's diaries are cited by Gustafson, *Tolstoy, Resident and Stranger*, pp. 183-84.

120. Gustafson, *Tolstoy, Resident and Stranger*, pp. 100-101. Tolstoy was not always consistent in his panentheism. While he sometimes wrote with confidence of God as Love, as late as 1904, he wrote in his diary that "God is for me ever *Deus absconditus*, unknowable." These moments of viewing God as unknowable were likely influenced by what can fairly be called a "low christology" in Tolstoy's thought. While Tolstoy maintained that the teachings of Jesus were authoritative, he rejected attempts to understand Jesus as a unique incarnation or manifestation of God. See Leo Tolstoy, *The Gospel in Brief*, ed. F. A. Flowers III, trans. Isabel Hapgood (Lincoln: University of Nebraska Press, 1997), pp. 19-20. Tolstoy's denial of the divinity of Jesus was one of the factors precipitating his excommunication from the Russian Orthodox Church, but truth be told, his radical social and political views may have been greater factors still.

121. Tolstoy, *Kingdom of God*, p. 103.

122. See Gustafson, *Tolstoy, Resident and Stranger*, pp. 397-98.

123. Tolstoy, *Kingdom of God*, pp. 5-33.

124. Troyat, *Tolstoy*, pp. 559, 586-88.

125. On the assassination and Tolstoy's letter, see Otto Friedrich, *The End of the World: A History* (New York: Fromm International Publishing Corporation, 1986), pp. 225-27.

126. Troyat, *Tolstoy*, p. 539.

127. George Woodcock, "James Mavor, Peter Kropotkin, Lev Tolstoy and the Doukhobors," in *Spirit Wrestlers: Centennial Papers in Honour of Canada's Doukhobor Heritage*, ed. Koozma J. Tarasoff and Robert B. Klymasz (Hull, Quebec: Canadian Museum of Civilization, 1995), pp. 95-99. In the same volume, see also David C. Elkinton, "The Quaker-Doukhobor Connection," pp. 109-22. Elkinton traces the mediating role that was played by the American Friends Service Committee in the 1950s in negotiations between the Canadian government and a Doukhobor group known as the "Sons of Freedom." Ironically, the Sons of Freedom group had been charged with acts of terrorism. In order to express total opposition to the war-making capacity of Canada, the Sons of Freedom took to burning buildings and destroying power pylons and railroad tracks with dynamite. Few were convinced by the claims of the Sons of Freedom that they were still pacifists since they made sure that buildings were vacant before they burned them and they held prayer meetings to assure that no one would be injured when their dynamite exploded!

128. Tolstoy also perceived the unraveling of power in the response to the witness of Yevdokim Nikititch Drozhin, a young peasant who died in prison following his refusal of military conscription. In a postscript that he wrote for a biography of Drozhin, Tolstoy noted how the powerful were terrified: "And wonderful to relate, all this vast potential

mass of men, armed with all the powers of human authority, trembles and hides itself, feeling its fault, and shakes in its very being, and is ready at any minute to crumble and fly into powder, at the appearance of a single man like Drozhin who would not yield to human demands, but obeyed the law of God and was faithful to it." Leo Tolstoy, "Postscript to the 'Life and Death of Drozhin,'" trans. Vladimir Tchertkoff, in Tolstoy, *On Civil Disobedience and Non-Violence* (New York: New American Library, 1967), p. 265.

129. Nikolai Berdyaev, *Slavery and Freedom,* trans. R. M. French (New York: Charles Scribner's Sons, 1944), p. 135.

130. From his diary, Tolstoy is quoted by Gustafson, *Tolstoy, Resident and Stranger,* p. 12.

131. The story of Day's visit to Koinonia is told by William D. Miller, *Dorothy Day: A Biography* (New York: Harper & Row, 1982), pp. 440-42.

132. Maurin, quoted by Miller, *Dorothy Day,* p. 244.

133. Day's view that the Catholic Worker movement "just happened" is summarized in the introduction to Robert Ellsberg, ed., *By Little and By Little: The Selected Writings of Dorothy Day* (New York: Alfred A. Knopf, 1984), p. xxviii.

134. In his play, *Major Barbara,* George Bernard Shaw reviewed what he considered to be the high points and low points of the Salvation Army. In Act III, one of Shaw's characters observes, "It is cheap work converting starving men with a Bible in one hand and a slice of bread in the other." Such a characterization may not even fit the Salvation Army, but it is certainly foreign to the spirit of the Catholic Worker. Shaw, *Major Barbara* (Baltimore: Penguin Books, 1959), p. 142.

135. Peter Maurin, *The Green Revolution: Easy Essays on Catholic Radicalism,* 3rd ed. (Chicago: Chicago Catholic Worker, 1976), p. 4.

136. Bloy's position is summarized and his words are quoted by William D. Miller, *A Harsh and Dreadful Love: Dorothy Day and the Catholic Worker Movement* (Garden City, N.Y.: Image Books, 1974), p. 45.

137. The reaction against Catholic Worker pacifism is reviewed by Jim Forest, "Dorothy Day: A Radical Simplicity," in *Cloud of Witnesses,* ed. Jim Wallis and Joyce Hollyday (Maryknoll, N.Y.: Orbis Books and Washington, D.C.: Sojourners, 1991), pp. 9-14. A convert from early association with communism to Roman Catholicism, Dorothy Day became a fairly "conservative" Catholic. She regularly prayed the rosary, she disliked many of the liturgical changes introduced by Vatican II, and she held priests and ecclesiastical authorities in high esteem. Nonetheless, she was willing to take positions that contrasted with those of church leaders. She supported the 1949 strike of the gravediggers' union against the Archdiocese of New York, even as Cardinal Spellman denounced the strike as "an anti-American, anti-Christian evil." When ecclesiastical authorities became sharply critical of Worker pacifism, Day was undoubtedly sincere when she stated that she would shut down all Catholic Worker kitchens and hospitality houses if Spellman ordered it, but then she added with a twinkling in her eye, "There are many ways to handle a Cardinal." *The Dorothy Day Book: A Selection from her Writings and Readings,* ed. Margaret Quigley and Michael Garvey (Springfield, Ill.: Templegate Publishers, 1982), p. 3.

138. Cited by Miller, *Harsh and Dreadful Love,* p. 199. The biblical text is Luke 9:54-55, relying on a variant reading found in some ancient manuscripts.

139. Quoted by Ellsberg, ed., *By Little and By Little,* p. 311.

140. The leaflet is quoted by one of the participants, Ammon Hennacy, *The Book of Ammon* (Salt Lake City: Hennacy, 1965), p. 287. Hennacy was one of a rich variety of colorful characters who have been members of Catholic Worker communities. Some have detected egocentrism in Hennacy's references to himself as "a one-man revolution." But if his style was less communitarian than that of others in the Workers movement, he certainly offered helpful perspectives on Christian anarchism and lively accounts of his numerous sojourns in jail.

141. Day's comment appears in her article on Cuba, "A Revolution near Our Shores," in Ellsberg, ed. *By Little and By Little*, p. 304.

142. Cited in *Voices from the Catholic Worker,* compiled and edited by Rosalie Riegle Troester (Philadelphia: Temple University Press, 1993), p. 183.

143. *The Dorothy Day Book,* pp. 41-42.

144. A brief overview of the history is provided by John Webster in his introduction to Desmond Tutu, *Crying in the Wilderness: The Struggle for Justice in South Africa,* ed. John Webster (Grand Rapids: Eerdmans, 1982), pp. 13-23.

145. The testimony is summarized by Nancy Scheper-Hughes, "Undoing: Social Suffering and the Politics of Remorse in the New South Africa," *Social Justice: A Journal of Crime, Conflict, and World Order* 25, no. 4 (Winter 1998): 131.

146. Desmond Tutu, *No Future Without Forgiveness* (New York: Doubleday, 1999), p. 130.

147. "Necklacing" was a brutal form of murder in which a tire doused with petrol was placed around the neck of a suspected informer and then set afire. At one point, Tutu threatened to leave South Africa for good if necklace murders continued. He understood his defense of the lives of informers and police and protesters alike to be part of the larger struggle for freedom in South Africa. When he intervened to negotiate a peaceful end to one standoff during the Defiance Campaign in Cape Town in 1989, Tutu told a group of protesters, "The prize for which we are striving is freedom, is freedom for all of us, freedom for those people standing outside [the police], freedom for them!" Desmond Tutu, *The Rainbow People of God: The Making of a Peaceful Revolution,* ed. John Allen (New York: Doubleday, 1994), p. 181. Freedom and justice were the goals for people of all colors. When Tutu traveled to Mobutu's Zaire, he was bold in denouncing a "postcolonial" situation in which only the complexion of the oppressors had changed. Tutu, *Rainbow People,* pp. 157-59. See also John Parratt, *Reinventing Christianity: African Theology Today* (Grand Rapids: Eerdmans and Trenton, N.J.: Africa World Press, Inc., 1995), pp. 138-39. Indeed, after the end of apartheid in South Africa, Tutu was also fully prepared to criticize the new ANC government. When some within the ANC opposed the release of the report of the Truth and Reconciliation Commission, Tutu was outraged. "I didn't struggle in order to remove one set who thought they were tin gods and replace them with others who are tempted to think they are. . . . The price of freedom is eternal vigilance, and there is no way in which you can assume that yesterday's oppressed will not become tomorrow's oppressors." Quoted by Mark Gevisser, "Two South Africas," *The Nation* 267, no. 17 (November 23, 1998): 7.

148. The resonance between Tutu's vision and King's "beloved community" is noted by Sheila Briggs in *The Kairos Covenant: Standing with South African Christians,* ed. Wil-

lis H. Logan (New York: Friendship Press and Oak Park, Ill.: Meyer-Stone Books, 1988), p. 91.

149. Tutu, "Deeper into God," in *Cloud of Witnesses,* p. 77.

150. Antjie Krog, *Country of My Skull: Guilt, Sorrow, and the Limits of Forgiveness in the New South Africa* (New York: Times Books, 1999), p. 206.

151. Green, quoted by Krog, *Country of My Skull,* p. 207.

152. See Parratt, *Reinventing Christianity,* pp. 155-56. It was appalling to Tutu that churches in South Africa could be divided along color lines and that some "white churches" could be proponents of apartheid. He wrote, ". . . a Church that does not suffer, cannot be the Church of Jesus Christ. I do not mean we should be masochists. Suffering will seek us out. It is part of the divine economy of salvation." Desmond Tutu, *Hope and Suffering: Sermons and Speeches,* ed. John Webster (Grand Rapids: Eerdmans, 1984), p. 187.

153. The struggles over these two options and the development of a "third way" are summarized by Tutu, *No Future Without Forgiveness,* pp. 15-32.

154. The abandonment of the punitive spirit was further reflected in some of the policies of the new government. Among his first acts in office, President Nelson Mandela supported an end to capital punishment and an end to the South African nuclear weapons program. Among the honored guests at Mandela's inauguration was his former prison guard. But the approach of the Truth and Reconciliation Commission has not been without its critics. Wole Soyinka, Nobel laureate for literature, has maintained that the effort to present "Africa's humanity" as superior to the "soulessness" of the history of apartheid and European colonialism has created an unrealistic standard by which Africans are expected to abide. Soyinka contrasts the way in which the U.S. has denied entry to suspected terrorists and "terrorist money" (e.g., Libyan contributions to the Nation of Islam) with the manner in which the new South African government has granted free access to the country for many of its opponents, including David Duke, a former member of the Ku Klux Klan who visited South Africa in order to support the racist proponents of a "Free Boer Republic." Soyinka argues that truth is a necessary condition for reconciliation, but not a sufficient condition. He makes the case for reparations and restitution and against "impunity." In fact, the government of South Africa has adopted a plan for reparations to the victims who are survivors of apartheid, but with the money coming from the government and not from those accused of wrongdoing. Financially, the program is inadequate. But what amount of reparations would *not* be inadequate? If some of Soyinka's arguments seem to make concessions to juridical definitions of "justice" and governmental understandings of "security," he nonetheless presents a cogent perspective on "forgiveness" that is at variance with the position held by Tutu and others. Some of the differences in perspectives may be attributable to the fact that Soyinka makes no claim to offering a specifically "Christian" position. Indeed, he questions the effort to have public policies too heavily influenced by specific understandings of spirituality. In some senses, Tutu is beholden to a different point of departure with a different outcome. Wole Soyinka, *The Burden of Memory, the Muse of Forgiveness* (New York: Oxford University Press, 1999).

155. These stories are full of anguish. Truth and reconciliation are not easy and the stories are not pretty, but some are well told in the article by Scheper-Hughes, "Undoing," *Social Justice:* 114-42.

359

156. Ngewu, quoted by Krog, *Country of My Skull*, p. 142.

157. See Tutu, *Hope and Suffering*, pp. 162-63, 166. In commenting on the last apartheid ruler of South Africa, F. W. de Klerk, Tutu said, "You see, we can't go to heaven alone. If I arrive there, God will ask me: 'Where is De Klerk? His path crossed yours.' And he also — God will ask him: 'Where is Tutu?'" Quoted by Krog, *Country of My Skull*, p. 210.

158. Clarence Jordan, *The Substance of Faith and Other Cotton Patch Sermons*, ed. Dallas Lee (New York: Association Press, 1972), p. 29.

159. The point here does not have to do with the historicity of the specific story about the killings of the children in and around Bethlehem, a story that has not been confirmed nor refuted definitively. The accounts of Josephus certainly indicate that Herod was capable of such brutality. After Herod had three of his own children executed, Augustus is said to have remarked of the Jewish leader, "I would rather be Herod's pig than his son." Peter Richardson, *Herod: King of the Jews and Friend of the Romans* (Columbia: University of South Carolina Press, 1996), pp. 297-98.

160. The "illegality" of the resurrection and the irony of the governing authorities remembering Jesus' promises better than the disciples are both noted by Bill Wylie Kellermann, *Seasons of Faith and Conscience: Kairos, Confession, Liturgy* (Maryknoll, N.Y.: Orbis Books, 1991), pp. 184-88.

161. On the significance of the Jewish refusal to separate body and spirit, see N. T. Wright, "The Transforming Reality of the Bodily Resurrection," in Marcus J. Borg and N. T. Wright, *The Meaning of Jesus: Two Visions* (San Francisco: HarperSanFrancisco, 1999), pp. 111-27.

162. Vernard Eller, ed., *Thy Kingdom Come: A Blumhardt Reader* (Grand Rapids: Eerdmans, 1980), pp. 127-28.

Bibliography

This bibliography does not offer an exhaustive list of resources, but only a list of those books and articles cited in this study. The resources have been arranged under topical headings that correspond to the chapter divisions of "newspaper," history, and biblical reflection. While each source is listed only once, it is clear that several of the titles could have been placed under more than one of the headings. Finally, it should be noted that reference to a particular work does not necessarily mean that I agree with that author's perspectives nor (I am sure many of these authors would want me to add) that he or she agrees with mine.

Terror and Counterterror in Contemporary Society

Abanes, Richard. *American Militias: Rebellion, Racism, and Religion.* Downers Grove, Ill.: InterVarsity Press, 1996.

Ahmad, Eqbal. "Just What in the World Makes Terrorism Tick?" In *Terrorism: Opposing Viewpoints.* Edited by Bonnie Szumski. Opposing Viewpoints Series. St. Paul, Minn.: Green Haven Press, 1986.

Anderson, Sean, and Stephen Sloan. *Historical Dictionary of Terrorism.* Historical Dictionaries of Religions, Philosophies, and Movements, no. 4. Metuchen, N.J.: Scarecrow Press, 1995.

Anderson, Terry. "Painful Lessons: Hostage-taking and US Foreign Policy." *Harvard International Review* 20, no. 4 (Fall 1998): 62-65.

Archer, Dane, and Rosemary Gartner. *Violence and Crime in Cross-National Perspective.* New Haven: Yale University Press, 1984.

Arendt, Hannah. *Eichmann in Jerusalem: A Report on the Banality of Evil.* Rev. ed. New York: Penguin Books, 1977.

"Assembly-Line Justice." *Le Monde*. September 3, 1998. Translated and reprinted in *World Press Review* 45, no. 11 (November 1998): 12.

Atkins, Stephen E. *Terrorism: A Reference Handbook*. Contemporary World Issues Series. Santa Barbara, Calif.: ABC-CLIO, Inc., 1992.

Beinin, Joel. "Palestine and Israel: Perils of a Neoliberal, Repressive *Pax Americana*." *Social Justice: A Journal of Crime, Conflict, and World Order* 25, no. 4 (Winter 1998): 20-39.

Berger, Maurice. "Visual Terrorism." In *Violent Persuasions: The Politics and Imagery of Terrorism*. Edited by David J. Brown and Robert Merrill. Seattle: Bay Press, 1993.

Binkley, Timothy. "Consensus and the Justification of Force." In *Reason and Violence: Philosophical Investigations*. Edited by Sherman M. Stanage. Totowa, N.J.: Littlefield, Adams & Co., 1974.

Blum, William. "A Brief History of U.S. Interventions: 1945 to the Present." *Z Magazine* 12, no. 6 (June 1999): 25-30.

———. *Killing Hope: U.S. Military and CIA Interventions since World War II*. Monroe, Maine: Common Courage Press, 1995.

Callahan, David. *Unwinnable Wars: American Power and Ethnic Conflict*. A Twentieth Century Fund Book. New York: Hill and Wang, 1997.

Camus, Albert. *The Rebel: An Essay on Man in Revolt*. Translated by Anthony Bower. New York: Vintage Books, 1956.

Chalk, Frank, and Kurt Jonassohn. *The History and Sociology of Genocide: Analyses and Case Studies*. Published in cooperation with the Montreal Institute of Genocide Studies. New Haven: Yale University Press, 1990.

Chomsky, Noam. *The Culture of Terrorism*. Boston: South End Press, 1988.

———. *Necessary Illusions: Thought Control in Democratic Societies*. Boston: South End Press, 1989.

Clark, Ramsey. "Beyond Terrorism." In *Violent Persuasions: The Politics and Imagery of Terrorism*. Edited by David J. Brown and Robert Merrill. Seattle: Bay Press, 1993.

Clutterbuck, Richard. *Protest and the Urban Guerrilla*. New York: Abelard-Schuman, 1974.

Cockburn, Alexander, and Jeffrey St. Clair. *Whiteout: The CIA, Drugs, and the Press*. New York: Verso, 1999.

Coughlin, Dan. "Haitian Lament: Killing Me Softly." *The Nation* 268, no. 8 (March 1, 1999): 20-23.

Crighton, Elizabeth H. "Beyond Neoliberalism: Peacemaking in Northern Ireland." *Social Justice: A Journal of Crime, Conflict, and World Order* 25, no. 4 (Winter 1998): 75-89.

Dillon, Martin, and Denis Lehane. *Political Murder in Northern Ireland*. Baltimore: Penguin Books, 1973.

Bibliography

Dobson, Christopher, and Robert Payne. *The Terrorists: Their Weapons, Leaders, and Tactics*. New York: Facts on File, 1982.

Dower, John W. *War Without Mercy: Race and Power in the Pacific War*. New York: Pantheon, 1986.

Drekmeier, Charles. "Knowledge as Virtue, Knowledge as Power." In Nevitt Sanford, Craig Comstock, and associates. *Sanctions for Evil: Sources of Social Destructiveness*. The Jossey-Bass Behavioral Science Series. San Francisco: Jossey-Bass, 1971.

Fanon, Frantz. *The Wretched of the Earth*. Translated by Constance Farrington. New York: Grove Press, 1963.

Fisk, Robert. "Talks with Osama bin Laden." *The Nation* 267, no. 8 (September 21, 1998): 24-27.

Flanders, Laura. "Chemical Arms Scam." *The Nation* 265, no. 21 (December 22, 1997): 5.

Fujimori, Alberto. "Terror, Society, and Law: Peru's Struggle Against Violent Insurgency." *Harvard International Review* 20, no. 4 (Fall 1998): 58-61.

Gevisser, Mark. "Two South Africas." *The Nation* 267, no. 17 (November 23, 1998): 7.

Gibson, James William. *Warrior Dreams: Violence and Manhood in Post-Vietnam America*. New York: Hill and Wang, 1994.

Gioseffi, Daniela, ed. *On Prejudice: A Global Perspective*. New York: Anchor Books, 1993.

Goldson, Annie, and others. "Terrorism and the Role of the Media: A Symposium." In *Violent Persuasions: The Politics and Imagery of Terrorism*. Edited by David J. Brown and Robert Merrill. Seattle: Bay Press, 1993.

Gourevitch, Philip. *We Wish to Inform You That Tomorrow We Will Be Killed with Our Families: Stories from Rwanda*. New York: Farrar, Straus and Giroux, 1998.

Guelke, Adrian. "Wars of Fear: Coming to Grips with Terrorism." *Harvard International Review* 20, no. 4 (Fall 1998): 44-47.

Hartung, William D. "Gold-Plating the Pentagon." *The Nation* 268, no. 8 (March 1, 1999): 6-7.

Herken, Gregg. *Counsels of War*. New York: Alfred A. Knopf, 1985.

Herman, Edward S. *Beyond Hypocrisy: Decoding the News in an Age of Propaganda*. Boston: South End Press, 1992.

————. *The Real Terror Network: Terrorism in Fact and Propaganda*. Boston: South End Press, 1982.

————. "Terrorism: Misrepresentations of Power." In *Violent Persuasions: The Politics and Imagery of Terrorism*. Edited by David J. Brown and Robert Merrill. Seattle: Bay Press, 1993.

Herman, Edward S., and Gerry O'Sullivan. *The Terrorism Industry: The Experts and Institutions That Shape Our View of Terror*. New York: Pantheon, 1990.

Hitchens, Christopher. "The Clinton-Douglas Debates." *The Nation* 267, no. 16 (November 16, 1998): 8.

Hoffman, Bruce. *Inside Terrorism*. New York: Columbia University Press, 1998.

Hoffman, David. *The Oklahoma City Bombing and the Politics of Terror*. Venice, Calif.: Feral House, 1998.

Holler, Elizabeth. "Grief Upon the Earth: Faces of War in the Former Yugoslavia." *Sojourners* 22, no. 3 (April 1993): 20-25.

Human Rights Watch. *Slaughter Among Neighbors: The Political Origins of Communal Violence*. New Haven: Yale University Press and Human Rights Watch Books, 1995.

Jacoby, Susan. *Wild Justice: The Evolution of Revenge*. New York: Harper & Row, 1983.

Janis, Irving L. *Groupthink: Psychological Studies of Policy Decisions and Fiascoes*. 2nd ed. Boston: Houghton Mifflin, 1983.

———. "Groupthink Among Policy Makers." In Nevitt Sanford, Craig Comstock, and associates. *Sanctions for Evil: Sources of Social Destructiveness*. The Jossey-Bass Behavioral Science Series. San Francisco: Jossey-Bass, 1971.

Klare, Michael T., and Peter Kornbluh, eds. *Low Intensity Warfare: Counterinsurgency, Proinsurgency, and Antiterrorism in the Eighties*. New York: Pantheon, 1988.

Kornbluh, Peter. "Chile Declassified." *The Nation* 269, no. 5 (August 9/16, 1999): 21-24.

Kramer, Michael. "Why Guns Share the Blame." *Time* (May 8, 1995): 48.

Krog, Antjie. *Country of My Skull: Guilt, Sorrow, and the Limits of Forgiveness in the New South Africa*. New York: Times Books, 1999.

Laqueur, Walter. *The Age of Terrorism*. Boston: Little, Brown, 1987.

———. *The New Terrorism: Fanaticism and the Arms of Mass Destruction*. New York: Oxford University Press, 1999.

———. *Terrorism: A Study of National and International Political Violence*. Boston: Little, Brown and Company, 1977.

———. "Terror's New Face: The Radicalization and Escalation of Modern Terrorism." *Harvard International Review* 20, no. 4 (Fall 1998): 48-51.

Lens, Sidney. *The Day Before Doomsday: An Anatomy of the Nuclear Arms Race*. Boston: Beacon Press, 1978.

Lifton, Robert Jay. *Destroying the World to Save It: Aum Shinrikyō, Apocalyptic Violence, and the New Global Terrorism*. New York: Metropolitan Books, 1999.

Lipschutz, Ronnie D. "Beyond the Neoliberal Peace: From Conflict Resolution to Social Reconciliation." *Social Justice: A Journal of Crime, Conflict, and World Order* 25, no. 4 (Winter 1998): 5-19.

Lorenz, Konrad. *On Aggression*. Translated by Marjorie Kerr Wilson. New York: Harcourt Brace & Company, 1974.

MacDonald, Eileen. *Shoot the Women First.* New York: Random House, 1991.

Mackenzie, Angus. *Secrets: The CIA's War at Home.* Berkeley: University of California Press, 1997.

Mander, Jerry. "Facing the Rising Tide." In *The Case Against the Global Economy: And for a Turn Toward the Local.* Edited by Jerry Mander and Edward Goldsmith. San Francisco: Sierra Club Books, 1996.

McGowan, David. *Derailing Democracy: The America the Media Don't Want You to See.* Monroe, Maine: Common Courage Press, 2000.

McKnight, Gerald. *The Terrorist Mind.* Indianapolis, Ind.: Bobbs-Merrill, 1974.

Merleau-Ponty, Maurice. *Humanism and Terror: An Essay on the Communist Problem.* Translated by John O'Neill. Boston: Beacon Press, 1969.

Merrill, Robert. "Simulations and Terrors of Our Time." In *Violent Persuasions: The Politics and Imagery of Terrorism.* Edited by David J. Brown and Robert Merrill. Seattle: Bay Press, 1993.

Merrill, Robert, and others. "Case Studies in Terrorism: A Symposium." In *Violent Persuasions: The Politics and Imagery of Terrorism.* Edited by David J. Brown and Robert Merrill. Seattle: Bay Press, 1993.

Milgram, Stanley. *Obedience to Authority: An Experimental View.* New York: Harper Torchbooks, 1975.

Mokhiber, Russell, and Robert Weissman. *Corporate Predators: The Hunt for Mega-Profits and the Attack on Democracy.* Monroe, Maine: Common Courage Press, 1999.

Morgan, Robin. *The Demon Lover: On the Sexuality of Terrorism.* New York: W. W. Norton, 1989.

Nadle, Marlene. "The Myth and Milosevic." *The Nation* 268, no. 14 (April 19, 1999): 5-6.

Nelson-Pallmeyer, Jack. *School of Assassins: The Case for Closing the School of the Americas and for Fundamentally Changing U.S. Foreign Policy.* Maryknoll, N.Y.: Orbis Books, 1997.

—————. "Wise as Serpents, Gentle as Doves? The Challenge to Nonviolence in the Face of Pleas for Intervention." *Sojourners* 22, no. 3 (April 1993): 10-13.

Netanyahu, Benjamin. *Fighting Terrorism: How Democracies Can Defeat Domestic and International Terrorists.* New York: Farrar, Straus and Giroux, 1995.

Norberg-Hodge, Helena. "The Pressure to Modernize and Globalize." In *The Case Against the Global Economy: And for a Turn Toward the Local.* Edited by Jerry Mander and Edward Goldsmith. San Francisco: Sierra Club Books, 1996.

Nordstrom, Carolyn. "The Backyard Front." In *The Paths to Domination, Resistance, and Terror.* Edited by Carolyn Nordstrom and JoAnn Martin. Berkeley: University of California Press, 1992.

Oliverio, Annamarie. *The State of Terror.* SUNY Series in Deviance and Social Control. Albany: State University of New York Press, 1998.

Opton, Edward M., Jr. "It Never Happened and Besides They Deserved It." In Nevitt Sanford, Craig Comstock, and associates. *Sanctions for Evil: Sources of Social Destructiveness.* The Jossey-Bass Behavioral Science Series. San Francisco: Jossey-Bass, 1971.

Parenti, Michael. *Against Empire.* San Francisco: City Lights Books, 1995.

Payne, Richard J. *The Clash with Distant Cultures: Values, Interests, and Force in American Foreign Policy.* Albany: State University of New York Press, 1995.

Perdue, William D. *Terrorism and the State: A Critique of Domination Through Fear.* New York: Praeger, 1989.

Pinkney, Alphonso. *The American Way of Violence.* New York: Vintage Books, 1972.

Rapoport, David C. "Fear and Trembling: Terrorism in Three Religious Traditions." *American Political Science Review* 78, no. 3 (September 1984).

Said, Edward W. *Covering Islam: How the Media and the Experts Determine How We See the Rest of the World.* New York: Pantheon, 1981.

Sanford, Nevitt H., and Craig Comstock. "Sanctions for Evil." In Nevitt H. Sanford, Craig Comstock, and associates. *Sanctions for Evil: Sources of Social Destructiveness.* The Jossey-Bass Behavioral Science Series. San Francisco: Jossey-Bass, 1971.

Scheper-Hughes, Nancy. "Undoing: Social Suffering and the Politics of Remorse in the New South Africa." *Social Justice: A Journal of Crime, Conflict and World Order* 25, no. 4 (Winter 1998): 114-42.

Schmid, Alex P., Albert J. Jongman, and others. *Political Terrorism: A New Guide to Actors, Authors, Concepts, Data Bases, Theories, and Literature.* New Brunswick, N.J.: Transaction Books, 1988.

Shorr, Ira. "Nuclear Insecurity." *In These Times* 23, no. 16 (July 11, 1999): 10-12.

Sivan, Emmanuel. *Radical Islam: Medieval Theology and Modern Politics.* Enlarged ed. New Haven: Yale University Press, 1990.

Sluka, Jeffrey A. "The Anthropology of Conflict." In *The Paths to Domination, Resistance, and Terror.* Edited by Carolyn Nordstrom and JoAnn Martin. Berkeley: University of California Press, 1992.

Sorel, Georges. *Reflections on Violence.* Translated by T. E. Hulme. New York: Peter Smith, 1941.

Soyinka, Wole. *The Burden of Memory, the Muse of Forgiveness.* New York: Oxford University Press, 1999.

Sterling, Claire. *The Terror Network.* New York: Holt, Rinehart, Winston/Reader's Digest, 1981.

Stern, Kenneth S. *A Force upon the Plain: The American Militia Movement and the Politics of Hate.* New York: Simon & Schuster, 1996.

Suárez-Orozco, Marcelo. "A Grammar of Terror: Psychocultural Responses to State Terrorism in Dirty War and Post-Dirty War Argentina." In *The Paths to Domi-*

nation, Resistance, and Terror. Edited by Carolyn Nordstrom and JoAnn Martin. Berkeley: University of California Press, 1992.

Taussig, Michael. *Shamanism, Colonialism, and the Wild Man: A Study of Terror and Healing.* Chicago: University of Chicago Press, 1987.

Van Atta, Dale. "Carbombs and Cameras: The Need for Responsible Media Coverage of Terrorism." *Harvard International Review* 20, no. 4 (Fall 1998): 66-70.

"Victory for the Real IRA." *The Economist.* August 29, 1998. Reprinted in *World Press Review* 45, no. 11 (November 1998): 12.

Walter, Eugene Victor. *Terror and Resistance: A Study of Political Violence with Case Studies of Some Primitive African Communities.* New York: Oxford University Press, 1972.

Wilkinson, Paul. *Terrorism and the Liberal State.* New York: New York University Press, 1986.

Wilmer, Franke. "The Social Construction of Conflict and Reconciliation in the Former Yugoslavia." *Social Justice: A Journal of Crime, Conflict, and World Order* 25, no. 4 (Winter 1998): 90-113.

Wright, Kevin. *The Great American Crime Myth.* New York: Praeger, 1987.

Wright, Robin. "Address the Causes, Not Just the Effects." In *Terrorism: Opposing Viewpoints.* Edited by Bonnie Szumski. Opposing Viewpoints Series. St. Paul, Minn.: Green Haven Press, 1986.

————. *Sacred Rage: The Crusade of Modern Islam.* New York: Linden Press/Simon & Schuster, 1985.

Wright, Scott. *Promised Land: Death and Life in El Salvador.* Maryknoll, N.Y.: Orbis Books, 1994.

Zinn, Howard. "Their Atrocities — and Ours." *The Progressive* 63, no. 7 (July 1999): 20-21.

Zuckerman, Edward. *The Day after World War III.* New York: Avon Books, 1984.

History

The Antinomian Controversy, 1636-1638: A Documentary History. 2nd ed. Edited by David D. Hall. Durham, N.C.: Duke University Press, 1990.

Arnold, Eberhard. *The Early Christians after the Death of the Apostles.* Translated by the Hutterian Society of Brothers. Rifton, N.Y.: Plough Publishing House, 1972.

Avrich, Paul. *Anarchist Portraits.* Princeton, N.J.: Princeton University Press, 1988.

————, ed. *The Anarchists in the Russian Revolution.* Documents of Revolution. Ithaca, N.Y.: Cornell University Press, 1973.

Bacon, Margaret Hope. "By Moral Force Alone: The Antislavery Women and Non-resistance." In *The Abolitionist Sisterhood: Women's Political Culture in Antebel-*

lum America. Edited by Jean Fagan Yellin and John C. Van Horne. Ithaca, N.Y.: Cornell University Press, 1994.

Bainton, Roland H. *Christian Attitudes Toward War and Peace: A Historical Survey and Critical Re-evaluation.* Nashville: Abingdon Press, 1960.

Bakunin, Michael. *God and the State.* New York: Dover Publications, 1970.

Barber, Malcolm. *The Trial of the Templars.* Cambridge: Cambridge University Press, 1980.

Barnet, Richard J. *Roots of War.* Baltimore: Penguin Books, 1972.

Bernier, Olivier. *Words of Fire, Deeds of Blood: The Mob, the Monarchy, and the French Revolution.* New York: Anchor Books, 1990.

Billington, James H. *Fire in the Minds of Men: Origins of the Revolutionary Faith.* New York: Basic Books, 1980.

————. *The Icon and the Axe: An Interpretive History of Russian Culture.* New York: Vintage Books, 1970.

Blanc, Olivier. *Last Letters: Prisons and Prisoners of the French Revolution, 1793-1794.* Translated by Alan Sheridan. New York: Farrar, Straus and Giroux, 1989.

Blockson, Charles. *The Underground Railroad.* New York: Prentice-Hall, 1987.

Bloom, Harold. *The American Religion: The Emergence of the Post-Christian Nation.* New York: Simon & Schuster, 1993.

Bookchin, Murray. *The Third Revolution: Popular Movements in the Revolutionary Era.* Vol. 1. New York: Cassell, 1996.

Brandt, Nat. *The Town That Started the Civil War.* Syracuse, N.Y.: Syracuse University Press, 1990.

Brinton, Crane. *The Anatomy of Revolution.* New York: Vintage Books, 1956.

Brinton, Crane, John B. Christopher, and Robert Lee Wolff. *A History of Civilization.* Vol. 2: *1715 to the Present.* 2nd ed. Englewood Cliffs, N.J.: Prentice-Hall, 1960.

Brock, Peter. *Freedom from War: Nonsectarian Pacifism, 1814-1914.* Toronto: University of Toronto Press, 1991.

Brodie, Fawn N. "Born out of Violence." In *Violence in America: A Historical and Contemporary Reader.* Edited by Thomas Rose. New York: Vintage Books, 1970.

Brooke, Rosalind and Christopher. *Popular Religion in the Middle Ages: Western Europe 1000-1300.* London: Thames and Hudson, 1984.

Brouwer, Steve, Paul Gifford, and Susan D. Rose. *Exporting the American Gospel: Global Christian Fundamentalism.* New York: Routledge, 1996.

Brown, Peter. *Society and the Holy in Late Antiquity.* Berkeley: University of California Press, 1989.

Buber, Martin. *Paths in Utopia.* The Martin Buber Library. Syracuse, N.Y.: Syracuse University Press, 1996.

Burns, Thomas S. *Barbarians Within the Gates of Rome: A Study of Roman Military*

Policy and the Barbarians, ca. 375-425 A.D. Bloomington: Indiana University Press, 1994.

Canavan, Francis, S.J. "Edmund Burke." In *History of Political Philosophy.* Edited by Leo Strauss and Leo Cropsey. Rand McNally Political Science Series. Chicago: Rand McNally, 1972.

Carey, John, ed. *Eyewitness to History.* New York: Avon Books, 1987.

Chamberlin, E. R. *Antichrist and the Millennium.* New York: Saturday Review Press/ E. P. Dutton, 1975.

Cheetham, Nicolas. *Keepers of the Keys: A History of the Popes from St. Peter to John Paul II.* New York: Charles Scribner's Sons, 1982.

Clastres, Pierre. *Society Against the State: Essays in Political Anthropology.* Translated by Robert Hurley and Abe Stein. New York: Zone Books, 1989.

Clebsch, William A. *Christianity in European History.* New York: Oxford University Press, 1979.

Cochrane, Arthur C. *The Church's Confession under Hitler.* Philadelphia: Westminster Press, 1962.

Cohn, Norman. *The Pursuit of the Millennium: Revolutionary Millenarians and Mystical Anarchists of the Middle Ages.* Rev. ed. New York: Oxford University Press, 1970.

Cordingly, David. *Under the Black Flag: The Romance and the Reality of Life Among the Pirates.* New York: Harcourt Brace & Company, 1995.

Cross, Whitney R. *The Burned-Over District: The Social and Intellectual History of Enthusiastic Religion in Western New York, 1800-1850.* Ithaca, N.Y.: Cornell University Press, 1950.

Deane, Herbert A. *The Political and Social Ideas of St. Augustine.* New York: Columbia University Press, 1963.

de Grazia, Sebastian. *Machiavelli in Hell.* Princeton, N.J.: Princeton University Press, 1989.

Delumeau, Jean. *Sin and Fear: The Emergence of a Western Guilt Culture, 13th-18th Centuries.* Translated by Eric Nicholson. New York: St. Martin's Press, 1990.

Diacon, Todd A. *Millenarian Vision, Capitalist Reality: Brazil's Contestado Rebellion, 1912-1916.* Durham, N.C.: Duke University Press, 1991.

Donat, Alexander. "The Holocaust Kingdom." In *Out of the Whirlwind: A Reader of Holocaust Literature.* Edited by Albert H. Friedlander. New York: Schocken Books, 1976.

Dörries, Hermann. *Constantine the Great.* Translated by Roland H. Bainton. New York: Harper & Row, 1972.

Douglass, Frederick. *Narrative of the Life of Frederick Douglass, an American Slave.* Edited by Houston A. Baker, Jr. New York: Penguin Books, 1982.

Durnbaugh, Donald F. *The Believers' Church: The History and Character of Radical Protestantism.* New York: Macmillan, 1968.

Edwards, Jonathan. "The Latter-Day Glory Is Probably to Begin in America." In *God's New Israel: Religious Interpretations of American Destiny*. Edited by Conrad Cherry. Englewood Cliffs, N.J.: Prentice-Hall, 1971.

Ehrenreich, Barbara. *Blood Rites: Origins and History of the Passions of War*. New York: Henry Holt and Company, 1997.

Elkinton, David C. "The Quaker-Doukhobor Connection." In *Spirit Wrestlers: Centennial Papers in Honour of Canada's Doukhobor Heritage*. Edited by Koozma J. Tarasoff and Robert B. Klymasz. Hull, Quebec: Canadian Museum of Civilization, 1995.

Engels, Friedrich. *The Peasant War in Germany*. Translated by Moissaye J. Olgin. New York: International Publishers, 1966.

Erickson, Carolly. *The Medieval Vision: Essays in History and Perception*. New York: Oxford University Press, 1976.

Ferguson, John. *War and Peace in the World's Religions*. New York: Oxford University Press, 1978.

Foucault, Michel. *Discipline and Punish: The Birth of the Prison*. Translated by Alan Sheridan. New York: Vintage Books, 1979.

Fox, Richard G. *Gandhian Utopia: Experiments with Culture*. Boston: Beacon Press, 1989.

Fox, Robin Lane. *Pagans and Christians*. New York: Alfred A. Knopf, 1987.

Franklin, John Hope. *From Slavery to Freedom: A History of Negro Americans*. 3rd ed. New York: Vintage Books, 1969.

Friedrich, Otto. *The End of the World: A History*. New York: Fromm International Publishing Corporation, 1986.

Fukuyama, Francis. *The End of History and the Last Man*. New York: Avon Books, 1993.

Gager, John G. *The Origins of Anti-Semitism: Attitudes Toward Judaism in Pagan and Christian Antiquity*. New York: Oxford University Press, 1985.

Gaustad, Edwin S. *Faith of Our Fathers: Religion and the New Nation*. New York: Harper & Row, 1987.

"The Good Old Days": The Holocaust as Seen by Its Perpetrators and Bystanders. Edited by Ernst Klee, Willi Dressen, and Volker Riess. Translated by Deborah Burnstone. New York: The Free Press, 1991.

Grant, Michael. *Constantine the Great: The Man and His Times*. New York: Charles Scribner's Sons, 1994.

Gratus, Jack. *The False Messiahs*. New York: Taplinger Publishing Company, 1976.

Hall, David D. *Worlds of Wonder, Days of Judgment: Popular Religious Belief in Early New England*. New York: Alfred A. Knopf, 1989.

Harrison, J. F. C. *The Second Coming: Popular Millenarianism, 1780-1850*. New Brunswick, N.J.: Rutgers University Press, 1979.

Hatch, Nathan O. *The Democratization of American Christianity.* New Haven: Yale University Press, 1989.

Hattersley, Roy. *Blood and Fire: William and Catherine Booth and Their Salvation Army.* New York: Doubleday, 1999.

Haven, Gilbert. "The War and the Millennium." In *Slavery Attacked: The Abolitionist Crusade.* Edited by John L. Thomas. Englewood Cliffs, N.J.: Prentice-Hall, 1965.

Hennacy, Ammon. *The Book of Ammon.* Salt Lake City: Hennacy, 1965.

Heresies of the High Middle Ages. Translated by Walter L. Wakefield and Austin P. Evans. Records of Western Civilization Series. New York: Columbia University Press, 1991.

Heyrman, Christine Leigh. *Southern Cross: The Beginnings of the Bible Belt.* New York: Alfred A. Knopf, 1997.

Hill, Christopher. *Antichrist in Seventeenth-Century England.* Rev. ed. New York: Verso, 1990.

———. *The English Bible and the Seventeenth-Century Revolution.* New York: Penguin Books, 1994.

———. *The World Turned Upside Down: Radical Ideas During the English Revolution.* New York: Penguin Books, 1975.

Hilton, Rodney. *Bond Men Made Free: Medieval Peasant Movements and the English Rising of 1381.* New York: Methuen, 1973.

Hitti, Philip K. *Islam and the West: A Historical Cultural Survey.* Princeton, N.J.: D. Van Nostrand, 1962.

Hobsbawm, E. J. *Nations and Nationalism since 1780: Programme, Myth, Reality.* 2nd ed. Cambridge: Cambridge University Press, 1992.

———. *Primitive Rebels: Studies in Archaic Forms of Social Movement in the 19th and 20th Centuries.* New York: W. W. Norton, 1965.

Hochschild, Adam. *King Leopold's Ghost: A Story of Greed, Terror, and Heroism in Colonial Africa.* Boston: Houghton Mifflin, 1998.

Jefferson, Thomas. *Notes on the State of Virginia.* Edited by William Peden. New York: W. W. Norton, 1972.

Johnson, Paul. *A History of the Jews.* New York: Harper & Row, Publishers, 1988.

———. *Intellectuals.* London: Weidenfeld and Nicolson, 1989.

Joll, James. *The Anarchists.* New York: Grossett & Dunlap, 1966.

Jones, A. H. M. *Constantine and the Conversion of Europe.* Rev. ed. New York: Collier Books, 1962.

Kantorowicz, Ernst H. *The King's Two Bodies: A Study in Medieval Political Theology.* Princeton, N.J.: Princeton University Press, 1957.

Katz, Solomon. *The Decline of Rome and the Rise of Medieval Europe.* Ithaca, N.Y.: Cornell University Press, 1955.

Kelly, J. N. D. *The Oxford Dictionary of Popes*. New York: Oxford University Press, 1988.

Klaw, Spencer. *Without Sin: The Life and Death of the Oneida Community*. New York: Allen Lane/The Penguin Press, 1993.

Lambert, Malcolm. *Medieval Heresy: Popular Movements from the Gregorian Reform to the Reformation*. 2nd ed. Oxford: Blackwell, 1992.

Langmuir, Gavin I. *History, Religion, and Antisemitism*. London: I. B. Tauris, 1990.

Lapham, Lewis H., with Peter T. Struck, eds. *History: The End of the World*. New York: History Book Club, 1997.

Laqueur, Walter. *The Terrible Secret: Suppression of the Truth about Hitler's "Final Solution."* New York: Henry Holt and Company, 1998.

Lasch, Christopher. *The True and Only Heaven: Progress and Its Critics*. New York: W. W. Norton, 1991.

Levin, Bernard. *A World Elsewhere*. London: Sceptre, 1995.

Lewis, R. W. B. *The American Adam: Innocence, Tragedy, and Tradition in the Nineteenth Century*. Chicago: University of Chicago Press, 1955.

Lunn, Eugene. *Prophet of Community: The Romantic Socialism of Gustav Landauer*. Berkeley: University of California Press, 1973.

Luther, Martin. "An Open Letter on the Harsh Book Against the Peasants." Translated by Charles M. Jacobs. In *Luther: Selected Political Writings*. Edited by J. M. Porter. Philadelphia: Fortress Press, 1974.

Lynd, Staughton, ed. *Nonviolence in America: A Documentary History*. Indianapolis: Bobbs-Merrill, 1966.

Maalouf, Amin. *The Crusades Through Arab Eyes*. Translated by Jon Rothschild. New York: Schocken Books, 1984.

Machiavelli, Niccolò. *The Prince*. Translated by Thomas G. Bergin. New York: Appleton-Century-Crofts, 1947.

MacMullen, Ramsay. *Christianizing the Roman Empire (A.D. 100-400)*. New Haven: Yale University Press, 1984.

Manschreck, Clyde L. *A History of Christianity in the World: From Persecution to Uncertainty*. Englewood Cliffs, N.J.: Prentice-Hall, 1974.

Marsden, George M. *Fundamentalism and American Culture: The Shaping of Twentieth Century Evangelicalism, 1870-1925*. New York: Oxford University Press, 1980.

Marty, Martin, and R. Scott Appleby, eds. *Fundamentalisms and the State*. Chicago: University of Chicago Press, 1993.

Mattingly, Harold. *Christianity in the Roman Empire*. New York: W. W. Norton, 1967.

Mayer, Henry. *All on Fire: William Lloyd Garrison and the Abolition of Slavery*. New York: St. Martin's Press, 1998.

McFeely, William S. *Frederick Douglass*. New York: W. W. Norton, 1991.

McGinn, Bernard. *Antichrist: Two Thousand Years of the Human Fascination with Evil.* New York: HarperCollins, 1994.

————. *The Calabrian Abbot: Joachim of Fiore in the History of Western Thought.* New York: Macmillan, 1985.

McLynn, Neil B. *Ambrose of Milan: Church and Court in a Christian Capital.* Berkeley: University of California Press, 1994.

Miller, Perry. *Errand into the Wilderness.* New York: Harper & Row, 1964.

————. *The New England Mind: The Seventeenth Century.* Cambridge, Mass.: Harvard University Press, 1982.

Miller, William D. *Dorothy Day: A Biography.* New York: Harper & Row, 1982.

————. *A Harsh and Dreadful Love: Dorothy Day and the Catholic Worker Movement.* Garden City, N.Y.: Image Books, 1974.

Morais, Vamberto. *A Short History of Anti-Semitism.* New York: W. W. Norton, 1976.

Mullett, Michael A. *Radical Religious Movements in Early Modern Europe.* Early Modern Europe Today Series. London: George Allen & Unwin, 1980.

Narrative of Sojourner Truth: A Bondswoman of Olden Time, with a History of Her Labors and Correspondence, Drawn from Her "Book of Life." The Schomburg Library of Nineteenth-Century Black Women Writers. New York: Oxford University Press, 1991.

Newhall, Richard A. *The Crusades.* Rev. ed. Berkshire Studies in European History. New York: Holt, Rinehart and Winston, 1963.

Niebuhr, H. Richard. *The Kingdom of God in America.* New York: Harper & Row, 1959.

Nirenberg, David. *Communities of Violence: Persecution of Minorities in the Middle Ages.* Princeton, N.J.: Princeton University Press, 1996.

Noll, Mark A. *One Nation under God? Christian Faith and Political Action in America.* New York: Harper & Row, 1988.

Norwood, Frederick A. *Strangers and Exiles: A History of Religious Refugees.* 2 vols. New York: Abingdon Press, 1969.

Oldenbourg, Zoé. *The Crusades.* Translated by Anne Carter. London: Weidenfeld & Nicolson, 1998.

Paine, Thomas. *Common Sense and Other Political Writings.* Edited by Nelson F. Adkins. Indianapolis, Ind.: Bobbs-Merrill, 1953.

Painter, Nell Irvin. "Difference, Slavery, and Memory: Sojourner Truth in Feminist Abolitionism." In *The Abolitionist Sisterhood: Women's Political Culture in Antebellum America.* Edited by Jean Fagan Yellin and John C. Van Horne. Ithaca, N.Y.: Cornell University Press, 1994.

Parrinder, Geoffrey, ed. *World Religions: From Ancient History to the Present.* New York: Facts on File Publications, 1971.

Partner, Peter. *God of Battles: Holy Wars of Christianity and Islam.* Princeton, N.J.: Princeton University Press, 1997.

Perry, Lewis. *Radical Abolitionism: Anarchy and the Government of God in Antislavery Thought.* Knoxville: University of Tennessee Press, 1995.

Porter, Bruce D. *War and the Rise of the State: The Military Foundations of Modern Politics.* New York: The Free Press, 1994.

The Power of the People: Active Nonviolence in the United States. Edited by Robert Cooney and Helen Michalowski from an original text by Marty Jezer. Philadelphia: New Society Publishers, 1987.

Raymond of St. Giles, Count of Toulouse. "The Capture of Jerusalem by the Crusaders." Translated by D. C. Monro. In *The Medieval World: 300-1300.* Edited by Norman F. Cantor. New York: Macmillan, 1963.

Riley-Smith, Jonathan. *The Crusades: A Short History.* New Haven: Yale University Press, 1987.

Robert the Monk. "Speech of Pope Urban II at the Council of Clermont, 1095." Translated by D. C. Monro. In *The Medieval World: 300-1300.* Edited by Norman F. Cantor. New York: Macmillan, 1963.

Rohrlich, Ruby. "The Shakers: Gender Equality in Hierarchy." In *Women in Search of Utopia: Mavericks and Mythmakers.* Edited by Ruby Rohrlich and Elaine Hoffman Baruch. New York: Schocken Books, 1984.

Rose, Paul Lawrence. *Revolutionary Antisemitism in Germany from Kant to Wagner.* Princeton, N.J.: Princeton University Press, 1990.

Rosenthal, Erwin I. J. *Judaism and Islam.* London: Thomas Yoseloff, 1961.

Ruether, Rosemary Radford. *The Radical Kingdom: The Western Experience of Messianic Hope.* New York: Harper & Row, 1970.

Runciman, Steven. *The First Crusade.* Cambridge: Cambridge University Press, 1992.

———. *The Medieval Manichee: A Study of the Christian Dualist Heresy.* Cambridge: Cambridge University Press, 1982.

Sagan, Eli. *At the Dawn of Tyranny: The Origins of Individualism, Political Oppression, and the State.* New York: Alfred A. Knopf, 1985.

Said, Edward. *Culture and Imperialism.* London: Chatto & Windus, 1993.

Sale, Kirkpatrick. *Rebels Against the Future: The Luddites and Their War on the Industrial Revolution, Lessons for the Computer Age.* New York: Addison-Wesley, 1995.

Schama, Simon. *Citizens: A Chronicle of the French Revolution.* New York: Alfred A. Knopf, 1989.

Schelling, Thomas C. "Some Questions on Civilian Defence." In *Civilian Resistance as a National Defence: Non-violent Action Against Aggression.* Edited by Adam Roberts. Baltimore: Penguin Books, 1969.

Schmookler, Andrew Bard. *The Parable of the Tribes: The Problem of Power in Social Evolution.* Boston: Houghton Mifflin, 1984.

Schwartz, Hillel. *Century's End: A Cultural History of the Fin de Siècle from the 990s through the 1990s.* New York: Doubleday, 1990.

Stampp, Kenneth M. *The Peculiar Institution: Slavery in the Ante-Bellum South.* New York: Vintage Books, 1956.

Starkey, Marion L. *The Devil in Massachusetts: A Modern Enquiry into the Salem Witch Trials.* Garden City, N.Y.: Doubleday, 1969.

Stewart, James Brewer. *Holy Warriors: The Abolitionists and American Slavery.* New York: Hill and Wang, 1976.

Stock, Catherine McNicol. *Rural Radicals: Righteous Rage in the American Grain.* Ithaca, N.Y.: Cornell University Press, 1996.

Strayer, Joseph R. *Western Europe in the Middle Ages: A Short History.* New York: Appleton-Century-Crofts, 1955.

Strout, Cushing. *The New Heavens and New Earth: Political Religion in America.* New York: Harper & Row, 1975.

Talmon, J. L. *Political Messianism: The Romantic Phase.* London: Secker & Warburg, 1960.

They Fought Back: The Story of Jewish Resistance in Nazi Europe. Edited and translated by Yuri Suht. New York: Schocken Books, 1975.

Thomas, Paul. *Karl Marx and the Anarchists.* London: Routledge & Kegan Paul, 1980.

Thompson, Damian. *The End of Time: Faith and Fear in the Shadow of the Millennium.* Hanover, N.H.: University Press of New England, 1996.

Thompson, E. P. *The Making of the English Working Class.* New York: Vintage Books, 1966.

Troeltsch, Ernst. *The Social Teaching of the Christian Churches.* 2 vols. Translated by Olive Wyon. New York: Harper & Row, 1960.

Troyat, Henri. *Tolstoy.* Translated by Nancy Amphoux. Garden City, N.Y.: Doubleday, 1967.

Tuveson, Ernest Lee. *Millennium and Utopia: A Study in the Background of the Idea of Progress.* New York: Harper & Row, 1964.

van Creveld, Martin. *The Rise and Decline of the State.* Cambridge: Cambridge University Press, 1999.

———. *The Transformation of War.* New York: The Free Press, 1991.

Venet, Wendy Hamand. "'Cry Aloud and Spare Not': Northern Antislavery Women and John Brown's Raid." In *His Soul Goes Marching On: Responses to John Brown and the Harpers Ferry Raid.* Edited by Paul Finkelman. Charlottesville: University Press of Virginia, 1995.

von Grunebaum, Gustave E. *Medieval Islam: A Study in Cultural Orientation.* 2nd ed. Chicago: University of Chicago Press, 1961.

Wagar, W. Warren. *Good Tidings: The Belief in Progress from Darwin to Marcuse.* Bloomington: Indiana University Press, 1972.

Walker, Williston, Richard A. Norris, David W. Lotz, and Robert T. Handy. *A History of the Christian Church.* 4th ed. New York: Charles Scribner's Sons, 1985.

Wallenstein, Peter. "Incendiaries All: Southern Politics and the Harpers Ferry Raid." In *His Soul Goes Marching On: Responses to John Brown and the Harpers Ferry Raid.* Edited by Paul Finkelman. Charlottesville: University Press of Virginia, 1995.

Walzer, Michael. *Just and Unjust Wars: A Moral Argument with Historical Illustrations.* New York: Basic Books, 1977.

―――. *The Revolution of the Saints: A Study in the Origins of Radical Politics.* Cambridge, Mass.: Harvard University Press, 1965.

Weber, Eugen. *Apocalypses: Prophesies, Cults, and Millennial Beliefs Through the Ages.* Cambridge, Mass.: Harvard University Press, 1999.

Weber, Max. *The Protestant Ethic and the Spirit of Capitalism.* Translated by Talcott Parsons. New York: Charles Scribner's Sons, 1958.

Wilken, Robert L. *The Christians as the Romans Saw Them.* New Haven: Yale University Press, 1984.

Wills, Garry. *Under God: Religion and American Politics.* New York: Simon & Schuster, 1990.

Woodcock, George. *Anarchism: A History of Libertarian Ideas and Movements.* 2nd ed. New York: Penguin Books, 1986.

―――. "James Mavor, Peter Kropotkin, Lev Tolstoy, and the Doukhobors." In *Spirit Wrestlers: Centennial Papers in Honour of Canada's Doukhobor Heritage.* Edited by Koozma J. Tarasoff and Robert B. Klymasz. Hull, Quebec: Canadian Museum of Civilization, 1995.

Zinn, Howard. *A People's History of the United States.* New York: HarperPerennial, 1990.

Biblical Studies and Theological Reflection

Anderson, Robert A. *Signs and Wonders: A Commentary on the Book of Daniel.* International Theological Commentary. Grand Rapids: Eerdmans and Edinburgh: The Handsel Press Ltd., 1984.

Aukerman, Dale. *Reckoning with Apocalypse: Terminal Politics and Christian Hope.* New York: Crossroad, 1993.

Augustine. *Concerning the City of God Against the Pagans.* Translated by Henry Bettenson. New York: Penguin Books, 1984.

―――. *The Confessions of Saint Augustine.* Translated by Edward B. Pusey. The Modern Library. New York: Random House, 1949.

Bailie, Gil. *Violence Unveiled: Humanity at the Crossroads*. New York: Crossroad, 1995.

Balz, Horst, and Günther Wanke. *"phobeo, phobos."* In *Theological Dictionary of the New Testament*. Vol. IX. Edited by Gerhard Friedrich. Translated by Geoffrey W. Bromiley. Grand Rapids: Eerdmans, 1974.

Barth, Karl. *Action in Waiting for the Kingdom of God*. Translated by the Hutterian Society of Brothers. Rifton, N.Y.: Plough Publishing House, 1979.

———. *Church Dogmatics*. Vol. 4, pt. 3, second half: *The Doctrine of Reconciliation*. Translated by G. W. Bromiley. Edinburgh: T. & T. Clark, 1962.

———. *The Humanity of God*. Translated by John Newton Thomas and Thomas Wieser. Richmond, Va.: John Knox Press, 1960.

Baumann, A. *"charadh."* In *Theological Dictionary of the Old Testament*. Vol. V. Edited by G. Johannes Botterweck and Helmer Ringgren. Translated by David E. Green. Grand Rapids: Eerdmans, 1986.

———. *"chyl."* In *Theological Dictionary of the Old Testament*. Vol. IV. Edited by G. Johannes Botterweck and Helmer Ringgren. Translated by David E. Green. Grand Rapids: Eerdmans, 1980.

Behm, Johannes. *"anamnesis."* In *Theological Dictionary of the New Testament*. Vol. I. Edited by Gerhard Kittel. Translated by Geoffrey W. Bromiley. Grand Rapids: Eerdmans, 1964.

Berdyaev, Nikolai. *Slavery and Freedom*. Translated by R. M. French. New York: Charles Scribner's Sons, 1944.

Berkhof, Hendrik. *Christ and the Powers*. Translated by John H. Yoder. Scottdale, Pa.: Herald Press, 1977.

Berrigan, Daniel. *Ezekiel: Vision in the Dust*. Art by Tom Lewis-Borbely. Maryknoll, N.Y.: Orbis Books, 1997.

———. *Jeremiah: The World, the Wound of God*. Minneapolis: Fortress Press, 1999.

———. *Minor Prophets, Major Themes*. Marion, S.D.: Fortkamp Publishing/Rose Hill Books, 1995.

———. *The Nightmare of God*. Photo etchings by Tom Lewis. Portland, Ore.: Sunburst Press, 1983.

Bloch, Ernst. *Man on His Own*. Translated by E. B. Ashton. New York: Herder and Herder, 1971.

Boehme, Jacob. *The Way to Christ*. Translated by Peter Erb. The Classics of Western Spirituality. New York: Paulist Press, 1978.

Braaten, Carl E. *Christ and Counter-Christ: Apocalyptic Themes in Theology and Culture*. Philadelphia: Fortress Press, 1972.

Brandon, S. G. F. *Jesus and the Zealots: A Study of the Political Factor in Primitive Christianity*. New York: Charles Scribner's Sons, 1967.

Bright, John. *Jeremiah*. Anchor Bible, no. 21. Garden City, N.Y.: Doubleday, 1965.

Brown, Dale. *The Christian Revolutionary*. Grand Rapids: Eerdmans, 1971.

Brown, Francis, S. R. Driver, and Charles A. Briggs. *A Hebrew and English Lexicon of the Old Testament.* Oxford: Clarendon Press, 1972.

Brown, Robert McAfee. *Religion and Violence: A Primer for White Americans.* Philadelphia: Westminster Press, 1973.

Brueggemann, Walter. *The Prophetic Imagination.* Philadelphia: Fortress Press, 1978.

————. *A Social Reading of the Old Testament: Prophetic Approaches to Israel's Communal Life.* Edited by Patrick D. Miller. Minneapolis: Fortress Press, 1994.

————. *Theology of the Old Testament: Testimony, Dispute, Advocacy.* Minneapolis: Fortress Press, 1997.

Caird, G. B. *The Language and Imagery of the Bible.* Philadelphia: Westminster Press, 1980.

————. *The Revelation of Saint John.* Black's New Testament Commentaries. Peabody, Mass.: Hendrickson Publishers, 1966.

Cairns, Ian. *Word and Presence: A Commentary on the Book of Deuteronomy.* International Theological Commentary. Grand Rapids: Eerdmans and Edinburgh: The Handsel Press, 1992.

Calvin, John. *Institutes of the Christian Religion.* Edited by John T. McNeill. Translated by Ford Lewis Battles. The Library of Christian Classics. Vol. XX. Philadelphia: Westminster Press, 1960.

Camara, Dom Helder. *Spiral of Violence.* Translated by Della Couling. Denville, N.J.: Dimension Books, 1971.

Campbell, Will D., and James Y. Holloway. *Up to Our Steeples in Politics.* New York: Paulist Press, 1970.

Childs, Brevard S. *The Book of Exodus: A Critical Theological Commentary.* The Old Testament Library. Philadelphia: Westminster Press, 1974.

Cohn, Norman. *Cosmos, Chaos, and the World to Come: The Ancient Roots of Apocalyptic Faith.* New Haven: Yale University Press, 1993.

Comblin, José. *The Church and the National Security State.* Maryknoll, N.Y.: Orbis Books, 1979.

Cone, James H. *The Spirituals and the Blues: An Interpretation.* Maryknoll, N.Y.: Orbis Books, 1992.

Cullmann, Oscar. *The State in the New Testament.* New York: Charles Scribner's Sons, 1956.

The Dead Sea Scrolls: A New Translation. Translated by Michael Wise, Martin Abegg, Jr., and Edward Cook. New York: HarperCollins, 1996.

de Vaux, Roland. *Ancient Israel.* Vol. I: *Social Institutions.* New York: McGraw-Hill, 1965.

The Dorothy Day Book: A Selection from Her Writings and Readings. Edited by Margaret Quigley and Michael Garvey. Springfield, Ill.: Templegate Publishers, 1982.

Edwards, George R. *Jesus and the Politics of Violence*. New York: Harper & Row, 1972.

Edwards, Jonathan. *The Nature of True Virtue*. Ann Arbor: University of Michigan Press, 1960.

Eichrodt, Walther. *Ezekiel: A Commentary*. Translated by Cosslett Quinn. The Old Testament Library. Philadelphia: Westminster Press, 1970.

Eller, Vernard, ed. *Thy Kingdom Come: A Blumhardt Reader*. Grand Rapids: Eerdmans, 1980.

Elliott, Neil. *Liberating Paul: The Justice of God and the Politics of the Apostle*. The Bible & Liberation Series. Maryknoll, N.Y.: Orbis Books, 1994.

Ellsberg, Robert, ed. *By Little and By Little: The Selected Writings of Dorothy Day*. New York: Alfred A. Knopf, 1984.

Ellul, Jacques. *Anarchy and Christianity*. Translated by Geoffrey W. Bromiley. Grand Rapids: Eerdmans, 1991.

―――. *Apocalypse: The Book of Revelation*. New York: Seabury Press, 1977.

―――. *Hope in Time of Abandonment*. Translated by C. Edward Hopkin. New York: Seabury Press, 1973.

―――. *Violence: Reflections from a Christian Perspective*. Translated by Cecelia Gaul Kings. New York: Seabury Press, 1969.

―――. *What I Believe*. Translated by Geoffrey W. Bromiley. Grand Rapids: Eerdmans and London: Marshall Morgan and Scott, 1989.

Fiorenza, Elisabeth Schüssler. *The Book of Revelation: Justice and Judgment*. Philadelphia: Fortress Press, 1985.

―――. *In Memory of Her: A Feminist Theological Reconstruction of Christian Origins*. New York: Crossroad, 1988.

Ford, J. Massyngberde. *Revelation*. Anchor Bible, no. 38. Garden City, N.Y.: Doubleday, 1975.

Forest, Jim. "Dorothy Day: A Radical Simplicity." In *Cloud of Witnesses*. Edited by Jim Wallis and Joyce Hollyday. Maryknoll, N.Y.: Orbis Books and Washington, D.C.: Sojourners, 1991.

"The Fourth Book of Ezra." Translated by B. M. Metzger. In *The Old Testament Pseudepigrapha*. Vol. 1. Edited by James H. Charlesworth. Garden City, N.Y.: Doubleday, 1983.

Frye, Northrop. *The Great Code: The Bible and Literature*. New York: Harcourt, Brace Jovanovich, 1982.

Fuhs, H. F. "*yare'*." In *Theological Dictionary of the Old Testament*. Vol. VI. Edited by G. Johannes Botterweck and Helmer Ringgren. Translated by David E. Green. Grand Rapids: Eerdmans, 1990.

Garrett, Susan R. "Revelation." In *The Women's Bible Commentary*. Edited by Carol A. Newsom and Sharon H. Ringe. Louisville: Westminster/John Knox Press, 1992.

Glenthøj, Jørgen. "Dietrich Bonhoeffer's Way Between Resistance and Submission." In *A Bonhoeffer Legacy: Essays in Understanding.* Edited by A. J. Klassen. Grand Rapids: Eerdmans, 1981.

Goldstein, Jonathan A. *I Maccabees.* Anchor Bible, no. 41. Garden City, N.Y.: Doubleday, 1976.

Gordis, Robert. *The Book of God and Man: A Study of Job.* Chicago: University of Chicago Press, 1965.

"The Gospel of Thomas." Translated by Thomas O. Lambdin. In *The Nag Hammadi Library.* 3rd ed. Edited by James M. Robinson. New York: Harper & Row, 1988.

"The Gospel of Truth." Translated by Harold W. Attridge and George W. MacRae. In *The Nag Hammadi Library.* 3rd ed. Edited by James M. Robinson. New York: Harper & Row, 1988.

Gottwald, Norman K. *All the Kingdoms of the Earth: Prophecy and International Relations in the Ancient Near East.* New York: Harper & Row, 1964.

———. *The Hebrew Bible: A Socio-Literary Introduction.* Philadelphia: Fortress Press, 1987.

———. *The Tribes of Yahweh: A Sociology of the Religion of Liberated Israel, 1250-1050 B.C.E.* Maryknoll, N.Y.: Orbis Books, 1979.

Greenberg, Moshe. "Job." In *The Literary Guide to the Bible.* Edited by Robert Alter and Frank Kermode. Cambridge, Mass.: Harvard University Press, 1990.

Gustafson, Richard F. *Leo Tolstoy, Resident and Stranger: A Study in Fiction and Theology.* Princeton, N.J.: Princeton University Press, 1986.

Hanson, Paul D. *The Dawn of Apocalyptic: The Historical and Sociological Roots of Jewish Apocalyptic Eschatology.* Rev. ed. Philadelphia: Fortress Press, 1979.

Hartshorne, Charles. *Omnipotence and Other Theological Mistakes.* Albany: State University of New York Press, 1984.

Hauerwas, Stanley. *Against the Nations: War and Survival in a Liberal Society.* New York: Winston Press, 1985.

Hauerwas, Stanley, and Jeff Powell. "Creation as Apocalyptic: A Homage to William Stringfellow." In *Radical Christian and Exemplary Lawyer: Honoring William Stringfellow.* Edited by Andrew W. McThenia, Jr. Grand Rapids: Eerdmans, 1995.

Hengel, Martin. *Judaism and Hellenism: Studies in Their Encounter in Palestine During the Early Hellenistic Period.* Translated by John Bowden. Philadelphia: Fortress Press, 1981.

Heschel, Abraham Joshua. *God in Search of Man: A Philosophy of Judaism.* Northvale, N.J.: Jason Aronson, Inc., 1987.

———. *The Prophets.* 2 vols. New York: Harper Torchbooks, 1975.

Hornus, Jean-Michel. *It Is Not Lawful for Me to Fight: Early Christian Attitudes Toward War, Violence, and the State.* Rev. ed. Translated by Alan Kreider and Oliver Coburn. Scottdale, Pa.: Herald Press, 1980.

Horsley, Richard A., and Neil Asher Silberman. *The Message and the Kingdom: How Jesus and Paul Ignited a Revolution and Transformed the Ancient World.* New York: Grossett/Putnam, 1997.

Horsley, Richard A., with John S. Hanson. *Bandits, Prophets, and Messiahs: Popular Movements at the Time of Jesus.* New Voices in Biblical Studies. New York: Harper & Row, 1985.

Howard-Brook, Wes, and Anthony Gwyther. *Unveiling Empire: Reading Revelation Then and Now.* The Bible and Liberation Series. Maryknoll, N.Y.: Orbis Books, 1999.

Hunsinger, George, ed. and trans. *Karl Barth and Radical Politics.* Philadelphia: Westminster Press, 1976.

Isaac, Jules. *Has Anti-Semitism Roots in Christianity?* New York: National Conference of Christians and Jews, 1961.

Jordan, Clarence. *The Substance of Faith and Other Cotton Patch Sermons.* Edited by Dallas Lee. New York: Association Press, 1972.

The Kairos Covenant: Standing with South African Christians. Edited by Willis H. Logan. New York: Friendship Press and Oak Park, Ill.: Meyer-Stone Books, 1988.

Kaufman, Donald D. *What Belongs to Caesar? A Discussion on the Christian's Response to Payment of War Taxes.* Scottdale, Pa.: Herald Press, 1969.

Kautsky, Karl. *Foundations of Christianity.* Translated by Henry F. Mins. New York: Russell & Russell, 1953.

Keel, Othmar. *The Symbolism of the Biblical World: Ancient Near Eastern Iconography and the Book of Psalms.* Translated by Timothy J. Hallett. New York: Seabury Press, 1978.

Kellermann, Bill Wylie. *Seasons of Faith and Conscience: Kairos, Confession, Liturgy.* Maryknoll, N.Y.: Orbis Books, 1991.

Kellermann, Bill Wylie, ed. *A Keeper of the Word: Selected Writings of William Stringfellow.* Grand Rapids: Eerdmans, 1994.

Kellermann, Diether. *"gur, ger."* In *Theological Dictionary of the Old Testament.* Vol. II. Rev. ed. Edited by G. Johannes Botterweck and Helmer Ringgren. Translated by John T. Willis. Grand Rapids: Eerdmans, 1977.

Kittel, Gerhard. *"eschatos."* In *Theological Dictionary of the New Testament.* Vol. II. Edited by Gerhard Kittel. Translated by Geoffrey W. Bromiley. Grand Rapids: Eerdmans, 1964.

Kuhn, Karl Georg. *"proselytos."* In *Theological Dictionary of the New Testament.* Vol. VI. Edited by Gerhard Friedrich. Translated by Geoffrey W. Bromiley. Grand Rapids: Eerdmans, 1968.

Küng, Hans. *Eternal Life? Life after Death as a Medical, Philosophical, and Theological Problem.* Translated by Edward Quinn. New York: Doubleday, 1985.

Laytner, Anton. *Arguing with God: A Jewish Tradition.* Northvale, N.J.: Jason Aronson, Inc., 1990.

Littell, Franklin H. *The Crucifixion of the Jews: The Failure of Christians to Understand the Jewish Experience.* New York: Harper & Row, 1975.

Malherbe, Abraham J. *Social Aspects of Early Christianity.* 2nd ed. Philadelphia: Fortress Press, 1983.

Martens, Elmer A. *Jeremiah.* Believers Church Bible Commentary. Scottdale, Pa.: Herald Press, 1986.

Mather, Increase. "Man Knows Not His Time." In *The Puritans: A Sourcebook of Their Writings.* Vol. I. Rev. ed. Edited by Perry Miller and Timothy H. Johnson. New York: Harper & Row, 1963.

Maurin, Peter. *The Green Revolution: Easy Essays on Catholic Radicalism.* 3rd ed. Chicago: Chicago Catholic Worker, 1976.

McFague, Sallie. *Models of God: Theology for an Ecological, Nuclear Age.* Philadelphia: Fortress Press, 1987.

McGinn, Bernard, ed. and trans. *Apocalyptic Spirituality.* The Classics of Western Spirituality. New York: Paulist Press, 1979.

Meeks, Wayne. *The Moral World of the First Christians.* Library of Early Christianity, no. 6. Philadelphia: Westminster Press, 1986.

————. *The Origins of Christian Morality: The First Two Centuries.* New Haven: Yale University Press, 1993.

Mendenhall, George E. *The Tenth Generation: The Origins of the Biblical Tradition.* Baltimore: Johns Hopkins Press, 1973.

Merton, Thomas. *Conjectures of a Guilty Bystander.* Garden City, N.Y.: Doubleday, 1968.

Metz, Johann Baptist. *Faith in History and Society: Toward a Practical Fundamental Theology.* Translated by David Smith. New York: Seabury Press, 1980.

Moltmann, Jürgen. *Theology of Hope: On the Ground and the Implications of a Christian Eschatology.* Translated by James W. Leitch. New York: Harper & Row, 1967.

Morris, Leon. *Apocalyptic.* Grand Rapids: Eerdmans, 1972.

Morrison, Clinton. *The Powers That Be: Earthly Rulers and Demonic Powers in Romans 13:1-7.* Studies in Biblical Theology, no. 29. Naperville, Ill.: Alec R. Allenson, 1960.

Mott, Stephen Charles. *A Christian Perspective on Political Thought.* New York: Oxford University Press, 1993.

Müller, H.-P. "*nabi.*" In *Theological Dictionary of the Old Testament.* Vol. IX. Edited by G. Johannes Botterweck, Helmer Ringgren, and Heinz-Josef Fabry. Translated by David E. Green. Grand Rapids: Eerdmans, 1998.

Musurillo, Herbert A. *The Fathers of the Primitive Church.* New York: New American Library, 1966.

Nanos, Mark. *The Mystery of Romans: The Jewish Context of Paul's Letter*. Minneapolis: Fortress Press, 1996.

Newsom, Carol A. "Job." In *The Women's Bible Commentary*. Edited by Carol A. Newsom and Sharon H. Ringe. Louisville: Westminster/John Knox Press, 1992.

Niditch, Susan. *Underdogs and Tricksters: A Prelude to Biblical Folklore*. New York: Harper & Row, 1987.

Otto, Rudolf. *The Idea of the Holy*. Translated by John W. Harvey. New York: Oxford University Press, 1958.

Pagels, Elaine. *The Gnostic Gospels*. New York: Vintage Books, 1981.

Palmer, Parker. *To Know As We Are Known: A Spirituality of Education*. New York: Harper & Row, 1983.

Parratt, John. *Reinventing Christianity: African Theology Today*. Grand Rapids: Eerdmans and Trenton, N.J.: Africa World Press, Inc., 1995.

Pelikan, Jaroslav. *The Christian Tradition: A History of the Development of Doctrine*. Vol. 3: *The Growth of Medieval Theology (600-1300)*. Chicago: University of Chicago Press, 1978.

———. *Jesus Through the Centuries: His Place in the History of Culture*. New Haven: Yale University Press, 1985.

Plöger, Otto. *Theocracy and Eschatology*. Translated by S. Rudman. Richmond, Va.: John Knox Press, 1968.

Pope, Marvin H. *Song of Songs*. Anchor Bible, vol. 7C. New York: Doubleday, 1977.

Porteous, Norman W. *Daniel: A Commentary*. The Old Testament Library. Philadelphia: Westminster Press, 1965.

Rauschenbusch, Walter. *Christianity and the Social Crisis*. Edited by Robert D. Cross. New York: Harper & Row, 1964.

Richardson, Peter. *Herod: King of the Jews and Friend of the Romans*. Columbia: University of South Carolina Press, 1996.

Risher, Dee Dee. "The Log in Our Eye: Is 'Islamic Fundamentalism' a Projection of Ourselves?" *The Other Side* 29, no. 3 (May-June 1993): 50-51.

Roper, Melinda. "'Do This in Remembrance of Me': Discipleship in the Face of Evil." *Sojourners* 19, no. 10 (December 1990): 17-18.

Ruether, Rosemary Radford. *Faith and Fratricide: The Theological Roots of Anti-Semitism*. Minneapolis: Seabury Press, 1974.

———. *Gaia and God: An Ecofeminist Theology of Earth Healing*. New York: HarperCollins, 1992.

Russell, D. S. *The Method and Message of Jewish Apocalyptic*. The Old Testament Library. Philadelphia: Westminster Press, 1964.

Russell, Jeffrey Burton. *The Devil: Perceptions of Evil from Antiquity to Primitive Christianity*. New York: New American Library, 1979.

Sanders, E. P. *Paul, the Law, and the Jewish People*. Minneapolis: Fortress Press, 1983.

Schmidt, Thomas E. *Hostility to Wealth in the Synoptic Gospels.* Journal for the Study of the New Testament Supplement Series 15. Sheffield, England: Sheffield Academic Press, 1987.

Scholem, Gershom. *The Messianic Idea in Judaism.* New York: Schocken Books, 1971.

Schwager, Raymund, S.J. *Must There Be Scapegoats? Violence and Redemption in the Bible.* Translated by Maria L. Assad. New York: Harper & Row, 1987.

Schweitzer, Albert. *The Quest of the Historical Jesus: A Critical Study of Its Progress from Reimarus to Wrede.* Translated by W. Montgomery. New York: Macmillan, 1968.

Schweizer, Eduard. *The Good News According to Matthew.* Translated by David E. Green. Atlanta: John Knox Press, 1975.

Sloan, Robert B., Jr. *The Favorable Year of the Lord: A Study of Jubilary Theology in the Gospel of Luke.* Austin: Schola Press, 1977.

Smith, Daniel L. *The Religion of the Landless: The Social Context of the Babylonian Exile.* Bloomington, Ind.: Meyer-Stone Books, 1989.

Soelle, Dorothee. *The Strength of the Weak: Toward a Christian Feminist Identity.* Translated by Robert and Rita Kimber. Philadelphia: Westminster Press, 1984.

Stendahl, Krister. *Paul Among Jews and Gentiles and Other Essays.* Philadelphia: Fortress Press, 1976.

Stringfellow, William. *Conscience and Obedience: The Politics of Romans 13 and Revelation 13 in Light of the Second Coming.* Waco, Tex.: Word Books, 1978.

——. *The Politics of Spirituality.* Philadelphia: Westminster Press, 1984.

Teilhard de Chardin, Pierre. *The Phenomenon of Man.* Translated by Bernard Wall. New York: Harper & Row, 1965.

Tipler, Frank J. *The Physics of Immortality: Modern Cosmology, God, and the Resurrection of the Dead.* New York: Doubleday, 1994.

Tolstoy, Leo. *The Gospel in Brief.* Edited by F. A. Flowers III. Translated by Isabel Hapgood. Lincoln: University of Nebraska Press, 1997.

——. *The Kingdom of God Is Within You.* Translated by Leo Wiener. New York: Farrar, Straus and Giroux, 1961.

——. "Postscript to the 'Life and Death of Drozhin.'" Translated by Vladimir Tchertkoff. In Leo Tolstoy. *On Civil Disobedience and Non-Violence.* New York: New American Library, 1967.

Trocmé, André. *Jesus and the Nonviolent Revolution.* Translated by Michael H. Shank and Marlin E. Miller. Scottdale, Pa.: Herald Press, 1973.

Tutu, Desmond. *Crying in the Wilderness: The Struggle for Justice in South Africa.* Edited by John Webster. Grand Rapids: Eerdmans, 1982.

——. "Deeper into God." In *Cloud of Witnesses.* Edited by Jim Wallis and Joyce Hollyday. Maryknoll, N.Y.: Orbis Books and Washington, D.C.: Sojourners, 1991.

————. *Hope and Suffering: Sermons and Speeches.* Edited by John Webster. Grand Rapids: Eerdmans, 1984.

————. *No Future Without Forgiveness.* New York: Doubleday, 1999.

————. *The Rainbow People of God: The Making of a Peaceful Revolution.* Edited by John Allen. New York: Doubleday, 1994.

VanderKam, James C. "The Dead Sea Scrolls and Christianity." In *Understanding the Dead Sea Scrolls: A Reader from the Biblical Archaeology Review.* Edited by Hershel Shanks. New York: Random House, 1992.

Van Houten, Christiana. *The Alien in Israelite Law.* Journal for the Study of the Old Testament Supplement Series 107. Sheffield, England: Sheffield Academic Press, 1991.

Vawter, Bruce, and Leslie J. Hoppe. *A New Heart: A Commentary on the Book of Ezekiel.* International Theological Commentary. Grand Rapids: Eerdmans and Edinburgh: The Handsel Press Ltd., 1991.

Villa-Vincencio, Charles, ed. *Theology & Violence: The South African Debate.* Grand Rapids: Eerdmans, 1988.

Voices from the Catholic Worker. Compiled and edited by Rosalie Riegle Troester. Philadelphia: Temple University Press, 1993.

von Rad, Gerhard. *The Message of the Prophets.* Translated by D. M. G. Stalker. New York: Harper & Row, 1967.

Ward, Benedicta, ed. and trans. *The Desert Christian: The Sayings of the Desert Fathers.* New York: Macmillan, 1975.

Weil, Simone. *Waiting for God.* Translated by Emma Craufurd. New York: Harper & Row, 1973.

Wengst, Klaus. *Pax Romana and the Peace of Jesus Christ.* Translated by John Bowden. Philadelphia: Fortress Press, 1987.

Wiesel, Elie. *Five Biblical Portraits.* Notre Dame: University of Notre Dame Press, 1981.

Wink, Walter. *The Powers.* Vol. 1: *Naming the Powers: The Language of Power in the New Testament.* Philadelphia: Fortress Press, 1984.

————. *The Powers.* Vol. 2: *Unmasking the Powers: The Invisible Forces That Determine Human Existence.* Philadelphia: Fortress Press, 1986.

————. *The Powers.* Vol. 3: *Engaging the Powers: Discernment and Resistance in a World of Domination.* Minneapolis: Fortress Press, 1992.

Wright, N. T. *Christian Origins and the Question of God.* Vol. 1: *The New Testament and the People of God.* Minneapolis: Fortress Press, 1992.

————. "The Transforming Reality of the Bodily Resurrection." In Marcus J. Borg and N. T. Wright. *The Meaning of Jesus: Two Visions.* San Francisco: HarperSanFrancisco, 1999.

Yoder, John Howard. *The Original Revolution: Essays on Christian Pacifism.* Scottdale, Pa.: Herald Press, 1971.

————. *The Politics of Jesus.* Grand Rapids: Eerdmans, 1972.

Zelizer, Gerald L. "Churches Give Hell a Makeover." *USA Today* (February 21, 2000): 15A.

Zobel, Hans-Jürgen. "*'emah.*" In *Theological Dictionary of the Old Testament.* Vol. 1. Rev. ed. Edited by G. Johannes Botterweck and Helmer Ringgren. Translated by John T. Willis. Grand Rapids: Eerdmans, 1977.

Other Sources

Alterman, Eric. "Speaking Truth to Power." *The Nation* 266, no. 9 (March 16, 1998): 5-6.

Ansbro, John J. *Martin Luther King, Jr.: The Making of a Mind.* Maryknoll, N.Y.: Orbis Books, 1982.

Balmer, Randall. *Mine Eyes Have Seen the Glory: A Journey into the Evangelical Subculture in America.* New York: Oxford University Press, 1989.

Baudrillard, Jean. *Looking Back on the End of the World.* New York: Semiotext(e), 1989.

Berger, Peter, and Thomas Luckmann. *The Social Construction of Reality.* Garden City, N.Y.: Doubleday, 1967.

Berry, Wendell. *Sex, Economy, Freedom, and Community: Eight Essays.* New York: Pantheon, 1993.

Campbell, Will. *Brother to a Dragonfly.* New York: Seabury Press, 1977.

Camus, Albert. *The Just Assassins.* In *Caligula and Three Other Plays.* Translated by Stuart Gilbert. New York: Vintage Books, 1958.

Coles, Robert. *The Spiritual Life of Children.* Boston: Houghton Mifflin, 1990.

Covington, Dennis. *Salvation on Sand Mountain: Snake Handling and Redemption in Southern Appalachia.* New York: Penguin Books, 1995.

Du Bois, W. E. B. *The Selected Writings of W. E. B. Du Bois.* Edited by Walter Wilson. New York: New American Library, 1970.

Edwards, David. *Burning All Illusions: A Guide to Personal and Political Freedom.* Boston: South End Press, 1996.

Eliade, Mircea. *Cosmos and History: The Myth of the Eternal Return.* Translated by Willard R. Trask. New York: Harper & Row, Publishers, 1959.

Ellul, Jacques. *Autopsy of Revolution.* Translated by Patricia Wolf. New York: Alfred A. Knopf, 1971.

————. *Propaganda: The Formation of Men's Attitudes.* Translated by Konrad Kellen and Jean Lerner. New York: Vintage Books, 1973.

————. *The Technological Society.* Translated by John Wilkinson. New York: Vintage Books, 1964.

Festinger, Leon, Henry W. Riecken, and Stanley Schachter. *When Prophecy Fails: A*

Social and Psychological Study of a Modern Group That Predicted the Destruction of the World. New York: Harper Torchbooks, 1964.

Foucault, Michel. *Power/Knowledge: Selected Interviews and Other Writings, 1972-1977.* Edited by Colin Gordon. New York: Pantheon, 1980.

Gandhi, Mohandas K. *An Autobiography: The Story of My Experiments with Truth.* Translated by Mahadev Desai. Boston: Beacon Press, 1957.

Gray, Francine du Plessix. *Adam & Eve and the City: Selected Nonfiction.* New York: Simon & Schuster, 1987.

Herman, Judith Lewis, M.D. *Trauma and Recovery.* New York: Basic Books, 1992.

Hitchens, Christopher. "The Divine One." *The Nation* 267, no. 4 (July 27/August 3, 1998): 8.

Kuhn, Thomas S. *The Structure of Scientific Revolutions.* 2nd ed. Chicago: University of Chicago Press, 1970.

Kundera, Milan. *The Book of Laughter and Forgetting.* Translated by Michael Henry Heim. New York: Penguin Books, 1981.

Lewis, Bernard. *The Political Language of Islam.* Chicago: University of Chicago Press, 1991.

Mencken, H. L. *Prejudices: A Selection.* Edited by James T. Farrell. New York: Vintage Books, 1958.

Mythologies of the World: A Concise Encyclopedia. Edited by Rhoda A. Hendricks and Max S. Shapiro. Garden City, N.Y.: Doubleday, 1979.

Nakazawa, Keiji. *Barefoot Gen.* Translated by Project Gen. Tokyo: Project Gen, 1978.

Occhiogrosso, Peter. *Through the Labyrinth: Stories of the Search for Spiritual Transformation in Everyday Life.* New York: Viking, 1991.

Pilger, John. *Distant Voices.* New York: Vintage Books, 1994.

Plato: The Collected Dialogues. Edited by Edith Hamilton and Huntington Cairns. Bollingen Series LXXI. New York: Pantheon, 1961.

Quinby, Lee. *Anti-Apocalypse: Exercises in Genealogical Criticism.* Minneapolis: University of Minnesota Press, 1984.

Schwarz-Bart, Andre. *The Last of the Just.* Translated by Stephen Becker. New York: Atheneum, 1960.

Seuss, Dr. *The Butter Battle Book.* New York: Random House, 1984.

Sharp, Gene. *The Politics of Nonviolent Action.* 3 vols. Boston: Porter Sargent Publishers, 1973.

Shaw, George Bernard. *Major Barbara.* Baltimore: Penguin Books, 1959.

Sontag, Susan. *Illness as Metaphor.* New York: Farrar, Straus and Giroux, 1988.

Spiegelman, Art. *Maus.* 2 vols. New York: Random House, 1993.

Strozier, Charles B. *Apocalypse: On the Psychology of Fundamentalism in America.* Boston: Beacon Press, 1994.

Suzuki, D. T. "General Characteristics of Buddhism." In *Readings in Eastern Reli-*

gious Thought. Vol. 2: *Buddhism.* Edited by Allie M. Frazier. Philadelphia: Westminster Press, 1969.

Twain, Mark. *The Adventures of Huckleberry Finn.* New York: Washington Square Press, 1950.

Vargas Llosa, Mario. *The War of the End of the World.* Translated by Helen R. Lane. New York: Viking Penguin, 1997.

Washington, James M., ed. *A Testament of Hope: The Essential Writings and Speeches of Martin Luther King, Jr.* New York: HarperCollins, 1991.

Wiesel, Elie. *Night.* Translated by Stella Rodway. In *Night/Dawn/Day.* Northvale, N.J.: Jason Aronson, Inc., 1985.

Wiesel, Elie, and Philippe de Saint-Cheron. *Evil and Exile.* Translated by Jon Rothschild. Notre Dame: University of Notre Dame Press, 1990.

Wolin, Richard. *The Politics of Being: The Political Thought of Martin Heidegger.* New York: Columbia University Press, 1990.

Zaehner, R. C. *Hinduism.* New York: Oxford University Press, 1966.

Index of Names and Subjects

Index of Scripture References